D0977021

The Education of
JULIUS
CAESAR

The Education of
JULIUS CAESAR

A BIOGRAPHY, A RECONSTRUCTION

Arthur D. Kahn

SCHOCKEN BOOKS · NEW YORK

First published by Schocken Books 1986
10 9 8 7 6 5 4 3 2 1   86 87 88 89
Copyright © 1986 by Arthur D. Kahn

All rights reserved

Library of Congress Cataloging-in-Publication Data
Kahn, Arthur David.
The education of Julius Caesar.
Bibliography: p.
1. Caesar, Julius.   2. Rome—History—Republic,
265–30 B.C.   3. Heads of state—Rome—Biography.
4. Generals—Rome—Biography.   I. Title.
DG261.K34   1986   937'.05'0924 [B]   85–26148

Designed by Nancy Dale Muldoon
Manufactured in the United States of America
ISBN 0–8052–4009–8

CONTENTS

v

PREFACE

IN 1921 Matthias Gelzer, dean of German historians of Rome, published a biography in which he assembled all the reliable source material about Julius Caesar. Reissued in numerous editions and translated into English, this work remains a standard reference. Scholarly, precise, extensively annotated, cautious in interpretation and chary of speculation, Gelzer's work does not require redoing, and in this book I have sought rather to explore the interaction between Caesar and his times and to define how the times shaped him and set the direction of his career; and how, in turn, he shaped his times and helped to redirect the course of history.

Such an objective presupposes an investigation of all aspects of life during the last years of the Roman Republic.

Since the publication of Matthias Gelzer's biography of Caesar more than sixty years ago, historians have elaborated or rendered more precise new disciplinary approaches to the analysis of past societies—anthropology, sociology, econometrics, etc. On the Late Republic there has been a spate of studies on the roles of women, slaves, bankers and freedmen along with investigations of working conditions, technology, land use and military recruitment.* Prosopography (the study of the influence on political events of clan, marital and other relationships) has also enriched the understanding of Roman politics.[1] Recently psychohistorians have sought new insights into the past through psychological interpretations of motives and actions. For Caesar's early years a cautious application of the theories of Erik Erikson (a founder and leading exponent of the psychological investigation of history) regarding crises and incremental psychological adaptations within life cycles as well as the insights in his psychohistorical studies of Gandhi and Luther offer modes for amplifying the data in ancient sources.

A scholar's initial impression is of astonishment at the amount of ancient source material for the Late Republic. Further probing, however, exposes major

---

*Each new issue of the annual bibliography of Classical studies, *L'année philologique*, offers a swelling flood of titles of articles, monographs and books on Caesar and on varied aspects of the Late Roman Republic. Indeed, had I listed in the bibliography all the titles examined during the dozen years spent in preparing this biography, any publisher would have cried halt, appalled at the number of pages to be added to an already lengthy manuscript. Accordingly, of the three thousand or so modern works of scholarship in a half dozen languages, I have made a limited selection.

gaps in documentation, a paucity of specific data and a necessity for creative reconstruction. Ancient historians vary, of course, in reliability and all reflect the influence of their rhetorical training, but even the least precise of them possessed an abundance of primary and secondary sources and a sense of the times that modern historians cannot hope to recapture, and all must be utilized.*

In any comprehensive exploration of the interaction between Caesar and his times a biographer must be bold in speculation, and, indeed, Michael Grant, the distinguished British historian, proposed defining the book as "a biography: a reconstruction." This is an appropriate description, and one that enjoys the sanction of the greatest historian of antiquity, Thucydides, who in the preface to his Peloponnesian Wars advised "the reader [to] consider [his] *reconstruction,* based on the clearest evidence available, as accurate as can be expected for ancient history."

In approaching the problems in such a reconstruction, I have sought guidance in Isaiah Berlin's counsel that "historians [who] have commanded the most lasting admiration are neither the most ingenious, nor the most precise, nor even the discoverers of new facts or unsuspected causal connections, but those who (like imaginative writers) present men or societies or situations in many dimensions, at many intersecting levels simultaneously: writers in whose accounts human lives and their relations both to each other and to the external world, are what (at our most lucid and imaginative) we know that they can be."[2] As for concerns regarding scientific objectivity and precision (particularly acute in history based on limited sources), the late British historian Edward Hallett Carr offered a commonsensical and profound observation:

> When we call an historian objective, we mean, I think . . . that he has a capacity to rise above the limited vision of his own situation in society and in history—a capacity to recognize the extent of his involvement in that situation, to recognize, that is to say, the impossibility of total objectivity . . . [and] we mean that he has the capacity to project his vision into the future in such a way as to give him a more profound and more lasting insight into the past than can be attained by those historians whose outlook is entirely bounded by their own immediate situation. . . . Some historians write history which is more durable and has more of this ultimate and objective character, than others; and these are the historians who have what I may call a long-term vision over the past and over the future. The historian of the past can make an approach towards objectivity only as he approaches towards the understanding of the future.[3][†]

---

*This book, addressed to a broader audience than Gelzer's, is not annotated with references to modern works of scholarship. The task would have required the expenditure of more additional years of life than the author could spare. References are provided, however, for quotations from ancient sources and, occasionally, for esoteric details, to modern sources.

†Carr was, of course, familiar with the famous declaration in Thucydides' preface that his work was "meant for those of any period who want to study the true course of past events and therefore of the similar or analogous events that are likely to occur in the future, according to all human probability."

Theodor Mommsen, the outstanding Roman historian of the last century, observed similarly that "history is the record of human life; you cannot learn to realize the life of the past but by experience of the present and by independent thought." As Mommsen suggests, a historian maintains a constant dialectic of comparison and contrast with the past for the extrapolation of general patterns and typical reactions. On the one hand, the historian recognizes that the varied (and typical) responses to tyranny in Aeschylus' Prometheus Bound are as meaningful for the twentieth century as for the fifth century B.C. On the other hand, the historian finds in the strategy and tactics of a Joe McCarthy in the mid-twentieth-century United States a model for investigating repressive conformism in the past. Only a Mussolini, fearing the illumination in such a confrontation, would proclaim that "fascists have lived too much contemporary history to be obliged to know the past with any profundity."

In selecting a biography of Caesar as a mode for an *implicit* confrontation between the ancient and modern worlds, I do emphasize Caesar's decisive role at a turning point in Western history. I by no means subscribe, however, to the Great Man theory of history, according to which it is the historian's task to record the deeds of men of heroic proportions who supposedly shape events to their private will. Rather, in exploring the interaction between Caesar and his times, I follow Hegel's dictum: "The great man of the age is the one who can put into words the will of his age, tell his age what its will is, and accomplish it. What he does is the heart and essence of his age; he actualizes his age."

Investigation of the Roman experience for an illumination of contemporary experience enjoys a long tradition in the United States. The Founding Fathers idealized the Roman Republic as the unique model for their own oligarchic republic. John Adams, for example, proclaimed that "the Roman constitution formed the noblest people and the greatest power that has ever existed."

Because of their decisive role in the present and for the future of mankind and because of their increasing uncertainty in regard to the aspirations and promises of their national heritage, Americans view the world with a more intense disquiet than other peoples. The generation that experienced the suffering and fraternity of the Great Depression and the pride and exhilaration of purpose of the Second World War and remembers when in many homes the Declaration of Independence was read aloud on July 4 and the Gettysburg Address was recited at Civil War monuments on Memorial Day—this generation of Americans knows what hopes the United States held forth and how swift and bewildering has been the decline in its democratic idealism. If for these Americans the Roman experience evokes especial poignancy, for succeeding generations it bears far more urgent significance. Ill-informed as to their heritage and deprived of insight into "the past as a political and psychological treasury from which we draw the reserves . . . that we need to cope with the future," the youth of the United States stand numb and impotent before an onrushing and seemingly unavoidable catastrophe. Indeed, "our culture's indifference to the past—which easily shades over into active hostility and rejection—furnishes the most telling proof of that culture's bankruptcy."[4]

Writing in 1961, at a time that then seemed turbulent but in retrospect seems like an age of innocence, Lewis Mumford warned that America was entering upon a degeneracy comparable to Rome's at the time of the collapse of that ancient republic. With the passage of years Mumford's prophecy has become ever more disconcerting:

> Wherever crowds gather in suffocating numbers, wherever rents rise steeply and housing conditions deteriorate, wherever a one-sided exploitation of distant territories removes the pressure to achieve balance and harmony nearer at hand, there the precedents of Roman building almost automatically revive, as they have come back today: the arena, the tall tenement, the mass contests and exhibitions, the football matches, the international beauty contests, the strip tease made ubiquitous by advertisement, the constant titillation of the senses by sex, liquor and violence—all in true Roman style. So, too, the multiplication of bathrooms and the over-expenditure on broadly paved motor roads and, above all, the massive collective concentration on glib ephemeralities of all kinds, performed with supreme technical audacity. These are symptoms of the end: magnification of demoralized power, minifications of life. When these signs multiply, Necropolis is near, though not a stone has yet crumbled. For the barbarian has already captured the city from within. Come, hangman! Come, vulture![5]

— — —

During the twelve years of research and composition of this biography, I have owed much to many people, some of whom are not aware how encouraging was their patience and confidence in my mustering the perseverance to continue with what became an ever larger and more complex project. Above all, Angus Cameron, formerly Chief Editor at Alfred A. Knopf, Inc., and one of the deans of American publishing, read through innumerable drafts, and his suggestions were crucial in the clarification of the direction of the biography. Michael Grant's enthusiasm for the work provided an impetus at a decisive moment, and his criticisms, too, have been astute. Professor Ernst Badian may not realize how useful were our informal conversations during the delightful summers we spent together at the Sulmona Institute in Italy. Professors Zwi Yawetz of Tel Aviv and Jacques Harmand of Clermont-Ferrand deserve gratitude, too, for their encouragement. My friend of many years, the talented caricaturist and painter David Levine, honors me with his jacket illustration. I owe special appreciation to the librarians at the New York Public Library, who were always eager to be of assistance during my many years of research there.

The Education of
JULIUS
CAESAR

I

AURELIA

EARLY one morning in a modest patrician house in the Subura, a street in a less than fashionable district of Rome, a four-year-old boy was awakened by shrill voices of slavewomen scampering at orders from his mother and sisters. The child realized that they were adorning his mother with jewels in her hair and with earrings, bracelets and rings, and fixing the brooches at her shoulders to hold the flowing stola, belted at the waist and reaching to the floor. Others would be combing the long hair of his two sisters before winding the tresses into buns at the back of their necks. The boy heard his father berating the vestiplicus, the wardrobe slave, because the folds of his toga were awry. Especially on such a day the senator would not be seen wearing this badge of Roman citizenship in slovenly disorder.

The boy's nurse raced into his tiny cubiculum exclaiming at his still being abed. She helped him from the footstool to the floor, washed his face and hands and had him rinse his mouth before his father entered with the vestiplicus, who carried a miniature toga. The slave folded the garment in half lengthwise and then draped it over the boy so that one edge fell in front from the left shoulder to the feet; the remainder of the bulky woolen blanket he wound under the child's right arm and threw over the left shoulder.

When the senator led his son forth, the entire household assembled to see the child in his own toga—the boy's mother and sisters and the household slaves as well as freedmen and other clients of the family. The mother reassured those who wondered whether such a little boy, particularly one so delicate, could support the heavy garment during long hours of waiting. Her child was aware how momentous a day this was for the family. A Roman child, particularly a scion of an ancient patrician clan, was not brought up to indulge himself.

The janitor opened the double doors to the corridor that led to the street, and the senator and his wife stepped forth. Over her head she drew an end of her outer garment of many colors, the palla. A slavewoman followed with her fan and parasol. The senator called to his son, now wearing a broadbrimmed hat like his father's, to take his hand, and the procession of family, slaves and clients advanced down the Subura. Barely fifteen feet wide, this major thoroughfare was thronged with hawkers and their customers. Both the street and the narrow alleys rang with the hammers of artisans and blacksmiths and the screeching of millstones as well as the bleating of sheep, snorting of swine and *honking of geese being driven to market. At the appearance of the senator and his household, women peering over flowerpots on windowsills called across to neighbors to see the nobleman and his family in their finery. It seemed only months earlier, on the principal day of the games to Apollo (July 13) in the six hundred and fifty-fourth year since the founding of Rome (100 B.C.), that they had seen the wreath on the door proclaiming the birth of a son in the house, and now he was parading like an adult in a toga.*

Past alleys stinking of urine and decaying garbage they walked, dodging lines of clothes hung out to dry by fullers. The senator's wife rubbed a small ball of amber and held it to her nose to dispel the stench. The Subura passed into the Argiletum, and an odor of leather emanated from bookstalls and cobblers' shops. The Argiletum opened into the Forum, an area for public assemblies and tribunals cluttered with monuments, statues, arches and colonnaded buildings. On the Sacred Way winding through the Forum the cortege encountered other aristocrats marching in state and turned with them into the Vicus Jugarius alongside the massive Temple of Saturn. Noisy commoners in holiday mood trooping through the narrow street yielded place to the great ones.

At the cattle market by the Tiber, the Forum Boarium, where stood a huge bronze ox, more intriguing to a four-year-old than temples and statues of heroes, the senator found his sister with her twelve-year-old son (the child's aunt and cousin). They were surrounded by magistrates with attendants bearing bundles of staves, the fasces, symbols of authority. At such gatherings, especially intriguing to a boy of four was the great variety in dress and symbols of status that proclaimed each man's place in a hierarchy of dignity and authority. Leading officials wore the toga praetexta with a purple border like that worn by the boy himself. Senators of lower rank were distinguished simply by a broad purple stripe visible on tunics under all-white togas. Resplendent in togas entirely of purple were the two censors. The boy knew that beaks of ships on the Rostra (the speakers platform in the Forum) were trophies of one of the censors, Marcus Antonius,* from a recent campaign against pirates. Equestrians, an order of aristocrats who were not members of the Senate, could be distinguished by narrow purple stripes on their tunics and by their gold rings. With senators and equestrians the boy was familiar, and he gaped rather at soldiers in breastplates and hobnailed boots, some displaying decorations for bravery on chains about their necks. Gentry arriving from the country maneuvered two-wheeled carts among artisans in dark tunics. People made way for an aged man hobbling on the arm of a slave—Aemilius Scaurus, the respected dean (princeps) of the Senate. One of the two consuls of the year, Publius Crassus, had brought his sons, older than the boy and already dressed in the plain white toga of manhood.[†] The senator's brother arrived as did his

---

*Grandfather to Caesar's future collaborator, Shakespeare's Mark Antony.
[†]One of these young men was Marcus Crassus, one day to be Caesar's close associate.

cousins and his wife's brother and her cousins. The dour Marcus Cicero was present with his two sons, Marcus and Quintus, schoolmates of the sister's son (the boy's cousin).

Meanwhile the boy eyed the children of other aristocrats, arrayed like him in adult finery—boys and girls with whom he played with the hoop, with tops or at blindman's buff or chanted in games jingles like:

> *If you do right, you will be king;*
> *but if wrong, you will be punished.*

These children were aware of their exalted place in the social hierarchy. Their ancestors were commemorated on tablets and monuments throughout the city; their parents could be distinguished by their dress, their speech, the architecture of their homes and by their self-assured air and the deference of their neighbors.

At a shout the crowd surged to the shore. A slave lifted the boy, and he saw a barge approaching upstream under the vigorous strokes of half-naked oarsmen. To the waving of white handkerchiefs on shore, a stern, broad-shouldered old man responded with a salute. As the craft neared the quay, the attendants raised the fasces to their shoulders and lined up at attention. The consuls advanced followed by the censors and by fellow augurs of the arriving hero (priests who discovered by the flight of birds or entrails of sacrificial animals whether the gods approved proposed actions of the state). The consuls welcomed the newcomer. He replied in a gruff voice. The boy's cousin stepped forward and kissed the old man's hand. The boy's mother led him forth, and the old man exclaimed with astonishment at the child he had seen two years earlier still in his mother's arms.

The old man stepped among the soldiers and the commons, addressing many by name. People cried: "Hail to the savior of Rome!"

Since no documentation exists for Caesar's childhood years, the foregoing account represents an imaginative recreation of an event crucial to Caesar's childhood and, indeed, to his entire life—the return to Rome from a pilgrimage in the East of his uncle by marriage, Marius, the outstanding general and political personality of the time. Through their marital alliance with the rough-and-ready military hero, Caesar's clan, the Julians, in decline for many generations, were enjoying a resurgence in their fortunes. His was a name Caesar heard constantly in the conversation of adults. He set an example for Caesar throughout Caesar's life, and during his last years when enemies compared him to old Marius, Caesar offered no denial.

AURELIA'S BOY

Marius was the most compelling personality of Caesar's childhood and youth, but it was customary for a boy to remain in his mother's charge until he was seven, and it was Aurelia who shaped his character and aspirations.* It was her task to mold him into a vir bonus (a good man, or, more precisely, a good Roman aristocrat). She was to indoctrinate him in the mos maiorum (the ways of the ancestors), training him in typical Roman virtues. An admiring Greek philosopher had recently described these virtues as "rugged endurance, a frugal manner of life, a plain and simple use of material possessions in general; a religion, moreover, wonderful in its devotion to deity; upright dealing and great care in avoiding wrongdoing in their relations with all men."[1]

In the crisis that had been overtaking the oligarchic republic since the previous century, a crisis that was to reach its culmination in Caesar's final years, attitudes and values in every aspect of life were being speedily transformed. Especially affected in this upheaval was the position of women. In comparison with the women of other Mediterranean societies, Roman women enjoyed exceptional privileges in marriage and divorce, in property rights and in public life. Such privileges are, of course, never granted out of generosity. In fact, only a half century before Caesar's birth, when women of the city and of the countryside demonstrated against a humiliating sumptuary law, the leading reactionary of the day, Cato the Censor, like reactionaries of every era, detected a revolutionary conspiracy behind the protest. He warned the Senate:

> Our liberty, destroyed at home by female violence, even here in the Forum is crushed and trodden underfoot; because we have not kept them individually under control, we dread them collectively. . . . Our ancestors permitted no woman to conduct even personal business without a guardian. . . . We (heaven help us) allow them now even to interfere in public affairs. . . . It is complete liberty or rather . . . complete license that they desire.[2]

Despite such mutterings against their supposed insolence, Roman women continued to expand their influence in public life. A generation before Caesar, Cornelia, mother of the Gracchan brothers, was accused of planning the radical measures promoted by her sons. Shortly before Caesar's birth, Catulus, a reactionary noble who was to play an important role in Caesar's life, delivered the first public eulogy of a Roman matron upon the death of his mother (mother also to Lucius Caesar and Caesar Strabo of the elder branch of the Julian clan). (As a young man Caesar would deliver eulogies of his aunt and of his wife in circumstances of greater political significance.) Caesar's mother seems actively to have advanced his career and encouraged him in his intellec-

---

*Roman men generally had three names: a praenomen or given name (clans traditionally limited their choice—the Julians employing Gaius, Lucius or Sextus); a nomen or clan name (Julius, for example); and a cognomen distinguishing the family within the clan or individuals of the clan (often according to some peculiar characteristic). Since father and son in this biography have identical names, Gaius Julius Caesar Maior (Senior) is referred to as *Gaius*, while Gaius Julius Caesar Minor is called *Caesar*. Their clansman Gaius Julius Caesar Strabo is referred to as *Caesar Strabo*.

In Caesar's day women were generally referred to simply by the feminine form of their clan name. Thus all the women of the Julian clan were named Julia; sisters were distinguished as Maior and Minor or Secunda, Tertia, Quarta, Quinta, etc., in the event of a large number of sisters.

tual interests, and throughout his life Caesar collaborated with ambitious and politically astute noblewomen.

The Sabine people from whom Aurelia's family originated, mountaineers in the Apennines northeast of Rome, were renowned for their devotion to the ways of the ancestors. Aurelia's father and brother did not disguise their country accents when addressing the Senate, the courts and assemblies. It was all the more remarkable, therefore, that Aurelia spoke a precise and cultivated Latin that delighted men like her husband's cousin Caesar Strabo, a playwright, orator and famous wit. Aurelia was not so conservative as those parents who raised their children as though in the days of their farmer-warrior ancestors, compelling their sons to endure heat and cold without complaint, to be content with a single tunic winter and summer and to bathe always in cold water. Nevertheless, she refused to entrust Caesar to a slave nurse. Instead she kept him on her lap and at her knee and sought "no higher praise than that she managed the house and gave herself to her children." She "regulated not only the serious tasks of her youthful charges but their recreations and games," taking care that they heard "no base word" and no untruth. She insisted that Caesar rise before his elders and cry good health when someone sneezed, and she refused to countenance outbursts of childish rage, offering Caesar "when he was quiet what she had refused him when he cried and reproving him whenever he misbehaved."[3]

Aurelia was to define for Caesar his place in the world. Initially this world consisted of the family, an entity to itself, confined within a house whose rooms all faced toward an atrium lit by an opening over a rain pool or onto a garden in the rear. Here Caesar was instructed in the relationship between the family and its gods. At dawn he attended a ceremony before the images of the household deities—the lares (embodiments of the spirits of the ancestors) and the penates (guardians of the pantry). He watched as with old-fashioned Roman gravitas (high-minded seriousness) Gaius, his father, raised his right hand to his lips and turned solemnly in a circle to cast a morsel of salted cake into the hearth, an offering to Vesta. Training in fortitudo (fearlessness in face of danger and hardship) also began in infancy. Three times monthly—on the calends, nones and ides—Caesar saw his father sever with a sacral stone knife the neck of a pig or a lamb while a slave clutched the screaming victim and directed its blood into an earthenware vessel.

Caesar took it for granted that the ancestors were part of the household. Images of forbears were stored in cupboards and adorned with wreaths on festival days. The birthdays of the dead were celebrated, and at certain holidays when all the Julians feasted at the clan tomb, Caesar became aware that his relationships extended beyond the family to a clan. The clan gathered also to deliberate on important matters—marital alliances, electoral campaigns or crimes among its members. Caesar was to emulate the great men of two clans: his father's, the Julians, divided into two families; and his mother's, the Aurelians, with numerous branches. Among famous Julians was a warrior who had killed an elephant in the first war against Carthage almost two centuries earlier, but transcending all other Roman heroes except perhaps Romulus, Founder of Rome, was Caesar's ancestor Aeneas, son of Venus, who had been driven from his Trojan homeland and had endured dreadful hardships on a long journey to Italy; and Aeneas' son Ascanius, who founded Alba Longa, from which town the Julians had migrated almost six centuries earlier to become senators at Rome.

As newcomers whose first consul had been elected only a century and a half earlier, the Aurelians did not rival the Julians in dignity. They did enjoy prestige, however, as hereditary priests of an ancient sun god and for exploits against Hannibal and in campaigns in Gaul and Sardinia. An Aurelian had built a major highway (still called the Via Aurelia), and in recent generations numerous Aurelians, including Aurelia's father, had won election as consuls.

Beyond the clan was the senatorial aristocracy in which Caesar would one day take his place. Many of the senatorial families claimed descent from heroes, and in bedtime stories Caesar heard of Romulus and Remus, who were suckled by a wolf; of Horatius, who stood off Samnite champions and then stabbed his sister for grieving for an enemy fiancé; and of Regulus, who, sent to Rome by his Carthaginian captors to negotiate peace, urged the Senate rather to press on with the war. Upon returning to Carthage, as he had sworn to do, Regulus was tortured to death. Above all, however, the four-year-old Caesar was to emulate a living hero whose name he heard day after day—Marius. Aurelia could relate many tales of the great general—how as a young officer he had engaged a Spanish champion in hand-to-hand combat; and how one evening at dinner, when someone asked Scipio Africanus to whom the republic could turn in case of a misfortune to Scipio, that mighty hero had looked around at his officers and asked, "What about Marius?" Years later, while Marius was fighting in Africa, a seer prophesied that the gods would grant him successes of "incredible magnitude and beyond his every expectation."[4]

Aunt Julia had discovered a Syrian clairvoyant who, crouching at her feet, predicted the winner of each combat in gladiatorial games. Marius paraded this wise woman before his troops dressed impressively in a double robe of royal purple and bearing a spear wreathed with fillets. He assured the legionaries, terrified at the German hordes who had been victorius over five successive Roman armies, that he would undertake no action without the holy woman's counsel. Sure enough, Marius crushed the fearsome Teutoni at Aquae Sextiae (Aix-en-Provence), and his grateful soldiers gave over all the booty to him, including ninety thousand prisoners for sale as slaves. Several months after this victory a herald brought news that Marius had defeated the Cimbri, another German tribe, and citizens embraced in the streets and poured libations to Marius as though hailing the epiphany of a god; they acclaimed him a new Romulus for refounding the city they had thought doomed.

As supreme commander Marius should have marched alone in triumph through the city. Instead he generously invited his lieutenant Catulus (half-brother to the Julians of the elder branch) to join him in leading the procession of captives, wagonloads of plunder and bewreathed legionaries. In fact, even before the German campaigns, he had been promoting the careers of his wife's clansmen and connections. Through his influence Catulus was elected to a consulship; Caesar Strabo and Caesar's father, Gaius, were appointed commissioners for the establishment of a veterans colony in Africa; and members of the clan moved steadily in the progression to the highest magistracies.*

It was after celebrating his triumph over the Germans that Marius had journeyed to Asia Minor to pay a vow to the Great Mother goddess. Now, upon the old man's return, the Julians anticipated a further impetus to their fortunes.

Caesar could appreciate the fruits of military conquest on visits to the mansion Marius was constructing on the Palatine hill overlooking the Forum and the Senate house. As the slaves lifted the sedan chair up the steps behind the Temple of Castor, Aurelia could part the curtains, discreetly drawn as was proper for a Roman matron, and point out palatial residences on the slopes and at the summit of the hill belonging to noblemen whose names Caesar heard frequently in the conversations of his elders. Livius Drusus had just renovated his mansion at a cost of 240 thousand sesterces, a huge sum. When asked by the architect whether he would like it built "in such a way that he would be free from the public gaze, safe from all espionage and that no one could look down into it, Drusus replied [like a proper Roman nobleman], 'If you possess the skill, you must build my house in such a way that whatever I do shall be seen by all.' "[5] The house of Lucius Crassus, Rome's foremost orator, was called the Palatine Venus because of its columns of Hymettus

---

*The cursus honorum (course of honors or progress of magistracies) set the stages of senatorial careers. The initial office was the quaestorship, held some time between the ages of twenty-seven and thirty; quaestors administered finances both at Rome and at various Italian towns or served as assistants to provincial governors; in 80 Sulla increased their number from eight to twenty; Caesar subsequently doubled the number. Following upon a quaestorship, a man entered the Senate. After this office some senators entered their candidacy for a tribuneship, a magistracy not open to patricians and not essential for further advancement in the cursus honorum; the ten tribunes served as defenders of the plebs and had the right of intercession and veto of acts of magistrates, elections, laws, Senate resolutions and court proceedings. The aediles, commissioners of public works and supervisors of the archives, were of two kinds—the two curule aediles, originally patricians, and the two plebeian—but by Caesar's day the distinction between the two grades had disappeared; the office was optional but since the aediles were in charge of some of the more important festivals, advancement to the highest offices often depended upon generosity in this magistracy; full senatorial membership began with an aedileship along with the associated privilege of a senatorial image among a family's ancestors. The praetors, of whom there were six in Caesar's childhood, served as judges and, when necessary, as commanders of armies; following their terms in office they could become provincial governors; Sulla increased their number to eight. Of the two consuls at least one had to be a plebeian; the minimum age for election was forty-two; the consuls gave their names to the year of their tenure. The highest office was the censorship, a magistracy with a tenure of eighteen months; censors conducted the quinquennial census, enrolling citizens according to their property and other qualifications, a function which involved a supervision of morals and control of the membership of the equestrian and senatorial orders; censors also passed on leasing of public property; the two censors held the right of veto of each other's actions.

marble imported all the way from Athens. For an alert child Catulus' residence, with its splendid portico, provided an even more startling contrast to the primitive cottage with thatched roof resting on rough-hewn pilings preserved as the house of Romulus, Founder of Rome.

With its many colors, gilded statues, hand-carved tables, ornate lamp stands and mosaic copies of Greek paintings, Marius' new mansion proclaimed his wealth and dignity and exposed, in contrast, the gloomy impoverishment of the house in the Subura. Curiously, however, Marius had no images of the dead in his atrium. He was, it appeared, "a new man," the first of his family to achieve high office. In effect, he had no ancestors. Some of the Julians, indeed, spoke condescendingly of his birth as a simple farmer in a town that had been granted Roman citizenship only a few generations back.

The political education of a young oligarch began informally. It is likely, for example, that Caesar sat in on family and clan discussions regarding the engagement of his older sister to a Pinarian. Old ladies who rehearsed lineages of the great folk while knitting in the sun rejoiced in a union of Venus (ancestress of the Julians) and Hercules (who had entrusted the Pinarians with his altar near the Tiber). Once the patricians had been the ruling caste of the city, their estates worked by subordinate clans. Romulus had appointed patrician elders as priests, magistrates, judges and councilors, and their clans had preserved their prestige through the ages. Although the Pinarians had not held a consulship for centuries, the Julians welcomed a union with one of the original patrician families of Rome.

Far more significant, however, was the marriage of young Marius to Licinia, daughter of the Crassus who owned the mansion called the Palatine Venus. The Licinians traced their ancestry back more than three centuries and boasted a host of images of consuls, censors and triumphers. They were among the plebeian clans who by exploiting slave labor on their estates and venturing into usury and commerce had surpassed many of the patricians in wealth. Two or more centuries before Caesar's time they had compelled the patricians to share power with them in the commonwealth. Crassus was a member of the inner circle of the Senate. His wife's family, the Scaevolae, were renowned jurisconsults whose reception halls were thronged with people seeking legal advice. One of their ancestors, a bedtime-story hero, caught in an attempt upon the life of an enemy Etruscan king, had defiantly thrust his hand into a sacrificial fire. By this bold act he had so astonished the king that the king lifted a siege of Rome. Henceforth the Mucians bore the cognomen Scaevola (left-handed). Crassus and the Scaevolae had solicited the marriage with a son of a "new man" in ratification of a truce between two opposing oligarchic factions.

Following upon Marius' marital alliance with these prestigious nobles, Gaius' cousin Lucius and Gaius' brother Sextus were elected to successive praetorships. Caesar's father expected to advance to the magistracy after them.

Caesar's lessons in oligarchic maneuvering and intrigue had begun.

II

GAIUS

AT the age of seven, according to Aristotle, a child can differentiate between good and evil; and among the Romans at seven a son passed from his mother's to his father's tutelage. Henceforth at dawn a paedogogus, a slave with whom Caesar spoke Greek to ensure his mastery of the empire's second language, hurried him through his ablutions so that he should have time for household prayers, to kiss the hands of his mother and father and to gulp down an apple and a chunk of bread before racing off to school.

Grown-ups bantered about their mischievous behavior at school and boasted about martinets who tweaked ears or hoisted pupils on the back of the biggest boy and whacked their buttocks with a scutica (whip). Those who espoused old-fashioned education cited Cato the Censor, a dreadful know-all whom doddering biddies recalled from "the good old days" before the Gracchan brothers turned life topsy-turvy with their radical ideas. Cato refused to entrust his son to a Greek schoolmaster "for such a priceless thing as education," and he himself taught his son to read and coached him in hurling the javelin, fighting in armor, riding, boxing and swimming. He wrote a history of Rome, too, "that his son might have in his own house an aid to acquaintance with his country's traditions." In those days even Cato's foe Scipio, a notorious Philhellene, complained publicly about shocking Greek innovations he had observed in a visit to a dancing school, declaring:

> In the company of effeminate fellows and carrying zither and lute, they go to schools for actors, and there they learn to sing songs which our ancestors regarded as disgraceful in young people of good family. . . . When I was taken to the dancing school, I saw, upon my word, more than fifty boys and girls . . . among them . . . the son of a candidate for public office, a boy less than twelve years old, dancing with castanets a dance which it would have been improper for a shameless little slave to dance.[1]

In Caesar's childhood boys and girls were aware that the world had been much different in "olden times." Nowadays, with no sense of shame, boys of senatorial families like young Gabinius or the little Murena as well as girls like Sempronia were enrolled with Greek dancing masters. Scipio's protégé Terence had posed the contrast between old-fashioned and modern education in his comedy The Brothers. Terence's traditionalist parent insists that "authority

11

will last longer and work better based on force rather than affection," while the modern father replies: "A father's job is simply to train his boy to behave of his own free will and not because he's afraid of what someone may do to him. This is the difference between handling sons and slaves."[2] Nevertheless, though arguing passionately for change at social gatherings, in practice adults resisted modifications in the ways of the ancestors, and Caesar's school scarcely differed from that of his parents.

In a converted shop curtained off from the street, boys and girls sat on backless benches, ignoring, under threat of rod and whip, the cries of hawkers, barking dogs, whinnying horses and the haggling of customers and tradesmen. In singsong they chanted the Latin and Greek alphabets forwards and backwards and then proceeded to combinations of letters, to syllables and at last to whole words. At an order from the teacher they set wax tablets on their knees and traced letters with a stylus. Ever in competition for accuracy and neatness, they eventually copied entire sentences, sayings meant to inspire lofty moral thoughts:

> Men believe what they want to believe.
> Experience is the teacher of all things.
> On ancient ways and heroes stands the Roman state.
> A man with courage has every blessing.
> Accept tasks that bring praise and profit.

Among the Greeks Hesiod was a favorite, for his didactic poem on farming, Works and Days, appealed to Roman pride in farmer-warrior ancestors:

> Bestow your gifts on whosoever gives; to him
> Who grudges, give not.[3]

For practice in the traditional virtues of constantia and disciplina, no subject was more effective than arithmetic—adding, for example, XXVII to XLI or multiplying II by XII. The children used their fingers, figured in a tray of sand or jiggled the beads of an abacus. An exhausting chore was the memorization of the Twelve Tables, an interminable code of laws the patricians had been compelled to grant the rebellious plebeians three and half centuries earlier. So archaic was the language that words and phrases were no longer comprehensible. With various provisions the children felt at ease. They did not, for example, question the double fine for breaking the bone of a free man as against a slave's. Others provoked grins—like the sumptuary regulation limiting display in funerals to a paltry "three veils, a purple tunic and ten flute players." More complicated laws that one day would prove of importance in Caesar's career were memorized now without comprehension—restrictions on usury, the guarantee of equality of all citizens before the law and the right of trial before the people in capital cases. Awesome was a father's power of life and death over his children, and as recently as Marius' war with the Germans, Aemilius Scaurus, the dean of the Senate, had compelled his son to commit suicide for cowardice on the battlefield.

In memorizing the ancient code Roman children were made conscious of the uniqueness of their heritage and of their historical mission to bring peace and order to the world. Boys and girls who wore about their necks a bulla (the amulet of Roman citizenship) of gold instead of leather—children of the senatorial and equestrian aristocracy—these bore a heavy obligation to the dour ancestors who had left this precious legacy. Children with consular ancestors bore an even heavier burden.

What of a scion of a newly resurgent patrician clan with the daily example of a Marius before him and with an ambitious-mother like Aurelia?

THE EDUCATION OF AN OLIGARCH

Much of an aristocratic child's education occurred outside of school, and it was Gaius' duty to prepare Caesar for his responsibilities among the three hundred senators and two thousand equestrians whom the gods had appointed to dominion over an empire stretching to the ends of the Mediterranean. As a Julian and as Marius' nephew, Caesar could expect to serve as a priest in one of the sacred colleges, as a legionary officer, a magistrate and eventually as a governor of some overseas dependency. First, however, he would come to head a household and manage landed estates, and on days when he was not at school he might stand beside the high-backed chair on which his father sat dictating instructions for the chief steward to note in the household daybook or summarizing accounts for submission at the quinquennial census (when censors scrutinized the financial records to ensure that only those with sufficient wealth remained inscribed in the senatorial and equestrian orders). Cato, the epitome of the old ways, had admonished that "a man was to be admired and gloried like a god if the final inventory of his property showed that he had added to it more than he had inherited."[4]

For his introduction to politics, the particular vocation of a senatorial oligarch, Caesar was fortunate that Gaius was preparing for the praetorian elections. Since Roman oligarchs involved their children in such activities, it is likely that Caesar accompanied his father in his campaigning. Local festivals provided an excellent opportunity for soliciting the votes of the neighbors: the Day of the October Horse, the termination of the war season, when in a savage melee, an outburst of barbarous fury, men of the Subura battled with men of the Sacred Way for the head of the right-hand trace horse of the winning team in a chariot race; and the Compitalia, early in January, a joyous carnival of the commons, freedmen and slaves, with athletic competitions, mimes in masks, dancers with castanets and tambourines, tumblers, sword swallowers, men with trained apes, snake charmers and a procession of the local collegia— associations of craftsmen and of religious cults—with images of strange gods and men and women in exotic dress led by the magister vici, the chairman of the event, and his assistants, slaves or freedmen, strutting in regalia to the beat of drums and piping of flutes.

In city-wide festivals, some lasting as long as fifteen days, Caesar saw his clansmen and other connections marching in the priestly colleges, and he overheard people name them and their offices and the honors and exploits of their families. On February 15 the Lupercalia (a festival at which would occur an incident of grave significance at the end of Caesar's life) began at a cave on the western slope of the Palatine, where the she-wolf had suckled Romulus and Remus. The flamen Dialis (high priest of Jupiter) in his conical hat supervised the sacrifice of goats and a dog; and other priests, laughing hysterically, smeared their faces with the blood of the victims, stripped off goatskins for loin cloths and raced half naked through the streets flailing with strips of skin women who stepped forward in the hope that the lash would render them fertile.

Some festivals had long ago lost their significance. Few could explain the carousing on the Ides of March (the day on which a half-century later Caesar would be assassinated), when Anna Perenna, the goddess of the Year, was honored. On this holiday Gaius had to bring his family to the Campus Martius early in the morning. Romans believed they would live as many years as the number of goblets of wine they drained, and as the day progressed the people gave up singing songs learned in the theater and decorous folk dancing for brawling and orgies scarcely decent for the eyes of a Roman matron or an aristocratic child.

Encouraged by the maxim that "the master's face does more good than the back of his head," Gaius could transform inspection tours of his estates into campaign excursions. Cato had proclaimed: "It is from the farming class that the bravest men and the sturdiest soldiers come; their calling is most highly respected, their livelihood is most assured and is looked on with the least hostility; and those who are engaged in that pursuit were least inclined to be disaffected."[5] Caesar could hardly hope to encounter any farmer-warriors like the ancient patrician hero Cincinnatus, who was called away from the plow to assume emergency powers in a crisis of the Early Republic. Even in Cato's day the yeomanry were declining as an influential element in Roman life. Over the course of his eighty-five years, Cato had participated in the war against Hannibal and lived through the series of wars in the East and the West that had expanded Roman dominion over the Mediterranean. He had watched the enrichment of a clique within the Roman oligarchy through the appropriation of vast tracts confiscated from Italian towns and tribes that had collaborated with Hannibal. With the enormous booty and the hundreds of thousands of slaves captured throughout the Mediterranean, these leading oligarchs established systematically organized plantations for intensive production of wine and oil as well as large-scale grain production and animal husbandry. Thus enriched, a few families monopolized the highest magistracies and military commands and seized the decisive share of subsequent plunder, while aristocratic families that had previously provided the leadership of the republic fell into obscurity. The Julians had maintained their prestige through marriages with influential plebeian aristocrats, but they attained only one consulship during the century of the great imperialist conquests.

At the same time, the yeomen legionaries, often serving for years on distant battle fronts, were unable to maintain their homesteads, much less compete with the more efficient estates operated by slave gangs, estates producing for both domestic and overseas markets. In the generation after Cato's encomium on the yeomanry, so many peasants had abandoned or been expelled from their holdings that the Gracchan brothers proposed radical measures to restore them as the base for military recruitment.

At his estates Gaius would reminisce with the local farmers about families who had moved to towns or migrated to northern Italy or even as far away as Spain. He would inquire about men fighting as legionaries in distant lands, offer legal and personal advice and make loans to tide poorer neighbors through times of hardship.

As a youth Marius had worked in his father's fields. During Caesar's childhood, however, too extensive an expertise in farming might even be suspect in an aristocrat. Nevertheless, dependent upon bailiffs for the management of his estates, only a profligate absentee landowner would be "wholly ignorant of the nature of sowing and reaping or of the lopping of trees and pruning of vines or of the times of the year for doing these things or how they were done." Farm management meant, primarily, slave management. Fortunately, Cato had left detailed instructions on the subject. He distinguished, of course, between domestic and farm slaves although, in general, he treated all "like beasts of burden, using them to the uttermost, then, when they were old, driving them off and selling them . . . like shoes or pots and pans, casting them aside when they are bruised and worn out with service."[6] With domestic slaves Cato had advice on how and when to praise, threaten, reprimand or reward. To prevent conspiracies he promoted dissension and rivalry among them. He entrusted the chief steward with major responsibilities and permitted him to be shaved by the local barber, to gossip with other stewards in taverns and brothels, to participate in neighborhood clubs, to play ball and to attend the theater. The more willing and cunning slaves he encouraged to buy slaves of their own to train and to sell at a profit. The slovenly and the lazy he flogged.

Farm slaves, distinguished as "speaking tools" from "mute" tools (animals) and "lifeless" tools (equipment), were to be worked to the limits of their endurance and to be sold when they were no longer productive. The bailiff and perhaps a few specialists in viniculture and orchardry were permitted to marry. Most of the others were manacled and locked up at night. If caught stealing or stepping beyond the boundary stones or listening to itinerant astrologers (troublemakers who preached dangerous thoughts), they were to be beaten and assigned to hard labor. Habitual recalcitrants were hung overnight on a cross; captured runaways were branded on the forehead and locked in an iron collar inscribed with instructions for their return and an offer of reward. Incorrigible slaves were to be prodded to a place of execution, flogged and hoisted and nailed to a beam and left to strangle.

In general, the employment and treatment of slaves was a pragmatic question, and many slaveholders accepted Aristotle's judgment: "Every assistant is as it were a tool that serves for several tools; for if every tool could perform its own work when ordered or by seeing what to do in advance—thus shuttles wove and quills played harps by themselves—master craftsmen would have no need of assistants and masters no need of slaves."[7] On the other hand, slave rebellion was the greatest peril confronting society. A good citizen exhibited no sentimentality in face of such a threat.

ELECTIONS

With the frequent elections and public assemblies, a senator's son early became familiar with the workings of the Roman constitution. He knew that every citizen was registered in one of thirty-five tribes and that at election time a candidate looked first to his fellow tribesmen for support. Gaius conferred with officials of his own Fabian tribe and provided them with bribe money (largess within one's tribe was not only legal but even obligatory). Only elections to lower magistracies, however, were conducted through the tribes. Election to the higher magistracies was by centuries, the original companies of the city-in-arms organized according to property qualifications. The wealthiest citizens were registered in eighteen "equestrian" centuries (originally the cavalry of the city-state) as well as in a first class; the next wealthiest in a second class, for a combined total of ninety-seven centuries. The poorer citizens were divided into three additional classes and a catch-all category of proletarii (those who had nothing to offer the state except their progeny [proles])—for a total of ninety-six centuries. Since voting was halted as soon as a majority of unit votes was reached, an overwhelming number of citizens never cast ballots. Few Romans questioned the rationale for this undemocratic procedure, that "the greater number of votes belonged not to the common people but to the rich . . . those to whom the highest welfare of the state was most important."[8]

From daily experience Caesar early became aware that Roman society depended upon a system of granting and repaying favors. Oligarchs dealt with each other as they did with the gods—on the principle of do ut des (I give that you may give). Political life was not to be separated from social life, and as a child Caesar came to know the members of the oligarchy either through report or direct acquaintance. A coterie united through marriage, friendship or social, political and financial activities entertained each other, sat together at the games, at the theater and at public festivities, paraded together in processions and employed the same tutors for their children. They knew everyone of importance and patronized sculptors, architects, actors, writers, scholars and philosophers. Gaius and Aurelia might draw up a list of such persons from whom they anticipated electoral assistance on the basis of blood, marital or other ties or on the basis of past favors.

At dinner parties and other social-political gatherings Caesar was introduced to aristocratic decorum. (As an adult he would be renowned for his savoir-faire.) Arriving late in the afternoon, guests paused in the outer entranceway to allow slaves to remove their walking shoes and to lace sandals on their feet. Inside, they changed from street clothes to light, colorful dining gowns, syntheses, a refinement adopted from the Greeks that would have roused old Cato's ire. Gaius and Aurelia conducted the guests to their places, the men reclining three to each low couch, left arms supported by a cushion and feet turned at an angle to the right, the women sedately seated on chairs. After water bowls were passed, slaves in bright tunics, their hair long and curled, brought hors d'oeuvres (perhaps oysters from the beds of Sergius Orata, the enterprising businessman who had recently devised a method for heating breeding ponds with hypocausts—flues circulating hot air through columns of heat-absorbent bricks). Caesar might be allowed to serve the men with mulsum, a mixture of wine and honey, or even a single cup of Greek wine, ordinarily reserved as a medication. (Within little more than a decade thousands of flagons would be poured at public potlatches.) Ladies, of course, drank a nonalcoholic grape juice. Although the custom of singing ballads about clan heroes had fallen out of fashion, Caesar and his unmarried sister might be asked to recite poetry in Greek or Latin.

According to the Romans, maxima debetur puero reverentia[9] (the greatest reverence is owed to a child), and as Gaius and Caesar strolled through the Forum greeting potential voters, Gaius responded patiently to the flood of questions from his eight-year-old son. Here Caesar could learn much about Roman history, for monuments abounded from every age of the city—the statue of Romulus, the shrine of the double-faced Janus constructed by pious King Numa (its gates, open whenever Rome was at war, had been closed only once during the city's long history); busts of consuls and generals massed in every corner; statues of the first four kings atop the Capitol; and a gaggle of geese sheltered nearby, a reminder of the fowl that had roused the ancestors against a Gallic surprise attack.

At the Temple of Castor and Pollux, entrepreneurs conducted varied business operations. Marius' partisans, they crowded about the old general to press him with questions on Senate policies in regard to the provinces, about measures to allay discontent among the Italian allies (the independent towns and regions of the greater part of the peninsula) and about fiscal matters generally. They would accept his recommendation regarding Gaius' candidacy, as they had done previously with other relatives and connections of Marius' wife, and Marius would reassure them as to Gaius' sympathy for their problems.

During the final weeks of the campaign, dressed in a toga whitened with chalk (the toga candida of a candidate), Gaius left the house with a nomenclator, a slave trained to recognize men of importance—officials of collegia and of tribes, government clerks, directors of corporations, moneylenders and even auctioneers and slave dealers. Theoretically the people were sovereign, and Gaius was expected to approach even the humblest citizen with bowed head to beg for his support. (Embarrassed at the humiliation, Crassus the Orator had implored his father-in-law, the dignified Scaevola the Augur, not to accompany him as he campaigned.)

One morning Caesar awakened to a blast of trumpets on the city walls, the call to an electoral assembly. Consulars and other distinguished persons had gathered in the atrium, and outside, blocking traffic, were clients, local tradesmen, members of the Fabian tribe and Marius' veterans—all assembled to escort Gaius to the Campus Martius on this momentous day. At this open space beyond the city walls, the herald announced that the auspices were favorable, and after a prayer the presiding magistrate asked the assembly: "Among the candidates whose names I have retained, who are those whom you want to make praetors?" The herald cried: "Quirites,* discedite"; and the citizens dispersed into their centuries. The equestrian century chosen by lot to lead the voting passed over a narrow bridge (Marius had introduced this reform to prevent interference with voters as they cast their ballots) and dropped into urns tablets on which they had written the names of candidates. A tally was taken immediately, for the decision of the first century was considered an omen, and succeeding centuries rarely deviated from its lead. The voting of the remaining seventeen equestrian centuries and those of the first and second class proceeded rapidly (the centuries of the wealthy contained few voters). Upon the announcement of his election as one of the six praetors for the coming year, Gaius received the congratulations of his friends, and he and Caesar were escorted back to the Subura.

Next year Caesar's uncle Sextus would campaign for a consulship, and the year after, Gaius' cousin Lucius. The year after that . . . ?

III

THE PRAETOR'S SON

AFTER Gaius' installation on January 1, 92, Caesar could rarely claim his father's attention. At any hour in the day a praetor received senators and equestrians for consultations or to entertain requests for favors. At a fixed hour each morning he received men of lesser dignity and advised them on legal,

---

*Men of Quirinus (the deified Romulus), though the term may be derived from a word for lance—the man-at-arms—a common appellation for citizens.

financial and even private matters or promised employment, temporary shelter, relief from military service or surety for a debt. He apparently impressed upon Caesar that a senator's prime obligation was not to his family or clan but to his clients, for throughout his life Caesar rarely was neglectful of this duty, which, according to the Romans, secured the fabric of society. Clients repaid such fides (loyalty) with pietas (reverence), assembling daily outside the door to provide a retinue for the praetor as he proceeded to the Forum. Upon notice that Gaius was about to set forth, six lictors (magistrates' attendants), attired like Gaius in togas with a broad purple stripe on the hem, raised to their shoulders the bundles of birch rods tied with red cords (the fasces) and arranged themselves in single file. Caesar took his place between the last lictor and his father, a symbolic expression of his aspiration to walk in his father's path. "Date viam, de via discedite!" ("Give way, clear the road!") cried a viator, and neighbors doffed hats and horsemen dismounted out of respect.

A praetor's duties were primarily judicial. Awesome to a child was the solemnity of court proceedings—the preliminary sacrifice and taking of the auspices and the assembling of scribes, counselors and grave jurors (up to seventy-five in number). Justitia, one of the ancestral virtues, was a bulwark of the social order, of the power and wealth of the slaveholding aristocracy— "assigning each his own and maintaining with generosity and equity . . . human solidarity . . . [and] connected with it . . . dutiful affection, kindliness, liberality, goodwill, courtesy and the other graces of the same kind." Rome, according to orators on patriotic occasions, was a republic ruled by law, not by men, and law "was a thing without ears, inexorable, more salutary and serviceable to the pauper than to the great man; it knew no relaxation or indulgence if one exceeded bounds."[1] (Caesar would early come to realize that, in fact, the law was "without ears" and "inexorable" to the poor and entirely "salutary and serviceable" to the rich. To those who challenged the way things were it showed no indulgence.)

As praetor peregrinus, Gaius adjudicated disputes between Romans and noncitizens, and he could favor some of Marius' clients, men of affairs both Roman and foreign. Thus with Gaius' magistracy Caesar was not only introduced to Roman law and court procedure but also to problems arising between individual Romans and individuals of allied peoples as well as between Rome and allied states, problems with which he would concern himself throughout his life.

Although custom, law, civil institutions and skilful manipulation seemed to promise eternal hegemony to the oligarchy, internal contradictions, ever intensifying, threatened the unity between the senatorial aristocracy and the aristocracy outside the Senate. The complexity of interests among the oligarchs prevented a unified stand on many issues, and contradictions between personal sentiments and political positions arose constantly. Indeed, from such tensions the factional accord reached in the marriage between Marius' son and Licinia experienced immediate strain. It was a cause for disquiet when the two censors, Ahenobarbus, often an ally of Marius', and Crassus the Orator, began sniping at each other. Ahenobarbus charged Crassus with luxury ill-befitting a guardian of public morality and derided him for weeping at the death of a pet eel Crassus had trained to respond to its name. Crassus retorted that Ahenobarbus was a stony-hearted wretch who had buried three wives without a tear. "It was not surprising," he quipped, "that Ahenobarbus had a brazen beard since he had a face of iron and heart of lead."[2]

More ominous was an attack by both censors on a client of Marius', a schoolmaster engaged in writing a history of the old man's military campaigns. This man had opened a school of rhetoric in which children of the nouveaux riches would be prepared simply in Latin, able to compete in the courts and in public office with young oligarchs trained in both Latin and Greek. In charging that the schoolmaster had "no capacity to teach anything except audacity," the censors were actually warning that he was assigning to his students topics for declamations that they considered dubious, even "subversive." It was a reflection of the contradictions inevitable in times of rapid change that in insisting upon the teaching of Greek rhetoric, the conservative censors were rejecting the warning of their hero, old Cato, that "Rome would lose her empire when she became infected with Greek letters." Old-fashioned aristocrats like Marius' fellow townsman and distant relative, the equestrian Marcus Cicero, might grumble that contemporary Romans reminded him of "a Syrian slavemarket: the better knowledge they had of Greeks, the more worthless were their respective characters."[3] Nevertheless, Cicero insisted upon his two sons' undergoing intensive training in Greek as well as Latin rhetoric.

Dissension among oligarchs offers opportunities for the disgruntled. For generations the Italian aristocracy of the autonomous regions of the peninsula had been complaining that though they provided the majority of the troops for Rome's conquests, they could not hold Roman magistracies or participate in Senate debates regarding peace and war. They were dissatisfied at the fact that Roman citizens had been paying no taxes for almost half a century, running their city on foreign tribute and booty, while Italians enjoyed no such advantages. They resented the humiliation of their officials by Roman magistrates, the flogging and execution without trial of Italian soldiers and the expulsion of noncitizens from Rome a few years earlier by the consuls Crassus the Orator and Scaevola the Pontifex. A generation ago the consul Fulvius Flaccus, the father-in-law of Lucius Caesar, had proposed a bill to grant the franchise to the Italians. With the failure of his effort, the question had become ever more pressing.

As a "new man" untrammeled by the prejudices of the old nobility and a native of a town that had received Roman citizenship only in the days of his grandfather, Marius represented himself as the champion of the Italians. During the German war he had awarded citizenship on the battlefield to a thousand soldiers from Camerinum (a piazza in modern Camerino bears his name) and dismissed remonstrances from the Senate by declaring that "the clash of arms had prevented his hearing the voice of the law."[4]

Like other Roman children, Caesar knew that after a lengthy and bitter conflict the patricians had been compelled to share power with wealthy plebe-ians. Over the years they had united into a new patrician-plebeian oligarchy. Now the Italian aristocrats, active in imperial commerce and in control of much of the city's food supply, were demanding a share of the power and plunder.

Conflicts within the ruling coterie often arose from trivial private squabbles. When antagonists sought support outside their own circles, such quarrels were magnified into political and social struggles. During Gaius' praetorship ten-sions between the inner circle of the Senate and other senators along with aristocrats outside the Senate exploded in a spectacular court case that would be recalled during succeeding decades as a turning-point in the general crisis of the oligarchic republic. The issues posed in the trial were to give rise to ever more violent struggles during Caesar's lifetime. In the immediate circum-stances, as in other political crises during Caesar's childhood, Caesar's family was directly involved. The prosecutor, a certain Caepio, was a close friend to Aurelia's brother. He was also a Servilian, one of the clans that maintained a sentimental connection with the Julians since their migration to Rome together from Alba Longa centuries earlier. The defendant, a former consul named Rutilius, was a connection of Aurelia's (his sister was married to her uncle). The case involved, too, the administration of the province of Asia (the western third of Asiatic Turkey), where Gaius was to serve as governor in the coming year.

The Senate had dispatched Scaevola the Pontifex with Rutilius as his deputy to investigate reports of outrageous extortions in Asia that threatened to im-poverish the only province of the empire that provided a surplus to the commonwealth above the cost of its garrisons. Rutilius drafted a charter for the province that exemplified the precepts of a Greek philosopher with whom he had studied. According to this Stoic, Rome had been called to a divine mission to impose peace upon peoples incapable of maintaining peace of their own; Rome's rule over subject nations was to be compared to the rule of the gods over men, of the mind over the body and of reason over the passions. Inspired by such lofty ideals, the two consulars instituted Draconian punish-ments for venal Roman tax-gatherers and other extortionists. They were hailed as saviors by the grateful provincials.

The bankers who had contracted to collect tribute in Asia for the public treasury found an opportunity for revenge in Caepio's rancor.

What were Caesar and his schoolmates to make of adult complaints that Caepio was prosecuting Rutilius not only to advance his career (a justifiable motive) but also to revenge himself upon his divorced wife and her brother, Rutilius' niece and nephew? How could Gaius and Aurelia explain rumors that Marius, who also nursed an old enmity against Rutilius, was abetting Caepio and shielding Scaevola, Rutilius' superior, because Scaevola was related to young Marius' wife?

Gaius' advancement to a consulship depended on the support of both factions, and his involvement with the case would bring loss of the goodwill of one side or the other.

Only isolated details about Gaius' life have been transmitted in ancient sources, but subsequent events suggest that he did not participate in the breach between Marius and the inner circle of the Senate that began in the trial of Rutilius. To avoid involvement, he may have departed early to take up his provincial governorship, but whenever and under whatever circumstances Gaius left for Asia, Caesar suffered the absence of his father at a crucial period of his childhood.

Before his departure Gaius repaired to the Temple of Jupiter in order to sacrifice and take the auspices. Then with his family and friends he descended the long flight of steps and the winding path along the slope of the Capitol, turned left at the Temple of Saturn and right at the Sacred Way, past the Senate house and the shrine of Janus and the New Shops, where moneychangers might leave off clinking coins to attract customers in order to wish Gaius a safe journey; through the arch commemorating a victory over the Gauls; alongside the Regia, seat of the high priests, then the domus publica, residence of the Supreme Pontiff* Ahenobarbus, and the cloister of the vestal virgins, guardians of the sacred fire of the city. On the right rose the Palatine gleaming with mansions constructed with the plunder of many wars. Emerging through the Porta Capena out to the Appian Way, they arrived at the Temple of Mars. Here Gaius took an oath to protect his province and to administer it justly. Along both sides of the highway stood a series of tombs. On one of these a nobleman boasted with the pride appropriate to a scion of a great clan:

> My life has enriched the glory of my clan.
> I have brought forth children, I have sought
> To rival the exploits of my father.
> I have deserved the praise of my ancestors,
> Who have rejoiced to see me born for their glory.
> My honor has brought renown to my clan.[5]

Further on, at the first milestone, the limit of the sacred precinct of the city, they found young aristocrats who were beginning their careers by serving on Gaius' staff together with the quaestor who was assigned as his deputy, scribes, heralds and a military escort. While Gaius awaited the signal for departure, men approached him with letters to be delivered on his way. Scaevola the Pontifex and Rutilius had an opportunity to offer last-minute advice about Asia. Marius could remind his brother-in-law of some confidential request. Gaius, on the other hand, could deliver a final appeal to his relatives to protect his family.

---

*Head of the religious family of pontifices, vestal virgins and various priests. The title pontifex maximus (supreme pontiff) has been maintained by the pope as bishop of Rome.

The lictors set the axes of authority, symbols of Gaius' power of life and death outside the city, within their bundles of rods, donned their purple military capes and raised the fasces to their left shoulders. A slave draped a commander's cape about Gaius and fixed it with a brooch. Gaius embraced his family, gave his hand to slaves and freedmen to kiss, ordered a blast of a trumpet and mounted a carriage.

It was a farewell of both sorrow and hope.

Few senators advanced to provincial governorships, and rare was the family that attained more than one such post in a generation. The fortunate appointee expected to amass sufficient wealth to enrich his family for generations. Asia was the richest plum of all, and even a scrupulous governor would return with enormous sums that would be regarded as "legitimate" perquisites. The Julians had failed to obtain a generous share of the vast plunder of the previous century; now, as a result of their connection to Marius, they had an opportunity to catch up with wealthier rivals in the nobility.

The procession slowly disappeared—lictors, carriage, retinue and military escort, men on horse and on foot, followed by pack animals and muleteers. Gaius was setting out on a journey of many weeks, first to Capua, then to Brundisium (Brindisi), where he would embark for Dyrrachium (Durres in modern Albania) and from there to a distant land to govern strange peoples under Roman law. Perhaps he would win military glory; certainly he would return rich.

FORMATION OF AN INTELLECTUAL

In his mature years even Caesar's foes stood in awe of his intellect, his broad interests and his exquisite taste. Indeed, he grew up in an environment that fostered intellectual development. Apart from his mother, renowned for the refinement of her speech, he had numerous models of cultivation among relatives and connections. Crassus the Orator spoke Greek with exceptional fluency and grace, and his friend, Gaius' cousin Caesar Strabo, the leading intellectual among the Julians, was praised as an outstanding orator and as a dramatist second only to the tragedian Accius. At the podium he saw himself as a character in a drama, and his speeches revealed an interplay of passion and wit marred, however, by a certain flaccid, nerveless quality. His half-brother Catulus and Catulus' son were noted for the purity of their Latin. The elder Catulus called Aristotle "his most particular admiration." He served as patron to poets and wrote verse of his own in the Alexandrian style, newly in favor among Roman intellectuals. His lines in praise of an actor of the day were hardly in the spirit of the poets of the past:

> My soul has left me; it has fled, methinks,
> to Theotimus; he its refuge is.
> But what if I should beg that he refuse
> the truant to admit, but cast it out?

> I'll go to him; but what if I be caught?
> What shall I do? Queen Venus, lend me aid.[6]

Along with Crassus the Orator, Caesar Strabo and Catulus, Aurelia's cousin Gaius Cotta was among the best educated men of his generation. These aristocrats exemplified a flowering of Hellenism that was to reach its culmination in Caesar himself. In a society organized about extended families, Aurelia would be expected to appeal to Julians and to her own relatives to act as surrogate fathers in Gaius' absence. In the ten-year-old Caesar, men like Caesar Strabo and Gaius Cotta had an apt listener as they discussed politics, philosophy and art, slipping back and forth between Latin and Greek, brightening conversation with snatches from Homer, Euripides and Plato.

Rome provided unrivaled opportunities for studying painting and sculpture, for the city was a vast museum with masterpieces plundered from all parts of the Mediterranean. Scattered throughout the Forum, atop the Capitol and in temples and colonnades were statues and paintings of all periods, Etruscan as well as Greek. In the previous century one general had carried off from Macedonia alone 785 bronze statues and 230 of marble. He had been followed by a second conqueror, who paraded through the city two hundred and fifty wagons loaded with Macedonian paintings and statues. After the sack of Corinth, another victorious oligarch stocked not only Rome but towns as far away as Spain with works of art. In this environment, with his cultivated relatives and connections Caesar gained an early sophistication in the arts.

Another figure influential in Caesar's intellectual formation was his tutor, Marcus Antonius Gnipho. (His name suggests that he was possibly manumitted by, or granted citizenship through, Marius' collaborator, the former censor Marcus Antonius.) "A man of great talent, of unexampled powers of memory . . . [in] disposition . . . kindly and good-natured,"[7] Gnipho was to achieve fame for a commentary on the works of Rome's greatest poet, Ennius, and for a monograph on the Latin language and as a teacher of rhetoric from whom distinguished orators would seek instruction.

Literature provided the core of education. Students practiced reading aloud, attending both to meaning and pronunciation and committing to memory ever longer passages of poetry. (Romans marveled years later that Caesar read without even moving his lips!) In addition, boys and girls interpreted epigrams embodying traditional values, values in Caesar's early years still granted perfunctory respect—exhortations like Appius Claudius':

> Be master of your soul lest your untamed nature bring forth deceit or disgrace.

or such lofty admonitions as Cato's:

> Bear in mind that if through toil you accomplish a good deed, that toil will quickly pass from you, the good deed will not leave you as long as you live; but if through pleasure you do anything dishonorable, the pleasure will quickly pass away, that dishonorable act will remain with you forever.

or inspiring sentiments from the comedian Terence like:

I am a man, I hold that nothing human is alien to me.[8]

Universally admired among parables providing moral lessons was the Choice of Hercules in the Memorabilia of Socrates' disciple Xenophon. In a young man's dream of a competition between Pleasure and Virtue, Virtue responds to Pleasure's enticement of the youth with "all the sweets of life" by warning:

> I know your parents and I have taken note of your character during the time of your education. Therefore I hope that if you take the road that leads to me, you will turn out a right good doer of high and noble deeds. . . . Of all things good and fair, the gods give nothing to man without toil and effort. If you want the favor of the gods, you must worship the gods; if you desire the love of friends, you must do good to your friends; if you covet honor from a city, you must aid that city; if you are fain to win the admiration of all Hellas for virtue, you must strive to do good to Hellas; if you want land to yield you fruits in abundance, you must cultivate that land; if you are resolved to get wealth from flocks, you must care for those flocks; if you essay to grow great through war and want power to liberate your friends and subdue your foes, you must learn the arts of war from those who know them and must practice their right use; and if you want your body to be strong, you must accustom your body to be the servant of your mind and train it with toil and sweat.[9]

Gnipho was an ideal tutor for encouraging Caesar's all-encompassing curiosity. Having studied in Alexandria, the major center of Hellenistic culture, he could bring to life the Egyptian antiquities in Herodotus' Histories, a standard text in Roman education, and rouse Caesar's patriotic envy with descriptions of the Museum, a research center founded by one of Aristotle's disciples to which the pharaohs invited scholars and scientists from all over the Greek world. Whether Gnipho stimulated Caesar's interest in geography and ethnology is a matter for speculation. (As an adult Caesar displayed an ecumenical view unique among Roman oligarchs, trapped as they were in a city-state parochialism.) He could describe the peoples of many lands who arrived by caravan and ship from as far off as India and China (the alternation of the trade winds that permitted rapid sailing to India and back had only recently become known to the Egyptians).

With its plunder and tribute, its expanding overseas commerce and flood of foreign slaves and immigrants, Rome was becoming cosmopolitan, and the city afforded lessons in more than history and the arts. At the Temple of Virtue, for example, Gnipho could demonstrate the movements of the seven heavenly bodies with the orrery constructed by the greatest scientist of antiquity, Archimedes of Syracuse, a device with which eclipses of the sun and moon could be predicted and the length of the year precisely calculated.

Rome was not dependent upon the Greek world for all its accomplishments. With the influx of hordes of slaves during the previous century new construction methods had been devised for the employment of unskilled and unwilling workers. Prefabricated sections of wall made of rubble and cement were set within wooden frames for the rapid building of huge structures like the recently completed mammoth granary composed of three rectangular courts 28 by 118 meters in extent, surrounded by shops and encompassing an area of almost 9,000 square meters. In addition, no cities in the Mediterranean world could compete with the magnificent aqueducts that supplied Rome with a volume of water not to be matched again in the city until the twentieth century. The Aqua Marcia alone, built by Gaius' maternal grandfather (or great-uncle), brought 187,000 cubic meters of water to the city daily, and it was only one of several aqueducts.

Throughout the city Caesar encountered ready evidence of Rome's cultural and commercial ties with the rest of the world. Atop the Aventine hill in a temple of Diana, Caesar saw a many-breasted statue of a fertility goddess, a copy of similar images at Massilia (Marseilles) and at Ephesus in Asia. At the riverside, dockers, chanting to ease their labor, unloaded into magazines constructed by Gaius Gracchus grain from Sicily, Sardinia and Africa for the gruel and gritty bread that provided the mainstay of the commons and of the slaves. On the Vicus Jugarius, running from the Forum to the Tiber, Aurelia purchased scents and unguents from Arabia. On the Sacred Way shops displayed luxuries from all corners of the world—jewelry, fine linens, spices, cloth of gold, swords with inlaid handles, furs, glassware, amber, embossed bronze, silver and gold, precious stones, vases, paintings and statuary. In cages or on platforms at the Temple of Castor, Caesar saw human merchandise—men, women and children, nude and with their feet whitened with chalk: docile Greeks from Asia Minor and Syria, kidnapped by pirates; grim Spaniards, wreathed to indicate capture in battle; Scythians from north of the Black Sea who had been sold by their chieftains; and stalwart Nubians, excellent runners with sedan chairs. The poet Horace recorded a typical pitch of a slavedealer:

> Here's a handsome boy, comely from top to toe;
> You may take him to have and to hold for eight thousand sesterces;
> home-bred he is, apt for service at his owner's beck,
> knows a bit of Greek learning and can master any art.[10]

Prospective buyers read sale tickets listing, as the law prescribed, defects, diseases and histories of attempts to escape. They examined slaves for scars and deformities, pinching muscles and peering into eyes, throats and ears. They ordered potential purchases to turn about, to jump or even to recite verses.

Like any child of an imperial society, Caesar came to believe that not only the products of all the world but even the peoples of the world existed for the benefit and comfort of Rome. To supply an insatiable slave market, Romans engaged in constant warfare. Slavehunting, slave dealing and day-by-day converse with slaves helped shape the Roman character and nurtured in Romans an arrogant and ferocious chauvinism.

War was Rome's major occupation as well as its major source of income. Military training began early. In the Campus Martius, outside the walls, young men raced chariots, galloped on horseback, played ball, wrestled and drilled with weapons. Youngsters like Caesar ran with hoops, raced, played tag and blindman's buff and perhaps begged youths like young Marius for a try at tossing a javelin or heaving a discus. Frail and sickly, Caesar had to strive hard to keep up with his companions. His later stamina and master horsemanship were the rewards of early perseverance.

More important than the arts and literature and as fundamental as war in a young oligarch's education was politics—the defense of the hegemony of the ruling clique. Every issue posed in the Forum or in the Senate, every shift in political alignments, every rumor of maneuvers and intrigues was of importance to Aurelia, the guardian of Gaius' career during his absence from Rome. The developments in the Rutilius case were of especial concern to her since they were decisive not only to Gaius' but also to Caesar's future.

Caesar's experience with these events helped to shape his political outlook for the rest of his life.

IV

THE GRAND DESIGN

THE Rutilius trial impelled a series of events that was to bring slaughter and devastation to Italy and the provinces, exile and violent death to Caesar's relatives and connections and mortal danger to Caesar himself. Years later, in similar circumstances, Caesar would recall the suffering, unrelieved anxiety and even terror of that grim decade of his youth. In the days of the trial, however, any ten-year-old would admire Rutilius, who, like a Roman Socrates, was exploiting the occasion to appeal for a revival of the old virtues. Viewing "the world and all its parts [as] set in order at the beginning and . . . governed for all time by divine providence," the old Stoic rejected any tampering with established institutions, whether the supremacy of the landed aristocracy, property rights in general or Roman imperial dominion. In regard to his own trial, confident that "reason possesses an intrinsic element of dignity and grandeur suited rather to require obedience than to render it,"[1] he scoffed at suggestions for theatrics to entertain the audience or for emotional appeals and bribery to win over the jury, and he addressed the court with the systematic order, epigrammatic brevity and unimpassioned tone of a Stoic preacher. His colleague Scaevola the Pontifex followed with comparable restraint, and his nephew, Aurelia's cousin Gaius Cotta, awed at his responsibility and frustrated by Rutilius' strictures regarding defense tactics, could scarcely be heard over the mounting din. In contrast, to the delight of the equestrian jurors and their friends (Gaius Gracchus had transferred control of the courts to the equestrians from the Senate) the prosecutor Caepio vilified the dour sexagenarian with hyperbolic accusations of adultery, unnatural sexual license and rapacious profiteering.

Although convicted and sentenced to a loss of civil rights and a fine that was equivalent to his purported extortions, Rutilius enjoyed the irony of his choosing exile in Asia, the very province where he had supposedly committed his depredations. His associates were less impressed, however, with the triumph of Stoic reason and perfect virtue. They feared new aggressive actions from their opponents and the exploitation of popular discontent in the city and of rebellious sentiment among the Italians. Convinced that a swift, bold response was required to avert peril to the senatorial order through civil disorders and even civil war, a coterie of leading senators elaborated a many-faceted reform program. In their plan they demonstrated a long-range vision rare among oligarchs and not to be seen again at Rome until Caesar's consulship. For the consulars participating in this effort, the program represented a reversal of previous policies. With an obstinacy worthy of a Rutilius, all of them had resisted change and excoriated reformers. Catulus, for example, proclaimed "that the memory of anyone who should adopt a policy ruinous to the republic should be utterly erased from the vision and the minds of men";[2] and to that end he constructed a portico over the site of the mansion of Gaius Gracchus' collaborator Flaccus (father-in-law to Catulus' half-brother, Lucius Caesar). Aemilius Scaurus had mobilized right-thinking citizens to lynch the radical tribunes Saturninus and his followers. With oligarchic arrogance, Crassus the Orator and Scaevola the Pontifex, as consuls, had expelled noncitizens from Rome. Now they were reversing themselves.

To implement their program the distinguished noblemen selected three young protégés of Crassus the Orator to hold successive tribuneships: Rutilius' nephew Livius Drusus in 91; his other nephew Gaius Cotta in 90; and a certain Sulpicius Rufus in 89. On December 10, 92, upon his installation in office, Drusus exposed the grand design: enrolment of three hundred equestrians into the Senate and transfer of control of the courts to the redoubled Senate; a grain subsidy and a distribution of public lands for the commons and the franchise for the Italians. On the other hand, rancorous at Rutilius' conviction, Drusus insisted upon the prosecution of equestrian jurors previously guilty of malfeasance.

On January 1, 91, in a momentary pause in factional maneuvering, the Julians marched through the Forum in a procession led by Caesar's uncle, Sextus Caesar, one of the new consuls. After prayers and sacrifices at the Temple of Jupiter on the Capitol, they watched Sextus and his colleague, Philippus, enter the temple for their inaugural session with the Senate. That afternoon the Julians honored their first consul in three generations. With Lucius Caesar about to enter his candidacy for the coming year, it appeared that once again consulships were prerogatives of Caesar's clan and that in this century the Julians might be one of the clans to monopolize the high office as the Scipios, the Fabians and the Fulvians had done in the previous century.

Drusus seemed an ideal advocate for the new program—wealthy, energetic and enjoying repute as the son of a tribune who had undermined Gaius Gracchus' influence by co-opting Gracchus' reforms. On the other hand, brusque and arrogant, he was incapable of the patient persuasion required for such a task especially insofar as opposition to Drusus and his program arose as much out of personal malice and opportunism as out of questions of principle. In an ominous portent, Sextus Caesar's consular colleague, Philippus, considered an ally to Drusus, abruptly reconciled himself with Drusus' foe, Caepio, with whom Philippus, too, had long been at enmity. "Free and outspoken in his language, with a large fund of humor . . . clever in the give-and-take of debate," Philippus was a dangerous and unpredictable opponent. Years earlier as a young tribune seeking popular favor, he had publicly complained that of the four hundred thousand Roman citizens scarcely two thousand possessed any property. (Oligarchs always condemn as irresponsible any such demagogic exposure of social realities.) Now, as presiding officer of the Senate, he goaded the Drusus faction. Playing upon Catulus' name [puppy], for example, he snapped, "What are you barking at?" "I see a thief," replied Catulus.[3] It was, of course, the ill-will underlying such childish repartee that roused Aurelia's anxiety. Any intensification of factional conflict jeopardized Gaius' future.

Opposed to all reform, as a young man Caepio had led a mob in breaking up an assembly convened to vote on a grain subsidy by the radical tribune Saturninus. Now a praetor, Caepio commanded considerable support. Many senators resisted any enlargement of their order, while equestrians, preoccupied with money making, rejected Drusus' offer of enrolment into the Senate and were indignant at his proposals to take the courts out of their hands and to prosecute former equestrian jurors. Aristocrats of both orders bridled at grain subsidies and land distributions. They feared, too, the strain on city-state institutions from a sudden increase in the city's territory and citizenry; and the commons, gulled by oligarchic demagogy, resented any sharing of their "sovereignty" over the empire through the extension of the franchise to the Italians.

Drusus summoned Italians to the city in support of his legislation. Recalling similar invasions by followers of the Gracchi and Saturninus, when, for the moment, the common people had become conscious of their strength, Drusus' opponents responded with an ultimate oligarchic defense—omens: of blood gushing from loaves of bread at Arretium (Arezzo), of stones and sherds raining from the sky elsewhere and of sweat oozing from Apollo's image at Cumae (a standard response of ancient deities to popular protest). The priests entrusted with the Sybilline prophetic books reported a timely oracle foretelling the most horrendous peril of all—dissensions between masters and slaves—

and warning against an ambitious individual who would waste his own patri-
mony and covet the wealth of others (presumably by proposing a grain subsidy
and land distribution).

Oligarchs, Caesar was learning, reversed positions repeatedly and without
apology, according to their self-interest. In the past, members of the Drusus
faction had rebuffed with contempt Italian demands for the franchise, and the
Italians had looked to Marius to promote their aspirations. Now, resentful of
the fame and clientship accruing to Drusus for advocating citizenship for the
Italians, Marius was conspiring with Philippus and Caepio to block the measure. In addition, oligarchs took advantage of factional strife to vent personal
animosities. The praetorian Sulla, a staff officer to Marius in the African war,
unveiled a gilded statue depicting his capture of the enemy African king, proclaiming, in effect, that he and not Marius had been the victor in that conflict.
Caesar knew the memorials to his uncle's victories—a fountain on the Esquiline, a temple to Honor and Courage together with war trophies on the Capitoline and a huge shield embossed with a German warrior with contorted body
and protruding tongue in the Forum. In the Regia, the house of the high
priests, Caesar had read Marius' name six times in the lists of consuls, a
number matched only once in Roman history. (Caesar would remember this
attack on his uncle's dignity and would defend his own even with arms.)

Publishing an oath of loyalty supposedly sworn by Italian aristocrats to Drusus, Caepio accused the tribune of aspiring to a throne, the ultimate denunciation against those who violated the principle of oligarchic collegiality. In con-
frontations with wayward noblemen of overweening ambition, oligarchs would
recall the oath that Brutus, the expeller of Rome's last king, had compelled the
citizens of his day to swear—to "suffer no king in Rome, nor any man who
might be dangerous to liberty"—liberty as defined, of course, by the oligarchs.[4]

When Philippus sought to block a vote in a public assembly, Drusus ordered
his arrest, and Drusus' attendant grappled wth the consul so ferociously that
blood gushed from Philippus' nostrils. Drusus suddenly fell ill, and it was
rumored he had been poisoned. With Drusus incapacitated, Philippus announced that he could not carry out his responsibilities in a Senate that had
abdicated its authority to a king. Contemptuously, he ordered Crassus the
Orator to silence. Crassus retorted: "You would have to cut out this tongue of
mine, although when it had been torn from my throat, my breath on its own
would serve my liberty for the refutation of your license." Upon these words he
clutched his side and pitched to the ground. In a few days the faction's most
eloquent spokesman died of pleurisy. In the tribunician elections, Gaius Cotta
suffered defeat. Philippus bullied the Senate into annulling Drusus' legislation.
One day, walking home from the Forum, Drusus was stabbed in the groin with
a cobbler's knife. As he expired, he exclaimed: "O my relatives and friends,
will my country ever have another citizen like me?"[5]

Thus ended a last-minute, comprehensive effort to undo decades of short-
sighted policies and to shore up the hegemony of the landed aristocracy. (Four

decades later, after Caesar attained supreme power in the commonwealth and attempted to effect a reconstruction of the republic, his associates would urge him to heed the lessons of Drusus' experience. But no more than the unfortunate tribune would Caesar be able to restrain his wrath at hostile goading. His oligarchic opponents, too, would reject reforms aimed at preserving their privileges and power, and they would kill Caesar as they had killed Drusus.)

The Italians took Drusus' murder as a signal for revolt. A praetor sent to Picenum, a region of central Italy along the Adriatic, to investigate reports of warlike preparations, was lynched. Instead of attending to the mobilization of the legions, however, Philippus and Caepio prompted a tribune named Varius to pass a law for the prosecution of those who had provoked rebellion by promoting false hopes among the Italians. With the courts once again under equestrian control, the Drusus faction could anticipate no mercy. The former censor Marcus Antonius fell on his knees to plead for his life. The aged dean of the Senate rose from a sickbed, hobbled to the Forum and shaking a palsied finger at Varius cried: "Varius accuses Aemilius Scaurus of rousing the Italians to war. He offers no witnesses. Whom do you believe, the Spanish-born Varius or Aemilius Scaurus?"[6] Lacking Antonius' and Scaurus' prestige and confronting special hostility as a relative to Drusus and to Rutilius, Gaius Cotta could not escape conviction. After inveighing against the equestrians who were promoting the prosecutions, he went into voluntary exile.

Thus in dramatic and violent incidents the world of the house in the Subura was overturned. Marius' alliance with the inner circle of the Senate foundered. Rutilius suffered conviction, Drusus assassination and Gaius Cotta exile, and Rome was caught up in a desperate war provoked by personal rancor and factional rivalry. Caesar had seen with what fury oligarchs resist reforms, even reforms aimed at their own salvation. He had had his first lesson as to the courage required to confront this fury as well as to the necessity of a precise calculation of the relationship of forces before promoting any program for change.

V

THE ITALIAN REVOLT

SOME forty years later, at the most momentous decision of his life—to embark upon a civil war—Caesar knew the horrors he was bringing upon Italy. Since the day when he saw the red flag on the Capitol, the signal for general mobilization against the Italian rebels, through the succeeding decade, he experienced the savagery of civil war among his own neighbors and relatives. It was not that he had been unfamiliar with war before that time. War was the principal activity of the commonwealth, and a major annual event was the enrolment of fresh legions by the consuls. With other young-sters Caesar watched as military tribunes at the Campus Martius walked among conscripts lined up according to tribe and took turns in selecting recruits. Upon the enrolment of a legion, officers alternated in swearing allegiance to the commanders. Then a soldier selected by lot took the oath on behalf of his comrades, and finally the recruits stepped forward one by one to declare, "I likewise."

On this occasion, anticipating resistance to an unpopular conflict, the oli-garchs prepared the population for extraordinary levies with their ever-suc-cessful expedient—religious manipulation. Before a solemn Senate a matron of the prestigious Metellan clan recounted a dream in which Juno warned of her imminent abandonment of Rome because of the neglect of her sanctuar-ies. By her prayers the pious noblewoman had persuaded the goddess to delay her departure. Profoundly distressed by this well-timed vision, the Senate voted monies to Lucius Caesar, the newly installed consul, for the restoration of the Temple of Juno the Preserver in the produce market at the edge of the Tiber. Like other sacred edifices throughout the city, it had long been in decay. Greengrocer women used it as a privy, and a bitch, Metella dis-covered, had dropped a litter at the foot of the cult statue.

Roman oligarchs were masters of awesome spectacles with priests in varied garb, elaborate rituals and impressive processions and sacrifices. They could revive memories of pious ancestral heroines and astonish the commons by having Metella fall on her knees alongside her slaves to scrub out Juno's sanctuary. After inducing the goddess to remain in the city, the consuls were ready to institute levies among the sullen commons. As Caesar and his friends watched the legions march off to battle, they saw that the factions maintained their division in the commands. Departing for the northern front under the consul Lupus, a relative of Marius', were Drusus' opponents—Marius, Caepio, Pompeius Strabo (father of Caesar's future rival) and the newly retired consul, Sextus Caesar; the Drusus faction, on the other hand, took over the southern front under the command of Lucius Caesar.

With one hundred thousand resolute troops at the ready, the Italians seized communication centers and inflicted defeats on the Romans on all fronts. On June 11, 90, rejecting Marius' advice not to risk a major engagement before testing raw troops, the consul Lupus fell into an ambush. Marius saw corpses floating down the Tolenus river. He raced to the consul's assistance, routed the enemy and retrieved Lupus' body. Caesar heard the herald cry in the street: "The consul Publius Rutilius Lupus, son of Lucius, grandson of Lucius, is given up to oblivion. Let every citizen to whom it is convenient attend the funeral rites. He is being brought from his house." Such was the general demoralization that the Senate "decreed that henceforth casualties should be buried where they fell so that others should not be deterred by the spectacle from entering the army."[1]

Not yet of age for military service, Caesar went on with his formal education. Since he was expected to investigate literature as "a representation of our manners in the characters of others and [as] a vivid picture of our daily life," the war introduced complications into his studies. Homer had proclaimed: "The Muse puts upon the lips of the bard the ways of life," and in his epics he propounded an approach to life which all subsequent poets investigated, modified and enriched. Decisive to the Homeric view was the belief that only in this world can one achieve self-fulfilment. Thus, in response to the flattery of Odysseus, a visitor in the underworld, the shade of Akhilleus declares:

> Let me hear no smooth talk
> of death from you, Odysseus, light of councils.
> Better, I say, to break sod as a farm hand
> for some country man, on iron rations,
> than lord it over all the exhausted dead.[2]

Akhilleus himself exemplified a brief but glorious heroic existence, according to the Homeric view. On the other hand, Romans mocked the Greeks for their self-seeking and their treachery and boasted of their own superior civic responsibility. The Roman Homer, Ennius, put into the mouth of the ancient hero Decius Mus, about to sacrifice himself in battle to turn a rout into victory, this appeal to the gods:

> Ye gods, hear this my prayer a little while; just as from my body I breathe my last for the Roman people's sake, with foreknowledge and awareness, in arms and in battle.[3]

But what was Caesar to think of descendants of such heroes—like Caepio? In the cupboards of his atrium stood images of Servilian forbears whose exploits Ennius celebrated, but rather with the rancor of Homer's Akhilleus than with the patriotic devotion of Decius, Caepio had provoked a fierce civil war, and like the consul Lupus, mocking Marius' counsel of caution, Caepio died in shame amidst his annihilated legion.

On the other hand, victories won by the Julians brought glory to the clan and additional hope for Caesar's own career: Sextus Caesar surprised an enemy force, killed eight thousand soldiers and captured a large store of arms; and when Lucius Caesar crushed the Samnite hill people in a major battle, at Rome men doffed their war cloaks as a sign that the city was no longer in peril. Caesar Strabo, an aedile this year, was delivering "carefully prepared harangues almost daily,"[4] and Lucius carried a law granting citizenship to Italians not yet in rebellion or prepared to lay down their arms. Even children might wonder why a war had been necessary to achieve this result. When some three decades earlier Lucius' father-in-law, the consul Fulvius Flaccus, had proposed a similar franchise bill, together with Gaius Gracchus and hundreds of their supporters, he had been murdered and his house leveled as a warning to other radicals.

Although the Italian war, one of the bloodiest of the ancient Mediterranean world, more devastating than the long and ferocious war with Hannibal, subsided after two years, various regions (including some that had already possessed Roman citizenship) carried on the struggle, especially those that had suffered most grievously from the wholesale displacement of smallholders by slave-operated plantations and by large-scale herding. For decades these areas would remain discontented and rife with banditry, the population ever ready to spring up behind any banner of rebellion.

With its hundreds of thousands of casualties and enormous devastation, the war intensified the general crisis of the republic. Posing a grave and immediate threat was the rebel mobilization of twenty thousand infantry and a thousand horse among runaway or manumitted slaves, an action that impressed slaves with a consciousness of their power and provided an impetus for a mass servile uprising fifteen years later. War profiteering broadened the gap between the very rich and the miserably poor. Even men of old and distinguished clans accumulated fortunes—men like Calpurnius Piso, the owner of an armory (a portion of whose wealth would one day pass to Caesar in the dowry of his granddaughter, Caesar's third wife). The poor, of course, suffered severely. Smallholders expelled from their farms squatted in temples, in porticos and under bridges. At crossroads auctioneers set up spears, the symbols of their trade, and hawked the last possessions of the desperate.

A youth studying literature as "a vivid picture of our daily life" would find in Tiberius Gracchus' oration on the miseries of the dispossessed peasantry—a model of rhetorical art—impressive lessons for contemporary events:

> The wild beasts that roam over Italy have every one of them a cave or lair to lurk in; but the men who fight and die for Italy enjoy the common air and light, indeed, but nothing else; houseless and homeless they wander about with their wives and children. And it is with lying lips that their imperators exhort the soldiers in their battles to defend sepulchers and shrines from the enemy; for not a man of them has an hereditary altar, not one of all these many Romans an ancestral tomb, but they fight and die to support others in wealth and luxury and though they are styled masters of the world, they have not a single clod of earth that is their own.[5]

In fact, these "masters of the world" were not willing "to fight and die" in a pointless civil war. Draftees mutilated themselves to avoid military service, and commanders could not trust their troops. Mutineers clubbed a former consul to death; others showered an officious consul with missiles, and when he subsequently fell in battle, it was rumored that he had been slain by his own men. In the city fierce tensions erupted among certain elements of the population. With farms pillaged and burned, herds scattered, orchards and vineyards destroyed and slaves dispersed, landed aristocrats were hounded by greedy moneylenders. One day when a praetor who had revived an ancient law against usury was about to sacrifice at the altar of the Temple of Castor and Pollux, a tribune raised an arm in a signal. A mob stormed toward the praetor. Dropping his sacred implements, he fled into a shop. The crowd dragged him forth. Someone had slit his throat.

(Whether Caesar actually witnessed this incident is not significant. In his early years, he was already taking violence for granted in civil strife as well as on the battlefield.)

For a moment, however, the entire citizenry was diverted from the horrors of war and of civil discord by an equal sorrow—the death of Aemilius Scaurus, the venerable dean of the Senate. This pillar of oligarchic respectability had published memoirs that were hailed as a guide for young Roman aristocrats and acclaimed as of equal literary merit to the Cyropaedia (on the education of an ideal prince) by the Greek historian Xenophon. Scaurus exemplified the myth that advancement to wealth and high office was open to every Roman with capacities and perseverance. From his father, an impoverished patrician reduced to peddling charcoal, he had inherited a mere ten slaves and a paltry 35 thousand sesterces (more than the lifetime earnings of a laborer), but Catulus bought a Greek grammarian from Scaurus' heirs for 700 thousand sesterces, the price Scaurus had paid for the slave—twenty times Scaurus' original inheritance.

Through skilful exploitation of opportunities and connections (especially with his wife's family, a branch of the powerful Metellans), Scaurus had advanced from magistracy to magistracy until people declared that he ruled the world with a nod of his head. Awesome was the number of indictments from which he had escaped unscathed, including charges of accepting bribes from an enemy African king and, more recently, from Mithridates of Pontus, Rome's perennial foe in Asia Minor. Not so obtuse as to allow factional rivalry to interfere with personal profit, he entered into a partnership with Marius for the disposal of the latter's war booty. Cavilers might recall his appropriation of legacies by fraud (what oligarch was innocent of such peccadillos?) and other manipulations. Most Romans, however, preferred to remember him as a latter-day hero who had compelled his son to commit suicide for cowardice on the battlefield and had rallied the citizenry to massacre the radical tribune Saturninus and his subversive partisans.

Scaurus was a model whom aristocrats could urge Caesar to emulate.

MARIUS' MANEUVER

Sharing interests, values, ambitions and common foes, oligarchs operate with a minimum of discussion in behind-the-scenes intrigues, and in plotting and scheming Marius was the match of any of his contemporaries. Now Caesar had the opportunity to follow the old man's maneuvering to obtain a final battle command in the East to cap a long and glorious military career. During Caesar's infancy, when Marius set off on a pilgrimage to the East, only naive hero worshipers believed he was making this long journey simply to render thanks to the Great Mother goddess for her assistance in crushing the Germans. In fact, with the encouragement of entrepreneurs he sought to provoke a war for plunder and renown. Visiting Mithridates, king of Pontus, who was extending his realm along the northern and southern shores of the Black Sea, Marius challenged the monarch "either to strive to be stronger than Rome or to do her bidding without a word."[6] An empire builder himself, Mithridates understood Marius' aspirations, and he knew that Rome would eventually seek to subjugate his kingdom. He preferred to choose his own opportunity for the forthcoming conflict.

It was after Marius' visit to the East that the Senate dispatched Scaevola the Pontifex and Rutilius to set in order affairs in the province of Asia. By introducing measures to prevent milking the province dry, these old-fashioned landed aristocrats infuriated the usurers, tax-gatherers and other extortionists, Marius' partisans. In retaliation Marius conspired with Caepio in the prosecution of Rutilius.

Gaius' nomination to the governorship of Asia followed.

Despite Caesar's fame, historians scarcely mention Gaius, and he seems to have possessed neither outstanding capacities nor the aggression for winning a governorship of Rome's wealthiest province, and in the light of Marius' prior and subsequent scheming for a command in the East it is likely that Marius engineered Gaius' provincial appointment in order to promote his own ambitions. What discussions they had in advance of Gaius' departure and what maneuvers Gaius engaged in during his governorship remain oligarchic secrets. The Romans had long experience in espionage. They maintained agents at foreign courts and were old hands at provoking "aggression" by neighboring states and tribes. It can be assumed that Gaius kept Marius informed of Mithridates' diplomatic moves and warlike preparations.

One day following Gaius' return from the East, Nicomedes, the king of Bithynia, a buffer state between Pontus and the province of Asia, arrived at Rome as a suppliant. Upon reports of the initial victories of the Italian rebels, Mithridates seized the opportunity to expel Nicomedes from his throne. Nicomedes would have appealed to a recent governor of Asia to support his request for aid in the Senate. (Caesar may have met Nicomedes on this occasion; he would come to know him well in later years.) Of course, Marius represented the king's first recourse; they had had previous dealings.

When Marius retired from his command against the Italians, pleading the infirmity of age, not even the eleven-year-old Caesar would have believed that the vigorous old man was seeking a life of quiet repose. Marius' strategy began to emerge when the Senate appointed as special commissioner to restore order in the East a certain Aquillius, a colleague in one of Marius' six consulships; and as his deputy Aquillius was assigned a senator who as a tribune twenty years earlier had nominated Marius for the supreme command in the African war in place of the haughty Metellan.

As governor of Asia Gaius had promoted the interests of the entrepreneurs, Marius' partisans, as an inscription erected by oil men (olive) in Gaius' honor on the Aegean island of Delos attests. Leading Italian entrepreneurs, the Cossutii, were engaged in business at this free port and major commercial center of the eastern Mediterranean, and at about the time of Nicomedes' arrival at Rome, Gaius and Aurelia announced the engagement of their only son to an heiress of the Cossutii. During the same period Gaius and Aurelia married their daughters also to wealthy equestrians. Julia Maior, recently widowed (or divorced), was married to a Pedius (the Pedii also had commercial interests in the East). But Marius required senatorial allies as well as entrepreneurial supporters. The current consul (89) Pompeius Strabo, as ambitious a "new man" as Marius and an equally consummate intriguer, had collaborated with Marius in the past and had served with him against the Italians under Marius' relative, the consul Lupus. Their alliance was now confirmed in the marriage of Caesar's younger sister to Attius Balbus, son of Pompeius Strabo's sister and of a prominent equestrian.

Thus it was that the three children of Gaius and Aurelia, themselves of prestigious noble families, were engaged or married to equestrians and, in the case of Julia Maior, to a newly enfranchised Italian businessman.

Although old-fashioned patricians still maintained a sense of their social superiority to plebeian aristocrats even of long-established nobility, for many generations patricians had ben intermarrying with plebeians of the senatorial order (the prohibition against such marriages had been repealed some two and a half centuries earlier). For their older daughter, however, Gaius and Aurelia had chosen initially a Pinarian of a patrician clan of minimal political influence but of ancient lineage. Marriages with equestrians, even with newly enfranchised Italians, were, of course, acceptable to a "new man" like Marius, but the betrothal of all three children of a patrician house to people in trade must have provoked indignation among the other Julians and much gossip in Roman society. Only a generation earlier, the satirist Lucilius (maternal great-uncle to Julia Minor's bridegroom) had exclaimed: "To be a tax-collector in Asia, to gather pasture duties for the government instead of being Lucilius, never—never! I would not trade myself for the whole world." Even in his own time, however, Lucilius' snobbery was dated. His predecessor, Cato, had already come "to regard agriculture as more entertaining than profitable and invested his capital in business that was safe and sure. . . . He bought ponds, hot springs, districts given over to fullers, pitch factories, land with natural pasturage and forest, all of which brought him back in great profits."[7]

With the expansion of the empire during the previous century, Rome had become the financial and commercial capital of the Mediterranean world, and leading Roman entrepreneurs commanded colossal fortunes with holdings in various parts of the empire as well as in Italy. The Cossutii and the Pedii were representative of these wealthy circles. Though they avoided political careers for themselves, inevitably they exerted ever-increasing political influence, and intermarriage between the old landed aristocracy and the leading entrepreneurs was no longer a rarity. Among these new connections to his family, Caesar heard talk not so much of elections and magistracies as of directorships of corporations, of shipping, of interest and exchange rates, of grain futures, of bids on public contracts and of buying and selling of real estate. Throughout his life he would maintain close ties with these entrepreneurs. Like Marius he would seek support among them and defend their interests. In his later years he would find his major councilors and agents within their ranks.

Eager for new sources of profit these circles welcomed imperial expansion, and it is likely that the Pedii and the Cossutii shared Marius' excitement at the arrival of ambassadors from the East who complained that after Mithridates had acceded to Rome's demands, Marius' associate Aquillius had goaded Nicomedes into invading the king's domains. The envoys read a list of senators and magistrates receiving subventions from Mithridates and accused these men of betrayal of trust.

Apparently the gods shared the displeasure of Marius' foes at the warlike maneuvering on a distant frontier. It was reported that a trumpet blast sounded out of a clear sky. Soothsayers offered a dire reading: the sound, they said, heralded a new cycle in the destiny of Rome, a cycle of dissension and bloodshed. Even as they were delivering this fearful monition, lo! a sparrow flew into the hall, dropped a snippet of a grasshopper and sped away. The Senate recalled the soothsayers, Etruscan aristocrats who maintained a particularly oppressive dominion over their smallholders and could be counted on to provide interpretations in support of the landed interest. They consulted among themselves in their strange tongue and then announced that the omen foretold troubles between landowners and the city populace, "for the latter," they explained, "is vociferous like a grasshopper, while the former haunt the fields."[8]

The seers were quickly vindicated in their reading of the portents.

Mithridates invaded the province of Asia, welcomed as a liberator. At a prearranged signal, with a fury rivaling that of the Italian rebels, the provincials slaughtered, so rumor declared, eighty thousand Italians. As for Aquillius—after parading him on a chain behind a mounted guard, Mithridates poured molten gold down his throat in a symbolic gratification of Roman greed. Equally threatening as an example for the rest of the empire was Mithridates' manumission of slaves who killed or denounced masters, his remission of the debts of those who betrayed creditors, his punishment of extortionists and his five-year moratorium on provincial tribute.

Shares in tax-farming corporations plummeted. Moneylenders called in loans and refused new credits, and very likely the Pedii and the Cossutii were among the entrepreneurs who massed at the Temple of Castor to demand the dispatch of legions to punish the barbarian.

To the general dismay, it was reported that Mithridates had offered an alliance to the Italians still in rebellion.

Rarely cheered by news from their homelands, slaves from the East revived tales of a comet that had burned for seventy days at Mithridates' birth and reappeared at his coronation. They recalled, too, an oracle predicting the destruction of Rome from the East and hailed Mithridates as the reincarnation of the Persian god Mithras, Destroyer of Evil, or as a new Dionysos, the conqueror god who had appeared out of India.

Marius was prepared.

To the cheers of former legionaries and of the entrepreneurs, the old general announced his candidacy for a seventh consulship. Once again he would save Rome from a barbarian invader and liberate the commonwealth's prime source of imperial tribute.

VI

MURDERED CLANSMEN AND JUPITER'S PRIEST

TO oppose the old man in the consular elections, the inner circle of the Senate chose Caesar Strabo. Among his sponsors were his brother Lucius and half-brother Catulus, their connection Marcus Antonius (whose son had been betrothed to Lucius Caesar's daughter), Publius Crassus (Lucius Caesar's colleague in the censorship) and the new consul, Sulla (who had recently married Scaurus' widow, a Metella). These men were determined not to allow Marius to capture an unprecedented seventh consulship, and their resistance to his aspiration to a final command in Asia represented a continuation of the struggle between the entrepreneurs and the leaders of the Senate that had erupted in the trial of Rutilius. Forgetting how Marius had promoted their careers, Caesar Strabo's faction now recalled only his repeated defiance of the leadership of the Senate and the turbulence resulting from his alliance with the radical tribune Saturninus to win land bonuses for his veterans. They reminded him of his plea of infirmity upon retiring from the Italian war and advised him to withdraw to his seaside villa or to undergo a cure for his rheumatism at some spa.

Caesar had heard how Marius had refused to be bound when a surgeon sliced open varicose veins in one of his legs. Now he saw Marius at the Campus Martius, his paunch bulging over his perizoma (the underpants with which Roman athletes, unlike the immodest Greeks, covered their nakedness). Caesar knew Odysseus' vaunt when challenged by young athletes at Phaeacia:

Now pain has cramped me, and my years of combat
hacking through ranks in war, and the bitter seas.
Aye. Even so I'll give your games a trial.
You spoke heart-wounding words. You shall be answered.

As the modern Odysseus joined in wrestling, boxing and hurling the javelin
and the discus, his foes gave off hooting. In the Forum, however, Marius
responded ineffectively to badgering, alleging lamely, for example, that he
sought another consulship "to take part personally in the campaign [against
Mithridates] in order to give his son a military training."[1]

In the new factional confrontation once again personal and ideological motivations interacted. Sulpicius Rufus, selected three years earlier to be the third
in the succession of tribunes to implement the Drusus reform program, won
election for 88. Since the tribuneship was reserved to plebeians, Sulpicius had
transferred himself out of the patriciate (like a British lord aspiring to a seat in
the Commons). A strict constitutionalist, he was indignant that Caesar Strabo
was aspiring to a consulship without having held a prerequisite praetorship.
When he denounced Caesar Strabo's illegal candidacy in public meetings, the
witty tragedian mobilized thugs to disrupt the assemblies. "Never look
round," he quipped to a partisan wounded in the face during a melee, "when
you are running away."[2]

Always alert for opportunities (Caesar would match him in this ability),
Marius entered an alliance with the disgruntled tribune, and Sulpicius proclaimed himself a champion of the people in the tradition of the Gracchi and
Saturninus. Charging Saturninus "with timidity and hesitation in his political
measures," Sulpicius outdid Drusus in the boldness of his proposals. The
oligarchs had tricked the Italians by restricting new citizens to a small number
of tribes, preventing them thereby from exercising an influence proportionate
to their numbers. Similarly, freedmen were enrolled in only four of the thirty-
five tribes. Now in reward for their military service against the Italian rebels
(they had previously been forbidden to bear arms), the freedmen demanded
equal franchise with other citizens. With Marius' support, Sulpicius proposed
to enrol both the Italians and the freedmen into all the tribes, a reform that
would radically shift the balance of forces within the republic to the detriment
of the inner circle of the Senate. Sulpicius was a formidable advocate and
opponent. In his speeches he combined "extreme boldness and energy, a very
loud and resonant voice and unrivalled vigor of bearing and dignity of gesture
with a weight and flow of language." From Caesar's maternal uncle he had
adopted a country mannerism of substituting a full "e" for an "i" in his
speech, an idiosyncrasy that endeared him to the populace but offended ped-
ants like Catulus as being less in the spirit of "the orators of old days" than of
"farm laborers."[3] Sulpicius had no intention of suffering the fate of previous
radical tribunes. Very likely aided by young Marius, he assembled a bodyguard
of young equestrians dubbed by his enemies his "anti-Senate." Alarmed at
Sulpicius' popularity with the youth, the freedmen, the newly enfranchised

Italians, the entrepreneurs and Marius' veterans and anxious both at civil disorders in the city and reports of new victories by Mithridates, the inner circle of the Senate recalled the consul Sulla from his command against holdout Italian rebels and appointed him to a command in the East. The action was constitutional, and Marius' foes were confident that the rival consular candidates would now retire from the race. Caesar Strabo did withdraw, but Marius persisted in his candidacy, and Sulpicius pressed on with his radical legislation.

To block Sulpicius' legislation, Sulla and his consular colleague Pompeius Rufus (a clansman and distant relative to the previous consul, Pompeius Strabo) halted public business by proclaiming a religious holiday. When at a turbulent public meeting young Pompeius Rufus attempted to divert the attention of surly hecklers to enable his father and father-in-law, the two consuls, to slip off to safety, the crowd stampeded up the steps of the Temple of Castor and trampled the young man to death. Catching sight of Sulla running up the steps of the Palatine hill, the people took off in pursuit.

Sulla burst into Marius' mansion.

Emerging at length, Sulla announced the termination of the religious holiday and declared that he was returning to his legions at the siege of the rebel stronghold of Nola, near Capua.

For an oligarch dignity was sacred. Sulla would have revenge for these humiliations and outrages.

THE FIRST MARCH ON ROME

The turbulence at the Temple of Castor was followed by traumatic events that Caesar would remember to the end of his life.

Sulpicius convened a public assembly. He expelled all partisans of the opposing faction, and with a unanimous vote of the thirty-five tribes (the vote of only one man sufficed to represent a tribe) he extended the franchise of the Italians and the freedmen and transferred the command in the Mithridatic war from Sulla to Marius. For thus defying the inner circle of the Senate, many tribunes had suffered exile or assassination. Neither Sulpicius nor other Romans could have imagined, however, the circumstances under which he was to meet his death.

Two officers who arrived at Sulla's camp at the siege of Nola to announce that Marius had replaced Sulla as commander in the war against Mithridates were lynched. Fearful of punishment and resolved to restore their general's dignity, the legionaries demanded that Sulla lead them in a march on Rome. Appalled at the sacrilege to the gods and to the ancestors, Sulla's officers deserted—all except Lucullus, whose Metellan mother was related to Sulla's wife. Sulla reassured the troops, demoralized by these defections, with an announcement that the war goddess Bellona had appeared to him in a dream, set a thunderbolt in his hand and bade him smite his enemies. To two praetors sent by the Senate to order Sulla to turn back with his army, Sulla declared, "I am coming to deliver

Rome from her tyrants."[4] So successful was the goddess in restoring the spirits of the legionaries that they smashed the fasces of the lictors, stripped the praetors of their togas and chased them ignominiously down the Appian Way.

For the first time in the seven-century history of Rome, a consul (and a patrician as well) was marching on the city.

In response to this threat a Roman who had six times been consul and twice a triumpher joined with a tribune of patrician stock in calling upon the slaves of the city to take up arms against fellow-citizens.

An initial engagement took place at the Esquiline hill. Sulla summoned reinforcements and sent soldiers into the Subura to attack Marius and Sulpicius from the rear. All about Caesar's house unarmed citizens hurled stones and tiles from the roofs and temporarily halted Sulla's advance. When Sulla ordered archers to shoot firebolts into these buildings and seized a torch himself, resistance collapsed.

At dawn at Sulla's orders the senators reported to the Senate house. They found the building invested by legionaries. At Sulla's command the senators ranged themselves in support of a motion to outlaw "the tyrants"—a dozen of Sulla's enemies, including Caesar's uncle and cousin, Sulpicius, several other senators and some equestrians. No senator dared to oppose the outlawing and execution of citizens without trial—except the octogenarian Scaevola the Augur, maternal grandfather to young Marius' wife. Some forty-five years earlier another Scaevola had refused to assent to similar unconstitutional violence against Tiberius Gracchus, and thereafter the Augur himself had assisted Gaius Gracchus in drafting a law reaffirming the ancient right of provocatio enshrined in the Twelve Tables—the right to appeal to the people in capital cases. Now the jurisconsult and strict constitutionalist Scaevola rejected Sulla's maneuver of outlawing citizens in order to deprive them of their right to trial. When Sulla upbraided him for his obstinacy, the aged consular replied: "You may point to the troops with which you have surrounded the Senate house and menace me even with death, but you will never make me with the little old blood remaining to me judge Marius an enemy who is the savior of the city and of Italy."[5] (When at personal risk a quarter-century later Caesar defended the right of provocatio against Cicero, he would be confirmed in his resolve by recollection of the courage of the aged consular in seeking to save the lives of Caesar's uncle and cousin.)

Marius in flight sent his son for money and supplies to an estate belonging to Scaevola. A cavalry patrol approached. The bailiff hid young Marius in a wagonload of beans, yoked up a pair of oxen and drove him back to Rome. The young adventurer spent the night with his wife and then escaped to the coast to board a ship. Old Marius had sailed without him.

Caesar saw Sulpicius' head on the Rostra.

Sulpicius' mother and children knelt before the conqueror and begged for the tribune's body, but unlike Akhilleus at old Priam's plea for Hektor's corpse, Sulla did not relent and lift up the suppliants.

No Penelope to sit weeping in her room, Aunt Julia appealed to Sulla's wife to intervene for her husband and son. But Sulla was adamant. Fearing for his own safety once he departed for the war in the East, he annulled Sulpicius' legislation, curbed the ancient powers of the tribunes and prescribed prior Senate approval of all legislation submitted to a popular assembly. Thus within weeks he restored to the Senate prerogatives wrested from the oligarchs over decades of struggle centuries earlier.

Further to protect his rear in Italy while he fought Mithridates, Sulla compelled the consuls-elect to swear to uphold his acts. In addition, Sulla arranged for his consular colleague Pompeius Rufus to replace Pompeius Strabo as commander of an army engaged in fighting Italian hold-outs. Pompeius Strabo, however, took a lesson from Sulla. As his clansman Pompeius Rufus was preparing to sacrifice upon his arrival at the legionary camp, the troops mobbed him, beat him to death and served up his corpse as the offering.

With the series of events beginning with Sulla's march on Rome, Romans now appreciated the implications of Marius' reform of legionary recruitment some twenty years earlier. The ancestors had permitted only those with a stake in the commonwealth to bear arms, but the oligarchs had rejected the Gracchan land reform directed at restoring the yeomanry, and the number of potential recruits owning property declined drastically. By appealing for volunteers among the destitute, Marius transformed a citizen militia composed of men of property into an army of mercenaries who owed loyalty not to the city and to its oligarchy but to the commander from whom they expected booty and land.

Since Rutilius' conviction, Caesar had experienced outlawry, assassinations and bloody riots. In recent months he had lived through the violence between the Marians and the party of Caesar Strabo and the murders of a consul's son, of a tribune and of a consul as well as an invasion of the city by Roman legions, an appeal to slaves to take up arms, the flight of his uncle and his cousin and the usurpation of supreme power by an arrogant warload. It appeared, indeed, as though a new era had been inaugurated even as the Etruscan soothsayers had foreseen, an era of bloodshed and dissension. Such was the world for which Caesar was to prepare himself.

THE VENGEANCE OF ODYSSEUS

Because of the close relationship he developed with the new consul Cinna, Caesar would recall with particular clarity the events of this year and of Cinna's subsequent consulships as well as Cinna's tragic end. Like Pompeius Strabo, with whom he had served during the Italian revolt, Cinna followed Sulla's example in opportunism and treachery. Freed of a military threat by the murder of Sulla's consular colleague, Cinna disavowed his oath to Sulla, revived Sulpicius' legislation on the franchise of the Italians and the freedmen, proposed the recall of all political exiles and prompted a tribune to indict Sulla for the murder of Sulpicius. Sulla sailed off for the East, and the indictment was left pending.

Oligarchs who had resented Sulla's march on Rome and his later arrogance had not necessarily opposed his general policies. Led by the other consul, Octavius, they assaulted Cinna and his partisans, and the Forum was heaped with bodies and the sewers ran with blood. After a vain appeal to the slaves, Cinna fled with six tribunes and other magistrates. Priests entrusted with the prophetic books bought centuries earlier by one of the kings from the prophetess of Apollo, the Sibyl of Cumae, discovered an oracle promising lasting peace upon the outlawing of the wayward consul and the other recalcitrant magistrates. Ignoring the tabu against disclosure of the Sibylline verses, Octavius read the prophecy in the Forum. Furthermore, in violation of sacred law enjoining the priest of Jupiter from holding secular office, the senators nominated the flamen Dialis (as the priest was called) to replace Cinna as consul.

In such an atmosphere, with turbulent experiences following one upon another, Caesar was expected to continue his analysis of literature and his declamation of oratorical set pieces. His uncle and cousin, however, were undergoing trials more dramatic than those Caesar encountered in Homer's epic about Odysseus and Odysseus' son. Marius' ship had been blown ashore, and he had been flushed out of a marsh and dragged, naked and covered with slime, to a nearby town. When the old man bellowed to a German slave sent to kill him, "Do you dare to kill Gaius Marius?" the slave fled in terror.[6] Escaping with the aid of local clients, he sailed to Africa. Young Marius, too, reached Africa and was confined to house arrest by a prince until a concubine, captivated by the young daredevil, contrived his escape. He and his father reached a veterans colony founded many years earlier by Gaius and Caesar Strabo.

Learning that two legions Sulla had left at the siege of the rebel stronghold of Nola were disgruntled at their exclusion from the war against Mithridates, Cinna appeared at the camp. He mounted a podium, ordered his lictors to cast down their fasces and declared to the assembled troops: "From you citizens, I received this authority. The people voted it to me; the Senate has taken it away from me without your consent. Although I am the sufferer by this wrong, I grieve amid my own troubles equally for your sakes. . . . Where will after this be your power in the assemblies, in the elections, in the choice of consuls if you fail to confirm what you bestow and whenever you give your decision fail to secure it?"[7]

In fact, commoners had no voice in the nomination or election of consuls, and Cinna was simply engaging in a standard charade of every oligarchy: the oligarchs put on a grave expression and solemnly avow their devotion to democracy, and the commons make a pretense at believing them. In a time of primitive information media, leaders depended much upon eloquence and spectacle (arts of which Caesar would become an unrivaled master.) On this occasion, when Cinna tore off his consular toga and threw himself to the ground (the signal prearranged with suborned officers), the legionaries broke ranks with a shout of indignation. They lifted him up and implored him to resume his magisterial chair and to reclaim his fasces.

UNOCAL 76

2 6372 4783 001 8 01468

RONALD W ELBERT

GONE WITH...
TIBURON CA
1981

	PRODUCT	QTY.	PRICE	AMOUNT
F	76 SUPER			
E	76 UNLEADED			
L	76 LEAD. REG.	76 DIESEL		
	SUPER PREMIUM 20W/50			
	Diesel cond.	128.89	11 50	

DATE AUG 1989 112586 421413

SERVICE ORDER NO.

SALES TAX 3 00

TOTAL 14 [68?]

This transaction is subject to the terms and conditions (as may be modified from time to time with required notice) of the Unocal Credit Card Account Agreement as contained on the monthly statement.

SIGNATURE OF BUYER Ronald Elbert

AUTHORIZATION NO.

DRIVER'S LICENSE NO.

VEHICLE LICENSE NO. 68V812NY STATE CA SVC. BY

ORIGINAL INVOICE

FORM 3-2K95W
(REV. 5-85)

Within a period of months all vestiges of civic piety had evaporated. Whereas only a single officer had joined Sulla in his attack on Rome, now only one (Appius Claudius, whose Metellan wife was related to Sulla's) refused to take an oath to restore Cinna to his consulship.

The fortunes of the house in the Subura, however, depended upon Marius. Landing in Etruria with a force of veterans and some Berber cavalry (who would one day, out of loyalty to Marius' memory, come to Caesar's aid), Marius proclaimed manumission to all slaves and broke into stockades on country estates. He appealed also to veterans whom he had settled in the region as well as to tenants and smallholders, long embittered against their arrogant wealthy neighbors. Four armies converged on Rome under Cinna, Marius, Carbo (a praetor outlawed along with Cinna) and the popular war hero Sertorius. A professional soldier and a native of the Sabine country from which the Aurelians originated, during the German war Sertorius had accomplished exploits of extraordinary heroism. Marius had cited him for bravery after he reconnoitered an enemy camp in German dress. In the Italian war he had lost an eye. "Others," he boasted, "could not always carry about with them the evidence of their brave deeds, but . . . in his own case . . . when men saw what he had lost, they saw at the same time a proof of his valor."[8] Principled and courageous, he was greeted with applause whenever he entered the theater. (He would serve as a model for Caesar.)

Other men who had formed Caesar's childhood world prepared to defend the city, including his clansmen Lucius Caesar and Caesar Strabo. Marcus Antonius, Catulus and Catulus' son rode south to urge Metellus Pius to offer terms to Samnite hill folk still in revolt and to bring his legions back to Rome. When the Samnites rejected an armistice, Cinna and Marius entered into an alliance with them, and the Italian revolt coalesced with the new insurgency. Meanwhile, at Rome legionaries, with no heart for a power struggle among oligarchs, panicked at omens. Young Pompeius foiled an assassination attempt against his father, who had brought his army belatedly to the city and was rumored to be in secret negotiations with Cinna. Pompeius Strabo was subsequently felled by a plague. During the funeral a mob in the Subura snatched the corpse from its bier and dragged it on a hook through the gutter.

On this occasion slaves responded to an appeal from Cinna and streamed across the lines. They were followed by crowds of citizens. In a parley with Metellus Pius, Cinna gave assurance that he would not willingly be the cause of anyone's death, but Metellus caught Marius, long an enemy to Metellus' family, scowling behind Cinna's chair, and he fled from the city. The consul Octavius, a lethargic and superstitious ninny, reassured by a horoscope drawn by his Chaldean astrologers, set his chair on the Janiculum hill on the far side of the Tiber and, resplendent in his purple-bordered toga and ringed by lictors and senators, awaited the enemy onslaught. A patrol advanced at a gallop, and a horseman lopped off Octavius' head.

An admiring moneyer named Macer, with whom Caesar would one day associate himself, issued a coin depicting Marius as Odysseus returning home on a ship. Like Odysseus about to take vengeance on the suitors in Ithaca, Caesar's uncle advertised his wrath in his shabby clothing and unkempt hair and beard. People reported that troops slew any man whose greeting Marius ignored. Slaves rampaged through the streets, smashing doors, overpowering household slaves, murdering, looting and raping. Sertorius, who had been rebuking Marius for his vindictiveness and urging Cinna to restraint, halted the disorders by killing a great number of the rioters.

Sulla had beheaded only one of his enemies. Marius and Cinna acted with more assiduity. Marius granted no mercy to ingrates. Caesar Strabo was hacked into quarters like a sacrificial animal before the tomb of Varius, the tribune responsible for Gaius Cotta's exile (whom Caesar Strabo had subsequently prosecuted and convicted), and his head was tossed next to his brother's in the Forum. Their half-brother, Catulus, begged to be allowed to live out his last years in exile, but when Marius reportedly answered: "Let him die! Let him die!"[9] Catulus shut himself in a newly plastered room, lit a charcoal brazier and smothered to death. Learning that Marcus Antonius had been routed out of a client's farmhouse, Marius, it was said, leaped from his dining couch and was only with difficulty dissuaded from running off to kill his one-time ally. According to rumor, he embraced the assassin, dripping with blood though the man was, and set Antonius' head on a table to gaze upon as he feasted. Publius Crassus and his elder son, fleeing on horseback, were overtaken by Fimbria, the hotheaded son of one of Marius' consular colleagues. Publius plunged his sword into himself, and his son was cut down by the pursuers. Though he resigned his consulship, Merula, the high priest of Jupiter, could not escape Cinna's wrath. Ordered to trial, he repaired to the Temple of Jupiter, removed his conical cap, the insignia of his office, slit his wrists and died, bespattering the image of the god with his blood.

Whereas Sulla had proscribed twelve of his foes and executed only one, Marius and Cinna took the lives of five noblemen of consular rank, three of them former censors and two of them clansmen to Caesar.

What could the partisans of Marius and Cinna anticipate upon Sulla's return from the East?

MARIUS' TOOL

Marius was master of Rome—and, of course, of the fortunes of the house in the Subura. Elected consuls for 86, Marius and Cinna, with the cooperation of compliant censors, outlawed Sulla and his closest associates and auctioned off their properties. They advanced their own partisans to magistracies and priesthoods. In Merula's succession, they faced a problem. Enemies would exploit the suicide of a priest of Jupiter among the superstitious. Furthermore, circumscribed by tabus, the flamen lived more like a prisoner than a priest of the god, and in the past aristocrats had sometimes been drafted against their will for the post. It was expedient to select a clansman to the murdered Julians and desirable to reward the loyal branch of that clan. The Julian descent from Venus and Aeneas provided an additional fillip to appease the commons, fearful at Jupiter's wrath. The nominee had to be the son of a couple married according to the ancient rite of confarreatio. Renowned for their devotion to tradition, the Julians would have been among the last to maintain the rite. Since the priest had to be married to a patrician priestess, Marius dissolved Caesar's engagement to the equestrian heiress Cossutia and negotiated a new engagement to his colleague's daughter, a Cornelian, an engagement that ratified Marius' new alliance with Cinna.

Though he would not be installed before assuming the toga of manhood, Caesar, Marius' candidate, seemed assured as to his future.

On January 13, 86, however, while readying legions to replace Sulla's troops in the war against Mithridates, Marius died.

It was young Marius' responsibility to deliver the funeral eulogy—to praise the old man's rise from a simple country boy who had worked alongside the slaves in his father's fields to an officer singled out by the mighty Scipio and then to a general awarded two triumphs and hailed as "the savior of Rome." He was to review also the old man's political career—his passage as tribune of a law guaranteeing secrecy of the ballot, his election against powerful opposition to a consulship and then to six additional consulships, a number unprecedented in the history of the republic, his suppression of the subversive tribune Saturninus and his co-option into the college of augurs (a preserve of the most prestigious nobility). He had embellished Rome with monuments, exhibited generosity to soldiers and colleagues, accumulated great wealth and an extensive clientship in many parts of the world. He had maintained his courage and perseverance into old age, enduring flight and exile and returning heroically to embark upon a final campaign to save Rome from another barbarian invader.

Caesar had private memories of the old man. He had wondered at Marius' exploits, played Marius in make-believe battles and blushed at a nod from the old man at the Campus Martius. He had experienced indignation at Sulla's denigration of Marius' victory in Africa, pride at the old man's pluck in competing with youths in athletic contests and fear when the old man fled into exile. On the other hand, he would remember Marius' intrigues in the conviction of the self-righteous Rutilius; his appeal to slaves against Sulla and his loosing slaves in the city after his return from exile; his maneuvering to provoke a war in the East; and his display on the Rostra of the heads of seven noblemen, including two Julians. (The germination of Caesar's policy of clemency to enemies in his last years, a clemency so generous as to rouse the suspicions of his foes, began early in Caesar's life.)

During these fourteen years, Marius helped to shape Caesar's view of the world and to clarify Caesar's insights into the contradiction between illusion and reality in Roman life. Boasting of a commonwealth founded on law, the oligarchs subverted the courts to factional or private advantage, employed assassination and even wholesale murder for political ends, provoked rebellion by resisting inevitable reforms, fomented wars to win commands and booty and even led armies against Rome itself to advance private interests or to slake personal rancor.

In decrying evils of an earlier day, Ennius, the singer of Roman martial virtue and selfless patriotism, had spoken prophetically of the present time:

> Wisdom is driven from our midst, brute force rules the state,
> the honest orator is scorned, the rude soldier is worshiped.[10]

A cry of horror interrupted the funeral ceremonies. Fimbria, the officer who had pursued Publius Crassus and his son to their death, had struck the aged Scaevola with a dagger.

Did the blow against the supreme pontiff, Caesar's mentor in his initiation into the mysteries of the priesthood of Rome's patron deity, offer a portent of the world Caesar was about to enter?

VII

THE CONSUL'S SON-IN-LAW

EVEN in times of ceaseless civil discord, of violence and civil war and prospects of more suffering to come, ordinary aspects of life continue. Like other mothers Aurelia marveled at how her adolescent son glanced more frequently in a mirror of polished bronze and combed and perfumed his hair (he was to earn a reputation as a dandy). Caesar was at an age to banter with girls and grin at prostitutes ogling him from windows and doorways. Nevertheless, more than other young aristocrats he had to "seize the day" (he astonished his contemporaries with his discipline and assiduity), for in addition to completing a standard education he had to master the mysteries of his forthcoming priesthood. A flamen Dialis officiated alone, with vestals or with other priests at monthly sacrifices, rites of public expiation, the Lupercalia, the initiation of the grape harvest. Since any imperfection in a ritual invalidated an entire ceremony (an error in a single word rendered a prayer ineffective), a priest had to undergo intensive instruction and rehearsal.

As head of the religious family, the supreme pontiff exercised supervision over candidates for the flaminates. Scaevola, recovered from the wound he received at Marius' funeral, was an aristocrat and scholar who would command Caesar's respect. Erudite, industrious and renowned for his precision of expression, he frequently quoted his father's opinion "that no one could be a good pontiff without a knowledge of the civil law." He himself had earned a reputation as a scholar with an eighteen-volume treatise on civil law as well as books on religion. (His works would provide a primary source for the codification of Roman law that Caesar would sponsor at the end of his career.) Scaevola was also "the most unpretentious man in the world" and "not without kindliness and affability."[1] Above all, he enjoyed a reputation for personal integrity, a rare quality that would become even rarer at Rome as Caesar grew older.

In his prospective priesthood Caesar confronted a fundamental contradiction between ancient ideals and current political reality or, more particularly in Caesar's case, between superstition and the enlightened view he had assimilated from literature and from intellectuals like Caesar Strabo and Gaius Cotta. He had heard adults deriding the credulity of the commons and their simplicity in submitting to religious manipulation. (Caesar's nomination to the flaminate was merely a move in a general political maneuver by his uncle). Although the more respectable and representative philosophy among oligarchs was and would continue to be Stoicism, another Greek school that had evolved during the tumultuous upheavals following upon the Alexandrian conquests was attracting a considerable following in Italy. According to this philosophy, Epicureanism, the gods, if they existed at all, exercised no influence on the affairs of men. Reflecting this view, the patriotic poet of the previous century, Ennius, had written:

> I have always said and will go on saying, there is a race of gods in heaven, but I do not believe that they concern themselves with what the human race is doing: for if they did, good men would fare well and bad men ill, which is not the case.

It was by now apparent to Caesar that even Stoics who preached that the universe was divinely ordained with an "order and harmony . . . without compare"[2] demonstrated in their own behavior that good men often fared ill in this best of all possible worlds. All Roman intellectuals, including Stoics, reflected the influence of Epicureanism, which was becoming increasingly pervasive in intellectual life—like Marxism and Freudianism in the early twentieth century. Gaius Cotta had studied under a distinguished Epicurean in Athens. Crassus the Orator, father-in-law to young Marius, had undergone treatment by the most renowned physician of the day, a Greek who applied to medicine the Epicurean theory that the world was composed of atoms in continuous movement and conflict.

The hocus-pocus surrounding the priesthood of Jupiter embodied the most primitive of superstitions and represented much of what Epicurean enlightenment attacked with patient analysis and ridicule. Supposedly sharing in Jupiter's inviolacy, the flamen could not be touched by a slave or suffer the restraint of oaths or even of knots in his clothing. Prisoners who came into his view were immediately released from their bonds. As the priest of a god of the upper world, he could not be in the presence of animals associated with the underworld like dogs and goats or eat certain foods or hear funerary flutes or look at men in the panoply of war. He could not leave his room unless garbed in priestly attire or step beyond the boundary of Jupiter's city. For Caesar, who in later life would choose his closest associates among Epicureans and find his most obdurate enemies among the Stoics, submission as a youth to such superstitious restraints must have proved galling.

As pontifex maximus and as an enlightened intellectual, Scaevola confronted a similar contradiction. He had rationalized by distinguishing three categories of religion: that of the poets, to be dismissed as mere fancy; that of the philosophers, to be examined seriously by all thinking men; and that of the state, to be reverenced as the most effective means for maintaining civil tranquility and for controlling the commons and the slaves.

The problem, in any event, was not posed immediately. Caesar's installation as flamen Dialis lay two or three years in the future, a long time to a youth in his teens. Meanwhile, after months of nightmares, present fortune was to be savored in the house in the Subura. No longer merely a shadow to Old Marius, Gaius enjoyed respect as the "loyal" Julian and as a connection of the consul's, and Caesar was numbered among the young aristocrats of greatest promise at Rome. As the prospective son-in-law to the consul, Caesar had the opportunity to listen to discussions of policy and tactics. He had much to learn from Cinna that he would apply during the last years of his life. Aware of the tides in political developments and sensitive to the general yearning for a surcease in conflict, Cinna did not revive Sulpicius' controversial legislation for extending the franchise though he did promote a token land reform and sponsor a minimal grain subsidy. He ended factional court battling, recessing the courts altogether except for a trial of Pompeius—a warning against the young man's pursuing the opportunism of his father. With Cinna's associate Carbo as defense counsel and Pompeius' engagement to the judge's daughter, the young man won acquittal, and the audience cried "Talassio!"—the marriage greeting.

Cinna favored his entrepreneurial supporters by promoting measures to relieve the financial crisis resulting from the Italian revolt and the loss of provinces in the East to Mithridates. His new colleague, Marius' replacement Valerius Flaccus, proposed a bill to remit seventy-five per cent of all debts in an attempt to mitigate a critical and chronic problem plaguing all ancient and modern societies, and at the request of the ten tribunes the praetors drafted a measure to stabilize the currency. Cinna considered reconciliation with his enemies, however, to be his prime task. Though he did not lift the ban of outlawry against Sulla or restore his confiscated properties, he did permit Sulla's wife and children as well as a number of disgruntled senators to leave Italy. Reassured by Cinna's policies, sons of murdered noblemen, including the younger Catulus and Lucius Caesar, remained at Rome along with Gaius Cotta's younger brothers. Nevertheless, Cinna's foes merely tolerated him as the only man with sufficient authority to restrain the radicals and adventurers among his followers. (Though in his final years he would make a far more intensive effort at reconciliation, Caesar would meet with no more success with his enemies.) By occupying four successive consulships and promoting the careers of his own partisans, many of them "new men" or recently enfranchised Italians, Cinna denied members of the opposing faction an opportunity to advance their careers or, in some cases, even to initiate them.

In addition, Cinna proved incapable of controlling the opportunists in his party. Marius' nephew, the praetor Gratidianus, stealing a march on his fellow praetors, published their collective currency stabilization measure as his own and won instant popularity. But the most dangerous adventurer proved to be Fimbria, Scaevola's would-be assassin at Marius' funeral. Sent to the East as lieutenant to the consul Valerius Flaccus with the army that Marius had assembled to lead against Mithridates, Fimbria provoked a mutiny, murdered Flaccus and seized command. Without an army Cinna was helpless to defend his regime against Sulla, and behind the facade of tranquility during Cinna's years in power there loomed an eventual confrontation with the vindictive warlord who would one day return from the East with victorious legions. Anticipating resistance to new levies among a war-weary populace, Cinna and his new colleague Carbo (who had fled from Rome with Cinna and led one of the armies that recaptured the city) called upon trusted associates for assistance. Caesar's father went north to organize recruitment in Etruria, a Marian stronghold.

Once again in a general crisis Caesar suffered a private tragedy.

A messenger from Pisa reported that one morning while lacing his red patrician sandals, Gaius toppled to the floor, dead. Aurelia extinguished the fire in the hearth and set a funerary cypress bough outside the door. When Gaius' body arrived, she had it washed and embalmed. She placed a coin under Gaius' tongue to pay Charon's fare across the river Styx.

Upon returning from the clan tomb after the funeral ceremonies, Caesar, his mother and his sisters stepped over a fire to prevent Gaius' spirit from following them over the threshold, and to guarantee that Gaius' shade had been expelled Caesar swept out the house.

Gaius had hardly been a Marius.

It was for Caesar to achieve glory in the family.

MASTER OF THE HOUSE

Caesar dedicated to the household lar the purple-bordered toga of childhood and his bulla (the amulet of a freeborn child) and donned a plain white toga woven by Aurelia and the household slaves. In the Forum he was enrolled in the Fabian tribe, and at the Temple of Jupiter he made a sacrifice. Thus initiated into manhood, he was supposedly not only master of the house and the estates but also guardian of his mother, his sisters, the slaves, the freedmen and the clients. A day of good omen could now be selected for Caesar's marriage to Cinna's daughter.

The ancient rite of confarreatio, requisite for a future priest of Jupiter, was celebrated in a temple or other public place with the pontifex maximus officiating along with, on this occasion, a substitute for the priest of Jupiter. The awesome ritual was designed to impress bride, groom and witnesses with the indissolubility of the union. (In the near future, at great risk Caesar was to honor this solemn undertaking.)

On the evening before the wedding Cornelia surrendered her toga praetexta, her bulla and her childhood toys to her household gods. Before dawn she put on a white gown woven according to an ancient prescription and bound with a linen girdle tied in a double knot. She put on a veil, a mantle and shoes of flame color and adorned herself with necklaces and bracelets. Slaves parted her hair with the point of a spear and wove it into six braids pulled so as to cross at the back of her head—the coiffure of the vestals and symbol of her chastity—and she set on her head a wreath of flowers she herself had gathered.

In early morning after augurs took the auspices from flights of birds and the entrails of a lamb, ten witnesses from ten different clans watched the signing of the marriage contract. Caesar and Cornelia exchanged rings and made an offering of fruits and a portion of spelt cake (panis farreus, whence the name confarreatio), reserving a piece of the cake to share between them. After a sacrifice of an ox and an invocation to the god of marriage, the couple and the guests repaired to Cinna's mansion for a wedding banquet in the presence of the masks of the ancestors. A union between a consul's daughter and the son of the loyal Julian and nephew of old Marius represented a major social event at which magistrates, priests and scions of old aristocratic families would be in attendance as well as wealthy equestrians.

In the evening, at the appearance of the first star, Caesar snatched Cornelia out of the arms of her weeping mother and dragged her out of the house (a recollection of the rape of the Sabine women in the days of Romulus). After a procession, enlivened by obscene verses and sly banter of friends, Caesar turned to Cornelia at the door in the Subura and asked her her name. She replied with the formula, "Where thou art Gaius, I am Gaia."

The precise dates of Caesar's assumption of the toga of manhood and of his marriage are not supplied by ancient sources, but whenever they occurred within this general period Caesar and Cornelia began their marriage in a time of grim anxiety.

Sulla had made peace with Mithridates, extorting 2 thousand talents (48 million sesterces) as an indemnity from the king and an additional 20 thousand talents from towns of Asia that had collaborated with the monarch. Furthermore, he had suborned the legions under Fimbria's command and combined them with his own. It was reported that Sulla had assembled sixteen hundred ships to transport his army to Italy.

Cinna journeyed to Ancona on the Adriatic to dispatch newly recruited legions across the sea to head off Sulla in Macedonia or Greece. Storms swamped some transport vessels and drove others back to port. The troops were demoralized and sullen. During a review a soldier stepped out of the ranks and blocked Cinna's path. A lictor struck the man. When another soldier came to his comrade's defense, Cinna ordered arrests. The legionaries broke formation. Some hurled stones, others fell upon Cinna with their swords and slew him.

During the previous half-century, Rome had experienced a spate of assassinations (a symptom of the accelerating collapse of the oligarchic Republic). With the intensifying social and political conflicts, conspiracies and rumors of conspiracies became ever more common. During the siege of Rome by Marius and Cinna, it was said that Cinna had plotted the death of Pompeius Strabo. Young Pompeius had been present at Ancona with Cinna but had stolen away upon learning of some accusation against him. In the camp it was rumored that Cinna had slain the popular young officer. Some said that this rumor led to Cinna's assassination.

In the house in the Subura there was sorrow and dread. Caesar's wife mourned for her father. Caesar and his family had lost the guarantor of their safety.

VIII

PERIPETEIA

A LTHOUGH at the end of the second decade of his life Caesar commanded little influence, nevertheless he was a personality of significance because of his connections, and he was about to demonstrate what would become his characteristic uncompromising defense of his dignity. Following his father-in-law's death a confrontation between Caesar and the mortal foe of old Marius and of Cinna approached inexorably. While other Romans saw the major conflict of the day as between the "parties" of Marius and Sulla, in the house in the Subura the perspective was more limited. For this family not only the fate of Rome was about to be decided, but, more particularly, the fate of young Caesar.

Of a senatorial delegation dispatched to negotiate with him, Sulla demanded the restoration of his dignity and compensation for his confiscated properties and those of his associates. He warned, too, of his intention to wield supreme power in the commonwealth. The headstrong Carbo, in any event, rejected

N.B. Peripeteia—a complete overturning from one extreme to another.

negotiations, and to rally support he revived Sulpicius' legislation for enrolling Italians and freedmen in all the tribes. Thus he sought to transform the conflict from a struggle between ambitious individuals and factions into one between "populars" and conservative oligarchs.

Catulus' son, young Lucius Caesar, the younger Cotta brothers and others of the opposition faction fled from Rome.

The Senate, impotent, passed a resolution calling for the disbanding of all armies throughout the empire, and the men of property elected as consuls for 83 a patrician Scipio and an Italian aristocrat, both disposed to negotiate with Sulla.

Young Marius and young Cinna, Cornelia's brother-in-law Ahenobarbus, the tribune Marcus Brutus and Sertorius, now a praetor, reported for duty. As Marius' nephew, Cinna's son-in-law and son of the loyal Julian, Caesar had an obligation to serve. On the other hand, the forthcoming war represented a continuation of unresolved antagonisms dating to the trial of Rutilius. Victory for either side would bring no solution to the crisis of the oligarchic republic. Throughout his life Caesar avoided committing himself to hopeless causes.

Upon Sulla's landing in Italy, senators raced to join him and fugitives from everywhere in the empire hastened home, eager to share in Sulla's victory. Pompeius recruited a private army of three legions and led his troops over to the rebel general. As always in such moments of partisan fervor, the moderates were ignored. The Pontifex Maximus Scaevola declared that he would accept Sulla's restoration on almost any terms in preference to renewed civil war. Caesar could count on his protection. He could also look to various officers on Sulla's staff to defend him, including Aurelia's cousin Gaius Cotta. As a youth who had not yet held public office, he would hardly be considered a threat to Sulla. Indeed, Marius and Cinna had not proscribed young men of Caesar's age.

Because of the paucity of sources on this period of Caesar's life, all assertions regarding Caesar's attitudes and actions at this time remain speculative. Nevertheless, it must have seemed to Caesar's guardians, whoever were the men charged in Gaius' will with this responsibility, that with their outrage at the suicide of the last priest of Jupiter and their pretensions at defending ancient institutions the Sullans would hesitate to harm a new flamen Dialis. Despite apparently contradictory data, evidence does point to the likelihood of Caesar's installation as the high priest of Jupiter during these years. The pontifex maximus had originally "captured" the candidate for the flaminate; now it was for Scaevola to assemble the thirty lictors who represented the vestige of an ancient royal council. After their routine acceptance of Caesar for the office, the conical hat made of the skin of a newly sacrificed heifer was set on Caesar's head, a wand of olive entwined with wool was placed in his hand and a purple mantle draped over his shoulders. Henceforth he was not to transgress the boundary of the city or to look upon armed men, much less to participate in combat.

Sulla landed in 83, and the civil war continued for almost three years with extensive new devastation following upon that of the recent Italian revolt. The insurgents rarely suffered defeat. Sulla proclaimed his acceptance of full franchise for the Italians and then suborned the army of one consul and routed the army of the other. At Carbo's urging and despite his mother's appeal against vainglorious folly, Marius entered his candidacy for a consulship in 82. Though not eligible for the office by reason of his youth and his failure to have held prerequisite magistracies, he successfully maneuvered his election. On July 6, 83, Jupiter displayed his displeasure, destroying with a lightning bolt the temple on the Capitol. Young Marius rescued from the flames fourteen thousand pounds of gold and six thousand of silver from the temple treasures to serve as a war chest for his forthcoming consulship. Sertorius, the most competent and principled of the loyalist commanders, objected to young Marius' unconstitutional candidacy and considering the struggle hopeless departed from Italy to assume governorship of the two Iberian provinces.

Though acclaimed as the son of Mars and Venus for his valor, Caesar's cousin was routed in a battle near Rome and blockaded within the walls of Praeneste [Palestrina] to the south. Vindictive like his father, young Marius smuggled orders to a praetor in Rome to assassinate oligarchs suspected of negotiating with Sulla. In the Forum the aged pontifex maximus was cut down, and his corpse along with the corpses of Carbo's cousin and Pompeius' father-in-law were dumped into the Tiber.

On November 1, 82, at daybreak a host of seventy thousand Samnite highlanders, loyalist recruits and runaway slaves appeared within sight of the Colline Gate. After some skirmishes Sulla arrived with his legions. It was reported that in exhorting his countrymen, ancient enemies of Rome, the Samnite commander cried: "These wolves that make such ravages upon Italian liberty will never vanish until we cut down the forest that harbors them."[1]

At sundown Sullan troops stampeded through the gate into the city. In the first hour after nightfall, however, the commander of Sulla's right wing, Marcus Crassus, broke the enemy line and routed their army.

At dawn the next morning, Sulla assembled the Senate in the Temple of Bellona on the Campus Martius. As he addressed the senators, proclaiming the inauguration of a new era for the commonwealth, a terrifying sound, an eerie howling, was carried into the temple from the nearby Villa Publica, a huge enclosure where censors conducted the quinquennial census. "Let us attend to business, gentlemen of the Senate," declared Sulla. "Only a few seditious persons are being killed at my orders."[2]

Sulla announced the annulment of all acts since his own consulship.

By this decree Caesar was deprived of his flaminate.

The howling had come from the slaughter of six thousand prisoners captured the previous night.

THE FINAL SOLUTION

Sulla determined to end the cycle of proscriptions inaugurated after his first march on Rome and followed by those conducted by Marius and Cinna upon their capture of the city. His solution was to exterminate his enemies. He began by beheading the enemy commanders captured after the battle of the Colline Gate, including two praetors. Thereafter step-by-step the killings approached the house in the Subura. Unable to wreak vengeance directly on his inveterate foe, Sulla ordered Marius' tomb broken open and his bones scattered into the River Anio and his memorials and trophies overturned. Marius was to cease to exist as a figure of Roman history. The murder of Marius' nephew, the praetor Gratidianus, handed over to Catulus for retribution for the death of Catulus' father, exemplified the Sullan resolve to terrorize opponents. With the assistance of Gratidianus' brother-in-law, a former supporter of Marius named Catilina, who also betrayed his own brother and his sister's husband (or so his enemies would later charge), Catulus flogged Gratidianus through the streets to the Catulus family tomb. Here the two noblemen ordered Gratidianus' arms and legs smashed with rods, his ears cut off, his tongue wrenched from his mouth and his eyes gouged out. Finally, while he was still breathing, they had him beheaded and offered up his corpse as a sacrifice to the shade of the elder Catulus. It was reported that an officer who fainted at the horrors was slain under suspicion of disloyalty. Catilina conveyed Gratidianus' head to Praeneste, where he posted it on a spear along with the heads of officers captured at the battle of the Colline Gate as notice to young Marius of the hopelessness of continued resistance.

Sulla announced a bounty on the heads of his enemies, listing at first eighty senators and sixteen hundred equestrians. Though he singled out particularly the "sacularii" (moneybags—those who had profiteered on properties confiscated by Marius and Cinna), he aimed at destroying the entrepreneurs of the equestrian order as a political force. An indiscriminate slaughter began with thugs and newly manumitted slaves enriching themselves as informers and killers. Debtors freed themselves by hiring assassins to stalk and denounce creditors. In the gutters headless corpses were left to rot, and the heads of the murdered were heaped about the Rostra and at a fountain at a corner of the Forum. No one dared to remonstrate or to mourn. To beg mercy for others meant risking one's own safety. Wives denounced husbands; children, parents. Everyone feared the slaves.

Caesar and his family had lived through three years of anticipation of horrors since Cinna's assassination. Because of young Marius' illegal assumption of a consulship, they were all the more endangered. With the mass killing and the general savagery, what hope could they place in an appeal for mercy?

After killing a Samnite comrade in a suicide pact, young Marius ordered a slave to run him through. Renegades from the Marian party whom Sulla entrusted with the siege of Praeneste offered amnesty in return for surrender.

When the citizens emerged through the gates and prostrated themselves in supplication, however, Sulla ordered the execution of all the men of the town and of their Samnite allies to the number of twelve thousand. Upon being presented with young Marius' head, he scoffed, "First learn to row before you try to steer."[3]

In Sicily Pompeius captured Carbo. When Carbo, thrice a consul, knelt in his chains and begged to be allowed to empty his bowels, Pompeius called for the ax, and Carbo's head joined Marius' on the Rostra.

With the death of the two consuls, the Senate hailed Sulla as Felix (the Fortunate). In a display of magnanimity he announced that to protect the innocent he would henceforth post lists of those marked for death. The lists merely inspired new terror. Those suspected of Marian sympathies dared not examine the white tablets for fear of being accused of a bad conscience; those who ignored the tablets were charged with lack of enthusiasm for Sulla's cleansing of the body politic. Men were put to the sword in the street, unaware that their names had been posted. Others perusing the lists discovered their names and did not escape alive from the Forum. "Ah, woe is me!" cried one such unfortunate, "My Alban estate is prosecuting me!"[4]

On the other hand, Sulla's associates, too, were awakened by screams in the night and by the pounding on doors of neighboring dwellings. They, too, lost relatives and connections and suffered a sense of helplessness when people groveled in their path and tugged at their togas and wept for permission to bury sons and husbands. In the theater they, too, shuddered at a line in a new tragedy by Accius: "Let them hate if only they fear." Catulus, his wrath at his father's death appeased, cried: "If we kill armed men in time of war and unarmed men in time of peace, with whose help shall we finally conquer?" A Metellan appealed to Sulla, saying, "We do not ask you to free from punishment those you have determined to execute but to free from suspense those you have determined to save."[5]

Sulla set June 1, 81, six months to the day after the victory of the Colline Gate, for the termination of the proscriptions.

Only for another few weeks would the family in the Subura dread the posting of Caesar's name on the white tablets.

Nineteen is an age for heroics, when a youth confronts questions of identity, of values and of ideals and proclaims what he stands for and what he stands against. Could Caesar take pride in being ignored, in remaining alive? In the dreadful time of nearly universal opportunism and betrayal, would not people assume that the nephew, son-in-law and cousin of Sulla's paramount foes had made his submission like many other Marians? Indoctrinated in the ancestral virtues, posed with examples of the two Mariuses and with a responsibility to a clan descended from a goddess and bearing the dignity of serving as the earthly incorporation of Rome's patron deity until his recent illegal deposition—could Caesar opt for pusillanimous security while relatives and connections fought or fled into hiding?

What of the classics of literature that Caesar had studied as "incentives to
noble actions" and as "pictures of high endeavor"? What of the ideals of the
Greco-Roman heritage by which a civilized man was to steer his life?—as in
Prometheus' defiance of the king of the gods:

> Let it not cross your mind that I will turn
> womanish-minded from my fixed decision
> or that I shall entreat the one I hate so greatly,
> with a woman's upturned hands,
> to loose me from my chains: I am far from that.[6]

Sulla summoned Caesar.

Now all that had shaped him, all that made him Caesar was to be tested.
Arguments for prudence would not avail—admonitions regarding the fool-
hardiness of principle in a time of corruption, the vanity of young Marius'
bravado, Caesar's responsibility as an only son . . . Of no meaning were
warnings of the impotence of a nineteen-year-old in confrontation with an
autocrat just voted a gilded equestrian statue in the Forum (an honor never
before accorded a living Roman) and annual games in commemoration of the
victory at the Colline Gate and proclaimed dictator with an indefinite tenure
("until the Republic was reconstituted"). In his triumphal procession, men of
the most distinguished clans, including Julians and Aurelians, marched behind his chariot with their wives and children, acclaiming Sulla as their savior
and father. Besides the gold and silver captured from young Marius he displayed fifteen thousands pounds of silver and gold, booty from the East. All
wealth confiscated from his enemies as well as all war booty Sulla claimed as
his private property. Protected by a fraternity of ten thousand manumitted
slaves and by tens of thousands of veterans, he was invincible.

Caesar was brought to bed. Physicians diagnosed his illness as a quartan
ague, according to Hippocrates "the least fatal and least difficult [ague] of all,
but the longest of all."[7]

Sulla gazed with contempt at Caesar's loosely girt tunic, a youthful affectation
scorned as effeminate by the older generation. Caesar saw that at close view
Sulla scarcely resembled the pictures and busts at crossroads in the city. His face
had lost its military rigor—the cheeks sagged, lines radiated from the corners of
his eyes, the neck was sinewed like an olive trunk, and the once delicate complexion was blotched with mulberry patches. The aureole of blond hair, once his
vanity, was thin and wispy. "After all it was not a god who threatened Greece,"
Herodotus had written of the Great King of Persia, "but a man, and there neither
was nor ever would be a man who was not born with a good chance of misfortune—and the greater the man, the greater the misfortune."[8]

Caesar had been prepared for Sulla's demand: a demonstration of loyalty.
He was to divorce Cinna's daughter. At the dictator's command Marcus Piso
had divorced Cornelia's mother, Cinna's widow; Pompeius had divorced his
wife in order to marry Sulla's stepdaughter (whom Sulla had divorced from

her husband though pregnant with his child); and Marcus Lepidus had divorced the daughter of the radical tribune Saturninus, the mother of his grown children.

"Freedom is having a pure and dauntless heart," wrote the poet Ennius, "all else is slavery."[9] Odysseus had undergone twenty years of vicissitudes in order to return to his life's companion. No matter what others had done, saying yes to Sulla meant saying no to himself.

"Sulla, when the blood mantled his cheeks, was in his fiercest mood."[10] He reddened as he dictated to a scribe an order depriving Caesar of Cornelia's dowry and of his inheritance if the youth continued to resist his demand.

During succeeding generations memory of the Sullan Terror persisted as a nightmare much as the Great Depression in the United States, the far more dreadful nazi occupation of Europe and the unspeakable Holocaust. Anecdotes were invented or inflated about actions of leading personalities during those traumatic times. One such account held that Caesar dispatched slaves to summon the crowd milling in the Forum. He had much to say—of his "capture" by the late pontifex maximus and subsequent ordination as flamen Dialis. No dictator could annul the acts of a pontifex maximus ratified by augurs and the thirty lictors. No mortal could dissolve a marriage consecrated by confarreatio.

Aurelia ordered slaves to pack Caesar's clothes and to assemble provisions and remedies for his ague. She emptied the money chest and instructed Cornelia to dress Caesar in high boots, a paenula of shaggy wool with pointed hood and a heavy scarf. With a freedman summoned to accompany her son, Aurelia reviewed directions to farms and villas in the Sabine country, the homeland of the Aurelians. Gaius had had connections there, and Sertorius' mother lived in Nursia (Nocera Umbria).

Sulla's guards burst into the house. Ignoring Aurelia's remonstrances they searched for Caesar.

Aurelia sent for Gaius Cotta. She demanded that he save her boy.

IX

THE OAK WREATH

AFTER scurrying from one mountain hideout to another, the protégé of Marius, son-in-law of Cinna, relative to two recent consuls, priest of Jupiter—the hunted prey—was captured. The money Aurelia had entrusted to Caesar was for such a contingency, and with a bribe of two talents (48 thousand sesterces), the bounty for a proscribed man, he bought his freedom. Meanwhile, Gaius Cotta along with the brother of the murdered tribune Drusus induced the vestal virgins to join them in an appeal to Sulla. Cotta commanded prestige as one of the last survivors of the circle of Crassus the Orator, as nephew and defender of the exiled Rutilius and as an early victim of the strife between the Marians and Sulla's party. Drusus' brother had just been acclaimed for capturing an Italian stronghold by climbing the wall at night to open the gates to his troops. Sulla could not refuse to hear the plea of the vestals, the guardians of the sacred hearth of the city and its intercessors with the gods. It was said that he mumbled something about Caesar's being a slovenly, ill-girt fellow; then, recalling Caesar's connection to his own inveterate foe, he exclaimed: "Have your way and take him. Only bear in mind that the man you are so eager to save will one day deal the death blow to the aristocracy, which you have joined me in upholding; for in this Caesar there is more than one Marius."[1]

Sulla had murdered thousands. Although he deprived Caesar of Cornelia's dowry and a portion of Caesar's own inheritance, he did pardon Caesar. Still the humiliation Caesar had endured after years of brilliant promise generated in him a titanic rancor that would serve as a relentless goad, a rancor that prodded him to seek "power and dominion . . . all of his life."[2]* At this juncture the wait for the day of vengeance promised to be long delayed. The Marians appeared vanquished. With a small band Sertorius was driven out of Spain into Africa. From Africa Pompeius sent back the head of Cornelia's brother-in-law, Ahenobarbus, commander of the last Marian army. Italy lay prostrate from confiscations, expulsions and massacres. Sulla had declared that he would not rest "until either he had destroyed all Samnites of importance [the most stubborn of the Italian rebels] or banished them from Italy."[3] At Rome he played Marian deserters against his original associates, freeborn citizens against freedmen, veterans against civilians and Romans of old stock against newly enfranchised Italians. He rendered the Senate subservient by appointing as senators men of certain loyalty, including noncoms of his legions.

Under this repressive regime Caesar was reduced to the status of a "new man," suffering not from an ancestry without senators but from connections with men proclaimed as traitors and outlaws. His presence at Rome was merely tolerated, and it was Caesar's good fortune that an associate of Gaius Cotta's, the new governor of the province of Asia, accepted him on his staff. In

---

*In his biography of Luther, Erik Erikson declares: "I could not conceive of a young great man in the years before he becomes a great young man without assuming that inwardly he harbors a quite inarticulate stubbornness, a secret furious inviolacy, a gathering of impressions for eventual use within some as yet dormant new configuration of thought—that he is tenaciously waiting it out for a day of vengeance when the semi-deliberate straggler will suddenly be found at the helm, and he who took so much will reveal the whole extent of his potential mastery"—*Young Man Luther* (New York, 1958), p. 83. (Despite the gaps in documentation for Caesar's life, the evidence bears out the Erikson theory of an "articulate stubbornness . . . a furious inviolacy [leading to] a new configuration of thought" and a "waiting it out for a day of vengeance.")

Asia Caesar would be far from the dictator. He would establish contacts with his father's and Marius' clients, renew acquaintanceship with old Rutilius, gain military experience and perhaps even win glory and booty.

TELEMAKHOS' JOURNEY

Even as ten years earlier with Caesar's father, the household, relatives and connections now accompanied Caesar to the first milestone on the Appian Way to send him off to distant Asia. In following the traces of his father and undergoing his first test of manhood, Caesar was like Odysseus' son, and for Caesar, too, Athena's advice to the departing Telemakhos seemed appropriate:

> You need not bear this insolence of theirs,
> you are a child no longer. Have you heard
> what glory young Orestes won
> when he cut down that two-faced man, Aigisthos,
> for killing his illustrious father?
> Dear friend, you are tall and well set up, I see;
> be brave—you, too—and men in times to come
> will speak of you respectfully.

But if Caesar resembled Telemakhos, Gaius was hardly an Odysseus. The modern Odysseus was Marius, and Athena's further counsel pointed less to Caesar's father than to his uncle:

> The son is rare who measures with his father,
> and one in a thousand is a better man,
> but you will have the sap and wit
> and prudence—for you get that from Odysseus—
> to give you a fair chance of winning through.

For Caesar, however, this journey signified more than a search for a father or a testing of manhood. It represented a cultural pilgrimage. A Roman aristocrat's education was primarily Greek, and Romans admitted that it was through the arts, sciences and philosophy of the Greeks that they had been "rescued from barbarism."[4] In this, very likely his initial trip abroad, Caesar would visit places associated with Alexander and with famous poets, artists and architects as well as with philosophers who had first challenged the belief in a divine creation of the universe. In Asia modern medicine had evolved, history had been first composed and profound theories of mathematics and astronomy formulated. Here the Bard had been born, and here was the town whose capture he sang, the ancestral home of Caesar's line and of Rome itself.

Ephesus was the immediate destination, the chief town and administrative center of the province and birthplace of Heraclitus, who preached that all things were in flux, a theory Caesar could readily accept in light of his own experience. Impressive to any young Roman on his first overseas journey were the majestic public buildings in Ephesus, the attractive fountain house, the bath complex, the gymnasium with facilities for various sports, the theater built on a hillside (Rome possessed no theater) and, above all, the Temple of Artemis, one of the Seven Wonders of the world. Tourists gawked at the massive edifice, three hundred feet long and one hundred and fifty wide, encircled by one hundred and twenty-seven columns sixty feet in height.

At the time of Caesar's visit, Ephesus, ordinarily a busy center of manufacturing, like the rest of the province was in turmoil, and Caesar saw Roman imperialism at its most oppressive. Mithridates had unleashed the fury of the provincials, encouraging a massacre of the Italians and their collaborators. He had freed slaves, confiscated property, redistributed lands and cancelled debts. Sulla had returned the slaves to their masters, restored property to loyal provincials and imposed an enormous indemnity on communities that had collaborated with the enemy. He punished some towns by razing their walls and leaving them defenseless against pirates and other marauders. In others he stationed garrisons and required the citizens to provide billets, meals and clothing and even the wages of the occupation troops. The towns "mortgaged their theaters, their gymnasiums, their walls, their harbors and every other scrap of public property, being urged on by the soldiers with contumely."[5]

Aurelia, Cornelia and Aunt Julia were eager to learn of Caesar's career, and he had much to report. Marcus Thermus, the proconsul, entrusted him with a mission to King Nicomedes of Bithynia to obtain ships for an assault against Mitylene, a town on the coastal island of Lesbos, which had refused to subscribe to Sulla's armistice with Mithridates. On his way to Nicomedes' capital, across the Bosphorus from Byzantium, Caesar passed through Smyrna, where Gaius Cotta's uncle, Rutilius, remained in exile. The old man had left Rome during the governorship of Caesar's father, and like old Nestor relating Odysseus' exploits to Telemakhos he could tell Caesar of Gaius' able administration. He himself was writing memoirs in which he would castigate Marius and justify his own career. His town, Smyrna, exemplified the best urban planning of the Age of Aristotle and Alexander, and its main thoroughfare, more spacious than any at Rome, was roofed against sun and rain.

But Ephesus and Smyrna were not the only impressive cities in Asia. Proceeding northward Caesar came to Pergamum, a former royal capital, a city artistically disposed on a hill with rows of porticos linking successive terraces. A huge theater was carved into a steep natural recess. At the summit stood monumental structures far handsomer than those of the Forum—marble temples, a vast royal palace and a library with two hundred thousand volumes, second only to the library at Alexandria. (Rome possessed no library.) An altar to Zeus, one of the most impressive monuments of Hellenistic civilization, was adorned with a grandiose stairway and with a podium and colonnade extending some one hundred and twenty feet in breadth and one hundred and twelve in depth and to a height of almost twenty feet. The outer wall of the podium bore a frieze of the battle of the gods and the giants sculpted with the intense passion of Euripidean tragedy.

At Rome Bithynian kings were bywords for oriental luxury. They were pictured reclining in litters on cushions of transparent Maltese embroidery and pressing to their nostrils a fine-meshed bag with rose petals. Years earlier, however, King Nicomedes had stood on the Graecostasis, the platform for foreign dignitaries awaiting a summons by the Senate, dressed in rags as a suppliant and with the liberty cap of a manumitted slave on a shaved head. Now with Roman loans and extortions from his subjects he had revived the splendor of his court, playing host to poets, artists and musicians. Caesar so enjoyed his entertainment that he found a pretext for a second visit. Nicomedes surrounded himself with effeminate minions, and Caesar was to be embarrassed all his life by a charge of an illicit relationship with the monarch.

With couriers from Rome requiring months to reach Asia, Aurelia could hardly keep Caesar abreast of developments in the city. In any event, she could offer little hope of imminent improvement in Caesar's fortunes. Straitlaced aristocrats who had yearned for a revival of the old-fashioned morality that Cato the Censor had propounded a century earlier discovered that their champion, Sulla, spoke much of the past but lived entirely in the present. "He consorted with actresses, harpists and theatrical people, drinking with them on couches all day long" and bestowed on "handsome women, musicians, common actors and the lowest of freedmen the territories of nations and the revenues of cities." Particularly obnoxious among Sulla's favorites was a freedman of Egyptian origin with the appropriate name of Chrysogonus, "the Golden Born," who "paraded through the Forum with hair carefully arranged and reeking with perfume" accompanied by a crowd of sycophants and displaying contempt for everyone he met.[6] He had seized a mansion on the Palatine and was vying in luxurious display with the great noblemen.

While his wife lay dying of some strange malady, Sulla regaled the commons with a feast in honor of Hercules, slaughtering such a host of animals that rotting carcasses had to be dumped into the Tiber. At an order from the pontifices, he removed the ailing Metella from his house as a pollution and sent her a notice of divorce—an action certain to rouse antagonism in her branch of the powerful Metellan clan.

Caesar, meanwhile, was advancing his career. Thermus ordered him to Mitylene. The commander of the siege of the town, Lucullus, the son of a Metella and first cousin to Metellus Pius (currently Sulla's colleague in the consulship), had been the only officer not to defect during Sulla's first march on Rome. The author of a history of the Italian war composed in Greek verse, Lucullus passed his leisure hours with a philosopher. History would remember him, however, as the voluptuary who gave his name to a "Lucullan feast," and we can speculate that Caesar owed something of his own refined tastes to an association with this master of savior-vivre. In his military operations Lucullus was confronting problems. His legionaries had served overseas for some five years, paid irregularly and often forced to forage for food. They traveled with a horde of slaves, prostitutes and dealers in booty and provisions. While Sulla shrugged at disorder and connived at his soldiers' plunder and Pompeius wept and cajoled his men, the tall, imperious Lucullus "was . . . strict in his demands for work and inexorable in his punishments; he did not understand how to win over a man by persuasion or to attach him by mildness or to make a friend of him by conferring honors or bestowing wealth."[7]

Old Marius had maintained discipline by personal example and promoted an esprit de corps within his units, and it was no wonder that Sulla and his associates were alarmed at news that Sertorius, once an officer under Marius, had crossed into Spain from his refuge in Africa. He was responding to an invitation to lead a rebellion of Lusitanians, fierce tribesmen who in the previous century had often routed Roman legions in seven bloody wars.

Absent from Rome for seven years and dependent for advancement upon an aging dictator, Lucullus was eager to resume his political career. He required a quick victory, and Mitylene was disposed on a narrow peninsula and fortified by impregnable walls. It would have befitted Lucullus' style to challenge his philosopher companion and his staff officers as to the tactic Homer would have advised for a speedy reduction of the town. In any event, one morning at daybreak he embarked his forces, abandoning not a wooden horse but siege-works stocked with provisions. Like Homer's Agamemnon he sailed to a nearby cove and waited only long enough for the famished townspeople to stream out the gates to plunder the camp. Raising anchor, he pounced on the scavengers, killing five hundred and compelling the rest to surrender.

If Lucullus' entourage hailed him as a latter-day Odysseus for his cunning, he in turn could acclaim Caesar as a new Pyrrhus, Akhilleus' son, who had hidden in the Trojan horse and then proved his valor in Troy's overthrow. To the cheers of the legionaries, the governor Thermus as commander-in-chief set the corona civica, a wreath of oak leaves, on Caesar's head, an award instituted by Romulus for killing an enemy to save the life of a citizen. Caesar had fulfilled his duty to his ancestors, vindicated Aurelia's hopes and proved himself a worthy protégé of Old Marius. In addition, he had regained his self-respect and initiated that pattern of valor which in the future would evoke the admiration of legionaries and the wonderment of all Romans.

Before returning home Caesar experienced new Sullan outrages. En route to Cilicia, a province to the south of Asia, the aide to the new governor, a certain Verres, was engaging in systematic plunder. During the civil war, this scoundrel deserted to Sulla with a paymaster's chest and then profiteered scandalously in the proscriptions. Now at every stop he scrambled after statues, paintings, gold and silver. In Athens he seized treasures from the Parthenon. At Delos, the island birthplace of Apollo, he would have escaped with sacred objects from the sanctuary if the god had not frightened Verres' superior, the governor, by rousing a storm. (Upon returning a year later on the staff of the succeeding governor of Cilicia, Caesar would discover how thoroughly these two plunderers would fleece the province.)

During the long journey home Caesar could reflect on his year in the East. It had been one thing to listen to senators and equestrians talk about tax-gathering, investments and problems of overseas administration. It had been quite another experience to view Roman imperialism directly and at its most venal. Romans who orated in the Forum about Rome's mission to bring peace and justice to the world—these very men in the provinces plundered like pirates. They imposed tribute, lent money at high rates of interest to assure payment of the tribute and dispatched troops to collect the extortions. Usurers confiscated property and goods and goaded debtors into selling themselves or their children into slavery. Profiteers by the thousands from Italy amassed princely fortunes in treasure, tracts of land, herds of cattle and sheep, mines and workshops and wrested control of the commerce and industry of towns and of entire regions.

Because of such extortion and oppression, Mithridates had been welcomed as a liberator by the provincials. In remitting debts, dividing up the land and punishing exploiters, he had carried out, in effect, a "popular" program in Asia.

With the vindictiveness he was subsequently to display in Italy, Sulla had restored the old regime in the province.

The Asians and the victims in Italy suffered alike from the dictator. Caesar would not forget this illumination of his young manhood.

X

THE OUTSIDER

LIKE Homer's Telemakhos, Caesar departed a youth and returned a man. In his report to the Senate Thermus singled out the twenty-year-old for commendation and described the circumstances under which he had won the corona civica. Like Marius and Sertorius before him, Caesar could expect applause upon entering the theater. He could also take his place among seats reserved for senators, as he had done years earlier while priest of Jupiter. On the other hand, he could hardly command at Rome the instant respect he had enjoyed in Asia as a Roman aristocrat and especially as the son of a former governor. In addition, he looked at the city with new eyes, contrasting it with the orderly towns of Asia with their libraries, theaters, lecture halls, schools and athletic complexes. With thought only for quick profit, Roman oligarchs had been indifferent to the anarchic disorder of their capital. The Forum boasted not a single marble construction, and through the city the gods were begrudged dwarfish temples of sun-baked brick that were crumbling with neglect. Mansions huddled among grimy taverns and teeming hovels. After his impelling experience in the East Caesar caught an inkling of how, in exploiting conquered peoples and maltreating the enslaved, the sturdy and puritanical farmer-warriors had degenerated into avaricious buccaneers appropriating from all over the Mediterranean food, luxuries, amusements, gods and works of art as well as the services of scholars, priests, philosophers, architects, artists and artisans, soldiers and physicians. Brutalized by constant wars of aggression and by daily oppression of slaves and freedmen, the Romans took delight in bloodthirsty entertainments. Above all, masters of propaganda, they beguiled not only themselves but even those they enslaved into believing that they represented the defenders of liberty, justice and peace for all mankind.

In the physical appearance of the city, however, Caesar saw the beginnings of a transformation, for like some oriental potentate the dictator sought immortality through memorials to his greatness. In the Forum gangs of workmen were paving over areas of squalid trampled earth. Others were constructing a new Rostra and enlarging the Senate house into an edifice appropriate to the Senate's restored authority. The monument in which the dictator sought particularly to enshrine his fame was a new and magnificent Temple of Jupiter to replace the one destroyed by fire during the civil war. Furthermore, the fleetloads of plunder Sulla had disgorged upon Italy were impelling a general explosion of conspicuous consumption. Appius Claudius was setting shields with images of his forbears on the Temple of Bellona (erected by his ancestor Appius the Blind, builder of the Appian Way); and Marcus Aemilius Lepidus was restoring a basilica built by one of his ancestors and adorning the columns with shields bearing portraits of famous Aemilians. From Africa he imported blocks of Numidian marble, yellow with red veins, for the doorsills of his mansion. Not to be outdone, Lucullus ordered black marble from the island of Chios for his residence. But the most impressive edifice, a monument to the restored dignity of the landed aristocracy, the Tabularium (begun by Sulla and finished by Catulus), a public archives of mammoth proportions. To the left of the Temple of Concord and rising into the saddle of the Capitoline hill, it afforded a striking vista from down the Sacred Way and brought a sense of order to the jumbled Forum. Masons were mixing broken stone in a mortar of lime and sand, employing a technique for rapid construction unknown in the East, and huge cranes with compound pulleys powered by a treadmill hoisted massive rectangular blocks for an arcaded passage flanked by a row of rooms on the ground floor. Above a pediment almost two hundred and fifty feet long, these arcades were decorated with Doric half columns with capitals and architraves and metopes and triglyphs—all of imperial grandeur.

Sulla had transported to Italy vast quantities of paintings, statues, furniture and other treasures. (Among his chief prizes were the works of Aristotle seized in Athens, many previously unknown at Rome). Following his example, his associates were snatching up antiques, and agents were scouring the Greek world for statues, paintings, vases, gems, tables and tapestries. A horde of artists and craftsmen, captives or free immigrants, were transforming Rome into the art as well as the political and financial capital of the Mediterranean. The wealthy vied in expending fortunes for custom-made furnishings, including sideboards ornamented with tortoise shell. With murals of parks, flowered paths and porticos executed with a mastery of perspective behind trompe l'oeil columns or pilasters, painters produced an illusion of oriental luxury in mansions and villas. Everyone, it seemed, was having his portrait done. The fashionable painter Sopolis hired a small army of assistants to meet the demand, and Iaia, an emigrant some years earlier from Asia Minor, had a waiting list of rich matrons (who would not, of course, sit for a man).

A bystander to the frenzied extravagance, Caesar was also an outsider in politics. During the years of the Cinnan regime oligarchs of the opposing faction had been excluded from office. Some had not even been able to commence their careers. They were determined to recoup the lost time. Sulla had drawn up lists of candidates for years to come, favoring clansmen, other connections and his former lieutenants. They would not permit an outsider like Caesar to usurp their place.

MAGNUS!

Yet Pompeius offered hope. Returning to Italy with his legions in defiance of Sulla's orders, the young warlord demanded a triumph, an honor never granted anyone below praetorian rank (Pompeius was not yet of age even for a lowly quaestorship) and an honor certainly never granted for a victory over fellow-citizens. Backed by the consuls-elect and other leading nobles, Sulla rejected the request. When Pompeius warned, however, that "more worship the rising than the setting sun," the dictator yielded.[1] As the young warlord, riding at the head of his legions, came into view of the crowd awaiting him outside the city, he was welcomed with cheers. He appeared radiant, conscious of his athletic carriage, of his noble, frank, if squarish, face with its powerful chin and of the shaggy lock that pushed forward on his forehead (a boyish feature irresistible to women). (Unfortunately, upon closer view, beneath the high, empty forehead the features appeared disproportionately small—the tiny eyes, the potato nose, the ill-defined, wilful mouth.) To universal astonishment, Sulla rose, doffed his hat and hailed the young man as Imperator (the title of a prospective triumpher) and as Magnus (the Great). Fancying himself in youth and prowess a second Alexander and exaggerating the general trend toward self-aggrandizement in place of civic responsibility, Pompeius like Sulla (Felix) had chosen a cognomen of self-glorification instead of one commemorating either a victory over a foreign foe after the example of Scipio Africanus or a strategy that preserved the state as with Fabius Cunctator (the Delayer).

But the new Alexander hardly commanded unquestioning loyalty from his troops. At the announcement that he was donating a share of his booty to the public treasury, the legionaries rioted. In petulant fury, Pompeius hurled his laurel-wreathed fasces at the troops, crying that they should begin their plundering with the symbols of victory. After reaching a settlement with the mutineers, he suffered a further humiliation: the city gate proved too narrow to admit the elephants drawing his gilded chariot. While the Great Man champed and the crowd tittered, harried attendants replaced the huge beasts with the traditional white horses. Even with such embarrassments no one could deny Pompeius' glory, rarely, if ever, equalled in Roman history. Caesar certainly could not hope to emulate the success of this warlord only six years his senior. He not only commanded no private army of his own, but he was also incapable of Pompeius' opportunism. Throughout his life no enemy ever accused Caesar of betrayal of friendship; no admirer ever praised Pompeius for loyalty.

It was advantageous, however, for Caesar to seek an association with the new Alexander, with whom he enjoyed a connection through the marriage of his younger sister to Pompeius' first cousin. Powerful noblemen had reached a similar decision. The consuls-elect, Appius Claudius and Servilius Vatia, had denounced Pompeius for his presumption in demanding a triumph, but after his braving of the dictator they sought a reconciliation and even counseled him in his dispute with his mutinous legionaries. These proud noblemen were connected through ties of blood and marriage with a branch of the Metellans, the most powerful of the aristocratic clans. Since Sulla's divorce of Metella and her subsequent death, they felt no more personal loyalty to the dictator than Pompeius after the recent death of his wife, Sulla's stepdaughter. More important, however, was their resentment at the autocratic power of a man of undistinguished family, at the indeterminate tenure of his dictatorship (traditionally limited to six months) and at his packing the Senate, that Council of Princes, with men of low birth. They resolved to give Sulla a warning. Too prudent to drive him to retaliate in defense of his dignity or to endanger the new order for which he and they had fought, they decided to attack him obliquely, through one of his minions. They found their opportunity upon the mysterious murder of a country squire, a certain Roscius. Two of the squire's relatives had persuaded Sulla's favorite, the flamboyant freedman Chrysogonus, to insert the murdered man's name retroactively in the list of the proscribed, and subsequently at the auction of the "proscribed" man's property Chrysogonus purchased for a mere two thousand sesterces ten farms valued at six million, while three other estates fell to the share of the two relatives. To protect themselves the three conspirators indicated Roscius' son for the murder. The plot was outrageous. The proscription lists had long been closed, and Roscius, in any case, had been a Sullan partisan.

Young Roscius fled for sanctuary to the home of one of Rome's most venerated matrons, the Metella who at the outset of the Italian war proclaimed her dream of Juno's displeasure and persuaded the Senate to appease the goddess. She called upon her nephew, Metellus Nepos, to arrange for Roscius' defense.

Nepos was a nephew also of the wife of Appius Claudius and a cousin to the other consul-elect, Servilius.

The great nobles associated in this maneuver were loath to expose themselves in the court proceedings, and one of their number offered the post of chief defense counsel to Marcus Cicero.

Caesar was acquainted with Cicero, who like Pompeius was six years his senior. As a fellow townsman and distant relative to Marius and schoolmate of young Marius', Cicero had gained entrance to the circle of Crassus the Orator and the Scaevolae. Though hardly impelled like Caesar by a profound rancor, he had a desperate yearning as a "new man" for acceptance among the nobility. Neither a patrician, a nephew to Marius nor a son-in-law to Cinna and never a priest of Jupiter, Cicero had not watched relatives parade in the priestly colleges on festival days or celebrated electoral victories of his immediate family. In his childhood, family talk of imperial politics rarely involved close connections. On the other hand, about to enter his candidacy for the first office in the progress of magistracies, Cicero confronted more immediate career pressures than Caesar. Although, unlike Caesar, he labored under no damaging personal associations, he could hardly expect favors from the dictator. During the previous turbulent decade he had lived in what he called "harmony with the real state of affairs," and in a handbook on rhetoric published during the Cinna years he offered a rationale for his political neutrality, asserting that

> it is often necessary to weigh [honor against security] . . . so that although honor is superior to security, it may be a question which it is preferable to follow. . . . One should take thought for security in a case in which though honor is lost for the moment while consulting security, it may be recovered in the future by courage and diligence. . . . In such circumstances it will be proper to yield to another or to meet another's terms or to keep quiet for the present and await another opportunity, provided only that some attention is paid to the question whether this cause which conduces to our advantage is worth a loss in glory and honor.[2]

Often criticized for vacillation, Cicero would rarely be censured for inconsistency in regard to this youthful statement of principles. On the present occasion, both security and honor counseled association with the oligarchic clique engaged in prudent opposition to the dictator. Some months earlier during a court case Cicero had called attention to himself by decrying the violence of the recent proscriptions. "No honorable man," he said, "even if he is within his rights, wants to put a citizen to death; he would prefer that it should be remembered that he spared when he could have destroyed than that he destroyed when he could have spared."[3] (Sixteen years later, as consul, aping Sulla, Cicero would forget this sentiment; and thirty-five years later he would recall his rebuke to Sulla in expressing admiration for Caesar's clemency to enemies.)

Slender, of delicate constitution, he projected his voice in a tense monotone and suffered fatigue quickly. From the long, thin neck emerged tones ranging from the humility appropriate to the son of an undistinguished equestrian to the righteous indignation of the spokesman for powerful oligarchs. Cicero's patrons desired no censuring of Sullan policies. They forbade comments on proscriptions and confiscations, and they sought Roscius' acquittal on the murder charge but not a return of his property. They posed no restrictions, however, on his assault on the Egyptian freedman, and Cicero denounced Chrysogonus and his ilk as scoundrels "commanding dangerous and intolerable power" and announced that the oligarchs would no longer endure the insolence of such men. Following instructions, Cicero did not directly attack Sulla. The dictator's "eminent virtues," he asserted, "at all times have exonerated him of blame for the corruption and cruelty in the commonwealth." Nevertheless, in a significant variation on the standard apology for all dictators, he spoke of crimes "of which Sulla *partly* disapproved and *partly* was ignorant, owing to the magnitude of his undertakings." (Sophisticates like Caesar would note the implication in the repeated word.) The focus of Cicero's oration was on the dictatorship. Indeed, it was inconceivable that a scion of the Claudians, notorious for their haughtiness, or an old-fashioned nobleman like Servilius Vatia should accept orders from a dictator during their consulship. Through Cicero they proclaimed that "while it was necessary and the state of affairs demanded, one man alone possessed all power; but after he created magistrates and established laws, everyone's sphere of duty and authority was restored to him."[4] The source of the confidence with which these men were challenging Sulla was exposed subtly, through an otherwise inexplicable digression—a comparison between the murder of the insignificant country squire Roscius and the assassination at young Marius' orders of the distinguished nobleman and pontifex maximus, Scaevola. Those keyed like Caesar to courtroom innuendo recalled that Metellus Nepos, the assistant defense counsel, was Scaevola's stepson and half-brother to Scaevola's daughter, Mucia.

Mucia had just been betrothed to Pompeius.

By his aside Cicero was advising the audience and the dictator that a clique of Metellans and sons and husbands of Metellans had rallied with Pompeius in a cabal against the dictator.

THE EVANESCENCE OF POWER

One day at gladiatorial games a radiant young beauty paused and plucked a bit of nap from Sulla's cloak. "It's nothing of importance," she remarked saucily, "but I too wish to partake a little of your good fortune."[5] No Roman aristocrat suspected that the removal of the lint or the witty play on Sulla's epithet Felix prompted the subsequent marriage of the dictator to this Valeria. More likely, the lady's half-brother Hortensius and her brother-in-law Catulus had seen an opportunity in Sulla's estrangement from a branch of the Metellans and in his eagerness for an association with another oligarchic coterie.

Sulla announced his support of Catulus for a consulship in the coming year. Pompeius was preparing for still another challenge to the dictator, assembling a private faction among aristocrats from Picenum, the Adriatic region where he had recruited his legions, as well as among officers on his father's staff during the Italian war. One of these officers was Marcus Aemilius Lepidus, like Pompeius a renegade Marian. Formerly of preeminent influence in the commonwealth, the partician Aemilians had not held a consulship for two generations. When Lepidus announced his candidacy for the high office, Pompeius immediately proclaimed his support, and the campaign developed into a sequel to the struggle in the trial of Roscius. Lepidus not only distributed generous bribes with monies extorted during his recent governorship in Sicily but also attacked the dictator and his policies with astonishing bravado. When Sulla's partisans heckled him about his own profiteering during the proscriptions, he silenced them by declaring that he had participated only through fear of otherwise being accused of disloyalty. They gasped when he proclaimed his readiness to restore properties he had seized and his determination to scrutinize other confiscations.

Without Pompeius' backing and the support of a segment of the senatorial as well as elements of the nonsenatorial aristocracy, Lepidus would hardly have dared to go beyond Cicero's call for an end to the dictatorship and the restoration of all authority to the people and to their magistrates. He chided "men bearing great names, made great by the deeds of distinguished ancestors" for their subservience to Sulla and his satellites.[6]

Very likely assisted by a recommendation from the consul presiding at the elections (either Appius Claudius or Servilius Vatia), Lepidus emerged first in the voting, ahead of the two candidates sponsored by Sulla. Catulus won second place, and a sobered dictator came over to Pompeius and declared: "I see, young man, that you rejoice in your victory; and surely it was a generous and noble thing for Lepidus, the worst of men, to be proclaimed by a larger vote than Catulus, the best of men, because you influenced the people to take this course." A master of manipulation himself, Sulla warned Pompeius: "Now, however, it is time for you to be wide-awake and watchful of your interests. You have made your adversary stronger than yourself."[7]

Soon after the elections, from the Rostra, where two years earlier heads of the proscribed had advertised Sulla's triumph and vengeance, the dictator dismissed his lictors and resigned his office. He declared his readiness to render an accounting to any citizen of his stewardship of the republic. Ancient sources do not report any acceptance of this offer. It was said that Sulla murmured to associates: "I have lifted the Senate into the saddle; let us see if it can ride."[8]

According to an anecdote reflecting both Sulla's faltering influence and the fearlessness Romans came to associate with Caesar, Caesar encountered the former dictator one day in the Forum and began to rail at the old man. To the astonishment of onlookers Sulla listened in silence. Upon retreating into his mansion, however, he remarked: "This young man will prevent any future holder of such power from laying it down."⁹ The story may well have been invented years later by Caesar's enemies, but, in any event, Caesar was spared further sight of Sulla, for the dictator retired to Campania to live among colonies of his veterans and to write memoirs in justification of his career.

Overseas defeats afforded further evidence of the instability of Sulla's new order. Balkan tribes were raiding deep into Macedonia. Pirates ranged unchecked on the seas. In Spain the one-eyed Sertorius, compared by the Iberians to the one-eyed Hannibal (who had invaded Italy from Spain), was raiding towns throughout the peninsula. Respected for his just administration during his earlier governorship, he now proclaimed himself the leader of the revived Marian cause and won to his standard both Iberian tribesmen and Italian settlers, especially those whose families orginated in regions of Italy sacked by Sulla. Metellus Pius, dispatched to crush the rebellion, proved helpless before Sertorius' guerrilla tactics.

The ferment within the Sullan camp offered no immediate opportunities to Caesar. His best hopes lay in further service overseas. Perhaps through his connection to Pompeius he obtained a post with the retiring consul Servilius Vatia, appointed governor of Cilicia with a task of rooting out pirate bases on the southern coast of Anatolia. Servilius had accepted two other aristocrats connected to Pompeius: Labienus, an equestrian from Pompeius' client region, Picenum; and Catilina, a patrician who had served with Pompeius' father. On such assignments young aristocrats established friendships useful for their careers, and both these officers would figure in Caesar's future.

An oligarch of the old school who still applied the rod to his grown son, Servilius elicited respect by his fairness, attendance to detail and his personal integrity. For Servilius the style of portraiture newly popular among Roman aristocrats was appropriate. In the revival of influence of oligarchs of ancient lineage, sculptors represented contemporary Roman aristocrats as worthy descendants of hardy, austere, strongwilled farmer-warrior ancestors—displaying naturalistic details of warts and scars and defining them precisely as individuals. Coins portrayed forbears with similar unromanticized verism.

Servilius had the difficult task of regaining the loyalty of demoralized provincials, for the preceding governor and his subordinate, the renegade Marian Verres had impoverished the Cilicians by their extortions. Caesar did not, however, remain with Servilius to share in the latter's victories and plunder.

Sulla died and the consul Lepidus invited Caesar to return to Rome.

Railing at a local official for procrastinating with an assessment for the reconstruction of the Temple of Jupiter, Sulla fell into an apoplexy, vomiting blood and phlegm, and died. Lepidus resisted a Senate resolution granting the dictator the first state funeral in the history of the Republic, but he was forced to yield when Pompeius sided with the other consul, Catulus. At the ceremony, the dictator's will was read. Sulla singled out Lucullus, entrusting him with his unfinished memoirs and with the guardianship of his small children. He nominated Catulus to complete the restoration of the Temple of Jupiter and, as was the custom, listed other noblemen to whom he wished to express affection, omitting his one-time son-in-law, Pompeius—a presage of future conflict.

Recalling how Sulla had broken open Marius' tomb and scattered Marius' bones in a river, the wily Philippus advised cremation instead of burial (traditional in the Cornelian clan). As thousands streamed past the pyre a strong wind fanned the flames, and the nostrils of the mourners smarted from the burning spices. The dictator's felicity held even in death: all day the sky had been threatening, but only after the corpse had been consumed did a downpour terminate the ceremony.

Sulla was interred in the Campus Martius after a funeral more appropriate for a pharaoh than for an oligarch of the "restored" Republic. Caesar could appreciate the epitaph the dictator had chosen for himself: "No man ever surpassed him in benefaction or enemy in severity."[10]

Upon his arrival in Rome, Caesar found that in obedience to a Senate decree ordering the women of Italy to wear mourning for an entire year, Aurelia, Cornelia and his aunt were dressed in black.

Poor Aunt Julia! Never permitted to mourn her only son, she now wore black for the man who had posted her son's head on the Rostra as an offering to the goddess of vengeance.

XI

DEBUT IN THE FORUM

A classic counterrevolutionary, Sulla was certain that by terror he could retard, even reverse, the trend of history. But though he slaughtered entrepreneurs and usurers, he could not stay the expansion in commerce and banking that had been proceeding apace for more than a century. With his plunder he had given an impetus to the trade in luxury goods, and though he eliminated the grain subsidy, he did not end the importation of grain to feed a city of almost a million people. In subsequent decades shipping magnates would construct vessels two hundred meters in length; and ships of eighty-seven tons with a capacity of seven thousand amphorae of wine or oil and accommodations for hundreds of passengers would not be uncommon. Neither these businessmen nor the entrepreneurs who exploited mines, forests and salt works, supplied equipment and material to the legions or collected tribute in the provinces could be excluded indefinitely from policy-making in the empire. Above all, by expanding the holdings of his senatorial associates and dispossessing tens of thousands of peasants to provide land for his veterans, Sulla magnified the tensions in the countryside and impelled a mass migration into the towns. Finally, having provided the example of successful defiance of the Senate and the constitution by the use of a private army, could he believe that by fiat and murder he had restored indefinitely the hegemony of the landed aristocracy and shored up their constitution?

While Sulla lived, divisions within the ruling oligarchy were already exposing problems unresolved or intensified under his new order. Upon his death peasants in Etruria raided their former homesteads to expel veterans Sulla had settled in their place. Although the consuls easily dispersed the poorly armed countryfolk, Lepidus adjudged the uprising as a sign of the readiness of disgruntled elements for a new overturning. He refused to disband his legions and demanded that the Senate yield to the primary aspiration of the opposition elements—the restoration of the tribunician powers. Centuries earlier after generations of struggle the people had compelled the oligarchy to create a college of public defenders. By a single decree Sulla had deprived the tribunes of most of their authority.

The Senate rejected a motion to censure Lepidus and enjoined both Catulus and him to swear to complete their consulships without disorders. Emboldened by this vacillation, Lepidus proposed a comprehensive program of popular reform, including bills for a grain subsidy, for recall of political exiles, for restoration of the civil rights of the children of the proscribed and for compensation for properties confiscated during the Terror. He exhorted the citizenry to overcome "the utter demoralization of the republic" and to "look upon freedom united with danger as preferable to peace with slavery."[1]

Among the opponents to the late dictator who rallied to Lepidus' side were Caesar's brother-in-law Cinna and the praetorian Marcus Brutus, husband of Caesar's future mistress, Servilia. Caesar had not joined his cousin Marius against Sulla, and with his cousin's fate he had learned the necessity of a precise calculation of the relationship of forces in times of crisis. Now after returning home at Lepidus' invitation following Sulla's death, he would not commit himself to the consul's "party." History offered abundant evidence of the oligarchy's acceptance of divisions and even heated controversy within its ranks. Once oligarchs sense a threat to their hegemony, however, they unite swiftly, granting no mercy to defectors. In the name of religion, patriotism and the constitution and with unsentimental ferocity they harry, torture, exile and massacre all whom they suspect of "subversive" thoughts or associations. Furthermore, Caesar was wary of opportunists. In the year of Caesar's birth, Lepidus had joined in the massacre in which his father-in-law, the radical tribune Saturninus, was lynched along with hundreds of partisans. In the recent civil war after defecting from the Marians, he had divorced his wife, Saturninus' daughter, as a warrant of his loyalty to Sulla. The dictator had allowed him to profiteer during the Terror and then rewarded him with the governorship of Sicily, where he had plundered with typical Sullan rapacity. At the present juncture, only if the demoralized and decimated enemies of the Sullan order were ready to take up arms for their rights could Lepidus hope to push through his radical legislation.

Although the events of the previous decade had produced a ferment pervading every aspect of Roman society, no one could yet foresee the precise contours of the transformation in progress throughout the peninsula. With the transfer of holdings to tens of thousands of veterans and the confiscation of the properties of almost five thousand proscribed citizens, a major redistribution of land had taken place. Those who had profiteered not only in land but also in treasure now could exploit their market-oriented plantations on a far larger scale and with increased efficiency. Managed with ruthless rationalization, the Roman villa resembled an agricultural manufacturing complex rather than an old-fashioned farm. Slaves in gangs of ten were assigned specific, limited tasks and worked under strict norms. Complex operations were left to specialist slaves. Free labor, either migratory workers or local smallholders, were hired temporarily for the harvest or for tasks that might endanger the costly "speaking tools." Associated industry was developed to occupy the slaves during the off-season—basket weaving, the manufacture of amphorae for the shipping of oil and wine, brickmaking, etc. Richer landowners owned their own ships for exporting the products of their estates and engaged in large-scale overseas commerce. Neither men with sizable holdings who lacked the funds to invest in equipment and manpower or the capacity to organize such agricultural factories nor smallholders could hope to compete with these efficient enterprises.

In addition, the extension of the franchise to all Italy up to the Po had impelled a major political restructuring. The ancients considered the city-state as the ideal form of political organization, and Italy became, in effect, a union of municipalities in which people held citizenship both in local towns and at Rome. Since most Italians, however, lived either in hamlets or on isolated farms, a vast civic construction program was initiated—subsidized, in part, by the treasure Sulla had drained from the East—not only to repair the immense destruction from the civil wars but also to establish municipal administrative and commercial centers for rural areas. Local aristocrats, often Sullan profiteers, sought to establish a political base for themselves by underwriting the construction of walls, marketplaces, fountains, theaters and other public buildings and amenities. Thus the construction in the capital was matched throughout the peninsula, employing thousands, including many of those dispossessed during the Sullan regime. A segment of the population was enjoying a previously unimaginable standard of living, and Romanization and urbanization were proceeding apace.

It was a question whether in this ferment Lepidus was properly assessing the desperation of the dispossessed and their readiness to take up arms for the redress of their grievances.

At first it did appear that Lepidus had calculated correctly. As he advanced northward to assume the governorship of the Gallic provinces, thousands rallied to his banner. It was reported that he was recruiting troops in Transalpine Gaul and that Marcus Brutus was conducting levies in Cisalpine Gaul,* and Lepidus had supposedly opened negotiations with Sertorius in Spain. Despite these reports Catulus was unable to persuade the Senate to act. The senators would do no more than summon soothsayers for consultation and dispatch emissaries to discover Lepidus' intentions. When news of warlike preparations persisted, however, the senators could not resist the exhortations of old Philippus. In a speech he assigns to the elder statesman for this occasion, Sallust captures the tone and argument of a typical reactionary responding to a challenge to oligarchic privilege. Sallust has Philippus thunder: "These are the men who rouse rebellion after rebellion, war after war, followers now of Saturninus, then of Sulpicius, next of Marius . . . and now of Lepidus."[2] Understanding that the Sullans of every age denounce killings by their foes as wanton slaughter but extol their own massacres as necessary police actions aimed at restoring law and order, Sallust has Philippus omit from his list the name of the most ferocious fomenter of civil bloodshed—Sulla. His Philippus goes on to warn not of a renewal of the horrendous Sullan mass terror but of "the crime of Cinna, upon whose return to our city the flower of this [senatorial] order perished." Philippus evokes the standard bugaboos, denouncing traitors "eager to renew the pillage and fire and once more to arm their hands against the country's gods." So soon after the bloody Sullan repression, what senator would risk suspicion of sympathy with pillagers, arsonists and sacrilegious "terrorists"? Yielding to Philippus' prodding, the senators enacted the ultimate decree of martial law, calling upon Catulus and "others who have military power" (only Pompeius held an official command) to take arms in defense of the republic.

Caesar's reluctance to commit himself to Lepidus' putsch was quickly vindicated.

Catulus routed Lepidus outside Rome, and Pompeius drove Brutus within the walls of Mutina [Modena].

In these years of social and political upheaval, Brutus' wife suffered losses equal to Caesar's—the assassination of her uncle and guardian (the tribune Drusus) and the death of her father, Caepio, a casualty of the Italian war. Now she experienced the murder of her husband. After granting Brutus safe-conduct in return for surrender, Pompeius, an epitome of oligarchic cynicism denounced by his foes as "the Young Butcher," immediately ordered Brutus' execution. Servilia resolved to train up her son, the eight-year-old Marcus Brutus, for vengeance. She invited into her house as tutor for the boy and children of close friends a certain Staberius, an enemy to tyranny who accepted without tuition children of the proscribed as his pupils. (In old age Servilia would see her son side with his father's murderer against her lover and join

---

*The Romans divided their Gallic dependencies into Gaul across the Alps and Gaul this side of the Alps, that is, the greater part of Northern Italy.

Gaius Cassius, another of Staberius' pupils, in assassinating Caesar though Caesar, like a surrogate father, granted Brutus clemency and advanced his career.)

Now it was Pompeius' turn to refuse to disband his legions.

Unlike Lepidus, the warlord posed no principled demands—requiring a proconsular command against Sertorius with authority equal to that of Sulla's consular colleague Metellus Pius, the supreme pontiff and head of the most powerful clan in Rome. After employing a flippant witticism on his own name (Philip was father to Alexander the Great), Philippus rejected all objections to granting Pompeius such a command, declaring: "I give my vote to send him not in place of a consul but in place of both consuls!"[3]

To universal relief Pompeius departed without more ado.

Following upon his father and his one-time father-in-law, Sulla, Pompeius was inaugurating a new mode of oligarchic advancement. Without ever submitting to an election, he had attained first a triumph and now a proconsulship. Of course, more than command of an army was required for such self-aggrandizement. Lepidus' defiance of the Senate, for example, ended in disaster. Fleeing to Sardinia, he died supposedly of a broken heart upon news of the infidelity of the woman he had divorced at Sulla's behest. Many of his followers, including Caesar's brother-in-law Cinna, escaped to Spain to join Sertorius, the last of the Marians still in arms.

IN THE COURTS

Reconciled to pursuing the standard career of a young aristocrat, Caesar entered the Forum. Though forbidden to charge fees (a regulation preserving the oligarchic monopoly of the courts) advocates could win public attention and assemble personal clientships. Prudent newcomers like Cicero accepted the role of defender but avoided prosecutions for fear of alienating powerful individuals or factions, and in times of intense political antagonism, a tyro had to assess with care his choice of clients. Ever fearless, though rarely imprudent, Caesar decided that Lepidus had misjudged the tempo of developments but not the breadth of resentment against the clique in power. Those who had believed that the repression would end with Sulla's death had, in fact, discovered in Lepidus' colleague Catulus a tyrant far crueler than the dictator. Despite their easy victory over Lepidus, Sulla's successors were hardly secure. They had collapsed before Pompeius' defiance, and they could not suppress the agitation for the restoration of the tribunician powers; and a tribune was able to compel the new consuls to express themselves publicly on the issue. In his idiosyncratic manner, the consul Curio swayed and nodded as he delivered his opinion. (Caesar Strabo had quipped about him: "Who is the fellow there talking from a skiff?") When Curio finished, the tribune, "a man of coarse and hilarious wit," remarked to the other consul, who sat like a mummy swathed in bandages and reeking from gout ointment: "You can never thank your colleague enough, Octavius, for if he had not thrashed about in his way, the flies would surely have eaten you alive right here and now."[4] The tribune's hilarity did not assure passage of the bill, but agitation on the issue would continue until a reinvigorated popular movement (of which Caesar would be a leader) overwhelmed Sulla's successors.

Throughout Italy, too, the Sullans were on the defensive. The countryside was harassed by bands of slaves unleashed by wealthy landowners against helpless smallholder neighbors, and throughout the peninsula "bandits," victims of the Sullan Terror and other outcasts, waylaid travelers and raided farmsteads. Abroad the Sullans were proving equally incapable of maintaining order. Sertorius mocked Pompeius as "Sulla's schoolboy" and boasted that he would need only "a cane and whip for this boy were he not in fear of that old woman, Metellus."[5] The young warlord suffered a rout in which he lost his baggage train and he himself, struck in the thigh by a spear, escaped capture only because Sertorius' Iberian auxiliaries fell to quarreling over the costly trappings of his mount.

Ominous, too, were Sertorius' experiments with the native peoples. "By introducing Roman arms and formations and signals he did away with their frenzied and furious displays of courage and converted their forces into an army instead of a huge band of robbers." He dressed the children of the chiefs in togas and presented them with bullae, the amulets worn by Roman children, "and set over them teachers of Greek and Roman learning . . . with the assurance that when they became men he would give them a share in administration and authority."[6] (A quarter-century later Caesar would find support in his struggle against the senatorial oligarchy among Iberians previously allied to Sertorius.)

Unable to resolve crises at home and abroad and eager to postpone any explosion beyond their consulships, Curio and Octavius diverted popular attention by dispatching with much fanfare commissions throughout the Mediterranean to assemble prophetic writings as replacements for the Sibylline verses destroyed six years earlier in the burning of the Temple of Jupiter. After centuries of indoctrination the Roman populace responded with an automatic reflex to religious manipulation. (Even with the shift in attitudes during the next generation, Roman oligarchs would still boast that "in the special wisdom which consists in the recognition of the truth that the world is swayed and directed by divine approval, we have excelled every race and every nation."[7]

In this atmosphere of ferment and uncertainty, Caesar entered the Forum.

Caesar did not take risks without calculation. In challenging the Sullans in the courts, he could be confident of avoiding vigorous retaliation, for with the current judicial corruption it was unthinkable that he could win a conviction against the distinguished personage he chose to prosecute. The defendant, a certain Dolabella, was charged with extortion during his recent proconsulship in Macedonia. A long-time associate of Sulla's, he had been selected by the dictator for a consulship upon the conclusion of the civil war and had thus presided over the Terror. Since in prosecuting this corrupt mediocrity Caesar could call to judgment the worst crimes of the dictatorship, the Sullans set their most formidable orators, Gaius Cotta and Hortensius, against the twenty-three-year-old novice. "Relaxed and quiet, constructing his sentences smoothly and easily, without the language of metaphor" and especially astute in analyzing complex arguments, Aurelia's cousin appealed to sophisticates in the audience. Hortensius, some years younger, on the other hand, was a master of histrionics. Actors attended his trials to study his gestures, and he delighted the public with his prodigious memory. Once after spending a day at an auction he listed all the transactions in sequence as the astonished auctioneer checked the articles, prices and purchasers against an account book. When orating Hortensius sometimes ticked off arguments on his fingertips to display the orderliness of his ratiocination. "Ornate, vivid . . . lively in diction and delivery,"[8] he exploited the exuberance of what was called the "Asiatic" style, with sentences in conscious balance set off by pointed phrases, a style more adapted to bedazzlement than to elucidation and thus much admired in the courts of the day.

Against these veterans Caesar acquitted himself admirably. "Tall of stature, with a fair complexion, shapely limbs, a somewhat full face and keen black eyes," a long, delicate neck with a prominent Adam's apple, hair slightly curling and combed forward toward the right over a high forehead, nose a trifle upturned, well-defined cheekbones within taut cheeks, a full mouth set over a sturdy chin, Caesar had the appearance as well as the bearing of a patrician. He spoke "in a high-pitched voice with impassioned action and gestures, which were not without grace." He delighted Romans (appreciative of eloquence) with the purity of his speech and his precise diction. "By joining to [a] careful selection of Latin words . . . the characteristic embellishments of oratorical style, he produced an effect as of placing a well-painted picture in a good light." Suetonius reports that early in his career (perhaps in this maiden speech) Caesar "transferred some passages word for word" from Caesar Strabo's classic oration against a governor of Sardinia also accused of extortion—a tribute to a famous clansman and a reminder of Caesar's connection to the distinguished man of letters. But Caesar did not require arguments from Caesar Strabo for an assault against a corrupt provincial governor. He could recall from his childhood the trumped-up charges against Rutilius and the honors his father had won as a just administrator. He had seen the results of Roman oppression in the East and knew that the enthusiastic welcome accorded Mithridates in Asia and Sertorius' victories in Spain exposed a crisis in Roman imperial government. As one who had maintained his personal integrity at the risk of his life, he did not need prompting in regard to Dolabella's association with the Sullan Terror. Indeed, Caesar apparently pressed the defendant to the point of desperation, and Dolabella retaliated by deriding Caesar for his supposed seduction by King Nicomedes of Bithynia, sneering at him as "the queen's rival, the inner partner of the royal couch."[9] (The charge, the more plausible because of Caesar's childlessness after years of marriage, was to pursue him all his life.)

To no one's surprise, Dolabella was acquitted.

Only months earlier the senators serving as jurors had voted to honor Dolabella with a triumph for victories over Balkan tribesmen. They would not readily convict him, in any case, of extortion in a province, a crime most senators yearned for an opportunity to commit. Besides, patricians still commanded awe, and Dolabella's conviction would have brought retroactive disgrace upon his Cornelian ancestors. Furthermore, at Rome, as in all other oligarchies, justice was skewed to protect the powerful. The citizenry admired politicians who committed crimes on a grandiose scale, and as applicable in Caesar's day as in the twentieth century is the lament of Cato the Censor a century before Caesar: "Those who steal from private individuals spend their lives in stocks and chains; those who steal from the public treasure go dressed in gold and purple." But decisive in all trials was bribery. In an extortion case of the time, a provincial governor complained "that a man of praetorian rank could not decently be convicted for less than three million sesterces" (the sum supposedly distributed to obtain his conviction).[10] Neither the Macedonian plaintiffs nor Caesar could match Dolabella's millions.

Tantalizing to the crowd that had assembled at the trial as at a theatrical entertainment was Cotta's diffidence. Caesar graciously avowed that he had failed to obtain a conviction because of Cotta's superiority as an orator, but the audience noted that though Cotta "was employed as the chief advocate, yet Hortensius played the leading role." Romans could wonder whether Cotta's irresolution reflected contempt for the ignominious Dolabella or eagerness to assure his cousin a brilliant entree into the Forum. In any event, Dolabella's acquittal represented no serious setback to Caesar. The prosecution of one of Sulla's closest associates by the nephew of Marius and son-in-law of Cinna afforded the kind of drama that titillated the populace. In addition, after years of frustration Caesar had appeared before Rome in a heroic stance, displayed his capacities as an orator and won a clientship in Macedonia that would prove useful in later years. A young man's first trial was an event of moment, and the prosecution of Dolabella helped to stimulate Caesar's life-long defense of provincials. His next case was also a prosecution on behalf of oppressed provincials. Unlike Dolabella, the defendant was accused of no recent crime but of acts committed in Sulla's service a full decade earlier, and the factional implications of the case were obvious. The trial matched Dolabella's in sensationalism, for the defendant, Antonius Hybrida, was the son of a censor executed by Marius and Cinna, with Caesar, the prosecutor, the nephew and son-in-law of the executioners. This trial had a different outcome. The younger of the Lucullus brothers used his authority as presiding praetor to facilitate the prosecution, and crying that he could not "compete in a fair trial in Rome against a Greek [the plantiff],"[11] Antonius won the intervention of a tribune and escaped conviction.

Nevertheless, once again Caesar enjoyed a succès d'estime, and though only in his twenty-fourth year he had already acquired "a great and brilliant popularity by his eloquence" and a broad following among "the common people for the friendliness of his manners in intercourse with them since he was ingratiating beyond his years."[12]

JULIA

During the period of Caesar's entrance into the Forum superstitious neighbors began to urge Cornelia to loosen the knots in her clothing and to let her hair hang free when she made offerings to Juno, goddess of childbirth, and they prodded Caesar to untie his belt and to wrap it about Cornelia's waist while repeating the formula, "I bound, and I too will unloose." Many Romans believed that a man could ease his wife's labor pains also by hurling over the house a stone or missile that had been used in killing a human being, a boar and a bear or by carrying into the house a spear drawn from a human body without touching the ground. The forest god Silvanus was to be warded off by having three men circle the outer doors at night and strike the lintels with an axe and a flour pestle and sweep the lintels with a broom. Evil spirits were to be appeased with food offerings and with lighted candles set on a couch in the atrium.

Such was the world of spirits and demiurges in which Caesar lived. Throughout his career, out of respect for tradition and out of antiquarian interest he honored religious beliefs and practices although disowning divine influence in his own activity. As the parent of a child long desired, he could welcome the custom of lifting the newborn infant from the floor in an acknowledgment of paternity. Until her untimely death some twenty years later, Caesar and his daughter enjoyed a relationship of loving affection.

The new Julia's arrival served to spur Caesar's ambition. In a few years he would have to provide her with a dowry befitting her station and his dignity.

XII

THE PONTIFEX

IN 76, in his twenty-fifth year, Caesar had an enviable opportunity for further political apprenticeship. It was Gaius Cotta's turn as a Sullan lieutenant to campaign for a consulship. Unlike Lepidus, who confused the voters by injecting serious issues into his electioneering, Cotta followed what twentieth-century campaign managers would call a standard "game plan." The cardinal principle in such orthodox vote getting is: The Man not the Issues. A "past master of electioneering,"[1] Cotta did not distract voters from the decisive question: his personality. He projected an image of sincerity, dedication and moderation. He reminded audiences of his unfailing generosity in defending clients in the courts and in entertaining petitions from citizens of every rank. He reassured the public by vaunting of his exploits on the battlefield and in the Forum and of his association with important personalities of a past era. He could safely recall his collaboration with the ill-fated tribune Drusus, his "pious" defense of his uncle Rutilius, the Roman Socrates, and his own unjust exile as an early victim of the Marians, but he was too astute to harp on his collaboration with the late dictator, for recollection of Sulla roused irrelevant controversy.

Cotta attracted to his entourage young men eager to learn the tricks of vote getting from a master politician. Among such aspirants to public careers were the Cicero brothers, and a dozen years later in a manual on tactics drafted for Marcus' campaign for a consulship, Quintus Cicero offered Cotta as a model to emulate. He recalled how Cotta

> used to promise his help to all, but give it to those in whom he expected he was making the best investment; he refused nobody ... if one undertook only what one could be sure to perform, one's house would be empty [of clients and partisans] ... and ... the anger of the man to whom one lied would be the last event in the series—for if you do promise, the anger is uncertain, not immediate and occurs in fewer cases; but if you refuse you are sure to rouse antagonism at once and in more people.[2]

Unlike the Ciceros, Cotta was no "new man," and for a scion of a famous noble family and a leading collaborator with the dictator, election was assured; and in a period devoid of statesmen of distinction, he stands out as one of the least mediocre. His task as consul, difficult enough as a result of Sulla's legacy of unresolved problems, was complicated by famine, the result of poor crops in the grain-producing provinces. One day as he and the other consul were walking through the Forum, a crowd advanced upon them shouting for bread. Famished men and women pushed against the lictors. The magistrates and their entourages fled into the house of Cotta's colleague.

Convinced that any concession will open the way to further demands and even to a questioning of the entire social order, the initial reaction of oligarchs to public "disorder" is not to yield to extralegal pressure. In addition, they avoid measures that may provoke division within their own ranks. Thus the consuls wasted no time discussing the suppression of the pirates who were intercepting grain ships or advocating curbs on speculators profiteering in the crisis. Nor did it occur to them to revive the grain subsidy abolished by Sulla or to propose a distribution of land from the public domains to some of the thousands of farmers evicted by Sulla who had flooded into the city. As successors to the dictator, the consuls understood their first responsibility: to stay the course—through cajolery and manipulation to delay or divert pressures for any modification in the new order established through their victory in the recent civil war.

Cotta undertook to win the starving citizenry back to reason by an appeal in the Forum. According to the speech recorded or invented by Sallust, Cotta not only appeased the wrath of the rioters but even evoked a sense of shame among them for their unpatriotic behavior. He appeared on the Rostra dressed in mourning, not out of grief, however, for the misery of the hungry men, women and children but rather at a sorrow more personal and poignant—the ingratitude of the mob toward him, their dedicated consul. Had he endured so "many dangers at home and abroad," he asked, only to arrive at old age without "hope for an honorable death," adjudged as he was a traitor to the city?[3] Had any Roman ever found him unreceptive when people "needed [his] voice, counsel [or] purse?" Surely no one had ever suspected that he "practiced a calculating eloquence" to mislead the citizenry, he whom the people had rewarded for his dedication and honesty with "a return from exile and election to high office." As for those who had grieved him by rioting, were they not aware of the "dire straits" of the republic, beleaguered by Sertorius in Spain and compelled to maintain defense garrisons on many distant frontiers? Did they not know that the public revenues "barely suffice[d] for a part of [the city's] expenditures so that even the fleet which [it kept] upon the sea [was] much smaller than the one which formerly safeguarded [its] supplies"?

Yet Cotta was a man of patient understanding. Although he found his fellow citizens in error, he did not judge them to be beyond correction. "Why," he asked in an appeal to their sense of propriety, "do you resort to acts unworthy of you, of us and of our country?" If they believed that the present "state of affairs had been brought about by treason or negligence," it would be proper for them to demand the punishment of their chief magistrates. He himself was prepared to suffer death if with his life he could bring an end to the present ills. What man, he asked, would desire to remain in high office if blamed "for the vagaries of fortune, for the uncertainties of the sea and for war brought on by others"?

Reassured as to the receptivity of his audience to a recall to reason, Cotta exhorted the crowd "to endure adversity and take thought for [their] country." They were never to forget that they bore special responsibilities as rulers of an empire and as a people with the unique mission of bringing peace and justice to a troubled and often ungrateful world. "The price of supreme power," he reminded them, "is great anxiety, many heavy burdens. It is vain for you to attempt to avoid them and to look for peace and prosperity, when all the provinces and realms, all lands and seas are devastated or exhausted by wars."

Since Roman citizens never doubted the sincerity of their leaders and never questioned the special mission of their republic, Cotta could easily persuade the famished men and women that in the fulfilment of Rome's sacred responsibility in the world the welfare of the commons was patently a secondary, an irrelevant, consideration of a chief magistrate. Who could question the allocation to the armed forces of the last funds of a nearly exhausted treasury? Patriotism required sacrifice. With the oligarchs and entrepreneurs exerting their energies to defending and magnifying the glory and plunder of empire, was it not proper that the impoverished and brutalized commoners accept a disproportionate share of sacrifice? Nor was it for the commons to question wars or supposed threats of wars. All wars Rome fought were noble; all rebellions by oppressed and terrorized provincials were evil, motivated by ingratitude and prompted by demagogues playing upon ignorance and base instincts.

Thus without a hint at relief of suffering or a word of compassion, Cotta recalled the commons to duty.

Fortunate the republic that can boast a statesman of such eloquence!

In the emergency Hortensius, the renowned orator and brother-in-law to the late dictator, came to Cotta's assistance. Romans had gasped at his expenditure of 144 thousand sesterces on a work by a famous Greek artist and of an additional huge sum for a shrine at his Tusculan villa to house the masterpiece. Now he won applause by distributing a week's supply of grain to every male citizen of Rome, a gesture that would guarantee his advancement to the higher magistracies, at a cost hardly disproportionate to the expenditure on his painting and its enclosure.

Neither Cotta with his eloquence nor Hortensius with his largess had achieved more than a brief stay in the disorders, and further to distract the hungry mob Cotta proposed a radical reform. To render the tribunate, a potentially dangerous office, unattractive to capable and ambitious young men, Sulla had deprived tribunes of the right to advance to higher magistracies. For seeking repeal of even this minor provision of Sullan legislation Cotta was denounced by fellow oligarchs and hailed as a "moderate" by other Romans. In such circumstances, good citizens shake their heads and murmur, "He did his best, the good man, they prevented him from doing more."

By standard criteria Cotta had conducted an exemplary consulship. He had pacified a riot without granting concessions and won a reputation as a reformer without instituting a significant reform. Now as a governor of Cisalpine Gaul he would goad Alpine tribes to war and celebrate a triumph. Then he would win election to a censorship and serve out his final years as a revered elder statesman.

Cotta offered Caesar an example of a successful orthodox politician. The new politics of the warlords represented the future and provided swifter advancement, but for Caesar with no military clientship Cotta's way required investigation. Experience with Cotta helped to prepare Caesar for maneuvering within the oligarchy. With the approaching collapse of the Republic, Cotta's hypocrisy and cunning would appear, in retrospect, ever more harmless and naive.

COTTA'S SUCCESSOR

With Gaius' recommendation and the assistance of a certain Cethegus, the second of the three Cotta brothers, Marcus, won election to a consulship. Marcus' backer, Cethegus, was a novel figure in Roman politics. Outlawed after Sulla's first march on Rome, he had fled into exile with Marius. Upon Sulla's invasion of Italy he had switched sides and taken part in the siege of young Marius. In the political turmoil following upon the dictatorship, Cethegus displayed "a complete mastery and profound understanding of affairs of state."[4] Taking advantage of the breakdown of old clientships as a result of the vast shifts in population and the enfranchisement of the Italians, Cethegus established himself as a political kingpin with contacts among officers of the electoral tribes and of fraternal and professional organizations as well as among leading equestrians and small-town aristocrats. He dispensed bribes and patronage and manipulated elections and legislative assemblies. Rare was the bill enacted without his support.

Cethegus promoted Marcus Cotta's career, of course, with a view to sharing in the profits of office, and Marcus began to remark portentously that the conflict with Mithridates "had not come to an end but merely to a pause."[5] To his good fortune, Nicomedes of Bithynia died and bequeathed his kingdom to the Roman people. (Through loans and exactions—the price of Roman "protection"—Roman oligarchs and entrepreneurs already controlled the country.) Immediately shares in a new Bithynian corporation to manage the royal estates and to collect tribute went on sale at the Temple of Castor. Cethegus arranged that Marcus Cotta should hold the governorship of the new province at the end of his consulship.

Meanwhile, Caesar set out for the East ostensibly to further his education. Study abroad was newly in fashion among Roman aristocrats, but with oligarchic maneuverings conducted behind closed doors, Romans could only speculate on a possible connection between Caesar's journey and Marcus Cotta's prospective proconsulship in Bithynia. The oligarchs were always shorthanded and wary of inviting outsiders to share their authority and plunder. With his experience in Asia and Cilicia, his connections in Bithynia and his proven capacities in diplomacy, on the battlefield and in the Forum, Caesar could render useful service to his cousin.

Sea travel during the post-Sullan years was perilous. Pirate vessels marshaled into squadrons and even entire fleets threatened Roman communications on the seas. The pirates had been in alliance with Mithridates and were now allied to Sertorius. Gaius Cotta, in fact, had suffered a defeat in an encounter with them off the coast of Spain. Thousands of freebooters—men displaced by wars, deserters, runaway slaves, bankrupts and motley adventurers—preyed upon every cove of the Mediterranean. They laid coastal towns and islands under tribute. They dared to raid Italy, striking at Brundisium (Brindisi), plundering the Temple of Hera near Croton and sacking Misenum near Naples. Their spies mingled with sailors on the docks and in taverns listening for talk of cargoes, sailing dates and sea routes.

Offshore from Miletus at the eastern edge of the Aegean, Caesar's ship was overtaken, and he was captured.

Roman captives who proclaimed their citizenship, haughtily demanding immediate release, might be encouraged to don their togas and to accept passage home by walking the plank. Displaying the resolution and courage that was to characterize him throughout his life, Caesar defied his captors. When they proposed a ransom of 20 talents (ten times the bounty for a proscribed man during the Sullan Terror), he scoffed and insisted he was worth at least 50 talents. Confident that they would be solicitous of such a valuable prisoner, Caesar behaved like a prototypical Roman patrician. He ordered silence when he lay down to sleep, mocked the pirates if they failed to applaud his declamations of poetry or orations and warned them as he participated in their games that one day he would hang them all. When his ransom had been assembled, he compelled them to provide hostages as a warrant for his release.

Freed at Miletus, Caesar commandeered warships and fell upon his former captors and seized ships and prisoners. When the provincial governor procrastinated in executing the men, calculating a profit from ransom or from their sale to slavedealers, Caesar crucified them himself. With a compassion rare among Roman oligarchs, however, he slit their throats so that they would not die in slow strangulation.

Richer from his booty and exultant at outwitting the pirates, Caesar arrived at his destination, Rhodes. The island city, handsome and immaculate, rose within a semicircle of hills in a checkerboard of broad avenues intersecting into six-hundred-foot squares. The city boasted an impressive theater, stately temples and a colonnaded market, all adorned with statues and paintings. The colossal bronze statue of the sun god Helios, one of the Seven Wonders of the world, overturned by an earthquake, lay prostrate since an oracle had warned against its restoration. (More likely, having lost its former prosperity, the city lacked funds for such an undertaking.) After the bread riot at Rome, Caesar could appreciate the rational welfare system under which the state here guaranteed the food supply, with wealthy citizens required to contribute to the support of the needy. Once the leading maritime city of the Eastern Mediterranean, Rhodes remained a center of art, literature, philosophy and rhetoric.

There was much at Rhodes to inspire Caesar's interest. Throughout the city stood monuments to great thinkers who had lived in Rhodes, and the most famous philosopher of the day, the polymath Posidonios, was a native of the city. He had calculated the circumference of the earth, constructed an orrery to demonstrate the movement of the celestial bodies and propounded theories regarding the influence of the stars on human affairs, theories discussed eagerly by the increasing number of Romans dabbling in astrology. (Later in his career Caesar would consult Posidonios' ethnographical studies on Gaul and Germany and his investigation of the relationship of the tides to the phases of the moon.) Oligarchs enjoy easy access to the famous, and Posidonios, who had visited Rome as an ambassador to Marius and Cinna, would hardly refuse an audience to a young patrician with Caesar's connections. Like other cultured Romans, Caesar was acquainted with the Greek thinker's political theories. According to Posidonios, a Stoic, Rome as the earthly manifestation of the divine commonwealth had a mission to bring the world of men into harmony with the transcendent order. But Posidonios was not uncritical. He deplored the loss of the ancestral austerity and warned of Roman laxity in regard to piracy and the related slave trade and of the unbridled exploitation of provincials. A fellow student of Posidonios' in their youth, Rutilius had drafted his charter for Asia with similar thoughts.

It was, however, to study with Apollonios Molo that Caesar had come to Rhodes. Cicero, previously under the renowned rhetorician's tutelage, praised Molo as "particularly skilful in criticizing and correcting faults and wise in his whole system." Molo encouraged his disciples "to repress . . . redundance and excess . . . marked by a youthful impetuousness and lack of restraint,"[6] instruction Caesar seems to have assimilated into his own style. Abruptly Caesar's studies were interrupted by reports from the mainland. Mithridates had invaded Bithynia, routed Marcus Cotta, newly arrived as governor, captured the Roman fleet and driven Cotta within the walls of a fortified town. Sertorian officers arriving from Spain under a treaty of alliance with Mithridates were leading a force against Ephesus. With the new proconsul of Asia, Lucullus, unprepared to resist the invaders, Caesar, with obligations to both proconsuls, mobilized Roman citizens in Rhodes and, crossing to the mainland, rallied local militia. (His speed and resolution seem to confirm the speculation that he had been sent to the East with the prospect of service with the two governors.) At Tralles, a town commanding the valley of the Meander less than fifty miles east of Ephesus, he met the enemy force and routed it.

With the rescue of the Asian metropolis, Caesar's military adventure ended.

Returning from Gaul to celebrate a triumph over Alpine tribesmen, Gaius Cotta had died suddenly from the hemorrhaging of an old wound. Cotta's colleagues in the college of pontifices selected his young cousin as his successor. Their action was extraordinary. By tradition a plebeian pontifex like Cotta was to be replaced by another plebeian, not by a patrician. Election in absentia, too, was almost without precedent. Furthermore, election was by unanimous vote, and all the pontifices had been supporters of Sulla; several had risen to the priesthood through the dictator. In his testament Cotta might have appealed to his colleagues to give preference to his young cousin, but no recommendation could erase Caesar's relationship to Marius and to Cinna or his defiance of Sulla, his prosecution of leading Sullans, his sympathy for Lepidus or his connection to a brother-in-law in Sertorius' rebel army.

Responsibility for Caesar's success lay ultimately with Aurelia. It was for her to solicit the pontifices, one by one, enlisting the aid of friends and relatives in the effort. She could be confident of the support of several of the priests. The brother to the murdered tribune Drusus, for example, had joined Cotta in appealing to Sulla for Caesar's life. Servilius had been Caesar's commander in Cilicia and would harbor till his death an affection for his younger associate. Marcus Lucullus would have been grateful for Caesar's assistance to his brother in the engagement with the Sertorians in Asia. Aurelia could appeal to priests related to Metellans on the basis of the long friendship between the Aurelians and the Metellans. As for Catulus, Aurelia's brother had been a friend to his father.

Aurelia would not have succeeded in overcoming so many obstacles, however, if the Sullan pontifices had not been desperate for allies. So far had they declined in authority that they were compelled to submit to Cethegus' insolence. The haughty Lucullus had had to attend upon the political boss's mistress like a suppliant in order to obtain a command in the East. Pompeius, too, had threatened the Senate again. "Unless you come to our rescue," he had written in a complaint about the failure to send supplies and reinforcements, "against my will but not without warning from me, our army will pass over into Italy bringing with it all the war in Spain."[7]

Though Caesar had hardly achieved a position of influence, the Sullans were eager to win to their side such a young man of proven courage and ability.

Only oligarchs of the highest nobility gained entrance into the college of pontifices. Several of the priests were of consular rank; the others were confident of attaining the high office.

For Caesar the election represented a revolutionary turn in his career.

At his mother's instructions Caesar set out for Rome.

XIII

WARLORDS

WITH the eagerness of any twenty-six-year-old hastening home to an infant daughter too long unseen and to new honors eagerly awaited, Caesar raced over the Via Egnatia from Thessalonica, at the northern extremity of the Aegean, to the Adriatic port of Dyrrachium (Durres in Albania). Here he did not tarry for a merchant ship but embarked in a four-oared dinghy with two friends and ten slaves for Brundisium. Toward the end of the journey Caesar saw a line of vessels blocking the way in the distance.

The Adriatic swarmed with freebooters.

Resolved not to undergo a second captivity, Caesar removed his outer garments and bound a dagger to his thigh.

What from afar had seemed masts of ships proved to be a row of trees on the mainland.

At Brundisium, however, Caesar learned that on the way to Rome he faced no such imaginary peril. A band of gladiators had escaped from barracks at Capua and holed up on Mt. Vesuvius. Slipping through encirclement, they routed a praetor. Slaves from nearby plantations and shepherds from the sheep and cattle trails, notorious for their ferocity and horsemanship, were rallying to the gladiators. Unchecked, they ranged over Campania, plundering country houses and villages. "Show me a slave," ran an old proverb, "and I'll show you an enemy." What, indeed, was the purpose of a state if not, as the Greek Xenophon had noted centuries earlier, to enable "citizens [to] ward one another without pay from their slaves and from evil doers to the end that none of the citizens may perish by violent death?"[1]

In Italy slaves probably constituted a third of the population, concentrated primarily in limited areas. In recent years they had become conscious of their power. They had fought in the Italian and civil wars. Marius had appealed for their aid against factional enemies and allowed them to rampage through Rome. Sulla had manumitted ten thousand and formed them into a private guard with license for violence and depredations. With the large-scale transfer of property during the Sullan Terror, many slaves acquired new, absentee owners, and with the extension of a rationalized market-oriented agriculture they were subjected to ever more intensive exploitation. Desperate, they threatened devastation to a peninsula not yet recovered from the wars of the previous decade.

Terrified at the peril in the countryside, diehard senators forgot their uncompromising resistance to any modification in the late dictator's policies and, disregarding admonitions about military priorities, bankrupting the treasury and encouraging idleness among the poor, they enacted a new grain subsidy to appease the urban plebs. Though the measure benefited a small percentage of the citizens and afforded less than subsistence, it signaled the undermining of the Sullan order. For Sulla's successors only the news from their commanders in Spain, Metellus Pius and Pompeius, offered encouragement. The Sertorians were in retreat, exhausted after years of intense warfare and weakened by dissension. Proclaimed imperator by his troops because of his successes, an exultant Metellus, like an oriental potentate, banqueted in triumphal garb, crowned with a wreath, while "victories made to move by machinery, descended and distributed golden trophies and wreaths, and choirs of boys and women sang hymns of victory in his praise."[2]

Victory meant Pompeius' return to Rome, and no one could predict what new humiliations he was preparing for the Senate.

In such an atmosphere Caesar celebrated his induction into the pontifical college. With his aristocratic demeanor, easy courtesy, sophisticated wit, literary and artistic erudition, precise diction and facile conversation—in short, his urbanity—Caesar found himself among great nobles. Throughout his life he would seek allies among them, sometimes displaying an uncharacteristic naiveté in granting them his trust. At ceremonies like an induction into a priestly college the oligarchs reveled in their imperial glory. Although no record remains of the banquet in honor of Caesar's installation, Macrobius, the compiler of a fifth-century miscellany, preserves an account of a similar banquet tendered four years later to a new flamen of Mars. Among those present on that occasion were Caesar, his clansman Lucius Caesar (the officiating augur), several vestals as well as the flamen's wife and mother-in-law. The menu evidenced the new plantation specialization in game, exotic fruits, vegetables and poultry as well as in fish and seafood from hatcheries for the expanding luxury market. According to Macrobius:

> They were served for the preliminary service sea urchins, unlimited raw oysters, scallops, cockles, thrushes on asparagus, fattened fowls, a dish of oysters and scallops, acorn fish (both black and white), then another service of cockles, mussels, sea nettles, figpeckers, haunches of venison and boar, fattened fowls in pastry, more figpeckers, murex and purple fish. For the main dishes they were served sow's udders, boar's head, stewed fish, stewed sow's udders, duck, boiled teal, hares, roasted fowl, creamed wheat and rolls in the style of Picenum.[3]

Henceforth, recognized as one of a select coterie of notables, Caesar would appear before the public at innumerable solemnities in a pontifical toga edged with purple and with thigh wrappings drawn closely around his hips (the feminalia). No aspect of an oligarch's life, of course, was divorced from politics, and all offices, sacred and secular, served as posts of hegemonial defense and as bases for factional and personal aggrandizement. In 73, the year of Caesar's installation, the pontifices were wrestling with a religious scandal, a charge of adultery involving two vestals. (Caesar knew the spot in the city walls where in a similar factionally inspired scandal, a great-aunt of his had been entombed with two other vestals.) Mere suspicion of immorality among the priestesses roused alarm. On this occasion, noting that the trials fell on the tenth anniversary of the burning of the Temple of Jupiter, a catastrophe followed by the Sullan Terror, people wondered what new calamities would befall the city. Two distinguished noblemen were accused as adulterers: Catilina, a fellow officer of Caesar's on the staff of Servilius in Cilicia; and Marcus Crassus, son of a censor executed by Marius and Cinna and the victor at the decisive battle of the Colline Gate during the civil war.

Making his debut into public life by prosecuting Catilina was a young patrician profligate named Publius Clodius (he affected an archaic spelling of his clan name, with an "o" instead of "au"). Defending Catilina were Catulus, who, according to rumor, had enjoyed Catilina's assistance in the savage execution of Marius' nephew during the Sullan Terror, and Marcus Cato, half-brother to Caesar's friend Servilia. Twenty-two and already esteemed for comportment as dour as his great-grandfather's (the renowed Censor), Cato announced that he was intervening for the sake of the city itself, and with self-righteous invective he routed Clodius.

Crassus suffered the handicap of his enormous riches. During the proscriptions Sulla had reprimanded him for exaggerated zest in profiteering. Old-fashioned aristocrats resented his open consorting with men in trade. As long ago as the Hannibalic war, conservative senators fearing a division of interest within their ranks along with entrepreneurs seeking to check competition from landed aristocrats had promoted a law forbidding senators to engage in large-scale business ventures. Senators, of course, did not accept for long restraints on opportunities for quick profits, and the measure proved of little effect. Nevertheless, tradition weighed heavily at Rome, and regardless of their own private commercial activity oligarchs publicly maintained that "every form of profit-seeking was . . . unsuitable for senators." Those who envied Crassus for his wealth or resented his business acumen muttered against him for "taking bribes for his voice in the Senate, wronging the allies, circumventing weak women with his flatteries and aiding base men to cloak their iniquities," and Cicero, who as a "new man" proclaimed the old-fashioned virtues with particular passion, would denounce Crassus as one who thought "no mode of profit-making base" and would without compunction "cheat and trick and ask and bargain and plunder and snatch . . . defraud partners and pillage the treasury."[4] Of course, by twentieth-century standards the manipulations of a magnate of a pre-industrial society appear ridiculously petty. Crassus chased fires in order to offer distraught property owners minimal compensation for burning buildings. Upon completing a deal, he either set his slaves to extinguishing the blaze or subsequently employed his crew of five hundred workers and architects to build new structures. While thus acquiring a substantial portion of the city real estate, Crassus squandered no millions on mansions for himself. In fact, he evoked indignation by his contempt for those who bankrupted themselves in the mindless prodigality of the day.

Whether Caesar participated in the trials of Catilina and Crassus, both of whom won acquittal, cannot be established. He did subsequently borrow large sums from Crassus and perhaps his first loan from the millionaire was actually a bribe for a vote in Crassus' acquittal. Within a few years, too, he was to enter a political alliance with both Crassus and Catilina. Meanwhile, priestly duties were not all-consuming, and exploiting both the dignity of his new office and the perfected oratory achieved in his studies at Rhodes, Caesar resumed his career in the courts.

In an era with primitive communications but with intense competition for office and riches, oligarchs sought quick recognition by cultivating some dramatic singularity. One noble family affected wearing the toga off-shoulder. A patrician orator practiced a rustic pronunciation. The Claudians were renowned for their haughtiness. Cato represented himself as the reincarnation of his moralistic great-grandfather. The Julians pretended a stubborn reverence for tradition, and Caesar proclaimed his particular devotion to the ancient virtues of pietas (the duty owed a father by a son, the commonwealth by a citizen and the gods by mortals) and of fides (the respect of a superior for his dependents—of a father for a son and of a patron for a client). According to Aristotle, a virtue, like a musical instrument, is mastered through practice, and Caesar had had much practice in both pietas and fides.

In a court case he undertook at this juncture, Caesar confronted a dilemma in regard to his emblematic virtues. The plantiffs were Bithynians, for whom Caesar entertained a sense of obligation, while the defendant (the provincial governor who had procrastinated in the execution of the pirates captured by Caesar) was a connection of Aurelia's. Custom prescribed priority to clients, and addressing the defendant, Caesar declared: "In consideration of my guest-friendship with King Nicomedes or my relationship to those whose case is on trial, Marcus Iuncus, I could not refuse this duty [as prosecutor]. For the remembrance of men ought not to be obliterated by their death as not to be retained by those nearest to them, and without the height of disgrace we cannot forsake clients to whom we are bound to render aid even against our kinsfolk."[5]

Caesar further displayed Julian reverence for tradition by entering his candidacy for a military tribuneship, an elective legionary post that had been held both by his father and by Caesar Strabo. After centuries of unremitting warfare and the near annihilation of entire generations of young men, "the profession of arms [was] falling out of fashion among the youth," and lengthy duty with the legions was no longer a prerequisite for public office. In campaigning for this office Caesar had an opportunity to present himself to the citizenry in a new capacity and to demonstrate that co-option into the college of pontifices had not caused him to change his political orientation. Obtaining "proof of the people's good will" by winning the election,[6] he immediately employed his new influence in promoting a bill for the restoration of the tribunician powers.

The leader of the agitation for this measure was Licinius Macer, a friend of Crassus' and the minter who had greeted Marius' reentry into Rome with a coin representing the Old Man as Odysseus returning to Ithaca. Macer commanded Caesar's respect as a representative of a new school of historians who were investigating Rome's past for sources of its current troubles and as an astute, principled and courageous statesman. Reviving Gracchan radical oratory, Macer gave voice to the discontent of those Sulla had deprived of influence or excluded from public life. His enemies sneered at his "life, his character, even his very face," but they could not deny his effectiveness as a public speaker. "His language," Cicero would later recall, "was not copious nor yet meagre, nor brilliant nor again crude" and his "voice, gestures, his whole delivery were without charm," but "upon invention and arrangement of matter he bestowed an extraordinary care . . . scarcely . . . surpassed in anyone."[7] In effect, Macer disdained the rounded periods, theatrical gestures and circus display of a prodigious memory of the outstanding reactionary orator of the day, Hortensius. A principled political leader, he attended instead to the matter of his speeches, seeking to clarify, to educate and to mobilize—hardly Hortensius' forte.

The speech Sallust assigns to Macer in the Histories synthesizes the language and aspirations of the reviving popular movement in the late seventies and reflects the most advanced thinking of the day, Epicureanism, especially in its vision of a universe, including human institutions, in constant flux. As a historian, Macer sought to define the trend of the times as well as the stage of development within the long-range political movement. Confident that from recent experiences the citizens realized "the difference between the rights left [them] by [their] forefathers and [the] slavery imposed upon [them] by Sulla,"[8] his task, he informed his partisans, was "to encourage [them] and to precede [them] on the road which . . . leads to the recovery of [their] liberties." Several previous tribunes had suffered trial and exile for agitating for the restoration of the tribunician powers, and only in the preceding year, for the first time since Sulla's dictatorship, had a tribune even dared to address the people from the Rostra in the Forum. Macer was mindful "how great [was] the power of the nobles" and how "powerless" he was "to drive them from their tyranny by the empty semblance of a magistracy." Nevertheless, emboldened by his long historical view and determined to make history rather than merely to submit supinely to events, Macer proclaimed that "defeat in a struggle for liberty is for a brave man better than never to have struggled at all." He warned that by promoting hysteria over supposed threats to national security, "a few men [had] taken possession of the treasury, the armies, the kingdoms and the provinces." On the other hand, the people, demoralized and confused, "like so many cattle [yielded themselves] a multitude, to single owners [aristocratic patrons] for use and enjoyment." They had been tricked into believing themselves sovereign in the commonwealth because they were allowed in elections to "choose [not their] defenders, [but their] masters." At the present stage of political development Macer could not persuade the commons of the overwhelming power they possessed if they acted "with a united purpose." Do you think, asked Macer, recalling the demagogy of Caesar's cousin, "it was from another motive than fear that Gaius Cotta, a consul chosen from the heart of the aristocratic party, restored some of their rights to the people's tribunes?" By fraudulent appeals for civil tranquility, the oligarchs had suppressed agitation for the restoration of the tribunician powers, and in noisy but vacuous political squabbles they pretended to battle over questions of principle when, in fact, "the real object was [merely] to determine who should be [the people's] masters." "Do not change the names of things," Macer urged his followers, "to suit your own cowardice and give to slavery the title of peace." If the people did not maintain a constant struggle for their rights, the oligarchs would "hold [them] in tighter bonds."

Macer did not attempt to exhort the demoralized commons to imitate "the manly deeds" of ancestors who had compelled the creation of the office of tribune and had wrested equal power with patricians for the plebs. On the other hand, as an Epicurean disbelieving in divine intervention in human affairs, Macer advised the commons not to expect help from Jupiter or any of the other gods. Instead, he issued a call for civil disobedience. If the oligarchs refused to restore the powers of the tribunes, Macer urged resistance to the military levies. "Let them hold their offices and administer them in their own way," he declared, "let them seek triumphs, let them lead their ancestral portraits against Mithridates, Sertorius, and what is left of the exiles, but let those who have no share in the profits be free also from dangers and toil." Macer chided the commons for expressing gratitude at the recent "hastily enacted law for the distribution of grain . . . by which they have valued all your liberties at five pecks [monthly] per man, an allowance actually not much greater than the rations of a prison." Even this pittance the oligarchs granted out of fear, for they were terrified that Pompeius, soon to return from Spain, might exploit the general discontent. Apparently privy to the maneuverings of Pompeius' agents at Rome, Macer assured his audience that "Pompeius prefers to be the leading man of the state with your consent, rather than to share in their mastery." He regretted, however, that the commons were so disorganized and demoralized as to have to rely on the power of a warlord to achieve their aspirations, and he chided his audience: "You have given up everything in exchange for your present slothfulness, thinking that you have ample freedom because your backs are spared and because you are allowed to go hither and thither by the grace of your rich masters."

The most profound crisis in the commonwealth, according to Macer, concerned "the country people, who are cut down in the quarrels of the great and sent to the provinces [as legionaries] as gifts to the magistrates. Thus they fight and conquer for the benefit of a few, but whatever happens, the commons are treated as vanquished." Dispatched to distant countries for campaigns of indefinite duration, the peasants won booty and hordes of slaves for their commanders, while their families at home were often driven out of their farmsteads by usurers or powerful neighbors. With their loot aristocrats displaced Italian peasants with slave gangs of peasants transported as captives from frontier lands. (In the decades following upon the Sullan expulsions and resettlements, one half of the rural population of Italy would leave the countryside, their lands appropriated for vineyards, olive groves, orchards and herds of cattle and sheep. It was this momentous social upheaval accompanied, of course, by unimaginable suffering, scarcely alluded to by public figures or historians of the day, that underlay the tensions that would ultimately lead, in Caesar's final years, to the overthrow of the oligarchic Republic.)

Thus, in the latter years of the seventies, Caesar gained invaluable political experience, achieving insights into "popular" issues and tactics and into the manipulations of the oligarchy. He was learning to calculate more precisely the relationship of forces in political struggles and was confirming that characteristic resolution in action with which he would repeatedly disconcert his opponents.

Late in the year Caesar departed for Greece to take up a post as military tribune on the staff of Marcus Antonius.

MILITARY TRIBUNE

Dependent upon the pirates for a sizable portion of the slave supply (ten thousand were supposedly auctioned off daily on the Aegean island of Delos alone), the senators responded tardily and with little enthusiasm to the pressure of shipping magnates and traders for action against the freebooters. Through the maneuvering of Marcus Cotta and the political boss Cethegus, a feckless nobleman had been awarded an extraordinary command with unlimited powers to crush the pirates throughout the Mediterranean. Son and namesake of a renowned orator and censor and victor over pirates, Marcus Antonius himself was simply a good-natured bungler. (In past centuries the senatorial oligarchy had justified its hegemony by claiming particular qualifications for leadership in war. When senators began avoiding lengthy military service, however, few could claim competence as generals, and commands were won through political maneuvering and not on the basis of ability.) It is likely that his wife, an ambitious noblewoman of the elder branch of the Julian clan, was instrumental in maneuvering Caesar's assignment to his staff, astutely recognizing the usefulness to her incompetent husband of her clansman with his corona civica, his experience with pirates and his exploits in repelling a Mithridatic incursion into Asia. Antonius had proclaimed the elimination of the freebooters from the Western Mediterranean, while actually dallying in Sicily and like a pirate plundering the island.

At Gytheum, a fishing village at the southeastern tip of the Peloponnesos, Antonius had established a headquarters for an assault on pirate strongholds on Crete. Gytheum offered no attractions other than a small theater and an altar where Orestes, driven mad after murdering his mother Clytemnestra, had, according to legend, found a cure, but Antonius and his officers pursued other interests than antiquities. Reserving for themselves the Senate campaign appropriation, they practiced such ferocious extortions as to compel the village elders to negotiate a loan with Roman moneylenders at forty-eight per cent interest. Caesar found Antonius with no conception of the ferocity of his foes. He was blithely loading ships with manacles for the prisoners he expected to capture for sale to slavedealers. After a brief struggle Antonius was compelled to accept a humiliating armistice. Nevertheless, friends in the Senate (undoubtedly prodded by the indefatigable Julia) hailed him as Creticus, conqueror of Crete. Thereafter, "while doing much and planning to do more to ruin [Rome's] allies and damage [Rome's] provinces, in the midst of his career of greed and injustice [Antonius] died suddenly."[9]

Meanwhile, in Italy, the consuls, as feckless as Antonius, were being routed by the horde of "living tools" under the leadership of the gladiator Spartacus. A praetor had fallen in battle, and the slaves had humiliated imperial Rome by exhibiting three hundred legionaries in funerary gladiatorial games. The host pressed toward the Alps, stripping fields, denuding storehouses, burning, looting, raping and killing—creating a swath of destruction through the peninsula. Abruptly, inexplicably, the slave armies halted their northward progress and veered south. With all citizens between seventeen and forty-six already under arms (one-eighth the male population), old men and boys manned the walls of Rome.

THE MILLIONAIRE

Marcus Crassus, one of the most prosperous of the slaveholders, proposed a variant of the ancestral principle that the wealthy, those with the most at stake, should bear the greatest burden in war. "No man is rich," he declared, "who cannot support an army out of his own substance." He announced his readiness to recruit new legions on his own. He had a reputation as a competent commander and was respected for his severitas and gravitas. When a tribune notorious for railing at leading noblemen was asked why he shied at attacking Crassus, he replied that the millionaire had "hay on his horn" (the warning against an ill-tempered ox).[10] Though wary of promoting the fortunes of a new warlord, the Senate had no choice but to accept Crassus' offer, and once more in appointing a powerful individual to an extraordinary command in place of the elected magistrates, the Senate was admitting the ineffectiveness of the oligarchic constitution.

With experienced officers scattered throughout the Mediterranean on many fronts, Crassus could not easily assemble an effective cadre, and he would have been eager to add an officer of Caesar's ability to his staff. Although no source specifically confirms Caesar's service in the servile war, a passage in Caesar's commentaries on his conquest of Gaul of two decades later implies his participation.[11] If Caesar did enter Crassus's service, he found the millionaire no doltish Antonius. In his forties, bald but with a manly handsomeness, Crassus honored the old ways. As custom prescribed, he had married his brother's widow. Like his famous grandfather, nicknamed "the laughless" and said to have laughed only once in his life, he lived frugally. On the other hand, he greeted even humble citizens by name, warmly clasping their hands, always receptive to their petitions. Caesar could discuss Aristotle with him, for Crassus was conning the sage's works with a house philosopher.

Spartacus had withdrawn to the south, to regions of Italy which had maintained resistance longest during the Italian war and had not been pacified, regions where herding was a major industry and the peasants either were under pressure to give up their smallholdings before the expanding latifundia or were already transformed into half-starved migrant workers. In these regions alone had Spartacus succeeded in capturing towns, encountering sympathetic support among the poor.

As a leading slaveholder, Crassus conducted the war with particular ferocity. Determined to crush the uprising before Pompeius, summoned by the Senate from Spain, arrived to usurp the victory, he flogged and executed every tenth man in a detachment that panicked in battle, and to blockade Spartacus within the toe of Italy he hounded his troups into digging a ditch fifteen feet wide and deep and backed by a rampart along a thirty-five-mile line. At a report that Pompeius was approaching the Alps, Crassus provoked the slaves to battle and destroyed their army, estimated by ancient historians (notorious for exaggeration of figures) at ninety thousand men. Pompeius did intercept several thousand fugitives at an Alpine pass and reported to the Senate that "Crassus had conquered the gladiators in a pitched battle but he himself had extirpated the war entirely."[12] Crassus vented his fury on his prisoners, crucifying six thousand along a one-hundred-fifty-mile stretch of the Appian Way. Nevertheless, the name of the slave commander has been commemorated through the ages, even to the twentieth century, whereas Crassus' victory is scarcely remembered.

It is difficult to estimate the impact of the Spartacan uprising, for ancient historians concerned themselves with slaves only when this substantial segment of the population rebelled against their masters. In the Spartacan war, up to one hundred thousand slaves may have fallen or run away from their owners. There is evidence that during the subsequent period manumissions became especially common and that, increasingly, large estates were worked by freeborn tenants. Profit-conscious landowners like the renowned polymath Varro modified old Cato's savage slave management practices and sought to encourage slaves to greater productivity by paternalist inducements, allowing more of them to enjoy family life and setting them up in independent trades and facilitating their buying their freedom. Fears of slave rebellion, however, remained intense for generations. (A quarter-century later, perhaps as a result of his participation in the servile war, Caesar in his own struggle against the senatorial oligarchy forbade enrolment of slaves in his legions and excoriated his enemies for endangering the common security by arming slaves against him.)

It was no longer the fashion for generals to disband armies after victory, and neither Pompeius nor Crassus would dismiss his troops before the other.

Pompeius posed the greater threat. To appease him and to win his support against Crassus, the Senate acceded to his demands for a triumph and for the privilege of running for a consulship despite his lack of qualifications in age and in prior magistracies. Thus Pompeius initiated his senatorial career with an unconstitutional act. Repeatedly thereafter, often with the pretense of defending the constitution, he would violate it. Alarmed at his isolation, Crassus appealed for an alliance. Delighted to bestow a favor on a nobleman of ancient lineage and to confound his enemies in the Senate, Pompeius announced to the citizenry that "he should be no less grateful to them for the colleague than for the office."[13]

Caesar hardly commanded sufficient influence to play one warlord against the other. With Pompeius pretending to champion the cause of the populars, however, Caesar could support the new consuls without compromising himself. During their consulship he would at least enter his candidacy for the first office in the progress of magistracies. With the favor of the two warlords, his election was assured.

XIV

THE OLD MAN'S SUCCESSOR

EVEN before Sulla's importation of previously unknown manuscripts of Aristotle roused new interest in the sage, the Greek philosopher had been "the most particular admiration" of the elder Catulus. He was the delight of Crassus' leisure. More than any of his contemporaries, however, Caesar exemplified the Aristotelian ideal of "a life concerned with action belonging to the rational part of man . . . activity of soul in conformity with excellence" over the course of "a complete lifetime." Even as a youth Caesar was formulating decisions, as Aristotle recommends, "from choice, not from desire . . . [choice] deliberated about beforehand."[1] In the transition from adulescentia (the age between the assumption of the toga of manhood and the inauguration of a political career) Caesar was already evidencing a maturity of vision, a certainty of purpose, a rationality of calculation and an ability to grasp the decisive moment and to define the decisive factor within evolving circumstances—all coupled with a disdain both of self-delusion and of opportunistic compromise.

The consulship of Pompeius and Crassus afforded particular opportunities for Caesar. Upon his election, questioned by a tribune primed for the occasion, Pompeius proclaimed his support for a restoration of the tribunician powers and went on to warn: "Our provinces have been wasted and laid desolate. Our law courts are behaving scandalously and wickedly." He promised to "take steps" to deal with these evils. At the same time the Sullans were demoralized. Their spokesman, Catulus, had repeatedly warned of "the worse trouble and evils that change might bring." Now he lamented that it was because the senators had proved such "ineffective and immoral guardians of the courts of justice" that the people "felt so acutely their loss of the tribunes' powers." Caesar participated in the victory of the restoration of these powers and assisted, too, in passing a bill to grant amnesty to political exiles, another measure resisted by the Sullans. On the latter occasion Caesar proclaimed once again his pietas and fides, for a beneficiary of the bill was young Cinna, his brother-in-law. "To me, indeed," Caesar vaunted, "it seems that as our kinship demanded I have failed neither in labor, in pains nor in industry."[2]

On the other hand, association with Pompeius meant accepting a role of dependency and adapting to Pompeius' purposes. While Caesar, Marius' nephew, could not be content for any length of time with such an association, Cicero, aware that the old nobility, jealous of its monopoly of the highest magistracies, would block the advancement of a "new man," solicited Pompeius' support in his candidacy for an aedileship. He was prepared to commit himself without reservations to the warlord, for Pompeius seemed both irresistible and resolute in pursuing his present course. Newly elected censors, the first since Cinna's day, fourteen years earlier, blacklisted sixty-four of the six hundred senators, expelling men of low rank appointed by the dictator, men compromised by corruption or bankruptcy and enemies of the two consuls. Among the victims of the purge were such distinguished noblemen as the consular Lentulus Sura, a patrician of the Cornelian clan recently married to Julia, Marcus Antonius' widow; and Marcus Antonius' brother, whom Caesar had prosecuted unsuccessfully five years earlier.

Pompeius was engaged in a power struggle with a coterie of leading Sullans in a trial of the despicable Marian turncoat Verres, whose depredations Caesar had experienced in Asia and in Cilicia. Recently as proconsul in Sicily, Verres had insulted, robbed and even put to torture clients of Pompeius'. He was confident of acquittal. While governor he boasted that he had parceled out his plunder, setting aside the take of the first year "to increasing his own fortune and reversing the profits of his second year to his advocates and defenders [Hortensius and some Metellans] . . . and the whole of the great third year, the richest and most profitable of the three, for his judges."[3]

For the first time in his career Cicero dared to undertake a prosecution, and of a personage with powerful connections. He counted on Pompeius' backing and on a sympathetic audience at the trial, for the populars had demonstrated in protest against Verres' oppression of the Sicilians and of Roman entrepreneurs with interests on the island. Persuaded of Pompeius' determination to reform provincial administration, Cicero decided to make an example of Verres. Echoing his mentor, Cicero declared: "Our provinces have been ravaged and plundered and utterly ruined; the allies and dependents of the Roman nation have been brought down to the lowest pitch of wretchedness."[4] On this occasion, however (as on even more critical occasions in the future), Cicero misjudged Pompeius' resolve. After humbling his opponents and winning acclaim from entrepreneurs, small-town aristocrats, shopkeepers and moneylenders, Pompeius lost enthusiasm for reform. He and Crassus began a feverish competition for popularity.

With Pompeius preoccupied with preparations for games in honor of his victory in Spain and Crassus with arrangements for a mammoth public banquet to Hercules, the Sullans, generously supplied with campaign funds by Verres, mobilized their clients and oligarchic allies, and in the elections Hortensius and a Metellan won consulships for the coming year. As Hortensius was being escorted home after his victory, near the Arch of Fabius at the edge of the Forum, the ex-consul Curio bawled out to Verres for all to hear: "I hereby inform you that today's election means your acquittal."[5] Indeed, against Verres' wholesale bribery and the opposition of Verres' powerful friends, Cicero barely won election as aedile, and only with difficulty did he block postponement of the trial to the coming year, when a praetor sympathetic to Verres would preside over the extortion court.

Despite the consuls' indifference, however, the momentum of the popular program continued. In daily harangues, Lucius, the youngest of the three Cotta brothers, a praetor this year, was proclaiming that "political stability [was] unattainable unless the courts [controlled by the senators since Sulla] were handed back to the equestrian order." Caesar assisted his cousin in promoting this judicial reform though aware that Lucius was motivated by a personal concern; his career was threatened by the opprobrium his brother Marcus had brought on the family in a shameful defeat by Mithridates and in sacking a city long allied to Rome. In his desperation, Lucius denounced his Old Guard colleagues with invective that would have dismayed Gaius Cotta and won applause from the radical tribune Macer. "There is," he proclaimed, "a senatorial method of extorting money that is common to the whole order and by now all but its admitted right. By this method our allies [the provinces and other dependencies] are with gross injustice being robbed of vast sums. The offenders run no risk of prosecution in courts composed of senators."[6]

The courts had lost all credibility. Romans joked about jurors who accepted bribes from both plantiffs and defendants. In a recent trial Hortensius had distributed colored ballots among the senatorial jurors in order to guarantee that they voted as paid. In another instance "senators were found to vote against a man whom they were condemning without having attended his trial." So intense was popular indignation that Cicero warned the senatorial jurors in the Verres trial that a verdict of acquittal would assure passage of Cotta's reform bill and deprive them of their judicial monopoly. In face of popular hostility, Cicero's eloquence and the overwhelming evidence Cicero had assembled, Hortensius abandoned the defense, while Verres fled into exile to suffer conviction in absentia and to maintain possession of most of his loot. Cicero published the additional speeches he had been unable to deliver at the trial, exhibiting in them the boldest championship of the "popular" program of his entire career. The political agitation of the radical tribune Macer and others (including Caesar) had so transformed the political atmosphere that the prudent Cicero dared to compete with Lucius Cotta in bravado. "Year after year," proclaimed the orator, "we have seen all the wealth of all the world become the property of a mere handful of men . . . none of these persons conceals his cupidity."[7] Macer could not have been more forthright.

As for Lucius Cotta, a skilful politician like his brother Gaius, he pretended to yield to overwhelming odds and accepted a compromise bill under which juries would henceforth be composed of senators, equestrians and a third category of wealthy citizens. His reform posed no serious threat to senatorial hegemony. The equestrian order, especially since Sulla's purge, consisted in great part of sons and relatives of senators along with other landed aristocrats and entrepreneurs not averse to sharing extortions and bribes with senators and equally as committed to the defense of property. After decades of turbulence, many senators were resigned to sharing judicial power with other elements of the oligarchy so long as senators preserved their monopoly of the executive power. Furthermore, increasingly, senators were engaging in banking and commercial ventures in association with nonsenatorial colleagues, and, except for diehard reactionaries like Cato, few senators were interested in renewing old struggles with the other aristocratic order.

In August Pompeius diverted the commons with victory games, and in September Crassus eclipsed the late dictator in the prodigality of his public banquet, heaping forth food on a thousand tables and distributing a three-month grain ration. Sated with glory and eager to pass on to other ventures, both consuls declined provincial governorships for the coming year. At the ceremony at which they relinquished their magistracies, in their antagonism the two men refused to look at each other. Suddenly an equestrian of the Aurelian clan (a maternal relative of Caesar's?) pushed through the crowd crying that Jupiter had appeared to him in a dream and bidden him to admonish the consuls not to depart from office without reestablishing their friendship. Unimpressed by divine injunctions that did not conform to his own will, Pompeius stood unmoved, but Crassus, probably privy to the maneuver, extended his hand. "I think I do nothing ignoble or mean, my fellow citizens," he declared with disarming ingenuousness, "in yielding first to Pompeius, whom you were pleased to call Magnus when he was still beardless and to whom you decreed two triumphs before he was a senator."[8]

Pompeius could never resist flattery, and he yielded for the moment. (A decade later, in a maneuver aimed at advancing his own career, Caesar would promote a lasting reconciliation between the millionaire and the warlord. It is to be suspected that he participated in this earlier maneuver as well.)

THE DECISION

Like Marius before him, Caesar appealed to the elements of the population that periodically coalesced into a popular opposition. During the consulship of Pompeius and Crassus, he enjoyed an opportunity he had not known previously. The restoration of the tribunician powers, the reform of the judiciary and the amnesty for the political exiles provided an impetus to the popular movement. Furthermore with the registration of tens of thousands of Italians, the citizenship rolls swelled from 463,000 to 910,000. The new citizens along with other elements uncommitted to the old senatorial aristocracy were looking for champions of their interests. With Pompeius and Crassus making no attempt to assemble an enduring faction of their own or to ensure their succession by reform candidates, the Sullans regained control of the consulship, and the popular movement found itself leaderless at the moment of its revival.

Caesar won election as one of the sixteen quaestors, officials assigned to supervising the treasury or to service with provincial governors. Commanding minimal authority, the magistracy, nevertheless, represented the formal initiation of an oligarch's political career and offered an occasion for evaluation of past experiences and for formulating new goals and strategies. With Caesar, a young man of insight, a stormy and eventful past, including assassinations, civil violence, war, proscriptions, personal humiliation and threats to his life, impelled a precocious definition of self and of his role and aspirations.

Assigned to the staff of the new governor of Further Spain, Caesar would have no opportunity to advance his influence at Rome. He would be forgotten by the citizenry during his two-year absence from Rome. How could he impress himself upon their memory?

Caesar would be departing for the land where Sertorius, the last of the Marian leaders, had maintained heroic resistance to the Sullans for the better part of a decade. Caesar's brother-in-law Cinna and other Sertorian officers amnestied by Pompeius and by the law Caesar helped to promote undoubtedly recounted to Caesar their experiences with this extraordinary Roman. Even Sertorius' enemies could not deny his greatness as a man, a general and a statesman. Like an ancestral hero he disdained luxury and displayed moderation in eating and drinking. He "would not consent to see or hear anything that was disgraceful but held his associates to the practice of indulging only in mirth and merriment that was decorous and restrained."[9] As a leader, inspiring fanatical devotion, he drove his troops to the limits of their endurance. It was, however, as a statesman that he made his impress on history. He not only exposed the crisis of empire in the West as Mithridates had done in the East, but he also pointed to the transformation that would ultimately preserve the empire. Untrammeled by the city-state mindset of the myopic oligarchy, with unparalleled vision he offered the varied peoples of the Iberian peninsula a prospect of eventual citizenship. Unready for such a radical policy, his Roman associates assassinated him.

With Sertorius' death, opposition elements everywhere in the empire lost their last champion.

On the eve of Caesar's departure for Spain another connection to Old Marius died—Caesar's Aunt Julia. With neither husband nor son surviving her, it fell to her nephew to arrange her funeral.

Julia's death closed an era.

Caesar used her funeral to initiate another era.

Old Marius had been dead for fifteen years, and Romans were eager to forget the ferocious antagonisms of past decades. At the funeral nobles hostile to Marius could signify their readiness to terminate the old conflict (especially since they considered themselves victorious). Some would attend out of particular obligations, men like Quintus Marcius Rex, a candidate for the coming year's consulship and a relative to Julia's mother, and Catulus, whose father's half-brothers had been Julia's cousins. Descendants of the Trojan clans that had migrated to Rome with the Julians and Caesar's colleagues in the college of pontifices would also be present. Especially eager to pay homage to the widow of the man seven times consul and the victor over German invaders would be equestrian survivors of the proscriptions, sons of the proscribed, freedmen, clients, household slaves and, above all, veterans who had served under the Old Man or his son.

Suddenly in the procession—images of Marius!—"seen for the first time since Sulla had proclaimed Marius and his friends public enemies. When some cried out against Caesar . . . the people answered them with loud shouts, received Caesar with applause and admired him for bringing back after so long a time, as it were from Hades, the honors of Marius into the city."[10]

Caesar's was no act of childish defiance but a calculated test of the will of those who had suffered under the dictator and his successors. By this bold maneuver, too, Caesar was reaffirming his loyalty to the man whose memory still roused hope among the populars, and he was offering himself as Marius' successor. But he was not content to be merely a successor even to such a man, and in his eulogy of his aunt he proclaimed her (and himself) as a noble Roman of glorious lineage, declaring:

> The family of my Aunt Julia is descended by her mother from the kings and on her father's side is akin to the immortal gods; for the Marcii Reges go back to [King] Ancus Marcius, and the Julii, the family of which ours is a branch, to Venus. Our stock therefore has at once the sanctity of kings, whose power is supreme among mortal men, and the claim to reverence which attaches to the gods, who hold sway over kings themselves.[11]

In this vaunt Caesar was speaking as much to himself as to his audience, defining who he was and what he could and would become. He was choosing anew his ancestors, his heroes and his ideals and reaffirming his connection to the founding of Rome, to the goddess-mother of Aeneas and to a benevolent king of the time of the ancestors. In heritage he surpassed the plebeian millionaire and the upstart warlord and the haughtiest of the patricians. Implicit in his boast was a rededication to pietas and fides—a proclamation of continuing association with Marius and defiance of Sulla and reassertion of his will to persevere as a champion of popular causes. He was a man, he was telling Rome, who would shape his own destiny. Unlike Crassus and Pompeius and other oligarchs of established prestige he was free of contamination with the dictator and the proscriptions and confiscations.

Cornelia's death followed upon Julia's.

It was not the custom to deliver eulogies for young women, but at Julia's funeral Caesar had abandoned caution: at Cornelia's he ignored tradition and set precedent. On this occasion Caesar could confirm the message he had delivered at Julia's funeral and assert with greater conviction his dedication to the virtues of pietas and fides. He could recall events poignant to those of his own generation in the audience—the assassination of Cornelia's father, the civil war, the proscriptions, the Lepidan revolt and the Sertorian war. He could remind Romans of the dictator's vain attempt to force him to divorce Cornelia and of Sulla's confiscation of her dowry. Caesar had shared the despair and suffering of the innumerable victims of the past decades. Yet he had maintained his dignity. People recalled his corona civica, his repulse of an invasion in Asia, his prosecution of associates of the dictator, his support of the radical tribune Macer and his agitation over the years for the restoration of the tribunician powers, for amnesty for political exiles and for reform of the courts.

In the two eulogies Caesar demonstrated that he had attained the age at which in young men of great promise there emerges the capacity to "care in a sense which includes 'to care to' do something, 'to care for' somebody or something, 'to take care of' and 'to take care not to' do something destructive." The women who heard him would be especially moved by his caring—a virtue much to be prized in times of corruption and opportunism. Indeed, Plutarch reports that the eulogy for Cornelia "brought him much favor and worked upon the sympathies of the multitude so that they were fond of him as a man who was gentle and full of feeling."[12]

In order not to be forgotten during his absence in Spain Caesar had required some spectacular action before his departure. In the two funerals he had found and embraced his opportunity. The eulogies would not be forgotten, for Caesar had evoked both a profound response among broad elements of the citizenry and a respect that confirmed his earlier popularity. In the orations he bade Rome a temporary farewell and inaugurated a new era in his life and, as the future would show, in the life of Rome itself.

XV

ALEXANDER

CAESAR'S defiance of the Old Guard, his assertion of his dignity on par with the most powerful nobles and warlords and his claim to leadership of the Marian party appeared as childish pretension before the gigantic victory monument Pompeius had erected at the pass leading to Spain through the Pyrenees. In imitation of Alexander's famous victory monument, Pompeius had placed an inscription below his statue proclaiming his capture of eight hundred and seventy-six towns from the Alps to the Ocean. As in the servile rebellion, when he had denigrated Crassus' decisive effort, here he ignored the contribution to victory of his associate, Metellus Pius. Proceeding south on the Via Herculea along the Iberian coast, Caesar encountered at every hand reminders of Pompeius' glory. Northeastern Spain had been a Sertorian stronghold and an area of fierce struggle. Osca, Sertorius' capital, Tarraco (Tarragona) and other towns had withstood lengthy sieges, and Calagurris (Calahorra) had not capitulated until the townspeople had first resorted to cannibalism. The haughty Celtiberians in cloaks of black wool Caesar met prancing on spirited horses or strutting with a swagger had either been generously rewarded by Pompeius for assistance in the recent war or as generously pardoned for fighting under Sertorius. The Celtiberians were renowned for loyalty to the death to leaders and patrons, and twenty years later, in a war against Pompeius, Caesar would discover that "those [states] which in the earlier war had taken the side of Sertorius and had been conquered feared the name and authority of the absent Pompeius and those which had remained loyal, having received great kindnesses, were devoted to him."[1]

Caesar had had repeated experiences in Rome's eastern provinces; here he found himself in another world. The Romans had arrived in Spain a century and a half earlier. The ways of the ancestors prescribed no morality in the treatment of "barbarians," and nowhere else in the Mediterranean world had the Romans practiced such unconscionable treachery or massacred and enslaved with such savagery. Nevertheless, over the generations Spain had become the most Romanized part of the world outside Italy, a land of opportunity, an El Dorado for tens of thousands of legionaries and other settlers. Whereas in the East Italians adopted Greek as their language and assimilated local customs, here colonists spoke Latin and Romanized their neighbors. Unlike other provincials, too, the Spaniards participated directly in Italian conflicts, and the Sertorian war represented a continuation of the Italian revolt and the civil war, a transfer of Italian conflicts to Italians living in Iberia.

Further Spain, the province in which Caesar was to serve his quaestorship, encompassed the south and southwest of the peninsula. Unlike Nearer Spain with its limited Italian settlements in the valley of the Ebro and along the coast, Further Spain was almost thoroughly Romanized. Despite a marked accent in their speech, the people of the provincial capital, Corduba, considered themselves more Roman than the Romans. The aristocracy spoke Greek in addition to Latin and patronized scholars, poets and artists. Much of their wealth derived from nearby mines, and they boasted that Spain was preeminent in the Mediterranean world for the variety and abundance of its minerals—gold, silver, iron, copper, lead, cinnabar, mercury and tin. Employing an advanced technology, mineowners extracted huge profits from ferociously exploited slaves. Already a century earlier forty thousand were employed in silver mines near Carthago Nova (Cartagena) alone. Of their working conditions, Diodorus Siculus, a contemporary of Caesar's, reported: "No respite or pause is granted them . . . but compelled beneath blows of the overseers to endure the

severity of their plight . . . indeed death in their eyes is more to be desired than
life."² With the high mortality among the miners, a stream of replacements had
to be assured by purchase, capture and kidnapping from unsubjugated tribes.
The industry brought huge returns not only to the proprietors of the mines but
also to dealers in timber, sacking, rope, tools and machinery, to contractors for
transport and provisions and to owners of foundries and metalworks as well as
to shipping magnates.

Assigned to conduct the assizes, the periodic tribunals held in major centers,
Caesar had an opportunity to gain insights into the social, political and economic life of this populous and wealthy region and to begin to assemble a
personal clientship there. The richest region of the province lay along the
Baetis (the Guadalquivir), an agricultural zone recalling the Campanian plain
south of Rome in the fertility of the soil, the variety of the crops and the
advanced technology in farming and herding. As in Central Italy medium-sized
plantations predominated, worked by slave gangs under rigid discipline. The
wheat of the province was of a superior strain, the olive oil the finest in the
Mediterranean and the livestock in such abundance that the provincials relied primarily on meat for their diet. Some years before Caesar's arrival, the
Rhodian philosopher Posidonios had pronounced the country preeminent in
"the entire inhabited world in respect of fertility and of the goodly products of
land and sea."³ The sea provided wealth to the coastal towns, especially to the
chief port of the Baetis valley, Gades (Cadiz), the largest city in the Western
Mediterranean after Rome. Founded by Phoenicians centuries before Rome
existed, the city had entered into alliance with Rome during the Hannibalic
war and supported Rome in subsequent conflicts. Although the population
spoke Punic, many townspeople were fluent in Latin and Greek (the lingua
franca of the Inland Sea). Caesar found the quays and streets thronged with
seamen of all hues and tongues and saw a harbor crowded with the largest fleet
of merchant ships and fishing smacks in the Mediterranean world. The majority of the male population was always at sea, sailing outside the Pillars of
Hercules down the coast of Africa or northward to Britain. Gaditan salt fish
and fish sauce (garum) reached Ostia and Puteoli in Italy in seven days in ships
loaded with grain, wax, pitch, dyes, ores, wool, hams, olives and linens. The
ships often returned with Campanian pottery. The economies of the two pe-
ninsulas had been growing ever more interdependent.

Since Roman aristocrats often traveled with letters of introduction, it may
have been thus that Caesar made the acquaintance of a wealthy Gaditan
named Balbus with whom he established a friendship that would last for the
rest of his life. Balbus had served under both Metellus and Pompeius and could
provide Caesar with another view of the recent Sertorian war. Controlling
much of the shipping and commerce of the province, Punic aristocrats shared
the Sullan sympathies of wealthy Italian settlers and of the more prosperous
Romanized indigenous people and freedmen. Jealous of their privileges and
fearful of the poorer elements of the population, the men of property relied

upon the legions to protect them against civil disorders as well as against threats from unsubjugated tribesmen. They were dismayed when Sertorius returned to Spain to lead a rebellion of the Lusitanians, ferocious marauders from the west and north who often pillaged and terrorized the province. With the loss and exhaustion of Asia and other eastern provinces during the Mithridatic war, Further Spain had enjoyed a spurt in commerce with Italy. With his alliance with pirates, however, Sertorius endangered trade and shipping, and in rallying to his army Italian settlers in frontier regions as well as Celtiberian tribes, he threatened the social order. The provincial aristocrats were alarmed, too, at his challenging the imperial dominion by establishing a Senate-in-exile, and in the event of his victory they anticipated radical measures like the cancellation of debts and land reform.

Confronting opposition among the most influential elements of the province, Sertorius sought support primarily in Nearer Spain. Metellus, on the other hand, established colonies of legionaries in Further Spain to provide bulwarks of defense, and both he and Pompeius were generous in rewarding with Roman citizenship provincial volunteers like Balbus and tribesmen serving as mercenary auxiliaries. Pompeius, in particular, was aware of the value of a clientship among the vigorous and martial peoples in these "everlasting storehouses of nature [and] never-failing treasury of an empire."[4]

Sertorius had left a legacy. He had exposed the anachronism of city-state imperialism and offered a vision of a different future for the province. Even as in Italy, where the Italians had won citizenship and transformed Roman history into Italian history, so in Spain Italians and Romanized Punic aristocrats like Balbus would, inevitably, be demanding a share in imperial power. They would be joined by descendants of marriages between legionaries and Celtiberians and by Romanized Celtiberians who had adopted Latin as their language along with Roman names and the wearing of the toga.

In later years Caesar would continue Sertorius' challenge to the city-state concept of empire and develop further Sertorius' imperial view, and he would confront opposition among the elements most hostile to Sertorius. At this juncture, however, as a lowly quaestor arbitrating petty disputes over boundaries and water rights and fugitive slaves, Caesar could entertain no such perspectives. Indeed, he suffered a painful realization of his insignificance upon a visit to the Temple of Melkart, the Punic Hercules, some dozen miles from Gades. On the doors of the temple he beheld a depiction of the labors of the demigod, and he recalled Hercules' lament in the underworld to Odysseus regarding his many travails:

> Odysseus, master mariner and soldier,
> under a cloud, you too? Destined to grinding
> labors like my own in the sunny world?
> Son of Kronion Zeus or not, how many
> days I sweated out, being bound in servitude
> to a man far worse than I, a rough master!

> He made me hunt this place one time
> to get the watchdog of the dead: no more
> perilous task, he thought, could be.

Caesar could recount his own travails and the paltry meed of his quaestorship, and when he entered the temple and beheld a bust of Alexander, he "heaved a sigh as if out of patience with his own incapacity at having done nothing noteworthy at a time of life when Alexander had already brought the world to his feet."[5]

Odysseus, that man of many toils, scarcely awaiting the conclusion to Hercules' complaint:

> whirled then, made for the ship, shouted to crewmen
> to get aboard and cast off the stern hawsers
> . . . and the ship went leaping toward the stream of Ocean.

Similarly, Caesar "straightway asked for his discharge, to grasp the first opportunity for greater enterprises at Rome."[6] Apparently he had developed with the provincial governor a relationship of affection, for he obtained leave to depart without completing his assignment. Before setting out, however, Caesar made a pilgrimage to the temple of the Punic Venus just west of Gades, where priests interpreted dreams of worshipers who slept within the sacred precincts. To his dismay, Caesar had a vision of violating his mother. He had, of course, a particularly close relationship with her. As a youth Caesar had written a tragedy about Oedipus, the Greek hero who, unaware of his sin, had married his mother. Upon his father's death, when Caesar was fifteen, Aurelia, unlike many other widowed matrons, seems not to have remarried, devoting herself to promoting the career of her only son. During these days, certainly, Aurelia was much in Caesar's thoughts, serving as she was as his housekeeper, as mother to his daughter and as guardian of his fortunes. Confronted with the paltriness of his achievements, he was reminded of her. He had failed her.

Canny from centuries of experience, the priests reached a swift intuition and satisfied Caesar with an astute, if conventional, interpretation of his dream. "He was destined to rule the world," they said, "since the mother he had seen in his power was none other than the earth, which is regarded as the common parent of all mankind."[7]

To Marius, who had initiated his long career in Spain, an African seer had prophesied successes of "incredible magnitude and beyond his every expectation,"[8] but the priests serving Caesar's divine ancestress promised him mastery over the earth—like Alexander.

CISALPINA

Challenged by the prophecy, Caesar would lose not a moment nor fail to exploit a single opportunity, and passing from Transalpine to Cisalpine Gaul, Caesar discovered an extraordinary possibility for assembling a clientship among a population of political significance, for Cisalpina was in ferment at the delay in extending full citizenship to the greater part of the region. Encompassing the territory from the Alps to the Adriatic, Cisalpina was administered as a province separate from the rest of Italy. In climate, in fact, it was continental rather than Mediterranean, with sharply demarcated winters and summers and abundant rainfall. Especially along the three hundred miles of the Po river and its basin, it possessed unrivaled pasturage and thick forests as well as profitable quarries and mines.

In a series of bloody wars following upon a Gallic sack of Rome more than three centuries before Caesar's day, the Romans had massacred or expelled various tribes and subdued the remainder. After the Hannibalic war, they conducted an intensive colonization program along the Po for defense against invasion from the north and built a dense network of military highways. The area south of the river, the Cispadane region, thoroughly Romanized, was awarded full citizenship in the eighties after the Italian revolt, but except for a few long-established colonies like the town of Cremona, the Transpadanes (people across the Po), Italians and Gauls alike, were granted only limited citizenship. With these changes in status both regions underwent a social, political and cultural upheaval even more profound than that in the central and southern regions of the peninsula. The territory was redistricted, and rural settlements and tribal areas were consolidated into municipalities. Following a mammoth survey, hundreds of square miles of land were marked into segments two iugera in size (240 Roman feet long and 120 wide—about five-eighths of an acre) within grids of a hundred parcels (thus the term *centuriation*). Highways formed the base of these grids, and secondary roads were laid out between centuries along with smaller intermediate access roads at regular intervals. Ditches were dug for drainage, and trees and hedges planted as windbreaks. In sparsely settled areas hamlets were razed and replaced by towns laid out in grid patterns like army camps to serve as administrative and commercial centers.

As a result of this social and political transformation, the Transpadane country began more and more to resemble the Romanized Cispadane region, and since the former area also provided a disproportionate share of legionary recruits, the inhabitants felt all the more resentful of their second-class citizenship. Inasmuch as Pompeius' father had carried out the enfranchisement of Cispadana during the Italian revolt, the Transpadanes had looked to Pompeius for full citizenship during his consulship—in vain. The domi nobiles, the local aristocrats, many of whom were among the most prosperous farmers, cattle dealers, industrialists and traders in Italy, were especially disappointed, for they were eager to compete for magistracies at Rome.

At the time of Caesar's arrival, the Transpadanes were engaged in vigorous agitation. The ferment offered Caesar a unique opportunity. By associating himself with this cause, Caesar could undermine Pompeius' influence and confirm his own reputation as a consistent opponent to the reactionary leadership of the Senate. He enjoyed the advantage of the local adulation of Old Marius, who had saved Cisalpina from devastation from German invaders. Word of Caesar's display of the hero's image at his aunt's funeral would have reached the north, for there was constant traffic between Rome and the province. On the other hand, in their character and attitudes, Caesar found the Cisalpiners congenial. Old-fashioned in their industriousness, sense of civic responsibility and local patriotism, the people, a pioneer folk, were nevertheless progressive. With an enormous communal effort they had rescued vast tracts of marshland by digging a network of drainage canals. Alone among the farmers of the peninsula, they employed the harrow in plowing and seeding, achieving high productivity without reliance upon the slave gangs of the plantations to the south. In construction, fifty years ahead of the rest of Italy, they were using baked instead of sun-dried brick.

Caesar had probably became aware of the vigorous cultural life of Cisalpina through his tutor Gnipho, a native of the region. Cisalpina offered promise of becoming the major center of Latin literature. Valerius Cato, a distinguished grammarian and the author of a poem entitled "Indignatio," a cry of outrage at Sulla's confiscation of his family's farm, served as mentor to a group of remarkable younger poets, some of whom, singers of a prosperous and cultivated society, were creating the first Latin lyric poetry, and it may have been during this first sojourn in the region that Caesar befriended at Verona a wealthy army contractor named Catullus,* whose teen-aged son was already exhibiting extraordinary poetic talent. (Vergil had been born at Mantua two years before Caesar's visit.) The Cisalpiners prided themselves, too, on their receptivity to advanced thinking, and one of the most effective popularizers of the radical Epicurean philosophy, a certain Catius, was a native of the region.

Scarcely a novice in political agitation, Caesar could make an impressive contribution to the Transpadane struggle for full citizenship. His task was facilitated by the cynical opposition of the pauci (the "few"—the obdurate clique of unreconstructed Sullans) to any extension of the franchise. In the Senate the consular Curio, for example, after granting that the demands of the people beyond the Po were just, arrogantly proclaimed: "Let expediency prevail."[9]

The campaign developed with such intensity that an alarmed Senate put the legions on alert. The Transpadanes had had enough of civil war, and Caesar had long since rejected adventurism. He had learned, too, that major issues are rarely resolved in a single effort. Inevitably citizenship would be extended up to the Alps. Meanwhile, he would be honored as a worthy nephew to the savior general and as a champion of the Transpadane cause; henceforth the people of Cisaplina would prove to be loyal supporters of his career and unwavering defenders of his dignity.

---

*This family, as the spelling of their name (CatuLLus) indicates, was not related to the influential noble family at Rome, who spelled their name CatuLus.

When, after an absence of about a year and a half, Caesar arrived at Rome, he had gained a profound appreciation of the political, military, economic and cultural potentials of the western provinces. He understood that the chief base of imperial power lay in the West, and he sensed the strategic role Cisalpine Gaul might play in Roman expansion across the Alps in Gaul, in Central Europe and in the Balkans. The flourishing agriculture and industry of the region required outlets, and the vigorous population would provide the troops to conquer markets and booty. Early in his career Caesar had already recognized Cisalpine Gaul as "the flower of Italy, the mainstay of the empire of the Roman people . . . the ornament of its dignity."[10]

XVI

POMPEIUS' ASSOCIATE

WITH the news of the Transpadane agitation Caesar heralded his return to Rome, reasserted his resolve to lead the opposition to the dominant clique of the Senate and gave notice that he would not be content to serve in the Senate as a mere pedarius, a senator of inferior rank entitled to vote with his feet in the divisions but rarely to express an opinion. Although not eligible for a consulship until 59, Caesar was already initiating his campaign for the high office. Long-range preparation was imperative. Prior to Marius' first consulship, seven years before Caesar was born, "although the commons could bestow the other magistracies, the nobles passed the consulate from hand to hand within their own order,"[1] and within the nobility a tiny coterie, to which the Julians did not belong, maintained a near monopoly of the high office. By winning five additional consulships, Marius had deprived five of this clique of the post. In 86 he had a held a seventh consulship, and in the eighties Cinna had retained the consulship for four successive years and Carbo three. During the years of civil war and bitter factional strife, with many nobles prevented from commencing their political careers, a sizable backlog of candidates had developed, and middle-aged aristocrats were now competing with younger men for all magistracies. Upon the enfranchisement of hundreds of thousands of Italians, Italian aristocrats entered the lists. In addition, some of the sixty-nine men expelled from the Senate by the censors in 70 were seeking rehabilitation by election to office. Thus few of the twenty-six quaestors elected each year could hope to advance even to an aedileship, much less to a praetorship or a consulship. In desperation, ambitious oligarchs schemed and conspired, engaging in wholesale bribery and even utilizing court indictments to eliminate rivals.

Sulla's former lieutenants, who considered the consulship a prize of their victory in the civil war, were divided not only by personal rivalries and animosities but even by superficial policy differences. Unable to control the vastly enlarged electorate, more and more they, too, were compelled to rely on bribery and fraud to preserve their monopoly of the highest magistracies. Few men of property could compete against the leading Sullans in manipulating clientships and in buying votes. Metellus Pius, Sulla's colleague in the consulship of 80, for example, had amassed so much wealth and property that during the recent war in Spain he had "made proclamation that to any Roman who should kill Sertorius he would give a hundred talents of silver [2,400,000 sesterces] and twenty thousand acres of land."[2] Piso, a member of the Sullan clique, employed bribery so blatantly to win the consulship for 67 that he subsequently had to distribute additional bribes to win acquittal of electoral fraud.

Especially for an outsider like Caesar, a political career entailed a dangerous gamble. In election campaigns fortunes were dissipated and landed estates encumbered with mortgages. Defeat at any stage in the progress of magistracies, however, meant bankruptcy, seizure of possessions, disgrace, political death and even the collapse of a family.

Upon arriving at Rome, with characteristic deliberation, Caesar set about extending his political alliances and augmenting his financial resources. A new marriage afforded possibilities in both matters. Although weddings among Roman aristocrats were simply affairs of money and politics, upon the announcement of Caesar's marriage to Sulla's granddaughter, many must have wondered whether Caesar was abandoning his former loyalties. Pompeia's father had been slain in a riot by followers of the radical tribune Sulpicius, Marius' ally. Her mother, Sulla's daughter, an avaricious profiteer during the proscriptions, had bought, among many other properties, a seaside villa of Marius' for 280 thousand sesterces and then sold it to Lucullus for ten million. Although almost certainly the richest woman in Rome, Cornelia was a notorious miser, and Aurelia must have bargained hard to win a substantial dowry for Caesar.

With this marriage Caesar acquired a new set of connections, but, more particularly, he reinforced his ties to Pompeius. His bride's brother maintained a close association with the warlord, oblivious of the fact that Pompeius' father had engineered the murder of his and Pompeia's consular grandfather; and Publius Sulla, a nephew of the late dictator and cousin to Caesar's new wife, had recently married Pompeius' sister. At this very time the Great Man was maneuvering for a new military command, and it may even have been at a report of the warlord's ambitions that Caesar hastened home from Spain and entered a marriage with Pompeius' clanswoman.

With Pompeia Caesar began a spree of fashionable prodigality. His foes scoffed that he was "purchasing a transient and short-lived fame at great price" and predicted gleefully that he would spend himself into bankruptcy, a prediction they would repeat many times during his career. Caesar's enemies, however, consistently failed to appreciate the long-range calculation in his every action. Caesar recognized that Sulla had confirmed the common belief that the wealthy had a claim to power and the wealthiest, to the greatest power. In return for their votes, from those who lived in princely magnificence Romans expected grandiose public entertainments and unlimited largess. Shopkeepers and neighbors would spread word of delivery to the Subura of cartloads of roses, violets and lilies, of baskets of Verona pears, Ravenna asparagus, mushrooms from far-off Bithynia and of braces of exotic fowl from Africa. Clients who lined up at the door for scraps from the banquet of a previous evening would boast of the refined palate and lordly extravagance of their patron. Caesar also pursued the reputation of a dandy. He never left the house unless faultless in dress and delicately perfumed. He sported a tunic with fringed sleeves reaching to the wrist—a daring fashion—and a toga almost sheer in its fine weave. His hair was not only "carefully trimmed and shaved," but he even had "superfluous hair plucked out."[3]

Caesar had to ensure that he was talked about politically, and it would be two years before he would be eligible to run for an aedileship. Plebeian aristocrats often entered their candidacies for a tribuneship after serving as quaestors, but that office was barred to patricians, and Caesar was too proud of his heritage to transfer himself to the plebs. Entering his candidacy for a highway superintendency, he won the choice post of curator of the Appian Way. Along this most ancient of Roman roads passed heavily laden ox carts and trains of pack animals from Puteoli (Pozzuoli), the chief port of Italy, as well as products from the metal shops of Capua and the potteries of Naples, mussels from private fish ponds and the varied harvest of the Campanian plain and of the vineyards and olive groves of the hills south of Rome. In dapper two-wheeled drays, in litters and in coaches or on horseback, the rich traveled to and from villas in the mountains or at seaside resorts and spas.

In his supervision of maintenance, repair and improvements of the road, Caesar, universally curious, had an opportunity to learn the techniques of surveyors, specialists in geometry and experts with the groma, a crosspiece on a vertical staff used in laying out lines at right angles. He could investigate engineering problems of elevation and of degrees of curves appropriate for heavy carts and study the principles of bridge building, gathering experience that would prove useful years later in his military career. Like any twentieth-century politician, Caesar expected that travelers seeing his name posted at sections of road under repair would recall his industry and public spirit at election time. During his superintendency, in fact, he "expended . . . vast sums of his own money."[4] The goodwill of the men of property who frequented the Appian Way was important. Caesar was not unaware, of course, that his uncle Marius and father-in-law Cinna had found much of their support among the industrialists and entrepreneurs who used this highway.

Although Caesar would not, unlike a growing number of aristocrats, seek to advance his career simply as one of Pompeius' clients, he had no choice but to enter unequal relationships with men of greater influence. During the two years of apparent retirement after his consulship, Pompeius had not been idle, and for 67 he had succeeded in promoting the election of two of his associates as tribunes. With them and others of his circle he evolved a carefully modulated strategy for advancing his career. The timing and dramatic invention in the campaign to win a new command for Pompeius betray, in fact, a particular contribution by Caesar. A two-fold strategy was pursued. While one of the newly installed tribunes, Cornelius, diverted the attention of the pauci (the "few"—the dominant coterie in the Senate) with a series of radical bills, the other, Gabinius, misled them into believing that Pompeius was seeking Lucullus' place as supreme commander in the continuing war against Mithridates.

Much of the power of the pauci rested on their control of overseas dependencies. Leading oligarchs reaped huge profits (as well as control over overseas dependencies) from loans to foreign envoys for bribing magistrates and senators. When Cornelius proposed a bill prohibiting such loans, the pauci mobilized successfully against it. During the period of elections, when legislative activity was forbidden, with a dispensation from the Senate they proposed a milder bill of their own in place of Cornelius' for increasing penalties for electoral fraud. Cornelius responded with a measure reserving to the people the right to grant such dispensations. The Senate voted the consuls a bodyguard. In a riot a crowd smashed the fasces of the consul Piso, a resolute and uncompromising reactionary, and would have lynched him if Cornelius had not dismissed the assembly. Compromises were found both on the electoral fraud legislation and on the question of Senate dispensations, and Cornelius succeeded in curbing the pauci's manipulation of the courts with a bill requiring praetors to honor the principles and procedures they established upon entering office and curbing their use of their unlimited judicial powers in favor of political allies and against foes.

Cornelius had fulfilled his mission. He promoted some reforms; above all, he provoked turmoil in challenging the Senate leadership and put the pauci on the defensive.

That Caesar collaborated with the other tribune, Gabinius, is attested in ancient sources. In attacking Lucullus, the commander in the continuing war against Mithridates, Gabinius' task was easier than Cornelius'. From the distant battlefields of Asia Minor, Lucullus was unable to defend himself, and he suffered also from the hostility of men of property, both senators and equestrians. The oligarchs regarded as a threat any disproportionate power of one of their number, and Lucullus was accumulating so much booty and enrolling into his personal clientship so many cities and principalities as to place himself out of competition with the other nobles. After the fall of the capital of Armenia, he distributed 192 million sesterces among his troops. So numerous were his prisoners that the price of slaves fell from the standard 1,200 to 2,000 sesterces to a mere 16, and he was able to replace at little cost some of the thousands of slaves he and his friends had lost during the Spartacan uprising. Three years earlier in his prosecution of Verres, Cicero had expressed the general indignation at such massive profiteering, declaring: "We have seen all the wealth of all the world become the property of a mere handful of men; and our readiness to tolerate and permit this is the more apparent because none of those persons conceals his cupidity, none is concerned to throw any doubt upon the fact of it."[5]

In the Forum Gabinius displayed a picture of Lucullus' villa at Tusculum, a building of oriental magnificence. When he described the porticos, formal gardens, the aviary, the libraries and sports facilities, Gabinius could count on a passionate response from his audience because of the desperate housing shortage in Rome. Speculators like Crassus bought up stretches of real estate and packed thousands of countryfolk swarming into the city into jerry-built tenements, stinking hovels without running water, heat or latrines. Since no laws protected tenants, landlords gouged them with exorbitant rents. Tenants dared not complain of leaking roofs or sagging floors or dangerous cracks in the walls (the tenements frequently crumbled with a great crash bringing sudden death to the inhabitants). If called by landlords "as witnesses in court, [they] were aware that if they made a mistake in a single word of testimony they might have no lodgings to which to return."[6]

More menacing to Lucullus was the rage of the men of property, particularly of the publicans, the most influential and best organized segment of the equestrian order. Upon his arrival in Asia seven years earlier, Lucullus had discovered that provincial cities "were forced to sell . . . their votive offerings, pictures and sacred statues. . . . Men had to surrender to their creditors and serve them as slaves, but what preceded this was far worse—tortures of rope, barrier and horse; standing under the open sky in the blazing sun of summer and in winter being thrust into mud or ice." The twenty-thousand-talent indemnity imposed upon the province by Sulla ten years earlier had sextupled because of the usurious interest exacted by bankers and moneylenders. Lucullus halted the depredations of the moneylenders and tax-gatherers. "Then he merely tried, by admonishing them, to make them more moderate in their demands."[7] His warnings ignored, the imperious nobleman instituted Draconian measures recalling Scaevola and Rutilius' during Caesar's childhood, and in less than four years Lucullus eliminated the provincial debt.

In retaliation, equestrians and senators engaged in banking and tax-gathering enterprises undermined Lucullus' authority. Year by year they whittled down his command. Simultaneously, Lucullus' brother-in-law, the patrician adventurer Publius Clodius, conspired against him within his own headquarters. Proclaiming himself "the soldiers' friend" and contrasting Lucullus' niggardliness in distributing war booty with Pompeius' well-known generosity to his troops (Clodius was a first cousin to Pompeius' wife), he asked the troops, some of them in overseas service for fifteen years: "Why then if our campaigns are never to come to an end, do we not reserve what is left of our bodies and our lives for a general in whose eyes the wealth of his soldiers is his fairest honor?"[8] Confronting mutiny, Lucullus was unable to prosecute the war.

(In Lucullus' ignominy Caesar learned an impressive lesson. For defending provincials against extortion and instituting measures to restore the provincial economy, he had suffered humiliation. In similar actions during his career, Caesar would employ a subtler style, seek to assure himself of broader support and strive to win consent through rational discussion—not always with success.)

It was not Gabinius' task to press for Pompeius' appointment as Lucullus' replacement. After weakening the haughty nobleman by moving the discharge of legionaries with long combat duty and assigning one of the current consuls to the governorship of one of Lucullus' two provinces, Gabinius proposed the measure for which he and Cornelius had actually been preparing the way, a bill for the appointment of a commander with extraordinary powers to eliminate piracy on the seas. Since the fruitless campaigns of Marcus Antonius, with whom Caesar had served as a military tribune, the pirate fleets had grown in numbers and daring. Defying Rome on every sea, the pirates burned a grain fleet in Rome's own harbor at Ostia. They seized Roman aristocrats for ransom and even captured two praetors with their entourages. Although they roused the fury of entrepreneurs engaged in overseas trade and rendered the commons desperate because of increases in grain prices, they also kept the slave markets supplied, and it was to be suspected that in this trade they acted in collusion with Roman equestrians and senators.

Upon a quick and enthusiastic adoption of his proposal in a public assembly, Gabinius nominated Pompeius to the command, and the people acclaimed his choice. The Senate, however, "preferred to suffer anything whatever at the hands of the freebooters rather than put so great a command into Pompeius' hands." "If Pompeius takes Romulus as his model," warned the consul Piso, "he will suffer the same fate [assassination for usurping autocratic power]."[9] Infuriated as much at Pompeius' appeal to the populars in the tribal assembly as at the prospect of a further enhancement of his power, the senators advanced on Gabinius. No one moved to the tribune's defense—except Caesar. He placed himself at Gabinius' side, and the two of them retreated out to the street. Here a crowd of their supporters surrounded them and rushed at the senators. Only the mulish Piso stood his ground. Gabinius rescued him.

Pompeius and his councilors were now prepared for the final scene of their charade. Gabinius assembled the people to present his nomination of Pompeius for a vote. He invited the Great Man to address the crowd, and to universal astonishment, Pompeius rejected the nomination, protesting that it was not fitting that he "should continually be in some position of command." He complained that from previous campaigns he was "worn out in body and wearied in soul."[10] He feared, too, the resentment of powerful noblemen, who in case of failure might indict him on some charge and in the event of success might harbor jealousy against him, a fear justified, indeed, by Lucullus' current experience. "Surely," he declared, "I am not the only one who loves you, nor am I alone skilled in warfare."

Upon this display of modesty, as Pompeius and his advisors had foreseen, senators who had been sounded on lucrative lieutenancies, bankrupt aristocrats hoping for posts as staff officers, entrepreneurs anticipating contracts for ships, materiel and provisions, commoners yearning for an end to the grain shortage and envisioning victory celebrations with generous largess and veterans still unrewarded with a land bonus for service in the Sertorian war and hungry for booty—all cried out in chagrin.

"You must not choose what is pleasing to Pompeius," declared Gabinius in a feigned rebuke to the coy warrior, "but what is of benefit to the state." Prompted by a claque distributed strategically in the crowd, the people joined Gabinius in pleading with Pompeius.

The optimates, equally adept at play acting, had also prepared for the occasion. A tribune of their faction announced that he would veto any vote taken that day. More than a half-century earlier, confronting a similar threat from a fellow-tribune, Tiberius Gracchus (whom the optimates blamed as the initiator of all current troubles) had proclaimed: "If he annuls the power of the people, he is no tribune at all . . . since he is destroying the very power which is the source of his own power."[11] For promoting the popular sovereignty against the authority of the Senate, Tiberius was murdered. The balance of forces had, however, shifted radically in three generations. Contemptuous of his opponents, Gabinius ordered the people to disperse into their tribes for a vote on the optimate tribune's impeachment. When seventeen of the thirty-five tribes had responded affirmatively, the obstructionist tribune withdrew his threat. A second optimate tribune raised two fingers to signify that two commanders should be elected. The people responded with such explosive fury that some people swore that a raven flying overhead plummeted to the ground, dead.

Pressing his victory, Gabinius invited to the Rostra the elder statesman Catulus. He warned against entrusting excessive power to a single individual. If the people considered that an emergency existed, he declared, they should call for the appointment of a dictator for the traditional six-month term. At the word "dictator," the audience hissed the hated name "Sulla." Unabashed, Catulus continued: "If Italy requires no such person, and you would no longer tolerate the fiction of the dictator but even the name—as is clear from your anger against Sulla—how would it be right for a new position of command to be created and that, too, for three years and embracing all interests both in Italy and outside?" Evoking no response, Catulus exclaimed: "If he fails . . . as not infrequently happens in many contests, especially on the sea—what other man will you find to take his place for still more urgent tasks?"

A wiseacre shouted and all the people chorused after: "You!"

Caesar saw Pompeius endowed with powers without precedent in the long history of the city, powers he himself could never realistically hope to achieve:

supreme authority on the seas and along all coasts to a depth of fifty miles, command of five hundred ships, one hundred and twenty thousand infantry-men and five thousand cavalrymen, authority to draw upon the common-wealth treasury and the privilege of appointing twenty-four lieutenants out of the Senate, men who would provide him with a nucleus of support to challenge the pauci in their own stronghold.

Immediately, the price of grain fell, and Pompeius' admirers boasted that "the very name of their hero had settled the war."[12] More likely, the grain merchants had been withholding supplies to pressure for the appointment of their hero. (Such behavior was not without precedent, and it would be re-peated in similar situations involving Pompeius.)

As the sole senator to side with Gabinius in defying the wrath of Pompeius' foes, Caesar had a claim to a lieutenancy with the Great Man. He had, how-ever, determined upon a long-range independent course for himself. He would forgo glory and booty and take advantage of Pompeius' absence to advance his own fortunes.

The struggle between the Great Man and his supporters in a temporary popular opposition coalition and the pauci had brought turbulence to Rome. Apart from the riots associated with the legislation promoted by Cornelius and Gabinius, other disturbances forced repeated postponements of magisterial elections, a phenomenon to recur ever more frequently as the political institu-tions of the city-state crumbled.

This year Caesar had seen once again that measures could be adopted in defiance of the pauci only by coalitions of broad elements in association with a warlord backed by an army or by well-disciplined veterans. He would remem-ber this lesson.

XVII

THE OLIGARCHY DIVIDED

FOLLOWING Pompeius' departure from Rome, the optimates regrouped to restore their authority, resentful of the warlord's manipulation of the com-mons to his own purposes. Of this subsequent period the historian Sallust (then a young man about twenty years of age) would write: ". . . the power of the commons was lessened, while that of the few increased. These possessed the magistracies, the provinces and everything else; being themselves rich and secure against attack, they lived without fear and by resort to the courts terrified the others in order that while they themselves were in office they might manage the people with less friction." Piso, the consul who had stubbornly resisted the two Pompeian tribunes, rejected the candidacy for the consulship of one of Pompeius' partisans, declaring that he did not believe the republic had sunk so low as to allow such a man to compete for the exalted office. Challenged as to what he would do if voters inscribed the man's name on the ballots, he retorted, "I would not proclaim him [as elected]."[1] In the fall upon taking up his post as governor of the Two Gauls Piso refused to levy troops for Pompeius' campaign against the pirates.

It was Caesar's tactic in circumstances of severe factional tension to test the will of the opposing sides. He found an opportunity at the end of the year when a newly installed tribune named Manilius revived a bill originally proposed more than twenty years earlier by the tribune Sulpicius for registering the freedmen in all thirty-five tribes instead of the four to which they were restricted. The freedmen represented a substantial and influential portion of the population of Rome and of towns throughout Italy. In wealth and influence they ranged from Sullan favorites who had enriched themselves during the proscriptions, officials of public corporations, agents for senators in business and financial enterprises, physicians, teachers, philosophers, engineers, architects and other professionals to skilled craftsmen, shopkeepers and laborers. Roman banking, commerce and industry depended upon them. Despite their diversity in wealth and social status, all suffered humiliations. All bore the names of their former masters, owed services to these masters and even were responsible for their masters' debts. Freedmen could not seek public office, membership in a priesthood or serve in the legions. Masters manumitted slaves out of self-interest—to avoid the burden of feeding, clothing and housing while enjoying the fruits of increased productivity from supposedly independent workers. The comic poet Plautus had summed up the pathos of many manumissions in a scene in which a "generous" master has difficulty in persuading a slave to accept freedom along with the gift of a cloak and a tunic. "What else will you give me," the slave exclaims, "for a slave must have something to live?"[2]

Freedmen predominated in the numerous and rapidly expanding collegia—the craft and religious fraternal associations. At New Year's the collegia celebrated neighborhood festivals, the Compitalia, and Manilius took advantage of the holiday to convene a public assembly at which he hastily passed his reform bill. The quaestor Domitius Ahenobarbus, a leading profiteer in the Sullan Terror and a violent foe to all reform, mobilized his clients and friends and attacked the assembly, killing a number of Manilius' partisans. The Senate congratulated Ahenobarbus for his civic spirit and annulled Manilius' law as improperly promulgated.

Frightened by threats from leading senators like Ahenobarbus, Manilius announced that he had promoted the franchise bill at Crassus' urging. Although Crassus scoffed and the senators, many of whom were in debt to the millionaire, denounced Manilius, it was not unlikely that Manilius was telling the truth. Crassus had close associations with the more distinguished freedmen engaged in banking, overseas commerce and in the public corporations. Furthermore, Crassus was always seeking to expand his clientship, and he was eager to exploit Pompeius' absence in order to augment his own authority. In the current political atmosphere, Manilius inevitably suffered a rebuff, but he did intensify the resentment of the freedmen against the pauci and rouse their eagerness to participate in a new opposition coalition. With the dearth of effective "popular" leaders, Caesar, who had confirmed his reputation as a champion of "popular" causes in his recent agitation for Transpadane citizenship, could offer to provide leadership to the freedmen in the future.

Cicero, elected to a praetorship for this year (66), was developing a strategy for his campaign for a consulship three years hence. He was apparently impressed with the new resolution of the pauci as exemplified in Piso's braving of Pompeius and in the Senate's prompt and decisive reaction to Manilius' maneuver. In a trial held in his praetorian court, he found an opportunity to curry favor with the Old Guard. The defendant was Macer, the radical tribune whose demands for the restoration of the tribunician authority Caesar had supported some seven years earlier. An agent of the pauci had indicted Macer, now of praetorian rank, on a charge of extortion during his tenure as a provincial governor. Macer was defended by his friend Crassus in a trial conducted in a spirit of intense factional antagonism. At the conclusion of the speeches on both sides, Macer returned home and "hastily trimmed his hair and put on a toga in the belief that he had been acquitted . . . but Crassus met him at the house door and told him that he had been convicted unanimously."[3] Macer reentered his house and died either of a heart attack or by suicide.

"Here in Rome my handling of C. Macer's case has won popular approval to a really quite extraordinary degree," Cicero wrote to a close friend. "Though I was favorably disposed to him, I gained far more from popular sentiment by his conviction than I should have gained from his gratitude if he had been acquitted." Of course, in this instance, the people to whom Cicero was referring were not the commons. Macer, indeed, "had great power in the city,"[4] but among people about whose opinions Cicero had not the least concern.

For Caesar, Macer's fate provided a further warning of the peril in seeking advancement as an opposition leader.

Frightened by the threats of the pauci and shaken by Macer's fate, Manilius turned for protection to the man with the army.

To the astonishment of the Mediterranean world, the war against the pirates, a war "so great and so protracted, so far and so widely extended, a war which pressed so heavily upon all nations and peoples, was by Gnaeus Pompeius organized at the end of winter, started at the beginning of spring and finished by the middle of summer."[5] With his great fleets and armies Pompeius was at the ready for yet another campaign. Manilius offered his services. He proposed (what Pompeius had probably been aiming at all along) that Lucullus be deprived of the meager authority remaining to him and that Pompeius be appointed governor of three of the provinces of Asia Minor and entrusted with the supreme command in the war against Mithridates.

On this occasion, Pompeius' opponents were divided. Indeed, four consulars declared their backing for Manilius' bill. Although Caesar enjoyed no direct advantage in an enhancement of Pompeius' power and prestige, he required the support of the warlord's partisans in his own election to an aedileship this year, and he was never averse to bearding the pauci. Cicero, often a good weathervane for the relationship of forces at Rome, had held aloof from the controversy over Pompeius' command against the pirates. Now, persuaded that it would be to his disadvantage to ignore the requests of the entrepreneurs, Cicero delivered the first speech of his career in support of a piece of legislation. (He had never risked alienating one faction or another by such partisanship.) Exuberant at addressing an enthusiastic audience of Pompeius' supporters, Cicero delivered an eloquent oration. In his speech he gave recognition to the augmenting influence of the men of affairs, his "good friends the Roman knights who [were] concerned for the great sums they [had] invested in the farming of [the people's] revenues." According to Cicero, all Romans had a stake in the defense of the eastern region of the empire. "While the revenues of our other provinces," he reminded the audience, "are barely sufficient to make it worth our while to defend them, Asia is so rich and fertile as easily to surpass all other countries in the productiveness of her soil, the variety of her crops, the extent of her pastures and the volume of her exports." Nor was it simply "the men of energy and industry . . . personally engaged in business in Asia [or those with] vast sums invested in the province" who required an energetic prosecution of the war. Repeating a shibboleth of every oligarchy, Cicero warned his audience that the prosperity of all citizens depended upon the prosperity of the millionaires, who could not "lose their property . . . without involving still greater numbers in their own ruin. . . . The system of credit and finance which operates at Rome, in the Forum," Cicero warned, "is bound up in, and depends on, capital invested in Asia."[6] This argument was persuasive. The Sertorian war, the depredations of the pirates and the loss of revenues from the East had brought a crisis of credit. Cash was in short supply, and more gold and silver was being drained out of Italy than was being collected in tribute. Moneylenders were chary of granting loans except on certain security, and smallholders and shopkeepers along with the land-rich were in desperate straits. Only the ultra-rich were secure.

Inspired by the enthusiastic response of his audience and confident of the sympathy of at least some of the pauci, Cicero dared to challenge Hortensius and Catulus. Turning to Hortensius, Cicero asked: "If . . . the Roman people had thought more of your opinion [regarding Pompeius' appointment to an extraordinary command against the pirates] than of their own welfare and their true interests, should we today be in possession of our present glory and our world-wide empire [or be able] to transact either . . . private or . . . public business overseas?" Though constrained to pay tribute to the "high character and position" of the esteemed elder statesman, Cicero derided Catulus' credo: "Let no innovation be made contrary to usage and the principles of our forefathers." Aware that Pompeius' enemies would retaliate against Manilius rather than against him, Cicero exhorted the tribune "with the authority of the Roman people behind [him] to stand by that proposal undeterred by violence or by threats."[7]

In December, upon the expiration of Manilius' tenure as tribune, the pauci moved an indictment against him. The case was to be heard before Cicero, whose praetorship was about to expire. He was loath to preside over the trial, fearing to offend one faction or the other, and at the initial hearing he abruptly ordered the trial to begin on the next day, denying Manilius the customary ten days to prepare a defense. At complaints of Manilius' supporters, tribunes haled Cicero before a public assembly. He pleaded that since only one day remained to his praetorship, he had sought to hold the trial under his presidency to Manilius' advantage. The commons applauded Cicero's generosity and demanded that he serve as Manilius' counsel after his praetorship. Compelled to accept the task, Cicero undertook his new and unwanted role with spirit, "mounting the Rostra [and] vigorously attacking the oligarchical party and those who were jealous of Pompeius."[8] The trial was disrupted by riots organized by Manilius' partisans, and for the moment Manilius was saved.

The Manilian law granting Pompeius a new extraordinary command was intensifying the divisions within the oligarchy. Factional conflicts would grow more complicated. Within three years Cicero would pass over to the faction of Hortensius and Catulus.

With ever greater difficulty, Caesar would maintain his independence.

XVIII

MARIUS AGAIN

IN times of social ferment, guardian deities were ever at hand to admonish the Romans to renew their faith in the ways of the ancestors, to obey the old laws sanctioned by the gods, to respect the nobility and the constitution, and, above all, to count their blessings as citizens of a city ordained by the gods to bring peace and prosperity to all mankind. In 65, the year of Caesar's aedileship, apparently persuaded that an especially impressive warning was required, the gods hurled a destructive blast at the Capitol, seat of Rome's divine patron, overturning images of Jupiter and of the wolf suckling Romulus and Remus and melting ancient bronze tablets of divinely ordained laws. Etruscan haruspices warned of "monstrous chaos and carnage"[1] and prescribed the erection of a new image of Jupiter to be set on a lofty column facing east so that the god might keep watch over the proceedings in the Forum and in the Senate house below.

The gods were closing ranks with the pauci against an inevitable confrontation with Pompeius. The Old Guard were resolved to suppress all divisions within the oligarchy and to respond decisively to disorders among the commons. After trials for electoral fraud, the two consuls-elect for 65 were convicted and declared ineligible for public office. One of these unfortunates was Publius Sulla, nephew of the dictator and brother-in-law to Pompeius. Violence attended the trials, and subsequently there were reports of an assassination plot against the newly installed consuls, a plot supposedly involving Crassus, a censor this year, Caesar, now an aedile, and Catilina, an adventurer who had been rejected as a candidate for the consulship because of a pending indictment for extortion while a provincial governor.

Unable effectively to exploit his connection to the distant warlord, Caesar turned to his cousin Lucius Cotta, one of the new consuls, who had probably assisted in Caesar's election to an aedileship; and to Crassus. A Mediterranean realm with fabled riches, a teeming population and unsurpassed productivity in agriculture and industry as well as a thriving commerce with distant lands to the south and east remained outside the Roman empire—Egypt. The leaders of the Senate maintained the ancient kingdom as a semi-independent protectorate, for they feared the power that would accrue to any nobleman who won its patronage, and they were unwilling to share the rewards of provincial administration with aristocrats outside their own narrow circle, already strained by the requirements of the current provinces. Furthermore, they enjoyed generous subventions from the pharaoh for recognition of his crown. The current pharaoh, who had been hailed (at a price, of course) as a friend and ally to the Roman people, had recently been overthrown by his subjects. As guardian of law and order throughout the world, Rome had an obligation to restore its hireling. On the other hand, in his will (possibly forged) the previous pharaoh had bequeathed the kingdom to the Roman people, and Crassus and Caesar saw an opportunity in a single stroke to rival the power and wealth of Pompeius. As censor, Crassus proposed the incorporation of the ancient kingdom into the empire, and Caesar, following Pompeius' recent example of bypassing the Senate to obtain a command, persuaded some tribunes to propose to the people his nomination for the task of transforming Eygpt into a Roman province. Although Catulus, Crassus' colleague in the censorship, vetoed the proposal, Crassus and Caesar had posed an issue that would preoccupy Caesar again and Rome for another generation.

At home an unresolved issue that offered opportunities for extending personal clientships was the franchise. The Transpadanes, among whom Caesar enjoyed considerable goodwill, remained eager to vote. Crassus announced his readiness as censor to register the Transpadanes into tribes and centuries as first-class citizens. Catulus once again interposed a veto, and the two censors, frustrated by their irreconcilable differences, eventually resigned without fulfilling their responsibilities.

Resentful at having been forced onto the defensive, the pauci displayed extraordinary vigor in reaffirming their control of the state. They determined first of all to provide a warning to future tribunes through prosecutions of Pompeius' agents, Manilius and Cornelius. In an initial prosecution, Manilius' partisans had disrupted the court. He was indicted a second time, and Ahenobarbus assembled a gang of toughs to protect the plaintiff. By a special resolution the Senate instructed the consuls to preside at the new trial and granted them an armed guard. This time Manilius was condemned to exile.

Having already antagonized the pauci by his defense of Manilius, Cicero had little to lose in undertaking the defense of Cornelius. The pauci mobilized their most awesome figures as character witnesses against Cornelius, including five former consuls. In response, recognizing that the tribunate itself was on trial, tribunes who had opposed Cornelius in 67 appeared in his defense. Cicero orated with such "sublimity and splendor" that the audience was "seized with a kind of frenzy and . . . burst forth spontaneously into a perfect ecstasy of delight,"[2] and Cornelius was acquitted upon the votes of all the jurors except the associates of the pauci.

Even with the intervention of five leading consulars the pauci could not overthrow the tribunician authority, so broad and firm was the support for this magistracy. (One day Caesar would proclaim his defiance of the leaders of the Senate in the name of the defense of the tribunate.)

Rebuffed in his attempt to secure a lucrative and prestigious assignment in Egypt and aware that the pauci were resolved to thwart him in his every endeavor, Caesar moved to confirm his popularity. The Roman Games conducted by the curule aediles during two weeks in September afforded Caesar an opportunity to display his genius for spectacle. In a characteristic bold gamble, he plunged himself recklessly into debt and compelled his optimate colleague Bibulus to match his extravagance. About the Forum they constructed temporary colonnades and decorated the entire center of the city. After the horse and chariot races, the combats of wild beasts, boxing bouts and dramatic presentations, to Bibulus' chagrin and the delight of the citizenry, Caesar announced that he would now offer funerary games in commemoration of the twentieth anniversary of his father's death.

Yielding place to the vestals and their aristocratic attendants (Aurelia honored especially as Gaius' widow), the people overflowed from the temporary bleachers in the Forum onto steps of temples and basilicas and roofs and galleries of buildings about the area. As presiding officer, Caesar sat on his curule chair (the backless ivory folding chair of a superior magistrate) wearing a wreath, bearing a scepter and dressed in the garb of a triumpher—a painted toga and a tunic ornamented with palms. Suddenly a cry of astonishment arose as a long line of gladiators came into view. They glittered in silver accoutrements, an unprecedented luxury. Caesar had ordered three hundred and twenty pairs, six hundred and forty men in all. As the gladiators performed warm-up exercises, tossing shields into the air, lunging and parrying with fearsome cries—the Thracians, brandishing scythes and small shields, in loin clothes with chests covered with silver and leather and legs and hips protected by coverings; the Samnites bearing enormous shields but scantily clad—men and women rose and stretched out their hands and waved white handkerchiefs in salute to Caesar.

Yet this momentous success did not cap Caesar's festival.

One morning word sped through Rome of an even more astonishing event. From everywhere people hastened to the Forum. Gleaming atop the Capitol they beheld gilded images of Marius and replicas of the Marian trophies Sulla had demolished. Caesar had had these fashioned secretly and carried up to the Capitol at night. Those who approached more closely saw that Caesar had inscribed a list of Marius' successes against the Germans, victories for which he had been hailed as a second Romulus, a Second Founder of Rome.

On an earlier occasion, at his aunt's funeral, Caesar, entering upon the progress of magistracies, defied the Sullan Old Guard and roused the cheers of the commons by displaying images of the two Mariuses. At that time Pompeius and Crassus had just concluded their consulships, and the populars found themselves without leaders. Caesar then proclaimed his readiness to champion their cause. Now, five years later, Caesar was not only showing reverence to his father but also reminding Rome that his father had been Marius' brother-in-law and the only Julian to remain loyal to the Old Man. After appearing to serve first as Pompeius' man and then as Crassus', Caesar was proclaiming once again that he was his own man, and once again he was offering leadership to any popular coalition in the continuing economic and social crisis. Whereas Caesar's action at Julia's funeral had been only momentary, soon forgotten, on this occasion in reestablishing the Marian trophies on the Capitol, Caesar was issuing an enduring challenge to the Sullans. Friends and enemies alike understood that "this proceeding was a test of the people," and in this test Caesar was not disappointed. While "some cried out that Caesar was scheming to usurp sole power in the state . . . the partisans of Marius encouraged one another and showed themselves on a sudden in amazing numbers and filled the Capitol with their applause. Many, too, were moved to tears of joy when they beheld the features of Marius, and Caesar was highly extolled by them and regarded as above all others worthy of his kinship to Marius."[3]

Bibulus remarked wrily: "Just as the temple erected in the Forum to the twin brethren [Castor and Pollux] bears only the name of Castor, so the joint liberality of Caesar and myself [during the previous months] is credited to

Caesar alone."⁴ Bibulus' irony scarcely reassured the pauci. After regaining confidence in their ability to suppress opposition upon the conviction of Macer and more recently of Manilius, they confronted a new and shrewder foe. Proclaiming himself once again Marius' heir, Caesar was rallying the people with a recollection of a figure who epitomized the opposition to Sulla and the Sullan order. Idealizing his memory, the people associated all their aspirations with the Old Man—land reform, extension of the franchise, grain subsidies, debt relief, recall of political exiles and a democratic spirit in political life.

Frightened by Caesar's assemblage of a small army of gladiators for his funerary games, the Senate, recalling the uprising of Spartacus' gladiators, passed a resolution limiting the number that might be displayed henceforth in the city. "No longer indeed by sapping and mining, Caesar," cried Catulus, "but with engines of war are you seizing power in the state."⁵

Caesar had achieved his purposes, affirming his independence and recon-firming his leadership of the populars. He had tested the sentiment of the opponents of the inner circle of the Senate and exposed the impotence of the Old Guard in numbers and spirit. But Caesar had learned that no popular coalition divorced from the military could challenge the authority of the Sen-ate. He had learned, too, that no political struggle proceeds with an untram-meled advance; and aware that his enemies would prefer not to magnify his present defiance, with quiet rationality he defended himself. The Senate ac-cepted his explanations, "whereupon his admirers were still more elated and exhorted him not to lower his pretensions for any man since the people would be glad to have him triumph over all opposition and be the first man in the state."⁶

O priests of Gades!

XIX

PRELUDE TO BATTLE

CAESAR had long ago assimilated the counsel of the Athenian sage Solon to the Lydian king of fabled riches—a standard school text: "As the years lengthen out, there is much to see and to suffer which one would wish other-wise. . . . The total of days for your seventy years is 26,250 and not one them is like the next in what it brings. You can see from that, Croesus, what a chancy thing life is."¹ The passage of Caesar's thirty-fifth year, the midpoint of life, served as a new reminder of how little he had as yet accomplished. On the other hand, if, in comparison with the careers of Pompeius, Crassus and Lucullus, Caesar's career appeared less than extraordinary, nevertheless, as a man he had achieved a personal integration beyond any of his contemporaries. Whereas during the previous two decades he had perforce merely reacted to circumstances, now events seemed rather to coerce him into actions which he himself willed. He had, in effect, made peace with necessity by choosing a direction in which history was moving. Within his own experience he had proven the Epicurean view of a universe of atoms in whose ceaseless turmoil every phenomenon underwent unremitting transformation; in constant struggle he had explored his capacities and transformed himself, honing his character to such definition that he and those who, like Aurelia, knew him well could predict what he would say and do in almost any situation.

Caesar shared, of course, the general tension at Rome, the premonition of impending catastrophe evoked during two decades of massacres and upheaval. If he experienced less anxiety than other oligarchs, it was because he accepted change and welcomed struggle. In addition, the trauma of the nearly calamitous setback he had suffered upon Sulla's victory still provided a relentless impetus to his ambition and fixed him within his opposition role as Marius' heir. The Sullans, on the other hand, ever confronting new challenges to their hegemony, labored under an uneasy sense that history was conspiring against them. Inasmuch as any analysis of the crisis adduced conclusions too disturbing to contemplate, they blamed the endemic instability on individuals—the "power-hungry" Pompeius, the "greedy" Crassus and, of lesser significance, the "unruly and demagogic" Caesar along with various "radical" tribunes and "rabble-rousers." They resented the "ingratitude" of the commons, who, according to one of the oligarchs' manipulative myths, shared equally with them in the blessings of the republic.

Nevertheless, with their monopoly of patriotism, their direct communication with the gods, their wealth, education, political and military traditions, their privileges enshrined in law and custom along with their network of relationships and clientships, the oligarchs appeared unassailable. It occurred to no one, including Caesar, to think of displacing them, but whereas Caesar recognized the necessity of sharing power with the Italian municipal aristocracy and the leading citizens of Cisalpina and perhaps eventually with Roman settlers overseas, the optimate leaders recoiled at any proposal for change. Like oligarchies of all times and places, they took seriously Aristotle's warning that "aristocracies are most liable to undergo revolution unobserved, through gradual relaxation . . . a small change may cause a revolution. For when they give up one of the details of the constitution, afterwards they also make another slightly bigger change more readily, until they alter the whole system."[2] The uncompromising commitment to the status quo was maintained not only by Sullan elder statesmen but also by a group of younger oligarchs. Outstanding among them was Cato, who took no step without asking himself how his great-grandfather, the renowned Censor, would have acted. A professed Stoic, he prided himself on his refusal to compromise or ever to change his mind. Like others of this school, abhorring superfluous verbiage, he addressed the Forum with abrupt laconicism, disdaining mere particulars and transforming his every intervention into a lecture on "weighty arguments drawn from philosophy."[3] His face reflected his energy, self-righteousness and obstinacy in a large nose with a distinctive aristocratic curve, heavy eyebrows and a formidable jaw. By peremptory rejection of all contrary opinions and assertive vaunting of his own incorruptibility, he intimidated many Romans into believing that a position on any issue was untenable unless he, the Man of Virtue, supported it.

As Caesar had long been aware, the pauci acted in unison only in face of what they considered a threat to their long-range hegemony. Otherwise their divisions allowed room for his maneuvering. Now he found an opportunity in a squabble between Cato and Catulus. Assigned as quaestor to supervision of the treasury, Cato provoked dismay by his meticulous scrutiny of the public accounts, by his dismissal of incompetent or dishonest clerks and by his institution of new procedures. When Catulus as defense counsel for a clerk indicted by Cato for malfeasance pleaded for the man's acquittal, Cato exploded. "It would be a shameful thing, Catulus," he exclaimed, "if you, who are the censor and should scrutinize our lives, were put out of court by our bailiffs."[4]

Upon the man's acquittal, Cato refused to restore him to his post.

Discovering that the exchequer was empty, Cato infuriated the pauci by demanding that those who had accepted bounties as informers or assassins during the Sullan Terror seventeen years earlier should now make restitution. Cato insisted that their bounties had been obtained "by unjust means and made [each of them] give [them] up, at the same time rebuking him with passionate eloquence for his illegal and unholy act." Alarmed at this revival of old rancor and challenge to Sulla's edict of immunity for crimes committed during the proscriptions, the Old Guard remonstrated with Cato. He, however, seized an issue like a mastiff; and when criticized he would respond with some Stoic maxim like: "The philosopher surmises nothing, repents of nothing, is never wrong, never changes his opinion." Now "with passionate eloquence" he denounced the Sullan informers and assassins as "accursed and polluted wretches."[5]

After Cato recovered the blood money from the informers, "they were at once charged with murder." Several of them appeared before Caesar, who was serving as a judge of the homicide court this year. He not only condemned two of the dictator's most notorious hirelings, but in a move of far greater significance he also rejected appeals by the defendants to the late dictator's edict of preemptive immunity for crimes committed during the Terror. Cato ignored Sulla's decree; Caesar, straining the authority of his office (a tactic he would often repeat), pronounced it unconstitutional. Profiteers from the Terror, who lived in constant fear of confiscation of their booty, suddenly saw themselves deprived of the protection of even this flimsy pretense at legality. Caesar's contemporaries sensed the implications of his action, and almost twenty years later, in a speech in defense of one of Caesar's foes after the civil war of the forties, Cicero recalled Caesar's courageous action. Sulla "ordered men to be murdered, though none accused," Cicero declared; "he lured men by bribes to commit murders; but his cruelty was requited years afterwards by" Caesar.[6] In ruling against Sulla's decree, Caesar was making more than a symbolic gesture; he was serving a warning to oligarchs who might contemplate a revival of Sullan lawlessness. By his action he enhanced his popularity among the innumerable Romans helpless to win redress of their many grievances and filled with rancor at the Sullan profiteers.

Caesar would need all possible support next year (63) when he would enter his candidacy for a praetorship. In the rapidly shifting currents of Roman political life, advancement, of course, was never assured, even for a patrician with Caesar's broad following. This year, however, Caesar enjoyed particular advantages. His clansman Lucius Caesar was serving as a consul, and his cousin Lucius Cotta had been elected a censor upon the resignation of the irreconcilable Crassus and Catulus. Cotta followed Crassus' example in announcing that he would enrol the Transpadanes as full citizens. Unfortunately, Cotta was an ineffectual tippler, and he and his colleague, at odds like their predecessors, resigned without holding a census. It was a further sign of the disintegration of the oligarchic Republic that for the next decades, until long after Caesar's death, no census would be ratified. During all these years Italians who had not succeeded in being registered as citizens by the censors of 70 remained deprived of the franchise. They joined the ranks of the disgruntled. The frustrations of so many varied elements of the citizenry offered opportunities for Caesar's maneuvering but intensified the insecurity among leading oligarchs and their impatience for repressive measures. The pauci were always fearful that some charismatic demagogue or "unprincipled" warlord would exploit the critical problems they themselves refused to address. Underlying the general anxiety, of course, was the threat from Pompeius. After advancing into little-known regions of the Caucasus, Pompeius sent his armies south to invade Syria—along with Egypt the last unsubdued Mediterranean kingdom and an additional power base for a warlord already commanding invincible power and wealth.

Caesar was collaborating with Crassus in assembling an opposition faction. In 64 they were backing two of their "friends" for the consulships of the next year, Catilina and Antonius Hybrida. As candidates, the two men were scarcely above reproach. Catilina was a scion of an ancient patrician clan that had not held a consulship for several centuries, a clan which had presumably participated even less than the Julians in the enormous plunder of the wars of the previous century. Determined to restore the wealth and influence of the Sergians, Catilina had switched allegiance opportunely during the civil war and been appointed to a command in Sulla's forces. Subsequently Caesar had served with him on the staff of the governor of Cilicia. Catilina's many enemies harassed him with indictments. In 73 he was accused, along with Crassus, of adultery with a vestal. Bankrupted by this trial as well as by his general profligacy, Catilina had sought to recoup his fortunes while governor of the province of Africa. Indicted for extortion in 66, he had been rejected as a candidate for the consulship. Although rescued by Crassus, who suborned the jury, Catilina emerged "as impoverished as some of his jurors were before the trial." This year he had been haled before a homicide court charged with murders during the Terror. Acquitted once again, he found himself more deeply in debt than ever. On the other hand, Catilina possessed a rare magnetism. A "complex and versatile spirit," he attracted followers among all elements of the populace, fascinating everyone with his appetite for "the monstrous, incredible, gigantic" and with his "great vigor of mind and body."[7] He had an especial appeal for other ruined aristocrats and, indeed, for all the numberless debtors.

Antonius Hybrida's chief distinction was that he was the son of the famous orator and censor executed by Marius. He was also the brother of the incompetent nobleman under whom Caesar had served in the campaign against the pirates. After escaping conviction when prosecuted for extortion by Caesar, he had been expelled from the Senate by the censors and then had exhausted his fortune in seeking rehabilitation through reelection to a praetorship. While in office he had ruined himself by presenting extravagant dramatic performances on a stage enclosed in silver ornamentation. Desperate and unprincipled, he was for sale.

Though alarmed at the enthusiasm for the candidates backed by the millionaire and the self-appointed new Marius, the pauci found no one among the other five candidates whom they could support with any confidence. Of these the only vigorous and eloquent competitor with a substantial following was Cicero, whom they deemed unworthy of the high office. As Cicero was always aware, "new men" were adjudged successful if they advanced a single step—from equestrian to senatorial status—but were condemned as presumptuous if they aspired to a consulship, and in three centuries no more than fifteen "new men" had risen to the high office. Six years earlier, at his election to an aedileship, Cicero lamented: "There is hardly one member of the old families, who looks kindly on our activity; by no services that we render them can we capture their goodwill; they withhold from us their interest and sympathy as completely as if we and they were different breeds of men."[8] Now at the decisive moment of his career, Cicero confronted directly the hostility of the old families, and it appeared that the patient labor of three decades would come to naught. Cicero's father had provided him with the best of educations; through his family's connection to Marius he had been able to serve his political apprenticeship with members of the inner circle of the Senate; through assiduous application he had successfully competed with the leading orators of the older generation and won the title of best orator at Rome; and through shrewd maneuvering and persistent solicitation of the goodwill of influential oligarchs of both aristocratic orders as well as of elements of the commons he had advanced without interruption through the progress of magistracies. Now, however, as he was about to achieve his ultimate aspiration, he faced a handicap not of his own making, a handicap unrelated to his capacities, a handicap against which his previous service and his eloquence proved of no avail.

No philosophical issue was involved. In two decades of intense court activity, Cicero had learned to promote either side of a question with equal skill and passion. So completely did he devote himself to each case at hand that he seemed utterly convinced of whatever position he was then defending. Cicero is not to be censured for lack of principle or opportunism. Behind the slogans and the frequently acrimonious factional conflicts in Roman politics only one issue was ever in question: the rate and tempo of the oligarchy's exploitation of the dependent or enslaved peoples of the city, the peninsula and the empire. Rare was the Roman oligarch who, like Caesar, approached this issue with serious probing.

A year earlier, in 65, desperately searching for allies, Cicero had offered to defend Caesar and Crassus' present candidate, Catilina, in the latter's trial for extortion. "We have the jury we want," Cicero wrote a close friend, "with full cooperation from the prosecution" (the patrician adventurer Clodius, who years earlier had prosecuted Catilina for adultery with a vestal and then had conspired against his own brother-in-law Lucullus in Asia). "If he is acquitted," continued Cicero, "I hope he will be more inclined to work with me in the campaign." In pursuing this alliance, Cicero "took [Catilina] for a loyal citizen, eager for the acquaintance of all the best men, and for a true and faithful friend."[9] Astutely, Cicero preferred to campaign with Catilina rather than against him. With the availability of Crassus' purse, however, the haughty patrician had no need of help from the eager "new man," and now, a year later, Cicero forgot his generous characterization of Catilina but not Catilina's rejection of his request for an alliance.

What backing Cicero could count upon would not guarantee his election. He looked first to clients—men he had defended in the courts and young aristocrats who attended him as apprentice orators—and influential heads of public corporations, whose goodwill he consistently solicited, as well as country squires and other men of property. He required, however, at least the acquiescence of the pauci to his candidacy, and he regretted his past inconsistency in seeking their favor. It was true that he had used his influence as praetor to accomplish the conviction of the former radical tribune Macer, and by mid-65 he was speaking of Domitius Ahenobarbus, Cato's brother-in-law, among the most violent and pigheaded of the pauci, as one "on whom my hopes of success depend beyond any other man."[10] He had also established a good relationship with Piso, the consul of 66, the obstinate opponent to Pompeius. Others in the Senate leadership Cicero had imprudently antagonized.

Cicero was aware that the pauci were in despair at the prospect of the election of the candidates backed by Crassus and Caesar. Cicero also recognized the increasing coincidence of interest since Sulla's death between the entrepreneurs and the senators who defied the prohibition against senatorial participation in commerce, banking and in the public corporations. Having achieved their major aspirations in recent years, the non-senatorial aristocrats were determined to resist "unreasonable demands" by the commons, with whose voices and fists they had regained their political influence. With shrewd maneuvering Cicero might achieve a coalition of all the men of property and win recognition as their agent and spokesman.

No one could assist Cicero more effectively in assembling such a coalition than Titus Pomponius, an old school friend and the brother-in-law of Cicero's younger brother. As a young man, appalled at Sulla's execution of the radical tribune Sulpicius Rufus (a connection of his), Pomponius had given up ambitions for a political career. Like many other Roman aristocrats revolted by the corruption and violence in public life, he embraced the Epicurean counsel to avoid politics, refusing to

> trust himself to the waves of civic strife since he thought that those who had delivered themselves up to them had no more control of themselves than those who were tossed on the billows of the sea. He did not seek offices . . . because they could not be canvassed for in the traditional way nor gained amid such unlimited bribery and corruption without violence to the laws, nor administered to the advantage of the state without risk in so debauched a condition of public morals. In public life he so conducted himself as always to be and to be regarded as being on the side of the best men [the optimates].[11]

Nevertheless, Pomponius assisted victims of civil strife within both factions, at one time even coming to the aid of the younger Marius (who, like Cicero, had also been a schoolmate). As a result, he gained a reputation for fairness and generosity, and his advice on political matters was sought by men of influence. During the civil strife of the eighties, he moved to Athens, where he was soon honored as a benefactor of the city. So thoroughly had he assimilated Athenian ways that he was called Atticus. A man of refined tastes, he dabbled in history and served Roman oligarchs as purchasing agent for Greek works of art. With his investments in various parts of the empire, his loans to numerous provincial communities, his estates, herds and gladiatorial school, Atticus was one of the wealthiest of the equestrians. In the Epicurean manner, however, he lived frugally and did not compete with other rich men in squandering his money on luxurious mansions and villas.

Cicero had long relied upon Atticus' counsel, and in July 65, a year before his candidacy in the consular elections, he appealed for help. "I need you home pretty soon," Cicero wrote. "There is a decidedly strong belief abroad that your noble friends are going to oppose my election. Clearly you will be invaluable to me in gaining them over."[12]

In the six years since Cicero's despondent complaint about the disdain of the nobles for "new men," circumstances, if not attitudes, had changed to Cicero's advantage. "Most of the nobles," Sallust would note in an account of the consular election in 64, "were consumed with jealousy and thought the office [of consul] in a way prostituted if a 'new man,' however excellent, should obtain it. But when danger came, jealousy and pride fell into the background."[13] Oligarchies are always prepared to recruit leaders from outside their ranks to protect them from threats, whether external or from below.

As the consular elections approached, Quintus Cicero drafted a manual for his brother summarizing their private discussions of strategy and tactics. As the initial and fundamental precept, Quintus set down the following rule: "Consider what city this is, what is it you seek, who you are. Every day or so, as you go down to the Forum, you must repeat to yourself: I am 'new'; I seek the consulship; this is Rome."[14] In the remainder of the document Quintus enumerated standard campaign procedures and proposed tactics for overcoming the "new man" handicap. Like other candidates, Cicero was to mobilize all his acquaintances, even his slaves, obtain endorsements of illustrious individuals and develop strategies for gaining the support of tribes and centuries as well as private electoral clubs "run by men of great influence in electioneering." No potential vote was to be ignored. To impress the electorate he was "always [to] have a crowd about [him]." He was to attend to details—"a memory for names, an ingratiating manner, constant attendance, generosity, publicity, a fine political image."

In regard to the key factor in the campaign—"to mobilize the support which nobody has ever possessed without the good graces of the highest personages"— Cicero was to "send friends to persuade them that [his] political sympathies [had] always been with the optimates" and that if he had ever appeared "to have spoken in a 'popular' way, [he] did it with the purpose of attaching Gnaeus Pompeius to [himself] in order to have him with his very great power, as a friend in [his] canvass or at least not an opponent." Quintus emphasized that it was essential that the "Senate deem [Cicero] to be *in future* an upholder of its authority; the Roman knights and men of worth and substance [to deem him] to be devoted to peace and quiet times [or in twentieth-century terms, to law and order]."

Reassuring and winning over the two aristocratic orders was Atticus' responsibility. Although handicapped by Cicero's reputation as a trimmer, Atticus could draw upon much in his friend's past to persuade the incredulous of Cicero's "true" political propensities. He could match Cicero's occasional lapses into "popular" sloganeering with examples of his propagation of oligarchic shibboleths. Thus in the year when Cicero had spoken in support of Pompeius' appointment as commander in the Mithridatic war, he had also solemnly proclaimed his faith in a hackneyed myth exploited by every oligarchy to maintain its hegemony. "Never, I maintain, has a state offered so much as does ours," he declared, "wherein if a man of humble birth shows in his life a character such as to support the high standing which rank confers, his advancement is dependent only on hard work and a blameless record." (The corollary to this bromide, of course, is that any citizen who fails to advance to wealth and power has only himself to blame.) The pauci who were unsympathetic to Cicero were primarily concerned, however, with his attitudes regarding the Sullan order, and for them Atticus could recall how even in his prosecution of Verres, a protégé of Hortensius and of members of the powerful Metellan clan, Cicero had defended the Sullan order with the very rationale employed by the esteemed elder statesman Catulus. "The whole system that [Sulla] set up," Cicero had declared, "is not only in force today but supported against change by the authority of the state, in our fear of the worse troubles and evils that change might bring."[15]

In the campaign manual Quintus concentrated his attention on tactics for defeating Antonius and Catilina inasmuch as the other candidates posed a minimal threat. Although Cicero had entered an electoral alliance with Antonius in their campaign for praetorships and had offered to defend Catilina in his trial on a charge of extortion, now he was to attack both without restraint. Quintus set the tone, denouncing them as "two assassins from boyhood, both libertines, both paupers." Antonius was a lesser threat, "afraid of his own shadow" and unable even to "call people by their names without a prompter." Catilina had "greater manliness" and offered a more serious challenge, and Quintus proposed that Cicero play upon the fears of optimates in regard to Catilina's indebtedness, his wilfulness and propensity to violence by deriding him as "born in his father's beggary, bred in his sister's debauchery, grown up in civil slaughter, his first entry into public life was a massacre of Roman knights [during the Sullan Terror]."

The vitriol which in his consulship a year later Cicero would direct against Catilina was brewed in the election campaign—"actors and gladiators as his accomplices . . . lust . . . crime . . . polluted by his mere wickedness . . . such skill and efficiency in his lust that he has raped children in smocks practically at their parents' knees . . ." Reassuring his brother in regard to his "new man" handicap, Quintus insisted: "It will not be a hard contest with these competitors who are by no means as eminent in birth as they are notable in vice."

Despite Cicero's vigorous assault, citizens flocked to the support of the two men, especially the charismatic Catilina. When he marched into the Forum, he was followed by a great crowd of enthusiastic and confident partisans.

The "best" citizens recalled how in 70, 67 and 66, radical tribunes had mounted demonstrations and packed assemblies by calling out the collegia. Mobilizing these fraternal organizations of freedmen, slaves and free poor, Manilius had attempted to extend the franchise of the freedmen, and with their members he had disrupted his first trial. Now the collegia provided a nucleus of Catilina's support.

By a Senate decree the pauci dissolved all but a few "trustworthy" collegia and dispersed thereby a base of the "popular party."

To deprive Catilina of his impressive entourage, a bill was passed limiting the number of attendants on candidates.

Against this counterattack Caesar, Crassus and Catilina could mount only limited resistance, and when, in vetoing a bill against electoral fraud aimed at Catilina and Antonius, a "popular" tribune sneered at Cicero as unworthy to hold a consulship, Cicero recognized his opportunity. His eloquence whetted both by rancor at the tribune's insults and by his desperation in this last chance to convince the pauci of his usefulness and loyalty, Cicero denounced the tribune as the agent of a dire conspiracy. In the uneasiness inspired by Catilina's rallying of disgruntled elements and by the insolence of his exuberant followers, Cicero could be confident of the receptivity of the leaders of the Senate even to outlandish innuendo and character defamation of those they believed threatened their hegemony and, therefore, the security of the commonwealth. Cicero intensified the general alarm. Subversion was his theme and would remain his theme for the rest of this year, for the year of his consulship and for much of the rest of his life—subversion of the oligarchic Republic, subversion as defined by those who resisted all reform.

In an atmosphere of anxiety at mounting popular discontent, the cry of subversion is irresistible, and Cicero was able to inflate a purported electoral bribery scheme into a diabolical subversive conspiracy. No one challenged Cicero to reveal the source of his report that on the previous evening Antonius and Catilina had met at the home of a distinguished but unnamed nobleman to distribute a vast sum to bribery agents for the purchase of votes. When he recalled an accusation against Catilina two years earlier of participation in a conspiracy (supposedly promoted by Crassus and Caesar) to murder the consuls-elect, no one objected that one of the intended victims, contemptuous of the charge, had offered to defend Catilina in a subsequent trial.

Now, Cicero was suggesting, in league with powerful, unnamed nobles, Catilina was engaged in a new conspiracy.

In these unnamed noblemen Cicero had ready subjects for his fearsome wit. He could mock the association of the new Marius (Caesar) with a Sullan murderer (Catilina); and of a young and idealistic prosecutor (Caesar) with a corrupt defendant (Antonius) who had escaped conviction more than ten years earlier through a shabby maneuver. What of the support by the victor over Spartacus (Crassus) of an impecunious nobleman (Antonius) who, so Cicero charged, had announced his intention to rouse a slave revolt if brought to ruin by his creditors? What of the general threat to men of property from two bankrupts like Antonius and Catilina? Would they promote a cancellation of debts? And thereafter . . . agrarian reform? . . . new proscriptions? . . . civil war? Could there be, as Quintus had asked rhetorically in his campaign handbook, "a citizen so vile as to want to unsheathe with one vote, two daggers against the state?"

As for Caesar and Crassus' candidates, what could they respond to such a farrago of insinuation, speculation and anonymous recrimination?

Catilina mustered a feeble sneer at Cicero's ignominious birth and chided the orator for his insolence as a "new man" in assailing a patrician of heroic ancestry. Antonius emitted a mellifluous but ineffectual rejoinder. "I do not fear him as an accuser," he declared, "for I am innocent; I do not dread him as a rival candidate, for I am Antonius; I do not expect to see him consul, for he is Cicero."[16]

By his last-minute appeal to the pauci as well as through Atticus' maneuvering, Cicero triumphed in the election. Antonius, favored by the renown of his censor father, condemned to death by Marius, and aided very likely by his one-time brother-in-law, the consul Lucius Caesar, overcame Catilina by the vote of a few centuries for second place.

Caesar and Crassus had succeeded in promoting the election of the weaker and less reliable of their two protégés.

What course would the impetuous Catilina now pursue, desperate at the prospect of ruin by his creditors?

Would Cicero, having won his consulship by warnings of a conspiracy, press his assault on the populars by rousing further hysteria against subversion?

In face of the momentous shift in the balance of forces resulting from the union of the men of property of both orders against a supposed threat of subversion, what strategy was Caesar to adopt to advance his own career?

What would be Pompeius' stance upon his triumphant return from the East?

XX

LEADER OF THE RESISTANCE

THE struggle of the next two decades in Roman politics would essentially be between those who recognized that in societies with blatant inequities in wealth, privilege and power, tension and conflict are endemic; and those who believed, despite constant experiences to the contrary, that movements for change can be indefinitely repressed. Each of these groupings, of course, encompassed a spectrum of degrees of conviction and of aggressiveness. With more consistency and perspicacity than other Romans, Caesar epitomized the forces accepting a reality of unremitting struggle; while Cicero served as the spokesman for and, occasionally, as the agent of the defenders of the status quo. During Cicero's consulship, in 63, the contradiction emerged in clear definition, a contradiction that would eventually be resolved with the destruction of the oligarchic Republic. In this respect—and certainly not in the respect for which he lauded it ad nauseam for the rest of his life—Cicero's consulship represented a turning point in the final years of the Republic. The events of this year were to shape Caesar's strategies in the immediately succeeding years and were to provide lessons and warnings for the last years of his life.

With the warlord's every victory, the pauci experienced new alarm. Even before Cicero's election they had been evolving, not necessarily with conscious deliberation, a strategy to prevent, upon Pompeius' return, a recurrence—this time at their own expense—of the kind of social upheaval that had resulted from the seizure of lands to settle tens of thousands of Sullan veterans and from other wholesale confiscations during the Terror. If with indictments and with violence they had failed to undermine the authority of the tribunes, they did succeed in thwarting attempts at extending the franchise, in outlawing the collegia and in blocking the election as consul of a dangerous adventurer. With the return from the East of Lucullus, enraged at his humiliation by Pompeius and at a tribune's vetoing of a triumph, the pauci received a new impetus to crush insolence and to restore law and order. If upon arriving at Rome the victorious Pompeius found the "best citizens" united in repression of "subversive" elements, he would either collaborate in the patriotic endeavor or be denounced as a collaborator with "revolutionaries." Despite his repeated solicitations of the populars, Pompeius had always sought above all else the respect of the nobility and he yearned to be acclaimed by them as the chief defender of the republic. He would not side with outcasts.

Following such a strategy—and who could stop them?—the leaders of the Senate would both suppress unruly elements and curb the arrogant warlord. With Pompeius far from Rome, with the entrepreneurs satisfied with recent gains and the populars at bay, the Old Guard saw an opportunity to reverse their retreat since the death of the dictator and to inaugurate a new era of civil tranquility. They preferred to avoid the unpleasant exaggerations of another Sullan Terror. A limited bloodbath, swift and decisive, might achieve the same end with less likelihood of a subsequent unmanageable upheaval that the opportunistic warlord might exploit.

Caesar alone had consistently opposed the Old Sullans, but never since the beginning of his political career had his role appeared so hopeless. An oligarch who derived his support from anti-senatorial elements could hardly prevail against the hysteria of a campaign against "subversion." Undismayed, Caesar and his associates evolved a counterstrategy to expose the actual goals of the anti-subversive campaign and to provoke debate about real rather than factitious issues. The fundamental problem in the ancient world, as in the underdeveloped regions of the modern world, was agrarian reform. In Italy since Sulla the smallholders had undergone the most severe crisis in the peninsula's history. The sufferings of the yeomanry had become a theme for poets. Caesar's contemporary, Lucretius, lamented:

Now the ancient ploughman shaking his head sighs many a time that the labors of his hands have all come to nothing, and comparing times present with times past

often praises the fortunes of his father and grumbles how the old world full of piety
supported life with great ease on a narrow domain.

Horace, born the year of Caesar's aedileship, knew the despair of the farmer
harried by his rich neighbor:

> What that thou tearest down each neighboring post that marks thy farm
> and in thy greed dost overleap the boundaries of thy tenants!
> Man and wife are driven forth bearing in their arms their household
>   gods and ragged children.[1]

With several of the tribunes-elect, other magistrates about to take office, the
consul-elect Antonius and very likely Crassus and Catilina, Caesar drafted a
comprehensive agrarian bill. Learning of the preliminary deliberations, Cicero
asked to participate in the discussions, asserting that "if the law seemed . . .
likely to be useful to the Roman plebeians [he] would support and help to pass
it." The drafters of the bill rejected the request, asserting that the consul-elect
"could never be brought to approve any kind of largess" to the people.[2] To
promote the bill, the sponsors selected the tribune-elect Rullus, whose father
had gained renown as the first Roman ever to serve an entire boar at a banquet
(a generation earlier such a modest display still evoked astonishment). Rullus'
only other recommendation for the responsibility was that his father-in-law
had been a major profiteer in the Sullan proscriptions, a fact that would
reassure other such profiteers that their holdings would not be threatened by
his measure. On December 12 (64) upon his installation as tribune, Rullus read
the bill aloud in the Forum. A bumbling speaker, he lost his audience (so
Cicero declared) as he droned through more than forty clauses of legal termi-
nology. When the bill was posted, as the law required, Romans saw that the
drafters had attended meticulously to details and provided in this single measure a wide-ranging program of social reform. By granting allotments to the
landless poor as well as to veterans, they sought both to resettle the demoralized indigent hordes crowding into Rome and, like the Gracchi, to reconstitute
the yeomanry as a source of legionary recruits. Allotments were to be made out
of public lands and from lands purchased from owners willing to sell. Sullan
profiteers were thus not threatened, and land-rich aristocrats overwhelmed by
debts were guaranteed a fair price for their holdings despite current depressed
land values. Anticipating the standard optimate warning against bankrupting
the treasury through social programs, the promoters of the bill proposed to
raise funds through the sale of property confiscated by the state in overseas
dependencies and from war booty (with Pompeius' current plunder excluded).
In proposing sale of public lands overseas, the sponsors hoped to win support
of entrepreneurs eager for profitable investments. In addition, through the sale
of war booty, they would inaugurate at last a rational system for disposing of
plunder. In its comprehensiveness and rationality, the law betrayed a decisive
contribution from Caesar and represented a forerunner of legislation he would
promote in the future.

Proponents of the agrarian bill could not take it for granted that Cicero would oppose unequivocally a measure so advantageous to many elements among the citizenry and to Pompeius as well. In his inaugural address on January 1, 63, Caesar and his associates awaited the new consul's response. Cicero would expose not only his attitude regarding the measure at hand but also the political line and tactics he intended to pursue during his year in office.

In his address to the Senate and in two subsequent orations in the Forum, Cicero rejected the Rullan measure out of hand. He found nothing to salvage in it, offered no constructive suggestions and proposed no substitute. Exuberant at his acceptance into the councils of the most prestigious nobles and confident that with the backing of the pauci he would rally all men of property behind his campaign to recall disgruntled elements to reason—Cicero delivered himself over to his mentors without reservation and committed himself with the passion of a new believer to their credo: "Let no innovation be made contrary to usage and the principles of our forefathers"—a credo he had mocked only three years earlier in promoting Pompeius' command against Mithridates.

Paragons of hyperbolic obfuscation, unabashed distortion and shameless disregard of principle, Cicero's speeches against the Rullan land bill remain as models of reactionary oratory with a claim to the attention of men of any era equally eager to repress efforts at mitigating social misery. His councilors would grant no redress to the desperate, yield not an iota to any challenge to their authority and entertain no reforms with which they might prolong their own outmoded hegemony. Like entrenched oligarchs of every other era, they fixed their eyes on an illusory past and preferred repression of discontent and eventual overthrow to slow retreat with dignity preserved.

Cicero adapted his speeches to his different audiences, repeating certain charges in all the speeches, though with varying emphases, as well as eliminating or adding charges from speech to speech. Common to all were ad hominem attacks, standard for all crusaders against subversion. He singled out Rullus. "As soon as he was elected," Cicero declared, "he practiced putting on a different expression, a different tone of voice and a different gait; his clothes were in rags, his person was terribly neglected, more hair about him now and more beard, so that eyes and aspect seemed to protest to the world the tribunician power and to threaten the republic." He accused the backers of the agrarian bill of seeking personal gain, charging Rullus especially with seeking to safeguard the holdings his father-in-law had seized during the Sullan Terror. Rullus' associates Cicero denounced as "a band of scoundrels."[3]

Appealing to Pompeius' partisans both in the Senate and among the citizenry, Cicero pictured the land reform commissioners, "enemies of Pompeius," entering "the general's camp" determined "that his army, resources and his reputation may be diminished." Representing himself as Pompeius' spokesman at Rome, he announced: "Pompeius rejects Rullus' offer."[4] On the other hand, the self-appointed champion of the warlord elaborated no alternate proposal for a land bonus for Pompeius' veterans.

Cicero repeated the standard arguments of every oligarchy against social reforms. No matter how enticing they appeared, he insisted, they were impossible of realization "without draining the treasury."[5] He complained of the loss of revenues from public lands to be distributed without mentioning the concern of wealthy landowners regarding plots they or their forbears had appropriated illegally, lands for which many of them avoided paying rent to the treasury. (Cicero's wife paid no taxes on public forest land she exploited.)

Cicero's major charge, constantly reiterated before both audiences, was that the bill was merely a blind for "pernicious designs by nefarious men." It was, he warned, the intention of the sponsors, operating through the ten elected commissioners (exercising, according to Cicero, "royal" power), to settle their partisans in key regions of Italy and then to seize control of the peninsula and to transfer the seat of empire away from Rome. "To Capua," he declared to the Senate, "they would have colonists conducted; that is the city they would have once more in opposition to this city [it had sided with Hannibal against Rome a century and a half earlier]; this is whither they would remove their wealth and the name of our empire."[6] The name of the city evoked memories of the Spartacan revolt as well as of the civil war when the city had supported Marius and Cinna.

Before the Senate Cicero proclaimed himself the spokesman for the pauci, a defender of law and order and a resolute foe of "subversion." Impressed with the grandeur of his mission, he adopted the prophetic magniloquence of the newly popular Eastern mystical cults which preached an eternal war of "the armies of light against the forces of darkness" and promised initiates eternal happiness after death through the grace of divine redeemers. "You have given hope," Cicero charged Rullus, "to the wicked and inspired the good with fear." But the champion of righteousness was at hand to repel the forces of evil. "In the midst of this confusion and disturbance of men's minds and affairs," Cicero proclaimed, ". . . the voice and authority of a consul has suddenly brought light into utter darkness for the Roman people."[7]

On the other hand, Cicero admitted to a grievous handicap in his effort to rally even senators to his campaign against "subversion." Unlike Gaius Cotta, who could quell bread riots by exhorting the citizenry to patriotic sacrifice in face of threats to the republic from external enemies, Cicero had to admit that because of Pompeius, "there [was] no danger from without . . . the evil [was] confined within [the] gates, it [was] internal and domestic." He warned of civil war. "The republic when it was handed over to me," he declared, "was full of anxiety, full of fear. . . . All kinds of seditious plots against the present form of government and against your quiet were reported to be already in progress, some to have been entered on the moment we were elected consuls."[8]

In the Senate Cicero attacked the agrarian bill as spokesman of the pauci; in the Forum he rejected it as a "popular," as "a consul of the people," the first "new man" in many years to hold the high office. Since a substantial portion of

Cicero's audience in the Forum was sympathetic to agrarian reform, Cicero could not dismiss Rullus' measure so arbitrarily as he had done before the Senate. His tactic was to accept the principle but to impugn the motive. What, he asked, employing a time-honored manipulation, were the actual intentions of those who "promise lands to the Roman people"? They were, in fact, "darkly engineering something different." Of course, if the allegation of an unfathomable "secret purpose" behind reform measures that otherwise immediately recommend themselves is accepted, no reform could ever be proposed, much less passed. Cicero was equating change with subversion. He warned, too, that he would accuse of advocacy of revolution any who proposed measures to mitigate misery and despair. On the other hand, as "the people's consul," Cicero assured his audience that he did not "disapprove of every kind of agrarian law in itself"! He recalled, in fact, that "the most illustrious citizens, the most able and the most devoted friends of the Roman people, Tiberius and Gaius Gracchus, settled plebeians in public lands." (On other occasions, Cicero, expressing his private opinion, would number the two popular heroes "among those whose murder was justifiable.") Despite their protestations of concern for the people's welfare, according to Cicero, the drafters of the Rullan bill, unlike the honest Gracchi, "assembled privately . . . in darkness and solitude . . . in secret meetings," and their purpose was not to benefit the people but to gain control "of the treasury, the revenues, all the provinces and the entire republic, of friendly kingdoms, of free nations."[9]

The urban plebs of 63 hardly resembled the resolute yeomen who had rallied behind the Gracchi. As Cicero's contemporary, the learned Varro, noted regarding the countryfolk of the day: "Practically all the heads of families have sneaked within the walls abandoning the sickle and the plow and would rather busy their hands in the theatre and in the circus than in the grainfields and the vineyards." Like every other society in dissolution, Rome harbored a numerous underclass that lived by its wits, robbery, violence and sale of votes, voices, fists and bodies. They menaced the security, morality and health of the city. Alienated and demoralized, they formed a second world within the city as against the world of the senators and equestrians and the rest of the tiny minority of men of property. Each world hated the other, with fear and contempt on the side of those who ate regularly and fear and rancor among those who were always half-starved. Feigning indignation, "the people's consul" quoted Rullus as declaring "that the common people of the city had too much power in the republic; that they ought to be drained off," as though, Cicero commented, "he were speaking of sewage instead of estimable citizens." Cicero exhorted the former farmers: "Keep possession of the influence you enjoy, of your liberty, of your votes, of your dignity, of your city, of your forum, of your games, of your festivals and all your other enjoyments."[10] The consul and his mentors offered circuses, but no bread.

Upon the successful rebuttal of his arguments by his opponents, Cicero was compelled to deliver a second speech in the Forum. Sarcastically he remarked:

"It has been dinned into your eyes and minds, O Romans, that I wished to gratify the seven tyrants [the dominant coterie of Old Sullans in the Senate]." After rehearsing his previous arguments, he challenged Rullus: "What then does this Marian tribune say, who is dragging us Sullans into unpopularity?" By alluding to the old Marian-Sullan conflict, Cicero was pointing to Marius' self-appointed heir. He was wary of naming Caesar and Crassus as prime movers of the agrarian law, but his audience knew whom he meant when he charged that the bill was proposed "to satisfy the insatiable avarice of certain individuals . . . some of [whom] . . . never think they have enough to keep [Crassus] and [some of whom] . . . never think they have enough to squander [Caesar]." At the end of his first speech in the Forum, implicitly addressing Caesar and Crassus, Cicero proclaimed "the unanimity which I have established between myself and my colleague to the great dislike of those men who said that we were and would be enemies . . . during our consulship." With an offer of a lucrative provincial governorship, Cicero had suborned the bankrupt and disreputable Antonius into betraying his former alliance. Exultant, Cicero gave warning. "I have wisely made provision for and taken precaution against all emergencies," he declared, "and tried to bring those men back to their allegiance. I have also given the tribunes notice not to stir up sedition during my consulship."[11]

Before the Senate Cicero boldly exposed the goal of his campaign against subversives like the proponents of the Rullan land bill. "If, conscript fathers," he announced, "you promise me your zeal in upholding the common dignity, I will certainly fulfill the most ardent wish of the republic, that the authority of this [senatorial] order, which existed in the time of our ancestors, may now, after a long interval, be seen to be restored to the State."[12]

The voice was Cicero's, but the words were Sulla's: renewal of the authority of the Senate and return of the republic to its condition before the Gracchan reforms. The "long interval" during which the Senate had lost its authority was, of course, the fifteen or more years since the dictator's death. Cicero was promising the restoration of the Sullan order, the ultimate aspiration of his mentors!

From the first weeks of January, during the remainder of his consulship and throughout his career, the defender of the commonwealth against the threat of reform would define his role not in terms of opposing points of view regarding measures to delay or avert or resolve a crisis in the republic but in terms of a war between the forces of good and evil. Of the problems of the homeless, the indebted, the jobless, the disenfranchised and the starving, not a word. Proponents of reform Cicero denounced as dangerous conspirators prepared "to throw the government into confusion by seditious speeches, by turbulent decrees of the Senate, by unjust exercise of authority and to seek some excuse for revolution."[13] For redress of grievances Cicero and his associates offered no alternative other than riots and rebellion.

Cicero roused hysteria, the pauci mobilized their clients, an optimate tribune threatened a veto, and Rullus' bill was either withdrawn or defeated in an assembly vote. Nevertheless, Caesar's faction had posed a pressing issue. Those who anticipated relief from misery through the agrarian bill swelled the ranks of the desperate. By repressing all moves for reform, Cicero and his mentors would intensify discontent. The danger was that the pauci might provoke a premature uprising in order to crush their opponents in a single bloody action. Then they would confront the victorious warlord confident in their prestige as saviors of the republic.

In Cicero, Caesar and his associates faced a cunning and eloquent foe. Caesar would have to exert all his genius in political maneuvering to counter the anti-subversive campaign. It was as though he faced Sulla once again. This time, however, Caesar was no helpless adolescent.

XXI

COUNTERATTACK

CAESAR had heard the slogans before—"the plot against liberty," "pernicious designs of nefarious citizens" and "seditious plots against the present form of government." These had been the battle cries of the Old Guard against the Gracchi, Saturninus, Drusus, Sulpicius, Marius and a series of radical tribunes since the death of the dictator. Some of these reformers had been assassinated or exiled; the followers of the "most dangerous" had been massacred. In his warnings against "passionate men, always disposed for violence, ready for revolution," in his assertion that it was his duty as consul "to exercise the most serious care and attention in protecting the republic" and in his solemn admonition to the tribunes "not to stir up sedition during [his] consulship,"[1] Cicero was implementing a plan of action directed toward an invocation of the ultimate decree of the Senate, a declaration of martial law permitting summary execution of outlaws and the suspension of provocatio (the ancient right of appeal to the people in capital cases). Rightly adjudging provocatio as their ultimate defense against oligarchic lawlessness, the "populars" had always contested the constitutionality of the ultimate decree of the Senate. When during the previous year, as president of a homicide court, Caesar invalidated the preemptive amnesty for crimes committed during the Sullan Terror, he was providing a warning to those who contemplated future "cleansings" of the republic, but Caesar held no magistracy this year (63), and he confronted an atmosphere of prejudice and hysteria in which any proposal for the reinforcement of constitutional rights would be denounced as a cover for conspiracy.

In such crises Caesar's tactic was to mount theatrical coups to prod the populace to a new awareness and to disconcert his enemies. He found a collaborator in the tribune Titus Labienus, a country squire from Pompeius' base of power in Picenum and a fellow officer of Caesar's many years earlier on the staff of the governor of Cilicia. Together they evolved a scenario far more imaginative and complicated than the charade with which Pompeius won a command against the pirates. The SCU (Senatus consultum ultimum—the ultimate decree of the Senate) had last been evoked to sanction a mass slaughter in the case of Saturninus and his followers. Over the decades the memory of Saturninus persisted among the people, and oligarchs were aware that the "very name" of the murdered tribune could still "inflame the passions of the unsophisticated multitude."[2] Among those slain at the side of Saturninus was an uncle of Labienus'—a coincidence that may have inspired Caesar and Labienus to concoct their wily maneuver. The victim they selected could hardly have been more appropriate for their purposes, an elderly, disreputable senator named Rabirius who over the years had been brought to trial for embezzlement, sacrilege, destruction of public records, illegal detention of slaves and scourging and even murder of citizens. In charging Rabirius with the murder of Saturninus, Caesar and Labienus were posing the issues of the inviolability of tribunes and of the right of appeal to the people in capital cases.

To draw attention to the antiquity of the constitutional guarantees involved in the case and to preempt the optimate monopoly of tradition, Caesar and Labienus revived a judicial procedure instituted six centuries earlier by King Tullus for the trial of the legendary hero Horatius, who had murdered his sister for bemoaning the death of her fiancé, an enemy Horatius had killed in battle.[3] A praetor, substituting for a king and acting in collusion with Caesar and Labienus, appointed as the two judges for the trial Caesar's clansman Lucius Caesar, a consul of the previous year, and Caesar himself! Pursuant to the ancient procedure, Labienus erected a cross on the Campus Martius and made preparations for scourging Rabirius before crucifying him.

The success of such a coup de theatre depends upon a consistent tension between melodrama and farce. In his eagerness to expose the cruelty of his self-righteous foes, Caesar failed to conceal his animosity. With such venomous delight did Caesar pronounce the formula—"Gaius Rabirius, I adjudge you a traitor; go, lictor, bind his hands, veil his head, hang him to the tree of shame"[4]—that the spell of the charade was shattered and the sympathy of the audience shifted momentarily to the defendant.

According to the legend, as the lictor approached with a rope to bind him, Horatius at a signal from the king cried, "Provoco!" ("I appeal"); and in a subsequent trial before the people he won acquittal.

Now the rascal Rabirius cried, "Provoco!"

For the new trial the optimates assigned their stellar orators, Hortensius and

Cicero (henceforth associates, no longer opponents). No one epitomized more graphically than Hortensius the effete defenders of outmoded traditions and institutions. Romans giggled at how one day as he proceeded like a peacock through the Forum, restraining his gait so as not to disturb the fall of his toga, a colleague brushed against him. Hortensius brought an action against the culprit for violation of his dignity, asserting that the disarrangement of a single fold of his toga represented a criminal affront.[5] Already discomfited by Labienus' imposition of a half-hour limit on defense speeches, Hortensius became further distressed by gibes at his meticulous toilet and studied theatrical gestures, for a vast concourse, including elderly populars who remembered Saturninus, members of the recently dissolved collegia and other disgruntled citizens, had assembled to vent their fury at the arrogant nobles.

Cicero, too, despaired of weaving a spell of obfuscation in a mere half hour. Unable, despite his ever-fertile imagination, to conjure up virtues in the scoundrel he was defending, once again he cried "subversion." The trial, he declared, represented no less than "an attempt to abolish from the constitution that chief support of our imperial dignity handed down to us by our forefathers [the SCU, the ultimate decree of the Senate], to make the authority of the Senate, the power of the consuls, the concerted action of good citizens impotent henceforward to combat the curse and bane of our country, which in the process of overturning these institutions, has prompted this attack upon my client." He exhorted "good and courageous citizens . . . to block all approaches of revolution."[6]

As the trial proceeded, jurors and audience came to appreciate the astuteness of the men who had promoted the indictment. To defend Rabirius against execution, Cicero was compelled to appeal to the right of provocatio as renewed in a bill passed after the murder of Tiberius Gracchus. "Gaius Gracchus carried a law," Cicero proclaimed, "forbidding sentence to be passed on the life of a Roman citizen without your consent." Indignant at the delight of the audience at his championship of provocatio, a bulwark of popular liberty, Cicero snapped: "Would that my case gave me the chance to proclaim that my client's was the hand that struck down that public enemy, Saturninus." In his anger Cicero had upset his customary unerring sense of timing. The shift from praise of Gaius Gracchus' law of civilized justice to praise of the murder of Saturninus in violation of that law was too abrupt. The audience hooted. Experienced in Forum manipulations, Cicero recovered himself and responded with a sly stratagem. Pretending that all who kept silent approved his words, he declared: "The outcry I hear does not perturb me . . . it consoles me, for it shows that there are some uninstructed citizens but not many."[7] (Cicero would repeat this stratagem later in the year on an equally grave occasion.)

Addressing himself henceforth to the "instructed," "good" citizens, Cicero attacked Labienus with the time-honored charge of guilt by association. Pointing to a portrait of Saturninus Labienus had displayed to the court, Cicero recalled that after Saturninus' assassination a jury "branded as a worthless citizen unfit to remain in the citizen body anyone who, by keeping the portrait of a man whose sedition made him a public enemy, either did honor to his death or by exciting the pity of the uninstructed [as Labienus was presumably now doing] caused them to regret him or showed an inclination on his own part to imitate such villainy."[8]

The "people's consul" now declared his readiness to promote another massacre of "revolutionaries." "What should I do," he asked rhetorically, "if Titus Labienus, like Lucius Saturninus, caused a massacre of the citizens, broke from prison, seized the Capitol with an armed force? I should do as Gaius Marius did. I should bring a motion before the Senate, exhort you to defend the republic and take arms myself to oppose with your help an armed enemy."[9]

Cicero was adapting history to his own purposes.

Empowered by the ultimate decree, Marius as consul had besieged Saturninus and his followers, but he had guaranteed them protection and a trial before the people in return for surrender. Desiring no public hearings, the leaders of the Senate incited the populace, particularly young aristocrats like Rabirius, to massacre the tribune and his partisans as they cowered within the Senate house, unarmed and trusting in Marius' pledge. In threatening Labienus now, Cicero offered no such constitutional guarantees as Marius had promised Saturninus. (Later in the year, empowered by an ultimate decree of the Senate, Cicero would arrest conspirators and execute them without trial.)

Suddenly a shout arose in the crowd. At the ancient fort atop the Janiculum hill across the Tiber someone was lowering the red flag. According to tradition, at this signal of the approach of an enemy, public business was to cease. In disuse for centuries, the signal climaxed the archaic drama mounted by Caesar and Labienus. The praetor Metellus Celer, Pompeius' brother-in-law and a personal enemy of Cicero's, had adjourned the trial by this exotic maneuver. Caesar and Labienus required no verdict. They had compelled Cicero both to acknowledge the law of provocatio and to announce his intention to violate it. He had proclaimed his readiness to prosecute opponents on a charge of guilt by association and declared his satisfaction at the murder of such "subversives."

For the moment Caesar and his faction dissipated the hysteria Cicero had inspired during the debate on the Rullan land bill and revived the morale of the populars with a theatrical trial of a brutish senator, a spectacle enlivened by ritualistic hocus-pocus. They exposed Cicero's readiness to put to death men accused not of armed rebellion but merely of advocacy of radical reforms and to pronounce men guilty by association for possession of a picture or a statue of a "popular" hero. (In antiquity as in the twentieth century, a major constitutional issue revolved about the distinction between advocacy—thoughts or intentions—and acts.)

To keep Cicero and his mentors off-balance, Caesar and his associates mounted new actions. Caesar prosecuted Piso, the ultra-reactionary consul of 67 who had resisted even with violence Pompeius' appointment to a command against the pirates. Cicero, displaying untiring zeal in his new post as agent of the pauci, undertook Piso's defense. "Subversion" and "revolution" and secret aspirations of "nefarious men" once again were his themes. Upon his client's

acquittal, Cicero exulted that "Piso had been preserved for the state uncondemned because he had been a courageous and steadfast consul,"[10] an assertion that would hardly endear Cicero to the absent warlord.

In the current resurgence of the pauci, Caesar could not hope to win a
conviction of Piso. He succeeded, however, in once again diverting Cicero
from advancing his campaign against "subversion." In addition, he strengthened his tie with Pompeius by prosecuting one of the warlord's most resolute
foes. Important for his future, too, was the goodwill Caesar won among the
Allobrogians, the Gallic plaintiffs against the former governor. He also confirmed his patronage of the Transpadanes by denouncing Piso for illegally
executing a native of the country beyond the Po.

Simultaneously, Labienus and other tribunes of the opposition faction kept
the optimates on the defensive by promoting additional reform legislation.
Oligarchs took it for granted that agrarian bills like Rullus' were forerunners
to other "subversive" measures, and now "popular" tribunes proposed bills
for the relief of debtors and for the restoration of civil rights to the sons of the
proscribed (excluded by Sulla from holding office). The stock objection of the
optimates to bills for debt relief was that such measures inevitably led to a
cancellation of debts and represented an attack on the rights of property and
an "undermining of the foundations of the commonwealth." In rejecting the
measure for the rehabilitation of the children of the proscribed, Cicero employed a subtler approach. "What fate could be more cruel," cried the
"people's consul," "than that the children of men of good birth and the descendants of distinguished ancestors should be excluded from participation in
public life?" Nevertheless, as he subsequently admitted, "at the cost of enmity
to myself, I deprived of the privilege of candidature at the elections young men,
who, though brave and patriotic, had passed through experiences which would
probably have led them to shatter the constitution, had they obtained office."[11]
The Sullans feared vengeance from these victims of the dictator. They would
demand the return of confiscated properties, and they would intensify the
already furious competition for magistracies.

Caesar's faction found an opportunity to enter a direct contest with the
pauci upon the death of Metellus Pius. Son of a confirmed enemy to Marius,
Sulla's colleague in the consulship after the civil war and Pompeius' associate
in the war against Sertorius, Metellus Pius was one of the most prestigious,
wealthy and influential of the pauci. Through Sulla's favor he had succeeded
Scaevola as supreme pontiff, head of the college of pontifices and of the sacred
family of high priests and vestals. With his death this exalted post fell vacant.

Shortly before Caesar's birth a tribune, the father of the obstreperous and
violent Ahenobarbus, had passed a law providing for the election of pontifices
by seventeen of the thirty-five tribes chosen by lot (a procedure aimed at
diminishing the possibility of bribery and long employed in the election of the
supreme pontiff). For sponsoring this democratic legislation, the citizens had
rewarded Ahenobarbus by electing him pontifex maximus. Sulla restored co-
option by the college, and Caesar was elected a pontifex by the priests them-

selves. Now Labienus posted a bill to repeal Sulla's measure and to revive Ahenobarbus' procedure for popular election of the priests. The bill passed.

An office of enormous prestige, the supreme pontificate, like the censorship, was considered a reward for long and outstanding service to the republic. No one was surprised when Catulus, a former consul and censor, supervisor of the reconstruction of the Temple of Jupiter and a leading spokesman of the pauci, announced his candidacy. The entrance of Servilius Isauricus into the competition provoked excitement among the oligarchs. A consular surpassing Catulus in military glory (he had celebrated two triumphs) and in reputation for devotion to the old virtues, Servilius harbored a long enmity for Catulus' ally and marital connection, Lucullus. He had supported the Manilian law to replace Lucullus with Pompeius as supreme commander against Mithridates. He maintained a patronage of a group of younger aristocrats of "popular" sympathies who had served on his staff during his governorship of Cilicia a dozen years earlier—Caesar, Labienus and Catilina, all associates of Pompeius'.

When a third candidate entered his name, Rome was astounded. The optimates were shocked at the insolence of one so young and of mere aedilician rank in aspiring to such an exalted office. The populars, on the other hand, welcomed this new display of defiance. Once again Caesar was declaring his political independence and his leadership of the opposition. Through his candidacy he was affording citizens an opportunity to express their resentment of optimate insolence and their rejection of Cicero's anti-subversive hysteria.

The optimates justly feared Caesar's skill as a campaigner and his popularity, newly reinforced in the trials of Rabirius and Piso and by his promotion of the recent series of reform bills. Caesar could advance a special claim to the high priesthood, arguing that it was time, after a lapse of seventy years, for a patrician once again to hold a post that in the days of the ancestors had been restricted to patricians; but he possessed a more persuasive and dramatic claim to the office—a legend recently revived by his clansman, the distinguished antiquarian Lucius Caesar, according to which Trojan Aeneas' first-born son had surrendered the throne to his half-brother in exchange for the spiritual leadership of the people, changing his name simultaneously from Ascanius to Iulus. "And to Iulus," reports Dionysios of Halicarnassus, possibly quoting from Lucius Caesar's writings, "instead of sovereignty, a certain holy power and an honor was given preferable to the royal dignity both for security and ease; which his posterity enjoy even to this day and are called Iulii from him."[12] Romans of all segments of the population, except perhaps aristocratic intellectuals or hard-nosed politicians, reveled in such poppycock, and Caesar knew how to drain full advantage from hoary legend. Caesar was a dangerous rival also because once determined upon a course he would risk life itself to achieve his goal. His enemies never understood his practice of embracing struggles in a mortal grappling. Judging Caesar by himself, Catulus was astonished when Caesar rejected his offer to pay all Caesar's debts and save him from bankruptcy if he retired from the race.

On the day of the election, Aurelia accompanied Caesar to the door. She wept. Caesar kissed her and said, "Mother, today you will see your son either pontifex maximus or an exile."[13]

When the herald proclaimed the tally, Rome learned that even in their own tribes, from which they had a claim to loyalty, Caesar had polled more votes than Catulus and Servilius had received in all the tribes taken together. The citizenry in the aristocratic orders and of the commons had rallied to the man of pietas and fides! The victory, spectacular and unexpected, represented a vindication of the long-range strategy of Caesar's adult life!

In the inaugural procession a sober-faced Catulus along with other optimates marched in Caesar's honor among the pontifices, vestals, flamens, augurs and magistrates. From his deposition as high priest of Jupiter, his installation in place of his cousin as a pontifex, his display of the portraits of the two Mariuses at his aunt's funeral, his commemoration of his father, the loyal Julian, his restoration of the Marian trophies and his annulling of the dictator's decree of preemptive amnesty, Caesar had emerged victor over the leader of the Sullan party and at the very moment when that party was plotting a restoration of the Sullan order.

Aurelia supervised the transfer of the household gods to the official residence of the pontifex maximus, the domus publica, and Caesar established himself in the heart of the city close to the Temple of Vesta, the temples of Castor, Saturn and Concord, the Gate of Janus, the Senate house and the meeting places of the assemblies, of the courts and of the bankers and entrepreneurs. Caesar now held responsibility for the sacred treasury, the priestly chronicles, the regulation of the lunar calendar, the interpretations of sacred law, the judgments of religious courts, the rites of purification and the testaments and adoptions of the great families. Henceforth, and for the rest of his life, he would speak in the name of the patron deities of Rome and officiate at the innumerable sacrifices, processions and celebrations at which they were honored or propitiated or rendered thanks. Not yet a praetor he was, nevertheless, a nobleman of surpassing prestige and authority. For his enemies he was becoming almost unassailable.

XXII

CATILINA'S TORMENT

ALTHOUGH the optimates resented Caesar's "insolence," they considered him more of a nuisance, a gadfly, than a major threat. No individual or faction without the support of an army had ever challenged the pauci for long. For them Pompeius represented the danger. His communiqués promised an imminent conclusion to a war that had drained the treasury at Rome and the manpower of Italy for almost a generation. The inner circle of the Senate had only months to prepare for the reception of the unpredictable warlord. Caesar and his associates had distracted them with his prosecutions, reform bills and his campaign for the supreme pontificate. For Caesar, Cicero, Crassus and the pauci, the remainder of the year would be a time of scrambling for position.

Catilina, on the other hand, could not wait for a change in his fortunes. He confronted bankruptcy, disgrace, ruin. While the sniveling Antonius had won a reprieve from moneylenders through his election to a consulship and the certainty of a lucrative governorship, Catilina was running out of expedients for holding off his creditors. "The man whose property has been sold," Cicero had once declared regarding a client threatened with bankruptcy, "who has seen not only his rich possessions but even the necessaries of food and clothing ignominiously put up for sale under the hand of an auctioneer—that man is not only banished from the company of the living but is relegated to a position lower than the dead, if that be possible."[1]

Catilina shared this peril with innumerable fellow-citizens. (The problem of debt was as critical at Rome as in every other society, before or since.) In a speech he assigns to Catilina, Sallust captures the rancor of these desperate men:

> Ever since the state fell under the jurisdiction and sway of a few powerful men, it is always to them that kings and potentates are tributary and peoples and nations pay taxes. All the rest of us, energetic, able, nobles and commons, have made up the mob without influence, without weight, and subservient to those to whom in a free state we should be an object of fear. Because of this, all influence, power, rank and wealth are in their hands or wherever they wish them to be; to us they have left danger, defeat, prosecutions and poverty.[2]

It was as much out of desperation as out of ambition and pride that Catilina, thwarted for three consecutive years in his aspiration to a consulship, entered his candidacy yet once again.

Caesar and Crassus had to deliberate carefully whether to support Catilina in another campaign. Sensitive as to his dignity, Catilina was not a man receptive to advice. Impetuous, he could not be trusted to exercise restraint. In the current tensions, it was hardly likely that any candidate who defied the pauci and aroused fears among broad segments of the aristocracy could win election. Crassus would not provide money nor Caesar support to a candidate who did not enjoy the favor of bankers and entrepreneurs.

For Cicero and his mentors Catilina's candidacy offered both a threat and an opportunity—a threat that Catilina might succeed in mobilizing a new popular coalition too massive to suppress; and an opportunity to crush once and for all just such a rally of the disgruntled elements. In Catilina's candidacy Cicero might discover "the conspiracy" against which he had been warning—a conspiracy not merely to promote a series of reform bills and to assemble menacing clientships but to advocate an entire new order of things with massive transfers of property and with the establishment of a new power group in control of the commonwealth. Against such a threat Cicero saw the possibility or rather the duty to mobilize all "good citizens" into a grand coalition in defense of law and order, morality, the gods and the constitution.

To no one's surprise Cicero proclaimed Catilina's candidacy a threat to the commonwealth, and the consular electoral campaign took on a frenzied air. All five candidates except one, Servius Sulpicius, a straitlaced jurisprudent backed by the virtuous Cato, ignored the law passed in 64 limiting the size of entourages. The Forum was jammed with candidates and their partisans. The candidates erected grandstands for meetings of entire tribes and held banquets for huge crowds. They distributed tickets for the circus or the games as well as generous bribes. To the dismay of Cicero and his mentors, Catilina outshone all the other candidates in his appeal to the electorate. A consummate politician and magnetic personality, he knew how "to attach many by friendship, to retain them by devotion, to share what he possessed with all, to be at the service of all his friends in time of need with money, influence, personal exertion . . . to guide and rule his natural disposition as occasion required and to bend and turn it this way and that; to be serious with the austere, gay with the lax, grave with the old, amiable with the young." Catilina found a response among all the varied elements in opposition to the Old Guard, from senators and equestrians to slaves. All those who had been thwarted in their aspirations saw Catilina as their champion—the Italians who had never been registered as voters, the freedmen who had been denied full citizenship, the potential beneficiaries of the defeated land bill, the debtors who had failed to obtain relief and the sons of the proscribed whose rights had not been restored. Forming a sizable contingent of Catilina's entourage also were bankrupt aristocrats and motley adventurers. They did not accept Sulla's new order as the final and eternal apportioning of property and power and yearned for another new order of things with a new division of wealth and prestige. Catilina found support, too, among men and women of the aristocratic orders who professed the Gracchan doctrine that the commonwealth was responsible for the welfare of all its citizens. Typical of women of this circle was Sempronia, a lady of distinguished family and wife of a consular. "In birth and beauty, in her husband also and children," Sallust recounts, "she was abundantly favored by fortune; well read in the literature of Greece and of Rome, able to play the lyre and dance . . . of no mean endowments, she could write verses, bandy jests and use language which was modest or tender or wanton; in fine, she possessed a high degree of wit and of charm." Although to twentieth-century readers, Sallust's description appears laudatory, the historian was suspicious of such attainments in a lady of Sempronia's station. He notes, for example, that she was "able to play the lyre and dance more skilfully than an honest woman need." Sempronia was representative of a class of "modern" aristocratic ladies who were insisting upon expressing themselves in a variety of hitherto forbidden ways and were participating actively and aggressively in every aspect of life. Graybeards scoffed that "you could not easily say [with such a woman] whether she was less sparing of her money or her honor."[3] Sempronia was, of course, a woman in whose company Caesar would delight. In the future he would treat her son, Decimus Brutus, with as much affection as a son of his own. (Twenty years later Decimus would join his distant relative Marcus Brutus, another of Caesar's favorites, in engineering Caesar's assassination.)

Exasperating to the optimates was the enthusiasm Catilina engendered among the youth, including scions of great houses who scoffed at warnings of nefarious plots and of threats to old institutions and to "the ways of the ancestors." Cicero mocked them "with their hair combed, sleek fellows, either beardless or abundantly bearded, with tunics that reach to the ankles and the wrists, clad in veils, not in togas." He dismissed them contemptuously as "gamblers, adulterers . . . unclean rascals" who spent their lives studying "not only to love and be loved, not only to dance and sing, but also to wave daggers and sprinkle poisons."[4]

What confirmed to Cicero and his councilors their own warnings of a menace of subversion was the rallying of hundreds of Sullan veterans to Catilina's banner. Failures as farmers, harried by creditors, disillusioned in their expectations, these old soldiers paradoxically found themselves allied to farmers dispossessed of their holdings for the veterans' benefit. Nothing frightened the "best" people more than the prospect of a coalition of soldiers with the rural and urban plebs.

To counter the danger from the veterans, Cicero and his faction overcame the opposition of the Pompeian tribunes and won authorization of a triumph for Lucullus, a triumph which Lucullus' enemies had blocked for three years. The only optimate who could vie with Pompeius in military glory, Lucullus transformed the Circus Flaminius at the edge of the Campus Martius into a vast exhibition area for captured weapons and engines of war and paraded through the streets horsemen clad in mail, princes in scythe-bearing chariots, 110 bronze-beaked ships of war, a life-sized gold statue of Mithridates as well as the king's shield glistening with precious stones, 20 litters of silver vessels and 30 of gold beakers, armor and coin along with mules laden with golden couches, 56 ingots of silver and 2,700,000 pieces of silver coin. On placards Lucullus advertised the great sums he had contributed to Pompeius' campaign against the pirates, the riches he had delivered into the public treasury and the 950 denars (three years' pay of an ordinary laborer) he had distributed to each of his legionaries. Finally, Lucullus entertained the entire citizenry at a mammoth banquet. Recalling that his father had never served more than a single cup of Greek wine to a guest at even the most lavish banquet, Lucullus furnished the people with more than 100,000 amphorae of wine. Even the oldest citizens could not remember a triumph of equal magnificence, except perhaps Sulla's.

Not only did Lucullus' festivities interrupt the momentum of Catilina's election campaign, but now also Lucullus' veterans, hitherto awaiting the triumph outside the city, were available to vote for Murena, one of the candidates and a lieutenant to Lucullus.

While many oligarchs were preoccupied with the consular elections, the more astute, unimpressed by Cicero's incessant warnings of domestic plots and conspiracies, were concerned about an imminent threat to the very hegemony of the pauci. Cato had set out for a vacation at his estates in the south accompanied by philosophers and trunks of manuscripts. Within days, he was back with books, philosophers and an un-Stoical ill-temper. Along the Appian Way he had encountered a baggage train tended by a host of muleteers. Pompeius' brother-in-law Metellus Nepos was hastening home from the East to enter his candidacy for a tribuneship. Immediately Cato ordered his attendants to turn about. "Do you not know," he grumbled in response to Servilia's remonstrances, "that even by himself Metellus is to be feared because of his infatuation? And now that he comes by the advice of Pompeius, he will fall upon the state like a thunderbolt and throw everything into confusion. It is not time, then, for a leisurely sojourn in the country, but we must overpower the man or die honorably in a struggle for our liberties."[5]

After the elections the delighted pauci congratulated the Man of Virtue on his success, while Pompeius' followers hailed Metellus Nepos, also elected a tribune, as the spokesman and agent for their hero.

In the consular election campaign, Cato supported the pedantic patrician Servius Sulpicius. Servius would engage in no flamboyant electioneering and proclaimed his strict adherence to the laws against electoral fraud. Ignoring social issues, he sought to win votes among "respectable" citizens with a lofty program of constitutional reforms. He revived, for example, a Gracchan proposal to replace unit voting by tribes and centuries with individual balloting, a radical and utopian measure that would threaten oligarchic control of the legislative and electoral assemblies. He called, too, for a change in procedure in jury selection with the aim of reducing corruption in the courts, a measure equally as objectionable to the aristocratic orders. With Cicero's cooperation he enacted a new law against electoral fraud mandating a penalty of ten years of exile. Then with Cato at his side he strode through the city dictating notes to his amanuensis on violations of the election laws. The two moralists condemned Catilina most of all for his campaign tactics, and Cato infuriated Catilina by threatening him with prosecution.

On September 22, the day before the consular elections, Cicero convened the Senate in emergency session.

In the predawn hours before the Senate assembled, a messenger brought word to the house of the pontifex maximus that Caesar's niece Atia, daughter of Caesar's younger sister and of Pompeius' cousin, had given birth to a son in her house in the street of the Ox Head on the Palatine. For Caesar this was both a gratifying and sobering event. At his present age (he was in his thirty-eighth year), his own father had a son about to assume the toga of manhood while he, more than twenty years after his first marriage, was still without a male heir. Gaius Octavius, the infant's father, a country squire priding himself on old-fashioned promptness, arrived late that morning at the Senate. He reported that a fellow senator, Nigidius, the outstanding practitioner of the Chaldean arts at Rome, had cast his son's horoscope and announced that "the ruler of the world had been born."[6]

Cicero solemnly reported to the Senate that at a meeting of his close associates the previous evening Catilina had declared that "no faithful champion of the wretched could be found except one who was himself wretched; that those who were down and out ought not to trust the promises of the solvent and the fortunate; so let those who wished to refill their empty purses and recoup their losses see what debts, what possessions, what daring he himself had; that he who was to be the general and standard-bearer of the unfortunate should himself be least timid and most unfortunate." To Cicero's chagrin, neither this report nor his further announcement of a plot by Catilina to assassinate him at the elections evoked alarm. Apparently, with his repeated warnings of conspiracies over the previous nine months Cicero had convinced few besides himself of an imminent threat to the republic. Because of the efforts of Caesar and his associates, many senators were wary of Cicero's accusations. On this occasion, "his announcement was not regarded as credible, and he was suspected of having uttered false charges . . . because of personal enmity."[7] Cicero did succeed, however, in winning a delay in the elections, a delay disastrous to Catilina, whose countryfolk supporters, including the Sullan veterans, with pressing harvest duties at home, could not tarry in the city.

At the subsequent session of the Senate Cicero challenged Catilina to respond to the charges of the previous day. Infuriated at the maneuvers to thwart his election to a consulship, Catilina cried that "there were two bodies in the state—one frail with a weak head, the other sturdy but without a head; this body if it deserved his support should not lack a head so long as he lived."[8]

Catilina spoke justly—the republic was split into "two bodies": the oligarchy, weak in numbers but strong in self-consciousness; and the great mass of the impoverished, strong in numbers but with no consciousness of its potential power. No state is secure with a broad disparity in wealth between rich and poor, and the disparity in Rome was enormous and growing apace. Although angry at Catilina's indiscretion in uttering such a dangerous truth, the senators rejected Cicero's request for special security measures. To Cicero's fury, Catilina "flung himself out of the Senate joyously triumphant though," according to Cicero, "he should not have left that place alive at all."[9]

Cicero was prepared to execute Catilina forthwith, but he would have to expend much effort yet to persuade most senators of the existence of a conspiracy to overthrow the Republic and, particularly, of a threat from Catilina. Resolved upon exposing and crushing such a conspiracy, Cicero gave out that Catilina was plotting to assassinate him as he presided at the consular elections. He alarmed the citizenry by appearing at the Campus Martius surrounded by an impressive bodyguard and wearing "beneath his clothing a breastplate, which he was careful to allow people to see."[10]

Cicero's maneuvers succeeded.

The herald announced the election of Junius Silanus, husband of Caesar's mistress Servilia and brother-in-law to Cato, along with Murena, Lucullus' former lieutenant.

Cicero could not suppress a boast that he had "kept [Catilina] from the consulship."[11]

It was all over, and it seemed as though it had never even taken place—the processions, rallies, banquets, shouting and brawling. The graffiti and placards on the walls and the handbills strewn in streets and alleys seemed the debris of some long past event. Catilina's partisans dispersed, numb and disconsolate, the young aristocrats tearful. Sullan veterans and dispossessed farmers (those that had remained at Rome after the postponement of the elections) trudged out the city gates, wondering how they would find a solution to their despair. For Catilina defeat meant both the loss of the last chance to save himself from ruin and disgrace as well as a blow to his pride beyond endurance. With Catilina's defeat Cicero also lost a bogeyman against whom to maintain his warnings of revolution.

In the praetorian elections following upon the consular elections even as in his election as pontifex maximus, Caesar's strategy of the year—his sponsorship of reforms, his prosecutions of Rabirius and Piso and his prudence in avoiding open support of Catilina's candidacy—was vindicated, and Caesar advanced to the highest office attained by his father. In three years he would enter his candidacy for a consulship. If he continued to display the political acumen he had exhibited this year, he would capture that office, too.

XXIII

THE CONSPIRACY OF CICERO AND CATILINA

UPON the assassination of Mithridates and the capture after a three-month siege of the Temple at Jerusalem (crammed with treasure but curiously devoid of a divine image), the war in the East was over. Fearful that he had miscalculated in associating himself so completely with the warlord's foes, Cicero proposed a public thanksgiving of unprecedented length; but Caesar and Labienus undercut Cicero's peace offering. Over Cato's vehement protests they passed a bill granting the vainglorious conqueror the unique privilege of

wearing a laurel wreath and a commander's cloak at public games and triumphal garb at the races. The alarm of the pauci at Pompeius' imminent return
was intensified when the augur Appius Claudius conducted the Augury of
Safety, a solemn request of the gods for permission to appeal for the general
prosperity, a rite celebrated only when peace reigned on all frontiers. Observing birds approaching from an unlucky quarter of the sky, Appius warned that
"a grievous and violent civil war was at hand."[1]

Thus did the gods (and their representatives on earth) recall the wavering
consul to his responsibilities.

With only three months remaining to the year, Caesar and his associates
knew that Cicero required a spectacular coup to assure lasting glory for his
consulship. He needed a scapegoat for the mounting social distress (to which
he had attended not at all during his term in office). For scapegoats oligarchs
prefer men too weak to offer effective resistance but sufficiently prestigious to
seem credible menaces. Although Caesar was aware that some of the pauci
were eager to involve him in any crackdown on "subversion," he could be
confident of comparative security because of his broad popularity, because of
his consummate skill in political maneuvering and because it was assumed that
he was Pompeius' agent. Crassus was too wealthy and too well entrenched
with his varied clientship and alliances. Catilina was an ideal scapegoat, well
known because of his tempestuous personality and spectacular election campaign but vulnerable because of the dissolution of his party after his electoral
defeat, because of his desperate financial circumstances and because of his
volatile and impetuous nature.

Cicero's problem was to persuade the citizenry that Catilina was engaged in
a subversive conspiracy.

Although desperate and wracked with fury, Catilina was an experienced
officer and no fool. He recalled as vividly as Caesar (and Cicero) how swiftly
Catulus and Pompeius had crushed Lepidus; and Lepidus, unlike Catilina, a
proconsul, commanded his own legions. In the event of an attempted putsch,
Cicero could immediately deploy two consulars awaiting triumphs outside
Rome, and, as consul, Cicero could quickly mobilize fresh legions. Pompeius,
too, would rejoice at "saving" the republic with his victorious army.

During the year Cicero had roused anxiety among "respectable" citizens
about some vague threat to the commonwealth. Because of widespread disaffection throughout Italy and continual riots and demonstrations at Rome during
recent years, Cicero's alarms appeared convincing. It was time for the next act in
the anti-subversive drama Cicero had initiated in his own election campaign and
advanced in his speeches against Rullus and in every subsequent move.

The evening of October 18 a messenger knocked at the door of Crassus'
mansion on the Palatine, handed the doorkeeper three sealed scrolls and disappeared. Crassus was at supper. After opening the scroll addressed to him, he
immediately dispatched slaves to the other recipients with a request that they
meet him directly at Cicero's house.

After consultation with the three noblemen, Cicero sent heralds to summon senators to a meeting at daybreak.

Awed by Cicero's grim demeanor and the anonymous warning in the three letters to flee the city before a massacre of leading members of their order, no senator, including Caesar, suggested an investigation of the strange event or asked questions that would have been posed under calmer circumstances:

Were the anonymous letters a hoax?

If so, who stood to gain from the alarm they roused?

Why had these three men in particular received the warning?

Why were the letters delivered to Crassus?

Skilled in political theatrics, Caesar could wonder whether Cicero had forged the letters. What better maneuver could be imagined for smoking out the sentiments of the recipients and for rousing panic among the senators generally?

Whereas a month earlier the Senate had refused to accept Cicero's announcement of a plot against himself or to take alarm at his report of an inflammatory speech supposedly delivered by Catilina to his followers, now, following upon Cicero's donning a breastplate and filling the Forum with a private bodyguard and the arrival of these menacing letters, rational discussion and inquiry were no longer possible.

Events followed rapidly one upon another.

Three days later, on October 21, a senator read aloud a letter he had received from Etruria (notorious as a center of disaffection) reporting that Sullan veterans were massing at Faesulae (Fiesole) for a march on Rome on October 27. Simultaneously, so the letter declared, revolutionaries were to set fires within the city and to kill leading senators. On November 1 other rebels were to seize Praeneste (Palestrina), a town south of Rome where young Marius had suffered his final defeat and Sulla had massacred thousands of townspeople. The senator who brought this letter to the Senate's attention was a close associate of Caesar's. Was Caesar seeking to clear himself of suspicion regarding an imminent putsch?

No one called for an investigation of the reports in the letter.

No one suggested that the Sullan veterans, middle-aged men who had not seen combat for almost twenty years and were worn out by labor on their farms and by anxiety over their debts, might be marching on Rome simply to petition for succor. Although the reports of imminent violence were based on mere hearsay and no individuals were outlawed as on all previous occasions, with no debate, apprehensive and cowed, the senators yielded to Cicero's demand for the passage of the ultimate decree—"Let the consuls take measures to assure the safety of the state." Cicero had succeeded at last in stampeding the Senate into unquestioning support of his campaign against "subversion." With the declaration of martial law he enjoyed a general mandate for crushing the enemies of his mentors. By stationing a garrison on the Capitol, deploying patrols throughout the city and appearing himself with a bodyguard under

Atticus' command so numerous that it filled the Forum, Cicero terrified the entire populace. Senators and wealthy citizens fled the city, their wagons and pack animals clogging the gates. Prices of shares in the corporations collapsed. Moneylenders called in loans and refused to advance new credits, and the Senate voted a resolution of commendation to a patriotic senator who announced that he would not profiteer on the blood of the citizenry by demanding payment of 15 million sesterces on his books.

In crises Caesar never lacked for expedients, and after their long experience with him, perspicacious oligarchs could suspect a cunning maneuver by Caesar when, to Cicero's dismay, Lepidus Paullus indicted Catilina on a charge of fomenting violence against the republic. The elder son of the Lepidus who had attempted a putsch against the Senate fifteen years earlier was eager either to clear himself of suspicion of sympathy with supposed revolutionaries or to assist Catilina (once a fellow officer of Paullus' father) by affording him a chance to clear himself in court. In a trial Catilina could compel Cicero, who had pursued him with obvious personal vindictiveness, to produce informants for cross-examination and could pose questions about the anonymous letters and the other letters and rumors. Above all, he could forestall Cicero from outlawing him without a trial under the ultimate decree. Immediately upon Lepidus Paullus' indictment, Catilina offered to place himself in custody in Cicero's house so that the consul might supervise his comings and goings. Cicero declined the embarrassing offer as did the praetor Metellus Celer, but Celer's brother, the tribune-elect Metellus Nepos, accepted him in his house. Since Nepos was Pompeius' brother-in-law and agent at Rome, Catilina seemed to be placing himself under the warlord's protection.

When on October 27 no army appeared at the gates of Rome and no arson or massacre occurred in the city and on November 1 no uprising took place in Praeneste, Cicero could boast, of course, that he had averted these perils by timely precautions. His credibility was strained, however, upon the arrival of a letter from the leader of the Sullan veterans, a former centurion (non-commissioned officer), a letter addressed to one of the consulars Cicero had ordered to march against the "rebels." Manlius appealed for an avoidance of bloodshed. "We have taken up arms not against our fatherland," he wrote, "nor to bring danger upon others but to protect our own persons from outrage; for we are wretched and destitute, many of us have been driven from our country by the violence and cruelty of the moneylenders, while all have lost repute and fortune." He complained that debtors found no protection in the courts, and he denied that he and his followers were seeking a new order of things. "We ask neither for power nor for riches," he assured the consular, "the usual causes of war and strife among mortals, but only for freedom, which no true man gives up except with his life." He concluded with a plea to senators and magistrates "to take thought for your unhappy countrymen . . . and not to impose upon us the necessity of asking ourselves how we may sell our lives most dearly."[2]

Manlius and his followers were appealing for a redress of grievances. They left the choice of violence or peaceful negotiation to the magistrates and the Senate.

The consular to whom the letter was addressed, a stalwart member of the Old Guard, rejected the plea. He called upon the "rebels" to lay down their arms and made no effort to appease the wrath of the desperate men. "The Senate and the Roman people," he advised Manlius, "had always been so compassionate and merciful that no one had ever asked it for succor and been refused."[3] The haughty nobleman was repeating the outworn myth of equality before the law and of the availability of redress of grievances to every citizen regardless of his station.

With the failure of the predictions of an assault upon the city and of arson and massacre, Cicero faced a loss of momentum in his campaign as well as a threat of a court inquiry into the spate of strange events and rumors.

On November 8, twenty days after the passage of the ultimate decree, Cicero summoned the Senate again into emergency session. To convey a sense of peril he convened the meeting in the Temple of Jupiter the Stayer, a fortresslike structure removed from the Forum. When Caesar walked down the Sacred Way past the cloister of the vestals and turned right on a path leading to the Palatine, he descried armed men drawn up before the six Corinthian columns and within the porch of the temple. After a sacrifice the senators followed Cicero inside. No sooner had Catilina taken his place on a bench than other senators scurried away as from the carrier of a plague. "How long," cried Cicero, "will you abuse our patience, Catilina?" and, pointing to the scowling patrician, he proclaimed: "He singles out and marks with his glance each one of us for murder." Cicero recalled that two generations earlier "Publius Scipio, the pontifex maximus [was Cicero contrasting the behavior of that 'patriotic' pontifex maximus with Caesar's?], . . . killed Tiberius Gracchus, who was only slightly undermining the foundations of the state. . . . Shall we, who are consuls," he asked rhetorically, "put up with Catilina, who is anxious to destroy the whole world with murder and fire?"[4]

With passionate hyperbole, Cicero was giving warning that, armed with the ultimate decree, he would execute without trial men he adjudged subversives; and like subversive-hunters of every age, he was transforming a possible minor police action into a crusade in defense of society against universal cataclysm! "You should be executed," continued Cicero, rendering explicit his intention to repeat the lynchings employed against the Gracchi and Saturninus, "when no one so depraved, so abandoned, so like yourself, can be found who does not admit that this was done justly." (Cicero was warning "sympathizers" with "subversives.") "The eyes and ears of many shall watch you," he admonished Catilina, "although you may not know it, as they have done heretofore." Cicero was watching other senators, too. "In this most sacred and dignified council of the whole world," he noted, "are men who plan for the destruction of all of us, who plan for the destruction of this city and even the destruction of the whole world."[5] Having induced fear and suspicion into the Senate, Cicero now presented his evidence of the conspiracy to "destroy the whole world"—a tale of a meeting in a house on the street of the Scythemakers at which Catilina had supposedly assigned men to raise rebellion in various parts of Italy or to take charge of burning Rome district by district. At the meeting, or so Cicero reported, two knights had volunteered to assassinate him the next morning. These very men, he declared, did appear at his door and were turned away.

In the hushed and tremulous atmosphere, neither Caesar nor anyone else interrupted to ask Cicero why, instead of merely refusing admission to the "assassins," he had not arrested them for the possession of arms, illegal within the city. Nor did anyone ask what advantage conspirators would achieve by murdering Cicero. (What if the two equestrians had come simply to negotiate an agreement with Cicero? Why did Cicero not produce them and his anonymous informant for questioning?)

"Since this is the situation, Catilina," proclaimed Cicero, "go whither you had intended, depart from the city; the gates are open; get on your way!"[6]

This was the action for which the consul had been preparing the Senate with his warnings of an impending world catastrophe! Yet for all the passionate invective, Cicero waffled on Catilina's guilt. "Depart and free me from this terror," he exclaimed, "if it is well founded that I may not be overwhelmed; if it is false that now at last I may cease to fear."[7]

Sensing Cicero's vacillation and the mixed emotions in the Senate, Catilina called upon Cicero to express himself explicitly. "Is it to be exile?" he demanded of the consul. Receiving no reply, he insisted that the Senate take a stand, declaring: "Refer the matter to the Senate, and if this body votes that I should go into exile, I will obey."[8]

As presiding officer, Cicero was in control. He would not comply with Catilina's inconvenient demand, and, with more cunning than principle, he employed a variant of his stratagem at the Rabirius trial. Then, when hissed for expressing approval of the murder of Saturninus, he had pretended that those who kept silent approved his words. Now instead of calling for a vote on Catilina's request, he asked instead for a vote on the exiling of the revered elder statesman Catulus. At an uproar of indignation, Cicero exulted: "In your case, Catilina, when they say nothing, they express their approval; their acquiescence is a decree." Having overcome his momentary embarrassment by this shabby maneuver, Cicero resumed an ad hominem invective against Catilina and repeated his warnings against guilt by association. Among the enemies of the republic, he declared, were those who had "fostered the hopes of Catilina by mild measures and . . . strengthened the growing conspiracy by not believing in its existence."[9] For Cicero anyone who doubted the "evidence" he presented or insisted upon respect of the civil rights of the accused was also to be suspected of treason!

Cicero was uneasy at his failure to link Catilina to Manlius' Sullan veterans, especially since his aim was to goad all "subversives" into emerging in the open so that "not only this plague rampant in the state but even the roots and seeds of all evil [would] be obliterated." Implicitly admitting the flimsiness of the evidence for his charges, he promised the senators that with continued energy by himself and his consular colleague, with assertion of senatorial authority, with courage among the equestrians and with "such cordial agreement among all patriotic men . . . after the departure of Catilina [they would] see all things made clear, brought to light, suppressed and punished."[10]

Only a man with Catilina's audacity would have risen to respond to such an eloquent denunciation and such consummate manipulation. Confident of his innocence, Catilina called to witness his patrician ancestors and his own exploits in behalf of the republic. The senators listened, aware that no court could convict Catilina on Cicero's makeshift charges, but once Catilina took to assailing Cicero as a mere "new man," a mere "lodger in the city," unconstrained by an ancient heritage like his own, the optimates hooted and called him a traitor and assassin. Goaded by the outcry, Catilina roared: "Since I am brought to bay by my enemies and driven desperate, I will put out my fire by general devastation."[11]

When Caesar was a child, his father had been compelled to vote with all the other senators—with the exception of the heroic old Scaevola the Augur—for the outlawing of Marius. Now Caesar himself had kept silent as the "new man"consul, confident in the authority of his office, the support of the pauci and his intimidation with the threat of guilt by association, traduced, badgered and goaded to rebellion a haughty patrician sensitive of his dignity and desperate at the prospect of ruin by his creditors. Caesar had sat silent, posing no questions or objections and submitting even to insinuations regarding his own loyalty.

The next day Caesar stood by as Cicero proclaimed to the people "proof" of Catilina's "guilt"—Catilina's flight from Rome early that morning. According to Cicero, Catilina had departed "blazing with audacity, breathing forth crime, wickedly plotting the destruction of his country, threatening you and this city with sword and fire." Aware that he was not addressing an audience as sympathetic as the Senate, Cicero proceeded not with a straight line of logical argument but cyclically, expounding ideas briefly, shifting to new points and then returning to the earlier thoughts, insinuating his views into the consciousness of his listeners. "Catilina ought long ago to have been put to death," he announced. At fault for his continued liberty were Cicero's listeners. The action appropriate for the criminal, he declared, "was not approved . . . by all of you . . . if I had punished him with death as he deserved I should have been overwhelmed with odium." As for the conspirators, cautious of alarming his audience, Cicero dismissed them as "a collection of ruined old men, of boorish high-livers, of rustic spendthrifts" united in an "incredible alliance of crime" by desperation over their debts.[12]

"Never were measures for the repudiation of debts more strenuously agitated than in my consulship," Cicero would recall almost two decades later. "Men of every sort and rank attempted with arms and armies to force the project through." Cicero sought no resolution of the crisis through timely reform measures. Instead, as he noted with pride, "I opposed them with such energy that this plague was wholly eradicated from the body politic." From the first day of his consulship Cicero had rejected all "innovations" and refused to entertain any proposal for relieving distress among the populace. He recognized only one response. "If my consulship is to destroy these men," he proclaimed, "since it cannot cure them, not some short time but many ages will be added to the life of the state."[13] The solution for Cicero and his mentors: repression, even massacre.

Cicero did entertain a grave fear. If Catilina went not to Manlius' camp, as Cicero had challenged him to do, but into exile, as Catilina had declared to friends he would do, "men will say," Cicero admitted, "not that this man was stripped of his armor of audacity by me, not that he was dazed and terrified by my vigilance nor thwarted in his hope and purpose but uncondemned and innocent he has gone into exile, driven out by the force and threats of a consul; and if he follows this course there will be those who will wish to think him not a criminal but an object of pity and me not a most watchful consul but a most cruel tyrant." Ignoring the warning from Caesar and Labienus in the Rabirius trial against the suppression of discontent by unconstitutional means and exultant in his power and his victories, Cicero vaunted: "On this side fights modesty; on that shamelessness; on this chastity, on that wantonness; on this honor, on that fraud; on this righteousness, on that crime; on this steadfastness, on that madness; on this honesty, on that deceit; on this self-restraint, on that lust; and finally on this side justice, temperance, fortitude, prudence, all the virtues, contend with injustice, extravagance, cowardice, recklessness, all the vices; lastly, abundance with poverty, good reason with bad, sanity with insanity and, finally, fair hope fights against deepest despair."[14]

Such language would recall to Caesar and to other intellectuals in the audience a classic description by Thucydides of class violence in the Greek world, when "words had to change their ordinary meaning and to take that which was now given them" according to the side employing them. "Reckless audacity," declared Thucydides, employing a term frequent in Cicero's recent orations, "came to be considered the courage of a loyal ally; prudent hesitation [for which Cicero pretended to take himself to task], specious cowardice; moderation [a virtue which Cicero rejected in his call for Catilina's summary execution] was held to be a cloak of unmanliness; ability to see all sides of a question [Cicero blocked investigation of charges], inaptness to act on any. . . . The advocate of extreme measures was always trustworthy; his opponent a man to be suspected [according to Cicero, of guilt by association].

"To succeed in a plot was to have a shrewd head, to divine a plot a still shrewder [Cicero!]; but to try to provide against having to do either was to break up your party and to be afraid of your adversaries [Cicero had warned such doubters]. In fine, to forestall an intending criminal or to suggest the idea of a crime where it was wanting was equally commended. . . . The fair proposals of an adversary [Catilina's offer to place himself in protective custody and his demand for a vote on his exile] were met with jealous precautions by the stronger of the two and not with a generous confidence."[15]

Thus the greatest of Greek historians characterized for all generations to come the distortion in language in times of repression of discontent, a distortion exemplified in Cicero's harangues.

Unlike Cicero, Thucydides recognized a class basis of morality and traced civil strife to class conflict. He spoke of "the lust for power arising from greed and ambition" which pitted two parties against each other: "On the one side with the cry of political equality of the people, on the other, of a moderate aristocracy," each seeking "prizes for themselves in those public interests which they pretended to cherish and recoiling from no means in their struggles for ascendancy. . . . Meanwhile," Thucydides continued, with an observation of particular import to Caesar and his associates, "the moderate part of the citizens perished between the two [opposing factions], either for not joining in the quarrel or because envy would not suffer them to escape."

Cicero's aim was clear. By goading the desperate to rebellion, he hoped to repeat Sulla's restoration of the authority of the inner circle of the Senate but without proscriptions and confiscations (and before the expiration of his consulship) and before Pompeius' return. Resorting once again to apocalyptic language, he prophesied to the people that "the greatest perils will be averted without any tumult and a rebellion and a civil war, *the greatest and most cruel within the memory of man,* will be suppressed by me alone, a leader and commander wearing the garb of peace."[16]

Caesar knew that the world was not so orderly. Cicero's plans were hardly certain of accomplishment, and he, Caesar, would do his best to see that Cicero's success, if achieved, would be of brief duration.

XXIV

THE PROMISE OF EVERLASTING PEACE

EN route to Massilia Catilina dispatched letters to explain his decision to go into exile. He had been "beset," he wrote, "by false accusations and unable to cope with the intrigues of his enemies." He repudiated "the terrible crime with which he was charged" and declared that he had left Rome "in order that his country might be at peace and that no dissension might arise from a struggle on his part." The restraint of the language, the selflessness of the action and the plausibility of the argument reinforced suspicions regarding Cicero's truculence and chicanery. Catulus, long a friend of Catilina's, read to the Senate a letter in which Catilina expressed despair at the repeated rebuffs he had suffered in seeking the consulship, admitted that in campaigning he had taken up "the general cause of the unfortunate" and described himself as "an outcast because of baseless suspicion . . . threatened with violence." He appealed to Catulus to look after his wife. "Protect her from insult," he wrote, "I beseech you in the name of your own children."[1]

Abruptly, Catilina turned off the Via Aurelia and made his way to Manlius' camp.

Apparently brooding over the humiliations he had endured and grieving at the prospect of vegetating in provincial Massilia while his estates were auctioned off by his creditors to the disgrace not only of himself but of his patrician clan, the haughty nobleman resolved to regain his honor on the battlefield. He would win renown even in defeat as champion of the oppressed instead of being remembered as a pitiful fugitive who had stolen out of Rome like a criminal.

Catilina's impulsive action rescued Cicero from embarrassment. Now, more than a month after the enactment of the ultimate decree, he was at last able to prod the Senate into outlawing both Catilina and Manlius. A deadline was fixed for other rebels to lay down their arms and a reward was posted for information regarding subversive activities. Nevertheless, even after eleven months of harangues and alarms, Cicero had not persuaded of the existence of a peril to the republic all those from whom he expected unconditional support. Cato, for example, had begun his political career ten years earlier defending Catilina against a charge of adultery with a vestal. He remembered the calumny Catilina had suffered then. Very likely, too, he found Cicero's megalomania offensive. Determined to restore righteousness to the Forum and deprived of a prime target (Catilina), the wilful Man of Virtue joined the defeated consular candidate Servius in indicting the consul-elect Murena for election fraud. They were indifferent to Cicero's discomfiture at a diversion from the anti-subversive campaign in a trial of Lucullus' lieutenant.

Although already overburdened in warding off "the destruction of the entire world," Cicero undertook Murena's defense. Unable to deny his client's guilt, Cicero transformed the trial into a comedy. He derided the learned Servius as a political innocent who had foolishly attempted to run a campaign on controversial issues and as a pedantic jurist ensnared in hair-splitting legalisms. In his rebuttal to Cato, "addressing a jury not an audience of scholars," Cicero "play[ed] to the gallery." To Cato's charge that in defending Murena he was not demonstrating the same devotion to the law as in his attack on Catilina, Cicero responded by mocking Cato as a philosopher "who reduces life to the fixed pattern of a system." With insolent condescension, he assured the jurors that the Stoic, with his exaggerated adherence to the letter of the law, would be "changed by experience, softened by time and mellowed by age." Cicero bantered with such gusto that Cato was overheard to remark, "My friends, what a droll fellow is our consul!"[2]

In a graver tone Cicero turned to the theme of his consulship. He was dismayed, he said, that he alone understood the danger to the state (a common complaint of crusaders against "subversion"). "The infection of [Catilina's] crime," he exclaimed, has "spread more widely than anyone thinks." In despair at Cato's blindness he cried: "The Trojan Horse is within, within the city, I say." In the event of the conviction of the consul-elect, he admonished the jurors, "the man who may check the rising tide of sedition and turmoil, that monstrous, insatiable curse of Catilina will burst out anew, it will spread rapidly over the territory about the city; madness will stalk on the speakers' platform, terror in the Senate house, conspiracy in the Forum, an army in the Campus Martius, desolation in the country; in every dwelling and in every place we shall fear sword and fire."[3]

What juror would want to promote such a disaster, especially when generously bribed to accept such melodramatic nonsense?

Patently guilty, Murena was acquitted. He fared far better than Catilina.

At the end of November, with only a month remaining to his consulship, Cicero had scarcely assured himself of mention in the annals of history. Within ten days new, hostile tribunes would be installed; three weeks thereafter the unpredictable Caesar would enter his praetorship.

Not a single conspirator had accepted the Senate's offer of clemency.

Not a single informer had claimed a reward for information of subversive activities.

If this intolerable state of affairs continued, Romans might suspect that no conspiracy had ever existed!

To Cicero's further chagrin, his consular colleague Antonius was dawdling in marching his legions against Catilina. "Had Catilina once made his escape from those frost and snowbound Apennines with a whole summer before him," Cicero later recalled, "had he begun to seize in advance the Italian sheep walks and herdsmen's huts, he would never have been overthrown without much bloodshed and most terrible devastation throughout Italy." In addition, by spring Pompeius would arrive in an Italy still in rebellion. He would crush the rebellion and claim all credit. Cicero instructed the quaestor Sestius, his informant and agent on Antonius' staff, to "rouse, exhort and urge Antonius on."[4] Fortunately, the gods did not abandon the beleaguered consul. They sent an impressive variety of evil portents as signs of their displeasure. At Pompeii a man was supposedly struck by lightning out of a clear sky; at Spoletium (Spoleto) buildings collapsed in an earthquake; and here and there eerie lights were seen in the heavens.

On December 3 Cicero summoned the Senate once again into emergency session, this time at the Temple of Concord. Erected three centuries earlier to commemorate the newly established harmony between patricians and plebeians, the temple was an appropriate site for celebrating the concordia ordinum (harmony of orders), the alliance of senators and equestrians Cicero boasted of forging in the defense of property and plunder. Furthermore, the temple had been reconstructed in celebration of the massacre of Gaius Gracchus and his partisans. In fact, an ironic verse carved at that time beneath the dedication stone remained legible: "A work of mad discord produces a Temple of Concord."[5] At the Senate meeting Cicero scarcely suppressed his exultation— he was at last transcending his equestrian origin to take a deserved place among nobles of ancient lineage, and he was inviting the world to look at him anew. For the moment he displayed that balanced inner tension, the strength tempered in generations of dominion, the unselfconscious assurance of men of exalted birth. It was as though Cicero for the first time was aware of his deeply lined, expansive brow, his heavy eyebrows drawn close together, his large eyes taking in all about them, his firmly anchored nose with generous nostrils and his large mouth with heavy but expressive lips. On this occasion men did not note that the nose was too fleshy and the chin, though defined, somewhat diminutive. Below it was a suggestion of a double chin and of sagging, middle-aged flesh. In the broad neck protruding muscles betrayed a humbler country past, as did the stocky body beneath. The expressive mobility in the countenance often permitted an uncontrollable collapse from defiance to uncertainty, but in the instant Cicero was certain.

Cicero recounted how he had infiltrated informers into a coterie of aristocratic conspirators. Acting on his agents' information, he had stationed two praetors with armed men at the Mulvian bridge on the highway leading northward from the city. At three o'clock this very morning, the praetors ambushed a party composed of Allobrogian envoys along with a suspected conspirator named Volturcius. Incriminating letters were discovered in their possession.

Exhausted by months of hysteria and false alarms, the senators listened as Cicero described how a certain Umbrenus, an entrepreneur active in commerce and moneylending in Gaul and "personally acquainted with many of the leading men of the [Gallic] states," had approached Allobrogian envoys in Rome to petition for relief from extortions of officials and usurers. Expressing sympathy with their plight, Umbrenus invited the Gauls to a conference at the home of the lady Sempronia, the cultivated matron who had supported Catilina during the recent electoral campaign. At this meeting Umbrenus supposedly disclosed a plot to overthrow the republic and, according to Cicero, "named the participants and, to give the envoys greater courage, included many guiltless men of all classes."[6] Fearful, with good reason, that the voluble Umbrenus might prove to be an agent provocateur, the Allobrogians consulted their senatorial patron. He, in turn, informed Cicero.

The Allobrogians were only too well acquainted with the consul. Several years earlier, in defending a governor whom the Allobrogians had accused of extortion, Cicero won an acquittal by demanding of the jurors whether "the most honorable native of Gaul [was] to be set on the same level with even the meanest citizen of Rome" and attacking the very complaint as "a savage and unconscionable assault of barbarism." Earlier this year Cicero won acquittal of another governor accused of extortion in Gaul, Pompeius' foe Piso, with Caesar serving as the prosecutor. In the last week the Allobrogians had listened as Cicero defended yet another recent governor of Gaul, the consul-elect Murena, and they heard him praise Murena for "justice and energy" in enabling Roman usurers and traders to collect debts in Gaul "which they had already written off."[7] Murena, in effect, had collaborated in the very extortions for which the Allobrogians were now seeking redress.

The Gauls were trapped, and when Cicero instructed them to ask for names of other Romans who "were of the same way of thinking" as Umbrenus, they had no choice. It was to be suspected that Umbrenus himself was in Cicero's hire, and Volturcius, the conspirator captured along with the Gauls, was almost certainly a paid informant. He had only recently joined the conspiracy and, upon capture, with inordinate alacrity offered to turn state's evidence. He corroborated not only the testimony of the Gauls but the whole spate of horrors Cicero had been warning against for so long. He swore, for example, that at a signal for an uprising on December 19 (during the Saturnalian revels), youths of noble families were to murder their fathers. (Cicero did not press Volturcius to name any of the prospective patricides.)

One by one four conspirators arrested that morning were brought into the hall. Each acknowledged the seal on his own letter among the correspondence captured with the Allobrogians. Cethegus,* a hotheaded young patrician, was asked to read his letter aloud. Addressing the Allobrogian people and their senate, Cethegus had written that he would carry out his promises to their envoys and asked them to execute the orders he was transmitting through their envoys. The letter offered no confirmation of the Allobrogian allegation that Cethegus had requested the dispatch of Gallic cavalry into Italy. Caesar and other incredulous senators listening to the testimony could note that the envoys would hardly have arrived home in time to dispatch cavalry into Italy for an uprising planned for the festival of the Saturnalia. When Cethegus fell silent after reading his letter, Cicero was certain that he was "overwhelmed and stricken by the force of conscience."[8] Others in the Senate could as readily have concluded that Cethegus, like Catilina before him, recognized the hopelessness of defending himself in the hostile atmosphere.

The letters of two other conspirators revealed no more precise evidence of criminal intent.

Cicero experienced a disquieting moment when his prize catch, Lentulus, attempted to cross-examine the Gauls and Volturcius. A consular expelled from the Senate by the censors in 70, Lentulus had regained his seat by winning election to a praetorship this year. He was a patrician of the Cornelian clan and the husband of the ambitious Julia, widow of Marcus Antonius (brother to

---

*The relationship of this man to the political boss with whom Marcus Cotta collaborated a decade earlier is not known.

Cicero's colleague), sister to last year's consul, Lucius Caesar, and clanswoman to Caesar. To Lentulus' questioning the Gauls responded that he "had assured them that the Sibylline books and soothsayers had promised him that he was that third member of the Cornelian clan to whom the rule and the sway of this city was fated to come; Cinna and Sulla [both Cornelians] had preceded him."[9] He noted, they said, a fateful coincidence in that this year was the twentieth anniversary of the burning of the Temple of Jupiter and the tenth of the trial of two vestal virgins for adultery. This year, he had supposedly declared, Rome would be destroyed.

Lentulus was further incriminated by a letter he had addressed to Catilina, which Volturcius was to have delivered. "You will know," Lentulus wrote, "who I am from him whom I am sending to you. Be brave and consider into what situation you have brought yourself; and see what you now need and take care to secure for yourself the aid of all, even of the lowest classes." Although the first sentence of this letter belied the charge of a carefully coordinated conspiracy involving Catilina and the remaining sentences would not have sufficed for conviction in court, in the current atmosphere neither the senators in the temple nor the equestrians listening at the doors required further evidence. When Volturcius went on to declare that Lentulus had also entrusted him with an oral message urging Catilina to arm slaves for an attack on Rome to be coordinated with the uprising within the walls, Lucius Caesar, Lentulus' brother-in-law, rose in indignation. Lucius' maternal grandfather, Flaccus, Gaius Gracchus' collaborator, had been killed in the massacre of the Gracchans. "Look at this man who lives and has my sister as his wife!" cried Lucius. "My grandfather was killed by order of the consul and this man lives!" Lucius recalled, too, how "his uncle, though but a youth and though sent by his father as an envoy [to seek peace], had been put to death in prison." What act of his grandfather or of his uncle, he demanded, "was going to be compared with the deeds of the conspirators?"[10]

Lucius Caesar had exposed it. Cicero was following the example of those who had lynched Gaius Gracchus and his followers. Cicero's goal, like theirs, was to crush all opposition to the leaders of the Senate.

Once the deposed praetor and the three other prisoners were led away, senators leaped up to give further evidence of a conspiratory and to praise the consul. The consul-elect Silanus declared that Cethegus had named to him three senators of consular and four of praetorian rank marked for death. (Silanus was not asked to explain why he had not reported that startling information earlier.) The consular Piso, that corrupt and pigheaded member of the Old Guard, confirmed Silanus' report. Catulus hailed Cicero as "Father of His Country"; and another optimate proposed a corona civica for Cicero as though the consul had risked his life in battle to save the life of a citizen. Caesar's cousin, the former censor Lucius Cotta, moved a thanksgiving to the gods, "the first ever granted to a man in a civil capacity." Cotta proclaimed that through Cicero's "courage, counsel, forethought . . . he had saved the city from fire, the citizens from slaughter, Italy from war."[11]

Caesar had never been accused of failing in courage, and he could not have been proud of his silence on this occasion, but it would have been foolhardy to pose questions in the current frenzy. To any senator retaining a modicum of common sense it was clear that the hullabaloo was out of all proportion to the events. A group of bumbling dilettantes very likely urged on by agents provocateurs had been playing at conspiracy.

For all the tumultuous outcry, only nine men were arrested.

In an appeal for unity in the "grave hour" and as a warrant of his confidence in two opponents of influence, Cicero entrusted one of the prisoners to Caesar's and another to Crassus' custody.

Cicero showed himself a worthy rival to Caesar in theatrical manipulation. In the morning he had arranged, for example, for the unveiling on the Capitol of a new statue of Jupiter—the image ordered two years earlier by Etruscan seers as a replacement for one destroyed by lightning. As they had ordained, the new statue looked "out upon the rising sun, the Forum and the Senate house," and when Cicero gave his report that afternoon to the people, he could ascribe the disclosure of the conspiracy to the god himself, who had seen everything from his vantage atop the hill. Calculating that the relief of the populace at his averting another civil war would dispel all questions about the events, the newly acclaimed Father of His Country boasted that "in this war, *the very greatest and most cruel within the memory of man* . . . I have so conducted myself, citizens, that you all are safe and when your enemies thought that only those citizens would remain who survived an indiscriminate slaughter and only as much of the city as the flames could not envelop, I have preserved both city and citizens safe and sound."[12]

Cicero's wonderment at the accomplishments of the day expanded as he spoke. Though he sought "no reward of courage, no insignia of honor, no monument of praise except the eternal memory of this day," he was confident that his deeds would be cherished in the memories of the citizens, "enhanced by the talk of men," and "in the monuments of literature . . . wax old and strong." Yet Cicero wanted more than posthumous glory. He called attention to the fact that "at one time in this state there have been two men, one of whom [Pompeius] fixed the borders of your empire not by limits of the earth but by the limits of the sky, the other preserved the home and abiding-place of this empire."[13] Now Cicero was finding the role of spokesman and agent for the "seven tyrants" too confining for a "Father of the Country." He would share the aribership of the empire with Pompeius!

As though spokesman for Jupiter himself, Cicero concluded his address by proclaiming to the populace: "You may dwell in everlasting peace."[14]

When Cicero mourned that he could "see no loftier honor that [the Roman people] have to bestow nor any higher pinnacle of glory to which [he might] ascend," Caesar could only be reassured. Neither bedazzled by Cicero's exposure of a puerile, makeshift conspiracy nor confident that Rome would ever achieve "everlasting peace," Caesar could predict mounting disdain among Cicero's mentors at his vainglory. They would use him so long as he was useful. They would never accept him in their mansions as an equal. As for Pompeius, he would not forgive Cicero's claim to glory on par with his.

On December 4, just one day after his presentation of "incontrovertible" proof of "the very greatest and most cruel war within the memory of man," Cicero suffered a reminder of the limits of his authority. One of Cicero's informers, a man expelled from the Senate during the consulship of Pompeius and Crassus, charged that Crassus had entrusted him with a message of encouragement for Catilina. To Cicero's astonishment senators who had been swept along in the hysteria of the previous day recognized the threat to themselves in Cicero's hunting of "subversives." They shouted in indignation. Cicero retreated.

Catulus, resentful of his defeat in the election for supreme pontiff, and Piso, angry at his prosecution by Caesar earlier in the year, pressed Cicero to loose an informer against Caesar. When Cicero demurred, Catulus and Piso made the charge themselves, denouncing Caesar with passion but without effect. The prisoners, however, did not enjoy the authority of the millionaire or of the pontifex maximus. With Catilina still at large and unlikely to be captured or killed while Cicero was still in office, Cicero required the execution of his prisoners to provide a culmination to his struggle for the supposed salvation of the commonwealth and to forestall any subsequent investigations into his actions during recent months. All year he had been preparing the Senate and the people for such an execution in his praise of the lynchings of the Gracchans and of Saturninus and in his expressions of remorse at his failure to execute Catilina. Caesar, on the other hand, who had seen his own relatives executed without trial, had repeatedly given warning of his resolve to defend traditional civil rights. On the issue of a summary execution of the conspirators, Caesar would not maintain silence. He would initiate a long-range counterattack against the subversive-hunters that would not reach its culmination until four years later.

XXV

CAESAR GIVES WARNING

BEFORE daybreak on December 5, 63, clients gathering in the antechamber of the domus publica, Caesar's residence as pontifex maximus, had already learned of an extraordinary event. The previous evening after strengthening the garrison on the Capitol and the guard in the Forum, Cicero had retired for the night in the center of the city, for his wife Terentia was officiating at home at the annual festival of the Bona Dea, a goddess worshiped in rites restricted to women. During the night, accompanied by vestal virgins, Terentia marched to the house where Cicero was sleeping. She reported that after the sacrifice a flame had suddenly shot up from the dead ashes. The ladies had been terrified, but the holy virgins, one of whom was Terentia's half-sister, had bidden Terentia, "a woman of no mild spirit nor without natural courage," to hasten to Cicero to "tell him to carry out his resolutions in behalf of the country since the goddess was giving him a great light on this path to safety and glory."[1] Immediately, Cicero dispatched heralds to every crossroad to summon the citizens to the Forum, and he instructed the praetors to administer the oath of enlistment to all men of military age as though an enemy were marching on the gates of Rome.

Setting out for the Temple of Concord, Caesar passed a vast throng awaiting word regarding the emergency proclaimed by the consul. At Caesar's every step down the Sacred Way were reminders of civil bloodshed—at the Temple of Vesta of the slaying of the pontifex maximus Scaevola at the order of young Marius; at the Temple of Castor of the lynchings during Caesar's childhood of a praetor by moneylenders infuriated at the revival of an old law against usury and then of the father of Caesar's present wife by followers of the tribune Sulpicius; on the Rostra Caesar had seen first the head of the tribune Sulpicius, murdered at Sulla's orders, and then the heads of his clansmen Lucius Caesar and Caesar Strabo, killed at the orders of Marius and Cinna, and still later the heads of young Marius and of hundreds of other victims of Sulla's fury. In the Senate house, Caesar knew, in the year of his birth Saturninus and his followers had been stoned to death. Atop the Capitol in front of the Temple of Jupiter Tiberius Gracchus had been beaten to death. Below stood the Temple of Concord, a monument to the massacre of Gaius Gracchus and his partisans. All about the Forum were grim memorials to the violation of the constitutional right of provocatio, memorials to lynch justice.

At the Temple of Concord, directly ahead, an imposing structure dominating the Forum from a shelf at the base of the Capitol, Caesar descried armed equestrians under Cicero's friend Atticus massed on the broad steps, between the massive columns and within the capacious porch. They and the crowd overflowing the Forum awaited the final scene of the drama Cicero had set in motion a year and a half earlier in his pre-election warnings against revolutionary plots.

Cicero opened the session of the Senate by reminding the senators of the intention of the conspirators "to burn the city, to murder all of [the senators], to welcome Catilina" back to Rome and to seduce Gauls and slaves to rebellion. He exhorted them to act this day without "vacillation or delay." Prudently, however, he announced his decision: "to refer the whole matter to you, Conscript Fathers, as if it were still an open question, both for your judgment on the deed and your decision about the punishment."[2] To ensure against

future misinterpretation of the day's debate, he distributed throughout the hall
clerks instructed in shorthand and assigned, in addition, several magistrates to
record the deliberations. Then, proceeding according to protocol, he called
first upon the consul-elect Silanus, Servilia's husband and Cato's brother-in-
law. "Quid censes?" ("What is your opinion?") asked Cicero. Silanus rose and
demanded the ultimate penalty for the conspirators, and all the senators assumed that Silanus was expressing the will of the optimate faction. Cicero then
turned to the other consul-elect, Murena, and after him to the consulars. All
concurred with Silanus. Next followed the eight praetors-elect. When it came
Caesar's turn, he stood and in a speech carefully premeditated and delivered
with the dignity appropriate to a pontifex maximus he addressed not only the
several hundred senators within the cavernous temple but also the equestrians
straining to hear at the huge doorway flooded with the early morning sun.

To recall the senators to rational deliberation, Caesar appealed to history,
citing instances when prudent statesmen, particularly the revered elder Cato,
dissuaded the Senate from rash and vindictive actions. He urged the senators to
take heed of the dignity of their order and to avert all suspicion of cruelty.
Precisely because of their awesome power, he declared, was it incumbent upon
them to adhere to a strict interpretation of the law.[3]

Thucydides' account of the events that led to the downfall of the Athenian
empire were being studied by Romans for lessons regarding the crisis of their
own empire, and the more learned in Caesar's audience would have been
reminded of a Thucydidean speech in which a statesman appealed to the
Athenians to reverse a hasty decision to massacre inhabitants of an allied city
that had wavered in its loyalty. "The good citizen ought to triumph," Thucydides' orator declares, "not by frightening his opponents but by beating them
fairly in argument. . . . Though I prove [the accused] ever so guilty," the orator
continues, "I shall not, therefore, advise their death unless it be expedient."[4]
Persuaded by his arguments, the Athenians resolved to bring to trial those
responsible for the rebellion and to retract their previous order for a general
massacre in the disloyal city.

Like Thucydides' orator, Caesar preached expedience, playing upon the fear
of Cicero and of the senators of being called to account one day for executing
citizens without trial. If despite the terror inspired by Cicero's inflammatory
oratory, his massing of a bodyguard at the entrance and his mobilization of the
able-bodied men into a defense militia, Caesar could induce the senators to
reflect upon the events of the previous day, they would realize that the ultimate
decree of the Senate provided no authorization for the execution of the men
Cicero had arrested inasmuch as they had not been captured in an armed
uprising, formally outlawed by the Senate or caught in treasonable acts, nor
had they confessed to treason. The charges against them were based on statements of witnesses of dubious reliability, and the accused had not been able to
confront their accusers.

Caesar reminded the senators of the many overturnings in Roman politics during their lifetime, noting that some powerful oligarch at the head of an army (the unpredictable Pompeius?) might cite the proposed violation of law and tradition as a precedent to be used against those voting a death penalty on this occasion. Constitutional rights, he warned, were not to be granted and withdrawn for factional advantage. Finally, Caesar traced the evolution of Roman law from primitive vendetta justice to a humane system exemplifying the best in the Greco-Roman heritage, a system that even permitted men convicted of capital crimes to choose exile instead of execution. Summary execution, Caesar declared, represented a retrogression in civilized practice, and he proposed that the prisoners be distributed for custody among Italian towns and placed under heavy guard until the termination of hostilities. In a concession to the passion of the moment, he suggested a confiscation of their property.

By his calm delivery and persuasive argument, Caesar transformed the atmosphere and shook the confidence of his opponents. The consul-elect Silanus rose. In demanding the ultimate punishment, he declared, he had not meant execution without trial. He was followed by others of consular and praetorian rank, including Cicero's brother Quintus, like Caesar a praetor-elect—all of whom supported Caesar's proposal. Dismayed at the crumbling of the antisubversive hysteria he had been cultivating so long and uneasy at Caesar's admonitions, Cicero admitted that if he adopted Caesar's motion he himself would "have to fear less popular disfavor because it is [Caesar] who proposes and supports it." Aware of Caesar's broad influence among elements of the population hostile to himself, Cicero spoke of him with deference, calling him "this most kindly and humane man." Of Caesar's "popular" inclinations, he declared respectfully: "It is well known what a difference there is between the fickleness of demagogues and a mind really democratic [popular], devoted to the safety of the state." He contrasted Caesar, too, with others who were absent from the Senate on this occasion "because they do not wish to vote on a capital charge involving Roman citizens."[5] Every senator had remarked that Crassus was not present, and his absence was ominous. Also absent were Publius Clodius (who may already have been entertaining the idea of replacing Catilina as a leader of the disgruntled at Rome) along with Piso Caesoninus and Gabinius, relatives of two of the imprisoned conspirators, for whose fate they would eventually seek revenge.

But Cicero's most susceptible audience was always himself, and the longer he spoke, the more he encouraged himself to pursue the policy of his consulship to a conclusion. He had been characterizing the conspiracy as one of the most monstrous and dangerous plots in history. If Caesar's advice were taken, at a trial in a calmer day he might be exposed to ridicule. Thus to Caesar's warnings he responded with the standard optimate argument that any man outlawed by the Senate automatically lost his constitutional rights. Such rights, he implied, could be annulled retroactively to the time of the planning of a conspiracy. His own spirit restored, Cicero harangued the Senate with visions

of "general conflagration . . . wretched unburied heaps of citizens, assault on
the vestal virgins," children murdered by rebellious slaves, houses burned,
Gauls striding triumphant "amid the ruins of the city." To encourage waverers, Cicero called attention to the presence in the Forum of "men of every
order, of all classes, even of all ages." (He had instructed the praetors to order
every able-bodied man to report for a muster.) With the union he had forged
between the two aristocratic orders, "hereafter no civil and domestic strife," he
assured his audience, "will come to any part of the state." Cicero claimed to
have won over all men of property, even shopkeepers and artisans. Freedmen
who had agitated only a few years earlier for full citizenship and had suffered
the dissolution of the collegia—even they had rallied behind the consul and the
Senate. Though the servile rebellion remained fresh in memory, there was "no
slave," Cicero proclaimed, "provided his condition of slavery is tolerable, who
does not shudder at the boldness of [the conspirators], who does not wish [the
present state of things] to abide."[6]

Catulus signaled his eagerness to speak. He sputtered in indignation at those
who buckled before Caesar's admonitions, but it was Cato, the self-appointed
scourger of corruption, who emerged as the new and aggressive spokesman for
the optimates. Mindful of the complaint of his famous great-grandfather that
"it is a hard matter to save a city in which a fish sells for more than an ox," he
excoriated the other senators for valuing "their houses, villas, statues and
paintings more highly [than] their country" and exhorted them to "wake up at
last and lay hold of the reins of the state." Weaklings like Caesar, he sneered,
prated of generosity, clemency and mercy while the commonwealth collapsed
about them. He was particularly exercised at Caesar's adducing Epicurean
doctrine in arguing against the death penalty—evidence enough for the rigid
Stoic of Caesar's subversive sympathies. Caesar had asserted that since in
death body and soul disintegrate into their component atoms, execution
merely brings "relief from toil and trouble." As a passionate defender of
"established truths," Cato derided Caesar for "regarding as false . . . the tales
which are told of the Lower World, where they say that the wicked take a
different path from the good and dwell in regions that are gloomy, desolate
and full of fears." Almost a century earlier Polybius had exposed the oligarchic
exploitation of religion that Cato was advocating. Since "every multitude is
fickle and full of lawless desires, unreasoning anger and violent passion,"
Polybius declared, "the only resource is to keep them in check by mysterious
terrors and scenic effects of this sort."[7]

Alternating between vituperation of the conspirators and of Caesar and
castigation of effete senators, Cato recalled his audience to a recognition of
who they were and what was to their interest. He wasted no words on
objective problems of the commonwealth. For him as for Cicero only moral
issues were at stake—the way things were was moral; change was immoral.
To insist upon a distinction between intentions and acts was to quibble. "Let
those who have confessed," he proclaimed, "be treated as though they had

been caught red-handed in capital offenses and be punished after the manner of our forefathers."

When, abruptly, Cato ceased and sat down, consulars and other senators thronged about him, praising his courage and chiding each other for their timidity. Cicero seized the moment and called for a vote on Cato's proposal.

Despite the charged atmosphere, Caesar rose once again. Like Scaevola the Augur refusing to assent to Sulla's outlawing of Caesar's uncle Marius, Caesar stood alone. Recognizing the hopelessness of rational argument, he urged the Senate not to inflict lasting sorrow on innocent families by depriving wives and children of property (as Sulla had done). He proposed a double vote—one on execution and another on confiscation of wealth. Infuriated at this maneuver to restore reason where none was desired, the senators hooted. At the doorway the equestrians brandished their swords. The tribunes stood silent. Caesar departed from the temple, and if Cicero had not signed to Atticus, the equestrians would have cut him down. Someone threw a cloak about Caesar and hurried him away.

That evening an armed guard arrived at the domus publica to fetch the prisoner left in Caesar's custody. Cicero himself called for Lentulus, the only magistrate among the condemned, and led him by the hand to the Tullanium, the dank prison at the foot of the Capitol close to the Temple of Concord. A crowd had gathered in the Forum, and young people, some of whom had no doubt campaigned for Catilina in the consular elections a few months earlier, too young to recall the Sullan Terror, watched "as though . . . they were being initiated with fear and trembling into some ancient mysteries of an aristocratic regime."[8] (In fact, the executions were neither without precedents nor would they lack successors throughout the ages.) After the public executioner had strangled the conspirators, one by one, Cicero, returning through the Forum, announced laconically: "Vixerunt!" ("They have lived!") On his way home he passed through streets lit by torches as though in celebration of some momentous victory.

Cicero had fulfilled the commitment of his inaugural address to the Senate on January 1. "If, Conscript Fathers," he had declared then, "you promise me your zeal in upholding the common dignity, I will certainly fulfill the most ardent wish of the republic, that the authority of this [senatorial] order, which existed in the time of our ancestors, may now, after a long interval [since the death of the dictator], be seen to be restored to the state."[9] Without wholesale slaughter and massive confiscations, he had apparently reconfirmed the hegemony of the pauci. By strangling a handful of foolish aristocrats he had with a swift, single coup intimidated the disgruntled and suppressed agitation for reform—or so he and his mentors believed.

Pompeius was about to return from the East.

Cicero's promise in the Forum the previous day of "everlasting peace" was a delusion of a man infatuated.

INITIATING THE COUNTERATTACK

The rout of Cicero and the pauci would require years of preparation, and their overthrow would not be completed in Caesar's lifetime. If at the moment Cicero was the hero of the "respectable" citizens, Caesar was the hope of the opposition. Admirers related with delight how during the impassioned session of the Senate on December 5 Cato glimpsed someone slipping a note to Caesar and "cried out that Caesar was outrageously receiving letters of instruction from the enemy. At this, a great tumult arose, and Caesar handed the missive . . . to Cato. Cato found . . . that it was a wanton bit of writing from his sister Servilia, and throwing it to Caesar with the words 'Take it, you sot,' turned again to the business under discussion."[10] The incident intensified the Stoic's hostility. Henceforth, even to his death, he would oppose Caesar's every action.

With his term as consul not yet expired, Cicero was discovering that if he had brought "everlasting peace" to Rome as a whole, he had scarcely achieved it for himself. Already on December 10, only five days after the execution of the conspirators, a newly installed tribune denounced Cicero as a tyrant for driving an innocent Catilina into exile, while another tribune, Pompeius' brother-in-law Nepos, castigated Cicero for executing citizens without trial. In vain he appealed to Mucia, Pompeius' wife and Nepos' sister, and to Clodia, Nepos' sister-in-law, to intercede with Nepos on his behalf. He was especially chagrined at the ingratitude of Nepos' brother, the outgoing praetor Metellus Celer. (To buy off Celer, Cicero had manipulated the lots to win him the governorship of the province of Cisalpine Gaul for the coming year.)

In a direct challenge to the pauci, Nepos posted a bill to recall Pompeius to restore order in Italy. He argued that Pompeius would see to it that no more Roman citizens were executed without trial. In response, an embittered Lucullus warned that Pompeius, "following his custom of alighting like a lazy carrion bird on bodies that others had killed and tearing to pieces the scattered remnants of wars," would once again claim unwarranted credit for a victory. Shunting aside Cicero as the agent and spokesman for the pauci, Cato, now also a tribune, moved to undercut Caesar and Nepos' support among the commons. Recalling his ancestor's remark that "it is a hard matter to argue with the belly since it has no ears,"[11] he offered a bill for increasing the number of recipients of subsidized grain by one-third, up to two hundred and seventy thousand. For the moment he forgot his Stoic maxims against ever changing one's mind and the traditional resistance of "respectable" citizens to "bankrupting the treasury" with programs of social welfare. With his bill he divided the urban plebs from the rural poor and undermined the support upon which Caesar and his associates had been relying.

But the momentum no longer lay with the pauci. On December 29, the last day of the Roman year, when Cicero mounted the Rostra to give an accounting of his expiring consulship, Nepos declared: "A man who had punished others

without trial ought not himself to be granted the privilege of making a speech."
He ordered Cicero to restrict himself to a recitation of the standard oath for
the occasion and then to step down from the platform. Cicero, who only weeks
earlier had been vaunting of saving the city from the worst calamity known to
history, humbly obeyed. At the end of the formula, however, in an outburst of
bravado, he exclaimed: "The safety of the state and this city is due to my
efforts alone."[12] His partisans chorused the declaration after him, and he did
not hear the jeers of the rest of the crowd.

If the optimates ever learned anything (a doubtful supposition), they should
have anticipated some dramatic coup by Caesar upon his installation as praetor.

On the morning of January 1, 62, senators and equestrians paraded up the
Clivus Capitolinus, accompanying the new consuls to the new Temple of
Jupiter. As the consuls were sacrificing at the altar in front of the temple,
someone pushed through the crowd and whispered to the consuls. Immediately
the consuls, the other magistrates, the senators and all the other "best" citizens
scurried down the steps into the winding path that led to the street below. At
the Rostra Caesar was rousing a crowd with witty sallies, denouncing the elder
statesman Catulus for mismanagement in the reconstruction of the Temple of
Jupiter, still unfinished after almost twenty years. He proposed that Catulus'
name be erased from the inscription above the entrance and Pompeius' be
substituted as the new official to complete the task.

Trembling at this "insolence" and at the prospect of Pompeius' once again
appropriating last-minute glory not only on the battlefield but even in the heart
of the city, the aged Catulus mounted the platform. Caesar barred the way and
ordered the former censor to speak from the steps below. At an outcry from
the "good" citizens, Caesar adjourned the meeting. He had achieved all that he
could hope to achieve in the current political atmosphere—interrupting the
installation of the optimate consuls and avenging himself on Catulus for accusing him of conspiracy with Catilina and rendering this leader, one of the
"seven tyrants," ridiculous. In addition, he had fueled the discord between the
optimates and Pompeius, inspired new spirit among the opposition elements
and won further respect as a leader of the opposition.

Caesar always pressed his enemies to a critical decision. Two mornings later
his attendants unfolded his curule seat on the lofty platform atop the steps of
the Temple of Castor, and Nepos set his tribunician bench beside him. At the
foot of the temple steps Nepos posted a guard of gladiators, and milling about
were Pompeius' and Caesar's partisans. Nepos instructed a herald to read his
bill to recall Pompeius from the East. As the herald unrolled the scroll, however, Cato elbowed his way through the multitude, pulling another tribune
behind him. They cried, "Veto!" Cato set his tribunician bench between Nepos
and Caesar. Nepos seized the scroll from the dismayed herald and began to
read. Shouting that "while he lived Pompeius should not enter the city with an
armed force," Cato snatched the document from Nepos' hands.[13] Nepos continued to recite from memory. The second optimate tribune clapped his hand

on Nepos' mouth. Nepos broke free and called out to the gladiators. Emboldened by Cato's daring, a crowd of optimates advanced with their clients to the
fray, and in the melee of fists, clubs and stones, the consul Murena threw his
cloak about the Stoic and drew him off to safety within the temple.

At an emergency session of the Senate that afternoon, Cato warned of "a
revolutionary movement set on foot by the poorer classes [whose] hopes were
fixed upon Caesar,"[14] and the pauci forced the adoption once again of the
ultimate decree of the Senate. Furthermore, recalling Caesar's warnings on the
day of the execution of the conspirators, they passed a resolution outlawing
anyone who called into question the legality of that execution (repeating the
preemptive immunity decreed by Sulla for those guilty of crimes during the
Terror—an immunity nullified only two years earlier by Caesar). Finally, the
Senate suspended Nepos and Caesar from office.

Infuriated, Nepos rushed out to the Rostra and announced his immediate
departure for the East. He would summon Pompeius to avenge this violation of
tribunician immunity. Caesar, on the other hand, called his praetorian court
into session in defiance of the Senate suspension. To general amazement, however, as soon as the optimates massed about his tribunal and proceeded to
denounce him, he dismissed his lictors, descended from the platform, walked
off to the nearby domus publica and shut the door behind him. During the
remainder of the day Caesar's people dispatched runners to knock on doors of
his friends and clients and of leaders of craft and neighborhood associations
(of the few remaining authorized collegia and of those dissolved two years
earlier). At dawn the shopkeepers joined a horde of slaves, freedmen and
free-born poor in a march on the center of the city. Massing at the domus
publica, they called for Caesar and cried out his title as praetor.

Caesar recognized the universal weariness with violence. He had succeeded in
rousing panic among the senators. He was certain that they regretted their haste
in impeaching Pompeius' brother-in-law and that they were dismayed at Nepos'
threat to summon Pompeius to punish them. Caesar had demonstrated that
violence belonged to the pauci; that his party merely responded with violence
when provoked. Emerging from the house of the pontifex maximus, he thanked
the people for their support, assured them that their assembly in such great
numbers provided a warning to his enemies and urged them to disperse so that
the injustice committed against him not serve as a signal for bloodshed.

As Caesar had foreseen (or prearranged), upon a report that at his bidding
the crowd were retiring to their homes and work places, senators cried out
with joy, extolling Caesar for saving the republic from a new crisis and demanding that he be restored to his former dignity. They dispatched a delegation to the domus publica to invite him to resume his seat in the Senate and his
functions as praetor.

In the space of a single day Caesar had goaded the pauci into an impetuous
passage of the ultimate decree and an undignified rescinding of the decree.
"As to stratagems, no man could claim Odysseus' gift for these."[15]

XXVI
POMPEIUS MISCALCULATES

EARLY in the new year Catilina achieved vindication in defeat. With a heroism that belied Cicero's contemptuous dismissal of them as undisciplined scoundrels, Catilina and his ragged band fought with the valor of men so desperate as to welcome death in a final moment of glory. The optimates wanted no survivors, no living martyrs, no embarrassing witnesses to bad faith and lack of compassion, and "out of the whole army not a single citizen of free birth was taken during the battle or in flight." It was reported that "almost every man covered with his body, when life was gone, the position which he had taken when alive at the beginning of the conflict." Even his enemies admitted that Catilina died "a death which would have been glorious had he thus fallen fighting for his country." He had taken his stand with his freedmen beside the standard, a standard of a Marian legion during the war against the Germanic Cimbri, and he was "discovered far in front of his fellows amid the dead bodies of his foes."[1]

The Senate decreed a public thanksgiving for the victory, but it was Catilina who would remain in the memory of the people.

The pauci had apparently achieved their goal. They had suppressed the general discontent by crushing a mere putsch, and they had rebuffed attempts by Pompeius' partisans, including Caesar and Nepos, to entrust the warlord with the restoration of civil peace. Now, confident in their restored prestige and reconfirmed hegemony, they proceeded to a final elimination of their opponents. They were handicapped, of course, by the loss of their scapegoat, for Cicero and "that monstrous insatiable curse of Catilina" had formed an inseparable pair. To keep alive the memory of the "traitor," they circulated atrocity stories about him, alleging, for example, that Catilina had compelled associates to take an oath with human blood mixed with wine. "Patriots," of course, accepted such tales, but "others thought that these and many other details were invented by men who believed that the hostility which . . . arose against Cicero would be moderated by exaggerating the guilt of the conspirators whom he had put to death."[2]

Cicero's informers now emerged to claim their rewards. Their characters scarcely added luster to the victory in what Cicero continued to call "the very greatest and most cruel war within the memory of man." A certain Curius, for example, a bankrupt expelled from the Senate seven years earlier, "a man of no mean birth but guilty of many crimes . . . as untrustworthy as he was reckless . . . could neither keep secret what he had heard nor conceal even his own misdeeds [and] was utterly regardless of what he did or said."³ A courtesan to whom he boasted of an imminent end to his poverty and of a new career of influence had recounted his tale of conspiracy to Terentia, Cicero's wife, and at Terentia's insistence Cicero enrolled both the courtesan and her lover in his private intelligence service. Now acclaimed a hero, Curius was voted a generous honorarium out of the public funds. An even more reckless prattler was a certain Vettius, an equestrian who had profiteered outrageously in the Sullan proscriptions. Granted immunity as a confessed conspirator, Vettius grew so giddy at his notoriety as a bloodhound that after submitting a long list of names he requested the privilege of adding still more, embarrassing even the pauci with his zeal in defense of the gods and the republic.

It was a seller's market in denunciations, and Rome was at the mercy of informers, and those who were named suffered for years. (Sixteen years later, when Caesar held supreme power, one informer, a certain Fadius, admitted to Cicero that he had given false testimony. "If what you reported to me," replied Cicero, " . . . was not true, what do I owe you? If true, you are the best witness of what the Roman people owe me."⁴)

A special court of inquiry was established to root out the remnants of the "subversion," and Cicero, no longer a magistrate, served as an unofficial inquisitor. His atrium was crowded with petitioners seeking assistance against indictments. Clearance from a charge of disloyalty cost money, and it was rumored that from one suspect Cicero had obtained enough to buy a country house at Tusculum, and from another, for a house at Pompeii. When Publius Sulla, Pompeius' brother-in-law and kin to Caesar's wife Pompeia, was charged with association with the conspiracy, Cicero undertook his defense in return for a "loan" of two million sesterces, which he used as down payment on Crassus' mansion on the fashionable Palatine, where Cicero was eager to "make a respectable show in the world" befitting his dignity as savior of the republic.⁵ It was said that he expected to obtain the remaining million and a half sesterces of the purchase price from a share in Antonius' pickings as governor of Macedonia.

With the optimates exultant in their unchallenged power, Caesar awaited his turn. Against him the optimates set their prize informers. In the Senate Curius testified that he had heard Catilina name Caesar as a fellow conspirator, and before the special court of inquiry Vettius, not to be outdone, proclaimed that he possessed an incriminating letter to Catilina in Caesar's hand. Caesar was not so helpless as he had been against Sulla, and neither bought exoneration nor sued for mercy. He called on "the savior of the republic" to bear witness in his favor, and Cicero, fearful of the broad support Caesar enjoyed among the citizenry, testified that Caesar had furnished evidence against the conspirators. Disavowed by his mentor, Curius was denied a reward for his testimony. From the Rostra Caesar denounced Vettius as a liar and a scoundrel, and the people mobbed the informer and would have trampled him to death if Caesar had not ordered his lictors to rescue the reprobate and convey him to prison. (This would not be Caesar's last encounter with this scoundrel.) Exercising his authority as a praetor, Caesar then arrested the commissioner of the court of inquiry for illegally arraigning a magistrate of superior rank.

Although successful in demonstrating once again that he was a personality not lightly to be assailed, in the repressive atmosphere, Caesar could accomplish little as a praetor. Rome awaited the arrival of Pompeius, and Caesar's chief concern was to confirm his relationship to the warlord. In March of 62 Pompeius announced the formal termination of a war against an enemy who had defied Rome for two generations. In a communiqué he vaunted of "having rescued the sea coast from pirates, restored to the Roman People the command of the sea" and subjugated or liberated a long list of states, peoples and potentates, obtaining the surrender of almost thirteen million people, sinking or capturing more than eight hundred ships and receiving the capitulation of more than fifteen hundred towns and fortresses. He had "found Asia the remotest of provinces," he boasted, "and made her a central dominion of his country."[6] After distributing 6 thousand sesterces to each of his legionaries, 120 thousand to each centurion and 720 thousand to each military tribune, he had reserved 200 million sesterces for the public treasury and a further sum, huge beyond all imagining, for bonuses for his quaestors and lieutenants.

Everywhere in the East, Pompeius was hailed as a second Alexander. Cities revised their calendars, basing them henceforth on a Pompeian era; they stamped his portrait on coins and erected statues to him as savior of the world on land and sea. Imitating the great Macedonian he founded towns (thirty-nine in all) and patronized the arts. At Mitylene he presided over a contest of poets, who competed in singing of his victories, and the town renamed a month in his honor. On the island of Rhodes he paid homage to the "new Aristotle," Posidonios, and attended debates of local rhetoricians, rewarding each with princely largess. At Athens he donated 1,200,000 sesterces toward the restoration of monuments destroyed during the Mithridatic war.

Characteristically, Pompeius gave no hint of his long-range intentions, and the nearer he approached Italy, the more Rome was panicked by rumors. Fearful regarding his own future, Cicero proposed a ten-day thanksgiving for Pompeius' victories, unprecedented in its length except for the previous thanksgiving voted a few months earlier on Cicero's initiative. An obsequious Senate delayed the consular elections to grant one of Pompeius' lieutenants time to return to register his candidacy. Few dared to object when the warlord's agents seized for his triumph two chieftains from the triumph of a Metellan, a victor over Cretan pirates.

With all talk only of Pompeius, Caesar required a new theatrical coup to remind the city of his presence. He found an opportunity in supporting the petition of a pretender to the throne of the African kingdom of Numidia. This Masintha was related to a former king who had been an ally of the Marians during the civil war. The current king, appointed by Pompeius, had held Caesar's cousin under house arrest when young Marius fled to Africa after Sulla's first march on Rome. Thus in undertaking Masintha's cause, Caesar was representing himself once again as Marius' heir and as leader of the Marian party. He pressed his advocacy with such passion that "in the dispute he caught the king's son Juba by the beard."[7] Ordered by the Senate to submit to the present king, the pretender faced certain execution, and Caesar, proclaiming his responsibility to a client, wrested the prince from his guards and spirited him to sanctuary in the domus publica. By this coup he once again transformed a defeat into victory, capturing the imagination of the populace and confirming, with bravura, his pietas and his independence as a political figure.

Caesar's enemies had long been prophesying bankruptcy and disgrace for him. They recalled his prodigality in commemorating his father's death and in restoring Marius' trophies and his recent squandering of a fortune in promoting his candidacy for the supreme pontificate. Respectable citizens, they charged, could have no confidence in such a wastrel. It was very likely at this time in response to his detractors that Caesar carried off a characteristic coup. "Having laid the foundations of a country house on his estate at Nemi [in the Alban hills southeast of Rome] and finished it at great cost, he tore it all down [proclaiming that] it did not suit him in every particular."[8] Who could lack confidence in a nobleman capable of such a grand gesture?

A NEW MIRACLE FROM THE BONA DEA

In December 62, at the end of a praetorship remarkable rather for Caesar's success in defending himself against his enemies than for constructive accomplishments, Caesar became embroiled in a diversionary melodrama involving Publius Clodius Pulcher. A pacesetter in a circle of high-stepping young aristocrats, Publius had commenced his political career by indicting Catilina for adultery with a vestal; thereafter he had fomented mutiny among the legions of his brother-in-law Lucullus, served as a fleet commander in the East under another brother-in-law, suffered captivity with pirates and almost lost his life in a mutiny while in command of a military expedition against Arab marauders for the king of Syria. A few years earlier he had invited Crassus to buy him off as prosecutor of Catilina in an extortion case, and last year on the staff of the governor of Transalpine Gaul he had enriched himself by his extortions. He was suspected of involvement in the Catilinarian conspiracy. In fine, Publius was a cynosure of patrician youth, a buccaneer with panache.

Gossip had it that Clodius was engaged in a liaison with Caesar's wife. Such philandering was almost too commonplace to evoke comment. Two of Publius' sisters were notorious for their infidelity to their husbands and their inconstancy with their lovers. Caesar himself had supposedly engaged in more intrigues with married women than most other aristocrats, and he was suspected of affairs even with the wives of Crassus and Pompeius. Everyone knew of his long-standing relationship with Cato's half-sister Servilia.

This year the annual festival of the Good Goddess took place in Caesar's residence under Aurelia's supervision. Since the rites were restricted to women, Caesar left the house for the night. As the noble ladies were gagging on the smoke from the sacrificial fire and grappling clumsily (wine formed part of the ceremony) with a squealing piglet whose neck they were to slit with a stone knife, a slavegirl screamed, "A man!" Aurelia ordered lamps and covered the sacred objects. Apparently a man had stolen into the house disguised, it was said, as a female lute player with a frontlet on his head, a saffron robe with a breastband, women's slippers and purple hose. Losing his way in the darkness, he asked directions of a slavegirl and betrayed himself with his voice. The matrons and vestals called for their cloaks and departed in a huff. By morning all Rome knew that Publius Clodius had attempted an assignation with the wife of the pontifex maximus during the rites of the Bona Dea.

Bumptious dandies could quip that Clodius had at least exposed the old wives' tale that any man desecrating the ceremony would be struck blind by the Good Goddess. Cynics, recalling the flame that burst from the sacrificial embers the previous year in Cicero's mansion, an omen inspiring him to execute the conspirators, could proclaim a second miracle in Publius' epiphany as a transvestite. Society giggled at the pontifex maximus' narrow escape from cuckolding during a sacred ritual at which his wife, mother and sister were among the celebrants. Old-fashioned citizens, however, murmured at the disgrace of a scion of the patrician Claudians engaging in a lark certain to undermine the piety of the commons. The matter was raised in the Senate and referred to the vestals and the pontifices. The vestals repeated the major portion of the ritual, and Caesar reported the judgment of the pontifices that a sacrilege had been committed. The Senate instructed the consuls to convoke a court of inquiry.

"My wife ought not even to be under suspicion," declared Caesar in his notice of divorce to Pompeia.[9] Sophisticated Romans remarked, however, that after five years of marriage Pompeia had not provided Caesar with an heir and that the marital alliance offered no continuing advantages. Just at this time, in any case, the attention of all Romans was diverted to an event of far greater import—Pompeius' landing in Italy and a notice of divorce he dispatched to his wife from Brundisium. Like Caesar with Pompeia, Pompeius made no charges against Mucia. Recalling the Homeric legend of how Aegisthus usurped Clytemnestra's bed in Agamemnon's absence during the siege of Troy, gossips whispered of Caesar as the Aegisthus to a latter-day Agamemnon. With every previous change of spouse, Pompeius had reoriented his policy. With this new divorce he would certainly seek a new political alignment. Mucia's half-brothers, the former praetor Metellus Celer and the former tribune Metellus Nepos, openly proclaimed their enmity, denouncing Pompeius for abandoning a wife who had borne him two sons and a daughter, all of marriageable age.

With Servilia Caesar could discuss strange negotiations between Pompeius and Cato. Summoning a close associate of the Stoic, Pompeius proposed marriages for himself and his elder son with women of Cato's family. During the negotiations, as a sign of his peaceful intentions, Pompeius assembled his legions, thanked the officers and men for their service and dismissed them with instructions to rally at Rome upon announcement of his triumph. Having "achieved a greatness which exceeded both his own hopes and those of his fellow-citizens and in all his campaigns surpassed the fortune of a mere mortal,"[10] the vainglorious warlord assumed that his claim to leadership of the oligarchy would be undisputed.

On the contrary, of course, without his army the optimates no longer entertained trepidation of the warlord.

"Go, Munatius," Cato instructed his friend, "and tell Pompeius that Cato is not to be captured by way of the women's apartments although he prizes Pompeius' goodwill and if Pompeius does justice [he] will grant him a friendship more to be relied upon than any marriage connection; but he will not give hostages for the glory of Pompeius to the detriment of his country."[11]

In his procession through Italy, "when the cities saw Pompeius the Great journeying along unarmed and with only a few intimate friends as though returning from an ordinary sojourn abroad, the people streamed forth to show their goodwill and escorting him on his way with a larger force brought him with them back to Rome, where, had he proposed any revolutionary changes at that time, he had no need of the army that he had disbanded." Absent from Rome during five turbulent years, however, Pompeius had no grasp of developments or sentiments in the city. Before the gate he made a speech pitiful in its vacuity, "of no comfort to the poor or interest to the rascals; on the other hand, the rich were not pleased and the honest men were not edified."[12] Aspiring to be the arbiter of the commonwealth, above all factions and devoid of personal interest, Pompeius exposed himself as an innocent.

Overcoming their astonishment at the evaporation of a threat they had feared for so many years, the optimates moved to divert attention from Pompeius' homecoming by inflating the Bona Dea incident into a major affair of state. Cato provided the leadership, outraged at aristocratic wastrels, who, he said, "have never seen the sun rise or set"[13] and were forever scoffing at the ways of the ancestors. Indeed, these young prodigals thought of themselves as a new breed of revolutionaries. With no conception of the world they aspired to create or how change was to be achieved and too self-indulgent for the sustained effort required to overturn a society, they insisted upon change for its own sake.

The leadership of the jeunesse dorée Publius Clodius shared with one of his sisters. A Sybarite, Clodia rejoiced in music, repartee, good food as well as sleek, witty young men often many years her junior. Bewitched by Clodia's large, brilliant eyes and her irrepressible vivacity, the poet Catullus, whom Caesar had probably met several years earlier in Verona, squandered his allowance in keeping pace with her. He praised her under the name Lesbia:

> Now Lesbia has beauty, she is everything
> that's handsome, glorious,
> and she has captured all that Venus has to offer
> in ways of love.[14]

Cato was suspicious of these young wastrels not only because of their loose ways but also because they played at being Epicureans. Serious disciples of the philosophy, of course, dismissed the flippant indulgences of these youths, and the Epicurean poet Lucretius berated them for their wanton hedonism:

> They consume their strength and kill themselves with the labor; add this, that one lives at the beck of another. Meanwhile wealth vanishes and turns into Babylonian coverlets; duty is neglected, good name sickens and totters. For her, fine and flexible Sicyonian slippers laugh on her feet, aye, great emeralds flash their green light set in gold, the sea-purple tunic is ever in wear and well used to absorbing the sweat of Venus. The well-won wealth of his fathers becomes coronets and girdles, or it may be a cloak of silks from Alinda and Cos. Banquets are prepared with magnificent trappings and rich fare, entertainments, bumpers in abundance, ointment, garlands, festoons; but all is vanity since from the very fountain of enchantment rises a drop of bitterness to torment even in the flowers; either when a guilty conscience chances to sting him with the thought that he is passing his life in sloth and perishing in debauches or because she has shot and left a word of doubtful meaning, which fixed in his yearning heart, keeps alive like fire because he thinks that she makes eyes too freely and gazes at another man, while he sees in her face the trace of a smile.[15]

To provide a lesson to the wilful young aristocrats and simultaneously to divert attention from Pompeius and from pressing social issues, Hortensius offered a bill mandating appointment of jurors by a praetor instead of by lot for the special court trying Clodius. The optimates hoped to assure a jury hostile to Clodius and impervious to bribery.

Expecting Pompeius to oppose Hortensius' motion, Pupius, a former lieutenant to Pompeius, prompted a tribune to sound him out on the subject. Pompeius equivocated. Questioned subsequently in the Senate by the other consul, Pompeius astonished the senators by responding that "in all matters he held and had always held the Senate's authority in the highest respect."[16]

For more than a year the optimates had awaited with apprehension Pompeius' declaration on the execution of the conspirators on December 5, 63. They had accepted Nepos' condemnation of the action as representing Pompeius' opinion. Now, publicly, whether with deliberation or by clumsy inadvertence Pompeius gave implicit consent to the deed. Dreading isolation in a reconciliation between Pompeius and the optimates, Crassus jumped up and eulogized Cicero, asserting that it was to the orator that "he owed his status as a senator and a citizen, his freedom and his very life. Whenever he saw his wife or his house or the city of his birth," he declared, "he saw a gift of [Cicero's]." Cicero, overwhelmed by this sudden release from a long torment, gave rein to a flow of "periods, clausulae and enthymemes and raisonnements" and all his other oratorical tricks and "brought the house down" with his time-worn themes of "the dignity of [the senatorial] order, concord between senators and knights, unison of Italy, remnants of the conspiracy in their death throes . . ." He wrote to his friend Atticus: "You know by now how I can boom away on such topics."[17]

Caesar had often witnessed panic and elation in the Senate, and he understood that having disbanded his army, Pompeius was at the mercy of his enemies. He realized, also, that Cicero no longer remained as an important political factor: the optimates had little more need of him; the populars despised him. For the immediate future, the major conflict within the oligarchy centered about Clodius.

Deadlocked on the sacrilege case, the Senate deferred all other business. Last year's praetors, including Caesar, were forced to await allotment of their governorships. But the optimates were becoming alarmed at unexpected dangers in the Bona Dea affaire, for Clodius was transforming his prank into a major challenge to the Senate, mobilizing to his support Catilina's former party. Hortensius yielded on the critical point in his jury-selection bill, and the Senate resumed its business. Lots were drawn for governorships, and Caesar was awarded Further Spain, where he had served his quaestorship six years earlier.

Before departing for his province, Caesar issued a statement on the Clodius case. He recognized in Clodius a potential ally of influence whom he did not want to antagonize. Clodius' wife could have served as an intermediary between the two men. A woman driven by ambition and politically astute, Fulvia was a half-sister to a Pinarius (son, grandson or other relation to Caesar's elder sister by her first marriage). Clodius had twitted Cicero for his "sensational discoveries" (the orator's repeated use of comperi—"I have discovered"—in connection with the Catilinarian conspiracy had made this a byword of scorn against him). Now Caesar evoked laughter by asserting that in the Bona Dea affaire *he* had "discovered" nothing.

When Caesar reported bandit incursions in his province and prepared to leave Rome, his creditors blocked his way. Caesar admitted that "he needed twenty-five million sesterces in order to have nothing at all."[18] In the current uncertain political situation, the prudent Crassus was not about to abandon an ally like Caesar. He offered surety for 830 talents (about 20 million sesterces), and Caesar departed for Further Spain.

XXVII

DEPRIVED OF A TRIUMPH

THE tale was told that as Caesar was passing through a squalid Alpine village, one of his companions exclaimed: "Can it be that here too there are ambitious strifes for office, struggles for primacy and mutual jealousies of powerful men?"

"I would rather be first here," Caesar was said to have mused, "than second at Rome."[1]

In fact, no one but Caesar's mother could believe that he would ever even be second at Rome, much less master of the world, as the priests of Gades had prophesied. Like any number of other Roman oligarchs, Caesar, in his thirty-ninth year, was proceeding at regular stages through the progress of magistracies. At a far younger age, Crassus, Lucullus and certainly Pompeius had achieved military glory, whereas Caesar's sole command, many years earlier, had been in a skirmish with Mithridatic invaders in Asia. Arriving late in Further Spain, Caesar could exploit no more than six months of the war season to win glory as well as booty to mollify his creditors and to accumulate a campaign chest for his candidacy for a consulship. More than a half century earlier in suppressing bandits while governor of Further Spain, Marius had acquired mining properties and established a clientship. Following his uncle's example, Caesar dispatched an ultimatum to warlike tribesmen in the Herminius mountains (the Sierra Estrella in northern Portugal) ordering them to cease their raids on the coastal lowlands and to come down from their fastnesses to settle as peaceful cultivators in the plains. The Lusitanians, fierce warriors, had wreaked many defeats on Roman legions during the previous century and a half. It was they who had summoned Sertorius to lead them in rebellion against a Sullan governor. With their black cloaks and masses of unshorn hair bound about their foreheads, they moved swiftly, covering distances without fatigue, sleeping on the ground and subsisting on acorns, dried, crushed and baked into a kind of bread, along with a little goat's meat. Captives they stoned to death or sacrificed. Some prisoners they covered with cloaks and stabbed in the belly so that priests could read auguries according to the way they fell and in examining their entrails.

Very likely assisted by Balbus, the wealthy Gaditan he had befriended during his quaestorship eight years earlier, Caesar recruited ten new cohorts, the equivalent of a single legion, some four or five thousand men, to reinforce the garrison of two legions. To instil confidence in the troops, Caesar followed the examples of Marius and Sertorius. Marius had reassured legionaries terrified by seemingly invincible German foes by parading a Syrian prophetess before them; Sertorius had heartened Iberian tribesmen by pretending to take counsel with the goddess Diana through a tame doe. Caesar, in turn, circulated tales of his strange mount with hoofs cloven into toes, an animal he had broken to the bit that would suffer no other rider. At its birth soothsayers prophesied that its master would one day rule the world. (Alexander had had his Bucephalus; Caesar, too, had a wondrous steed!)

Like Marius and Sertorius, Caesar exacted strict discipline from his men. When Lusitanians drove cattle ahead of them in battle to tempt Caesar's recruits with easy booty, he restrained the cohorts until an appropriate moment for attack. Having studied Sertorius' tactics, he outfoxed the Lusitanians in hit-and-run attacks, foiling their ambushes and matching them in spying out dispositions and movements. He displayed, too, a mastery of improvisation, swiftly constructing rafts, for example, to pursue tribesmen who had fled to islands off the coast. Nevertheless, he suffered a reverse when his rafts were swept out to sea by a sudden shift in the tide (tides were unknown in the Mediterranean) and part of the landing party was annihilated in hand-to-hand combat. Caesar sent a dispatch to Gades to obtain ships from the local merchants, and with this squadron he landed his army and crushed the last resistance, eliminating the threat from the marauding highlanders and restoring a section of Lusitania to Roman control.

In their letters from Rome, Caesar's mother and daughter could hardly match his news. Campaigning among rude barbarians who drank beer instead of wine, used butter instead of olive oil, cleansed themselves in saunas followed by plunges into cold baths, and danced to flute and trumpet with wild leaps and crouchings, Caesar must have found the gossip from the capital especially trivial—the younger Lucullus' divorce from a wife caught in flagrante delicto; Pompeius adorning his house on the Caelian hill with prows of vessels captured from the pirates and distributing bribes in his garden to guarantee the election to a consulship of one of his lieutenants; and Cato's muttering to the women of his household, "This evil would have belonged to us too if we had undertaken a marriage alliance with Pompeius."[2]

On the other hand, reports of Clodius' trial would have diverted Caesar and his officers. Clodius' partisans had jammed the Forum, cheered, hooted and shouted obscene threats. The aged Aurelia and Caesar's sister, the chief witnesses, were, of course, attended with the respect due ladies of their station, but the audience grew surly when Cicero gave testimony. A member of Cicero's bodyguard during the Catilinarian conspiracy days, Clodius relied upon the orator for an alibi, but eager to be counted among the optimates in this affaire, Cicero denied Clodius' contention that he had been more than two days' journey from Rome at the time of the Bona Dea ceremony. Cicero testified instead that on the morning of the sacrilege Clodius had consulted him at Rome on some legal matter. Truth was immaterial in a Roman trial, and gossips insisted that at rumors Cicero had been philandering with Clodia, Terentia had demanded he prove his fidelity by attacking Clodia's brother. In face of threats from Clodius' partisans, the Senate granted the jurors an armed guard. Despite generous bribes (reportedly 3 to 4 hundred thousand sesterces per juror or a total of 9 to 12 million sesterces), twenty-five jurors out of the fifty-six held out for conviction. Encountering one of the jurors after Clodius' acquittal, Catulus asked whether the jury had requested a guard out of fear of having their pockets picked.

The shenanigans were amusing, but of importance to Caesar was the fact that by usurping the leadership of the urban plebs, Clodius, allied to Crassus, had introduced a new force to Roman politics.

After their swift victory over the dread Lusitanians, Caesar's troops needed little haranguing to continue on to a further venture. Balbus and his Punic associates spoke of the unconquered country beyond the Herminius mountains up to the northwest cape of the Iberian peninsula as a land thickly populated, "blest in fruits, in cattle and in an abundance of gold and silver."[3] Posidonios had reported that tin was to be found there also, a metal essential for the manufacture of bronze and in short supply in the Mediterranean. Gaditan traders and metal workers in Campania would applaud Caesar's display of Roman might to natives controlling a source of the precious metal. Rome had marveled at Pompeius' penetration of the Caucasus, beyond the limits of the known world, but Pompeius had marched over land; Caesar was about to brave the fearsome wastes of Ocean. Possibly recalling Caesar's expedition, the poet Lucretius, singing of the monster guarding the legendary golden apples of the land of the setting sun (Hesperides), would sound the Roman dread of uncharted waters:

> What mischief, pray, could he do by the Atlantic shore and the pitiless seas, whither none of our folk ever goes and even the outlander dares not?[4]

Appearing suddenly out of the ocean and churning great breakers, Caesar's armada so astonished the people of Brigantium (La Coruna?) that they mounted no resistance. Caesar's forces hailed him as imperator, proclaiming, according to tradition: "It is you who have inspired us. The honor of victory is yours."

Caesar's communiqué to the Senate probably crossed letters from Rome describing Pompeius' triumph, his third and over the third part of the world (over the Marians in Africa, Sertorius in Europe and now Mithridates and other kings and princes in Asia as well as the pirates on the seas). The contrast between Caesar's bandit suppression and raiding expeditions and Pompeius' conquests would have depressed even a man of little ambition. Pompeius timed his triumph to coincide with his birthday (September 29). On September 28 Pompeius paraded plunder and lesser captives, including hundreds of Jews taken at the siege of the Temple at Jerusalem. Litters bore thirty-three crowns of pearls and a gaming board of mammoth dimensions made of precious metals and adorned with a gold moon weighing thirty pounds and innumerable other gold objects, including a representation of a mountain decorated with figures of deer, lions, fruit and ivy, and a monumental statue of Mithridates. The next day Pompeius rode in a gem-encrusted chariot with an entourage of the wife, sons and daughters of Mithridates, Scythian queens, a prince of Judea and the son of the king of Armenia followed by a huge portrait of Pompeius rendered in pearls. At the Capitol Pompeius dedicated a collection of precious stones. To the goddess Minerva he made an offering of more than 8 million sesterces and to Venus the Victorious he vowed a shrine atop what would be the first permanent theater in Rome. He announced that from the tribute of the newly conquered lands the annual income of the public treasury would nearly treble, rising from 200 million sesterces to over 540 million. On each of his quaestors he bestowed nearly 4 million sesterces.

But what kind of hero allowed admirers to proclaim that he had accomplished these wonders at the same age as Alexander, thirty-four, though as all Rome was aware, Pompeius was entering upon his forty-sixth year?

Despite the disparity in achievement, the Senate voted a thanksgiving also in honor of Caesar's victory, and the temples were thrown open and the statues of the gods displayed. Men wearing laurel wreaths and women with hair unpinned thanked the deities for the success of Roman arms on uncharted seas at the western tip of the world, a new region for Roman plunder and enslavement.

In the brief months remaining to his term, Caesar sought to consolidate his patronage in the province. He used the opportunity to apply theories derived from discussions during his childhood of the model charter drafted by Scaevola the Pontifex and Rutilius and of his father's administration of Asia as well as from his own prosecutions of corrupt provincial governors and from the examples of Sertorius, Lucullus and Pompeius. Whereas at Rome under Cicero's leadership the optimates blocked any rational approach to the crucial problem of debt, in Further Spain Caesar mandated payment of two-thirds of all debts in satisfaction of the original amounts, providing less relief than Lucullus had granted in Asia so as not to alienate bankers and moneylenders. In keeping with his own enlightenment, he "extirpated a kind of ingrained barbarity from the customs and institutions of the people of Gades"—human sacrifice[5] (outlawed at Rome only during Caesar's childhood, by Crassus' father). Caesar won the gratitude of the provincials by successfully petitioning the Senate for the abolition of a special levy imposed on the Spains during the Sertorian war.

News from Rome impelled Caesar to cut short his governorship.

The "eternal" harmony Cicero had established between the senatorial and equestrian orders was disintegrating, and Pompeius, Crassus and Clodius were each frustrated in their aspirations in separate conflicts with the optimates. Pompeius' protégé, the consul Afranius, a consummate social dancer, proved "a lazy, poor-spirited warrior" in promoting measures favored by his mentor, and his colleague Metellus Celer, hostile to Pompeius since the latter's divorce of his sister, joined with Lucullus and Cato in denying ratification to Pompeius' complex administrative settlements in the East. Crassus, delighting in Pompeius' discomfiture, sided with the optimates in insisting upon an examination of these arrangements one by one, a procedure that would drag on for years. When a tribune in Pompeius' service proposed a land bonus for Pompeius' veterans, Metellus denounced the measure with such vehemence that the tribune ordered him led off to prison. Belatedly Pompeius was learning "that he did not possess any real power but merely the name and envy resulting from his former authority, while in point of fact he received no benefit from it, and he repented of having let his legions go so soon and of having put himself in the power of his enemies"[6] (an error Caesar would not repeat).

Crassus could not gloat at Pompeius' frustration. Upon returning from his journey to the East, the millionaire had promoted a petition by the tax-farmers for remission of part of the Asian tribute. The economy of the war-ravaged province had not recovered sufficiently to enable the publicans to fulfil their state contract. Cato, an uncompromising champion of free enterprise, was indignant at the request of the corporation executives for the Senate to bail them out of a greedy miscalculation, and Cicero complained that the Stoic was once again showing "more resolution and integrity than judgment or intelligence" in blocking a vote on the issue. In Clodius' acquittal in the Bona Dea trial the previous year and the rebuff to the publicans this year, Cicero beheld "the overthrow of the two foundations of the constitution which [he] and [he] alone had established, the authority of the Senate . . . and the harmony of the [senatorial and equestrian] orders."[7]

Clodius had been rebuffed in his attempt to transfer from the patriciate to the plebs in order to run for a tribuneship. Fearing his influence with the commons in a position of such power, the optimates united against him, and his cousin, the consul Metellus Celer, actually declared that he was ready to slay Clodius with his own hand.[8]

With the contending factions and personalities at Rome at a stalemate, Caesar would exploit the deadlock to promote his election to a consulship. Ignoring the law requiring him to remain in his province until the arrival of his successor, he decided to return home and to reach the city in time to register his candidacy.

At a ceremonial farewell the elders of the city of Gades broke a tally and gave Balbus one half as a sign that he was to serve as their spokesman at Rome, and Caesar and his friend departed for Italy.

FIRST QUARREL WITH THE SENATE

Although enemies disseminated tales of his begging money from provincials to pay his debts and of his attacking towns after their surrender, in the current confusion no one indicted Caesar for extortion. In fact, the Senate acceded to his request for a triumph, and Cicero, under the illusion that since Catulus' recent death he was "holding to the optimate road without supporters or companions," was confident that he could "make Caesar, who," he said, "is riding on the crest of the wave just now, a better citizen."[9]

Establishing himself in the Villa Publica in the Campus Martius, the residence of generals awaiting a triumphal entry into the city, Caesar petitioned to register his candidacy for the consulship by proxy. Cato, not always consistent in his Stoicism, was unyielding in his rancor. On the day before the deadline for the registration of consular candidacies, the self-appointed watchdog of optimate interests filibustered until nightfall, when the Senate automatically adjourned. Caesar's petition failed to come up for a vote. Cicero was outraged. He complained that the Stoic "speaks in the Senate as though he were living in Plato's republic instead of Romulus' cesspool,"[10] a surprising description of Roman politics from a confirmed enemy of reform.

Caesar entertained no illusions about the distinction between the trappings and the realities of power. Surrendering his claim to a triumph and abandoning banners, floats, litters laden with booty and manacled prisoners assembled for his procession, Caesar threw off his military cloak and marched through the gate into the city to register his candidacy for the consular elections.

Despite their successes due, in part, to rivalries among the dynasts, the optimates themselves were in disarray. Elder statesmen were devoting themselves to "drinking bouts, banquets and revels, torch races and all manner of frivolity." Cicero sneered at them as "fools enough to expect to keep their fish ponds after losing constitutional freedom."[11] Pompeius' display of oriental luxury during his triumph had inspired intensified conspicuous consumption. Great houses were staffed with armies of slaves: chefs, scullions, bakers, confectioners, butlers, cupbearers, slaves attending on individual chambers. Rich Romans employed gardeners from the East in planting myrtle clipped in geometric shapes and in laying flowerbeds along paths among statues, fountains and benches. Even tradesmen were abashed if they could not serve guests on silver plates and bowls (often decorated with embossed reliefs or with gems) or offer wine in crystal or murrina (fluorspar or agate) cups.

Lucullus and Hortensius set the pace. North of Neapolis Lucullus "suspended hills over vast tunnels, girdled his residences with zones of sea and with streams for the breeding of fish," and Hortensius fed mullets with his own hands and was said to have wept at the death of a favorite lamprey. Catching Lucullus off guard in the Forum one day, Cicero and Pompeius declared, "We desire to dine with you today just as you would have dined by yourself." Upon their arrival at his mansion Lucullus instructed a servant to make ready the dining couches in the Apollo room, one of his most lavishly appointed apartments. His guests were not aware that he set a fixed allowance for each of his dining rooms, and they were astonished when he regaled them with a banquet costing 200 thousand sesterces.[12]

Appius Claudius, Publius' brother, related an equally amazing anecdote regarding Hortensius. During a dinner held in an enclosed platform within a game preserve at one of the orator's estates, Hortensius suddenly ordered that Orpheus be summoned. "When he appeared with his robe and harp and was bidden to sing," Appius reported, "he blew upon a horn. Whereupon there poured around us such a crowd of stags, boars and other animals that it seemed to me to be no less attractive a sight than when the hunts of the aediles take place in the Circus Maximus."[13]

In the atmosphere of feverish striving, empty show and prodigal dissipation, Romans, rich and poor, found no solace in the ancestral religion. In the street Caesar and his retinue were frequently forced to give way before processions of disciples of the Egyptian goddess Isis. Led by priests in white linen with razored heads, they marched to stately hymns and music of flutes and tambourines. According to legend, Isis had experienced the death of a loved one and was known as the Mother of Sorrows. She was forgiving of repentant sinners; in return for asceticism and attendance to rituals she offered the gift of eternal life. The number of Jews, that curious people, too, had increased. Because of their stubborn persistence in strange dietary laws and refusal to work on the sabbath, Pompeius' Jewish captives fetched minimal prices on the slave market, and fellow Jews, long residents of the city, manumitted them as a religious obligation.

Anticipating determined opposition from Cato's faction, Caesar organized his election campaign with the precision of a military operation. He entered an alliance with another candidate stipulating that the other man, who "had less influence but more funds . . . should in their common cause promise largess to the electors from his own pocket."[14] Conferring separately with Pompeius and Crassus, he promised the warlord assistance in ratifying his arrangements in the East and in obtaining land allotments for his veterans and undertook to win for the millionaire a reduction in the tax quotas assumed by the publicans in Asia. He could count on Clodius' gratitude for his refusal to testify at the Bona Dea trial, and he could help Clodius to transfer to the plebs in order to enter his candidacy for a tribuneship.

To deny Caesar, in the event of his election, a prestigious and lucrative governorship after a consulship, Cato and his faction voted to assign the consuls of the coming year a command for suppressing brigandage in Italy, a proconsulship offering opportunities neither for plunder nor for glory; and to counter the bribery by Caesar and his associate, the optimates amassed a huge campaign fund in support of their own candidate, Cato's son-in-law Bibulus. Setting in abeyance his Stoic virtue, Cato condoned bribery by his own faction "for the good of the commonwealth."[15]

With Pompeius' veterans, his own clientships and those of Crassus and Clodius, Caesar captured first place with an overwhelming vote of the centuries. Bibulus emerged as his colleague. Since either consul could veto the actions of the other, Romans could anticipate a year of wrangling and deadlock. In fact, the gods, anxious at the threat to their optimate favorites, sounded a warning. "Of a sudden such a storm descended upon the whole city and all the country that quantities of trees were torn up by the roots, many houses were shattered, the boats moored in the Tiber both near the city and at its mouth were sunk, and the wooden bridge was destroyed and a theater built for some festival collapsed, and in the midst of all this great numbers of human beings perished."[16]

Caesar had attained the highest magistracy, surpassing his father. He had scarcely matched the achievements of his uncle, Old Marius, and was far from having it all, all that the priests of Gades had prophesied.

XXVIII

POMPEIUS' CONSUL

IT was traditional for the consul-elect to pass the night before his inauguration out of doors. Caesar would not digress from the Julian devotion to ancient traditions—a pietas confusing to his enemies and reassuring to his more conservative supporters—and at dawn on New Year's well-wishers expected to find the domus publica wreathed with garlands to proclaim the good fortune of the household. Slaves assisted Caesar into a triumphal purple robe, and he stepped forth from the domus publica to mount a chariot, acknowledging cheers and the waving of handkerchiefs. Twelve lictors raised fasces and assumed a single file, double the number preceding Caesar's father when Caesar as a child had walked in a place of honor behind them. Relatives, clansmen and other connections, anticipating new prosperity from Caesar's assumption of the consulship, joined Caesar, Aurelia, young Julia and a crowd of clients for the procession to the Capitol. Caesar could boast of no heir to walk before him. His closest young male connections were the grown sons of his elder sister and his four-year-old grandnephew, Octavius.

As Caesar proceeded down the Sacred Way, citizens on steps of basilicas and temples and in galleries above the rows of shops removed their hats. Men and women pointed out to their children the patrician "friend of the people," who "surpassed all his fellow citizens in beauty of person,"[1] tall, lithe and well-featured, alertness and vigor shining in his blue-gray eyes. Proclaiming the breadth of his connections was the host of friends led by Pompeius, Crassus and Clodius.

After the procession had wound up the slope of the Capitoline, Caesar dismounted from the chariot and ascended the steps leading to the Temple of Jupiter. With his unfailing graciousness, he saluted his colleague Bibulus and Bibulus' optimate supporters. Attendants opened ivory folding chairs near the altar, and the new consuls took their places. After giving thanks to Jupiter for protecting the city during the previous year, they rose, covered their heads with a fold of their togas and supervised the sacrifice of heifers. Then Caesar, first chosen in the elections and consequently holding power during January, led the senators into the temple. As the senators advanced, they caught sight of the Marian memorials Caesar had set up six years earlier in defiance of the optimates. Trooping within the portals, they recalled how three years earlier Caesar had proposed the substitution of Pompeius' name for that of the optimate elder statesman Catulus on the dedication stone of the reconstructed edifice. All the senators had long since learned to respect the cunning and courage with which Caesar had often outmaneuvered his opponents. He never suffered total defeat, it seemed, but always wrenched advantage out of adversity. With his consular authority, his powerful allies and the divisions among his enemies, he was now an especially dangerous foe.

A crowd of equestrians massed at the broad opening to the temple, facing Caesar, who was seated on a curule chair at the far end. Senators took places on benches to either side. With the rejection of a land bonus for Pompeius' veterans, the refusal to remit the contractual obligations of Crassus' publican friends, the blocking of Clodius' transfer to the plebs and the denial of a triumph to Caesar, the senators could expect a session of bitter recriminations.

Four years earlier Caesar and his friends had awaited a pronouncement from Cicero on the agrarian bill they had drafted. Now the optimates were to hear

Caesar on a similar bill he himself was proposing. Caesar, however, sought no confrontation. He had sounded out the opinions of senators in advance and had even sent Balbus to invite Cicero, the apologist for the optimates and foe of all agrarian legislation, to join his advisory council. Under the illusion that he was still the chief defender of the optimate interests, Cicero declined the invitation.

In his inaugural address Caesar proclaimed an end to the demoralizing bickering of the last years. "He would propose no measure," he announced to his opponents, "which should not also be to their advantage."[2] As a gesture of goodwill he was reviving the tradition of having his lictors defile behind rather than ahead of him during the alternate months when his colleague Bibulus assumed leadership in the Senate. Furthermore, to subject Senate actions to public review, he was instituting a bulletin of its proceedings, the Acta senatus, along with a daily gazette of public events, the Acta diurna. These would be posted in the city and filed as a permanent record. Copies could be excerpted and transcribed for dispatch to officials and leading citizens throughout Italy and the empire. The major burden of Caesar's address, however, was devoted to a new agrarian law, which, he promised, "he would not introduce [for ratification by a popular assembly] unless it should be according to [the] wishes [of the senators]." Anticipating objections, Caesar had modified the Rullan bill of four years earlier. He provided once again for resettlement of part of the urban unemployed, prone to violence and prey to demagogy; for the redevelopment of desolate areas of the peninsula and for land bonuses for veterans. The booty from the Pompeian campaigns would be used to fund the program. All public lands in the peninsula would be distributed except those in Campania, either appropriated long ago by the wealthy or providing rents to the treasury. As with the Rullan bill, landowners embarrassed by debts and eager to sell holdings would be offered a fair price based on their tax assessments. To carry out the provisions of the bill, twenty commissioners (with Caesar himself specifically excluded as a candidate) were to be elected. In a further gesture of reconciliation, Caesar promised the senators an opportunity to express their opinions and to offer amendments to the measure.

"Nihil vos tenemus, patres conscripti!" ("We hold you, conscript fathers, to no further purpose!") announced Caesar in the formula for adjournment. The senators rose, and Caesar led them out of the temple. The senators as well as those listening at the three massive bronze doors could not but be struck by the contrast in tone between Cicero's vituperative polemic against the Rullan bill four years earlier and Caesar's calm delivery, cogent arguments and appeal to reason in advocating this new agrarian bill. What oligarch could recall an inaugural address so constructive, so imbued with a spirit of confident leadership and so persuasive in its appeal for a consensus on behalf of the general welfare?

Caesar sought to inaugurate a new era of rational discourse in Roman political life. He was appealing for negotiation and compromise, challenging the magnates and their factions to surmount parochial interests for the survival of the oligarchy as a whole. Recent decades of Roman politics offered little hope for a sudden triumph of reason. Caesar would have to persuade the oligarchs of the depth of the crisis to their dominion and to confront them with the sole realistic alternative: the institution of reforms that would limit excesses in plundering.

In Caesar's childhood a coterie of farsighted senators had drafted a comprehensive reform program aimed at prolonging oligarchic hegemony. Drusus, the promoter of the program, had suffered assassination. All but the youngest senators recalled the horrors of the ensuing civil wars. Could Caesar hope that Drusus' nephew and ward, the obdurate Cato, had learned the lesson of his uncle's abortive struggle? Or would Cato so resent the prestige accruing to Caesar from the new agrarian reform bill as to prefer intensification of the crisis of the republic to an increase in Caesar's authority? Was it naive to expect Cato and his friends to learn from the past? Would they not automatically, almost instinctually, revive the hysteria of the Catilinarian days and denounce all reforms as blinds for a sinister conspiracy?

Caesar was acting as though not yet convinced that an oligarchy that has outlived its usefulness will not learn from experience and is not receptive to rational investigation of expedients for prolonging its hegemony. Scrambling after the shrinking opportunities for plunder, the varied elements of such an oligarchy will entertain curbs on the excesses of others but not on their own; and confronting growing resistance among those they exploit, they envision no response other than terror.

Underlying current conflicts and transcending personal antagonisms was an unbridgeable ideological division. The Stoic Cato considered that the Roman Republic of the time of his famous ancestor—idealized in his imagination (and in Cicero's)—represented mankind's supreme political achievement. For him any modification of the institutions, laws and customs of that day represented a marring of perfection: subversion. Caesar, on the other hand, subscribed without dissimulation to the Gracchan theory that the state bore responsibility for the welfare of all its citizens; and he accepted as inevitable adaptations in concept and structure of inherited institutions and welcomed discussion of all issues of political, social and economic policy (except the fundamental issue, which no one of the time thought even to pose—the issue of slavery).

Caesar was no naif. He understood that the inner circle of the Senate feared, on the one hand, new proscriptions and confiscations to displace them from their seats of power and, on the other hand, the expansion of any discussion of reforms into a comprehensive proofing of the entire social order. Far easier was it to cry betrayal of ancestors, impiety to the gods, threats to temples and hearths and virginity—Cicero's repertory of shibboleths. The shortsightedness and selfishness of the oligarchs was matched by the lack of perspective for significant change among other elements in the society, heterogeneous, unconscious of common aspirations, demoralized and, in considerable measure, corrupt. Riots and lawlessness, factional bickering, political stalemate and repeated threats of military occupation of the city had kept all elements of the population in fear and anxiety for more than a generation. Caesar sought an end to this tension.

At the session of the Senate convened for discussion of the agrarian bill, Caesar honored Crassus by calling upon him first for an opinion. (Senators could murmur that the consul was making a first payment to his chief creditor.) When Caesar next called upon Pompeius, he was, in effect, reminding the senators of the thousands of veterans the warlord could rally in support of a bill that offered them a long overdue reward. Continuing down the ranks of the senators, Caesar encountered neither proposals for amendments nor opposition to his bill. Upon advancing at last to the senators of quaestorian rank, he realized that the optimates had appointed the Man of Virtue to present their response. Cato rose and invoked the dictum of his faction. He would, he declared, stand by things as they were and brook no innovations in the republic. Having delivered himself of this unequivocal rebuff to Caesar's invitation to negotiation and compromise, Cato launched into a filibuster, the tactic by which he had deprived Caesar of a triumph only months earlier.

Provoked by mulish unreason, Caesar often lost control. He ordered Cato to silence, and when Cato, defiant, continued his harangue, Caesar instructed an attendant to conduct the Stoic to the prison close by. Cato set off meekly, and the other optimates, as they had apparently prearranged, rose and filed out behind their spokesman. To Caesar's query as to where he was going, a praetorian, a close associate of Pompeius', replied: "I prefer, Caesar, to be with Cato in prison than to be here with you."

Victory in this encounter fell to Cato. He had provoked Caesar to anger and exposed the fragility of Caesar's offer of reconciliation. Above all, he had diverted attention from the agrarian bill to himself as a martyr to the optimate cause and to the cause of the ways of the ancestors.

Quick at recovery, Caesar signed to a tribune to release the Stoic. Then in a warning as to where power henceforth resided in the commonwealth, he announced: "I have made you judges and masters of this law so that if anything did not suit you, it should not be brought before the people, but since you are not willing to pass a preliminary decree [of authorization], they shall decide for themselves."[3]

CAESAR VS. THE OPTIMATES: FIRST BATTLE

The tribune Vatinius dispatched heralds throughout the city and posted announcements of a public meeting at the Temple of Castor.

Vatinius boasted of his connection to Caesar through his marriage to the daughter of the shrewd and aggressive Julia of the elder branch of the clan. He and Caesar planned close collaboration during their year in office. Vatinius would present bills to the popular assembly and mobilize resistance, if necessary, to optimate obstruction. Indeed, he gave public warning that he would repudiate any attempts at religious maneuvers to block passage of measures he supported. Vatinius was a formidable opponent. The optimates abhorred him as "a nobody sprung from mud and obscurity"[4] and as a boor who exulted in his vulgarity, flaunted his indifference to high birth and proclaimed unabashedly his lust for power and riches. He did not provide an easy target for the savage wit of a Cicero or a Cato, for he mocked his own ugliness with gusto, his enlarged goiter, ulcerous boils and gouty shuffle.

As Caesar advanced to the Temple of Castor, his lictors sank their fasces before the people, the supposed sovereign power in the city. On the podium Crassus and Pompeius ranged themselves on either side of him. Caesar's consular colleague, Bibulus, approached with a band of partisans. When Caesar called out to him to declare publicly his opinion of the agrarian law, Bibulus replied that he would "tolerate no innovations during his year in office." Pretending not to accept Bibulus' response as a final rejection, Caesar urged the crowd to join him in begging Bibulus to give way. "You shall have the law," Caesar warned, "only if he wishes it."[5]

"You shall not have this law this year, not even if you all want it," Bibulus responded with contemptuous defiance of the ancient right of the people to pass laws.

Turning to Pompeius, whose veterans were in no mood for interference with their land bonus, Caesar asked the warlord's opinion of the measure. Pompeius reviewed the law clause by clause and expressed his satisfaction with its every particular.

"In case any resistance should be made to the law," asked Caesar, "will you come to the aid of the people?"

"Yes, indeed," replied Pompeius, "I will come bringing against those who threaten swords both a sword and a buckler."[6]

Caesar turned to Crassus, and the millionaire declared his accord with Pompeius. Rome understood that Caesar had restored the one-time alliance between the two dynasts, an alliance directed once again against the inner circle of the Senate.

Caesar always followed up an assault, to complete the rout of his foe. In setting a day for a vote on the agrarian law, the tribune Vatinius stipulated that each senator was to take an oath to uphold the law after its passage. Forty years earlier the tribune Saturninus had prescribed a similar oath in defense of an agrarian bill for Marius' veterans. With this maneuver Saturninus and Marius drove into exile a Metellan of censorial rank, who refused to submit to the demand. Now Marius' nephew and another "subversive" tribune were posing the same challenge to the Old Guard.

The ultimate resort of the optimates was religion. Bibulus proclaimed that for the remainder of the year he would "watch the heavens." The obnuntiatio, as this procedure was called, merely signified that a magistrate was making himself available to receive a sign of the gods' will. No thunder or lightning was required for delaying public business. The obnuntiatio was honored by "respectable citizens" as "a bulwark and rampart of security and repose," but by staking their authority on this device, Cato's party risked a further undermining of their most effective defense. Romans would tolerate occasional religious interference with legislative activity but hardly a cynical "sky watch" throughout an entire year. The state religion was beleaguered. In recent decades the "godless" Epicureans had been proselytizing throughout Italy with extraordinary success, preaching that only out of ignorance do men assign to the gods responsibility for human affairs. The poet Lucretius, already engaged in the composition of an epic summation of Epicureanism, exhorted people to seek rational explanations for all phenomena and reject superstition:

> The law and aspect of the sky have to be understood; storms and bright lightnings have to be sung, what they do, and by what cause they are set in motion at any time; that you may not, like one senseless, divide up the heavens into quarters and tremble to see from which direction the flying fire has come or to which of the two halves it has passed hence, how it has penetrated through walled places and how after taking complete possession it has won its way out. Men are unable to see the cause of these works at all and think them to be done by divine power.[7]

Apparently, the optimates were not certain they could count on divine intervention to counter Caesar, and on the day set for the vote on the agrarian bill, as Caesar was delivering a preliminary address, Bibulus strode into the Forum accompanied by Cato, Lucullus, Metellus Celer and three optimate tribunes. The tribunes interposed a veto on the proceedings, and Bibulus, preceded by his lictors, advanced toward the podium, warning against a violation of his sky-watching. Strong-armed guards posted by Vatinius about the Temple of Castor moved on the consul. Baring his neck, Bibulus defied Vatinius' men to strike. "If I cannot persuade Caesar to right," he cried, "I will affix upon him the guilt and stigma of my death."[8] Vatinius' roughnecks accepted Bibulus' invitation. They seized the consul, hurled him down the temple steps and smashed the fasces of his lictors. According to one report, in the melee someone dumped a basket of excrement on the consul's head. Friends wrenched Bibulus free and hustled him off past the compound of the vestals all the way to the Temple of Jupiter the Stayer. Two tribunes were wounded. The optimates fled, all except Cato. Elbowing through the crowd, he bellowed threats until Vatinius' toughs swung him above their heads and carried him off, kicking and shouting.

Once the Forum was cleared of the optimate party, Vatinius dismissed noncitizens and ordered the voters to line up by tribe within aisles marked off by ropes from the podium. Down these passages and over raised platforms men advanced to cast ballots marked with a "U" (Uti rogas—as you request—for an affirmative vote) or, unlikely to be employed on this occasion, with an "A" (Antiqua malo—I prefer the old ways—for a negative vote). The measure passed, of course, with a unanimous vote of all thirty-five tribes.

The leaders of the Senate could not ignore the exposure of the ineffectuality of their religious tactic or the humiliation to their order. Bibulus demanded an annulment of the vote, charging that the agrarian bill had been passed by violence. Intimidated by the mood of the populace, by the presence of Pompeius' veterans and by the disclosure of the renewed alliance between Crassus and Pompeius, even optimate senators failed to support Bibulus' motion. Bibulus did give warning that under changed circumstances (and Roman politics were ever in flux) the optimates, as they had done repeatedly against other "subversives," would annul Caesar's acts and indict him for employing violence in passing the laws. (For the rest of his life Caesar's political actions would be conditioned by this warning from his optimate opponents.)

As the day approached for the senators to swear to uphold the provisions of Caesar's agrarian law, the consular Metellus Celer, Pompeius' confirmed enemy since his divorce of Celer's sister, announced he would follow the example of his uncle, Marius' enemy, and go into exile rather than submit to such an oath. He was joined, of course, by the Man of Virtue, and in vain did Cato's womenfolk beg the Stoic to yield. Only when Cicero insisted that the republic would not survive without the presence of its most dedicated champion did Cato abandon his commitment to martyrdom.

At the Temple of Saturn at the foot of the Capitol, the senators, including Metellus Celer and Cato, one by one, repeated the oath to uphold the provisions of Caesar's agrarian law.

Now Caesar turned to his commitments to his other associates. On the question of relief for the Asian publicans, he confronted a delicate issue, for the directors of the corporations, who exacted returns as high as one hundred and twenty per cent on their investments, were, in effect, demanding that the commonwealth rescue them in the event of losses even when their losses were due to managerial incompetence and miscalculation, "a most shameless proceeding," as Cicero noted privately. If Caesar supported this demand, he risked antagonizing Italian entrepreneurial elements whose interests conflicted with those of the publicans, as well as provincial landowners and merchants, upon whom Rome relied in great part for maintaining its dominion. This very year Italian traders had joined Asian businessmen in protesting to the provincial governor Quintus Cicero duties the publicans were collecting on goods transported from one port to another within the province. Perplexed as to which group to favor, Quintus consulted his brother. "If we oppose [the publicans]," the consular replied, "we shall alienate from ourselves and from the commonwealth an order that has deserved extremely well of us and been brought through our instrumentality into close association with the commonwealth, and yet if we yield to them in everything, we shall be acquiescing in the utter ruin of those whose security and indeed whose interests we are bound to protect."[9]

With characteristic statesmanship Caesar resolved the dilemma. Warning that his action was to constitute no precedent, he sponsored a bill releasing the corporations from a third of their obligations, while simultaneously exacting a commitment from the directors to remit to the provincials a share of the taxes already collected under the original contract. Thus he granted relief both to the publicans and to the provincials. Frustrated by Cato's resistance to their petition for more than a year, the publicans were delighted. "They extolled Caesar to the skies."[10]

The publicans and entrepreneurs rallied in support of the en bloc ratification of Pompeius' arrangements in the East, anticipating boundless returns from the exploitation of the territories their hero had opened to Roman penetration. The optimates, in turn, united in opposition behind Lucullus, vindictive at Pompeius' usurpation of his command against Mithridates. The leaders of the Senate resented, with justification, Pompeius' arrogant dismissal of senatorial commissioners dispatched to supervise administrative arrangements in liberated and conquered territories; and they feared that Pompeius' rationalization of provincial administrative procedures would inhibit their exploitation of dependent territories.

Caesar summoned Lucullus and hinted at a revival of an old indictment for misappropriation of booty during the Mithridatic war. Involved in such a court case, the aging nobleman would hardly have time to finish laying out his luxurious gardens on the Pincian hill and adorning his mansions and villas with fish ponds, art collections and libraries. Would it not be more prudent for Lucullus to devote himself to nurturing the cherry trees he had introduced into Italy from the East? Fearing the kind of vindictive punishment he and his associates were plotting for Caesar, Lucullus fell on his knees and pleaded that he was an old man ready to retire from public life and eager to pass his last years in peace.

Having eliminated the threat from Lucullus, Caesar and Vatinius steered the ratification of Pompeius' Eastern arrangements through an assembly with no difficulty.

With his opponents in disarray, Caesar easily passed a resolution recognizing the claim of the king of Egypt to his throne. Ptolemaios XII, nicknamed "the Piper" by irreverent subjects, an illegitimate son of the monarch who had allegedly bequeathed his kingdom to Rome, had had to bribe Roman senators over the previous twenty years to maintain his crown. Six years earlier Crassus as censor had proposed the incorporation of Egypt into the empire, and Caesar had persuaded tribunes to nominate him for the task of reorganizing the realm into a province. To defend himself the king ingratiated himself with Pompeius by supplying eight thousand horse for Pompeius' campaign in Syria and Judea and by feasting Pompeius' officers at a banquet where a thousand guests were served new gold goblets at every course. Alarmed at Caesar's election to a consulship, the king had hastened to Rome and floated loans totaling 144 million sesterces for buying the goodwill of Pompeius, Caesar and their associates.

HUNTING THE HUNTERS

Caesar had rebuffed his enemies, but upon his departure for a provincial governorship they would regroup to annul his legislation and to destroy him. Leading the counterattack would be Cato and Cicero. In the few months remaining to his consulship, Caesar would have to render them impotent.

Even during his most bombastic outbursts of self-praise, Cicero had had a premonition of the dangers he might face for his execution of the Catilinarian conspirators. On December 5, 63, he declared to the Senate that he had made for himself "as many enemies as there are conspirators." At Caesar's warning of retribution upon a shift in the power balance in the commonwealth, Cicero expressed fear that "that band, incited by the mad fury of someone, [should] have more power than [the] prestige [of the Senate] and [the] prestige of the state."[11]

That time was now at hand.

Resistance to the subversive-hunters had long been mounting. Now Caesar inaugurated a comprehensive assault on the leaders of the repression of 63 and 62. As his first target he chose the despicable Antonius Hybrida, who, as consul in 63, had betrayed Caesar and Crassus on a bribe from Cicero and commanded the legions that had annihilated Catilina's outnumbered and ill-equipped army. A protégé of both Crassus and Cicero, a young man named Caelius, was selected to indict Antonius for extortion while governor of Macedonia.

History remembers Caelius as the lover who replaced the passionate poet Catullus in the affections of Clodius' sister. The mortified poet rendered Caelius' name immortal in a poem of indignation against an erstwhile friend:

> You had broken your way into my very soul, tearing at
>   my entrails, your hands upon my soul itself.
> Look, my life has been left empty and good fortune
>   vanishes with you.
> You are the curse that falls upon the grave of all I
>   love and all that's dear to me.[12]

A youth of wit and talent, Caelius attacked the wretched Antonius with exultation, fearless in confronting his former mentor, the formidable Cicero. With a victim as pathetic as Antonius, Caelius easily transformed the trial into a comedy. More than a century later the rhetoretician Quintilian would cite as a masterpiece of rhetorical description Caelius' account of what Antonius' officers discovered upon racing to his tent to warn him of a surprise attack by Balkan tribesmen:

> They found him lying prone in a drunken slumber, snoring with all the force of his lungs and belching continually while the most distinguished of his female companions sprawled over every couch and the rest of the seraglio lay around in all directions. They, however, perceived the approach of the enemy and half-dead

with terror attempted to arouse Antonius, called him by name, heaved up his head, but all in vain, while one whispered endearing words into his ear and another slapped him with some violence. At last he recognized the voice and touch of each and tried to embrace her who happened to be nearest. Once wakened he could not sleep but was too drunk to keep awake and so was bandied to and fro between sleeping and waking in the hands of his centurions and his paramours.[13]

Exasperated by Caelius' witty attack and by the raucous laughter of a hostile audience, Cicero failed to rouse the court with his standard bombast about the "glorious" victory over Catilina in that "greatest of all wars in the history of mankind." In his frustration he recklessly denounced Caesar for seeking to overturn all that had been achieved on December 5, "the second birthday of Rome," the day of the execution of the conspirators.

At noon the jury returned its verdict: exile and loss of civil rights for Antonius.

By two o'clock, informed of Cicero's attack against him, the pontifex maximus convened the thirty lictors who represented the obsolete curiate assembly, and with Pompeius serving as augur Caesar performed the ceremony of adoption by which Clodius was transferred from the patriciate to the plebs. Omitting the prescribed investigation by the college of pontifices and the posting of a public notice three market days in advance and ignoring Bibulus' sky-watching, Caesar pronounced the formula of adoption. Encouraged, no doubt, with generous bribes, the lictors could announce their consent without smiling. Fonteius, Clodius' new adoptive father, was only twenty years old, fifteen years younger than his newly adopted son. Immediately upon completion of the ceremony, he liberated Clodius from all filial obligations, and Clodius never adopted his "father's" name, as custom required.

By this act Caesar unleashed an irreconcilable foe against Cicero, for Clodius was now eligible for election to a tribuneship. In that office with his extensive and aggressive following, Clodius would exact vengeance from the orator for the latter's hostile testimony at the Bona Dea trial.

That evening a crowd, jubilant at Antonius' conviction, decked Catilina's tomb with wreaths in a celebration of belated victory of the "subversives" over Catilina's destroyer. As they banqueted they prophesied vengeance against Catilina's remaining foes.

Caesar and his associates now turned on Pomptinus, one of the praetors who at Cicero's behest had waylaid the Allobrogian envoys and captured letters incriminating the conspirators. As governor of Transalpine Gaul, Pomptinus had suppressed a year-long revolt of the desperate Allobrogians (who had been granted a resolution of gratitude for serving as state's witnesses against the conspirators in 63 but no relief from the extortions of Roman moneylenders and officials). At a banquet in Pomptinus' honor, Vatinius displayed his contempt by arriving in dark street attire instead of formal white dress. He and Caesar blocked the resolution granting Cicero's former collaborator a triumph.

Calculating that after the conviction of Antonius and the rebuff to Pomptinus Cicero was susceptible to a new enticement, Caesar offered the orator an ambassadorship to Alexandria. Although Cicero recognized the danger which threatened him and was aware that Romans were weary of the sight of him and wearier still of his irrepressible vaunting, he was balked by a new complication in his old principle of balancing honor against security: fear of being accused, especially by Cato, of selling out to the enemy. "What will history say of me six hundred years hence?" he exclaimed to his friend Atticus.[14]

Caesar would devise new inducements and new threats for the vainglorious "Father of His Country."

Caesar's immediate concern, however, was a wavering Pompeius, upon whose support he would be compelled to rely against optimate attacks when he left Rome for a provincial governorship.

XXIX

FATHER-IN-LAW TO THE GREAT MAN

ALL Pompeius had ever wanted was recognition of his dignity as the first citizen of the republic, a dignity he was convinced he merited because of his contributions to the rout of the Marians, his victories over Sertorius, the pirates and Mithridates, his enlargement of the empire and his achievements as consul. Who could vie with such a record? Beyond recognition of his dignity, Pompeius yearned for affection. He was uncomfortable whenever any segment of the citizenry displayed hostility to him. It pained him that he had been compelled to pose as champion of one faction or another and had never been accepted universally as arbiter of the republic, above partisanship. Through what he considered to be his patronage of Caesar (he would one day boast that he had made Caesar and could just as easily unmake him) and his renewed alliance with Crassus, he had won a land bonus for his veterans and the ratification of his arrangements in the East. With his immediate aspirations achieved, his old yearning revived for universal recognition and affection. He chafed at the hostility of the optimates and was abashed at the tactics Caesar and Vatinius pursued to overcome optimate resistance, tactics they employed on his behalf.

For all his desire to be loved, Pompeius did not know how to act without dissimulation. He preferred to have associates express his intentions so that he could disown their assertions if they confronted resistance. If compelled to offer an opinion of his own, he equivocated, unwilling to give offense to either side in a quarrel. Thus he declared his approval of Caesar's legislation but insisted that Caesar would have to bear responsibility for the procedures employed in its passage. "He was," he said, "in favor of the agrarian bill [which benefited his veterans], but whether opportunity was given [the tribunes] for a veto was no concern of his. He was in favor of settling the king of Egypt's affaire at long last [especially since he enriched himself in the settlement], but whether or not Bibulus had been watching the skies at the time it was not his business to inquire. As for the tax-farmers, he had wished to oblige the equestrian order but could not be expected to prophesy all that would happen if Bibulus went down to the Forum at that juncture."[1]

Pompeius was, of course, signaling his receptivity to an accommodation with the optimates on condition of their recognition of his special status in the commonwealth. Simultaneously he was advising Caesar, Crassus and Clodius not to take him for granted and warning his opponents against threats to measures in which he had a direct stake. He would keep opponents in check, he declared, with Caesar's army (the legions Caesar was readying for his proconsulship in the coming year). On May 13, at a warning from Bibulus of an assassination plot against him, Pompeius panicked. It was astonishing that this man who had so often displayed valor on the battlefield should fall into utter distraction at a report of a possible attempt on his life at Rome. Those who, like Caesar, had long years of experience with the Great Man understood that he was exhibiting not so much fear as despair, the despair of a man rebuffed in his desire to be admired and respected. Confronted with such a blow to his esteem, Pompeius' reaction was unpredictable, and Caesar moved swiftly both to confirm his alliance with the warlord and to bolster his morale. He dissolved young Julia's engagement to a nephew of Servilia's, and negotiated her engagement to Pompeius, a man old enough to be her grandfather. At the next session of the Senate, Caesar called first upon his prospective son-in-law, ahead of Crassus, a gesture reassuring to Pompeius. Furthermore, in order to accelerate the assignment of allotments to Pompeius' veterans, Caesar proposed a second agrarian bill for the distribution of the last of the public lands in Campania. In this bill, too, with a vision unmatched since the days of the Gracchi, Caesar undertook to resolve a critical social problem: the declining birthrate among the freeborn poor and the disappearance of the yeomanry. He set aside plots for families with at least three children. Immediately twenty thousand applicants presented themselves.

Though never weary of praising their farmer-warrior ancestors, the optimates showed no inclination to revive a similar yeomanry. They sputtered outworn clichés about undermining the social order and rousing a threat of a general redistribution of wealth. They grumbled particularly at a clause requiring candidates in the forthcoming elections to swear to uphold the provisions of the new law though they, in fact, had rendered such a provision necessary by their threats to repeal Caesar's laws at the first opportunity.

Unlike Crassus and Pompeius, who had neglected to promote the election of their partisans to succeed them as consuls, Caesar, confronting grave threats from his enemies, had to explore every avenue for securing his legislation and his personal security after his consulship. Within days of the announcement of Julia's engagement to Pompeius, Romans read in the Acta diurna, the daily gazette instituted by Caesar, a notice of Caesar's engagement to a daughter of a wealthy nobleman of the Piso branch of the Calpurnians, a prestigious plebeian clan. The young woman's mother was a distant relative of Aurelia's.

Servilia, who had grown children and was probably somewhat older than Caesar, would not have provided Caesar with the male issue for which he still yearned. As a warrant of his affection, Caesar bestowed upon Servilia a pearl said to cost six million sesterces. With his share of the bribe extorted from the king of Egypt Caesar could afford such an extravagance.

In establishing an alliance with Calpurnius Piso, Caesar gained more than a handsome dowry (Piso's father had amassed a fortune by profiteering in armaments during the Italian war thirty years earlier). Piso was a serious disciple of Epicureanism, an intellectual who evoked respect by his grave mien and thoughtful interventions in senatorial debates. Personal enemies and foes of his philosophy scoffed at his unprepossessing appearance, his bushy eyebrows, hirsute cheeks and discolored teeth and mocked him for his carelessness in attire and disdain of pretension. At his house Caesar enjoyed no gala banquets served by sleek young slaves in livery. Calpurnius' servants were elderly and unattractive; one man served both as doorman and cook; he owned no baker and sent out to a nearby tavern for bread and wine. On the other hand, at Calpurnius' Caesar had a unique opportunity of conversing with both Calpurnius and his constant companion, the outstanding Greek poet of the day and renowned Epicurean, Philodemos (who had been a fellow student in Athens with Caesar's cousin and mentor Gaius Cotta). The well-read Caesar was, of course, conversant with Philodemos' work. Generally, Caesar would have delighted in the Epicurean spirit at Piso's home, a spirit celebrated in witty verses of an invitation Philodemos sent to his patron for a celebration of Epicurus' birthday:

> Tomorrow, dearest Piso, your friend, beloved by the Muses, who keeps our annual feast of the twentieth invites you to come after the ninth hour to his simple cottage. If you miss udders and draughts of Chian wine, you will see at least some friends and you will hear things far sweeter than in the land of the Phaeacians. But if you ever cast your eyes on me, Piso, we shall celebrate the twentieth richly instead of simply.[2]

Certainly in visits to Calpurnius' home Caesar engaged in more than small talk about the weather. Engaged at every moment in political struggle, Caesar was constantly confronted by the political implications of the two major philosophies of the day. Alien to Caesar was the Stoic doctrine Cato adduced as a rationale for his stubborn defense of the status quo: "Whether in nature, whose order and harmony are without compare, or whether in the works of man, is it possible to find anything better arranged and more firmly bound together or constructed? Is not the universe in all its parts so well organized and disposed that the shift of a single letter would cause it to collapse? It is in fact true that not a single element can be shifted."[3] In his daily experience, Caesar verified the contrary Epicurean doctrine that everything in the universe suffers unremitting change, that the atoms composing all matter are "in everlasting conflict, struggling, fighting, battling in troops without any pause, driven about with frequent meetings and partings." In his own struggles Caesar had proved that the world of men likewise was in constant transformation; he himself had never known rest, compelled since his youth ever to remain on the qui vive. He required no convincing that "the old order always passes, thrust out by the new, and one thing has to be made afresh from others." Change he knew never occurred without struggle nor struggle without pain:

No night ever followed day or dawn followed night but has heard mingled with . . . sickly wailings [of birth] the lamentations that attend upon death and the black funeral.

Above all, Caesar had tested in his own life the Epicurean theory of the survival of the fittest:

Whatever you see feeding on the breath of life, either cunning or courage or at least quickness must have guarded and kept that kind from its earliest existence.

From his earliest years, too, Caesar had learned scorn for superstition, mysticism and philosophic idealism. He found congenial the Epicurean rejection of religion under whose oppression "a great dread holds all mortals . . . in bond because they behold many things happening in heaven and earth whose cause they can by no means see, and they think them to be done by divine power."[4] In place of the Platonic world of immobile forms and ideas (the philosophic basis for the Stoic resistance to change), Caesar preferred the world of pragmatic investigation of Aristotle of the Politics and the Nicomachean Ethics. On the other hand, Caear could not accept the preference of the Epicureans for a life of contemplation and their rejection of political striving and military glory. Caesar would never abandon the Senate, the Forum and the legionary camp. So persuasive was he on this matter that he impelled his Epicurean father-in-law to enter his candidacy in the forthcoming consular elections.

ARMIES AND PROVINCES OF HIS OWN

The optimates had cause for disquiet in the consular candidacies of Calpurnius and Gabinius (the tribune of several years earlier who had won for Pompeius the extraordinary command against the pirates). Relatives of conspirators executed without trial on December 5, 63, both men would press Caesar's campaign against the anti-subversives of that time. To mobilize against their candidacies, Bibulus postponed the elections from July to October, a delay threatening to Caesar, who, in the event of a defeat of either of the two men, would have little time to take further measures in his own defense before departing for his province.

Caesar had restored in good time his alliance with Pompeius, whose spirits revived upon his marriage to Caesar's charming, intelligent and affectionate daughter. The Great Man rallied his veterans to an assembly at which Vatinius put to a vote a bill in effect annulling the previous Senate assignment of police duty in Italy to this year's consuls and granting Caesar instead the governor-ship of Cisalpine Gaul and neighboring Illyricum (much of modern Yugosla-via). Caesar was to enjoy a five-year term as proconsul instead of the standard two years and command a force of three instead of two legions. Impotent, Cato muttered that the people were establishing a tyrant in the citadel of the peninsula (Cisalpina). "It was intolerable," he declared, "to have the supreme power prostituted by marriage alliances and to see men helping one another to powers and armies and provinces by means of women."[5]

Upon the sudden death of the governor of Transalpine Gaul, Pompeius and Crassus promoted a resolution in the Senate assigning this province, too, to Caesar along with a fourth legion. With a five-year command stretching from the Atlantic to the far shores of the Adriatic, Caesar had an opportunity to win military glory second only to Pompeius'.

Caesar's enemies did not yield without resistance to his self-aggrandizement. Confident that he would not employ against them their most successful strat-egy, anti-subversive repression, they badgered him mercilessly. Rome's out-standing scholar, Varro, formerly a lieutenant to Pompeius, denounced the alliance among Caesar, Pompeius and Crassus as a "three-headed monster." From the seclusion of his mansion, where he had retired after the failure of his sky watching, Bibulus issued edicts for posting throughout the city. He roused mirth by snide accusations. "The queen of Bithynia," he sneered, reviving the twenty-year-old charge of Caesar's supposed illicit relationship with King Nicomedes, "of yore he was enamored of a king, but now of a king's estate."[6]

Eager for excitement and resentful of exclusion from high office by the triumvirs, who would promote the candidacy of their own followers, young aristocrats under the leadership of Curio, son of an optimate consular, rallied to the attack.*

Imperturbable before such attacks, Caesar replied in kind. Before a crowded Senate, matching his enemies' vulgarity with a salacious double entendre, he boasted of his success in winning a command over three provinces, declaring that "having gained his heart's desire to the grief and lamentation of his opponents, he would therefore from that time mount on their heads." The

---

*The term "triumvirate" for the alliance of Caesar, Pompeius and Crassus is a modern inven-tion. The later triumvirate of Antonius, Octavius and Lepidus, on the other hand, was officially recognized by the Senate.

sensitive Pompeius, however, quailed when the young poet Calvus not only took up the Bithynian scandal: "Whatever Bithynia had and Caesar's paramour . . ." but also taunted Pompeius: "With one finger he scratches his head. What do you think he wants? A man!" To guffaws at a public meeting, a demented individual saluted Pompeius as "king" and Caesar as "queen," and at the Apollonian games the audience cheered when an actor declaimed: "To our misfortune art thou great [Magnus]"; the people demanded an encore of the next lines: "But that manhood bitterly / In time to come shalt thou lament." The actor failed to complete the succeeding verse, for Caesar entered the theater, and the audience lapsed into hostile silence. Upon Curio's arrival, however, a great cheer arose.[7]

Vatinius was only too eager to respond to the sniping. He dispatched a herald to arrest Bibulus on the charge of impeding legislation with his skywatching. Though rescued by optimate tribunes, Bibulus suffered humiliation. Poor Pompeius! He flinched at this insult to a consul, and at a public meeting on July 25 the Great Man, who only weeks earlier had been strutting at popular adulation, embarrassed friends and foes by stuttering and wincing at catcalls.

Pompeius became utterly demoralized at a report of a new conspiracy to assassinate him.

An equestrian named Vettius, an informer who had terrorized Rome in the aftermath of the Catilinarian conspiracy, even lodging an accusation against Caesar, saw an opportunity for new notoriety. Adapting himself to the changed political situation, he represented himself not as a hundred per cent patriot informing on revolutionaries but as the exposer of a plot against the Great Man. Apparently, he had acted as agent provocateur for Cicero. Now he sought the same role on his own. He approached Curio, who was openly hostile to Pompeius, with a plan to assassinate the warlord. Curio reported the conversation to his father, who warned Pompeius. Summoned before the Senate, the unsavory intriguer, who could not distinguish fact from fancy or stick to a consistent story (no handicaps in his denunciations of supposed Catilinarians), denied ever meeting with Curio. At cries of indignation, he blurted out a tale of conspiracy involving several young nobles. As he spoke, senators recalled with dismay the terror of the Catilinarian time. Abruptly, however, at Vettius' declaration that Bibulus' secretary had brought him a dagger with which to kill Pompeius, the senators exploded with laughter. As though Vettius had been unable to procure a dagger on his own! Senators remembered, too, that only weeks earlier Bibulus had warned Pompeius of another assassination plot. Confronted by young Curio and reminded that one nobleman he had denounced had been abroad at the time of the supposed organization of the conspiracy, Vettius stood tongue-tied. The Senate ordered the scoundrel imprisoned pending an investigation.

Caesar saw an opportunity to expose the fraud and hypocrisy of the antisubversive hysteria of four years earlier and to afford the subversive-hunters a

salutary experience with indictments, trials and threats of exile from denunciations of a megalomaniacal informer. He and Vatinius plotted a scenario for
repeating the procedures of the anti-subversive campaign of Cicero's consulship. Vatinius haled Vettius before the people in the Forum. At Caesar's
prompting, Vettius added to the names he had listed before the Senate. (During
the inquest following the Catilinarian affaire Vettius had embarrassed the
optimates by requesting permission to add to his original list of conspirators.)
Now Vettius accused Lucullus and Ahenobarbus, leaders of the optimate faction, as well as a senator who had pressed the indictment of Clodius in the
Bona Dea affaire along with the son of an optimate candidate for the consulship. On this occasion, however, Vettius omitted the name of young Marcus
Brutus. The accusation against Brutus had seemed plausible, for Pompeius was
responsible for his father's death, and recently in a gesture aimed at the triumvirs, Brutus had issued a coin with representations of Liberty and of Brutus'
two tyrannicide ancestors. Wags snickered that a night had intervened since
Vettius' initial testimony, a night during which Servilia had presumably appealed on her son's behalf. When Caesar completed his interrogation, Vatinius
pressed for still more names, and Vettius, terrified but with imagination unim-
paired, named Cicero's son-in-law along with a senator who had withdrawn
his candidacy for a tribuneship rather than swearing to uphold Caesar's second
agrarian law. Vettius, who, as Cicero's paid agent, had been applauded in 62
for his ready recollection of "subversive" remarks by opponents to the optimates, now charged Cicero himself with asserting that the republic "stood in
need of a Servilius Ahala or a Brutus,"[8] Brutus' tyrannicide ancestors.

Pursuing the procedures of the Catilinarian affaire, Vatinius proposed the
appointment of a special prosecutor to investigate the informer's charges and
called for a reward for further information regarding assassination plots. At
Vatinius' behest the people assigned Caesar an armed guard, not so numerous
as Cicero's in 63, but equally intimidating.

The subversive-hunters exhibited little courage when confronted with their
own devices and pretended not to see the parallels between the current semi-
comic anti-subversive hysteria and that they had provoked four years earlier.
Seemingly oblivious to any irony, Cicero moaned: "We are . . . named by
informers, accusations are being invented against us, perils are being prepared
for us," and the poet Catullus expressed the rage of the young aristocrats in
Curio's circle in an invective against the informer:

> O Victius [Vettius], you stink.
> You if any man has earned what may be said
> against fools and bloated windbags, Victius.
> Go, use your tongue to some good purpose, clean the backsides
> and the boots of slaves who stand in gutters
> with this tongue of yours. You'd kill us all, your enemies—
> but not a word, open your mouth (O what an odor, Victius!)
> and we'll fall dead.[9]

Some Romans blamed Caesar as the instigator of this sordid affaire. Others noted that many of those denounced by the informer were enemies to Crassus and Clodius, both of whom stood to gain in reminding Pompeius of his vulnerability. The outlandishness of the incident, too, reflected Clodius' humor—or was it more like the Rabirius trial?

No matter who promoted the strange incident, Caesar exploited it in a masterly fashion to expose the shabby maneuvering of Cicero and his collaborators three and four years earlier.

One day Vettius was found dead in prison. He was mourned by no one, and neither Caesar nor his enemies pressed for an investigation. Vatinius did not pursue the proposal for establishing a special court of inquiry. It was not 63, and Caesar not Cicero was consul, and Caesar would permit no campaign against "subversives" and "conspirators" to divert attention from the real issues of the commonwealth.

Having attended to fundamental problems of the city and of Italy with his agrarian legislation, Caesar now turned to those of the empire, bringing to bear his varied experience in the drafting of a comprehensive bill with more than a hundred clauses for an overhaul of provincial administration. Even his enemies admitted that his bill represented a "just and admirable" achievement.[10] The law provided strict and precise curbs to corruption. It would evoke the gratitude of provincials as well as of Italian traders and investors in the provinces and of citizens at Rome weary of the reckless exploitation that was drying up sources of tribute upon which Italian prosperity depended. If enforced (scarcely a certainty with the disintegration of Roman political institutions), Caesar's code would end the cycle of extortions by, and indictments of, provincial governors, indictments generally inspired by factional rivalry and promoting corruption in the courts.

At the time of the promulgation of Caesar's law, Flaccus, one of the praetors who in 63 had waylaid the Allobrogian envoys at the Mulvian bridge, was under indictment for extortion as governor of Asia. In defending his former collaborator, Cicero rehearsed his time-worn theme, exhorting the jurors to recall "the gravest dangers to this city and empire [when] I saved your wives and your children from death, the temples, the shrines, the city and Italy from devastation." He charged that Flaccus' indictment represented another move in the campaign of retaliation against the subversive-hunters of his consulship, declaring:

> He [Antonius Hybrida, Cicero's colleague in the consulship] has been condemned who slew Catilina when he was leading troops against his country; then why should not he who drove Catilina from the city be afraid? He is hurried to punishment who secured the evidence of the universal plot [Flaccus, the current defendant]; why should he feel confidence who took care that these things should be brought to light and disclosed [Cicero himself]? Those who shared his counsels, his assistants and comrades are being attacked; what may the authors, the leaders, the chief men, expect?[11]

Now wary of attacking Caesar and the other powerful men backing the indictment, Cicero jeered instead at the Greeks and Jews who appeared as prosecution witnesses. Calling attention to the large crowds of freedmen who were noisily interrupting the court proceedings, Cicero muttered, "Men of those nations often throw . . . our assemblies into confusion." He sneered at the Greeks as "men to whom an oath is a joke; testimony a game; reputation empty shadows; for whom fame, profit, favor, goodwill all depend on shameless lying." The Jews Cicero mocked for their "barbaric superstition." He charged that the prosecutor had set the trial near the Temple of Castor so as to be close to where Jews ordinarily congregated. "You know what a big crowd it is," he exclaimed, "how they stick together, how influential they are in informal assemblies."[12]

Of course, it was not these slaves and freedmen who intimidated Cicero, but the noblemen at whose call they rallied so eagerly—Caesar and Clodius. "Those are not wanting," Cicero complained, "who would incite them against me and against every respectable man." It was these leaders, he insisted, who were responsible for the "uncertain times . . . turmoil and confusion." In accomplishing Antonius' conviction and promoting Flaccus' indictment they demonstrated, he declared, that "they do not think the state is sufficiently overturned unless they have involved the most deserving citizens in the same punishment with the criminals [the Catilinarians]." Nevertheless, after these bold remarks, with unwonted humility, Cicero appealed for mercy. "Let them keep their power," he exclaimed, "their offices, their complete control of other advantages, but let those who wished to save the state themselves be safe."[13]

Where was Cicero's vaunting now?

A jury of Roman aristocrats would hardly convict a nobleman, no matter how patent his guilt, whom Cicero described as "belonging to a family whose first consul was the first consul elected in this commonwealth, by whose courage the kings were expelled and liberty established in the republic, a family which has continually, even up to the present time, maintained its distinguished record of achievements in offices of honor and military commands."[14] Caesar, however, had long ago learned that total victory was not essential in every struggle; besides, no subversive-hunter, Caesar was not seeking death sentences or to inspire fear among the general population. It sufficed that Flaccus' career was cut short (he would never attain a consulship) and that the optimates were further intimidated.

On October 1 Calpurnius and Gabinius emerged victorious in the consular elections. In vain did a relative of Cato's attempt to indict Gabinius for electoral fraud. When at a public meeting he denounced Pompeius as a dictator, he was mobbed, barely escaping alive from the Forum.

For the coming year (58) Caesar was assured of two partisans as his successors in the consulship.

XXX
CONSOLIDATING DEFENSES

WITH his extraordinary proconsulship over three provinces, Caesar began a new phase in his career, one that offered opportunities for fulfilling the prophecy of the priests of Gades, opportunities hardly to have been foreseen a year earlier. The Balkans north of Macedonia and east of the Illyrian coast invited conquest. Since the vast expansion of Italian agriculture and manufacturing over the previous century, Italian merchants had been engaged in extensive trade in the region, displacing traders from the Eastern Mediterranean. With the spread of bronze and iron tools, production of goods had been increasing rapidly in the Balkans with a concomitant increase in population. Italian traders exchanged wine and oil, bronze tools and other manufactured goods for cattle, leather, furs, honey, beeswax and possibly lumber and gold. With the suppression of piracy on the Inland Sea and Pompeius' extension of the imperial frontiers, new sources of slaves were required. Participating in this commerce were entrepreneurs from Campania and Cisalpina, regions where Caesar enjoyed particular support.

A Dacian chieftain named Burebista had recently united the Dacians into a kingdom of considerable power and aggressiveness. Bursting out of the mountains of Transylvania, he had conquered most of the Balkan peninsula, including Greek towns along the Black Sea coast. Abetted by a charismatic seer, he destroyed vineyards and forbade the importation of wine, a policy naturally resented by Italian merchants. Employing Greek artisans and engineers, he was constructing powerful fortifications and improving his weaponry. Rome could not tolerate the existence of a powerful barbarian kingdom along the borders of the provinces of Illyricum and Macedonia. For several generations Roman proconsuls had waged fierce wars with Balkan tribes. It was time to subjugate the entire region, to liberate the conquered Greek towns and to provide protection to Italian traders and, of course, to reap plunder, capture slaves and win glory.

The Dacians threatened Rome on other frontiers, for they drove westward tribes living along the midcourse of the Danube, impelling a general movement of semi-nomadic peoples. Under the leadership of a certain Ariovistus, Germans were flooding across the Rhine, and last year a Druid priest of the Aeduans, a tribe of Central Gaul long honored by the Senate as "brethren and kinsmen" to the Roman people, arrived at Rome to appeal for aid against the invaders. In the turmoil the Helvetians, among the most warlike of the Gauls, were preparing to migrate from their homes about Lake Geneva to occupy land near the ocean. Just before Caesar's consulship, in response to these events, the Senate proclaimed a state of emergency, enjoined the consuls to cast lots for the two Gallic provinces, ordered new levies and cancelled furloughs. Ambassadors were dispatched to investigate the situation and to convey a warning from the Senate and the Roman people to tribes threatening the peace. Upon the arrival of a mission from Ariovistus, Caesar, eager to secure his rear during his campaign in the Balkans, introduced the envoys to the Senate and promoted a resolution hailing the German as "a friend of the Roman people."

Before he undertook any Balkan campaign, Caesar had to secure his rear at Rome as well as in Gaul. In previous departures from the city, Caesar had mounted dramatic coups to ensure that he would not be forgotten during his absence. On this occasion his concern was that during his five-year command his legislation would be repealed and his career undermined. Over such a long period, he could hardly count on his three allies. Crassus and Pompeius maneuvered from situation to situation, and neither of them was about to hold a magistracy with authority. For the immediate future, despite his adventurism and the instability of the coalition he had assembled, Clodius represented Caesar's most effective ally.

Upon his installation as tribune on December 10, 59, Clodius proposed a series of measures drafted in consultation with Caesar. Two of Clodius' bills were designed to curb optimate obstructionism: one prohibited religious interventions against legislative and electoral assemblies, like Bibulus' sky-watching, while the other restricted the power of the censors to blacklist senators and equestrians for partisan advantage. Two other bills confirmed Clodius' power base: one reconstituted the collegia dissolved in 64 and permitted the organization of new collegia; and the other provided free grain to all citizens (Clodius was following Cato's example of winning popular favor with the dole).

Unable to prevent optimate tribunes from vetoing these measures, Caesar and Clodius counted on Cicero to assist them. They were confident that the orator, frightened by the recent prosecutions of the closest collaborators of his consulship and fearful of Clodius' enmity, would snatch at any reassurance regarding his own safety. They could hardly have anticipated, however, the alacrity with which Cicero agreed to their proposal. Exuberant at his deliverance from a nightmare, Cicero took no warning when Clodius forbade Bibulus to address the people upon laying down his consulship (the very humiliation Cicero had suffered four years earlier); or when Clodius revived the Compitalia, the New Year's festival of slaves and freedmen, which had been outlawed by Senate decree. On the other hand, he took exaggerated reassurance from Calpurnius' calling upon him in the Senate immediately after Pompeius and Crassus.

On January 4, pursuant to the agreement, Cicero persuaded the optimate tribunes not to veto Clodius' legislation, and the measures were adopted.

Immediately thereafter Cicero rashly supported a resolution for a review of Caesar's acts as consul. In three days of spirited debate Caesar routed his foes. Then, donning his scarlet military cape, he walked through the gate and established headquarters for his proconsular command outside the city. Simultaneously, armed with his new legislation, Clodius set up tables at the Temple of Castor and opened registration in new collegia organized by street and district under ward captains. Dockers, carters, masons, armorers, weavers, potters, tanners, tailors, fullers, wheelwrights, flute players, jewelers, house painters, smiths, common laborers and the unemployed—freeborn, freedmen and slaves—swarmed out of the alleys to enroll in Clodius' unprecedented political associations. Ignoring the muttering of the optimates, Clodius' assistants removed the steps to the lofty platform of the Temple of Castor and converted the edifice into a fortress command post. His enemies whispered that Clodius had cached arms within the sanctuary.

When the former tribune Vatinius, now a lieutenant on Caesar's staff, returned to the city to respond to an indictment launched by one of Caesar's enemies, Clodius massed his partisans at the trial and so intimidated the jurors that Vatinius was acquitted. By February Clodius was ready to deal with Cato and Cicero, the two major threats to Caesar's security.

Following a complicated strategy evolved with considerable deliberation, Clodius proposed the incorporation into the empire of the kingdom of Cyprus. With the sale of the royal estates and treasuries, he would underwrite the free distribution of grain at Rome. Appropriations for the dole had risen from 8 million sesterces twenty years earlier to 30 million under Cato's bill and now to 64 million. Fearing a test of strength on an uncritical issue, the optimates agreed to charge the provincials with the cost of appeasing the poor at home, a painless strategy by which they had long been buying off the commons. At the public meeting where he presented the Cyprus question Clodius also proposed more lucrative provincial assignments for the two consuls than those previously set by the Senate, Macedonia to Calpurnius and Cilicia to Gabinius (with the profitable responsibility of incorporating neighboring Cyprus into his province). Having thus assured himself of the consuls' cooperation, Clodius proposed a third bill formulated in a single sentence:

Whoever put to death a Roman citizen without trial should be condemned to exile.[1]

The bill named no individual and mandated a trial for anyone accused of the crime. Clodius could argue, of course, that his measure merely reaffirmed the ancient right of appeal to the people in capital cases, but Cicero, long anticipating his turn, adjudged the measure as the culmination of Caesar's campaign against the subversive-hunters of 63 and 62. Now, belatedly, he regretted his rejection of Caesar's successive offers of reconciliation: the invitations to join Caesar's advisory council, to undertake a diplomatic mission to Egypt and, most recently, to serve on Caesar's proconsular staff. He lamented especially his collaboration in the passage of Clodius' legislation. Although neither named nor indicted under Clodius' law, the orator, who had so long been wearying the citizenry with vauntings about his consular exploits, now wandered the streets dressed in mourning, appealing to passers-by for succor, "not being ashamed to annoy people who knew nothing about the business so that his doings excited laughter rather than pity."[2]

The citizenry failed to rally to the defense of "the Father of His Country." A group of equestrians did assemble on the Capitol and issue a call to all "good" citizens to put on mourning in sympathy for the beleaguered leader. They selected a delegation to present a petition to the Senate, which was meeting at the time in the Temple of Concord, in the very hall where, against Caesar's advice, Cicero had exhorted the senators to execute the conspirators on that "Second Birthday of Rome." Guarding the steps of the temple on this occasion were not armed equestrians under the command of Cicero's friend Atticus but members of Clodius' new collegia, commoners and slaves. The consul Gabinius denied the equestrian delegation admission to the Senate, and Clodius summoned the equestrians from the Capitol to the Rostra in the Forum. To shouts of approval from his partisans, he proclaimed that his law reaffirming the constitutional right to trial in capital cases was "abetted by Pompeius and instigated by Crassus. The consuls," he added, "had made common cause with him." If any citizens sought to obstruct the implementation of his bill, he would summon Caesar with his legionaries from outside the walls.[3]

Gabinius forbade the wearing of mourning in public and expelled from the city an equestrian who championed Cicero's cause with excessive ardor. In despair Cicero appealed to Calpurnius. Maladroitly, he and his son-in-law, a relative of the consul's, appeared in Calpurnius' atrium before noon on February 21, the morning after the monthly Epicurean festival, and a groggy Calpurnius greeted them in slippers, his breath heavy with wine and his head swathed in a hood. He responded lucidly, however, to Cicero's observation on the coincidence of Clodius' assigning provinces to the two consuls at the very public meeting where he proposed punishment for those convicted of executing citizens without trial. His colleague Gabinius, Calpurnius admitted, like Cicero's colleague Antonius, "was a beggar cast out from house and home who could not exist without a province."[4] Like Cicero with Antonius, he was catering to Gabinius by yielding to him the choice assignment of organizing Cyprus into a province. They had, of course, required Clodius' cooperation. As for Cicero, Calpurnius could proffer no better advice than to depart quietly from the city (Cicero's advice to Catilina in 63!).

A courier reported that the Helvetians, joined by a tribe driven west by the aggressive Dacians, were assembling to begin their migration across the Province (the common name for Transalpine Gaul). Thus pressured, Caesar had to accelerate the strategy he had evolved with Clodius. Clodius now posted a bill appointing Cato to a special command for the liquidation of the royal holdings in Cyprus. With sardonic irony he praised the Stoic "as the purest man of all the Romans," the only senator who could be trusted to render an honest accounting in the auction of the island king's property. When the Man of Virtue denounced the proposal as "a snare and an insult," Clodius quipped: "Well, then, if you don't think it a favor, you must make the voyage as a punishment."[5]

Next came Cicero's turn. Clodius convened a public meeting outside the walls in order to permit Caesar, now a commander in arms, to attend; and the Circus Flaminius on the far side of the Capitol rang with shouts not of chariot race enthusiasts but of Clodius' partisans and Caesar's legionaries.

It was the final scene of a six-year drama in which at last the orator himself was to play the victim.

Clodius called first upon Gabinius. The consul recalled that one of his relatives had been executed without trial on December 5. "He was gravely displeased," he said, "at the punishment of uncondemned citizens," and he warned the equestrians who had rallied to Cicero's support in 63 that they "would pay for the day . . . they had been on the slope of the Capitol in arms; that the hour of vengeance had arrived for those who had hitherto been in fear." Clodius called on Calpurnius next. He, too, noted that he had lost a relative among those executed. He insisted, however, that as an Epicurean "he had always been of a compassionate nature. . . . No deed of cruelty or sadness," he declared, "pleases me." Next Clodius invited Caesar to speak. "Everyone," said Caesar, "knew all that had been in his mind concerning the events of the time, as he had cast his vote in sparing their lives." Nevertheless, reaffirming his dedication to the law, he expressed doubts regarding ex post facto legislation. "It was not fitting," he suggested, "for any such law to be drawn up with regard to events now past."[6] Young Publius Crassus, an officer on Caesar's staff and long an admirer of Cicero's, represented his father. He praised Cicero but quoted his father's opinion that the matter should be left to the judgment of the consuls. Pompeius proved more circumspect, hiding away at his hillside villa at Alba, southeast of Rome, and sending neither a spokesman nor a message.

Calculating that his chief hope lay with Pompeius, Cicero journeyed as a suppliant to Alba. He should have had no illusions about the warlord, whom he had described two years earlier as "without largeness and loftiness in view, entirely given over to a mean pursuit of popularity."[7] At this moment Cicero regretted that during his consulship he had dared to place himself as "savior of Rome" on an equal plane with the Great Man, conqueror on three continents. Pompeius abhorred disagreeable encounters, and, according to one report, at Cicero's arrival he fled out a rear door, sending word that he was not at home. Another story held that when Cicero knelt before him, Pompeius turned away and did not bid him to rise. Pompeius did, however, subsequently receive a delegation of senators headed by a praetor and two consulars. Characteristically, he equivocated, declaring that he would not defy a tribune of the people but promising grandly that he would draw his sword if summoned to do so by the Senate. There was, as he and his visitors recognized, little likelihood of such a summons.

To a similar delegation Calpurnius declared with patent irony that "there was no need of arms nor of conflict; that it was in Cicero's power a second time to save the state, by bowing to the storm, that . . . resistance would mean endless massacre." Hortensius and Cato, from whom Cicero expected comfort and support, also urged him to "yield to the necessities of the times and become a savior of the city" by going off voluntarily.[8]

Aurelia, visiting Caesar outside the walls, could report how Cicero descended from his house on the ridge of the Palatine, proceeded along the street between the cloister of the vestals and the Temple of Castor toward the domus publica and turned down the Sacred Way into the Forum. Followed by slaves bearing a picture of Minerva from a shrine in his mansion, up the winding road to the Temple of Jupiter he went to dedicate the image as "Guardian of the City" during his absence. That very night he was espied stealing out of the Porta Capena with a small entourage, heading south.

The next day Clodius passed the bill that had impelled Cicero's flight. At the same time he put to a vote the bill on the consular provinces. No one objected to Gabinius' receiving Syria instead of Cilicia, in compensation for Cato' assignment to dispose of the royal holdings in Cyprus. Chastened by Cicero's experience, Cato announced that he would accept any duty imposed by the Roman people. Clodius refused to provide the dour Stoic with a ship, a bodyguard or any assistants beyond two clerks, one a notorious scoundrel and the other a client of Clodius'.

Caesar had achieved the banishment of his two most dangerous foes, the most resolute leaders of the anti-subversive campaign of 63 and 62.

Couriers brought word that the Helvetians and their allies had fixed the spring equinox for forcing the frontier of the Province.

Caesar hastened to depart. In leaving Rome he could take satisfaction in his accomplishments of the year. With his colleague shut up in seclusion, helplessly sky watching, people had come to speak of the consulship of "Julius and Caesar" and to recite a popular ditty:

> In Caesar's year, not Bibulus', an act took place of late,
> For naught do I remember done in Bibulus' consulate.[9]

Like Cicero's consulship four years earlier, Caesar's opened with consideration of an agrarian bill. Whereas Cicero set the tone of his year in office by rejecting all discussion and denouncing the bill's promoters as subversives, Caesar offered reconciliation to his enemies, deliberation in concert and compromise leading to a consensus. Cicero engendered an atmosphere of panic in order to stifle discontent and to suppress demands for reform. Caesar, warding off provocations, ignoring obstruction, humbling arrogant noblemen and exposing the vacuity and unpopularity of the optimates, enacted the most significant agrarian program since the Gracchi and the most comprehensive legislative reform of the provincial administration in Roman history. He had not de-nounced his opponents as traitors, accused their collaborators of guilt by association, harried them with informers (except for the bloodless object lesson in the Vettius affair) or curbed their freedoms by the imposition of martial law, much less executed them without trial. He had scorned resorting to omens, prodigies or other religious manipulations. He had exposed the injustice and hysteria of the anti-subversive campaign and rendered impotent, at least temporarily, the chief promoters of the recent assault on constitutional liberties. In place of Cicero's "eternal" harmony of the orders, a union of equestrians and senators in defense of plunder that had dissolved within months, Caesar mobilized a new coalition, and the elements that had rallied to Cicero in 63 dispersed as at a gust of wind when called to the orator's defense against Caesar and Clodius and their associates.

Romans maintained the illusion that Caesar was Pompeius' man, and it would take several years for them to realize how powerful Caesar had become on his own and how much respect he had earned as a man "exceedingly keen and vigorous of mind,"[10] unmatched in statesmanship and political cunning. On the other hand, primarily in struggling on behalf of Pompeius, Caesar had acquired powerful and embittered enemies sworn to his destruction. They raged at their impotence, at his humiliation of their leaders, at his denigration of the Senate and at his disregard of religious manipulations and tribunician vetoes. They would forget, of course, his offers of reconciliation and collaboration.

Few Romans sensed that in Caesar's consulship the commonwealth had reached a turning point; the old was dying, the new had not yet emerged.

In his proconsulship, from afar, Caesar would have to maneuver skilfully to preserve his security and to advance his influence and career.

The prophecy of the priests of Gades, though far from fulfilment, seemed less unlikely.

XXXI

MASTERING THE ARTS OF WAR

ASSURED of Cicero's exile and Cato's preoccupation in Cyprus, Caesar and his companions careered along the coast of Italy at almost a hundred miles a day to arrive after eight days at Lake Lemanus (Geneva). Caesar immediately ordered the destruction of the single bridge across the Rhone and with engineers surveyed the open terrain between the lake and the Jura range.

Learning of his arrival, Helvetian chiefs sought a parley. They assured Caesar of their peaceful intentions and promised to respect lives and property as they cut across a corner of Allobrogian territory within the Roman Province. War with the Helvetians, reputed to be the best fighters among the Gauls, was not to be equated with the police action against mountaineer marauders or the adventurous sally by sea Caesar had conducted three years earlier in Spain. Then he commanded three legions, whereas now he had at the ready only a single legion, some four thousand men, veterans of the recent suppression of the Allobrogian revolt. He had had no opportunity to establish rapport with them or to test them in battle.

With the Helvetians, Caesar confronted a complicated problem involving power relationships across Central Gaul. Some years earlier the Aeduans, the most powerful of the Gallic tribes, had engaged in a war over river tolls with their neighbors the Sequanians. The Sequanians had called in German mercenaries under the Suebian chief Ariovistus and inflicted a major defeat on the Aeduans. Subsequently, the Sequanians, themselves threatened by the Germans, sought a reconciliation with the Aeduans against the common foe. Two parties arose within both tribes, one proposing to solicit aid against the Germans from the Helvetians, and the other seeking Roman intervention. While the Romans were preoccupied with the revolt of the Allobrogians, neighbors to the Helvetians and the Aeduans, a Helvetian chieftain plotted with an Aeduan chief and a Sequanian chief for mutual assistance in seizing power in their respective countries. Such an alliance among the three Gallic tribes could not be tolerated by Rome, and, possibly at Roman instigation, the Helvetian, Orgetorix, was tried by his people and convicted of attempting to usurp supreme power. The Helvetians, however, continued their plans to migrate to the sea. With the general movement of semi-nomadic tribes in Central Europe, Rome feared the warlike Germans might occupy the Helvetian homeland. Furthermore, the territory where the Helvetians were planning to settle was close to both the Garumna (Garonne), a major route of the tin trade from Cornwall, and to a region rich in mineral deposits that were just beginning to be exploited. Above all, with the German intrusion and the Helvetian migration, the political equilibrium in the vast and little-known Gallic expanse was being disturbed, and Romans had not forgotten their catastrophic defeats in Gaul a half-century earlier.

Caesar could not initiate any military campaign in the Balkans without securing his position in the West, nor could he at the outset of his proconsulship permit any tribe within the Roman sphere of influence to challenge his authority. On the other hand, a military defeat would prove disastrous to his career. To gain time he instructed the Helvetian chiefs to return in a fortnight for his reply to their request to cross Roman territory.

At the start of his campaign against the Germans, Marius had inspired an esprit de corps among demoralized legionaries by setting them to dig a canal at the mouth of the Rhone. Following his uncle's example, Caesar distributed shovels, axes, saws and hammers to supplement the standard-issue entrenching tools, palisade stakes, ropes and pickaxes carried in backpacks on wooden frames (called "Marius' mules"). Recruited primarily in rural areas, the troops were familiar with farm crafts, and under the direction of engineers, surveyors, carpenters and smiths, the legionaries set to work on nineteen miles of fortifications between Lake Geneva and the mountains. While special details felled trees, transported and sawed timber, the rest of the legion dug a moat and erected a rampart sixteen feet high with towers placed at intervals for engines of war.*

With his thin line of troops secure behind these defenses, Caesar declared to the Helvetian envoys upon their return on April 13 that "following the custom and precedent of the Roman people, he could not grant anyone a passage through the Province."[1] The Helvetians were nonplussed. Apparently assured by Caesar's predecessor of Roman acquiescence to their migration westward, they had burned their homes and villages and stores. They had been counting, too, on the cooperation of their neighbors just over the frontier within the Province, the recently pacified Allobrogians, who had generous justification for rancor against Rome. The Allobrogians, however, trusted Caesar. He had prosecuted their extortionist governor Piso, opposed the faction of another corrupt governor (Murena, consul in 62) and blocked the triumph of a third (Pomptinus) in celebration of his crushing their recent revolt. They were informed of Caesar's comprehensive legislation against extortion in the provinces and were aware that Caesar enjoyed the goodwill of their patron in the Senate, Fabius (grandson of the conqueror of the tribe), who was at the moment campaigning for an aedileship with Caesar's backing.

Bewildered by Caesar's sudden arrival, his resolution in constructing a defense line and his adamant rejection of their petition, the Helvetians attempted unsuccessfully by day and night to cross the Rhone on rafts or with makeshift bridges. At last, repulsed by the missiles of the legionaries, they lost heart and ceased their efforts.

From Caesar's agents at Rome reports were reassuring. (For security reasons, in communications he employed a secret code of transposed syllables.) Upon Claudius' passage of a bill banishing him beyond a five-hundred-mile radius from Rome, Cicero had fled to Greece. Even the orator's former political allies were deriding him in his ignominy as "the most unstable of men, a suppliant to his enemies, insulting to his friends, an adherent now of one party and now that, loyal to no one, an unstable senator, a mercenary counsel."[2] The volatile Romans were diverted, in any event, from thoughts of either Cicero or Cato (on his way to dispose of the royal estates in Cyprus) by magnificent games conducted by Sulla's stepson Scaurus, who was squandering the fortune he had

*Napoleon (who traveled with Caesar's writings even as Alexander had traveled with Homer's) notes that since a soldier can dig three hundred and twenty-four cubic feet of an entrenchment in three days, a legion could fulfil Caesar's task in fifteen days. *Précis des guerres de Jules César*, dictated to, and edited by, M. Marchand; in Paris in 1836 (hereafter cited as *Napoleon*), p. 33.

amassed as a lieutenant to Pompeius. In a temporary theater accommodating eighty thousand spectators Scaurus constructed a three-storied stage adorned with three hundred and sixty columns, those of the lowest tier, thirty feet in height, of marble, those in the center of glass and those at the top of gilded beams. Three thousand statues, plunder from the East, were interspersed among the columns, and paintings by great masters embellished the walls. Performers glittered in cloth of gold, and Romans gaped at the first hippopotamus ever seen in Italy and at five crocodiles, one hundred and fifty female leopards and the skeleton of a sea monster seized from a museum in Jaffa, forty feet long with ribs larger than an elephant's and a spine a foot and a half thick.

Other aristocrats despaired of rivaling such munificence in advancing their careers. Henceforth only multimillionaires or candidates they supported would be able to aspire to high office. People gloated at news of a fire at Scaurus' villa in Tusculum with damage estimated at 30 million sesterces. (Such sums had been beyond imagination a generation earlier, before Sulla's dictatorship.) At the report, however, that slaves were suspected of arson, citizens became alarmed and cited an old maxim: "Slaves have eaten more masters than dogs." People murmured that crucifixion of all the slaves in the household would provide a useful warning.

THE FIRST CAMPAIGN

While Rome buzzed of such events, Caesar faced a new crisis. With the Sequanians, their neighbors to the northeast, the Helvetians secretly negotiated passage along the edge of Lake Geneva at the foot of the Jura, a route outside the boundary of the Province. Since a narrow defile admitted only a single wagon at a time, it would be weeks before the Helvetians broke out into open country, time for Caesar to summon Publius Clodius' elder brother, Caesar's lieutenant, with three legions poised at the Illyrian frontier for an invasion of the Balkans. The legion at Lake Geneva Caesar entrusted to Labienus, Pompeius' countryman and the tribune with whom Caesar had collaborated during Cicero's consulship. He instructed Balbus, his friend from Gades now serving as his aide-de-camp, to send to Spain for supplies and reinforcements. Pompeius Trogus, son of a Gallic prince granted citizenship by Pompeius during the Sertorian war and now serving as Caesar's secretary, was to levy auxiliaries among tribes within and outside the Province. Caesar himself sped across the Alps to recruit and train fresh troops in Cisalpina during the two months Gaius Claudius would be marching from the Adriatic into Gaul.

Within weeks, following the basic training refined by Old Marius, stern drillmasters, driving relentlessly, transformed recruits into legionaries. Lubberly Cisalpine farm boys submitted to barking centurions who wielded batons freely on laggards and in mock attacks cudgeled those who failed to race on the the double, while roaring a war cry. They hectored young men who stumbled in clumsy hobnailed boots, compelling them to march in cadence under sixty-pound packs. Mocking and praising by turns, they set the new recruits to battling with swords and shields twice the size and weight of the standard issue until all were "ready to endure toil and despise wounds."[3]

Caesar's enemies could snicker that his success in rallying craftsmen, shop-keepers and laborers at Rome offered no guarantee that he, an urbane sophisti-cate, would evoke respect from recalcitrant rawboned yokels. People recalled the difficulties in maintaining discipline of Sulla, Pompeius and Lucullus, men with far more military experience. No rough-and-ready soldier like Old Mar-ius, how would this haughty descendant of a goddess, who strolled about the Forum with a fold of his toga flapping effeminately, who on the Rostra or in the Senate sought to persuade with precise diction and aristocratically modu-lated voice—how would he manage these dolts? And in a war against one of the most bellicose of the Gallic tribes!

Consistently projecting their own incapacities onto Caesar, Caesar's enemies could hardly appreciate the rationale he applied in assigning responsibilities and his recognition of capacities other than birth or wealth. Officers and men noted, for example, that this patrician of Trojan ancestry, this pontifex maximus, appointed to his staff a coarse entrepreneur, Ventidius Bassus, an energetic and efficient contractor for mules and wagons, and entrusted him with important commissions. By his presence, carriage and mode of address Caesar set the tone of his army. Legionaries watched with admiration as Caesar galloped down the line, often with hands clasped behind his back. Centurions grinned when he addressed them by name. Tales of his wondrous mount, the steed with hoofs cleft like hands that accepted no other rider, made the rounds along with the prophecy that its rider would one day rule the world. Officers and noncoms emulated his self-control, precision and decisiveness and adopted his manner with their own subordinates, rebuking without anger and praising without effusion.

While Caesar was preoccupied with military preparations, his position at Rome was threatened by squabbling among his partners. At first, after Clodius' confiscation of Cicero's properties, all had gone well. Caesar's father-in-law Calpurnius seized marble columns from the orator's mansion on the Palatine, while Gabinius appropriated a country villa. Clodius, however, "set his heart upon building upon the Palatine a paved portico three hundred feet long with apartments opening from it and commanding a magnificent view, possessing a spacious colonnade and other such accessories with the intent to surpass all other men's houses in roominess and imposing appearance."[4] For this project Clodius required a vast sum of money, which he proceeded to raise by accepting huge bribes for installing a new priest at a wealthy shrine in Asia Minor and for arranging the escape of the hostage son of the king of Armenia. The displaced priest and the liberated prince, however, were clients of Pompeius'. In addition, in a fracas involving the prince, an equestrian friend of Pompeius' was slain. Enraged, Pompeius defied Clodius' prohibition on any discussion of amnesty for the orator and prompted associates to agitate for Cicero's return from exile.

The optimates saw their opportunity. In a shrewd maneuver, they offered to legitimize Caesar's consular legislation by resubmitting each measure to a vote held in accordance with religious prescriptions. Caesar would have to admit that his legislation had been passed illegally, and he would have to trust the optimates to fulfil their bargain. Simultaneously, the optimates could annul Clodius' transfer to the plebs and invalidate his subsequent election as tribune. Recognizing the attempt to alienate him from Clodius, Caesar dispatched a letter to the tribune, which Clodius read aloud in the Forum. Addressing him not as a proconsul writing to a tribune but saluting him informally—"My dear Pulcher"—Caesar congratulated Clodius on his recent political successes.[5] From a distance, however, Caesar could do no more than exhort Pompeius, Crassus and Clodius to renew the harmony amongst them.

To speed his return to the Province, Caesar did not embark his legions at Genua to sail to Nicaea (Nice) around the headland where the Alps jut out to the sea. Instead, he marched to the north through a pass where the headwaters of the Padus (Po) flowing eastward approach those of the westward-flowing Duria (Durance). On the way he tested his inexperienced recruits in engagements with marauding mountaineers. At Vienna (Vienne) on the Rhodanus (Rhone), he found envoys from the Aeduans, the Allobrogians and other tribes with complaints that the Helvetians were ravaging their lands. A Senate resolution mandated governors of Transalpina to defend the Aeduan allies, and Caesar had a pretext for transgressing the frontier of the Province.

Informed by scouts that the barbarian horde, except for a rearguard, had crossed the Arar (Saône) just above its confluence with the Rhodanus, Caesar launched a pre-dawn surprise attack and slaughtered many of the Tigurini, a clan of the Helvetians. During the remainder of the day, he transported across pontoon bridges twenty thousand troops and two thousand pack animals. Demoralized by the surprise attack and by Caesar's celerity in traversing the river, the Helvetians requested a parley. An aged chief of the Tigurini offered to lead his people wherever Caesar directed. (Caesar had forbidden the Helvetians to cross the Province; he had not ruled on their migration.) On the other hand, the chief, who as a youthful commander had fought in a battle in which Roman legions had been defeated and compelled to pass under the yoke, cautioned Caesar to "remember the earlier disaster of the Roman people and the ancient valor of the Helvetians."[6] In that catastrophe the grandfather of Caesar's father-in-law had lost his life along with the commanding consul. It was incumbent upon Caesar as a proconsul to avenge the humiliation to Rome and as a relative to avenge Calpurnius Piso's clan. Uncertain about his untested legionaries, Caesar merely demanded reparations for the destruction the Helvetians had caused on their trek and the delivery of hostages as a warrant against further depredations.

"It was the ancestral practice and the regular custom of the Helvetians," scoffed the old warrior, "to receive not to offer hostages."[7]

With the break-off of negotiations, Caesar adopted a tactic Marius had employed against the Germans. From sunrise to dusk at a distance of five or six miles he tracked the horde that stretched beyond the horizon, an interminable ribbon of creaking ox-drawn wagons loaded with infants, the sick and the aged as well as household goods and supplies. Tens of thousands of men and women herded pack animals, cattle, sheep, pigs and goats and innumerable children, while men-at-arms circled about as a mounted guard. Late every afternoon at a site readily defensible and accessible to water, timber, and forage, the legionaries constructed a fortified camp, each man performing a preassigned task so that within a half hour they had finished digging a trench fifteen to eighteen feet wide and nine feet deep backed by a twelve-foot rampart with towers of newly hewn timber.* Simultaneously other detachments gathered firewood and fodder or hauled water. Within the fort leather tents were arranged in rows according to rank and service, with the officers grouped about Caesar's command post. Pickets of cavalry and foot were posted at each gate as well as sentinels on the earthen mound behind the moat. The remaining troops prepared the evening meal, each man grinding a ration of grain in a mortar for a gruel, pancake or flat bread.

In Spain Caesar had conducted quick campaigns without supply problems. Now he confronted a grain shortage. Unlike his attack on the Lusitanian mountaineers, Caesar's pursuit of the Helvetians preceded the harvest, and he was compelled to draw on the reserves of his Gallic allies. Aeduan deliveries proved erratic, and upon investigation Caesar discovered dissension within the tribe. Commanding Gallic cavalry that had been worsted in an engagement with an inferior Helvetian force was a certain Dumnorix, the Aeduan chieftain who several years earlier had conspired with his Helvetian father-in-law and with a Sequanian chief for mutual assistance in seizing thrones in their respective states. It was Dumnorix also who had negotiated with the Sequanians for the passage of the Helvetians across Sequanian territory after Caesar had blocked the way across the Province. Dumnorix's connections were extensive also in other states of Central Gaul. Among his own people, Dumnorix held "paramount influence with the common folk" and commanded a sizable cavalry force drawn from among his clients. It was he who had exhorted the Aeduans to withhold their grain "on the plea that it was better for the Aeduans if they could not now enjoy the primacy of Gaul to submit to the commands of Gauls rather than of Romans."[8] Dumnorix's brother, Diviciacus, on the other hand, was leader of the pro-Roman faction among the Aeduans. Caesar summoned him, and with a young Romanized Gaul named Procillus as interpreter, "an intimate friend in whom he had the utmost confidence," he questioned Diviciacus about recent events. The Gaul burst into tears and begged mercy for his brother. Caesar confronted Dumnorix with what he had learned, and, uncertain about appropriate tactics among this unfamiliar people, he simply placed the ambitious nobleman under surveillance.

*Napoleon's estimate, based on the labor of twenty-four thousand infantrymen and eighteen hundred cavalry, p. 82.

Caesar further exposed his inexperience by misjudging the capacities of an officer who had served under Sulla and then under Crassus and been recommended by the latter as "a master in the art of war."[9] One night, after dispatching Labienus to seize a strategic height overlooking the Helvetian encampment, Caesar sent Crassus' protégé on a reconnaissance mission. Disoriented by the darkness and the unfamiliar terrain, the officer mistook Labienus' legionaries for Gauls and reported that Labienus had failed to occupy the position, and Caesar lost an opportunity for a decisive engagement.

With his grain supply nearly exhausted, Caesar broke off the pursuit and veered toward Bibracte (Mont Beuvray), the chief town of the Aeduans, some eighteen miles or a day's march to the east. Informed by Gallic deserters of Caesar's retirement, the Helvetians advanced to the attack. Caesar posted three lines of veteran legionaries in the van and stationed the new recruits and the Gallic auxiliaries on high ground as a guard for the baggage train. He ordered his own horse and the mounts of all the officers to the rear to remove all possibility of flight. After a brief exhortation to the troops, he signaled the trumpets to sound attack and the standards to lead the advance. The Helvetians, fearsome blond, white-skinned giants, full mustachioed, their hair stiffened with lime and pulled tight behind their heads in torques, came on with huge oval or figure-eight shields embellished with animals and monsters. Here and there prancing on a steed a chief in chain mail sported a helmet surmounted by a crest or a pair of horns. The two forward lines of legionaries moved at a trot to within twenty-five yards of the enemy, halted, gripped the leather thong at the point of balance of their javelins and hurled the six-foot shafts through the air. Then they drew their short double-edged pointed swords from the scabbard and, ringing a battle cry, raced to the attack. The barbarians responded with chilling whoops and the bray of bronze horns, but many of the warriors were struggling with shields pinned down by the javelins, for the soft tips of these weapons bent upon impact and could not be extracted. Some Gauls dropped their shields and exposed bare limbs adorned with bracelets of gold and silver. They brandished heavy, blunt-tipped sabres, and in close combat they were unable to wield their clumsy weapons, while the legionaries jabbed freely with their pointed short swords. At a sudden flank attack by the Gallic cavalry, the two rear lines of legionaries swerved, directed by their standards, to confront the mounted assault. Since even spirited and disciplined cavalry proves impotent against foot soldiers in close order unless the infantry panics at the awesome sight of screaming horsemen hurtling against them, the Gauls veered about before the serried ranks of legionaries. With the failure of the cavalry charge, the Gauls fell back on their camp and fought until dark among carts and wagons, cheered on by their women. At dusk most fled, and the remainder dropped to their knees, hands raised in supplication.

Caesar dispatched his Gallic cavalry to order neighboring tribes to round up Helvetian fugitives. Although exhausted from the all-day battle, the legionaries set up camp. Caesar moved among the wounded, consulting with veterans skilled in battle medicine and with officers experienced in treating the sick in their own households. Army physicians, few in number, separated the mortally wounded, abandoning them to their death. With the others, they cauterized wounds, extracted darts, set fractures, applied herbs and performed surgical operations. Three days later, with the troops rested, Caesar undertook pursuit of the Helvetian fugitives. Encountering a delegation of elders begging for mercy, he initiated a policy he would adhere to henceforth: hardening terms at persistent resistance. The Helvetians had rejected his demand for reparations and hostages. Now he ordered them not only to furnish hostages but also to deliver up their arms, to surrender slaves who had escaped from the Roman camp and, finally, to return to their homeland about Lake Geneva. Six thousand warriors who made a run for the Rhine after the capitulation, captured at his orders, Caesar sold at auction. The remaining Helvetians and other tribesmen, destitute of provisions, Caesar instructed the Allobroges to supply with grain. The Boians, refugees from Dacian aggression in Central Europe, he gave over to the Aeduans to settle as clients along an undefended border area on the Liger (Loire).

In a communiqué addressed to the Senate and published in the Acta senatus, Caesar reported the discovery in the barbarian camp of census tablets listing 263,000 Helvetians, 36,000 Tulingi, 14,000 Latobrigi, 23,000 Rauraci and 32,000 Boii, including 92,000 men-at-arms.[10] If Caesar had been initiating a standard two-year instead of an extraordinary five-year proconsulship, he might have requested a triumph for this victory, as the culmination of his service.

Not enough of the war season remained to transfer the legions across the Alps and Cisalpina to the Illyrian frontier for an invasion of the Balkans. Besides, Caesar had now embroiled himself deeply in Gallic affairs. He had become aware of the complex problems in any imperial intervention in this vast, varied and populous country, and he could not leave Gaul without completing the initiatives he had undertaken.

In this first Gallic campaign, Caesar had learned lessons. He had failed to inform himself sufficiently of the maneuverings in recent years among Aeduan, Sequanian and Helvetian chieftains. Because of an undeveloped intelligence service, he had been caught off guard by the Helvetian negotiation of a passage through Sequanian territory. Underestimating the conflict in which he was to be involved, he had procrastinated in summoning the bulk of his army from the Illyrian border and in recruiting reinforcements. Thereafter he had been compelled to abandon his pursuit of the enemy because of his failure to guarantee his food supply, and he had bungled an opportunity for inflicting a defeat on the enemy as a result of a misjudgment of the capabilities of an officer entrusted with a critical reconnaissance mission. If he was to intervene effectively in Gallic affairs, he would have to familiarize himself with personalities, factions, alliances and intrigues within the Gallic states with as much precision as he employed in political maneuverings at Rome.

Nevertheless, in this first major campaign Romans would adjudge that Caesar had acquitted himself well. Both partisans and foes looked with anticipation for his eloquent communiqués. Ever exploring dramatic possibilities even in minor details, Caesar broke precedent by sending his dispatches in book form instead of in the usual scrolls. In the reports, master of persuasion that he was, with a lucid but compelling style he beguiled with understatement and a disarming frankness. But the facts, in any case, spoke for themselves. With a vastly outnumbered army composed of troops new to his command and for the most part untested in battle, he had defeated a ferocious horde of barbarians and vindicated Roman honor for a humiliating defeat suffered a half-century earlier. Romans would be impressed with Caesar's punishment of barbarian arrogance and reassured at his elimination of a serious threat to the security of the Province and of Italy itself.

Roman aristocrats with military experience could appreciate the particulars of Caesar's achievement: the complex problems in recruiting, training, equipping and supplying an army that represented, in effect, a sizable city in movement. That Caesar had been able to levy two legions so rapidly in Cisalpina attested to the goodwill he enjoyed in that province, for recruiting officers in recent years had been encountering resistance to military service. Knowledgeable Romans understood the mastery of organization required in building lines of fortifications, bridging rivers, constructing camps, coordinating the movements of supply barges and mule trains and perfecting an intelligence service (dispatch of scouts, maintenance of order of battle information, interpretation of prisoner of war interrogations and map making). They recognized, too, Caesar's genius for timing, for adapting to sudden changes of circumstances and for evoking an esprit de corps among his troops.

In the Province, Cisalpina and throughout Italy, relatives and friends of officers, legionaries and auxiliary troops read in letters from their menfolk how Caesar infused his men with a sense of pride and responsibility and how he was training them for precise coordination in maneuvers, in swift and automatic responses to commands and in mastery of their weapons. Caesar had demonstrated his prudence in not committing troops rashly for the sake of personal glory, in avoiding premature deployment of new recruits and in abandoning the pursuit of the enemy when confronting a shortage of grain. Provincials would note that Caesar entrusted Romanized Gauls with sensitive assignments. Troops and families rejoiced at the division of booty and captives.

Caesar had initiated a process that would transform his legions into the finest military force the Republic had ever known, if not the finest army anywhere until his day.

Caesar was compelled to concern himself about developments at Rome as well as in Gaul. Dispatches became more and more disquieting. Caesar could enjoy the irony in Clodius' consecrating a shrine to Liberty on the ground of the razed mansion of the consul who had executed citizens without trial as well as in a portion of the portico erected by the elder Catulus more than forty years earlier over the foundations of the house of Gaius Gracchus' closest collaborator with the intention of erasing the memory of a popular hero. Unfamiliar with the ritual, Clodius' brother-in-law Pinarius, recently elected a pontifex with Caesar's support, stammered awkwardly in reciting the formula of consecration for the sanctuary. Hardly so humorous was Clodius' baiting of Pompeius and his open break with the consul Gabinius.

Clearly, during the five years of his governorship Caesar would be waging campaigns at Rome as well as at the frontiers of his provinces.

XXXII
APPRENTICESHIP IN IMPERIALISM

B Y crushing and resettling the Helvetians, reputed to "excel the rest of the Gauls in valor,"[1] Caesar established himself as the arbiter of independent Gaul. Even as at Rome when senators rushed to associate themselves with any oligarch or faction that achieved dominance, so now chieftains from the states of independent Central Gaul hastened to Caesar's headquarters to congratulate him on his victory. Implicitly acknowledging his authority, they requested permission to convene an assembly at which they might present petitions for his consideration. (Roman oligarchs were old hands at inspiring such "spontaneous" appeals.) The leading figure at the conference (and very likely the convener at Caesar's behest) was Diviciacus, the head of the pro-Roman faction among the Aeduans. Caesar and Diviciacus enjoyed more than the usual patron-client relationship, for the Gallic nobleman had assimilated Greek culture from the center of Hellenism in the West, Massilia (Marseilles), as well as Roman culture from the Province. As pontifex maximus Caesar was curious about local religious beliefs and practices, and Diviciacus, a Druid, could discuss with Caesar the teachings of the Gallic priest-philosophers, interpreters of the law and guardians of tradition. Originating among tribes in Britain about the time of the initial large-scale Roman intervention in Gaul three generations earlier, Druidism developed out of a social and political ferment among the Gauls. Caesar could question Diviciacus on the fundamental Druid teaching that "souls do not die but after death pass from one to another." With this doctrine, the Druids believed, "the fear of death is cast aside" and a warrior has "the greatest incentive to valor."[2] Of course, Caesar was motivated by more than intellectual curiosity in investigating Gallic religious beliefs; from the Pyrenees to the Rhine among some ninety jealous and warring states varying in population from forty to four hundred thousand, the Druids under an elective chief priest alone offered a potential leadership either in association with, or in opposition to, Rome.

At the end of an inconclusive conference, a delegation of chiefs sought a private audience with Caesar. They threw themselves in tears at his feet and appealed for protection against Ariovistus, the leader of the German mercenaries summoned some years earlier by the Sequanians in a quarrel with the Aeduans. Once established west of the Rhine, Ariovistus invited thousands of Germans to immigrate into Gaul. Torn by intertribal strife, domestic dissension and social unrest, the Gauls were incapable of resisting such a fearsome invader. Impressed by Caesar's crushing of the Helvetians and hopeful that Caesar, intent upon a campaign in the distant Balkans, would not seek to extend Roman rule over independent Gaul, the chieftains saw in him a potential savior against the other intruder. (They could hope, too, that the two foes would destroy each other.)

From the vantage of Central Gaul itself Caesar better appreciated the potentialities of the region both for the rapidly expanding trade in Italian wine, olive oil and manufactured goods and for the critical tin route from Britain that passed along the Sequana (Seine), the Arar (Saône) and Rhodanus (Rhone) to Massilia. Caesar had seen lines of barges laden with amphorae backed up in the Rhone awaiting the resolution of the Helvetian crisis before proceeding northward into the Saône.* As they penetrated ever further into independent Gaul, Italian merchants had become aware of the profitability in Massilia's monopoly of the river and land routes, and in the last generation a sizable portion of Eastern Gaul had replaced Massiliot with Roman currency. "Gaul is packed with traders," Cicero had proclaimed ten years earlier, "crammed with Roman citizens. No Gaul ever does business independently of a citizen of Rome; not a penny changes hands in Gaul without the transaction being recorded in the books of Roman citizens."[3] Wine and slaves predominated in the commerce between Italy and Gaul, slaves to shepherd the vast herds migrating back and forth according to the seasons along tracks through the mountainous spine of the peninsula, and additional slaves for the gangs working the plantations of west-central Italy with their ever-expanding production of wine and oil. It was a profitable trade, as Caesar's contemporary, the Sicilian historian Diodorus, noted:

> The Gauls are exceedingly addicted to the use of wine and fill themselves with the wine which is brought into their country by merchants, drinking it [unlike the peoples of the Mediterranean] unmixed. . . . They partake of this drink without

---

*"In 1869 a remarkable find of 24,000 amphorae ends was made at Chalons-sur-Saône while the river Saône was being dredged prior to the construction of a railroad bridge. As the dredging operation was limited to the area necessary for the bridge, this find represents only a small proportion of the Campanian wine-jars dumped into that Gallic river before the time of Caesar." (Cedric A. Yeo, "The Development of the Roman Plantation and Marketing of Farm Products," *Finanzarchiv*, NF 13, 1952, 340.)

moderation. . . . Consequently, many of the Italian traders, induced by the love of money which characterizes them, believe that the love of wine of these Gauls is their own godsend. For these transport the wine on the navigable rivers by means of boats and through the level plain on wagons and receive for it an incredible price; for in exchange for a jar of wine they receive a slave, getting a servant for the drink.[4]

In Italy Caesar's support rested in great part on entrepreneurs of Campania, Etruria and Cisalpina involved in Gallic commercial and banking activity. With disquieting developments at Rome, Caesar's future depended ever more upon their goodwill. Publicly humiliated by Clodius (abetted by Crassus), an infuriated Pompeius had opened negotiations with the optimates to recall Cicero from exile. On August 11 one of Clodius' slaves was apprehended in the Forum pushing his way toward Pompeius, dagger in hand. Recalling his experience as a youth in foiling an attempt on his father's life, the terrified warlord shut himself up in his house and announced that he would not emerge so long as Clodius held a tribuneship. Clodius' partisans besieged him, threatening to demolish his mansion and to construct a sanctuary in its place. (Clodius had found a new tactic of religious manipulation. He had replaced Cicero's mansion with a shrine to Liberty and had warned Gabinius of his intention to treat him similarly. Now it was Pompeius' turn.)

Young Julia informed Caesar that a hostile tribune was urging Pompeius to divorce her and to enter a marital alliance with some leading optimate.

Events in Gaul were intimately related to events at Rome.

Ariovistus had upset the political equilibrium of independent Gaul and endangered north-south and east-west trade routes linking the Mediterranean with the north countries. Nevertheless, if Caesar marched against the Germans, the optimates would denounce him for committing aggression against a chief hailed under Caesar's auspices as a Friend of the Roman People. They could argue, too, that at the request of the Senate, Ariovistus had ceased his threats against the Aeduans and had remained neutral during Caesar's campaign against the Helvetians. Actually, of course, Roman oligarchs were no more concerned than other imperialists about justice or morality in such circumstances. Injuries to an ally, an insult to a Roman citizen, a breach of a treaty or an old bugaboo like "the German peril" could always be adduced as a pretext for another plunder raid, slavehunt or war of aggression. Still, like twentieth-century imperial peoples, Romans insisted upon a pretense of morality in international affairs; and Roman children were taught that "when glory is the object of a war, it must still not fail to start from the same motives which . . . are the only righteous grounds for going to war." Conscious of the proprieties, Caesar merely "promised the Gallic chieftains that he would concern himself with [the German] matter; he had, he said, great hope that by his good offices and his authority he would induce Ariovistus to put a stop to his outrages."[5]

To justify his campaign against this Friend of the Roman People, Caesar formulated a scenario of intensifying arrogance from the German chieftain. According to Caesar, Ariovistus insisted that if Caesar had anything to discuss, he should journey to the German encampment. Although Roman proconsuls were accustomed to summoning mighty kings into their presence, Caesar overlooked the barbarian's insolence. He reminded Ariovistus of his intervention in the Senate in the German's favor and demanded merely an end of migration from across the Rhine and of oppressive actions against Roman allies and the freeing of Aeduan hostages. He cited a Senate resolution of three years earlier mandating the governor of Transalpine Gaul to "protect as far as he could do so with advantage to the state, the Aeduans and the other friends of the Roman people."[6]

In defiance, Ariovistus claimed as much right as Rome to dictate to those he had conquered and warned that "if challenged . . . he would teach Caesar what invincible Germans, highly trained in arms . . . could accomplish by their valor."[7]

Any Roman proconsul who submitted to such effrontery deserved the scorn of his countrymen. Every schoolboy knew the story of the senator dispatched to order the king of Syria to desist from an invasion of Egypt. Drawing a circle about the monarch, the senator declared: "Before you step out of this circle, give me an answer which I may take back to the Senate." Dumbfounded, the Syrian replied: "I shall do what the Senate decrees"; and he ordered his army to retire. With his challenge, Ariovistus had, in effect, stepped out of the circle Caesar had drawn about him. Resolved to humble the arrogant barbarian, Caesar advanced by forced marches to Vesontio (Besançon), the chief town of the Sequanians, a fortified market center dominating a trade route from the east on the river Dubis (Doubs). At a report that Ariovistus was summoning reinforcements from across the Rhine, however, within the legions "a panic arose from inquiries made by our troops and remarks uttered by Gauls and traders, who affirmed that the Germans were men of a mighty frame and an incredible valor and skill at arms; for they themselves (so they said) at meetings with the Germans had often been unable even to endure their look and the keenness of their eyes."[8] Gauls still frightened their children with tales of the invasion of the Cimbri and the Teutoni, when Germans roamed through the land, massacring, raping and burning. Among Romans, too, the Germans remained a by-word for ferocity and their annihilation of five successive Roman armies a half-century earlier was memorialized in a Black Day of mourning every October. It had been Marius, with a sixth Roman army, who had finally repelled and overwhelmed the invaders. Now it fell to Caesar to repeat his uncle's triumph.

The fear arose in the legions not on account of losses in the battles with the Helvetians nor on account of Ariovistus' crushing of a Gallic army far larger than his own nor on account of the perils in advancing far from the Province along unmapped tracks that dissolved into quagmires after rains. The instigators of the panic were young aristocrats "who had followed Caesar from Rome to court his friendship, without any great experience in warfare." Desperate over their debts, these young prodigals "were in a hurry to snatch the money and return home, just as if what [they] had brought the commander-in-chief was not a letter of recommendation, but a bill of exchange." Learning from home that the triumvirate was disintegrating, they wondered whether they would advance their careers through association with Caesar, and anticipating in this campaign no substantial booty except ferocious captives difficult to enslave, they "hid in their tents to complain of their fate. . . . Everywhere throughout the camp there was signing of wills."[9]

In face of such demoralization Caesar would not risk calling a general assembly. Instead he summoned to a council of war lieutenants, military tribunes and prefects (commanders of barbarian auxiliary detachments) as well as centurions (not just those of the highest grade, but all sixty from each legion).* Unlike Pompeius, Caesar did not weep before his subordinates, nor like Lucullus did he berate them with aristocratic hauteur. Addressing himself particularly to the centurions, most of whom were professional soldiers risen from the ranks, Caesar delivered a lesson in military virtue interpreted in accordance with Aristotelian ethics: "Excellence or virtue in a man will be the disposition which renders him a good man and also causes him to perform his function well."[10] Following Aristotle, Caesar established the criteria for judging both the commander and the commanded, ascertaining the function of each in the achievement of the common goal, victory, and posing, implicitly, such questions as: What is the end (goal or supreme achievement) of centurionship? What is the duty of the centurion as against that of the commander? How can a centurion fulfil his function with excellence? Step by step Caesar exposed, too, the illusions provoking the panic among the troops, asking regarding himself: "Why do you despair of your own courage or of my competence?" Reminding them whose nephew he was, he declared: "We made trial of this foe in the time of our fathers, on the occasion when, in the defeat of the Cimbri and Teutoni by Gaius Marius, the army was deemed to have deserved no less praise than the commander himself." He recalled, too, the defeat of Germans in the hosts of the servile rebellion and noted that the Helvetians, whom the legionaries had easily overwhelmed, had often worsted the Germans in battle. As for doubts regarding Caesar's judgment, was it the function of subordinates to determine the route of march or to concern themselves with problems of logistics?

Finally, Caesar employed his tactic of intensifying demands in face of recalcitrance and of gambling all in a crisis. "I intend to execute at once," he asserted, "what I might have put off to a more distant day and to break camp in the fourth watch of this next night to the intent that I may perceive at once

---

*A legion was commanded by a legate. At full strength it consisted of six thousand troops in ten cohorts under military tribunes, with each cohort composed of six centuries commanded by centurions.

whether honor and duty or cowardice prevail in your minds." In dismissing the assemblage, he announced: "If no one else follows, I shall march with the Xth legion alone: I have no doubt of its allegiance, and it will furnish the commander-in-chief's escort."[11]

Chastened by Caesar's resolution and stirred by his exhortation, officers and noncoms returned to their units to report the commander's messsage. In singling out the legion which had held off the Helvetians at Lake Geneva, Caesar displayed his incomparable ability to inspire emulation among his associates. The Xth expressed "thanks to Caesar through its tribunes for the excellent opinion he had formed of it and . . . affirm[ed] its complete readiness for active service. Then the remaining legions moved their tribunes and senior centurions to give satisfactory explanation to Caesar that they had felt neither doubt nor panic and had regarded it as the commander's business, not their own, to decide the plan of campaign."[12] (The legionaries were adopting Caesar's Aristotelian distinction between the functions of commander and subordinates.)

Having restored discipline, Caesar could readjust his plans without seeming to yield to pressure. In consultation with Diviciacus, he plotted a longer route of march through open country to avoid the danger of ambush. Before dawn he assembled his officers for the routine daily briefing. They passed on his orders to the centurions, and at a trumpet call, after the commander's and the officers' tents had been dismantled, the legionaries struck their own tents; at a second blast the pack animals were loaded; and at a third the column set out in predetermined marching order.

On the road Caesar was met by envoys from Ariovistus, and a parley was arranged to be held on horseback equidistant from both armies, each commander to be attended by a guard of ten men. Mistrustful of his Gallic cavalry, Caesar set men of the Xth legion on horses. At the meeting Caesar recalled his favors as consul to Ariovistus and cited in regard to the Aeduans the tradition of the Roman people to "desire that its allies and friends should not only lose none of their possessions but should enjoy increase of influence, dignity and distinction." Apparently well briefed, Ariovistus replied that he was aware that Caesar was breaking Roman tradition in crossing the frontier of his province without Senate authorization and in threatening a Friend of the Roman People. As for Caesar's concern for the Aeduans, he knew that "it was the practice of the Romans to make foreign friends of any people for whom they wanted to intervene on the score of friendship without being obliged to defend them as allies." The Romans, he noted, had not defended the Aeduans during their war with him some years earlier. "If he put Caesar to death," he boasted, "he would gratify many nobles and leaders of the Roman people"; so he had been advised by "messengers sent on behalf of all whose favor and friendship he could purchase by Caesar's death." On the other hand, in the event that Caesar abandoned this region of Gaul to him, he would "compensate [Caesar] by a great reward and . . . execute any campaigns he might wish to be carried out."[13]

Warned by one of the legionaries that Ariovistus' horsemen were edging toward the mound on which he and Ariovistus were conferring and were discharging stones and darts at Caesar's bodyguard, Caesar broke off the parley. When he disseminated a report of the conference, "the army was inspired with far greater eagerness and enthusiasm for battle."[14]

Upon a request from the German for a resumption of talks, Caesar dispatched two envoys, the Gaul Procillus, "a young man of exemplary courage and courtesy" whom Caesar employed as a confidential interpreter, and a Roman officer who had exchanged hospitality with Ariovistus in the past. The two men failed to return. When Ariovistus began parading his forces outside Caesar's entrenchments, Caesar, following Marius' example, restrained his troops, wary of the strange and dreaded enemy, from responding to the challenge. After five days of observing the wild disorder of the barbarians and their childish shouting and obscene gestures, the legionaries lost their terror and through their officers conveyed their eagerness for combat. Learning from prisoners that holy women had warned that victory would come to the Germans only on a new moon, Caesar ordered an attack. At the trumpet signal and at the advance of the standards, legionaries and Germans rushed at each other with such speed that the Romans had no time to hurl their javelins. Diminutive Italians leaped upon the huge shields and thrust down upon the Germans. After failing in a flank attack, the Germans broke into a rout, fleeing toward the Rhine, a few miles to the east. A great slaughter ensued.

In his defeat and massacre of the Germans Caesar demonstrated to tribes on both sides of the Rhine the folly of challenging Roman arms and gave warning against further migrations from the East disruptive of the equilibrium in independent Gaul and threatening to the security of the Province.

Only within Caesar's lifetime had the Italian peninsula achieved unity and become the largest political entity in the Mediterranean world. After six months beyond the Alps, Caesar had become aware that though more extensive in area, more populous, richer in resources and only slightly less advanced technologically than Italy, independent Gaul was weakened by division into numerous warring states varying in level of civilization according to their propinquity to the Province and Massilia, according to the number of generations since their migration from across the Rhine and according to the proportion of subjugated indigenous people within their borders. The country was undergoing rapid social change, and Caesar would know how to exploit the contradictions within the individual states.

Appointed to commands on account of birth and rank rather than military ability or experience, Roman generals often suffered initial reverses while mastering strategy and tactics, accustoming themselves to working with officers and men and gaining insights both into the enemy and into the character of the war in which they were engaged. Caesar, however, adapted to his military campaigns principles of conflict he had evolved in political struggles, particularly his appreciation of the necessity for a precise analysis of the relationship of opposing forces and for distinguishing between a superficial factor like numerical superiority and decisive factors like generalship, discipline, logistics, technology and morale. In the Forum he had gained insight as to how and when to intensify pressure so as to accelerate a crisis, and he had acquired a sense of timing for calculating the moment when application of concentrated force breaks enemy resistance. He had also evolved the tactic of hardening a negotiating stance in face of continuing resistance so as to persuade foes of his resolve and of the deliberation behind his decisions. Now he was beginning to coordinate diplomacy and war with the aim of substituting psychological warfare and political manipulation for military engagement.

In his communiqués Caesar kept himself before the attention of Rome and by subtle allusions evidenced his intention to maintain his influence in the city. Romans would appreciate, for example, his mention of a Fabius (grandfather to the current aedile-elect) in a comment on the conquest of the Province and his pointed omission of the grandfather of his foe Ahenobarbus, who had shared in that victory. By proclaiming his satisfaction in avenging the death in battle of Calpurnius' grandfather, Caesar reaffirmed his ties to his father-in-law; and to Marcus Crassus by commenting on the latter's victory over Spartacus and by commending the valor of young Publius Crassus. On the other hand, in reporting the disaffection of the legions before the battle with Ariovistus, Caesar recalled charges leveled against his foe Lucullus in a mutiny during the Mithridatic war, noting that "in any cases where an army has not obeyed its general, either fortune has failed because of some actual blunder or else some crime has been discovered and a charge of avarice has been brought home."[15] Above all, Caesar exposed the machinations of foes at Rome in promoting a mutiny among his officers and in conspiring with Ariovistus for his destruction. (This would not be the last occasion in which they would conspire with an enemy against him.)

All who read Caesar's communiqués would note his astuteness in singling out the Xth legion for praise at Vesontio and inspiring emulation thereby among all his units. By witty indirection Caesar warned that unlike Pompeius four years earlier he would brook no opposition to rewards for his troops upon the completion of their service. In reporting his setting men of the Xth legion on horseback for the conference with Ariovistus, Caesar took note of a seemingly trivial witty remark by a legionary, that Caesar was enrolling legionaries as equestrians, a pun warning that Caesar would exalt deserving veterans even into the equestrian order, beyond rewarding them with a mere land bonus.

In his communiqués Caesar addressed himself particularly to the people of Cisalpina and the Province, whose support was decisive to his success. They would delight in Caesar's praise of the Romanized Gaul Procillus and at Caesar's account of the rescue of this youth, sent as an envoy to Ariovistus and imprisoned by the German chieftain. Riding in pursuit of the routed enemy, Caesar reported that he came upon Procillus being dragged off in chains. "Indeed," Caesar exulted, "it brought Caesar no less pleasure than the victory itself to see a most distinguished member of the Province of Gaul, his own close friend and guest, snatched from the hands of the enemy and restored to himself; and to feel that fortune had in no wise lessened, by the loss of his friend, his own great pleasure and gratification [in the general victory]."[16]

XXXIII

CONSOLIDATION IN GAUL AND AT ROME

FROM booty and the sale of thousands of captives the victorious Caesar had money to spare, and, encouraged by his agents, numerous senators journeyed to his winter headquarters in Cisalpina, supposedly to consult with him on matters of state. To each Caesar gave "what [each] wanted and sent all away in actual possession of some of his favors and hoping for more." On the other hand, dissension among Pompeius, Crassus and Clodius offered opportunities to Caesar's enemies. The issue of Cicero's recall provided a focus for disagreement, and to appease Pompeius, Caesar agreed to the orator's return on two conditions: that Cicero give assurance not to attack them or their associates and that the bill of exile be formally revoked by a popular assembly. (Caesar could be confident that for the immediate future Clodius' partisans would block the vote.) But Caesar could not appease Pompeius without offending Clodius, and the sly tribune gave Caesar warning against yielding on the Cicero issue. Summoning Bibulus, Caesar's colleague in the previous year's consulship, Clodius asked "whether he had been assiduous in observing the sky while Caesar was introducing the laws. Bibulus replied in the affirmative. [Clodius] questioned the augurs as to whether legislation so carried had been validly carried; they replied that there was a flaw in the process."[1] Upon the augurs' ruling, Clodius announced his readiness to permit Cicero to return from exile provided that Caesar's consular legislation be invalidated. By this ploy Clodius not only warned Caesar but also threatened Pompeius with the loss of lands alloted his veterans through Caesar's agrarian bills. Even Caesar's five-year proconsulship was in jeopardy. Matching Clodius in wiliness, Pompeius prompted a tribune-elect to propose that Caesar be recalled for prosecution for acts committed during his consulship.

Thus two men upon whom Caesar had been relying to defend his interests were competing in pressuring him for their own ends.

In January 57, no longer a tribune, Clodius employed his ward organizations to disrupt an assembly convened to vote on a bill rescinding Cicero's exile. In the riot Quintus Cicero was struck down and escaped death only by huddling in a heap of corpses. In a subsequent fracas a tribune was seriously wounded. The leadership of the Senate was transforming the issue of Cicero's return into a test of strength in which they were playing Caesar, Pompeius and Clodius (supported by Crassus) against one another.

Meanwhile, from beyond the Alps Labienus reported that Belgian tribes, less civilized and more warlike than the peoples of Central Gaul, were exchanging hostages and accepting quotas for an army under a unified command. They suspected, with good reason, that having established a protectorate over the states of Central Gaul, Caesar would cross the Sequana (Seine) and Matrona (Marne) in order to secure the borders' bellicose neighbors. They were also aware that Caesar would heed appeals from Italian traders to invade their territory. Of all the Transalpine regions, the Belgian states were "least often visited by merchants introducing the commodities that make for effeminacy," and the more isolated tribes forbade any importation of wine.[2]

The Belgian states were not only warlike but very populous as well, and they would prove far more daunting a foe than the enemies Caesar had defeated during the previous year. Using the report of their preparations as a pretext and without seeking Senate authorization, Caesar recruited two additional legions in Cisalpina to bring the effective strength of his army to eight legions. He mobilized additional squadrons of cavalry among the Gallic tribes in the Province as well as in Spain and recruited four hundred German mercenaries along with contingents from states of Central Gaul. He also dispatched recruiting agents to hire archers in Crete, slingers in the Balearic islands and spearmen from Numidia in North Africa, thereby not only strengthening his army with varied weaponry but also building clientships for himself in disparate regions of the Mediterranean. In early spring Quintus Pedius, Caesar's nephew (son of his elder sister), a young man of devotion and reliability, marched the newly recruited XIIIth and XIVth legions across the Alps to join Labienus in the land of the Sequanians northwest of Lake Geneva. In May, having delayed as long as possible in Cisalpina in order to remain in contact with Rome, Caesar followed. To avoid supply problems this year, he halted in the Province and on his way up the Rhone to negotiate with dealers and barge owners for a steady flow of grain for the coming war season.

During the winter Labienus had engaged in diplomatic maneuvering, and when Caesar marched his legions to the Marne, he was met by a deputation from the Remi (Rheims), who offered to submit to his will. The southernmost and among the more civilized of the Belgians, the Remi maintained close connections with Central Gaul. Their land was astride the trade route to Britain, and, unlike most other Belgian tribes, they had fixed urban centers with well-established artisanries. Impressed by Roman military might and by the advantages accruing to the Aeduans as Caesar's foremost clients, they desired his patronage among the Belgians. From the Remi Caesar obtained more detailed intelligence than he had possessed at the commencement of the previous year's campaigns. He inquired regarding the leadership of the enemy tribes, the relations among the tribes and the numbers and quality of their forces. Contributions to the coalition, he learned, ranged from 7,000 warriors from the smallest tribe to 100,000 from the powerful Bellovaci (Beauvais), for a total of over 300,000 or almost eight times his own force.

When the Belgians attacked a Remi town, Caesar's reliability as a patron was put to the test, and he responded by dispatching light-armed mercenaries. Bewildered by the hail of arrows from the Cretan bowmen, the pellets of the Balearic slingers and the spears of the Numidians, the Belgians veered off to attack Caesar himself. So enormous was their host that the fires of their encampment extended more than eight miles. Caesar knew, however, that barbarians traveled with a minimum of supplies and were compelled to seek a swift decision. Once again Caesar followed the Marian tactic of delaying battle until his troops had tested the enemy in minor engagements. One night after a vain effort to entice Caesar to fight on unfavorable ground and an unsuccessful assault on his fortifications, the barbarians withdrew. Suspecting a ruse, Caesar did not order a pursuit. The next morning, however, his reconnaissance confirmed a general and chaotic retreat. Caesar marched to the attack and inflicted great slaughter on the disorganized bands. In war as in politics Caesar pressed his advantage, and he turned immediately upon the stronghold of the nearby Suessiones (Soissons). Advancing mantlets (screens protecting units employing battering rams and hooks for pulling down walls) and constructing a ramp and movable towers, Caesar so dismayed the defenders with his celerity and with Roman technological prowess that they sued for peace. Caesar demanded hostages and the delivery of all weapons and placed the tribe under the protection of the Remi.

Elders of the Bellovaci met Caesar at the borders of their country. At Caesar's request Diviciacus, Caesar's Druid counselor, had led an Aeduan force against this tribe. The chiefs who had provoked the war fled to Britain, where many of their fellow tribesmen were settled. Caesar demanded six hundred hostages and the surrender of all arms and placed the tribe under the protection of the Aeduans. With the capitulation of the Bellovaci, the coalition disintegrated, and only the barbarous tribes to the east remained in arms under the leadership of the Nervians (Namur). This tribe required a demonstration of Roman might, for it afforded "traders . . . no means of access to them, for they allowed no wine nor any of the other appurtenances of luxury to be imported because they supposed that their spirit was likely to be enfeebled and their courage relaxed thereby."[3] (Apparently, Romans had learned the effectiveness of alcohol in extending their sphere of influence among less advanced peoples.)

Although avoiding an ambush against which he had been warned by his intelligence service, more efficient this year than last, Caesar was caught off guard by a Nervian attack on an advance legionary contingent engaged in constructing a camp. Caesar "had everything to do at one moment—the flag to raise as a signal for a general call to arms; the trumpet-call to sound; the troops to recall from entrenching; the men to bring in who had gone somewhat farther afield in search of stuff for the ramp; the line to form; the troops to harangue; the signal to sound." This year, however, he could rely on "the knowledge and experience of the troops—for their training in previous battles enabled them to appoint for themselves what was proper to be done as readily as others could have shown them." On the basis of the experience of the previous year, too, Caesar "had forbidden the several lieutenant-generals to leave the entrenching and their proper legions until the camp was fortified. These generals, seeing the nearness and the speed of the enemy, waited no more for a command from Caesar but took on their own account what steps seemed to them proper." The sutlers (muleteers and baggage attendants) and the merchants accompanying the legions (sellers of provisions and purchasers of booty), however, panicked and fled helter-skelter. Fearing a general rout, Caesar seized a shield "and calling upon the centurions by name and cheering on the rank and file, he bade them advance and extend the companies that they might ply their swords more easily."[4] The newly recruited legions at the rear of the line of march heard the uproar from the distance and advanced to the fray, and Labienus committed the Xth legion at a decisive moment and turned the tide. Encouraged, even the wounded propped themselves up to continue the fight; the sutlers regained their spirit and though unarmed entered the combat. The cavalry regrouped, and the enemy gave way and fled.

Caesar and his lieutenants were sobered by this near defeat. Though the legionaries and the auxiliaries had mastered many skills and learned to react as effective entities, neither they nor the officers nor Caesar had developed sufficient resourcefulness to adapt quickly to novel tactical situations. Caesar had failed to foresee the danger, but he had shown himself an awesome exemplar of courage and coolheadedness in the continuing process of molding the legions into a single effective unit.

Against tribes that possessed no urban centers subject to destruction or occupation, the most secure and lasting defense was extermination or sale into captivity. Caesar, however, hoped that with a demonstration of mercy he might win the Nervians as clients and encourage other tribes to give up the struggle. Accordingly, when Nervian elders arrived at his camp to sue for peace, pleading grievous losses, Caesar "bade them . . . keep their own territory and towns and commanded their neighbors to restrain themselves and their dependents from outrage and injury." The Aduatucans, however, a remnant of the Cimbri and Teutoni defeated almost a half century earlier by Caesar's uncle, Marius, would not surrender. They withdrew into a natural stronghold atop a steep height. Neither Gauls nor Belgians possessed the technology, the logistical capabilities nor the stamina for lengthy siege operations, and to them the Aduatucan redoubt appeared impregnable. The Aduatucans jeered as the legionaries set to encompassing their fortress with a rampart fifteen thousand feet in circumference. When they beheld a many-storied tower advancing up a ramp, however, they took fright. "They supposed that the Romans did not wage war without divine aid inasmuch as they could forward at so great a speed engines of so great a height,"[5] and they sent deputies to capitulate. During the night, in violation of the armistice, the Aduatucans sallied forth from their gates. On this occasion, Caesar was not caught by surprise, and the battle was quickly over. The next day, in retaliation for the treachery and in accordance with his policy of intensifying his reaction to continuing resistance, Caesar gave over the stronghold to pillage and sold fifty-three thousand captives to the merchants accompanying the legions.

While Caesar was pacifying the region west of the Seine and north of the Marne, Publius Crassus, rewarded with an independent command for his valor in the previous year's campaigns, obtained the submission of the coastal states west of the Seine, along the Channel and the Ocean as far as the southern limits of Armorica (modern Brittany and a part of Normandy). Impressed by Caesar's victories during the two war seasons, the tribes along Publius' route offered no resistance.

Caesar's clemency to the Nervians and enslavement of the Aduatucans proved effective. Several tribes across the Rhine sent envoys with promises of hostages. From these deputies Caesar learned of intertribal rivalries among the Germans that he might eventually exploit. For the present, however, he had no time to deal with the Rhenish frontier, and he bade the envoys to come back at the beginning of the next war season.

RESURGENCE OF THE SUBVERSIVE-HUNTERS

In correspondence from Rome awaiting him after his return from Belgium, Caesar found disturbing reports. Two optimate tribunes, a certain Milo and Cicero's friend Sestius, were contesting control of the city with Clodius. In continuous street brawls their bands of gladiators and hired thugs were proving a match for Clodius' urban plebs. Both sides disrupted meetings and generally brought terror to the city. The crisis was complicated by another famine. It was rumored that profiteers were creating an artificial grain shortage. With Clodius acclaimed a "lucky Catilina," the hungry openly rebellious and the magistrates and Senate helpless to restore order, "respectable citizens" were looking for some effective alternative power. At theatrical presentations during the July Apollonian games they cheered lines that seemed to allude to Cicero's recall from exile. They were outraged when Clodius' followers invaded the theater shouting for bread.

Caesar knew Cicero's character and modes of operation. If permitted to return, the orator would forget his sniveling poltroonery before and during his exile and revert to his old megalomania. His promise not to attack Caesar or his allies would be forgotten. Once more he would revive the cry of "subversion," and Caesar would be among the first objects of his attack. In the Senate Pompeius was proclaiming that through Cicero's actions as consul "the republic had been preserved" and warning that Cicero's "cause stood or fell with the welfare of all." The Senate instructed the consuls to summon all citizens to Rome on August 4 to vote for the repeal of Cicero's exile, and in letters dispatched throughout Italy and in exhortations in the Forum, Pompeius revived the language of the anti-subversive campaign of 63, calling upon citizens "to uphold the authority of the Senate, the constitution of the commonwealth and the fortunes of a meritorious citizen." On the very day the Senate approved Cicero's recall, the price of grain plunged "to an unexpected cheapness," and the orator's partisans exulted that "the immortal gods had given a clear intimation of their approval."[6]

The vote on Cicero's recall was not held in the tribal assembly, where Clodius exercised decisive influence, but in the centuriate assembly, dominated by the rich. An unprecedented concourse of citizens from all Italy responded to Pompeius' call to restore the authority of the Senate and to defend the constitution, and the resolution to recall Cicero passed by an overwhelming vote. A month later, on September 4, eighteen months after he had slunk out of the city, Cicero reentered Rome in triumph. Dizzied by the cheers of welcoming crowds, he imagined himself back in the days of his victory "in the greatest war in the history of mankind." In orations delivered before the Senate and in the Forum, he blocked out all memory of his craven behavior before his exile and of his subsequent fits of weeping, threats of suicide and bathetic moan that his tragedy surpassed all others in history. In fact, he transformed his flight into an act of heroism and self-sacrifice. Many listened with open-mouthed incredulity as he turned events upside down. Then he whined, now he vaunted:

> Realizing as I did that the Senate was bereft of leaders, that the magistrates had either attacked me, betrayed me or deserted me and that slaves had been enrolled by name under plea of being formed into clubs, that all Catilina's forces with scarcely any change of leaders had been led to renew their hopes for opportunities of slaughter and incendiarism, that Roman knights were stirred by apprehension of proscription, the municipalities of devastation and all men by dread of violent death, then I might, conscript fathers, I say I might, have defended myself by armed force and have been supported in that policy by many gallant gentlemen; and indeed that same courage of which I have afforded you proof in the past was still with me then. But I saw that if I proved victorious over my immediate foe [Clodius] there would be still others, too [including Caesar], many others, whom I should have to vanquish; and if, on the other hand, I were defeated, many good patriots would shortly have to meet their doom with me, for me, even after me.[7]

Few, if any, in Cicero's audience remembered the circumstances of a year and a half earlier as Cicero described them, but all recognized the tone of the harangues of 63. Once again Cicero was posing as the defender of law and order, a martyr "torn without trial from the state." Maneuvering to effect a breach between Pompeius and Pompeius' former associates, Cicero, in Pompeius' presence, rounded on Gabinius and Calpurnius and even menaced Caesar. "There was another," he declared, "who hovered at the city gates with a large army and with a command which was prolonged to him for many years." (Cicero was threatening to move for a curtailment of Caesar's proconsulship!) "He I do not say was an enemy," he continued with a pretense at caution; but I do know that when he was stated to be my enemy he never uttered a word of denial."[8]

Those who had maneuvered Cicero's return to serve their own interests listened in silence as he proclaimed with megalomaniacal self-delusion that "in the universal judgment on one occasion [the republic] owed its preservation to the efforts of single man."[9] His warning of imminent vengeance on all who had betrayed him before his exile was so comprehensive as even to include not only Caesar and his associates but Cato and Hortensius as well.

Assuming the role of arbiter of the republic, Cicero pursued a strategy for undermining Clodius' influence and for controlling Pompeius. In collaboration with the consuls, he moved to deprive one of Clodius' collaborators of the supervision of the grain dole and to grant Pompeius extraordinary authority over the grain supply of the entire Mediterranean basin for a period of five years. On the other hand, to remind the warlord of the limits of his influence, Cicero joined other senators in rejecting a proposal by a tribune in Pompeius' hire to grant the warlord unrestricted access to the treasury, command of a sizable army and fleet and jurisdiction superceding that of the provincial governors. Nevertheless, upon Pompeius' nomination, the price of grain, artificially inflated, fell once again. Suddenly supplies were adequate.

Handicapped by his inability to respond to day-to-day shifts in city politics, Caesar confirmed his position among leading figures at Rome by distributing largess out of his share of the sale of the Aduatucan prisoners. Otherwise, he maintained his prestige through his communiqués. Although it was taken for granted that generals would embellish their accomplishments and underplay their reverses, no one could gainsay Caesar's exploits, for officers and legionaries corroborated his claims as did the flow of booty into Italy. Men of letters, always comparing Roman literary achievements with the Greeks', praised Caesar's style as equal to Xenophon's in the latter's journal of a march of Greek mercenaries through Asia Minor three centuries earlier. Certainly, Caesar matched the Greek historians in the objectivity of his representation of his enemies. Whereas, with typical imperialist chauvinism, Romans were unashamed of their ignorance of the geography and ethnology of the lands of the barbarians, Caesar, displaying a more enlightened attitude, distinguished among the various peoples, praising the Remi for their loyalty and the Nervians for their valor. In describing the battle that almost brought destruction to his army, Caesar expressed admiration that "even when their hope of safety was at end [the Nervians] displayed prodigious courage. When their front ranks had fallen, the next stood on the prostrate forms and fought from them; when these were cast down and corpses were piled in heaps, the survivors, standing as it were upon a mound, hurled darts on our troops or caught and returned our pikes."[10]

Unable to deprecate Caesar's exploits, Cicero played him against Pompeius. Upon receipt of the final communiqué of the war season, Cicero proposed a thanksgiving of fifteen days in honor of Caesar's victories, "an honor that had previously fallen to no man"[11] and five days longer than either of the thanksgivings Cicero had promoted for Pompeius at the conclusion of hostilities in the East.

With Pompeius' appointment to an extraordinary command in charge of the imperial grain supply, the equilibrium among the triumvirs and Clodius had been upset. To Cicero's dismay, the optimates allied themselves with the "people's leader." They applauded Clodius' baiting of Pompeius. After Pompeius ordered a scrutiny of the grain lists with a view to excluding thousands of slaves emancipated by owners so that they could be fed at public expense, Clodius burned the Temple of the Nymphs, the registry of the grain recipients. The optimates scarcely complained. Nor did they comfort Cicero when Clodius' partisans drove off workmen reconstructing Cicero's mansion and set fire to Quintus' house nearby.

Meanwhile, in Gaul after the repulse of an attack by mountain tribes at a pass "through the Alps by which traders had been accustomed to travel but at great risk and on payment of great tolls," Caesar reassured Italian merchants (for whose goodwill he was always concerned) regarding the security of the route. With Gaul stable, Caesar was able to set out for his other province, Illyricum, desiring "to visit the tribes there also and to become acquainted with the country."[12] As governor of Macedonia, Caesar's father-in-law Calpurnius had been hailed as imperator after overcoming fierce Balkan tribes in battle, and Caesar was very likely investigating the feasibility of a two-pronged invasion of the unsubjugated heart of the Balkan peninsula, with Calpurnius advancing from the south, while he himself moved down from the north, a venture they had undoubtedly discussed before Caesar's departure for his provinces two years earlier.

The expansion of the Dacians out of the mountains of Transylvania jeopardized Roman trade, and the townspeople of Aquileia, where Caesar established his headquarters, along with other Cisalpiners, would welcome a campaign to protect and expand their commerce, a commerce equal to, if not more extensive than, that with independent Gaul. A trading center at the head of the Adriatic on routes running both east and west and north and south, including the amber route to the Baltic, Aquileia, Caesar discovered, was also "an emporium for those tribes of the Illyrians that lived near the Ister [the lower Danube]; the latter loaded on wagons and carried inland products of the sea and wine stored in wooden jars (larger than houses) and also olive oil, whereas the [Italian traders] got in exchange slaves, cattle and hides."[13]

Caesar's tour of inspection was interrupted by a report from Publius Crassus of a conspiracy among the sea peoples of northwestern Gaul. The Veneti (Vannes), who controlled the trade with Britain, were alarmed at the expansion of Roman intervention in Gallic trade. They may have been particularly disturbed at an excursion by Publius Crassus to one of the tin-producing islands, during which he became aware of the possibility of profitable commercial operations. "The metals were being dug," he learned, "from only a slight depth and . . . the men there were peaceable." The Veneti were calling upon other tribes in independent Gaul "to choose rather to abide in the liberty received from their ancestors than to endure Roman slavery."[14] They detained officers sent by Publius to requisition grain and demanded the return of hostages previously delivered to him.

Caesar ordered the construction of warships on the Liger (the Loire) and the recruitment of oarsmen in the Province and of sailors and pilots elsewhere. He himself remained in Cisalpina concerned at the conflict developing between Crassus and Pompeius over the restoration of the king of Egypt. Expelled from Alexandria by subjects infuriated at his extortions to pay his debts to Roman moneylenders, Ptolemaios had fled to Italy and sought refuge with Pompeius. A delegation of a hundred leading citizens of Alexandria journeying to petition the Senate against the king was ambushed on the Appian Way and many were slain. When Pompeius attempted to address the people in the Forum, Clodius assembled his partisans and heckled the hero with a chorus of questions and responses:

"Who is the man that starved the people to death?" (An allusion to Pompeius' collusion with the grain merchants to advance his personal aspirations.)

"Pompeius!"

"Who is bent upon going to Alexandria?"

"Pompeius!"

"Whom do you want to go?"

"Crassus!"[15]

It was left to the gods to resolve the issue. Lightning struck a statue of Jupiter on the Alban Mount, a sanctuary sacred to the old Latin tribes, and priests entrusted with the interpretation of the Sibylline books (one of whom was Clodius) discovered an oracle warning against restoring the king "with a multitude" and decrying "anyone's wishing to go to Alexandria from a selfish desire for a military command. . . . Amazed at the coincidence between the verses and the events of the time," the Senate resolved to dispatch no army at all to Egypt, and Pompeius lost interest in the assignment. The Epicurean poet Lucretius sneered at such crass exploitation of superstition, exclaiming:

Why does [Jupiter] shatter holy shrines of the gods and even his own illustrious habitations with the fatal thunderbolt, why smash fine-wrought images of the gods and rob his own statues of their grandeur with a violent stroke? And why does he generally attack high places, why do we see on the mountain tops so many traces of his fire?[16]

In a frenzy of frustration, Pompeius cried that Crassus was planning to assassinate him, and to Caesar he complained that a series of plots were being hatched against his life, that the tribune who published the Sibylline verses was in collusion with Crassus and that Clodius had been suborned by Crassus and by leading optimates. Hard pressed by a populace "practically estranged from him, with a nobility hostile, a Senate unfairly prejudiced and the youth of the country without principle," to defend himself he was compelled to "call up men from rural districts." No one, he moaned, remembered his exertions in filling the seas with grain ships so that the semaphores never ceased blinking signals of the arrival of cargo vessels at the port of Puteoli. He won no gratitude for risking his life to guarantee the food supply though everyone had heard how when a captain refused to sail into a violent storm at a time of a grain emergency, Pompeius had proclaimed, "To sail is necessary, to live is not."[17]

CAESAR REVIVES THE ALLIANCE

At a distance of hundreds of miles, Caesar could only with difficulty fulfil his role as father-in-law, mollifying Pompeius as he had done during his consulship. Now he was hampered, too, by Cicero's maneuvering. Nonplussed at Clodius' new friendship with the optimates and under the illusion that the dissensions among powerful individuals and factions afforded him an opportunity to seize the leadership in the commonwealth, Cicero used his defense of the former tribune Sestius (indicted by Clodius in a politically motivated action) to remind Romans yet once again of his supposedly incomparable services to the republic and of his martyrdom as an exile. Reviving the slogans and charges of his consular orations, Cicero promulgated a new "harmony of the orders" in another attempt at rallying "the best people" against "subversion." This time he appealed not only to senators, equestrians and municipal aristocrats. "All are optimates," he proclaimed, "who are neither criminal nor vicious in disposition nor mad revolutionaries nor embarrassed by home troubles [debt]"; anyone was an optimate who sought civil "peace with honor" and was ready to defend "religious observances [like the sky-watching Caesar had defied during his consulship], the auspices, the authority of the Senate, the laws, ancestral custom, criminal and civil jurisdiction, credit, our provinces, our allies, the prestige of our government, the army, the treasury."[18]

As enemies of the republic Cicero classed all who "seek to cause revolution and changes of government; or who, owing to a sort of inborn revolutionary madness, batten on civil discord and sedition; or who, on account of embarrassment in their finances, prefer a general conflagration to their own ruin." Resisting all innovations, the "best people," Cicero insisted, "reject agrarian reform" as "an incentive to dissension" and out of the conviction that through any redivision of property "the state would be stripped of its champions by the eviction of the rich from their long-established tenancies"; optimates, according to Cicero, opposed the grain dole as "a call to the masses to desert industry for idleness and . . . a drain upon the treasury." (Caesar, of course, was the champion of the former and Clodius, of the latter "revolutionary madness.")

Persuaded that his recall from exile represented a mandate to renew the anti-subversive campaign of his consulship and oblivious to all the changes that had occurred since his consulship, Cicero once again lauded his crushing of the Catilinarians "as the grandest deed in the history of the human race." Reasserting himself as the Father of His Country, in his defense of Sestius he delivered a lengthy and vituperative diatribe against Caesar. Too prudent to assail Caesar directly, he attacked Caesar's collaborator Vatinius. Reviewing and rejecting all the legislation of Caesar's consulship, significantly Cicero singled out Vatinius' bill granting Caesar a five-year proconsulship—a warning to Caesar. Hardly Cicero's match in wit, Vatinius sneered at Cicero as "that consular buffoon" and mocked Cicero's boast that he had returned from exile on the shoulders of the people. "How then," asked Vatinius, "did you get those varicose veins in your legs?" (Cicero wore his toga long to hide his disfigurement.)[19] With such jibes Vatinius could not stem the general attack on Caesar which Cicero was provoking. Ahenobarbus, Cato's brother-in-law, a candidate for a consulship, declared his intention to recall Caesar from his command, and the optimates suborned a man from Gades to indict Caesar's agent Balbus on a charge of falsely claiming Roman citizenship.

With the triumvirate in dissolution, the optimates were able not only to threaten Caesar but also to attempt to neutralize Pompeius. When a temple on the Alban Mount supposedly shifted on its foundations; a blaze of light darted across the sky; a wolf was sighted in the city; thunderbolts struck citizens; and a subterranean rumbling signaled divine wrath—soothsayers warned against the triumvirs, particularly Pompeius, whom many were accusing of aspiring to a dictatorship. "Let not," declared the seers, "death and danger be wrought for the fathers [senators] and for statesmen by reason of the discord and division of the nobles and let them not be bereft of divine power; and let the state lapse not to the rule of one." With a variant of the optimate motto, they offered the admonition: "Change not the condition of the republic."[20]

With the diffidence of an Epicurean non-believer, Clodius, now in alliance with the optimates, seized upon the soothsayers' further warning that some god was angry because consecrated sites were being used as residences. He demanded that Cicero be brought to trial for razing the shrine to Liberty he had consecrated on the site of the orator's mansion. On April 4, as aedile in charge of the games to the Great Mother goddess, in a demonstration of his political power, Clodius assembled what Cicero described as "innumerable bands of slaves . . . from every quarter in the city" and loosed them in the theater during the performance of the sacred drama. Suddenly, according to Cicero, "from every archway and entry at a given signal they burst on to the stage" shouting for bread and reviling Pompeius, the commissioner of the grain supply, for the renewed famine.[21]

In a Senate debate "as rowdy as an open-air meeting,"[22] senators vacillated between fear of Clodius' rioters and alarm at bankrupting the treasury. Fear won out, and they appropriated 40 million sesterces to Pompeius for the replenishment of the granaries. To Balbus' dismay, a tribune in Pompeius' service complained of the loss of state revenues resulting from Caesar's distribution of the public lands in Campania and called for a review of Caesar's agrarian legislation. Cicero supported the tribune, and a debate was set for May 15, immediately after the spring recess.

Crassus departed from Rome.

Two days later Pompeius left the city. He informed Cicero he was going to Sardinia to expedite grain deliveries. Actually he journeyed north to Luca (Lucca), just across the border in the province of Cisalpina. Here he met with Caesar and Crassus along with Clodius' brother Appius and cousin Metellus Nepos. On hand, too, was a vast concourse of senators and magistrates (rumor spoke of two hundred senators and one hundred lictors), all eager to return to Rome "pockets full and hopes high."[23]

Renewing their alliance, the triumvirs divided the empire into spheres of influence and chose their candidates for magistracies for the next several years. To seal the agreement Pompeius engaged one of his sons to Appius' daughter and became thereby a connection of Clodius'. He also undertook the assignment of taming Cicero.

Upon the conclusion of the conference, assured of his security at least for the immediate future, Caesar, already overdue in repressing the rebellion of the Gallic sea peoples, set out across the Alps.

On May 15, the day appointed for a review of Caesar's agrarian legislation, Balbus reported that Cicero had absented himself from the Senate. The motion was tabled.

XXXIV
"SHATTER THE CONFINING BARS OF NATURE'S GATES . . ."

WITH the triumvirate restored, Clodius appeased and his enemies reduced to impotence, Caesar could return to what his foes called his policy of "alternately subduing the enemy with the arms of citizens and capturing and subduing the citizens with the money which he got from the enemy." Cicero, brought to heel by Pompeius, switched in attitude from insolent presumption to solemn subservience. Ignoring sneers from Caesar's enemies that "those who were getting so much money from Caesar urged the Senate to give him money as if he had none," Cicero steered passage of a bill authorizing the appointment of ten additional lieutenants to Caesar's staff as well as a special appropriation for the new legions Caesar had levied on his own during the previous two years, measures Cicero had denounced only a month earlier as "outrageous proposals." When Ahenobarbus moved the termination of Caesar's proconsulship, Cicero eloquently defended his new patron. In private, however, he chafed at his bonds. "Reckoned a madman if I speak on politics as I ought," he complained to Atticus, "a slave if I say what is expedient and a helpless captive if I say nothing—how am I to feel?" In the Senate, on the other hand, he offered no apology. "Can I," he asked of those who mocked him for his abrupt turnabout, "be the enemy of this man [Caesar] whose dispatches, whose fame, whose envoys fill my ears every day with fresh names of races, peoples, places?" Distinguishing between Caesar and others who had campaigned in Gaul, including his fellow townsman Marius, Cicero proclaimed that Caesar

> did not think that he ought to fight only against those whom he saw already in arms against the Roman people, but that the whole of Gaul should be brought under our sway. . . . From the very beginning of our empire we have had no wise statesman who did not regard Gaul as the greatest danger to our empire, but owing to the might and numbers of those peoples never before have we engaged in conflict with them as a whole. . . . Yet one or two summers and fear or hope, punishments or rewards, arms or laws can bind the whole of Gaul to us with eternal fetters.[1]

No patriotic Roman could oppose this aspiration!

"You have conferred many exceptional and almost unexampled honors upon Gaius Caesar," he noted in an attempt to inveigle other senators into sharing his "bondage." "If you did so because he deserved them," Cicero continued, "it was an act of gratitude; but if also it were to attach him most closely to this [senatorial] order, you therein showed more than mortal wisdom." Finally, in a display of humility that cost him dearly, he exonerated Caesar of blame for his exile and admitted that he himself had erred in rejecting Caesar's gestures of conciliation. "I have more reason to fear blame," he announced to an astonished Senate, "for my presumption in refusing his generous offers than he for the harm he did me notwithstanding our friendship."[2]

It appeared that Cicero had apprehended a new fact in Roman political life: henceforth no action would be taken in the city without regard to Caesar's wishes. The oligarchs had awaited with trepidation first Sulla's and then Pompeius' return as conquerors from the East; they now had to deal with a different military figure, one who maintained a dominating presence in the city even when far away.

Senators would hardly object to Cicero's declaration (certainly cleared in advance with Balbus) that after two years of campaigning Caesar had resolved to bind "the whole of Gaul with eternal fetters." In fact, like empire builders before and after him, Caesar discovered that the further he extended Rome's sphere of influence the more widely he had to range beyond the frontiers to assure the new Roman dependencies against potential aggressors. Of course, too, the further he advanced, the more Italian traders, who both preceded and followed the legions, pressed him to open additional territories. In addition, the more he encroached upon the ancient tin routes, the more resistance he could expect from states controlling these routes (prompted by their old trading partner, Massilia). In imposing Roman dominion over all of Gaul, Caesar anticipated ever-intensifying opposition. "All men," he declared in a statement that represented a personal credo as well as a political insight, "are naturally bent on liberty and hate the state of slavery."[3] Recognizing, therefore, the susceptibility of the Gallic states to the call of the sea peoples for a general revolt, Caesar divided his army, dispatching the lieutenant Sabinus against tribes along the Channel, Labienus to Belgian territory and Publius Crassus to Aquitania in the south. Following his practice of assigning ever greater responsibilities to young officers in whom he had particular trust, he appointed as commander of the newly constructed Roman fleet a young man for whom he, still without a son, harbored particular affection, Decimus Brutus, the twenty-five-year-old son of Sempronia, the cultivated lady who had opened her mansion to Catilina and the conspirators in 63.

The sea peoples proved a canny foe. As Caesar approached, the Veneti retired into strongholds erected at spits extending into the sea. As soon as Caesar readied assault engines, they withdrew at high tide on ships to a neighboring strongpoint, and Caesar was compelled to start anew with his siege works. Furthermore, advised of Caesar's concern about securing his food supply, they stripped their fields to deny him the possibility of living off the land. According to Caesar's intelligence, the sea peoples had assembled a fleet of some two hundred vessels. Decimus Brutus discovered that the speed of the oared Roman warships availed little against enemy vessels constructed of oak beams with crosspieces a foot thick fastened with nails "as thick as a thumb"—impervious to ramming. With their high prows and leather sails, the Gallic ships could "endure any violence and buffeting"[4] in stormy seas, and with their flat keels they could sail about even in the shallows. In addition, because of the lofty sterns of the Gallic craft, the Romans could not discharge missiles against them even from turrets erected on the decks of their warships. Caesar's previous victories had often depended upon Roman technology, and now legionary craftsmen contrived hooks affixed to long poles for grappling the halyards. When Roman oarsmen pulled forward at full speed, the hooked halyards would snap and the yards fall. Deprived of sail and tackle, the Gauls would drift helplessly.

Educated Romans would inevitably have compared Caesar's description of the naval engagement with the Veneti (the greatest ever fought on the Ocean) to Herodotus' description of the battle of Salamis. Even as Xerxes observed that titanic encounter between his Persian armada and the Greek fleets from a hill on the island of Salamis, so now "the engagement took place in sight of Caesar and the whole army so that no exploit a little more gallant than the rest could escape notice. The army, in fact, was occupying all the hills and higher ground from which there was a near view down upon the sea,"[5] and the legionaries serving as marines were aware that they were being watched by their fellows and by their commander. At first the battle raged indecisively, but suddenly the wind dropped; the oared warships converged on the Gallic vessels; the Romans drove hooks into the leather sails; and the legionaries boarded the enemy ships. Few escaped destruction or capture. The legionaries marveled at Caesar's fortuna, the good luck attending generals who enjoyed divine favor. Caesar and his staff, of course, recognized that Roman technological ingenuity had triumphed over Gallic conservatism. In decades of military decline the Gauls had proved not only incapable of unity against aggressors and deficient in perseverance for lengthy contests but also sluggish in evolving new strategies and in devising new weapons. On the other hand, in this campaign they had demonstrated that they had learned the folly of attempting a decisive engagement with the legions on land and had sought to exploit Caesar's logistical problems, insights that portended more effective resistance in future conflicts.

On the pretext that "the privilege of deputies [as he denominated the officers dispatched to requisition grain] might be more carefully preserved by the natives for the future," Caesar made a dreadful example of the Veneti; he "put the whole of their senate to the sword and sold the rest of the men as slaves." In the Channel states, where the legate Sabinus had won a victory at the same time as the naval battle, the uprising was directed not only against the foreign invader but also against the large landowners, and the commons led by ambitious nobles put to death their senators for opposing the rebellion. With thousands of the oppressed yearning for a cause or at least an opportunity to vent rancor and frustration, prosperous Gallic landowners confronted perils from both their own people and the foreign invader, and during the revolt of the sea peoples "from every corner of Gaul a great host of desperadoes and brigands . . . gathered whom the hope of plunder and the passion for war seduced from the daily toil of agriculture."[6]

While Caesar was pacifying the sea peoples, Publius Crassus was subjugating Aquitania. Very likely at their Luca conference in April Caesar and Marcus Crassus had discussed the potential profits from this mineral-rich region and had decided that Publius Crassus should be entrusted with opening the region to Roman exploitation. (In subsequent decades, the lands from the Pyrenees to the Garonne became a major supplier for Italy of silver, copper, lead, iron and gold.) Publius confronted a serious threat when the Aquitanians summoned from across the Pyrenees "men who had served . . . with Quintus Sertorius and were believed to be past masters of war,"[7] warriors who had adopted Roman practices like the construction of fortified camps and had also mastered guerrilla warfare. Through a ruse worthy of his commander-in-chief, young Crassus inflicted a devastating defeat upon his foes. With the conquest of the entire coast from the Gulf of Gascony almost to the Rhine, Caesar held command over nearly all the ports engaged in the tin trade, and Italian entrepreneurs at Narbo could hope to displace the Massiliots in this lucrative commerce.

Caesar still had to clear the coast westward from the Straits of Dover to the mouths of the Rhine. The primitive tribes of this region could not resist the Roman legions, nor could Caesar maintain control over peoples widely dispersed through difficult terrain. When the Gauls retreated into the wilderness, Caesar called upon his engineers. They cut swaths through the forest and constructed ramparts of timber to protect the flanks of Caesar's armies against enemy sorties. Caesar was handicapped, however, by the early arrival of autumn in this north country, and with the onset of seasonal storms he withdrew. To intimidate the tribes and to starve them into submission, he drove off their cattle, laid waste their fields and burned hamlets and isolated farms. Nevertheless, in this expedition Caesar had won no victory.

At the capital, denied his counsel, Caesar's partners were encountering stubborn resistance from their optimate foes. A hostile consul refused to register Crassus and Pompeius as candidates for the forthcoming consular elections, and when a tribune warned that he would retaliate by vetoing all elections for the remainder of the year, the consul exclaimed: "Applaud, Romans, as much as you still can. Soon you won't be able to do so without punishment." On the other hand, having disposed of the Cypriot royal holdings, Cato had returned. Informed that "all the magistrates and priests, the whole Senate and a large part of the people [had come] to the river to meet him so that both banks of the stream were hidden from view [and that] the consuls and praetors were at hand, he neither landed to greet them nor checked his course but on a royal galley of six banks of oars swept past the bank where they stood and did not stop until he brought his fleet to anchor in the dockyard."[8] After this boorish act of contempt for the magistrates and the populace, Cato rejected a Senate resolution awarding him an honorary praetorship and permission to wear a purple-bordered robe at all public spectacles. In a gesture of old-fashioned modesty, he requested as a reward for his services nothing more than the manumission of the former steward of the royal household, an act he could have undertaken on his own. He astonished the city by unloading for exhibition in the Forum several hundred crates, each containing fifty thousand sesterces in coin as well as varied treasures.

THE TRIUMVIRATE RESTORES ORDER

With Caesar at last free to attend to problems at Rome, the triumvirs could effect decisions taken at Luca. Caesar dispatched Publius Crassus to Rome with a detachment of legionaries to assure the election of his partners. In January 55, after the departure from office of the hostile consuls of 56, an interrex (a patrician senator selected by fellow patricians to hold belated consular elections) set a day for the vote. At dawn Ahenobarbus, the only candidate daring to compete against Pompeius and Crassus, set out for the Campus Martius accompanied by his brother-in-law Cato and a small entourage. On the way they were ambushed, their torchbearer slain and several of their company, including Cato, wounded. With Publius' legionaries standing guard, Pompeius and Crassus won election as consuls.

In the subsequent praetorian elections, upon the herald's announcement that Cato had carried the first century, Pompeius, who was presiding, declared that he had heard thunder and dismissed the assembly. During the next days by intensified bribery and intimidation, Pompeius and Crassus succeeded in gaining the election of Vatinius, the tribune who had collaborated so effectively with Caesar during Caesar's consulship. In a riot at the aedilician elections, Pompeius sent slaves home with garments drenched with blood. Julia, in advanced pregnancy, fainted at the sight and suffered a miscarriage. Thus the civil dissension cost Caesar his first grandchild and nearly deprived him of his only child. In their distraction, he and Pompeius (sincerely devoted to Julia, if to no one else) were united in a new bond of affection. Crassus and Pompeius, too, forgot old rivalries and took to visiting each other socially and to collaborating on every issue.

Following his consulship Pompeius was to receive the governorship of the Two Spains for a period of five years. He was to administer the provinces in absentia so that he might protect the interests of the triumvirate at home. Crassus obtained Syria, also for five years, with the right to conduct war against Parthia, a kingdom bordering upon Syria and the only great power threatening Rome on any frontier. When the tribune Trebonius presented a bill authorizing these special commands, Cato mobilized resistance. At dawn, the day the measure was to be put to a vote in a public assembly, Cato forced his way onto the Rostra. After a harangue of two hours, Trebonius sent an attendant to pull him down from the platform. Cato continued to shout from below, and Trebonius' men hustled him out of the area. When the Stoic pushed his way back, repeating the error Caesar had made several years earlier, Trebonius ordered him led off to prison. Accompanied by a great crowd, Cato went off willingly until Trebonius, belatedly, ordered his release. Voting was postponed. In a subsequent fracas the sexagenarian Crassus bloodied the nose of an optimate senator, several citizens were wounded and a few were slain. The bill did pass, as did another measure extending Caesar's proconsulship for an additional five years so that his command would continue as long as his partners'. Recalling Sulla's warning after Pompeius had assisted Lepidus to a consulship, Cato admonished the ever-suspicious Pompeius "that he was now taking Caesar upon his shoulders and that when he began to feel the burden, he would neither have the power to put it away nor the strength to bear it longer."[9]

With his position once again assured at Rome, Caesar returned to the task of securing the frontiers of his Gallic protectorate. With Gallic rebels soliciting reinforcements or seeking asylum beyond the Rhine and across the Channel, Caesar could not restrict his military operations to hostile border tribes. Lacking troops for investing thinly populated regions, he determined to make a show of Roman might to intimidate more distant peoples. When various rebellious Gallic states invited to their aid two German tribes, the Usipetes and the

Tencteri, who invaded the Rhine delta through a perfidious ruse (or so Caesar reported), Caesar summoned a conclave of Gallic chiefs. He announced a campaign against the Germans and assigned quotas of cavalry and grain.

With an arrogance like Ariovistus' three years earlier, envoys from the two German tribes announced that they would not "refuse the conflict of arms, for it was the ancestral custom of the Germans to resist anyone who made war upon them and not to beg off."[10] Caesar replied as the protector of newly subjugated Gaul, declaring that it was "not just for those who could not defend their own lands to seize those of others." He offered to settle the tribes beyond the Rhine in lands of another German people who had appealed for Caesar's protection against aggressive neighbors. Fearing treachery, Caesar rejected the request that he delay the advance of his legions. German cavalry surprised a squadron of Caesar's auxiliaries and bewildered the Gauls by leaping from their mounts to stab the Gallic steeds. In retaliation Caesar arrested a delegation of elders who came to apologize for the breach of the truce and immediately surprised the German encampment and slaughtered the men, women and children there.

Caesar's satisfaction at the swift conclusion to what he had feared would be a long and difficult campaign was dampened by news from Rome. With Pompeius preoccupied with preparations for the dedication of a huge theater complex he had begun to construct shortly after his return from the Mithridatic war and Crassus busy readying his campaign against the Parthians, the optimates elected Ahenobarbus to a consulship and Cato to a praetorship the following year, 54. Emboldened by these successes, enemies took to badgering Pompeius and Crassus. When at a trial of one of his close associates Pompeius arrogantly sneered that the plaintiff, a very old man, must have arisen from Hades to appear in court, the old man agreed and listed among the shades he had seen in the netherworld noblemen murdered by Pompeius during the civil war and the Lepidan revolt. The audience recalled Pompeius' old nickname, "the Young Butcher." Cicero undertook a scurrilous attack on Caesar's father-in-law, accusing Calpurnius, just returned from his governorship of Macedonia, of maltreatment of tax collectors and moneylenders and of military incompetence and mocking him with the stock charges against Epicureans. The young aristocrats who had badgered Caesar and Pompeius during Caesar's consulship renewed their sniping. Catullus, the poet from Verona, embittered at returning with an empty money chest after service with another provincial governor, reviled Calpurnius for similar niggardliness with Catullus' friends:

> From [Calpurnius] Piso's army, bankrupt, your equipment
> very light indeed (my Fabullus and best of
> good fellows, dear Veranius)
> you've served this keg of flat wine,
> this monster whose wages are starvation
> paid with winter's cold. How are your books, your ledgers!
> profits small? (Like mine, under my general . . .

Catullus resented the new men on Caesar's staff who flaunted their Gallic plunder, attacking particularly a certain Mamurra, who was adorning his house on the Caelian hill with a marble veneer, an ostentatious innovation:

> What a pair of pretty boys, Caesar and Mamurra,
> both decadent with secret lust . . .
> sick with the same diseases.
> See the loving twins abed,
> graced with the same learning and the same quick appetite
> for wives of other men. . . . [11]

A world away from the caviling and intrigues of the city, Caesar could not prod Crassus and Pompeius into displaying statesmanship beyond their capacities. He and his officers were exploring the strange country at the mouths of the Rhine; they found neither vines, olives nor fruit trees. The natives "fertilized the land with a white chalk" and employed instead of salt from mines or evaporated seawater "salty coals obtained by burning certain kinds of wood." Determined to exploit his recent victory, however, Caesar could not indulge his curiosity about such phenomena. "Even among the farthest tribes of Germany," he reported to the Senate, writing of himself, as was his custom, in the third person, "the renown and reputation of his army after the defeat of Ariovistus and the success of [his] last action" rendered tribes already under his protection "secure in the prestige and the friendship of Rome." One tribe across the Rhine, however, refused to deliver up fugitive Usipetes and Tencteri. "If he thought it unfair," they declared, "that the Germans should cross into Gaul against his will, why did he claim any imperial power across the Rhine?" [12]

Caesar determined that more than a military demonstration was required to impress these volatile and bellicose peoples. He decided to overawe the Germans with an unparalleled engineering feat, the report of which, he knew, would travel hundreds of miles on either side of the Rhine. He would construct a bridge at a point where the Rhine was four hundred yards wide and five to twenty-five feet deep (near modern Coblenz), an accomplishment beyond the imagination of the peoples of the region. Officers and men were assigned specific tasks, some to cut timber, others to construct machines—windlasses and cranes with block and tackle. Blacksmiths forged levers, spikes and nails. Piles eighteen inches thick, pointed at the end, were carried out on rafts and driven into the riverbed at intervals of two feet in parallel rows forty feet apart. Those downstream were slanted against the current, those upstream in the direction of the current. Couplings were so fixed that "the greater the force and thrust of the water, the tighter were the balks held in lock." [13] A further row of piles was sunk downstream to retard the force of the river and yet another row of fenders upstream to ward against ramming by logs or vessels released by the enemy.

Ten days after the felling of the first timbers the bridge stood ready, a marvel of Roman technological genius and an example of the superior efficiency of free men engaged in a common purpose over the forced labor of slaves. Establishing garrisons at both ends of the bridge, Caesar advanced across the river. Word of the wondrous engineering feat preceded him, and the peoples of the region, including the powerful Suebi, withdrew into the wilderness. Within days Caesar retired. He "had accomplished all the objects for which he had determined to lead his army across the Rhine—to strike terror into the Germans, to take vengeance on the Sugambri, to deliver the Ubii [his clients among the Germans] from a state of blockade."[14]

Caesar turned north, 'to the Channel. Although only a few weeks remained of summer in a part of the world where winters commenced early, he adjudged it "of great advantage to him merely to have entered [Britain], observed the character of the natives and obtained some knowledge of the localities, the harbors, and the landing places." For Italians the island was of incredible magnitude, while others "averred that its name and story had been fabricated since it never existed." Although Caesar interrogated traders from all parts, he could discover "neither the size of the island nor the number or power of the tribes inhabiting it, nor their manner of warfare, nor the ordinances they observed, nor the harbors suitable for a number of large ships." Resentful of Caesar's interference in the profitable tin trade, seamen and traders, Gauls and Massiliots, jealously guarded such information. Their silence merely encouraged Caesar. Like Odysseus riding off to the land of the Cyclops, he was eager to

> find out what the mainland natives are—
> for they may be wild savages and lawless
> or hospitable and god-fearing men.

Like his Homeric exemplar, Caesar dispatched a scout to reconnoiter along the coast. He himself marched his forces to ports at the point of "shortest passage to Britain"[15] and summoned ships from the neighboring coastal states along with the fleet he had employed against the Veneti.

Informed of Caesar's preparations, the Britons sent deputies to offer hostages and to express their willingness to accept Roman protection. In response Caesar dispatched Commius, a chief he had set as king over a Belgian tribe, a man with many connections in the island, where "his influence was reckoned to be of great account." Caesar embarked two legions on eighty transports and ordered the cavalry to follow on eighteen other ships awaiting a favorable wind down the coast. Sailing at midnight in fair weather, Caesar and his fleet reached Britain in the morning. He found the Britons massed on the cliffs. When he moved some seven miles down the coast, the Britons followed. The legionaries confronted novel battle conditions. Hampered by their packs as they pushed through the surf, the troops were harried by enemy horsemen and missiles. Caesar lined up warships along the enemy's flank and directed fire from scorpions, catapults for rapid firing of arrows (the Roman equivalent of machine guns), and ballistas, which hurled stone balls of fifteen or more pounds. What proved decisive, however, was the spirit of emulation Caesar had engendered among his men in four years of campaigning. The eaglebearer of the crack Xth legion cried out a prayer to the gods and then exhorted his comrades. "Leap down, soldiers," he shouted, "unless you wish to betray your eagle to the enemy; it shall be told that I at any rate did my duty to my country and my general." Thereupon he jumped from the ship and pushed forward. When they saw their eagle moving toward the beach, "the troops exhorted one another not to allow so dire a disgrace [as the capture of their standard] and leaped down from the ship with one accord. When the troops on the nearest ship saw them, they likewise followed on."[16]

With Caesar deploying small boats to bring assistance to hard-pressed units, the legionaries charged. The enemy fled. They requested terms and offered to deliver hostages. Commius, Caesar's Belgian envoy, who had been detained and thrown into chains, was released. The enemy chiefs blamed the commons for provoking the hostilities, and they dispersed their forces.

Even the most brilliant general has no command over the vicissitudes of fortune. A sudden storm dispersed the cavalry transports en route from the Continent and swamped many of the ships on the beach. Caesar had read Posidonios' observation that "the movement of the ocean is subject to periods like those of the heavenly bodies" and that "when the moon rises above the horizon to the extent of a zodiacal sign [thirty degrees], the sea begins to swell." This night, indeed, "the moon was full, the day of the month which usually makes the highest tides in the Ocean." Although men had speculated on the effect of latitude on climate and waters, no Greek or Roman had ever studied the tides or the weather on the Channel. Possibly inspired by Caesar's venture into the far north, the poet Lucretius asked:

> Do you not see also that novelty of climate and water affects any who travel far from home and country just because there is a great difference in these things? For what difference in these things must we suppose to be between the climate of Britain and that of Egypt, where the world's pole leans aslant?[17]

In his haste to invade Britain before the advent of bad weather, Caesar had failed to stock materials to repair storm-damaged ships or to assure a grain reserve. Legionaries sent to forage suffered harassment from the Britons, who hurled missiles from speeding chariots or leaped to the ground for hand-to-hand combat and then retired on their chariots to regroup for a fresh assault. Like Homeric Greeks, the Britons enjoyed both "the mobility of cavalry and the stability of infantry." They galloped down the steepest slopes, stopped short and whirled about. The warriors were able to "run along the pole, stand on the yoke and quick as lightning to dart back into the chariot."[18] In pitched battles, however, the legionaries easily worsted the Britons. Once again they sued for peace, promising hostages. Having repaired a sufficient number of his ships, Caesar weighed anchor late one night and brought all his transports and men-of-war safely across the Channel.

Despite the near misadventure, Caesar professed satisfaction with his achievement. As in the lands across the Rhine he had displayed Roman might, learned something of the country, of the people and of their mode of warfare. He would be better prepared for a more extensive incursion during the next year.

On the continent Caesar found letters describing the magnificent ceremonies in the dedication of Pompeius' theater. Seating almost eighteen thousand, the structure was an architectural marvel. Eminent artists had decorated the walls with reliefs, and the entire compound was adorned with statuary. In an adjoining portico, Pompeius exhibited masterpieces by famous painters. Fourteen mammoth statues representing the various peoples of the empire surrounded the theater with a statue of Pompeius in their midst. A temple to Venus the Victorious dominated the interior, while a meeting house for the Senate formed part of the lower area. (Here Caesar would be assassinated.)

Poor Pompeius, how often he fumbled in moments of triumph! Aesopus, the leading tragic actor of the previous generation, lost his voice on stage. Sophisticated Romans scoffed at the pretension in parading six hundred mules along with an army of infantry and cavalry during a representation of the Agamemnon legend and in drawing forth from a Trojan horse three thousand bowls. Although people delighted in the first rhinoceros ever exhibited in the city and in Gallic lynxes Caesar sent for the occasion and no one objected to the slaying of five hundred lions, in a battle between twenty elephants and Africans armed with javelins the spectators were terrified when the great beasts stampeded against the palisade enclosure. One elephant, forced to its knees by darts, crawled about and snatched shields from its tormentors and tossed men into the air; another, struck in the eye, fell dead with a terrifying crash. Men of sensibility wondered "what pleasure can it possibly be to a man of culture when either a puny human being is mangled by a most powerful beast or a splendid beast is transfixed with a hunting spear?" Most of the elephants refused to fight and strode about "with trunks raised toward heaven lamenting . . . and calling upon heaven to avenge them," and at the eerie wailing of the great beasts the public "bursting into tears rose in a body and invoked curses on the head of Pompeius," for the animals inspired "a certain compassion and a . . . feeling [of] fellowship with the human race."[19]

Unable to vie with Pompeius in splendid games or in the dedication of an imposing theater, Caesar roused wonderment in communiqués, penned as usual with consummate artistry, describing the rout of ferocious Germans and a peerless feat of engineering—the Rhine bridge. By crossing the mighty river into an uncharted wilderness and by braving waves and storms in a descent upon a mysterious and fearful land, Caesar challenged nature itself. With his compelling spirit he rallied stockish rustics who had never traveled beyond the nearest market town to share his zest in testing the world. To Epicureans, with their enthusiasm for exploration, Caesar seemed to rival the Master himself, Epicurus, of whom Lucretius sang:

neither fables or the gods could quell him nor thunderbolts nor heaven with menacing roar, nay all the more they goaded the eager courage of his soul so that he should desire first of all men to shatter the confining bars of nature's gates.[20]

Indignant at the rapture over Caesar's exploits, Cato rose in the Senate and accused Caesar of a breach of divine law in the massacre of the Usipetes and Tencteri. He demanded that Caesar be delivered over to the Germans in order to "purge away the violation of the truce in behalf of the city and to turn the curse therefore on the guilty man."[21] The Senate ignored the cantankerous Stoic and decreed a thanksgiving of twenty days in Caesar's honor, five days longer than the unprecedented thanksgiving of the previous year.

XXXV
"MIGHTY IN HONOR AND FAME"

CAESAR never learned to suffer fools gladly, and no one exasperated him more than the Man of Virtue, who had opposed his every action since his speech against the execution of the Catilinarian conspirators and continually threatened to annul his consular legislative program and to recall him from his command. In response to Cato's accusation of perfidy in connection with the massacre of the Usipetes and Tencteri, Caesar sent off a vituperative letter with snide remarks about a curious marital arrangement Cato had recently made with Hortensius. Cato had divorced his pregnant wife in order that the old orator, a widower, might marry her and father an heir (he was alienated from his only son). Cato dismissed Caesar's accusations as "childishness and vulgarity," and he used the occasion to warn "that it was not the sons of Germans or Celts whom [the senators] must fear but Caesar himself."[1]

Once again the triumvirs were on the defensive, with Crassus the chief object of optimate sniping. Ebullient as a schoolboy, the millionaire, a partially deaf sexagenarian, was boasting that in his forthcoming war against the Parthians he would "make the campaigns of Lucullus against Tigranes [king of Armenia] and those of Pompeius against Mithridates seem mere child's play." Intoxicated with visions of glory, he "flew on the wings of his hopes as far as Bactria and India and the Outer Sea." Suspicious of a new war of conquest affording disproportionate prestige and power to another warlord, especially one of the triumvirs, the optimates played upon the war weariness of the commons and encouraged resistance to new levies. Popular leaders exhorted the people to oppose a war against a state that had done Rome no harm. So intense was the hostility against him that Crassus appealed to Pompeius to walk with him as he departed from the city. At the gate they encountered a tribune with a blazing brazier into which he "cast incense and libations . . . and invoked curses which were dreadful and terrifying." Champing for combat, Crassus embarked his troops in November, after the sailing season. As legionaries filed into the transports at Brundisium, they were frightened at the cry of a hawker of Caunian figs, "Cauneas, cauneas," which sounded ominously like the Latin for "Beware of going."[2] In fact, in the stormy Adriatic Crassus lost several vessels with the legionaries on board.

Upon Crassus' departure, the optimates fueled Pompeius' jealousy of Caesar's military successes. At Rome Caesar's chief resource against Pompeius' instability was Julia, pregnant again and expecting to give birth in the summer. Of course, continuing victories in Gaul offered the firmest guarantee for Caesar's long-range security. Before leaving for winter quarters in Cisalpina, Caesar ordered the repair and construction of ships for a second expedition into Britain. From the war against the sea peoples and the invasion of Britain, Caesar had learned much about naval engineering, and he assisted in designing ships adapted to the winds and tides of the Channel. "For speed of loading and for purposes of beaching," he reported to the Senate, "he would build them somewhat lower than those which we are accustomed to use on our own sea— and the more so because he had learned that by reason of the frequent turns of the tides the waves off Gaul are generally smaller. For the transport of cargo and of the numerous draft animals, he would have the ships somewhat broader than those we use on the other seas. All of them he ordered to be fitted for oars as well as sails, to which end their lowness of build helped much."[3]

Having thus provided for another invasion of Britain, Caesar set out for Cisalpina to attend to the affairs of that province and to events at Rome. Appius Claudius, Publius' brother and father-in-law to one of Pompeius' sons, served as a counterbalance to the other consul, Caesar's foe Ahenobarbus. The winter was so bitter that senators could hardly sit still for squabbling, and on February 12 Appius adjourned the Senate in response to the whimpering of the few frozen senators who ventured forth that morning. In addition, Caesar now enjoyed almost universal admiration. Quintus Cicero, for example, resigned from Pompeius' grain commission to join Caesar's staff and urged his orator brother to shift his primary allegiance from Pompeius to Caesar. Informed of Quintus' counsel, Caesar instructed Balbus to grant Marcus Cicero, like other oligarchs always short of cash for real estate transactions and for expenditures on luxuries, a loan of 800 thousand sesterces at less than one per cent interest, and Caesar appealed directly to Cicero to propose protégés for commissions in the Army of Gaul. Always susceptible to flattery, Cicero, who had until then served Caesar with reluctance, made another of his reversals, assuring Quintus (who either reported his brother's words or showed his letters to Caesar) that he had "long been singing the praises of your friend" and called Caesar "my bosom friend." Caesar proceeded to overwhelm the orator with unsolicited benefactions. Cicero was captivated. "I was having quite a serious conversation at my house with our friend Balbus," he wrote to Caesar, "about this very Trebatius [a protégé of Cicero's], when I am handed a letter from you at the end of which were the words, 'As to the Marcus Rufus [another protégé] you recommend to me, I will e'en make him a king of the Gauls. . . . If you care to do so, send me somebody else to give a post to.' Balbus and I both raised our hands. So marvelously opportune was it that it struck us as something that was not mere luck but an intervention of the gods. [A cynic might have wondered how great was Balbus' surprise at this coincidence.] I therefore send you Trebatius."[4]

Extraordinary was the reversal of sentiment among the young intellectuals who had long been badgering Caesar in limericks and pamphlets. Wearying of anarchic rebellion and disgusted by the mulish resistance to change among the optimates and the incapacity of the reactionaries to make connections among disparate aspects of social and political life or to entertain imaginative reforms directed to their own long-range security, these young people had come to recognize that among the leading figures of the republic Caesar alone was receptive to new ideas and capable of a comprehensive view of a world in dynamic evolution. He revived their sense of the Roman historical mission in his expedition beyond the horizon of the known world to an island as mysterious as the moon, and he disarmed them by his good-humored response to their sniping and by his general civility.

Forty-six, Caesar would ordinarily have been accounted one of "the enemy" by young people suspicious of the older generation. No long-faced graybeard, however, Caesar matched any youth half his age in zest for life and in curiosity about the universe. A bon vivant and something of an exquisite when away from the front lines, Caesar was not given to lecturing young people on their behavior, values or aspirations. He left such preachments to Cato and Cicero. In a court speech of this time, ironically in defense of one of the fast young set, Cicero delivered a manifesto of the graybeards, proclaiming:

> For myself if there ever was a man of mind strong enough of character sufficiently virtuous and self-controlled, to despise all pleasures and spend the whole course of his life in bodily labor and mental exertion; to be insensible to the attractions of rest, of relaxation, of the pursuits of his friends, of love affairs and festivities; to think that nothing in life was worth striving for unless it was united with glory and honor—such a man, in my judgment, I hold to have been endowed and blessed with virtues greater than human.

But young intellectuals scoffed at "virtues greater than human" and aspired to "pleasures, rest, relaxation, friends, love affairs and festivities," and Cicero lamented that "virtues of this kind are no longer to be found in our manners, indeed, but rarely in our books." To his dismay, "some have said that they would do everything for the sake of pleasure, and learned men have not shrunk from this . . . statement."[5]

The "learned men" to whom Cicero was referring were, of course, the Epicureans, who posited pleasure as the prime motive in life and advocated an unremitting reevaluation of religion, morality, culture and life-style. Unlike Cicero, Caesar, in constant opposition in his own youth, appreciated the iconoclasm of the youth of the day. Alienated from public life and disillusioned about the greed, unbounded ambition and corruption of their elders, bright young aristocrats gave themselves over to immediate gratification, rejecting discipline, rootless, promiscuous, self-indulgent and socially unproductive. Except for the arts! In poetry and oratory, paradoxically, they practiced meticulous craftsmanship and displayed a learning bordering on pedantry. If they professed Epicureanism in defiance of the Stoicism of their elders, they employed it to effect a revolution in sensibility. They explored the gamut of emotions and defined and illuminated and expanded the scope of their passions and of their imaginations. Obsessed with the necessity for a radical transformation in social values and perceptions, they responded enthusiastically to Epicurean atomism, the theory of matter in constant change.

Caesar sensed a world in birth in the attempts of the young poets to force language to new levels of perception, to a revelation of reality behind slogans and pretensions. The visual arts, too, aspired to the representation of new dimensions of experience. Mural painters were exploring perspective and the interplay of light and shadow in subjects evoking deeper emotions and a new excitement about man and nature. In portraiture sculptors, eclectic in their searchings, were investigating the elusive in personality and evoking inner conflict and growth, strength mixed with weakness, distinguishing through selective detail the uniqueness of their subjects. Like poets and painters they probed for the essence of experience, as though exposing the atoms of which all matter was composed. In music the shift in taste was most apparent. Oldsters like Cicero observed in chagrin "that audiences which used to be deeply affected by the inspiring sternness of the music of Livius and Naevius [classic composers of the past], now leap up and twist their necks and turn their eyes in time with our modern tunes."[6]

In oratory Calvus, son of the radical tribune Macer, with whom Caesar had associated himself in his youth, was the chief exponent of a new direction, Atticism. Adopting as models not the magniloquent Demosthenes (Cicero's idol) but lesser Athenian orators renowned for the spare grace of their speech, Calvus and his friends aimed not so much at winning a case or manipulating an audience as persuading with rational argument. Like the artists in the other media they strove to expose the essence of reality. They found much to admire in Caesar. Second only to Cicero in the Forum, Caesar was renowned for "his force, his penetration and his energy" and accounted "as vigorous in speech as in his conduct of war," and "all these qualities [were] enhanced by a marvelous elegance of language," accomplishments certain to win the applause of Calvus' circle. Caesar's war communiqués exhibited similar strengths, affording an impression of "nude figures, straight and beautiful; stripped of all ornament of style as if they had laid aside a garment"; he delighted his audiences with "a brevity clear and correct."[7]

Whether impelled by a transformation in the mood of the times, by a new maturity as they grew older or by admiration for Caesar's exploits at the Rhine and in Britain, the "new" poets, as they were called, shifted in their attitude toward Caesar. (A Transalpine poet had already written a florid epic celebrating Caesar's first year in Gaul.) Apprized that Calvus desired his friendship, Caesar wrote and expressed an equal desire, and the two men forgot past harsh words. In Verona Calvus' friend Catullus, whose father was discomfited by the young man's acidulous verses about Caesar and Caesar's officers, apologized to Caesar and was immediately invited to dinner. Reconciled with these two, Caesar also won the friendship of others in their circle. These young people took seriously the Epicurean exaltation of friendship. Catullus, for example, devoted much of his verse to his friends. In one poem he described the talented litterateur Asinius Pollio (a young man in his early twenties) as "a pretty fellow, sweet, delicate and faultless in all his blandishments"; he spoke of his fellow poet as "the delightful Calvus" and expressed sorrow at receiving no communication from his "friend Cornificius," another young man of letters. He praised a long esoteric mythological poem by Helvius Cinna (a work of nine years' labor), speaking of it as "immortal music." (Asinius Pollio, Cornificius and Helvius Cinna were all to enter Caesar's service in posts of responsibility; Calvus and Catullus died early. Pollio rejoiced that though he was very young Caesar immediately "treated [him] as one of his oldest friends," and he himself reciprocated with an "esteem . . . based on the deepest devotion and loyalty.")[8]

Caesar (and the many Epicureans in his entourage) would eagerly discuss with Catullus and Catullus' friends the outstanding artistic event of the year, if not of the century—the publication of Lucretius' On the Nature of Things, the greatest scientific poem in the Latin language and very likely the greatest Latin poetic work until this time. In February Quintus Cicero had corresponded with his brother about Lucretius' six-book epic on the philosophy of Epicurus, and the orator, whose sympathies hardly lay with Lucretius' thought, replied to Quintus' exuberance with the restrained comment that the poetry exhibited "little original genius but much artistic skill." Although Caesar would respond with especial enthusiasm to the passion for scientific inquiry informing Lucretius' epic and would delight in the poet's wide-ranging speculations in support of the Epicurean atomic theory as well as his polemics against superstition, with Catullus it is more likely he discussed Lucretius' style and diction, subjects of intense interest to men whose education consisted primarily in the art of oratory. Unlike Catullus and the other "new" poets, Lucretius held to the Homeric dactylic hexameter and employed archaisms in diction and morphology (word forms), but in common with the younger poets, Lucretius strove to expand the expressive capacity of the Latin language and complained of "the poverty of our mother tongue" in comparison with the supple Greek.[9] Such questions Caesar and Catullus' circle would have investigated in relation to another significant work published only months earlier, Cicero's On the Orator, a Roman adaptation of the teachings of Aristotle and other Greek rhetoricians and a brilliant exploration of the style of oratory that had attained its zenith in Cicero's own practice, a style in which the decisive criterion was persuasion, with validity or equity as secondary considerations.

Differing fundamentally in world outlook from Cicero and perhaps inspired by conversations with intellectuals in Cisalpina, Caesar determined to compose a rejoinder. After years among peoples of minimal literacy, he must have participated with zest in exchanges with the young poets. Other circumstances, too, motivated him to write on language. Aurelia died. Renowned for her exquisite speech, she had inspired Caesar to make of himself, in Cicero's judgment, "the purest user of the Latin tongue." Upon news of her death, Caesar recalled, of course, his childhood and thought of his tutor of those years, Antonius Gnipho, the author of a work on the Latin language entitled On Analogy and a man who influenced Caesar "to bring to perfection the merit of correct speech by diligent and enthusiastic studies of a recondite and esoteric kind."[10] Nevertheless, Caesar devoted no time to any activity that did not provide political advantage, and he recognized that adding an intellectual dimension to his reputation would enhance his prestige among a significant segment of the citizenry, including but also transcending the circle of young intellectuals about Catullus and Calvus. Surely Cicero and Varro, the outstanding Roman intellectuals along with Caesar, would be impressed to find Caesar competing with them in their own specialized fields.

Before attending to this creative effort, however, Caesar journeyed to Illyricum to deal with barbarian incursions. Preceded by the fame of his recent exploits—the annihilation of tribes renowned for their courage and ferocity, the construction of a wondrous bridge across the Rhine and the descent with a great armada upon Britain—Caesar on this occasion did not have to demonstrate Roman might to barbarian tribesmen. The marauders sent an offer of reparations, and Caesar resolved a worrisome situation without the force of arms, a resolution of a problem he hoped to repeat in Gaul.

As he hastened back across Cisalpina and through the Alps into the Province, Caesar dictated the work upon which he had been meditating, two volumes entitled like Gnipho's study, On Analogy, "a careful treatise on the principles of correct Latinity" based on the concept "that the choice of words was the foundation of eloquence." Caesar exhorted Romans "to avoid as the sailor would a rock a strange and unfamiliar word" and proposed rules in grammar and syntax such as had been established centuries earlier by Greek scholars for their language. Cultivated Romans were alarmed at the deterioration of Latin as a result of a general lapse in intellectual discipline and of "the influx of many impure speakers coming from different places," for immigration into Italy had "created a situation which called for a purge of language and the invoking of theory as an objective control or touchstone not subject to change like the easily distorted rule of common usage."[11] Caesar expounded the analogist view of language, an approach congenial to Epicureans, as against the anomalist, which appealed to the Stoics. Characteristically, the Stoics viewed linguistics with philosophic idealism, preaching that language development followed a preexistent principle. Analogists, on the other hand, held the view that language like other phenomena was in constant flux, and they set linguistic evolution in a perspective of dynamic social change. In effect, Caesar reflected the thinking of forward-looking intellectuals like the young men of Catullus' circle. He expressed himself as their theoretician, producing for them a manifesto for refining language to achieve greater precision in reflecting reality.

Despite his ideological differences with Cicero, Caesar maintained good-humored banter with the orator during the weeks he was planning and composing his monograph. Thus in writing about a protégé he was sending to join Caesar's staff, Cicero noted amicably: "As to his character, I guarantee you this—not using that hackneyed expression which you rightly ridiculed when I wrote to you [recently] . . . but in the good old Roman style, which is the speech of men of the world." No dogmatist, Caesar recognized the orator's achievements, and with diplomatic finesse he dedicated his treatise to Cicero in a generous and modest statement that did not ignore the contradictions between them. "If to the task of giving brilliant and oratorical expression to their thought," he wrote, "some have devoted unremitting study and practice, where we must recognize that you, as almost the pioneer and inventor of eloquence, have deserved well of the name and prestige of Rome—yet are we therefore to look upon a mastery of the easy and familiar speech of daily life as a thing that now may be neglected?"[12]

Moved by Caesar's graciousness in dedicating to him a work produced "in the midst of the most absorbing activities,"[13] Cicero, now completely captivated by Caesar, informed Quintus of his intention of celebrating in an epic poem Caesar's forthcoming invasion of Britain.

XXXVI

NEW VICTORIES, NEW GLORY

IN planning a second invasion of Britain, Caesar's officers and men shared that spirit of adventure that Lucretius attributed, intellectually, to Epicurus: "Forth he marched far beyond the flaming walls of the heavens, as he traversed the immeasurable universe in thought and imagination." Arriving at the Channel, Caesar discovered that "by the exemplary energy of the soldiers and in spite of the utmost lack of all necessaries," six hundred transports and twenty-eight men-of-war were nearly ready for the expedition. On the other hand, Caesar faced new contumacy among the Gauls, for his interventions into the domestic politics of the states involved a delicate balancing that required constant attention. Among the Treveri (Trier), where a certain Indutiomarus and his son-in-law Cingetorix were competing for leadership, Caesar decided that it was "of great importance that the authority of one whose signal goodwill towards himself he had fully proved should be as strong as possible among his folk" and he supported the younger man.[1] Though Indutiomarus delivered hostages as a warrant of his submission, Caesar was aware that the old chieftain commanded considerable influence within the tribe and that he would nurture rancor for the rebuff.

To assure the loyalty of the Gallic states generally, Caesar ordered all the chiefs to join in the invasion, excepting only those few "whose loyalty towards himself he had proved . . . taking the rest with him by way of hostages because he feared a rising in Gaul during his own absence." Even among the Aeduans, his principal clients, he was encountering disaffection. Dumnorix, brother to Caesar's chief counselor among the Gauls, the recently deceased(?) Diviciacus, petitioned for permission to remain in Gaul, and Caesar's informants reported that he was warning other chiefs that Caesar was "stripping Gaul of all her nobility" so as "to transport to Britain and there slaughter all whom he feared to put to death in the sight of Gaul." At the time of embarkation the Aeduan chieftain fled with his clients. Caesar ordered pursuit, and Dumnorix was slain "crying repeatedly that he was a free man and of a free state."[2] His defiance provided a warning of the fragility of the loyalty Caesar enjoyed even within a favored state.

More than the tranquility of Gaul hung upon Caesar's success in this new invasion of Britain. Rome was in turmoil over the worst electoral scandal in its history. So lavish was the bribery in the consular election campaign that usurers drained their money chests, and on July 15, 54, interest rates doubled from four to eight per cent and credit evaporated. Pompeius' agents were whispering that a dictatorship afforded the only alternative to anarchy, and his son-in-law, Faustus Sulla, son of the late dictator, issued a coin showing a globe surrounded by three wreaths, one for each of the warlord's triumphs, topped by a fourth wreath jeweled and bound with a fillet, a symbol of royalty. Against the threat of a coup, Caesar could do nothing more from his command post on the Channel than to instruct Balbus to announce a vast public works program to confirm his prestige and the goodwill of entrepreneurs and construction workers. To assure himself of Cicero's continuing loyalty, Caesar invited the orator to collaborate with the banker Oppius in supervising the program, which included the construction of a new Forum adjoining the cluttered old one, a basilica in the old Forum and a vast marble hall to accommodate the voting assemblies in the Campus Martius, edifices that would remind Romans day by day of Caesar's claim to a leading role in the political life of the city.

In the new invasion of Britain, Caesar used to advantage the experience of the previous year. Not only was he well supplied with transports and warships of superior design and armed with information about winds, tides and the lay of the coast, but, in addition, he was not pressed for time and could proceed with prudent deliberation. As he approached the island with an armada of some eight hundred vessels, the awed Britons withdrew into the hinterland. Upon landing, Caesar advanced at once and routed the enemy. Again fortune intervened. In a violent storm anchors and cables gave way under wind and breakers, and forty vessels were destroyed.

Caesar found satisfaction in the impact at Rome of the news of his landing and initial success. Quintus Cicero, engaged in a fraternal controversy with Marcus as to which of them should record Caesar's exploits in verse, showed Caesar a letter in which his orator brother exclaimed: "What encampments, what natural characteristics of things and places, what manners and customs, what tribes and what battles you have to write about and, finally, what a man in your com- mander-in-chief himself!" Aware that Romans shared his own curiosity about the ethnology and geography of this mysterious country, Caesar included in his reports disquisitions about the people and the land, describing a matrilinear society in which men had wives in common and the population subsisted on milk and flesh, covered their nakedness with animal skins and dyed their skins with blue woad to terrify their foes. For the entrepreneurs back home Caesar expatiated on the tin, iron and timber resources. He noted that parts of the island were thickly settled with farmhouses one upon another. Cattle raising was a major industry, and the more advanced tribes employed bronze or gold coins or iron tallies. As to the particulars of the geography, Caesar's informants were vague. Checking the assertion of certain Greek writers that in islands off the coast "the midwinter night lasts for thirty whole days," Caesar "could discover nothing . . . by inquiries," but he was impelled by his own interest in the sciences and perhaps inspired by Lucretius' injunction:

> Wherefore we must lay down right principles concerning things celestial, how the courses of sun and moon come about and by what power all is done upon earth.[3]

He conducted an experiment on the relationship of latitude to the length of the day. Scientists in Alexandria had measured the diameter of the sun by compar- ing the quantity of water flowing from a water clock from the moment of sunrise to the complete appearance of the sun above the horizon with the amount collected during an entire day. By similar measurements Caesar deter- mined that summer nights in Britain were shorter than on the Continent.

Encouraged by the disaster suffered by Caesar's fleet, the Britons regrouped. The heavily armed legionaries could not pursue the chariots, and Caesar's cavalry was worsted when the Britons leaped from their chariots to fight as infantry. In response, Caesar coordinated the movement of cavalry and legionaries. Foiled by this tactic the Britons massed on the far side of the Thames, fortifying the bank and shallows with stakes, while Kentish chieftains assailed Caesar's coastal base and cut his communications with the mainland. Against the superstitious barbarians Caesar set in the van of his forces an elephant he had imported for just such a situation. Terrified by the élan of the legionaries and by the strange monster, the Britons fled. After deploying some four thousand chariots in a brief and unsuccessful attempt at guerrilla warfare and confronting defections promoted by Caesar's diplomacy, the leader of the Britons sued for peace. Caesar had accomplished his purpose. He had frightened the islanders from supporting rebellion on the Continent or from offering asylum to Gallic insurgents, and he had opened the island to Italian traders. A generation later the geographer Strabo reported: "[The Britons] submit so easily to heavy duties, both on the exports from there to Celtica [Gaul] and on the imports from Celtica . . . that there is no need of garrisoning the island."[4] Strabo mentions exports from the island of grain, cattle, gold, silver, iron, tin, slaves and hunting dogs.

Hastening to anticipate the autumn storms, Caesar sailed away with all his troops.

DISQUIETING PORTENTS

Caesar's satisfaction with his police action in Britain evaporated upon reading letters awaiting him on the Continent.

Julia had died in childbirth and her infant only days thereafter.

At the conclusion of the funeral service in the Forum, just as the bier was about to be transported to Pompeius' villa in the Alban hills, distraught citizens, moved by affection for Caesar and Pompeius or by an intimation of the threat to civil peace in Julia's death, seized the bier and carried it to the Campus Martius. Deaf to the admonitions of the consul Ahenobarbus that it was "sacrilegious for her to be buried in the sacred spot without a special decree," they honored Julia as only Sulla had been honored before her.[5]

Almost a decade earlier in his speech in opposition to the execution of the Catilinarian conspirators, Caesar had proclaimed the Epicurean view that death signified annihilation of body and soul. All matter was in flux, with birth and death an unremitting process. Sorrow availed not and represented self-pity rather than grief, and since death was a constant reality on the battlefield, Caesar could claim no special dispensation in his private loss. Indeed, he exhibited "courage and dignity in the midst of his intense sorrow."[6] In a letter to be read in the Forum, he promised funeral games in Julia's memory.

Meanwhile, at Rome in a series of factionally inspired trials oligarchs were employing the courts to conduct private vendettas. Out of private rancor, for example, Caesar's mistress Servilia was abetting the prosecution of Sulla's stepson Scaurus on a charge of extortion as governor of Sardinia. Tempers were short because of an intense heat wave. Cato, the presiding praetor, appeared at the tribunal barefoot and without a tunic, alleging that he was wearing the attire of the ancestors as represented in old statues, but enemies murmured that the Stoic was, as usual, inebriated. Scaurus distributed bribes and appeared before the court in squalid dress, weeping and appealing to his father's renown. The jury understood that without extortions in the provinces men like Scaurus could not repay debts incurred in lavish aedilician games and in campaigning for office, and they recognized the disgrace of convicting a son of a former dean of the Senate, a stepson of Sulla, and a scion of the patrician Aemilians. A group of consulars, including Pompeius, intervened to win acquittal for Scaurus, and despite the exposure of his utter corruption he was permitted to pursue his candidacy for a consulship.

A general electoral scandal exploded that summer. The chief culprit was Caesar's candidate for the consulship, Memmius, Lucretius' patron, an aristocrat "highly trained in letters, but only Greek, for he scorned Latin . . . an orator of the subtle ingenious type with a pleasing diction but averse to the labor not only of speaking but even thinking."[7] At Pompeius' prompting, Memmius confessed that in return for support in the elections he and another candidate named Calvinus (one day to become one of Caesar's most devoted lieutenants) had promised the consuls Appius Claudius and Ahenobarbus several million sesterces as well as help in obtaining lucrative governorships. In addition, Memmius and Calvinus had contracted to distribute 10 million sesterces within the first century in the balloting inasmuch as the vote of this century generally provided a lead for the succeeding centuries. Outraged more at the disclosure than at the corruption itself, the Senate demanded an investigation. Not only the two confessed culprits but all the other candidates as well were indicted for electoral fraud, and the elections were indefinitely postponed.

Quintus Cicero could show Caesar a despairing letter from his brother. "There is really no republic in existence," the orator lamented, "no Senate, no law courts, no position of authority held by any one of us." He was distraught at "an alarming rumor of a dictatorship," for Pompeius' agents were intensifying their agitation on behalf of their patron.[8]

It was not only because of the crisis at Rome that after three days of mourning for his only child Caesar "returned to his duties and conquered grief as quickly as he was wont to conquer everything."[9] Two states had overthrown kings Caesar had appointed over them—the Senones by expulsion, the Carnutes by assassination; and Labienus reported new stirrings among the sea peoples and the Belgians. Postponing his departure for winter quarters in Cisalpina, Caesar summoned the Gallic leaders to Samarobriva (Amiens). A drought intensified Gallic discontent. Although Caesar dispersed his legions over a wide area to minimize grain requisitions on individual states, the chiefs received the notice of new quotas with obvious displeasure.

In the midst of the meeting Caesar received word that a huge force of Belgians was besieging Quintus Cicero's camp. Quintus, whose pluck was out of all proportion to his diminutive stature and his poor health, had rejected an ultimatum and was mounting a heroic resistance. After two weeks of fighting he had at last succeeded in slipping a Gallic auxiliary through the enemy lines with a letter hidden in the hollowed shaft of a javelin. Caesar responded with resolution. He summoned young Marcus Crassus (a replacement for his brother Publius, now on his way to Syria to join his father against the Parthians) to assume defense of the grain supplies and the archives at Samarobriva and sent dispatches to the legates Labienus and Fabius to set out with their troops to Quintus' relief. Labienus replied that he was blockaded by the Treveri. He also sent details of a massacre of fifteen cohorts under the legates Sabinus and Aurunculeius. Roused by Indutiomarus, the chief rejected by Caesar as supreme leader of the Treveri, the Eburones, an equally warlike Belgian tribe, had burst out of the forest and surrounded their encampment. The commander of the attacking horde, Ambiorix, a chief who had served under Caesar and benefited from Caesar's favor, offered safe-conduct out of the territory, and Sabinus, convinced that "Gaul was incensed at all the insults experienced since it was brought in subjection to the authority of Rome,"[10] gave credence to Ambiorix' report of a general uprising and of the approach of German reinforcements. Overruling Aurunculeius, Sabinus accepted a truce. When the legionaries, mostly new recruits, marched out of the camp, they were ambushed and all but a handful were slaughtered. Among the five to six thousand casualties in this disaster were hundreds of new recruits from the Transpadane country, for whom Caesar felt particular responsibility. He vowed not to cut his hair or beard until the officers and legionaries were avenged. In his report to the Senate he paid especial homage to Aurunculeius, a splendid officer and a man of learning. He included echoes of Lucretius' poem, for like others of Caesar's officers, Aurunculeius had been an Epicurean.

Impelled upon vengeance for the slaughtered cohorts and upon the rescue of Quintus' beleaguered camp, Caesar and his men marched twenty-five miles a day. Caesar dispatched a Gallic runner with a message in Greek characters (unfamiliar to the Belgians) to be hurled into the camp on a spear. (The spear stuck in a tower and went unnoticed for two days.) Quintus read the message to his legion, and soon they descried smoke from burning fields and villages, a sign of Caesar's approach. When the besiegers withdrew from Quintus' camp to confront him, Caesar employed a ruse he had found unfailingly effective with the Gauls. To encourage them into making an impetuous assault, he constructed a small encampment as though for a limited force and refused battle as though frightened by the enemy's superior numbers. As he anticipated, the impetuous Belgians raced up the hill to the attack. Suddenly Caesar ordered the trumpets to sound, and the legionaries and auxiliaries poured forth from all the gates. The Gallic horde turned and fled and suffered a great slaughter.

At the liberated camp Caesar commended Quintus and cited for valor various centurions and tribunes. Nine out of ten of the legionaries had been wounded.

Henceforth Caesar was to confront a new threat—the application of Roman tactics by Gauls formerly in his service. Ambiorix had compelled prisoners to assist in encompassing the camp with a rampart nine feet high and a trench fifteen feet wide. Though forced to cut sod with swords and to carry earth in their hands and cloaks, because of their great numbers the Gauls completed in less than three hours an entrenchment five miles in circumference. They reinforced the works with towers, forged grappling hooks to pull down the Roman palisade and constructed shelters under which to approach the Roman fortifications.

At word of Caesar's victory, the Treveri gave up their siege of Labienus' camp, the sea peoples dispersed to their homes and the Senones sent envoys to offer excuses for the expulsion of the king Caesar had appointed over them. Caesar assembled a second conclave of chiefs, "and by frightening some with the announcement that he knew what was afoot and by encouraging others he kept a great part of Gaul in submission." On the other hand, he recognized "that this nation, which at one time surpassed all others in military courage, was grievously indignant to have lost so much of that estimation as to submit to the sovereignty of the Roman people."[11] Now that a trusted client like Ambiorix had taken up arms against him other clients would be denounced as collaborators and would become increasingly unreliable. Ominous, too, were the loss of Caesar's reputation for invincibility with the massacre of his fifteen cohorts as well as the Gallic apprehension that by attacking legions one by one they might expel him from their country.

On the other hand, Labienus succeeded in enticing Indutiomarus, the instigator of the uprising, into a rash attack and killed him, and for the moment, potential rebels were intimidated. Despite his setbacks, at Rome people continued to take it for granted that Caesar could easily defeat rebel tribes whose names had been unknown before his campaigns, and Caesar's invasion of Britain continued to evoke wonder. In the Province a coin was issued depicting the elephant that had terrified the Britons at the Thames, and at Rome another coin displayed scythe-bearing British chariots. Those who earlier had grumbled about the risks in an invasion of an island "guarded with astonishing masses of rock" and affording "no hope of booty except for slaves" of barbarous manners and without skills succumbed to Caesar's eloquent accounts of the expedition. In December Cicero wrote his brother: "For your promise about the slaves I heartily bless you; and it is true that both at Rome and on my estates I am short-handed."[12] Cicero would hardly be the only oligarch to share in the booty.

Anecdotes in letters from Caesar's officers and men circulated in the city and throughout Italy and the Province extolling his valor and genius. According to one tale, he had made his way to a beleaguered camp disguised as a Gaul; another reported that he had been captured in battle and released only because a Gaul misunderstood a command from a chief. Before his death, Caesar's faithful lieutenant Aurunculeius had written a testimonial to his commander noting that "the first man in the world to cross over to attack Britain, though he had a thousand ships, took as a retinue three slaves in all." Catullus, too, gave rein to his admiration, singing in a love poem:

> Even though he marches over Alps to gaze on
> great Caesar's monuments: the Gallic Rhine and
> Britons who live beyond torn seas, remotest
> men of distant lands . . .[13]

Such adulation evoked jealousy, particularly in Pompeius, and since Julia's death Caesar could no longer count on the Great Man's goodwill. To reassure the Great Man of his continuing devotion, Caesar joined him in urging Cicero to defend Pompeius' associate Gabinius (who as consul had helped to effect Cicero's exile). Indicted by publicans who resented curbs he imposed on them while governor of Syria, Gabinius was at first acquitted. Before a second trial got underway, however, the Tiber overflowed, undermining houses and sweeping people off the streets in a sudden avalanche of water. Gabinius' enemies reminded the citizenry that the Sibylline books had warned against military action to restore the king of Egypt to his throne, and people muttered that "heaven had become angry with them for [Gabinius'] restoration of Ptolemaios," and he was convicted and forced into exile.[14] (Years later Caesar would recall him to serve him as a loyal lieutenant.)

Troubled by continuing rumors of an impending dictatorship under Pompeius, Cicero was employing his leisure in composing a Roman version of Plato's Republic and, in fact, was already reading the first two books of this treatise to friends. He advocated the appointment of a supreme arbiter for the state, an ideal statesman entrusted with the task of reviving a sense of civic responsibility among the citizenry and of renewing the dignity and influence of the senatorial order. No one could expect the orator to exclude his own candidacy for such a post, but Cicero was sufficiently chastened by recent events to recognize that he possessed neither the influence nor the authority to aspire to such a role. Months earlier, at Quintus' urging, he had shifted his primary allegiance from Pompeius to Caesar and begun to serve as Caesar's chief spokesman at Rome. Generously rewarded for his services, Cicero spoke openly of his "delectable rapprochement with Caesar [as] the one plank left from the wreck [of his own and the republic's fortunes]." He was overjoyed at Caesar's kindnesses to Quintus. "Such distinction, such appreciation and favor," he exclaimed to Atticus. "I couldn't do more if I were commander-in-chief myself. He has just offered him the choice of a legion for the winter. . . . Wouldn't you love such a man? If not, then which of your fine friends?"[15]

Caesar's associates could speculate whether Cicero looked to Caesar as his ideal statesman. In defending a close associate of Caesar's at this time, Cicero delivered a panegyric that would inspire suspicion that Caesar was indeed Cicero's candidate for rector of the republic. "Many are the great and amazing virtues," Cicero declared, "which I have found in Gaius Caesar, but the generality of them are designed for display upon an ample theater and almost before the public gaze: to select a site for a camp, to set an army in array, to storm cities, to rout hostile forces, to endure extremities of cold and stress of weather such as we can scarcely support within the shelter of our city houses, to be pursuing the enemy at this very season when even the beasts of the field crouch in the covert of their lairs and when all wars are suspended by the general consent of nations." But Cicero's praise extended beyond Caesar's military genius. "Grant," he went on to say, "that his substantive achievements are great, as great indeed they are. . . . I, amid all his power and all his success, place his generosity towards his friends and his recollection of an old friendship above all his other qualities. This charity of his, so novel in its character, so rarely displayed by men of renown and preeminent power [never by Pompeius!], you, gentlemen, ought not merely not to despise and to discourage but to cherish and foster." If this effusive altitudo represented no more than standard courtroom grandiloquence, astute Romans noted in Cicero's new treatise a pointed reference to Caesar in an otherwise curious digression on a legend about Romulus, an allusion to a certain Proculus Julius, a supposed ancestor of Caesar's, who had proclaimed to the Roman people the deification of the founder of the city as the god Quirinus.[16] In effect, Cicero was extolling Caesar through his forbear and linking Caesar to the hero-founder of Rome.

All who knew Caesar would find no difficulty in associating with him Cicero's prescriptions for such an arbiter of the commonwealth:

He should be given almost no other duties than this one (for it comprises most of the others)—of improving and examining himself continually, urging others to imitate him, and furnishing in himself, as it were, a mirror to his fellow-citizens by reason of the supreme excellence of his life and character.[17]

The vacillating orator would, in any event, not persist in his admiration for his great contemporary. He would transfer his allegiance back to the untrustworthy Pompeius and eventually call for Caesar's death.

XXXVII
COLLAPSE OF THE TRIUMVIRATE

BECAUSE of a general immobilization of the Senate and the magistrates following upon the unprecedented scandal in the consular election campaign and the attendant trials of the candidates, the year 53 like 55 began without the installation of new consuls. A tribune, a cousin of Pompeius', proposed that the warlord be appointed dictator. As was his custom, Pompeius said nothing, awaiting a call from the people. The optimates were frightened. Marcus Brutus denounced his father's murderer, charging that "Pompeius' hands were stained and even steeped in civil blood." "It is better," he declared, "to rule no man than to be the slave of any man since one may live with honor without ruling, whereas life is no life for a slave."[1]

To Pompeius' maneuvering Caesar reacted gingerly. He was, of course, concerned with the implications for his own future in the increasing tempo in the disintegration of the institutions of the oligarchic republic; but able to intervene only belatedly and indirectly in events in the city, he could do no more than remind the citizenry of his existence. To expedite the construction of his public works at Rome, he summoned to Gaul the freedman assisting the Greek architect in charge of the project.

With the disaffected Gauls heartened by the massacre of the fifteen cohorts, Caesar "conceived it to be of greatest importance for the future as well as for the present to create an impression . . . that the resources of Italy were extensive enough not only to repair in a short time any damage incurred in the war but even to increase the establishment." To this end he levied two new legions and appealed to Pompeius (in an implicit reaffirmation of their alliance) to release a legion just levied in Cisalpina for duty in Pompeius' Spanish provinces. At Pompeius' acquiescence, Caesar praised him for a "concession to public service and private friendship." When Pompeius neglected to request Senate approval for the transfer of the legion, Cato cried: "Armies of this great size and arms and horses are now the mutual gifts of private persons." He went on to denounce Pompeius, too, for "managing factions at the elections as though he were directing games and contributing disturbances from which by way of anarchy he is seeking to win for himself a monarchy."[2]

Compelled by the accelerating tempo of events at Rome to hasten the pacification of Gaul, Caesar launched a preemptive attack on the Nervians. He seized herds of cattle and hundreds of prisoners, devastated the fields and distributed the booty among his troops as compensation for the hardships of a winter campaign. Thereafter he convoked an assembly of the Gallic chiefs at Samarobriva. When envoys from the Carnutes and the Senones, tribes which had dethroned the kings Caesar had set over them, failed to appear, he abruptly transferred the meeting to Lutetia (Paris), a village of the Parisii on an island in the Seine, close to the Senones, and while the chiefs were assembling, by a forced march Caesar surprised the Senones. They besought the intervention of the Aeduans; and, anticipating similar punishment, the Carnutes appealed to Caesar's other clients, the Remi; both delivered over hostages. Gaul was, however, clearly unstable.

At the conclave of the chastened Gallic chiefs Caesar demanded cavalry forces for a punitive expedition against Ambiorix, the Belgian leader responsible for the massacre of the fifteen cohorts. Caesar advanced against the Menapii in the lower Rhine, while Labienus marched into the land of the Treveri

(Trier) to the south, setting themselves in position for a pincers movement against Ambiorix, a fugitive in the forest of the Ardennes. Constructing causeways over marshlands, Caesar pursued the Menapii, burning their villages and dispersing their cattle until the tribe appealed for mercy. Simultaneously, Labienus enticed the Treveri into battle before the arrival of expected German reinforcements. Exhorting his legionaries to "display under our command the same valor that you have often displayed to the commander-in-chief and think that he is present and beholds this action with his own eyes," Labienus routed the Treveri with great slaughter, and their leaders fled across the Rhine.[3]

Since the first demonstration of Roman might had not intimidated the Germans from aiding Gallic rebels, Caesar ordered a second crossing of the Rhine. Utilizing their previous experience, the engineers constructed a bridge even more rapidly. When the Suebi, the most aggressive of the German tribes, once again withdrew into the forest, Caesar destroyed the eastern terminus of the bridge and posted a garrison at the Gallic end to guard against incursions. The portion of the bridge left standing would serve as a reminder of his ability to invade Germany at will.

News from Rome was mixed. After tricking Pompeius into a public denial of the charge that he was promoting civil disturbances with a view to seizing power in the state, Cato called upon the warlord to "devote himself to the cause of law and order,"[4] and Pompeius instructed the tribunes in his hire to cease obstructing the elections. Calvinus and Hortensius' nephew Valerius Messala, both participants in the election scandal of the previous year, were chosen consuls for the remaining half of the year with the immediate task of holding elections for 52. Cicero's friend Milo entered his candidacy for a consulship, and their enemy Clodius filed for a praetorship. Clashes between the armed bands of these two hotheaded aristocrats were certain to disrupt civil activity for another year.

Pompeius was waiting to exploit the turmoil.

If Caesar had not felt uneasy about events at Rome, he might have pursued a leisurely policy of conciliation in Gaul, patiently persuading the states to an acceptance of Roman rule, but the instability in the city prevented any slackening in his confirmation of Roman dominion over the vast territory. He resolved to respond with terror to the mounting disaffection. To distract the Gauls from thoughts of rebellion, he proclaimed the territory of the Eburones, the tribe responsible for the massacre of the fifteen cohorts, open to plunder, and "a great number [of Gauls] assembled speedily from every side."[5]

Leaving his baggage, his wounded and a legion of new recruits with Quintus Cicero in the camp previously occupied by the massacred cohorts, Caesar started off in pursuit of Ambiorix in the Ardennes. After seven days of fruitless searching, Caesar returned to Quintus' camp. To his chagrin, he discovered a large portion of the garrison slain and the remainder demoralized. Two thousand Germans who had crossed the Rhine to participate in the pillaging of the Eburones had swept out of the woods in a surprise attack. Against Caesar's orders, Quintus Cicero had permitted details to go out foraging. Cut off by the Germans, veteran legionaries succeeded in fighting back to camp, but new recruits, the greater part of two cohorts, were slaughtered. Had it not been for Baculus, a centurion who had earned commendations for heroism in previous battles, the garrison would have been annihilated. Convalescing from wounds and weak from fasting for five days, he rose from his bed, seized arms and stationed himself at the gate with other centurions and repelled the attackers.

Caesar resumed his scouring of the Ardennes. His account of the campaign reflects both his fury at the tribe responsible for the massacre of his legionaries and his desperate resolve upon a quick and final pacification of the country: "Every hamlet, every homestead that anyone could see was set on fire; captured cattle were driven from every spot; the corn crops were not only consumed by the vast host of pack animals and human beings but were laid flat in addition because of the rainy season so that even if any persons succeeded in hiding themselves for the moment, it seemed that they must perish for want of everything when the cavalry was withdrawn."[6]

The Eburones ceased to exist.

Caesar calculated that the annihilation of this people would intimidate other potential rebels, but events elsewhere in the empire, always reflected in developments in Gaul, upset his plans. In the East Crassus had suffered a debacle. The valorous Publius Crassus and the Gallic cavalry supplied by Caesar had been cut to pieces by mounted Parthian archers, employing battle tactics novel to the Romans and the Gauls. Publius had ordered a retainer to kill him. Marcus Crassus, however, had been captured along with ten thousand of his troops, and at a performance of Euripides' Bacchae held at the Armenian court to honor the victorious Parthian monarch, Crassus' head was displayed in lieu of the murdered king's in the play. The Parthians proclaimed themselves heirs to the Persians, who centuries earlier had nearly overwhelmed the Greeks, and Crassus' defeat represented the first rout of the West by the East since before the time of Alexander.

During two decades Caesar and the millionaire had collaborated. Crassus had rescued him from moneylenders, assisted him in his election to the consulship and defended him in his proconsulship. With the recent deaths of his mother and his only child, Caesar was increasingly alone, and he would miss Crassus as a friend and Publius as a comrade-in-arms. In his miserable demise, the millionaire would henceforth serve as an exemplum for the Epicurean teaching of the vanity of ambition. Lucretius had sung:

For when he [Epicurus] saw how mortals had ready for them nearly all that need demands for living and that life was established safe so far as it could be; saw how men were rolling in riches, mighty in honor and fame, proud in the good repute of their sons, while at home nevertheless each had an anxious heart; saw how they tormented their life in their own despite without any pause and were compelled to wax furious with lamentations—then he understood that . . . an inward corruption tainted all.[7]

Crassus had a further significance for Caesar—as a balance between him and Pompeius. Now Pompeius, no longer allied to Caesar through Julia, would consider Caesar his sole rival in military glory and the chief obstacle to his supremacy in the republic, and the optimates would maneuver to alienate Pompeius from him. One day, Caesar resolved, he would avenge his friend, regain the captured legionary standards and restore Rome's honor and prestige. For the moment, however, an enduring subjugation of the Gauls was Caesar's immediate task. Summoning a conclave of the chiefs at Durocortorum (Rheims) in the land of his clients, the Remi, he held a belated inquest into the overthrow of the kings he had appointed over the Senones and the Carnutes. The arch-conspirator in the assassination of the Carnute king he haled before the assembly in chains, and, to the horror of the chiefs, he "pronounced a heavier sentence than usual and executed punishment in the traditional [Roman] fashion," flogging the prisoner to death.[8]

LESSONS ON THE NEW DOMINIONS

Having abandoned all pretense regarding the incorporation into the empire of formerly independent Gaul, Caesar dispatched a lengthy communiqué describing the new regions Rome had taken under its rule. In his observations about the lands and peoples Caesar expounded an Epicurean view of social and cultural evolution, as a dynamic process within a materialist cosmology. The dominant philosophy among Caesar's staff officers was Epicurean, and its doctrines provided a frequent topic of conversation or at least set the tone of discussions. In February 53, in fact, Cicero wrote to one of his protégés at Caesar's headquarters: "Well, my friend Pansa [one of Caesar's councilors and an Epicurean] has let it out—you have turned Epicurean! . . . How on earth will you uphold the principles of civil law [the young man was serving as a legal adviser to Caesar] when your every act is for yourself alone [according to the Epicurean pleasure principle] and not for your fellow-citizens?"[9]

Involved in extending Roman dominion over a society in flux and transformation, Caesar and his aides concerned themselves, of course, with other aspects of Epicurean doctrine than personal ethics and the pleasure principle. Human progress, Epicurus taught, was the anthropological counterpart to evolution in nature. Inventions exemplified man's increasing mastery over the external world and were not gifts of the gods. Major inventions, evolved in the grappling with the environment, signaled the stages in man's advancement out of barbarism into civilization. In the disquisition about the Gauls he addressed to the Roman people, Caesar could apply Epicurean insights he found in Lucretius:

Ships and agriculture, fortifications and laws, arms, roads, clothing and all else of this kind, life's prizes, its luxuries also from first to last, poetry and pictures, the shaping of statues by the artist, all these as men progressed gradually step by step were taught by practice and the experiments of the active mind. So by degrees time brings up before us every single thing, and reason lifts it into the precincts of light. For their intellect saw one thing after another grow famous amongst the arts until they came to their highest point.[10]

Ethnographical and geographical writing, though known to the Greeks, was novel among the Romans, and in the objectivity which he brought to his account Caesar exposed an ecumenical view rare among his countrymen. Caesar's purpose was to demonstrate the feasibility of assimilating into the empire the regions he had conquered. Unlike the East with its ancient civilizations and well-established institutions, "long-haired" Gaul (as distinguished from previously subdued "trousered" Gaul, the Province) was politically and socially in a stage that Rome had passed through centuries earlier. It would be receptive to Roman institutions and culture.

Caesar did not expatiate on the Gallic economy. All Romans were aware of the high-quality iron and bronze weapons and implements produced in workshops in towns like Aeduan Bibracte—swords forged of layers of welded and tempered iron, carpenter's tools, horseshoes and armor. Italians had seen legionaries on leave sporting long-sleeved tunics, capes and pants bound at the ankles, some of heavy-textured Gallic plaids. People at home knew about the vast herds of cattle and sheep in Gaul from the imports of leather and wool products, especially the varied sandals and boots eagerly sought at Rome. Nor did Caesar need to speak of innumerable sanctuaries cluttered with statues and ex-votos and glittering with gold, for his plunder was flooding back to Italy.

In describing Gallic society Caesar offered implicit analogies to contemporary Rome. Of the chiefs, as proud and mettlesome as Homeric heroes (or contemporary Roman oligarchs), he noted that "before [his] coming this would happen well nigh every year—they would either be making wanton attacks themselves or repelling such." Their influence, like that of Roman aristocrats, rested upon a system of clientship, and populars at Rome would nod in recognition at Caesar's observation that Gallic common folk were "treated almost as slaves, venturing naught of themselves, never taken into counsel. The more part of them oppressed as they are either by debt or by the heavy weight of tribute or by the wrongdoing of the more powerful men commit themselves in slavery to the nobles, who have, in fact, the same rights over them as masters over slaves."[11]

Roman oligarchs, viewing religion as an instrument for manipulating the people, would share the interest of the pontifex maximus in Gallic religious organization and practices. Unlike the Romans, the Gauls maintained a priestly caste, the Druids, who met in annual conclave under an elective chief priest. Romans would recall the feverish competition that led to Caesar's election as pontifex maximus upon Caesar's observation that at the death of the Chief Druid, "either any other that is preeminent in position succeeds, or, if there be several of equal standing, they strive for the primacy by the vote of the Druids or sometimes even with armed force."[12] The influence of the Druids depended in part on their control of the education of young aristocrats, to whom they taught fear of the gods and personal morality and in whom they instilled martial ardor. Candidates for the priesthood trained for as long as twenty years, committing to memory innumerable verses containing the wisdom of the priesthood, for none of the sacred teachings was set down in writing and made available to the general population. Commanding the dread weapon of excommunication and acting as the ultimate dispensers of justice among states and powerful nobles, the Druids represented a potential unifying force among the Gauls.

Like Romans of centuries earlier, the Gauls practiced some barbarous customs, even sacrificing criminals to their gods. Funeral rites, however, generally resembled the Romans'. Gallic nobles, like Roman aristocrats, were buried in magnificent ceremonies, and the uncivilized practice had disappeared according to which "slaves and dependents known to have been beloved by their lords used to be burnt with them at the conclusion of the funeral formalities."[13] Gallic fathers exercised power of life and death over wives and children, but Gallic wives, like Roman women, enjoyed considerable rights in regard to dowries and inheritance. All in all, the Gauls were sufficiently similar to the Romans as to be susceptible to Roman manners and ways, especially insofar as they had a propensity to imitation.

In contradiction to Posidonios, who confounded Gauls and Germans, Caesar distinguished between the two peoples. Amongst the Germans the Romans found themselves in another world. These "noble savages" practiced archaic virtues long forgotten in Italy. They nurtured in their young stamina against the elements; they held chastity in repute and admired physical prowess. They worshiped natural forces rather than gods, walked about half-naked under animal skins and divided their lives between war and hunting. Their agriculture was primitive, and like other semi-nomads they subsisted primarily on animal products.

Caesar described in detail aspects of German social organization certain to evoke interest among Romans. "No man," he reported, "has a definite quantity of land or estate of his own. The magistrates and chiefs every year assign to tribes and clans that have assembled together as much land and in such place as seems good to them and compel the tenants after a year to pass on elsewhere." The rationale Caesar offered for German primitive communism represented, in effect, a critique of current Italian society: "the fear . . . that they may become zealous for the acquisition of broad territories, and so the more powerful may drive the lower sort from their holdings; that some passion for money may arise to be the parent of parties and of quarrels." Caesar noted that among German chiefs (quite unlike Roman oligarchs) "it is [the] aim to keep common people in contentment, when each man sees that his own wealth is equal to that of the most powerful."[14]

Demonstrating the futility of the subjugation of a semi-nomadic people whom the Romans could not police as well as the lack of trade opportunities among them, Caesar justified his fixing the Rhine as the frontier of his protectorate. Regarding Gaul, however, Caesar confirmed his intention, hinted at in earlier communiqués, to follow Sertorius' example in winning the loyalty of the indigenous population and encouraging Romanization among them. He employed Gauls from the Province in positions of responsibility and enrolled leading aristocrats into his personal clientship, promoting their careers and inviting them to share in the booty. Officers returning to Italy reported that in entertainments he regaled Gallic leaders and hostages with Alexandrian delicacies and vintage Italian and Greek wines to excite their eagerness to ape Mediterranean ways. To impress Gauls with the wealth of the south, he traveled with a marble flooring. Thousands of Gauls served in Caesar's army, and, inevitably, during the years of Caesar's campaigns numerous civilians formed friendships with Roman soldiers. Legionaries bought food, clothing and varied local products from the people, and Caesar's army had become an important factor in the Gallic economy. Gauls and Romans learned to communicate at least minimally in each other's language. In effect, the assimilation of the country into the empire was proceeding apace. If Caesar had held an indefinite proconsulship and had been able to dedicate years to a leisurely conciliation of the Gauls, he might have achieved greater success than Sertorius with the Spaniards. Ever prodding Caesar, however, was the mounting peril at Rome. His relations with Pompeius were deteriorating. He suffered an ominous rebuff when Pompeius rejected his proposal to divorce his great-niece Octavia and marry her to Pompeius if Pompeius divorced his daughter from Faustus Sulla for Caesar (who would divorce Calpurnia). Pompeius had ambitions in which Caesar was to play no part. He was awaiting an opportunity to seize power as Milo and Clodius, both candidates for office for the coming year, engaged in pitched battles with private armies. The consul Calvinus was wounded in a riot, and he and his colleague were unable to hold elections for the coming year.

As in 55 and in 53, Rome entered the new year (52) without consuls. New Year's fell on a market day, an evil portent, and many distressing prodigies were reported. "Wolves were seen in Rome. The mournful howling of dogs was heard by night. The image of Mars sweated. A thunderbolt strayed over the whole city, overthrowing many images of gods and taking people's lives."[15] Disciples of the Egyptian gods, partisans of Clodius who preached a vision of an egalitarian utopia, warned of peril to the city when a Senate decree ordered the destruction of the temples of Isis and Serapis.

The calamity fell suddenly.

In the third week of January a courier from Rome reported that on the 18th of the month Clodius, riding on the Appian Way with thirty armed retainers (no man of substance traveled in those turbulent days without a sizable entourage), encountered his foe Milo in a coach with his wife Fausta (Sulla's daughter) and some three hundred guards. In a fracas one of Milo's gladiators thrust a javelin at Clodius and wounded him. When Clodius' slaves carried him into a nearby inn, Milo ordered his men in pursuit. They killed the innkeeper and dragged Clodius out to the highway, stabbed him repeatedly and left his corpse on the road. A senator passing in a litter carried Clodius' body to Rome.

Fulvia, Clodius' widow, dispatched runners throughout the city, and a vast crowd massed outside Clodius' mansion on the Palatine. Fulvia's lamentations stirred their fury. The next morning, January 19, led by Fulvia and two tribunes, Clodius' partisans bore the corpse, naked so as to expose the many gashes, from the Palatine to the Forum and into the Senate. At the exhortations of Fulvia and the tribunes, the crowd heaped up benches and tables as well as scrolls from nearby bookstalls for a funeral pyre. The flames leaped high and ignited the ceiling beams of the Senate house; the building was destroyed.

Assembling on the Palatine, the terrified senators enacted the ultimate decree, calling upon Marcus Lepidus (the interrex elected by his fellow patricians in the Senate to hold belated consular elections), the tribunes and Pompeius (who held a military command as governor-in-absentia of the Two Spains) to see to it that no harm befell the republic. A levy was instituted throughout Italy.

With the death of Clodius, Caesar was deprived of another ally. No one else at Rome could mobilize the plebs as a counterweight to Caesar's senatorial foes. For the moment, however, Clodius' partisans took over the city. After celebrating a funeral feast in the Forum, mourners attacked the houses of Milo and of the interrex. Repulsed by archers at Milo's mansion, they established a siege at Lepidus'. Others seized the consular fasces from their storage place in the temple of the goddess of the dead and paraded to the houses of Scipio and Hypsaeus, candidates for the consulship allied with Clodius. They called upon these men to assume the high office. Still others massed at Pompeius' gardens outside the walls and with the confused notion that he would champion their cause against the Senate, they hailed him by turns as consul and as dictator.

In the turmoil Milo, informed of the indignation of men of property at the burning of the Senate house and at the general lawlessness, stole into the city and distributed bribes lavishly. The tribune Caelius, once a lover of Clodius' sister but long an enemy of both Clodius and Clodia, invited Milo to speak from the Rostra. A riot ensued, Caelius and Milo were driven from the Forum, and many people were killed. The commoners ranged through the city beating and murdering all whom they suspected of sympathy with their hero's murderer and wreaked their fury on the rich, attacking "especially those who wore fine clothes and gold rings."[16] The men besieging Lepidus' house stormed inside and ripped down the images of his Aemilian ancestors and the ancient weapons of heroes of his patrician clan, and Lepidus' family was rescued only by the timely arrival of Milo's gladiators.

Impotent to restore order and fearful that Pompeius would exploit the chaos to seize power, the optimates maneuvered to win him to their cause. Before a startled Senate, Bibulus, Caesar's colleague in the consulship and impassioned enemy, proposed the election of Pompeius as sole consul with the right to appoint a colleague after the restoration of order. (Three years after his second consulship, Pompeius was not eligible for another.) Pretending surprise at Bibulus' motion, the Man of Virtue, the self-appointed defender of the constitution and the old ways, "rose, leading everyone to think that he was going to speak against it, and when silence was made, said that he himself would not have introduced the proposed measure but since it had been introduced by another, he urged its adoption because he preferred any government whatever to no government at all and thought that no one would govern better than Pompeius in a time of such disorder."[17] Delighted at the unexpected recognition of his primacy in the republic, Pompeius expressed his gratitude for the trust of these leaders of the Senate and invited Cato to serve as his counselor in restoring order. Though barred from the city as a proconsul with a military command, he now passed through the gate. No one objected to his illegal retention of a proconsulship along with his unprecedented sole consulship.

Having achieved the recognition for which he had yearned for three decades, Pompeius had no further need of the alliance with his former father-in-law, and in Pompeius' marriage to the daughter of Metellus Scipio, a scion of the revered Scipio branch of the Cornelian clan and testamentary heir to Metellus Pius, Sulla's closest associate, Caesar saw his new isolation. Widow to Publius Crassus, Scipio's daughter Cornelia, the most eligible matron in Rome, combined beauty with birth and was "well versed in literature, in playing the lyre and in geometry and . . . accustomed to listening to philosophical discourses with profit." Gossips grumbled that her "youth made her a fitter match for a son of Pompeius," and others objected that in the parlous condition of the city Pompeius should be "decking himself with garlands and celebrating nuptials."[18]

With each of his four previous marriages Pompeius had embarked upon a new political course. What change would this fifth marriage bring?

Balbus encouraged tribunes friendly to Caesar to propose that he be appointed Pompeius' colleague. It was doubtful, of course, that Pompeius would share the office with a man of Caesar's vigor and statesmanship. Indeed, Caesar could not have accepted the office, for the crisis at Rome set off a new crisis in Gaul, a crisis that placed in jeopardy all Caesar's accomplishments of the previous six years.

XXXVIII

AT BAY

NEWS of a general levy in Italy and of the anarchy at Rome inspired Gallic chiefs to plot a rebellion. "The Gauls added . . . a circumstance of their own invention . . . that Caesar was detained by the commotion at Rome and, in view of discords so serious, could not come to the army. Such an opportunity served as a stimulus to those who even before were chafing at their subjection to the sovereignty of Rome, and they began with greater freedom to make plans for a campaign."[1] Caesar recognized the extent of the peril upon receiving a report from Labienus that Commius, a trusted client whom Caesar had appointed king of the Belgian Atrabates and had employed as an envoy to the Britons, was engaged in a conspiracy. Labienus laid a plot to kill Commius, but the Belgian escaped with a head wound. The circumstances were suspicious and recalled the tensions between Roman officers and Iberian chiefs that led to Sertorius' downfall. Caesar could take for granted the involvement of his factional opponents in the new Gallic disturbances. They had conspired with the German chieftain Ariovistus during his first year in Gaul. With his present renown and power, they would maneuver against him with greater zeal.

The Carnutes, who had murdered the king Caesar appointed over them, issued the call. At a conclave of chiefs in their territory, a Druid conducted the most solemn of Gallic ceremonies, the swearing of an oath of alliance before massed standards. On a day fixed at the assembly, the Carnutes slaughtered Roman merchants at Cenabum (Orléans). In the Gallic fashion, heralds shouted news of the massacre from hilltop to hilltop so that within hours word had traveled a hundred and sixty miles south to the land of the Arverni (Auvergne), bordering upon the Province. Although clients to Caesar's enemy Ahenobarbus (they had been subjugated by his grandfather), the Arverni had participated in no resistance movements, and a number of their chiefs had enrolled in Caesar's service, including a certain Vercingetorix (his name meant King of Heroes). Upon the report of the massacre at Cenabum, Vercingetorix called upon his fellow tribesmen to resume their ancient leadership among the Gauls. Expelled from the tribal fortress of Gergovia (south of Clermont-Ferrand) for stirring up rebellion, he defied the tribal elders and "held a levy of beggars and outcasts."[2] With popular support he cast out the chiefs who had expelled him and dispatched envoys throughout Gaul. Everywhere he was hailed as commander-in-chief of the patriotic forces.

Familiar with Caesar's tactics, Vercingetorix moved with resolution, demanding hostages from friendly tribes as warrants of loyalty and assigning quotas of troops. In his army, which rapidly swelled to a sizable force, he imposed discipline previously unacceptable to the individualistic Gauls, executing with fire and torture those guilty of major offenses and cutting off ears or gouging out eyes for lesser infractions. In levying troops he emphasized the cavalry, the best arm of the Gauls.

Despite reports of the gathering rebellion, Caesar tarried in Cisalpina to follow the crisis at Rome. With his new optimate allies Pompeius passed a series of emergency measures, each of which could be justified in the immediate crisis, several of which posed threats to Caesar. A special court of inquiry was established for the current crisis with Ahenobarbus—a stubborn foe to Caesar and the populars—as the judge and a panel of three hundred and sixty jurors chosen by Pompeius almost exclusively out of the optimate faction. On the other hand, Pompeius was not ready to jettison his alliance with Caesar, not out of any newly developed sentiments of loyalty but out of fear of losing his bargaining position vis-à-vis his new associates. Against Cato's dogged opposition, in association with all ten tribunes he passed a bill sponsored by Cicero at Caesar's request granting Caesar the privilege of registering his candidacy for a future consulship in absentia. Under this decree, Caesar would avoid the humiliation he had suffered from Cato years earlier, when he had had to forgo a triumph in order to enter his candidacy for a consulship. More important, he would not surrender his magisterial immunity between the termination of his proconsulship and his election to a consulship, an interval during which his enemies would otherwise hobble him with indictments.

Having won this minimal safeguard, Caesar crossed the Alps.

A MATTER OF SURVIVAL

Imitating Caesar's strategy and exploiting the experience of the recent Gallic uprisings, Vercingetorix moved against Caesar's legions one by one, aiming to crush those dispersed throughout the north before Caesar could make his way to the encampments through hostile territory and winter-bound roads. Caesar responded with calm calculation. He summoned his distinguished clansman, the consular Lucius Caesar, to assume command in the Province. He himself supervised the establishment of garrisons at key defense points and levied legionaries among the Roman citizens and auxiliaries among the Gallic tribes. With this force, he struck across the wintry Cévennes, clearing a road through six feet of snow. Since no traveler ever crossed the range at this season, Vercingetorix had taken no provisions against such a move. Suddenly Caesar appeared in the undefended country of the Arverni.

By this coup Caesar regained the initiative. Vercingetorix, marching northward, reversed direction. By the time he reached his home country, Caesar had vanished. Speeding by a circuitous route, Caesar arrived among his legions at the Belgian frontier ahead of the messengers sent to announce his coming. Without pausing he marched to the relief of a loyal Gallic town, captured the chief stronghold of a rebel state and stormed Cenabum, the site of the massacre that signaled the revolt. He plundered the town and burned it to the ground.

After years of campaigning, Caesar's intelligence service functioned with efficiency, and Caesar learned that Vercingetorix, fearing a collapse in morale among his impetuous but unstable allies, had proclaimed a new strategy. He had noted Caesar's insistence upon a guaranteed food supply before embarking upon a campaign and his policy of starving tribes into submission by driving off their cattle and burning their foodstuffs. Aware that on this occasion Caesar had not had time to assemble provisions or transport, Vercingetorix harassed Caesar's foragers and sought to cut Caesar's supply lines. Following the strategy adopted by the sea peoples several years earlier, he proposed a scorched earth policy to deprive Caesar of the possibility of living off the land. Within a single day Caesar received reports of the burning of more than twenty villages in the land of the Bituriges, and fires were descried beyond the borders of that tribe.

Caesar confronted a superior commander and a new set of circumstances in the current revolt. If the Gauls attained unity in opposing him, he might suffer a disaster. As it was, social and political contradictions worked to Caesar's advantage. For all Vercingetorix' magnetism and cunning, the Gauls could not overcome the divisions and irresolution that had enabled Caesar to conquer this land so much larger and more populous than Italy. After winning acceptance of his scorched earth strategy, Vercingetorix was compelled to yield to the pleas of the Bituriges against the destruction of Avaricum (Bourges), their chief city and one of the fairest towns in all Gaul. Protected by the Loire and by marshes with only a narrow approach to the walls, Avaricum, they said, was impregnable.

Vercingetorix had greater success in interrupting Caesar's food supply. It was an ill omen that the Aeduans were lax in providing grain. Cattle requisitioned in distant hamlets staved off famine, but meat was uncongenial to the cereal-eating Italians. Nevertheless, when Caesar walked among the men engaged in constructing siege works outside Avaricum and offered to lift the siege, they responded that "they had served for many years under his command without once incurring disgrace, without anywhere leaving a task unaccomplished; they would regard it in the nature of a disgrace if they relinquished the siege they had begun."[3]

Caesar's auxiliary troops could no longer be trusted, and from deserters Vercingetorix learned that Caesar was planning a counterambush to one he himself had devised. Arriving at the site, Caesar found the Gauls entrenched in an impregnable position. Incensed both at the Gallic defiance and at confronting massive resistance after so many years of exertions and ferocious struggle, the legionaries shouted for the signal. Now Caesar's problem was to restrain his troops from a rash assault. "When he saw them resolved to refuse no risk that might bring him renown," he declared, "he deserved to be condemned for the uttermost injustice if he did not count their life dearer than his own welfare."[4]

Vercingetorix' problems were more acute than Caesar's. Compelled to defend himself against a charge of treason because of the disclosure of his own ambush, he produced captured slaves, whom he had coached in advance. They reported hunger in Caesar's camp and legionaries too weak to complete the siege works at Avaricum. Caesar, they declared, had resolved to withdraw if he did not capture the town within three days. Upon this welcome testimony, the mercurial Gallic chiefs "clashed their arms in their peculiar fashion, as they always did for a man whose speech they approved." Resolving that "in keeping possession of the town rested almost the whole issue of victory,"[5] they voted to send ten thousand élite troops into Avaricum to assure its defense.

Capture of Avaricum was important not only for the war in Gaul but also for the maintenance of Caesar's influence at Rome.

The optimates failed to rescue Milo from conviction for the murder of Clodius. At his trial Fulvia and Clodius' daughter-in-law stirred the commons with tearful and dramatic testimonies. On the final day, when a "popular" tribune rallied Clodius' partisans, Pompeius responded by posting troops in the Forum. Cicero, the chief defense counsel, was so intimidated by the hostile crowd and the ranks of armed men that he could barely complete his address, but in a published version of the speech Caesar saw that Cicero had once again revived the slogans of 63. "When did [Clodius'] dagger," Cicero cried, "which Catilina had bequeathed to him, rest in its sheath? That it is which has threatened us." He accused Clodius of levying "armies of slaves to enable him to make himself master of the whole state and the private possessions of all." He proclaimed that Milo "stands unrivaled as the greatest public benefactor in history . . . the preserver of a great nation and the avenger of a great crime [Cicero's banishment]." Clodius' murder, he asserted, had been "for the sake of the general liberty," and Milo deserved the same praise as the murderers of the Gracchi and Saturninus and equal praise with Cicero himself (the destroyer of Catilina). For Cicero the prosecution of this assassin represented a continuation of the harassment he and his associates had endured in retaliation for rooting out "revolutionaries" almost a decade earlier. "What wicked thought did I entertain," Cicero inquired rhetorically, "what enormity did I commit when I tracked down, laid bare, dragged into the light of day and stamped out the symptoms of a universal calamity? That is the head and fount of all the sorrows that have overwhelmed my friends and myself."[6]

With Milo condemned and off to exile in Massilia, the optimates turned on Clodius' partisans with the fury they had employed in the past against the followers of the Gracchi, of Saturninus and of Catilina. Ahenobarbus' court of inquiry set about trying and condemning Clodius' closest collaborators on the charge of inciting violence upon their leader's death. It was a sign of the new direction in the state that the man in Milo's entourage responsible for Clodius' death was acquitted of murder.

Nor were events promising in Gaul. The defenders of Avaricum, men with experience in local iron mines, resisted Caesar with an ingenuity he had not previously encountered. They ensnared Roman grappling hooks and hoisted them with windlasses and dug mines under his ramp. The walls of the town, constructed of interlaced logs fastened with clamps and faced with stone, proved impervious to battering or to fire. By late-night sallies or by showers of hot pitch or pounding with great boulders, the defenders harassed legionaries working around the clock on siege works.

Despite the torment from the enemy and from early spring showers, in twenty-five days the legionaries completed a ramp three hundred and thirty feet wide and eighty feet high, the most massive siege work of all Caesar's campaigns. In a desperate attack the Gauls set several Roman engines ablaze, but Caesar, no longer easily caught off guard, repelled the attackers with artillery. Alarmed at a decision of the warriors to abandon the town, the women signaled from the walls that their menfolk were about to break out to join Vercingetorix, and the Gallic troops were forced to give up this plan. The next day, calculating that the demoralized garrison would not expect an attack in the midst of a downpour, Caesar ordered an assault. The legionaries, exasperated by weeks of hardship, broke into the town and rampaged through the streets slaughtering wantonly. Scarcely eight hundred of the forty thousand within the walls escaped to Vercingetorix's camp.

Before the demoralized chiefs Vercingetorix recalled his insistence upon the destruction of Avaricum and declared that the defeat demonstrated the necessity of a unified command and strategy. He promised to intensify his efforts to rally states still uncommitted to the rebellion and assured his associates that "with unanimity not even the world could resist" the Gauls.[7]

Caesar was unable to exploit his victory because of a crisis among the Aeduans. Two chiefs were battling over the highest magistracy. Caesar hastened into Aeduan territory to resolve the conflict. He ruled that according to the laws of the state only one of the contenders was eligible for the office. Although he feared that the unsuccessful candidate might defect to the rebels, he exhorted the Aeduans to unity and requested that they provide him with cavalry and ten thousand foot soldiers.

Henceforth within every state a Roman party and a freedom party would be struggling for supremacy, and Vercingetorix had mastered the art of exploiting such rivalries. Caesar sent Labienus against the Senones and Parisii to forestall a general uprising in the north. He himself marched south along the Elaver [Allier] towards Gergovia in Vercingetorix's home country. Within four days he and his legionaries descried the mountain fortress looming twenty miles in the distance. It rose abruptly from the plain twelve hundred feet high, fronted on the north and east with steep escarpments. Walls, some seven feet thick, reinforced the natural defenses.

While preparing the siege of Gergovia, Caesar received a report that an Aeduan chief leading reinforcements to Gergovia had murdered Romans traveling with him and then sent messengers throughout Aeduan territory to rouse the people to war against Caesar. "Without a moment's hesitation,"[8] Caesar marched forth with most of his infantry and all of his cavalry. He caught the insurgents and obtained their surrender. The ringleaders of the mutiny fled, and Caesar dared not exact a penalty for the murder of the Roman citizens. Resting his troops only three hours, he raced back to Gergovia with the Aeduan auxiliaries, arriving just in time to repel a heavy attack from the fortress.

Sobered by the Aeduan disaffection, Caesar resolved to abandon the siege of Gergovia. Just as he was about to march off, however, he was informed by scouts that a section of the hill was unfortified and undefended. He ordered a probing attack. So surprised were the Gauls at the sudden appearance of the legionaries that a chief napping in his tent barely escaped, half dressed, on a wounded horse. Sensing a decisive victory, the legionaries ignored the trumpet signal for retreat. Overextended and exhausted from climbing the steep height, they were routed in a massive counterattack. Only a last-minute maneuver by Caesar averted a disaster.

In this reckless assault Caesar recognized a new and more menacing manifestation of the impatience legionaries had displayed earlier. Confronting a breakdown in discipline, Caesar had to react with caution. At a general review the next morning, he sought to draw lessons from the defeat. (Some seven hundred soldiers, including forty-six centurions, had been lost.) He praised "the high courage of men whom no camp fortifications, no mountain height, no town wall had been able to check," but he cautioned that he required of his men "discipline and self-restraint no less than valor and high courage."[9] Unwilling to depart from Gergovia with a sense of defeat, Caesar drew up the legions in line of battle. As he anticipated, Vercingetorix refused to accept the challenge. The next day after repeating this maneuver, Caesar marched off into the territory of the Aeduans.

TRIUMPH IN GAUL

Upon news of the defeat at Gergovia, the anti-Roman faction among the Aeduans renewed its agitation. Caesar sent two young aristocrats, men whose careers he had advanced, to exhort their people to loyalty. He reminded them of his favors to the Aeduans, recalling "their humiliations at the time when he had received them—crowded into towns, deprived of fields, all their resources plundered, a tribute imposed, hostages wrung from them with the utmost insolence—the success and the distinction to which he had brought them with the result that they had not only returned to their ancient positions but to all appearance had surpassed the dignity and influence of all previous ages."[10] The Aeduan chiefs, as Caesar was aware, did not want to hear of past benefits. They yearned for glory and envied the renown of their ancient rivals, the Arverni, who had usurped the leadership of independent Gaul. Caesar's envoys defected. When at an Aeduan town on the Loire insurgents massacred a Roman garrison and Italian merchants and seized horses, provisions, money and hostages, Caesar's officers and men fell into dejection, and the impact of the news at Rome of the defeat at Gergovia and of the collapse of the alliance with the Aeduans was grievous for Caesar. The optimates now were confident that he would be entangled in a long conflict and might even lose all he had gained during the previous seven years.

As his colleague in the consulship, Pompeius appointed his new father-in-law, Scipio, who with Pompeius' assistance had recently escaped conviction for electoral fraud. A pompous and unscrupulous mediocrity, Scipio's only claim to fame besides his pedigree lay in his invention of a method of stuffing geese to swell their livers and then further enlarging the livers by soaking them in milk sweetened with honey. (In fact, an equestrian disputed the invention with him.)

When word of Caesar's defeat at Gergovia reached the north, the Bellovaci, the most powerful of the Belgian states, rose in rebellion, and Labienus was threatened with encirclement. By a skilful stratagem he maneuvered the Gauls into battle on ground favorable to the legions and broke free. The division of the Army of Gaul imperiled both forces, and it was a joyous day when the two armies came within sight of each other.

According to intelligence reports, all the states of Gaul except the Remi among the Belgians and the Lingones (Langres) in Central Gaul as well as the Treveri, preoccupied by a war with Germans, sent delegates to a Gallic assembly at the Aeduan town of Bibracte. Rivalry among the states once again threatened the unity of the insurgents. To the chagrin of the Aeduans, who demanded the supreme command as a reward for their defection from Caesar, Vercingetorix was retained as commander-in-chief.

In preparation for the decisive battle of the war, Caesar rested his legions, replenished his supplies and summoned reinforcements from across the Rhine, squadrons of cavalry supported by foot soldiers. Employing a standard and infallible ruse, Caesar pretended dismay at the gathering Gallic host and retreated southward toward the frontier of the Sequanians. (Actually he was shortening his supply line to the Province and entrenching himself in a region close to the friendly Remi and Lingones and not far from his German clients.) Heartened by Caesar's apparent pusillanimity, Vercingetorix announced: "The hour of victory has come," and the Gallic chiefs, brash, vain and impetuous, swore that "no man should be received beneath a roof, nor have access to children, or to parents or to wife who had not twice ridden through the enemy's column."[11] The next day the Gauls attacked. Caesar formed the legions into a square, impenetrable to the enemy cavalry, and the German horse routed the overconfident Gauls.

It was in character that from strutting and crowing the Gauls should collapse into despair. Once again Vercingetorix was compelled to reverse his strategy in order to revive morale. He ordered a retreat into the stronghold of Alesia some miles to the north. Caesar took up pursuit, inflicting heavy casualties on the disorderly columns. At Alesia he set to investing the town, hoping to bottle up the enemy commander and a sizable army. A metallurgical and commercial center astride a tin route from Britain to Massilia, Alesia stood on a plateau some six miles long and almost a half mile wide. It had never fallen to an enemy, and Vercingetorix could encourage his troops by recalling their victory at an equally impregnable stronghold—Gergovia. Caesar, on the other hand, could be confident that his legionaries had learned a lesson at Gergovia and would respond to orders with firmer discipline.

With engineers Caesar surveyed the site. "The bases of the hill," he noted, "were washed on two separate sides by rivers. Before the town a plain extended for a length of about three miles; and on all the other sides there were hills surrounding the town at a short distance and equal to it in height. Under the wall, on the side which looked eastward, the forces of the Gauls had entirely occupied all this intervening space and had made in front a ditch and a rough wall six feet high."[12] Caesar marked out siege works over a perimeter of eleven miles with camps at convenient intervals and with twenty-three forts along the line.

Apparently concluding that in their defeatism the Gallic cavalry would only exhaust the food stores in the town, sufficient at most for a month, Vercingetorix sent them away, instructing the departing chiefs to rouse the states of Gaul to a final, heroic effort by drafting all able-bodied men into a relief force that would crush Caesar from the outside, while he pressed from within. Both for the morale of the legionaries and for a defense against a two-fold attack, Caesar resolved to construct a double set of works, aimed inward and outward. After years of building bridges, ships and siege works, the legionaries knew their individual assignments and were proud of their skills. They were awed by Caesar's plan, for he ordered the digging of mile upon mile of a principal trench twenty feet wide with perpendicular sides along with two parallel rows of secondary trenches fifteen feet wide and deep at intervals of four hundred paces. He filled the innermost trench with water diverted from a stream, and behind the trenches he constructed a ramp revetted with a twelve-foot palisade reinforced by a breastwork and battlements. In the breastwork he set pointed stakes jutting out horizontally to prevent the enemy from climbing over the works. All about these defenses, at intervals of eighty feet, he established turrets for artillery. Here and there he sank ditches some five feet deep fitted with sharpened stakes upon which attackers would be impaled. Sporadically he dug camouflaged pits similarly armed. Other devices with iron hooks were set as traps for horses. Upon completion of these inner defenses, Caesar began a second series of similar entrenchments in a circuit of fourteen miles to face an enemy attacking from without. Meanwhile, from the Remi and the Lingones he collected grain and forage for a lengthy siege.

At a new conclave of Gallic chiefs Vercingetorix's appeal for a mobilization of all able-bodied Gauls was rejected and more realistic quotas were set for individual states. "They feared that with so large a host herded together they might not be able to preserve discipline, to distinguish their several contingents or to secure a supply of grain." In effect, the chiefs, in particular those who had served with Caesar, were demonstrating a grasp of problems of logistics and morale unprecedented for the Gauls. From the Aeduans and Arverni and their client states, the conclave demanded thirty-five thousand troops each; from all others, a further two hundred thousand. But the Gauls had not surmounted all their old weaknesses. The Bellovaci refused to furnish any troops, sending word that "they would wage war with the Romans on their own account and at their own direction and would obey no man's command."[13] Only at an urgent appeal from the defector Commius did they send two thousand warriors.

For a review in Aeduan territory the Gauls assembled some eight thousand horse and two hundred and fifty thousand infantry. (No such host had been assembled since the apogee of the Persian empire four centuries earlier; the tally was obviously inflated.) To oppose this enormous force Caesar commanded some fifty thousand troops, including Gallic and German auxiliaries,

a force not much greater than the garrison blockaded within Alesia. As supreme commanders for the relief army, the Gauls chose Commius, two Aeduan
chiefs and a cousin of Vercingetorix, that is, representatives of the Belgians,
Aeduans and Arvernians.

The mobilization of the Gallic horde required more than the thirty days
Vercingetorix had allotted for the food supply in Alesia. Because of the growing famine some leaders urged capitulation and others a desperate sortie to
break through Caesar's entrenchments. An aged Arvernian chief, however, a
certain Critognatus, denounced both proposals. Recalling the invasion of the
German Cimbri during his own childhood, he urged the besieged to "do what
our forefathers did in the war. . . . They shut themselves into the towns and
under stress of a like scarcity sustained life on the bodies of those whose age
showed themselves useless for war and delivered not themselves to the enemy."
He reminded the other chiefs that now the destiny of Gaul was being decided
for all time, and he contrasted the Romans to the Cimbri, who "devastated
Gaul . . . yet departed at length . . . and sought other countries, leaving us our
rights, laws, lands, liberty. . . . What else do [the Romans] seek or desire
than . . . to settle in the lands and states of men whose noble report and martial
strength they have learned and to bind upon them a perpetual slavery?"[14] (In
this speech, based either upon an informer's report or simply invented, Caesar
exposes his own insights into Roman imperialism and his appreciation of the
yearning for liberty of the Gauls.) One day a great number of women and
children and old people emerged from the gates of Alesia and approached the
Roman lines on their knees, weeping and begging to be accepted as slaves. In
response to Critognatus' exhortation, the war council was expelling all noncombatants to relieve the demand on the dwindling provisions.

Caesar ordered the suppliants turned back.

Scouts reported the vanguard of the relief army at a hill not more than a mile
from the Roman entrenchments, and the next day a great host of cavalry filled
a plain three miles wide, with the infantry ranged behind them. Sighting the
long-awaited succor, Vercingetorix marched his force out of the town and
commenced to fill in the nearest Roman trench.

Confronting each other were not merely two armies, but two civilizations.
The Gauls gazed in astonishment at a panorama of miles upon miles of defense
and siege works ribboning along valleys and hillsides, an achievement of organization, technology and resolution beyond their comprehension. Indeed, Caesar's siege works very likely surpassed any others ever constructed in the Mediterranean world. Within these fortifications, at the ready, stood the finest
military force ever assembled, and the crack legionaries were aware that they
served under perhaps the greatest military genius of all time. The legionaries
themselves were at the peak of morale, confident in the skill of their officers and
in the solidarity of their comrades and filled with pride at having girded this huge
plateau with trenches and networks of traps, ramparts and palisades as well as
towers bristling with artillery.

The squadrons of Gallic chiefs prancing on high-spirited steeds glittering with ornate panoplies no longer daunted Caesar's men, for they had tested and routed these braggart popinjays in battle after battle. They had contempt for the undisciplined mass assaults of the Gauls and the swift collapse of their morale at any reverse. Scouts reported that the tracks from Aeduan territory to Alesia were clogged with troops, horses and wagons blundering in each other's way, trampling croplands and fouling streams. Bumptious chiefs bridled at orders and snarled over questions of precedence, and the common levies plodded on to battle sullen, clutching at makeshift arms, almost as resentful of their brutal overlords as of the Roman invaders.

"Caesar disposed the whole army on both faces of the entrenchments in such fashion that, if occasion should arise, each man could know and keep his proper station."[15] He was confident that he could rely on the discipline and initiative they had acquired under his command over the previous seven years. They would have to display their full military competence not only because of the overwhelming numbers they confronted but also because in Commius and other chiefs who had served under Caesar they faced officers of considerable competence. Indeed, to guard against another rout of their cavalry, the Gallic commanders infiltrated archers and light-armed infantry within the squadrons, and in an initial skirmish Caesar's outnumbered cavalry was repulsed. Indignant at suffering a reverse from Gauls, the Germans wheeled about with such vigor that the Gauls turned and fled, abandoning their archers to be slaughtered. From his headquarters on a hill overlooking the Alesia plateau, Caesar saw Vercingetorix's force withdraw into the town, dispirited at the defeat.

Nevertheless, the Gauls, always demoralized after any setback, this time apparently realized that they could not afford to yield to despair. They prepared new tactics. After a day's delay, at midnight they stole up to the Roman entrenchments with hurdles, ladders and grappling hooks, and roaring a battle cry to alert their countrymen within the town, they began an assault with arrows and other missiles. The legionaries replied with artillery, and the two generals in command of the sector under attack deployed reserves at threatened points. The Gauls were impaled on stakes in the camouflaged pits and cut down by lances fired from engines in the turrets. At dawn, badly mauled, they retreated.

From local inhabitants the Gallic commanders learned that Caesar had not had time to complete defenses about one hill of very broad circumference. At night they assembled some sixty thousand troops against the two Roman legions stationed at this point. At midday the entire Gallic horde, supported by Vercingetorix's force, advanced on the Roman defenses. By attacking a vast arc of the Roman line while concentrating on the weak segment, the Gauls compelled Caesar to spread his troops thin and to face attacks from both inside and out. From his hilltop observation post Caesar watched the progress of the battle and dispatched runners with orders for deployment of reserves. At the weak point in the defenses the Gauls seized a height and began hurling missiles upon the Roman camp below. Because of their great numbers they were able constantly to commit fresh troops. They filled in the moat and engaged the exhausted legionaries, many of whom had used up their weapons. Caesar ordered Labienus to march to the relief of the embattled troops with six cohorts. Meanwhile, however, Vercingetorix's men overwhelmed several turrets and dismantled a portion of the rampart with grappling hooks. Caesar sent Decimus Brutus and Gaius Fabius to reinforce the line, and he himself descended to exhort the troops. Hastening to Labienus' aid, he withdrew four cohorts from a stable sector and ordered part of the cavalry to follow him and part to pass through the outer entrenchments to harry the enemy from the rear.

Caesar's arrival was signaled by his scarlet commander's cloak, "which it was his habit to wear in action as a distinguishing mark."[16] Upon his appearance, both sides raised a war cry that was echoed up and down the entrenchments. Heartened by the presence of their general, the legionaries plied their swords with renewed élan. While the cavalry struck the Gauls from the rear, relief cohorts advanced to the fray in military file. The enemy faltered and then broke. In the panic, slaughter ensued. Upon the sudden reversal of fortune, Vercingetorix withdrew into the town.

Caesar's men were too weary to pursue the tens of thousands of Gauls in flight, and only after midnight did Caesar send the cavalry after the fugitives. Many Gauls were captured or slain, and seventy-four standards were brought to Caesar.

The next morning a deputation arrived from Alesia to seek terms. Caesar ordered the surrender of all arms and the personal capitulation of the leaders. He set his seat in the entrenchments and waited. Abruptly, unannounced, "Vercingetorix appeared . . . and threw some who were present into alarm, for he was very tall to begin with and in his armor he made an extremely imposing figure."[17] All present were aware that they were participating in an event of momentous solemnity befitting the end of a seven-year war of conquest. (They could not appreciate, of course, the momentous significance for Western civilization of Rome's advance into the northwest of the continent.)

Some of Caesar's officers apparently wrote accounts of what they saw, accounts transmitted through various ancient historians. One reported that the Gaul declared to Caesar: "Receive these spoils, you yourself, bravest of men, have conquered a brave enemy." Another, however, declared that Vercingetorix."uttered no word but fell upon his knees with hands clasped in an attitude of supplication [and that] Caesar reproached him in this matter on which he most relied for his safety and by setting over against his claim of former friendship his recent opposition showed his offense to have been the more grievous. Therefore he did not pity him even at the time but immediately confined him in bonds."[18]

Conscious of their own glory in securing the fate of Gaul, the legionaries hailed Caesar as Imperator, and he, in turn, rewarded them with a prisoner apiece either to hold for ransom, to sell to slave dealers or to retain as servants.

In the exuberance, however, never unmindful of long-range policy, Caesar kept apart among the tens of thousand,s of prisoners the Arvernians and Aeduans, numbering twenty thousand, and gave them their freedom, confirming thereby his clientship over these two key states of Central Gaul, a clientship that would prove decisive to his future and to the future of Rome.

XXXIX
AN OUTSIDER ONCE AGAIN

CATO was defeated in the consular elections. Although Caesar's agents provided campaign funds against him and he himself refused to distribute bribes or enter into private alliances, his defeat reflected most especially the lack of support for a quixotic defender of outmoded values in the new heyday of market-oriented plantations and manufactures and of imperial banking interests. With Stoic aplomb and idiosyncratic cantankerousness, upon the proclamation of the polling results, Cato "anointed himself and practiced ball in the Campus Martius and after the midday meal, as was his wont, went down into the Forum without shoes or tunic and walked about there with his intimates."[1] Caesar knew the Man of Virtue too well to be beguiled by this pretense of sangfroid.

Cato's defeat was counterbalanced by Pompeius' increasing hostility. Upon protests that a bill he sponsored to require registration in person of all candidates for office contravened the law passed earlier that year granting Caesar the privilege of registering his candidacy for a consulship in absentia, Pompeius feigned dismay at his oversight, and without Senate approval or assembly ratification he affixed an amendment to the new law granting a specific exemption to Caesar. His action was of dubious validity. In the future *he* would decide which law he considered appropriate. Furthermore, with another law he mandated the appointment to provincial commands of consulars who had never held such posts. Many additional senators thus became eligible to replace Caesar. On the other hand, Pompeius prorogued his own governorship of the Two Spains for an additional five years, thereby assuring himself of a military command after Caesar's expired.

Pompeius and his new allies were preparing for a test of strength. Elated at their reassumption of power, the optimates proclaimed their intention to destroy Caesar, and in optimate-dominated courts jurors with cynical indifference even to a pretense at equity were convicting factional opponents of electoral corruption or of association with the violence following upon Clodius' murder. Cicero, formerly an enthusiastic prosecutor of "subversives," exclaimed to a client whom he failed to save from conviction and exile: "The condition of the laws, the law courts and politics in general with which it seems we are threatened is such that the man who has quitted this republic of ours with the lightest penalty would appear to have come off best."[2] Scipio, Pompeius' consular colleague and father-in-law, repealed Clodius' laws restricting religious obstruction of legislation and curbing the partisan exploitation of the censorship; restoring to the optimates by his first bill a religious weapon; by the second facilitating censorial expulsion of Caesar's friends from the senatorial and equestrian orders.

In this tense and menacing atmosphere, Caesar rejoiced in the arrival of Marcus Antonius to serve as his quaestor. The son of the ever-maneuvering Julia of the elder branch of the clan and of the Antonius with whom Caesar had served some twenty years earlier in the campaign against the Cretan pirates, Antonius joined the numerous relatives and connections on Caesar's staff: Caesar's nephew Pedius, Antonius' brother-in-law Vatinius, Sulpicius Rufus (son? of the tribune allied to Marius and murdered by Sulla), who was married to a Julia, as well as Antonius' uncle Lucius Caesar, Caesar's legate in command of the Province. With no hope of a grandson any longer, Caesar had been advancing the careers of young aristocrats like the lamented Publius Crassus and Decimus Brutus. Now Antonius was to enjoy his favor. A member of the set of young profligates at Rome, Antonius was given to flamboyant posturing. With his broad forehead, heavy mat of hair, full sideburns, carefully trimmed beard framing a face of power and energy, aristocratic slightly bowed nose and muscular physique, he affected a resemblance to Hercules, from whom he claimed descent. He sometimes appeared in public wearing a lion's skin. Adding to his flamboyance was his oratory with its exuberant magniloquence in what was called the Asiatic style. Above all, however, Antonius was valorous, as much a spendthrift of life as of money. Once in an assault against rebels in Judea, he had inspired his troops by being the first to mount the fortifications. In the expedition to restore the Egyptian king to his throne (a venture Antonius had encouraged Gabinius to undertake) he had exhibited similar dash. He was idolized by legionaries for his bravado, his willingness to share the hardships of the common soldiers, his camaraderie in drinking, brawling and whoring and his solicitation of the comfort and safety of his troops. From his father he had acquired an easy-going profligacy; from his mother, energy and ambition; but above all it was his braggadocio that roused wonder.

As driven as his legionaries to complete the pacification of Gaul, Caesar denied the scattered rebels time to regroup. On the last day of December he marched out of Bibracte into the territory of the unpacified Bituriges, surprising people at work in the fields and capturing thousands. He sent cavalry after those who fled into adjoining states and issued a proclamation declaring his determination "to keep friends loyal and to bring doubters by intimidation to terms of peace."[3] When he offered clemency to all who yielded forthwith to his authority, the demoralized Bituriges requested terms.

(For the account of the events of this final year, 51, of the Gallic campaigns, we are indebted to Caesar's loyal associate Hirtius, who in response to Balbus' importuning after Caesar's assassination added an eighth book to Caesar's Commentaries on the Gallic War. In a preface, after explaining the circumstances under which he agreed to provide a conclusion to Caesar's Gallic Commentaries, Hirtius declares:

> I trust that those who will read [this work] will understand how unwillingly I have undertaken the task of writing this Commentary; for so shall I the easier free myself from the charge of folly and of presumption for having intruded myself in the middle of Caesar's writings. For it is universally agreed that nothing was ever so elaborately finished by others that is not surpassed by the refinement of these Commentaries. They have been published that historians may not lack knowledge of those great achievements; and so strong is the unanimous verdict of approval as to make it appear that historians have been robbed of an opportunity rather than enriched with one.* Yet here is our own admiration greater than other men's; the world knows how excellently, how faultlessly, but we know also how easily, how speedily he completed his Commentaries. Caesar possessed not only the greatest facility and refinement of style, but also the surest skill in explaining his own plans.... We listen in different fashion to events which fascinate us by their wonderful novelty and to events which we are to state in evidence. Yet I doubt not that, in collecting every plea to excuse myself from comparison with Caesar, I incur a charge of presumption for imagining that there is anyone in whose judgment I can be set beside Caesar.[†])

Conscious of the weariness of the legionaries, Caesar granted a bonus of 200 sesterces to the troops and 2,000 to the centurions for campaigning in almost unendurable winter cold. To mitigate the strain on the men, Caesar rotated assignments. (They noted that he was unsparing of himself.) It was a tribute to the discipline of the legionaries and a warrant of their devotion to Caesar as well as of their conviction of fighting the final engagements in a momentous historical undertaking that they acquiesced in his prohibition against pillage, reacting like no other Roman army within memory. Caesar persuaded them that only with such restraint could he reconcile the Gauls to Roman rule and avert further rebellions.

Next Caesar struck at the Carnutes. Terrorized, they capitulated. Then in response to an appeal from the faithful Remi, Caesar turned on the Bellovaci. He "deemed it important not only to his honor but even to his security that no

---

*The ancients considered "commentaries" as mere notes to be transformed by scholars into full-fledged "history."

†Admired as a decent, modest and honorable man even by the ever-vacillating Cicero, Hirtius was apparently not troubled by the supposed distortions in Caesar's writings on account of which some twentieth-century scholars impugn "the myth" of Caesar's greatness.

disaster should come upon allies who had deserved exceedingly well of the republic." The Bellovaci had chosen as commanders a chief "to whom the name of the Roman people was most hateful" as well as Caesar's former protégé Commius. When the Bellovaci retired into the forests and marshlands and dispatched Commius across the Rhine for reinforcements, Caesar recognized "a prudence far removed from the recklessness of barbarians." Laying gangways of prefabricated sections on brushwood over a marsh, Caesar advanced and annihilated their forces in an ambush. Deputies appealed for terms, blaming their leader for rousing the untutored commons in defiance of the tribal elders. Caesar rejected this excuse, and in his account to the Senate Romans would recognize a pointed rebuttal to optimate propaganda blaming a single dead individual (Clodius) for civil dissension and disorders. "It was easy enough," Caesar declared, "to shift the blame of the offense on to the dead, but no one was so powerful if chiefs [analogous to the leadership of the Senate at Rome] and the council [the Senate at Rome] were in opposition and all good citizens adverse, he could excite and conduct a war by means of a feeble band of common folk [Clodius' partisans]."[4] (Caesar was suggesting, of course, that the disaffection in Italy was not to be blamed on any single charismatic leader but was to be traced to social and economic tensions within the society.)

At Rome it was now Caesar, not the murdered Clodius, who was being singled out as the danger to the commonwealth. The five-year prorogation of his proconsulship was about to run out, and the consul Marcus Marcellus (goaded out of his natural sluggishness by private rancor at Caesar) was insisting that in Gaul "the war was ended, peace was established and the victorious army ought to be disbanded, also that no account be taken of Caesar at the elections unless he were present." The majority of the senators resented Marcellus' refusal to discuss any other business than the displacement of Caesar, and they murmured approval when the other consul, the learned jurisconsult Servius, "urged the Senate" to draw lessons from the events of the previous generation when Roman politics had experienced "a ruthlessness hitherto quite unprecedented." He warned that under present circumstances "whosoever should succeed in the crushing of the republic by force of arms should display a tyranny far more intolerable."[5]

As determined now as in Cicero's consulship to crush all threats to their hegemony, the optimates sought to undermine Caesar's prestige with rumors, reporting imaginary disasters in Gaul: Caesar had lost his cavalry, the VIIth legion had been mauled, and Caesar himself had been cut off by the Bellovaci. In repeating such tales, Ahenobarbus, it was said, "puts his fingers to his lips before he speaks" as though about to disclose a state secret. When Caesar dispatched the XVth legion to Cisalpina as a garrison against incursions by Illyrian brigands, the optimates alleged that without consulting the Senate or the Roman people Caesar was conferring citizenship on the Transpadanes, and the consul Marcellus proposed that colonists Caesar had settled at Lake Como be deprived of their citizenship; he ordered a magistrate from the colony flogged and then advised him "to carry his scars and show them to Caesar."[6]

The citizenry was sated with squabbling and revolted by the stream of scandals in the courts, the elections and the provincial administrations. When Messalla, a consul of the previous year, indicted for bribery in the election campaign of two years earlier, the most venal Rome had ever known, was acquitted after flagrant subornation of the jury by his uncle and defense counsel, Hortensius, people called the verdict "the most discreditable thing that has ever happened,"[7] and Hortensius was jeered when he entered the theater. More outrageous were events surrounding the trial of Gaius Claudius, elder brother to the murdered tribune and formerly a legate to Caesar. A Claudian was not easily convicted, especially in this time of unabashed corruption, but, to universal astonishment, Gaius was condemned for extortion as governor of Asia. The mystery was resolved when Gaius' son indicted a member of his father's staff for absconding with the bribe money.

From Cilicia Cicero, newly installed as governor, sent indignant complaints about his predecessor, Appius, the eldest of the three Claudian brothers, who, Cicero charged, had "permanently ruined" the province. "I have heard of nothing," Cicero reported, "but inability to pay the poll taxes imposed, universal sales of taxes, groans and moans from the communities, appalling excesses as of some savage beast rather than a human being. In a phrase these people are absolutely tired of their lives."[8]

Gaius Marcellus, a cousin to the present consul and an equally embittered foe to Caesar, was elected consul for the coming year (50). As for Pompeius, people noted that "he thinks one thing and says another and yet is not quite clever enough to disguise his desires." Now openly hostile, he charged that "since Caesar's own means were not sufficient to complete the works which he had planned nor to do all that he had led the people to expect on his return, he desired a state of general unrest and turmoil."[9]

The intensifying opposition at Rome heightened the pressure on Caesar for a swift resolution in Gaul. He developed a threefold strategy aimed at destroying irreconcilable foes, at rendering rebels still in arms hateful to the rest of the population for prolonging a hopeless resistance and at winning goodwill by acts of clemency. He devastated the countryside where Ambiorix, unpunished for his annihilation of fifteen Roman cohorts, continued to elude search parties; and Labienus wrought similar havoc in the lands of the equally stubborn Treveri. On the other hand, Caesar was prevented from displaying clemency toward a certain Gutruatus, delivered over to him as the original inspirer of the general rebellion. Exasperated at the continuing Gallic resistance and at their own hardships, the legionaries demanded a ruthless punishment, and "in opposition to his own inclination [Caesar] was compelled to execute him by the troops, who gathered in a mighty crowd, for they attributed to him all the dangers and losses of the war. He was therefore scourged to death and then decapitated."[10]

Caesar calculated every act not only in terms of political expediency but also in regard to his vision of himself. In inaugurating a policy of terror, he confronted a danger of brutalizing himself, of imitating his troops rather than providing an example to them. This realization would influence his future policy.

Nevertheless, because of a potential morale problem with his war-weary army and the mounting crisis at Rome, Caesar judged that the obstinacy of rebels holed up in Uxellodunum in southwestern Gaul "must be visited with a severe punishment, for he feared that the Gauls as a whole might suppose that what had been lacking in them for resisting the Romans was not strength but resolution." Caesar's enemies at Rome, motivated more by rancor than by patriotism, were assuring Gauls still in arms "that there was one more summer season in his term of office" and "that if they could hold out for that [additional year], they had no further danger to fear."[11]

At Rome, convinced that Caesar would be preoccupied for months at the siege of Uxellodunum, a fortress atop a cliff within a bend of the Duranius (Durance, a tributary of the Garonne), the optimates prepared new moves against him. Pompeius' father-in-law Scipio proposed that the question of replacing Caesar as a proconsul "be brought before the Senate on the first of March [of the coming year—50] and that no other matter . . . be combined with it." At first Pompeius pretended to oppose the measure, but four weeks later, on September 30, having "definitely ascertained that Pompeius' inclinations were in the direction of having a decree passed that Caesar should quit his province after the first of March," the consul Marcellus in concert with Ahenobarbus, Scipio and the tribune-elect Curio formally moved Scipio's proposal.[12]

Caesar's foes were apparently confident that even as Lucullus' foes had undermined his authority while he was engaged in the war against Mithridates they could now deprive Caesar of his commands and then complete his humiliation upon his return to Rome. But Caesar was a far more astute and tenacious opponent. He kept abreast of events and maintained an effective corps of agents to defend his dignity at Rome. For the moment, avoiding a confrontation that might alienate uncommitted senators, Caesar's men did not resist the resolution to bring the issue of Caesar's provincial command before the Senate on March 1. They did, however, oppose three other resolutions: one prohibiting a tribunician veto in the discussion on March 1, 50 (a new optimate attempt at curbing the tribunician authority); another, a copy of a measure passed against Lucullus, permitting "soldiers now in the army of Gaius Caesar . . . who have served their full time or have pleas to advance, which pleas would entitle them to a discharge [to bring] their cases . . . before the Senate";[13] and a third, permitting Caesar's replacement by ex-praetors as well as former consuls, a measure making available a larger pool of individuals to take over Caesar's three provincial governorships.

At the session of the Senate at which the varied resolutions relating to the termination of Caesar's proconsulship were presented, Pompeius, suddenly transformed into a strict constitutionalist, expressed profound concern regarding possible violations of the constitution in regard to Caesar's position. When he announced that after March 1 he would defend whatever action the Senate held advisable, an optimate senator asked: "What if there were any [tribunician] vetoes interposed on that day?"

"It made no difference," replied Pompeius, oblivious to the cynicism with which he himself had repeatedly employed tribunes to contravene the will of the Senate, "whether Caesar was going to refuse to obey the Senate or whether he put up someone to obstruct its decrees."

"What if he is minded," insisted another senator, "to be consul and keep his army at the same time?" (a violation of the constitution of which Pompeius himself was currently guilty).

"What if my own son," declared Pompeius (formerly Caesar's son-in-law and still Caesar's publicly acknowledged heir) "should be minded to lay his stick across my shoulders?"[14]

Arriving at Uxellodunum, Caesar found officers and legionaries demoralized at the prospect of a long siege. Only by depriving the defenders of access to a spring outside the walls could they compel a surrender. Caesar "alone saw how it could be done," writes Hirtius, "and once again he inspired his men with his daring and imagination as well as his confidence in their capacities." In a technological tour-de-force, he advanced a ramp sixty feet in height upon which he pushed forward a ten-story tower from which legionaries could rain missiles upon townspeople who ventured forth for water. Simultaneously he dug a mine and diverted the spring. Awed by the massive constructions and desperate at the sudden drying up of the spring, the defenders concluded that these marvels were "due not to the device of man but to the act of god" and surrendered.[15]

Caesar decreed a punishment for the rebels captured at Uxellodunum that was at once dreadful and, for the times, merciful. "While granting them their lives, he cut off the hands of all who had borne arms to testify the more openly the penalty of evildoers." Returning to their homes throughout Gaul, these men would carry a sign of the wages of rebellion and serve as warnings to potential insurgents. On the other hand, by sparing their lives and not selling them into slavery, Caesar demonstrated his readiness for reconciliation. Immediately thereafter a fugitive rebel chief of the Senones, despairing of his cause, starved himself to death; and another chief, "a champion of revolution who always exercised great influence among the natives," was betrayed by an Arvernian with whom he had sought refuge, "a devoted friend of the Roman people [who] put him in bonds without hesitation and brought him to Caesar."[16] During these developments Labienus completed the pacification of the Treveri and captured the only Aeduan leader still in arms.

From Uxellodunum Caesar undertook a tour of Aquitania, subdued several years earlier by Publius Crassus. He was met by envoys of the states, who offered hostages as warrants of their loyalty. Next he turned into the Province and began a triumphal procession in celebration of the conclusion of the campaign of so many years and of the victory which brought the Province a promise of enduring security and prosperity. He rewarded tribes, communities and individuals who had contributed to the eight-year struggle. Finally, he journeyed north and established headquarters at Nemetocenna (Arras) in the country of the Atrebates, the people over whom he had set his one-time protégé Commius as king. It was a sign of the end of the war that Commius should now sue for peace and deliver hostages to Caesar's quaestor, Marcus Antonius. It was a sign, too, of the depth of rancor of chiefs whom Caesar had deprived of their power that Commius should set as a condition for his surrender "that he should not come into the sight of any Roman."[17]

Caesar understood the pathos of men committed to lost causes and outworn institutions. He acquiesced in Commius' demand, and the chief departed for asylum into Britain.

XL

RECONCILIATION IN GAUL, ISOLATION AT ROME

CAESAR decided to winter among the Belgians to confirm peace in that region, "for there was nothing which he desired less than to have the definite necessity of a campaign imposed upon him on the eve of his quitting his province for fear that when he was about to lead his army south he might leave behind a war which all Gaul would readily take up without immediate danger." Caesar could not risk the possibility of disorders at his rear while he dealt with the crisis at Rome. More than that, he had to be assured of support, even with sizable contingents, from recently subjugated Gallic states in the event of a contest with enemies at home. He had much to offer the Gauls: security of their borders against invaders and an end to the interminable warfare among and within the states. With their incorporation into the imperial system, the Gauls could anticipate, too, an upsurge in commerce with the entire Mediterranean world. "By addressing the states in terms of honor, by bestowing ample presents upon the chiefs, by imposing no new burdens, he easily kept Gaul at peace after the exhaustion of so many defeats, under improved conditions of obedience."[1] Cynics, of course, argued that circumstances required clemency, but they overlooked Caesar's experiences in his childhood and youth from which he learned the limitations of repression and

terror in maintaining imperial control over subjugated areas. He had undergone a new lesson, too, in regard to terror—that it inspires desperate resistance
and requires constant intensification to remain effective. Caesar was guided
also by the example of Sertorius twenty or more years earlier in Spain for the
institution of a new direction for the empire. Thus he imposed a modest annual
tribute of 40 million sesterces. (Sulla had imposed an indemnity on Asia of 480
million sesterces; shortly before his death Clodius had spent 15 million sesterces on a mansion at Rome; and as a praetor Caesar had personal debts
amounting to 20 million.) Caesar entrusted the collection of the tribute to the
states, protecting them from rapacious publicans. He neither confiscated large
tracts of land nor settled Roman colonists in the conquered territory. He
preserved local autonomy and respected laws and customs.

With the plunder from the final campaigns Caesar could shore up his influence in Italy. Over the years he had been "tempting people with his bribes and
contributing to the expenses of aediles, praetors, consuls and their wives."
Now he redoubled his efforts at buying support. "When he had put all Pompeius' friends under obligation, as well as the great part of the Senate, through
loans made without interest or at a low rate, he lavished gifts on men of all
other classes, both those whom he invited to accept his bounty and those who
applied to him unasked, including even freedmen and slaves who were special
favorites of their masters or patrons." So huge were his shipments of gold
across the Alps that the price of the metal fell by a quarter among the speculators in the Forum. The present crisis, however, involved more than a standard
competition between two ambitious proconsuls. Caesar and Pompeius were
rivals for the patronage of the Mediterranean world, and Caesar set out "to
win the devotion of princes and provinces all over the world, offering prisoners
to some by the thousand as a gift and sending auxiliary troops to the aid of
others . . . without the sanction of the Senate or People, besides adorning the
principal cities of Asia and Greece with magnificent public works, as well as
those of Italy and the provinces of Gaul and Spain." It was rumored that in
response to an appeal he had regaled Athens with 50 talents (1,200,000 sesterces), a report certain to incense Pompeius, who considered himself the patron of the famous city.[2]

Caesar's prize catch was the consul-elect Lepidus Paullus, elder son of the
Lepidus who had mounted a coup against the Senate twenty-five years earlier.
For a grant of 36 million sesterces (almost a year's tribute from the Gauls)
toward the reconstruction of the Basilica Aemilia, a great hall and center of the
moneychangers built by an Aemilian in the previous century, Caesar expected
Lepidus to neutralize his consular colleague, the second hostile Marcellus to
hold the high office. On the other hand, Caesar's negotiations apparently
broke down with the tribune-elect Curio, a leader of the young prodigals who
had badgered the triumvirs during Caesar's consulship. Curio had bankrupted
himself in grandiose funeral games for his father, astonishing Rome by present-

ing performances simultaneously in two theaters back to back and then revolving the stages on turntables to form an amphitheater for gladiatorial combats. Balking at the exorbitant price Curio demanded, Caesar confronted the handicap of having no competent tribune in his service.

On March 1, 50, the day fixed for a Senate debate on the termination of Caesar's proconsulship, the consul Gaius Marcellus moved that new governors be appointed for the Gauls and for Illyricum. His colleague, Paullus, remained strangely silent. The tribune Curio, as expected, spoke in favor of the motion. To the general astonishment, however, he added an amendment calling for Pompeius' simultaneous resignation as governor of the Two Spains and for the demobilization of Pompeius' legions along with Caesar's. No one could gainsay the logic in Curio's proposal. Under his motion all those apprehensive of Caesar's military power and of Pompeius' domination of the city would be reassured, and "the state would be free and independent." "Unless they both obeyed," Curio declared, "both should be voted public enemies and military force levied against them." The majority of the senators, previously leaderless and intimidated by the optimates and Pompeius, murmured their approval of Curio's evenhanded justice. Outside the hall, massed to learn the results of a momentous debate, the people, apprized of Curio's maneuver, greeted him with exultation and "escorted him home, scattering flowers as though he were an athlete and had won the prize in some great and difficult contest."[3] Curio had tapped a general yearning for peace.

Now, with hindsight, optimates recalled Curio's embitterment at their rejection of legislation he had proposed earlier that year. Some insisted that at the time of his election as tribune they had warned against him as "a man who never does anything according to plan." Others had dismissed him as "eloquent, reckless, prodigal alike of his own fortune and chastity and of those of other people, a man of the utmost cleverness in perversity."[4] Shrewder observers rebuked themselves for failing to take into account Curio's recent marriage. Curio had taken as his bride Clodius' widow, Fulvia. She was goading the brash, articulate and energetic Curio into daring ventures, even as she had done with her previous husband. She realized that Caesar needed Curio more than did the optimates and would pay a higher price for his collaboration. Besides, Fulvia had worked with Caesar in the past, and gossips might speculate that Marcus Antonius had helped to win Curio's cooperation, for in their youth the two men had paraded about openly as lovers. It was even bruited that Curio had long ago been suborned by Caesar and had disseminated the story of the breakdown of their negotiations in order to mislead Caesar's enemies. Caesar had experience in such maneuvers, and Fulvia was a woman capable of counseling her husband in such an intrigue.

Though now eligible, after the ten-year interval required by law, to enter his candidacy for a second consulship, Caesar had yet to complete the pacification of Gaul, and he dared not undertake an election campaign until the question of his privilege to register his candidacy in absentia was resolved. With his alliance with Curio, Caesar had room for maneuvering, especially since the optimates were not of a single mind.

At the moment Cicero was caught up in a striking example of the contradictions always emerging among oligarchs. For him as a "new man" a triumph represented the culmination of a career. His petition was opposed by Cato, who insisted that the orator's skirmishes with bandits in Cilician mountain villages did not fulfil the criteria in a law Cato himself had promoted. To win support among the leading nobles, Cicero was compelled to bear witness in favor of his predecessor, the venal Appius Claudius, indicted for the "robberies, outrages and indignities" that, according to Cicero, had brought ruin to the province of Cilicia. Appius had married one of his daughters to one of Pompeius' sons and another to Brutus, Cato's nephew, and Cicero dared not reject the importunings of such personages on Appius' behalf. On the other hand, Dolabella, Cicero's daughter's fiancé, a young patrician of the prestigious Cornelian clan (an impressive catch for the family of a new man), was seeking to advance his career as prosecutor against Appius. In this dilemma Cicero's confidant at Rome, the aedile Caelius, urged Cicero to utter "not a word" about the marriage negotiations for fear of jeopardizing his chances for a triumph.[5]

It could be argued that in the current general corruption a new man could be pardoned for scanting principle to achieve his supreme aspiration. Cicero's morality was strained, however, not only in regard to Appius Claudius. Upon a request from Appius' son-in-law, Marcus Brutus, for a squadron of cavalry to enable two moneylenders to collect a debt from the Cypriot town of Salamis, Cicero discovered that at Brutus' behest under Appius' governorship one of these moneylenders had besieged the town council until five of the elders starved to death. Furthermore, Cicero learned that the usurers were charging forty-eight per cent interest on their loan. When Cicero noted that a Senate decree set a limit of twelve per cent, the moneylenders produced another Senate decree granting an exemption from the interest regulations for this particular debt. Cicero proposed terms of settlement. The Salaminians agreed; the moneylenders demurred. To Cicero's astonishment, writing in "an arrogant, bold tone and uncivilly," Brutus confessed that he himself was the actual creditor. Cicero was "horror-stricken," for the terms of the loan "spelled ruin to the community." Fearful of alienating Brutus while his petition for a triumph was still pending, Cicero postponed the matter for resolution by his successor. On the other hand, he did prod a local princeling into paying Brutus some 2,400,000 sesterces on another loan. Discovering that the potentate was burdened also by a great debt to Pompeius, Cicero exclaimed that he had "never seen a kingdom more plundered." Pompeius, "an easy-going creditor willing to forgo his capital and content with interest," received an income of 800,000 sesterces a month from this single loan, and he held many such loans.[6]

Oligarchs extorting such sums from imperial dependencies would fight hard to defend their pelf.

Although Cicero submitted to the churlish insolence of Brutus' agents and dutifully supplied testimonials to assist in Appius' acquittal, Cato continued to oppose a triumph for him. Balbus recognized his opportunity. Just as Curio, out of pique over some unrelated matter, was about to veto the resolution for a thanksgiving on Cicero's victories, Balbus intervened, and Caelius wrote to Cicero: "I can speak highly of Balbus' assiduous efforts, for he had a heated interview with Curio."[7] Balbus could be confident that Cicero would remember that Caesar, too, had been prevented from holding a triumph by Cato and that he would contrast Caesar's sympathy for his aspirations with Cato's diffidence.

Pompeius fell ill at Naples with a stomach ailment. The optimates were in despair. They prompted towns throughout Italy to offer sacrifices for Pompeius' recovery, and upon his convalescence they mounted a triumphal procession to bring him back to Rome. "No place could contain those who came to greet him . . . but roads and villages and ports were filled with sacrificing and feasting throngs. Many also with garlands on their heads and lighted torches in their hands welcomed him and escorted him on his way, pelting him with flowers."[8] It was not difficult to account for the intense emotion of the populace. As they had demonstrated in their grief at the death of young Julia, the people were in terror of new civil dissensions and feared any disturbance in the political equilibrium. Many believed that Pompeius represented a bulwark against senatorial excesses and considered him still an ally of Caesar's.

With the solemnity appropriate to one recalled from death by the prayers of the citizenry, Pompeius announced his willingness to resign his commands before the expiration of their term. He expected once again a tearful appeal not to desert the republic, but Curio would have nothing to do with charades. Promises, he declared bluntly, resolved nothing. He demanded Pompeius' resignation forthwith. The warlord's friends hooted with indignation, but they could not secure a Senate resolution of censure against the contumacious tribune. On the other hand, the optimates succeeded in passing a decree requiring Pompeius and Caesar each to surrender a legion for service against the Parthians, reportedly massed for an invasion of Syria. Pompeius announced that he would give up the legion he had transferred to Caesar after the massacre of Caesar's fifteen cohorts. "Caesar, though there was not the least doubt about the intention of his opponents, nevertheless sent the legion back to Pompeius and on his own account ordered the XVth, which he had kept in Nearer Gaul, to be handed over in accordance with the Senate's decree."[9] The troops of the two legions Caesar rewarded with a bonus of two years' pay with a specially minted coin depicting Caesar's ancestor the Trojan hero Aeneas and his father Anchises, a common representation of pietas. Symbolically Caesar was promising the men his continued devotion and requesting their loyalty in turn.

The optimates had learned the necessity of constantly puffing up Pompeius' self-esteem. Appius Claudius' nephew, dispatched to lead Caesar's two legions into Italy, reported general disaffection among the troops and an eagerness for a transfer to Pompeius' command. Pompeius was exultant at the report. Upon learning that Caesar was recruiting Gauls in both the Province and among the newly subjugated states for a legion called the Alaudae (from the Gallic word for lark—the legion's insignia) and that Caesar was mustering additional Gallic and German auxiliaries, Pompeius sneered that Caesar was nothing more than his own creation and vaunted that "he would pull him down much more easily than he had raised him up." Giddy at the applause of the optimates, he further proclaimed, "In whatever part of Italy I stamp upon the ground, there will spring up armies of foot and horse."[10]

The optimates were elated also at their victory in the consular elections, for they overwhelmed Caesar's candidate and former legate, Galba, "though he had been far stronger in influence and votes alike because he was intimately connected with Caesar by personal friendship and by service as his lieutenant." Another Marcellan (the third in succession), husband to Caesar's great-niece Octavia but as hostile to Caesar as his cousin and brother before him, as well as Lentulus Crus, a bankrupt opportunist, "had been elected," the exuberant optimates announced, "to despoil Caesar of every office and distinction."[11]

Caesar had to disabuse both his former ally and his optimate enemies of any misapprehension regarding the breadth of his support in Italy and his determination to defend himself in any confrontation. To demonstrate his continuing influence among the electorate, he promoted the candidacy of Marcus Antonius against Ahenobarbus for a vacancy in the college of augurs. The election was as much a test of strength between Caesar and his opponents as his own election as pontifex maximus more than a decade earlier. While journeying across the Alps to exhort the Cisalpiners to travel to Rome to cast votes for Antonius, Caesar received word that the election had already taken place and that those "who desired by the defeat of Marcus Antonius to upset the influence of Caesar when he should retire from his province" had suffered a rebuff. Indignant at his defeat, Ahenobarbus charged that the priesthood "had been snatched away from him by an act of injustice." He was infuriated "that the people should have such joy at his discomfiture."[12]

Declaring his desire to thank the voters of Cisalpina for supporting Antonius, Caesar continued on his way. The Cisalpiners were aware of the attempts of the optimates to destroy their hero. They massed to demonstrate their loyalty, and his procession proved more splendid than Pompeius' after the latter's illness. Most of Caesar's legionaries had been recruited in Cisalpina, and the provincials considered Caesar one of their own. They sensed, too, the prosperity they would enjoy at the new frontiers Caesar had won for them and looked forward to further profits from his future campaigns. Thus "the arrival of Caesar was welcomed . . . with honor and affection beyond all belief. . . . The whole population with the children went forth to meet him, victims were sacrificed everywhere, festal couches duly spread [for images of the gods] occupied market places and temples so as to anticipate if possible the joy of the triumph so long, so very long expected. Such was the magnificence shown by the richer folk, such the eagerness of the humbler sort."[13]

Reassured, if indeed he required reassurance, of the devotion of the Cisalpiners, Caesar returned to Belgium for a review of his victorious legions, a ceremony of general celebration and of mutual congratulations. Glistening in arms inlaid with silver and gold, arms furnished by Caesar as fit accoutrements for élite troops who had brought Europe from the Ocean to the Rhine into the imperial sphere, the legionaries paraded before Caesar and hailed him as their commander and their comrade. The legates, military tribunes and prefects marched in elegant cuirasses, tight leather jerkins fitted with strips of bronze, silvered shin pieces and brilliant cloaks with metal insignia—wreaths, silver spearheads, gold crowns, miniature standards—according to their rank. Gallic and German auxiliaries pranced by in formation, corselets, helmets, shields and lances flashing.

Glorying in their splendor and might, legionaries and cavalrymen shouted greetings to Caesar as they passed the reviewing stand, proclaiming their pride in their excellence as soldiers and in the genius of their general and their confidence in vanquishing any foe against whom Caesar might lead them. Those who looked forward to retirement on some plot of ground Caesar would obtain for them as a bonus for years of devoted service could wonder whether they could submit to a life of tranquility and routine after the zest of peril, the exuberance of victory, the adventure of invading unknown corners of the world, the joys and sorrows of comradeship and the pride of association with Caesar.

So long as Caesar retained influence at Rome his officers could anticipate advancement in the progress of magistracies. Every year, indeed, Caesar had sent some of them back to run for office and had appointed to his staff cooperative magistrates upon the expiration of their terms. This year one legate had been elected a praetor; Caesar's close associate Pansa, an aedile; and Marcus Antonius, a tribune (as well as an augur). Caesar ordered Labienus, for so many years his second in command, to lead the XIIIth legion into Cisalpina as a replacement for one of the legions surrendered to the Senate for duty against the Parthians. Labienus was to campaign for a consulship with Caesar for the year after next (48).

In reward for their devotion and as a warrant of his future generosity, Caesar announced a doubling of the legionaries' pay.

If Pompeius and the optimates posed a challenge to his dignity and his future, Caesar would be prepared.

XLI

CIVIL WAR?

CATO and the other optimates harbored the illusion that in any crisis they could manipulate the citizenry to do their will. They believed that despite the exposure of corruption and ineptitude in every facet of political life they could still persuade the citizenry that the preservation of oligarchic hegemony was essential for the common welfare and that defense of the privileges of a tiny coterie was a divinely sanctioned, patriotic obligation. Caesar had deeper insight into the political dynamics of the commonwealth than his optimate opponents. He understood that the people had more pressing concerns than the defense of oligarchic privilege. Having experienced during the last decades the contemptuous indifference of the oligarchs to their problems, the citizenry had undergone a profound alienation. Over his lifetime Caesar could trace the erosion of respect for ancestral values and for established institutions. After more than a generation of almost unremitting civil strife, anti-subversive hysteria, cynical disregard of the constitution, scandals in elections, the courts and in provincial administration, and the substitution of bribery, assassination and gang warfare for rational debate and orderly political processes, the patriotic commitment to the republic that Caesar took for granted when growing up had all but evaporated even among the youth of the aristocracy. Cato proclaimed that the world would function well enough were it not for "troublemakers," that institutional reforms merely upset the divine order and that a return to the old virtues by the aristocracy would resolve all problems. The leaders of the optimates had so long monopolized power and influence in the commonwealth that they assumed, beyond argument, that their views represented an unassailable orthodoxy. The thoughts and opinions of Cato's clique were "good Roman thoughts and opinions," the contrary were at best outlandish, at worst "subversive," and fundamental political and social questions were rarely posed in the elections (that epitome of Roman oligarchic "democracy").

A few optimates did sense a need to restore the image of the oligarchy. As a newly elected censor, Appius Claudius, one of the most venal of the nobles, was supposedly "performing prodigies" in expelling corrupt individuals from the senatorial and equestrian orders. By "vigorous activity in the matter of statues and pictures, the amount of land held and debts"[1] (violations of sumptuary laws and of the financial qualifications for the two aristocratic orders), he gained a reputation as a scourger of profligacy, and the people, ever short of

308

memory, forgot Appius' shabby personal history. In fact, of course, Appius was not conducting a crusade for moral regeneration but a campaign for eliminating opposition to the optimate party.

More than a decade earlier, awaiting Pompeius' return from the East, the optimates had mobilized to crush all dissension; so now, too, as they prepared for a struggle with Caesar they were once again hunting out their enemies. Caesar's agents had promoted the election of Caesar's father-in-law as Appius' colleague in the censorship, but Calpurnius had no stomach for factional vendettas, and he proved ineffectual in resisting Appius' wholesale blacklisting. Appius' victims, like the victims of the optimate courts, saw hope of redress only in Caesar, and Caesar's agents sought to enrol them into his party. One of their outstanding catches was the aedile Caelius. As tribune in 52, an outstanding orator and wit without principles, he had defended Milo, Clodius' murderer. Now, in retaliation, Appius, Clodius' brother, charged Caelius with unnatural sexual appetites and threatened to expel him from the Senate. Caelius countered with a similar indictment of the censor. Cato rallied to Appius' defense. "Getting off his gelding," Cato sneered, "the fellow performs a step dance and pours out a flood of cheap patter. . . . What is more, he sings when so disposed, sometimes recites Greek verses, cracks jokes, varying the tone of his voice and performing a step dance." Caesar's agents were alert to the opportunity; Caelius was receptive. Writing to Cicero he declared that "so long as the struggle is carried on constitutionally and without recourse to arms [men] are bound to follow the more honorable and when it comes to war and taking the field, the stronger cause and to resolve upon that as the better course in proportion to its greater safety." In any prospective conflict he adjudged Caesar's army as "altogether above comparison."[2] A notorious spendthrift forever harried by moneylenders, Caelius suddenly purchased a handsome estate, undoubtedly out of Gallic booty.

Caelius was able to defend himself against Appius' blacklisting, but the censor succeeded in expelling from the Senate another former tribune, one with "popular" sympathies, Gaius Sallustius (who would win fame as the greatest Roman historian of his generation).* Appius revived an old scandal of Sallustius' being caught in flagrante delicto with Milo's wife (Sulla's daughter, a woman notorious for her promiscuity) and paying a substantial ransom after a thorough hiding. Sallustius announced his adherence to Caesar's party, and Caesar instructed Balbus and Oppius to discuss with Sallustius, a litterateur with a penchant for denouncing the degeneracy of his fellow oligarchs, the drafting of a party platform about which to rally support against the optimates. Caesar himself, though the most perspicacious statesman of the day, had not evolved a long-range, comprehensive program of reform for the regeneration of the republic. As consul he had promoted pragmatic measures to

---

*Cited previously as a source historian, Sallust was referred to by his common Anglicized name; henceforth as a participant in events he will be referred to by his Latin name.

alleviate social tensions domestically and in the empire. In the decade since his consulship, however, the alienation of the general population had deepened, and more and more elements of the citizenry were turning away from politics to engage in private searchings through astrology and mystical cults or were surrendering themselves to dissipation or mindless money making.

During the anti-subversion campaign of 63, Caesar had mounted opposition by promoting discussion of real and pressing issues. Now at a distance from the capital, he was compelled to employ a different strategy, publishing a party manifesto drafted by Sallustius in the form of an open letter to Caesar—a program of moderate reform that would appeal to a broad segment of the propertied citizenry. Affecting an archaic style reminiscent of Cato the Censor, Sallustius signaled a turn in Caesar's political strategy by directly attacking Pompeius. He exhorted Caesar to take heed "of the interests of the city" and "to restore the government by the same means by which [Pompeius] had overthrown it." "Insolently exercising a tyranny," Sallustius charged, Pompeius had granted "a few senators the absolute power of regulating the revenues, the expenditures and the courts," and with rhetorical hyperbole Sallustius, a victim himself, denounced the prosecutions and censorial blacklisting by which "Marcus Cato, Lucius Domitius [Ahenobarbus] and the others of that faction have butchered forty senators and many young men of excellent promise like so many sacrificial victims. . . . They have deprived some of their rank, others of their citizenship."[3]

Sallustius proposed to regenerate the republic by expanding participation in its institutions, by alleviating misery, by curbing the arrogance of the leaders of the Senate and by eliminating corruption in the courts and in the elections. He urged the extension of the franchise and the establishment of colonies for the landless and unemployed (planks in all previous popular programs). In language recalling the harangues of the radical tribune Macer some twenty years earlier, he warned Caesar of the "rage and tempests among the nobles, who [would] cry out [with the promotion of such reforms] that the very foundations of society [were] being undermined." He reminded Caesar of the fate Drusus suffered during Caesar's childhood, assassinated for promoting similar measures. Sallustius would reform the courts by selecting jurors from among all propertied citizens and not simply from among senators and equestrians. In regard to the elections, he urged the revival of a Gracchan reform under which the first century to vote in the centuriate assembly would be selected by lot from among the centuries of all propertied voters and not just from among the eighteen equestrian centuries. To break the grip of the inner circle of the Senate, he called for the introduction of the secret ballot and for an increase in the number of senators. On the other hand, like Cicero, Sallustius believed that the crisis of the republic could be cured only with a restoration of morality among the aristocracy, and he appealed to Caesar to curb the frantic pursuit of wealth, the cause of all social ills.

In his concluding exhortation to Caesar, Sallustius openly challenged Pompeius and the leaders of the Senate. "If you rescue almost from the brink of ruin the most famous and powerful of cities," he declared in a direct invocation to Caesar, "who upon the face of this earth will be more famous than you, who will be greater?"

CICERO'S NEAR TRIUMPH

On November 25, 50, returning from his governorship in Cilicia, Cicero landed at Brundisium. Absent from Rome for a year and a half, he had held aloof from the altercations between Caesar and the optimates. Learning of his arrival, Caesar instructed Balbus to solicit the orator's services as a mediator in the current conflict. He and his associates would appeal to the "Father of His Country" to avert civil war and once again to save the republic. Beyond the prospect of such glory, Caesar and his councilors could offer a tangible inducement—assistance in gaining Senate authorization for a triumph. To Cicero's chagrin Cato, who had opposed a triumph for him earlier in the year, now proposed a thanksgiving for his son-in-law Bibulus, governor of Syria, for victories over the Parthians. By awarding Bibulus a thanksgiving of twenty days, the optimates, in effect, were equating his achievements with Caesar's. As governor of a neighboring province, however, Cicero knew the truth about Bibulus' exploits. "So long as there was a single Parthian in Syria," Cicero muttered, "Bibulus did not stir a step further from the city gates than from his house when he was consul [then he had locked himself in his mansion in protest of the actions of his colleague, Caesar]."[4]

Like Caesar and others of their generation, Cicero recalled with horror the massacres and other outrages of the civil wars of their youth. He foresaw that an armed conflict between Caesar and Pompeius would be "the greatest struggle . . . that history has ever known."[5]

Balbus and Oppius and Caesar's other agents reassured Cicero regarding the hostile rumors circulating about Caesar. Inflating the news of the dispatch of the XIIIth legion for garrison duty in Cisalpina, for example, the optimates reported that on October 15 Caesar himself had arrived in Cisalpina at the head of four legions, prepared to march on Rome. In addition, they charged Caesar with inflammatory statements, quoting him as declaring "that now that he was the leading man of the state, it was harder to push him down from the first to the second than it would be from the second"—a remark certain to infuriate Pompeius, who would brook no rival. More alarming was the report that a centurion on leave in Rome upon learning that the Senate would not grant an extension of Caesar's proconsular command slapped the hilt of his sword and exclaimed, "But this will give it."[6]

Caesar and his associates could count on Cicero's undergoing an intensive education as he proceeded from Brundisium to Rome. He would be astonished at the tempo at which the peninsula was hurtling toward a catastrophic civil war and be sobered by the nearly universal anger and despair at the prospect of bloodshed and devastation. There was even the possibility that after his recent experiences with Appius Claudius, Brutus and Cato, Cicero would appreciate the resentment of the populace at the arrogance and corruption of the leaders of the Senate.

Within a week of Cicero's landing in Italy, the censor Appius Claudius announced Curio's expulsion from the Senate, proclaiming his defiance of Caesar's leading associate in the Senate, a tribune and the son of a Sullan general and consular. Prodded by the consul Paullus and by Caesar's agents, Calpurnius roused himself and vetoed his colleague's action. When Appius detailed his charges against Curio before the Senate, the impetuous tribune jumped at him and ripped his toga.[7] The consul Marcellus proposed a motion of censure, but noting the hesitation among the senators Curio responded with a tactic Catilina had employed in similar circumstances thirteen years earlier. "I am conscious of doing what is best and most advantageous to my country," he declared to the senators. "To you, however, I surrender both my body and life to do with as you please." The relationship of forces in 50 was different from that of 63, and Curio foiled Marcellus' maneuver. Denouncing Curio's mentor as a bandit and demanding that Caesar be outlawed if he did not forthwith lay down his command, Marcellus required each senator to express an opinion on two questions: "Shall successors be sent to Caesar?" "Shall Pompeius be deprived of his command?" In response to the first question, all but a few senators signified their approval. Curio, however, was too quick for Marcellus. With the support of Caesar's father-in-law and of the tribune-elect Marcus Antonius, he offered an amendment to Marcellus' second question, proposing a vote on a resolution calling upon both Caesar and Pompeius to lay down their commands.

In the division, three hundred and seventy senators took their place beside Curio; a mere twenty-two sided with Marcellus. Infuriated at Curio's cunning, Marcellus shouted: "Enjoy your victory, and have Caesar for a master."

Curio had exposed the weakness of the warmongering clique and succeeded in representing himself and Caesar as the parties eager for reconciliation. When Curio emerged from the Senate, a crowd pelted him with garlands and flowers. During the day, however, some senators and equestrians donned mourning to display their grief at an impending conflict.

The next morning Marcellus announced to the Senate that Caesar was crossing the Alps with ten legions. To defend the commonwealth he proposed that the two legions surrendered by Caesar for service against the Parthians (but actually retained in Italy) be dispatched to the north. In response, Curio charged Marcellus with rousing alarm with a false report and threatened to veto his proposal. "If I am prevented by the vote of the Senate," cried Marcellus, "from taking steps for the public safety, I will take such steps on my own responsibility as consul." Giving a sign to his faction, he led them out of the Senate house. They marched to Pompeius' mansion outside the walls. Marcellus summoned Pompeius to come forth, handed him a sword and declared: "I command you to march against Caesar and in behalf of your country, and we give you for this purpose the army now at Capua or in any other part of Italy and whatever additional forces you yourself choose to levy."

Although undoubtedly forewarned of the consul's intentions, Pompeius

feared to lose his bargaining power by breaking off all possibility of reconciliation with Caesar. He was aware, too, that without Senate and assembly approval or the passage of the ultimate decree of the Senate, Marcellus had no
constitutional authority to entrust him with an army or to order him to conduct a general levy. In effect, in collaborating in this maneuver, Pompeius and
his optimate allies could be accused of provoking a civil war without constitutional justification. Thus in accepting the consul's orders, Pompeius remarked
with an innuendo not lost on his audience, "Unless we can do better."

During these events Caesar received daily, if belated, dispatches from Rome.
Upon learning of the developments on December 1, the day prior to Marcellus'
offering Pompeius a sword and ordering him to hold a levy, Caesar sent his
trusted aide-de-camp Hirtius to Rome with a message for Pompeius. Alerted as
to Hirtius' mission, Balbus arranged a meeting with Scipio, Pompeius' father-
in-law and confidant, for December 7. Arriving on the evening of the 6th,
however, Hirtius learned of the events of December 2—Pompeius' acceptance
of the command of the legions at Capua and of the responsibility to conduct a
levy against Caesar. A good staff officer, Hirtius decided that his instructions
did not encompass the new circumstances, and unwilling to undertake negotiations without further orders from Caesar, he departed early the next morning
without conferring with Scipio. That evening (December 7) Curio, about to
lose immunity upon the expiration of his tribuneship and convinced that the
optimates were resolved upon war, also set out for Caesar's headquarters at
Ravenna. Upon arriving some days later, he confirmed Sallustius' contention
that the optimates would sooner "buy" Caesar's overthrow "at the cost of
their own lives and . . . do not feel so much pleasure in their supremacy as . . .
chagrin at [his] glory." Insisting that Pompeius outdid the optimates in eagerness for war, Curio urged Caesar to summon his legions from across the Alps
for a march on Rome. Concerned at an accusation of initiating a civil war,
Caesar determined to pursue negotiations. He did, however, order three legions to invest the passes of the Pyrenees against the seven legions Pompeius
maintained on a war footing in the Two Spains. Two other legions he summoned across the Alps into Cisalpina.

Caesar laid great store on Cicero's mediation in the mounting crisis. Cicero
not only enjoyed influence among men of property, but, in addition, his views
often reflected those of a significant element of the citizenry. As usual, Cicero
vacillated. Although alarmed at the belligerence of leading optimates and fearful of sharing a defeat with them, he was even more fearful of their hostility in
the event he failed to share in their victory. Always reluctant to separate
himself from the coterie of leading nobles, he early began to prepare rationales
for a break with Caesar. With petulance he declared to Atticus, to whom only
a few years earlier he had been praising Caesar as a nonpareil of magnanimity:
"Caesar has not been liberal to me considering my services and considering his
lavishness towards others." It salved his conscience to denounce Caesar as a
new Catilina, "a man who fears nothing and is ready for anything" with a
following among "all persons under legal sentence or censorial stigma and all

who deserve the one or the other . . . all the younger people, all the desperate city rabble, some sturdy tribunes . . . all the debt-ridden."[8] In this disingenuous letter Cicero omitted facts he knew at first hand—that few men deserved blacklisting more than the blacklisting censor Appius Claudius himself and that no defendant of the opposing faction could expect justice in a court in which Ahenobarbus presided over jurors as partisan as himself.

On December 10 Cicero emerged bewildered from a conference with Pompeius at the latter's villa at Cumae (near Naples). Pompeius was resolved upon war. He pointed to Hirtius' failure to keep the appointment with Scipio three days earlier as evidence that Caesar did not sincerely desire peace. Noting Cicero's dismay at his eagerness for a conflict, Pompeius urged Cicero to stay away from the Senate so as not to jeopardize his chances for a triumph in these days of acrimonious debate. Unconvinced as to the inevitability of war and confident that granted a second consulship Caesar would behave with moderation, Cicero was too discomfited to expostulate with Pompeius. Everywhere he encountered among equestrians and senators "the bitterest language about the conduct of affairs in general and this trip of Pompeius' [to take command of the legions at Capua] in particular." Men of property were unequivocal in their insistence upon a peaceful settlement and in their conviction that victory in a civil war would result in a despotism regardless of which side triumphed. Perhaps recalling the advice of the revered pontifex maximus Scaevola at the time of Sulla's return from the East that civil bloodshed was to be avoided at all cost, Cicero himself came to believe that it was "more expedient to concede to [Caesar's] demands than to join battle." Ever gnawing at him, however, was his fear of alienating the Senate leadership. While he reiterated that he would "vote for peace at any price," he also admitted that "it is yet another major misfortune for the country that for me especially there is in a way something wrong in dissenting from Pompeius on such high matters." While thus vacillating, he received word that without consulting him and "without mandate either from the Senate or the assembly," Pompeius, already taking command in a war that had not been declared, had assigned him to the defense of Sicily. In exasperation he cried, "The result [of civil war] will be proscription if beaten [by Caesar] and slavery if one wins."[9]

As he veered day by day closer to the optimate position, Cicero became ever more uncomfortable at Caesar's broad support even among the "respectable" citizens—"the tax farmers, never reliable, now warmly attached to Caesar or the capitalists [moneylenders] or the farmers, whose first prayer is peace," none of them "frightened of living under an autocracy . . . so long as they are left in peace." He reminded himself of Caesar's "eleven legions, all the cavalry he may want, the Gauls beyond the Po" as well as his numerous partisans in Rome and throughout Italy. On the other hand, he reassured himself as to the decision he was, in fact, already determined upon, by declaring "if the honest men are beaten, Caesar will be no more merciful than Cinna in the slaughter of leading men and no more temperate than Sulla in plundering the rich."[10]

In these tense circumstances Caesar was gravely handicapped by the prohibition against leaving his province and by the necessity of employing as spokesmen at Rome men motivated by aspirations not always consonant with his own. With the wily Curio out of office, Caesar now had to rely on the flamboyant Antonius, who displayed brash wilfulness as soon as he entered upon his tribuneship. After reading to the Senate and to the people an appeal from Caesar "not to take from him the privilege [of registering his candidacy for a consulship in absentia] which the people had granted him or else to compel the others in command of armies [Pompeius] to resign also," Antonius exploded into a personal diatribe against Pompeius. His outburst shook waverers like Cicero, and the orator listened sympathetically a few days later when Pompeius exclaimed to him privately, "How do you expect Caesar to behave if he gets control of the state when his feckless nobody of a [former] quaestor dares to say this sort of thing?" Cicero, now eager to be persuaded, nodded when the Great Man warned that "if Caesar is made consul, even after giving up his army, it will mean the subversion of the constitution."[11] (Neither the man who had advanced his career through repeated violations of the constitution, nor the one who had executed conspirators without a trial appreciated the irony in this remark.)

Noting Cicero's continuing apprehension, Pompeius offered assurance that Caesar would either back down before a display of resolution or suffer a swift defeat on the battlefield. Awed by Pompeius' self-confidence, Cicero praised the Great Man's counsel regarding "the dangers of a false peace." Two days later, after a few short weeks of indecision, Cicero shifted further in opposition to Caesar. Abruptly he felt nettled at the burden of his private debt to Caesar. "What irks me most," he informed Atticus, "is that Caesar must be paid his money and the wherewithal for my triumph diverted to that purpose."[12]

Informed of loss of will among "moderates" like Cicero, Caesar anticipated an aggressive move by the new consuls upon their installation on January 1, 49.

New Year's fell on a market day, an ill omen, and Romans whispered of dire portents for the coming year.

XLII

"THE DIE IS CAST"

IN a final effort for peace, Caesar dispatched Curio to Rome. Driving his mounts at a furious pace, Curio covered the 1,300 stades (nearly 160 miles) from Ravenna to Rome in a mere three days and arrived in time for the inaugural session of the Senate. As the new consuls were proceeding into the Temple of Jupiter, Curio handed them a letter from Caesar, making certain that other senators saw him deliver the scroll, for he feared that the consuls might otherwise ignore it. In fact, during the session Lentulus Crus, the presiding consul, neglected the communication until the tribunes Marcus Antonius and Quintus Cassius* demanded that it be read. In the letter Caesar repeated his insistence upon either the retention of his proconsular immunity until his installation as a consul or the immediate and simultaneous resignation of both Pompeius and himself from their military commands so that, as he phrased it, the Senate and the people might enjoy freedom of decision without fear.

Lentulus Crus refused to entertain any motions regarding Caesar's proposals or any discussion at all on Caesar's letter. Instead he issued a warning to the Senate, declaring that "he would not fail the republic if the senators were willing to express their opinions with boldness and resolution; but if they paid regard to Caesar and tried to win favor with him as they had done on previous occasions . . . he would consider his own interests and would not obey their authority." As to his remark about considering his own interests, the senators in the temple and the equestrians at the portals were aware that Caesar had rejected an offer of Lentulus' services because of the exorbitant price the consul demanded. Indeed, Lentulus went on to boast: "I, too, can shelter myself under the favor and friendship of Caesar." If he did not win approval of his policies, he would reach a private understanding with Caesar. So much for the consul's principles! Forbidden entrance to the city as a proconsul in command of an army, Pompeius expressed a similar threat through his father-in-law. "Pompeius," Scipio declared, "is inclined not to desert the republic if the Senate follows him; but if it delays and acts remissly, it will in vain solicit his aid should it wish to do so in the future."[1]

While charging Caesar with high-handed insolence, his enemies were delivering ultimata to the Senate.

In face of this bullying even Marcus Marcellus, who as consul two years earlier had initiated the campaign to recall Caesar, took fright. He urged a delay on decisions pending the mobilization of an army capable of defending the Senate. The praetorian Calidius, sympathetic to Caesar, supported by Caelius moved that Pompeius depart for his provinces as a conciliatory gesture. Lentulus refused to put Calidius' motion to a vote and hectored Marcellus into withdrawing his proposal. Cutting off discussion, Lentulus asked for a division on a resolution offered by Scipio ordering Caesar to disband his army by a certain date on pain of outlawry. Caesar's tribunes interposed a veto and moved to substitute Curio's motion of a month earlier for the simultaneous disbanding of the armies of both warlords. "Against a robber," cried Lentulus in reply, "there was need of arms, not votes,"[2] and he adjourned the meeting.

That evening, following a prearranged scenario, Pompeius, without any

*Probably a cousin to Servilia's son-in-law, Gaius Cassius (Caesar's future assassin).

constitutional authority to do so, summoned the senators outside the walls. Addressing them more like a monarch than a proconsul, "he praised the zealous and encouraged them for the future; the sluggish he reproved and stimulated."[3] Before dawn, with equal disregard for constitutional niceties, he dispatched troops within the walls. Undismayed by the optimate stampede, Caesar's father-in-law Calpurnius and the praetor Roscius, formerly a legate in the Army of Gaul, requested a moratorium of six days during which they would journey to Ravenna to negotiate with Caesar.

Their proposal was rejected.

On January 4, flattered by appeals from Balbus and Oppius, Cicero reached the gates. He was greeted by a great multitude (very likely mobilized by Caesar's people) and hailed as a peacemaker. Immediately he set to mediating between Pompeius and Caesar. Caesar had prepared a negotiating strategy, the reverse of his policy in Gaul of intensifying demands in face of continuing resistance. Seeking to detach Pompeius from the optimates, he instructed his agents to retreat step by step in dealing with his former son-in-law. By this tactic he hoped to persuade Pompeius and vacillating senators of the contradiction between his conciliatory flexibility and the obdurate belligerence of the optimates. First of all, in a concession to Pompeius' pride, he abandoned his insistence upon Pompeius' simultaneous resignation of his military command. He required merely that Pompeius depart for Spain (which had recently suffered a major revolt not yet suppressed) to govern his provinces in person. In return for recognition of his right to election in absentia, Caesar agreed to surrender his command in Transalpina and to discharge all but two of his legions. Thus he gave up control of the Province and of the lands he had conquered and released most of the army upon which his power depended. He was prepared to retain a force less than a quarter of Pompeius'.

Such terms did not admit of a flippant rejection, and Cicero emphasized Caesar's generosity. Furthermore, anticipating that Pompeius would be embarrassed at agreeing to terms too quickly after his recent bombastic pronouncements, Caesar authorized Cicero to grant a further concession, his surrender of Cisalpina and one of his two legions. With his retaining only the minor province of Illyricum and a single legion (along with proconsular immunity, of course), Pompeius could boast of a victory without a struggle, and Cato could no longer charge that Caesar posed a military threat to Rome. Rejection of this offer, on the other hand, would expose the optimates' resolve upon war and burden them with the guilt for hostilities.

For the inner circle of the Senate, greater than the fear of war was the fear of a reconciliation of the two giants. In fury the consul Lentulus demanded Caesar's unconditional surrender. "Cato cried that Pompeius was blundering again in allowing himself to be deceived," and the optimates mocked Cicero as "ill-informed as to the facts."[4]

On January 7, three days after Cicero's arrival at Rome, Cato exhorted the Senate "to fight to the death rather than allow the republic to accept a single dictate from a mere citizen." He "often declared and took oath too that he would impeach Caesar the moment he had disbanded his army." Everyone understood that if Cato had his way, Caesar would be tried "in a court hedged about by armed men." Ignoring Caesar's concessions and his own repeated threats to Caesar, Cato proclaimed: "Now these things are come to pass which I foretold to you, and the man is at last resorting to open compulsion, using the forces which he got by deceiving and cheating the state."[5] He adjured Pompeius to recall his own warnings against a false peace and of the threat to the constitution in the event Caesar obtained a second consulship.

Cicero's task was rendered the more difficult by the bellicosity not only of Cato's party but also of opportunists in Caesar's faction. Men like Curio, Caelius, Antonius and the tribune Quintus Cassius were calculating the power and wealth they hoped to win in a civil war. They were abetted by adventurers like those that had flocked to Catilina's banner, aristocrats "whose burden of guilt or of poverty was so heavy or who were so given up to riotous living that even [Caesar with his Gallic booty] could not save them . . . to these [Caesar] declared in the plainest terms that what they needed was a civil war."[6]

Just as Cicero was becoming desperate "in the midst of a throng of men mad with the lust of battle," the optimates made him an irresistible offer. "Amid all these disturbing occurrences," he exulted, "a full Senate nonetheless demanded that I should have a triumph."[7] About to attain his ultimate aspiration, Cicero lost zeal for mediation.

At the consul's demand, the Senate, demoralized and intimidated, voted the ultimate decree.

Three days later, on January 10, a courier brought news of the collapse of Cicero's efforts and of Pompeius' acquiescence in the optimates' decision for war. In voting the ultimate decree, the optimates were employing against Caesar the legislative weapon with which they had destroyed the Gracchi, Saturninus, Catilina and Clodius' followers after Clodius' assassination. As Caesar noted, never in the past, however, (except with Catilina, at Cicero's instigation) had the Senate enacted the ultimate decree "except in the case of pernicious laws, tribunicial violence, a popular secession or the seizure of temples and elevated positions." No such conditions, Caesar insisted, prevailed in the current circumstances "or had even been thought of."[8]

Nevertheless, with the passage of the ultimate decree the optimates outmaneuvered Caesar. If, in defiance of the decree, he took up arms to defend himself, he would bear responsibility for initiating a civil war. The populace would forget the events leading to the conflict, including Caesar's many concessions. They would ask only who had been the first to draw a sword. Caesar knew how decisive a role a civilian population played in any conflict. In jeopardy was the reservoir of goodwill he enjoyed throughout the peninsula. It was not merely that almost every family recalled the loss of kinsmen in the Italian war, the civil war, the Lepidan rebellion, the servile uprising or the Catilinarian revolt. In civil strife tens of thousands had been expelled from their homes, their property confiscated or their homesteads destroyed. In addition, after years of domestic peace, Italy was now enjoying unprecedented prosperity. The plantation system with its rationalized slave labor directed to domestic and foreign markets as well as similarly rationalized manufacturing in pottery and metalwork were reaching a zenith of productivity and profit. Trade throughout the Mediterranean as well as with regions beyond the imperial frontiers was flourishing. If the great mass of the population continued to exist on a subsistence level, a substantial segment (the segment that participated in elections and exercised political influence) was enjoying unprecedented prosperity. The most luxurious mansion in Rome at the time of Sulla's death was no longer even among the hundred most impressive residences a mere generation later. Men of property, great and small, wanted no interference with economic opportunities. The universal yearning for civil tranquility provided a constant theme for the poets. In an invocation to Venus, the procreative spirit, Lucretius had appealed to the goddess to exercise her wiles on her lover, the war god Mars:

> There he reclines, goddess, upon thy sacred body, do thou . . . pour from thy lips sweet coaxings and for thy Romans, illustrious one, crave quiet peace.

Lucretius bemoaned the unnatural horrors of civil strife, when men "amass wealth by civil bloodshed and greedily multiply riches, piling murder upon murder; cruelly they rejoice at the mournful death of a brother, they hate and they fear a kinsman's hospitality." Catullus echoed his older contemporary in a poem about the Trojan war:

> But then followed long years when earth was stained with
> blood and men released their souls to hell, justice
> a word forgotten; brothers dipped their fingers into brother's blood
>   and sons
> no longer wept over a father's body . . .[9]

Meditating on the alienation of the Italians and on the judgment of future generations, Caesar welcomed Curio, the two tribunes, Antonius and Quintus Cassius, along with Caelius. They reported that upon the passage of the Senate's final decree, Lentulus thundered at Antonius and Curio to leave the Senate before he employed his emergency powers against them. With Quintus Cassius and Caelius they hurried through lines of troops in the Forum, and at nightfall on January 7, disguised as slaves and in hired carriages, they fled from Rome.

The next day a courier confirmed the hysteria in the capital. On the morning of January 8, assembling outside the gates to enable Pompeius to participate in the deliberations, the Senate passed a series of resolutions in preparation for war. Freed of the threat of tribunician vetoes, the optimates annulled the privilege granted Caesar by the law of the ten tribunes and moved that Caesar "should enter the city as a private citizen and should as such submit himself to

the votes of the Roman people in his candidacy for the consulship."[10] In heady
exultation the optimates succumbed once again to the illusion that by a single
magical act, in this instance the passage of a series of decrees, they could
dissipate threats to their dominion. Scipio moved that Caesar be deprived of
his command. A general levy was decreed and monies appropriated to Pompeius for the defense of the republic. To assure control of the provinces, the
optimates assigned governorships to their own stalwarts, the first rewards of
an as yet unfought civil war. Populous and wealthy Syria fell to the bankrupt
Scipio; Transalpine Gaul to Ahenobarbus. Two eligible consulars were passed
over—Marcius Philippus (husband to Caesar's niece Atia and stepfather to
young Octavius) and Caesar's cousin, Lucius Cotta.

Upon reports of these warlike preparations, Caesar disguised his intentions,
for he did not want associates to influence a decision that would determine the
rest of Caesar's life and his place in history as well as the destiny of the republic
and the empire. From infancy he had been conscious of his responsibilities to
the Julian clan and as a patrician entrusted with Rome's world mission. Caesar
recalled, of course, his humiliation by the most awesome of the optimates,
Sulla; the menaces of the optimates upon his opposition to the execution of the
Catilinarians; Cato's depriving him of a triumph after his governorship in
Spain; the optimates' rejection of negotiation and compromise in regard to his
consular legislation; their repeated threats to annul his legislation and to bring
him to trial; their chicanery regarding his privilege of election in absentia.
Affronts to his dignity, above all, were their rebuffs to his recent concessions,
so generous as to confuse and infuriate them. Finally, their demand for unconditional surrender.

Yet Caesar nursed more than personal rancor. Associated with his dignity
were the fortunes of hundreds of thousands of clients—officers, legionaries,
provincials who had furnished him with troops and materiel, Transpadanes
who looked to him for full citizenship, young aristocrats and senators who
had exposed themselves as his partisans as well as the victims of optimate-
dominated courts and of Appius Claudius' censorial blacklisting. With his
overthrow legionaries would be deprived of land bonuses; officers, of advancement in their careers. As for the newly conquered Gauls, how would his
arch foe Ahenobarbus, his replacement as governor, treat Gallic leaders loyal
to himself? Ahenobarbus would annul treaties and ignore his arrangements
for fostering commerce and industry.

Overthrow!

How could the conqueror of Gaul, the invader of Britain and Germany
entertain an overthrow? Those whose slogan was "Let no innovation be made
contrary to usage and the principles of our forefathers" might submit to the
Stoic precept: "Do not ask that everything should happen as you wish, but
wish that it should happen as it does." Caesar had tested and proved that man
makes history, and he adhered to Lucretius' exhortation to "the will snatched
from Fate."[11]

Caesar ordered the single legion he had marched from across the Alps, the XIIIth, to proceed south to the frontier between Cisalpina and Umbria near the Adriatic. During the day he attended a theatrical performance, inspected plans for a gladiatorial school and went to a banquet. Outside his intimate circle no one divined his intentions. "It was not until after sunset that he set out very privily with a small company, taking the mules from a bakeshop hard by and harnessing them to a carriage; and when his lights went out and he lost his way, he was astray for some time but at last found a guide at dawn and got back to the road on foot by narrow bypaths." At the Rubicon, a stream forming the provincial border, he found the XIIIth legion along with a squadron of Gallic and German cavalry. "Halting in his course, he communed with himself a long time in silence as his resolution wavered." He was about to undertake no mere theatrical coup designed to bewilder opponents—no display of the portraits of the two Mariuses at Aunt Julia's funeral or restoration of Marian trophies at games in his father's memory or sensational archaic trial as during Cicero's consulship.

Returning to his friends, Caesar unburdened himself, "estimating the great evils which would follow their passage of the river and the wide fame of it which they would leave to posterity." This insignificant stream might become a watchword for all time. "Even yet we may draw back," he said, "but once cross yon little bridge, the whole issue is with the sword."[12] Then exclaiming a line from Menander, a Greek comedian he favored, "The die is cast," he ordered the advance.

XLIII
MORE THAN DIGNITY

AT dawn on January 12, 49, the XIIIth legion along with Gallic and German cavalry drew up in the town square at Ariminum (Rimini). The centurions barked commands, and the centuries and cohorts snapped to attention. Accompanied by four senators, Caesar in his scarlet commander's cloak strode to a podium. At Caesar's invitation the senators—two tribunes, Marcus Antonius (known to the troops as Caesar's quaestor in Gaul) and Quintus Cassius; the former tribune, Curio, and the former aedile, Caelius—related how a faction in the Senate had outlawed Caesar and threatened them with violence.

Then Caesar spoke. He addressed himself not only to his troops and to the townspeople but also to citizens throughout the peninsula, for he would send a copy of his speech to Balbus and Oppius for dissemination at Rome and throughout Italy. During the many years of his Gallic campaigns, in communiqués to the Senate Caesar had justified his policies, proclaimed his accomplishments and refuted attacks of his enemies. Henceforth, in the rapid shifts in the civil war, Caesar would issue policy statements at each new turn. His immediate task, of course, was to justify his invasion of the peninsula, to demonstrate that he acted in self-defense and to represent himself as the defender, not the violator, of the constitution. Thus he linked the question of his dignity and security to a betrayal by an old friend (Pompeius) and to his concern for the rights of the people's defenders (the tribunes) as well as for the old issues of the scope and validity of the ultimate decree of martial law now directed against him under circumstances contrary to all precedent.

In his speech Caesar rehearsed "all the wrongs done to him at various times by his enemies." Seeking to aggravate the suspicions between Pompeius and the optimates, he charged that the optimates had "seduced Pompeius and led him astray," whereas he himself had "always supported Pompeius and helped him to secure advancement and reputation." After earning "the credit of having restored" the powers of the tribunes of which Sulla had deprived them, Pompeius had now eliminated even the little authority left them by the dictator. Caesar ended his address with an appeal to the legionaries. "I have been your commander for nine years," he declared; "under my leadership your efforts on Rome's behalf have been crowned with good fortune; you have won countless battles and have pacified the whole of Gaul and Germany. Now I ask you to defend my reputation and standing against the assaults of my enemies."[1]

The legionaries would not permit insults to a commander who had shared their hardships and inspired them to heroic exploits for so many years. If he was overthrown, a senatorial faction that deprived tribunes of their prerogatives and wilfully instituted martial law would scarcely prove receptive to rewards for their long service. "The men of the XIIIth legion clamored that they were ready to avenge the wrongs done to their general and to the tribunes." After the dismissal of the assembly, a deputation of centurions appeared at the command post conveying a resolution from the troops that "one and all offered their service without pay and without rations, the richer assuming the care of the poorer."[2] The centurions, recently rewarded with handsome bonuses after the final Gallic campaigns, volunteered to supply with their own money a mercenary horseman apiece.

Ariminum, the first town Caesar seized beyond the Cisalpine border, was a well-chosen first objective. It was not just that Ariminum was a major port, market and center of pottery manufacturing for a prosperous wine region as well as a strategic point on intersecting highways, one of which led across a pass into central Italy and to Rome. In recalling his connection to Old Marius and his own opposition to Sulla, Caesar was assured of a sympathetic response here, for Marius was a hero; and Sulla had sacked the town. Besides, a sizable number of Caesar's legionaries were natives of this area, and with his characteristic foresight Caesar must have previously bestowed on this town a portion of his generous largess to Italian municipalities. In conferring with the anxious town councilors, Caesar could guarantee the discipline of legionaries who at his orders had refrained from plundering Gallic foes during recent campaigns. His soldiers understood that they were to treat Italians as countrymen, not as enemies, if only, as in Gaul, to shorten the war. Caesar appealed to the townsfolk for aid in levying troops so that he might end the conflict rapidly and with a minimum of bloodshed.

Word of Caesar's moderation and of the restraint of his legionaries as well as of the friendly reception he received at Ariminum would spread throughout Italy.

Making full use of his single legion, Caesar dispatched Antonius with five cohorts to the west to seize Arretium (Arezzo), a market center astride a strategic highway leading northward from Rome through the middle of the peninsula. Enemy troops advancing on this highway could cut Caesar off from Cisalpina. The other five cohorts he sent individually, with cavalry support, to seize towns on the highway along the Adriatic coast.

As Caesar had anticipated, when news of his crossing the Rubicon "came flying to Rome . . . the city was filled with tumult, consternation and a fear that was beyond compare." Like volatile Gauls, the overconfident optimates, who had been assuring each other that an intimidated Caesar would capitulate to their ultimata, collapsed into despair. The Senate in a body repaired to Pompeius' house, and a consular demanded an accounting of the number of troops Pompeius had at his disposal. To the senators' dismay, Pompeius replied that he had the two legions that had been given up by Caesar for a war against the Parthians. "You have deceived us!" cried the consular. Another senator reminded Pompeius of his boast "to stamp upon the ground and call up the forces" he needed.[3]

Pompeius bore the raillery calmly. "You will have [troops]," he declared, "if you follow me and do not think it a terrible thing to leave Rome, and Italy, too, if it should be necessary." At Pompeius' reply, the optimates were struck all at once with the fearful consequences of their policies. Cato, the most consistent and intransigent foe to Caesar, proposed, with characteristic irony, that in defense of the republic Pompeius be entrusted with "unlimited powers, adding that the very men who caused great mischief must also put an end to it."[4] The other senators, however, numb with fear and outrage, would grant him merely control of the public treasury, the right to sell votive offerings in the temples and the authority to conduct additional levies. When Pompeius declared he would consider any senator who failed to depart from Rome an enemy of the republic, only the surly Ahenobarbus, champing for war, spoke in his support.

News of Marcus Antonius' capture of Arretium, a mere six days' march from Rome, evoked general panic. On the evening of January 17 Pompeius set out with his wife and sons for his legions at Capua, and all night senators and equestrians loaded wagons and pack animals. While the gates leading to the south were backed up with families in flight from Rome, those at the north and east were choked with refugees fleeing before Caesar's advancing troops and spreading wild reports of Gauls and Germans galloping to occupy the city.

The cowardly flight from Rome and the abandonment of the Capitol, the Senate house and the Forum—the dwelling places of the tutelary deities and the seat of empire—intensified the demoralization among the optimates and roused dismay and disgust throughout Italy. Caesar did not march on defenseless Rome, aware that the power vacuum in the city worked to his advantage. Furthermore, upon word of Pompeius' threat to evacuate Italy and to carry on the war overseas, Caesar realized that only by preventing Pompeius' embarkation from Brundisium could he end the conflict quickly. Caesar knew Pompeius. Dreaming of a final, titanic campaign, a culmination of a long and glorious military career, Pompeius was contriving a vast pincers movement. From the West he would summon his army in the Spains, and in the East he would call upon his clients to assemble an armada and a horde of foreign troops. Like an Olympian god he would mobilize forces of unprecedented might for a cataclysmic conflict reaching from the Ocean to the Euphrates. He, Pompeius Magnus, would rally the power of the Mediterranean world and by his exploits cast into obscurity even the Macedonian.

While indulging in such megalomaniacal visions, in day-by-day maneuvering, Pompeius proved less venturesome. Following his tactic ever to play both sides in conflicts and to disguise his intentions, he dispatched two successive envoys to negotiate privately with Caesar, Caesar's clansman young Lucius Caesar, son of Caesar's legate in the Province and first cousin to Marcus Antonius, and the praetor Roscius, formerly a legate in the Army of Gaul. In his message Pompeius lectured Caesar like an officious schoolmaster. "He had," Pompeius declared, "always put the good of the country before the claims of personal friendship," and he urged Caesar to "subordinate his personal ambitions and grievances to the good of Rome and . . . not allow his anger against his personal enemies to lead him into damaging Rome in his efforts to do them harm."[5]

Pompeius offered no proposals for peace, and in his reply Caesar threw the onus for the conflict on his adversary. After rehearsing his grievances against the leaders of the Senate, Caesar declared: "I am prepared to resort to anything, to submit to anything, for the sake of the commonwealth." He repeated his terms for a settlement: Pompeius' departure for his Spanish provinces, a disbanding of armies, a discontinuance of levies and the cessation of "the regime of terror" in order that free elections might be conducted with "the Senate and the Roman people . . . in full control of the government." Employing his standard tactic of requiring new concessions after a refusal of previous terms, he now insisted upon a meeting with Pompeius to ratify terms by oath.[6]

By the time Lucius Caesar and the praetor Roscius returned to Campania with Caesar's proposals, the optimates had learned of the fall of Iguvium

(Gubbio), a strategic point in the Apennines, where at the approach of Curio with three cohorts, the garrison of five cohorts under an optimate praetor deserted and ran off to their homes. Caesar himself was marching south along the coast into Picenum, where twenty-five years earlier Pompeius had recruited a private army in support of Sulla. Alarmed at Caesar's unchecked advances and mindful now of Pompeius' unpreparedeness, Cato forgot his impassioned exhortations to war earlier in the month and, un-Stoically, changed his mind. Now he announced that he preferred "slavery to war."[7] At this moment the optimates might have acceded to Caesar's peace proposals if Fortune had not revived their illusions.

Labienus arrived at Pompeius' headquarters.

As a native of Picenum, Pompeius' client region, and a long-time protégé of Pompeius', Labienus hesitated to take up arms against his former mentor. Above all, he had waxed arrogant because of his exploits and booty in Gaul. He was also aware of the weariness among Caesar's legions and very likely believed that they would not engage with any will in yet another "final campaign." Since the decision to cross the Rubicon, Caesar had avoided employing Labienus in any operations. Now, to demonstrate his indifference to the defection of his former lieutenant, Caesar ordered Labienus' baggage and money chests sent after him.

Exhilarated once again as suddenly as they had fallen into despair, Pompeius and the leading optimates used Labienus' defection as a pretext for ignoring Caesar's proposals. As though it were Caesar and not they who were suffering defeat after defeat, they demanded that he retire into Cisalpina and disband his legions. They, meanwhile, would continue to conduct levies. Only after Caesar's compliance with these terms would Pompeius set out for his Spanish provinces. They ignored Caesar's request for a personal meeting with Pompeius, and Pompeius spoke grandly of mobilizing an army of overwhelming numbers once he set foot in Picenum, his loyal recruiting ground.

In plotting his advance into Italy, Caesar had taken into account the social and political conditions along the Adriatic. Unlike other parts of Italy the two-hundred-mile stretch from Ariminum south to Apulia (the heel of the peninsula) had not undergone the transformation from smallholdings to plantations or latifundia operated primarily by slave gangs although large estates did exist, worked in great part by tenant farmers. In these regions there was deep-seated suspicion of the senatorial and equestrian oligarchy with its market-oriented plantations and international commercial and banking interests. The countryfolk had long been resentful at providing a disproportionate share of the recruits for the legions. Here the Italian revolt had erupted, and resistance had been most obdurate. Here, too, Spartacus had found support among freeholders. Indeed, even in Pompeius' Picenum social, economic and political considerations proved decisive over the patron-client relationship with Pompeius.

When Lucius Caesar and Roscius caught up with Caesar with the reply from

Pompeius and the consuls, Caesar had already occupied Auximum (Osimo), a major Picene town and the headquarters of a former praetor sent to conduct local levies. Here Caesar enjoyed the effect of his war communiqués over the years. The town councilors of Osimo informed the optimate commandant "that while they were not competent to judge the issue, neither they nor their fellow townsmen could allow Gaius Caesar, a holder of a military command, a man who had served the state well and had many brilliant achievements to his credit, to be shut out of the town."[8] Their proclamation of neutrality in a region supposedly devoted to Pompeius was heartening to Caesar. After a skirmish, the recruits dropped their weapons and scattered to their homes or deserted to Caesar. To convey news of this grievous setback to the optimates along with a new peace proposal, Caesar set free a centurion, a veteran of Pompeius' service.

Bewildered at his miscalculation regarding Picenum, Pompeius fell into despondency; and as crestfallen as they had been elated only days earlier at Labienus' defection, the optimates now grumbled that their commander had "no courage, no plan, no forces, no energy." Especially disconcerting was the news that Cingulum (Cingulo), a town in Picenum built and settled by Labienus, had sent envoys to proclaim its loyalty to Caesar and to promise to send recruits at his request. Above all, the optimates were dismayed by the apathy everywhere in Italy to calls to the defense of the Republic. "Recruiting officers dared not show their noses [and] there [were] no volunteers."[9] Ordered by Pompeius to return to Rome to seize the public treasury, abandoned in the flight from the city, the consuls replied sarcastically that they would do so upon Pompeius' recapture of Picenum.

To exploit this defeatism and dissension, Caesar mounted a feverish letter-writing campaign both on his own and through his associates. He also sent heralds throughout Italy to proclaim his modest demands and readiness to conclude peace. News of the arrival from across the Alps of the battle-hardened XIIth legion reinforced his persuasion. When Caesar arrived at the fortress of Asculum [Ascoli Piceno], the consular Lentulus Spinther, "who was holding that town with ten cohorts, as soon as he hear[d] of Caesar's approach [fled] from the town . . . and [was] deserted by a great part of his men."[10]

At contradictory rumors the optimates veered from elation to despair. One day Cicero exclaimed to Atticus, "The rapidity of [Caesar's] movement is beyond belief," while the next day upon receiving a letter from some irrepressible optimist he exulted that Ahenobarbus had assembled "a strong army, that the cohorts [fleeing from Picenum before Caesar's advance] have joined Ahenobarbus, that Caesar may be, and is afraid of being cut off, that the honest men in Rome have taken fresh heart and the villains are pretty well floored." Later that week, the hopeful rumors having been confuted, Cicero was bemoaning "a cause in which there has at no time been any attempt to plan either peace or victory but always infamous and disastrous flight."

Whereas eight years earlier Pompeius and the optimates were able to rally the men of property throughout Italy to assemble at Rome to vote for Cicero's return from exile, now in the widespread alienation the leaders of the republic commanded no loyalty. Theirs was "a cause," Cicero admitted, which "aroused no passion in any order. . . . The feelings of the honest men . . . were as usual far from keen, whereas the populace and the lower orders sympathized . . . with the other side and many were eager for revolution."[11]

After thirty years (since Sulla) of unrestrained arrogance and corruption, selfish profiteering, indifference to misery and resistance to all reforms, the Cato faction remained uncomprehending at their loss of legitimacy. All these years they had striven to restrict power, prestige and wealth to an ever-shrinking coterie of profiteers, and now they were bewildered at the unwillingness even of men of property to spring to their defense.

PHASE TWO

Caesar's enemies were not only daunted by his speed and resolution and the élan and discipline of his troops as well as by the mass desertions on their own side. They were also resentful of Pompeius' miscalculations and of his decision, evidently long meditated, to withdraw from Italy. They recognized that they would be completely in his power overseas once he assembled his foreign client armies and navies. They feared, too, that in the event of victory he, like a second Sulla, would seize autocratic power in the commonwealth. For these reasons and out of his own vainglory, Ahenobarbus holed up in central Italy and rejected Pompeius' orders to withdraw to the south. He was determined to oppose Caesar on his own and to deprive Pompeius of the prestige of victory. During the Sullan Terror, Ahenobarbus had accumulated vast holdings in east-central Italy, and among his clients he mobilized some twenty cohorts. An additional thirteen cohorts he assembled from troops in flight before Caesar. Most of this army he concentrated at Corfinium (Corfinio). Almost precisely at the midpoint of the peninsula, at the junction of three highways, girded by mountains and rivers and enjoying the resources of a fertile valley, Corfinium had been selected by the Italians forty years earlier as the capital of their rebellion.

If Ahenobarbus had been a match for Caesar as a general and his raw recruits a match for Caesar's legionaries, he might have blocked Caesar's advance. As it was, by assembling an army in Corfinium like Vercingetorix at Alesia, he afforded Caesar an opportunity to destroy in a single engagement a major portion of the optimate forces. On February 14 Caesar's scouts routed a detachment Ahenobarbus had sent belatedly to destroy a bridge over a nearby river. Caesar advanced to the town and established a camp close to the walls. Ahenobarbus had committed the further error of dividing his forces among nearby towns, and in response to a report that the citizens of Sulmo (Sulmona), a major stop on the seasonal migration of the sheep herds, were prepared to surrender to him, Caesar sent Antonius there with five cohorts. The chief town

of the Paeligni, Sulmo had been a center of Italian resistance. Its most famous
son, the poet Ovid, as yet unborn, would boast:

> I shall be called the glory of the Pelignians, a race whom their love
> of freedom compelled to honorable arms when
> Anxious Rome was in fear of the allied bands.

Sulla had sacked the town; now an officer serving under Marius' nephew
approached the walls. "The people of Sulmo as soon as they saw our standards," noted Caesar, "opened the gates and sallied forth in a body, townsmen
and soldiers, to meet and congratulate Antonius."[12] The optimate officers
jumped from the walls, and one of them, brought to Caesar, was immediately
set free.

On February 17 the VIIIth legion arrived from Transalpina along with
twenty-two cohorts (the equivalent of more than two legions) newly recruited
in the Province and a squadron of horse from a chief of Noricum (part of
modern Austria), whose response to Caesar's appeal evidenced the effectiveness of Caesar's diplomacy during his proconsulship. With these reinforcements Caesar began the investment of the fortress. On February 18, however,
scouts reported sounds of fighting within the walls. The next day a deputation
from the garrison arrived at Caesar's headquarters. Although Pompeius had
sent word that he could not rely upon the two legions withdrawn from the
Army of Gaul, Ahenobarbus announced to his troops that Pompeius was
leading a relief force to Corfinium. Further to encourage his troops, he promised each man a sizable homestead out of his vast estates. Somehow the troops
had caught Ahenobarbus in the lie about Pompeius' notice. Caesar sent back
the envoys with instructions for a capitulation the next morning.

That night the consular Lentulus Spinther shouted from the wall that he
desired an audience with Caesar. Brought to Caesar's tent, he begged for his
life. Interrupting the distraught nobleman, Caesar observed, "I did not leave
my province with intent to harm anybody. I merely want to protect myself
against the slanders of my enemies, to restore to their rightful position the tribunes of the people who have been expelled because of their involvement in my
cause and to reclaim for myself and for the Roman people independence from
the domination of a small clique." In fact, as he proceeded southward, Caesar
had demonstrated his rejection of all rancor by setting free a number of captured officers, none, of course, of Spinther's rank. Astonished at Caesar's
generosity, quite different from the treatment the optimates were prepared to
mete out to Caesar and his associates, Spinther requested permission to return
into the town. "The fact that I have been granted my life," he assured Caesar,
"will bring great comfort and hope to the others; some have been so terrified
that they have been driven to think of violence against themselves."[13]

At dawn on February 20, Caesar summoned out of Corfinium some fifty
senators, many accompanied by grown sons, and a large number of equestrians and country squires. To shield them from the jeers of their troops, Caesar

drew them apart. Many he chided individually for returning his past benefactions with ill will. He did not single out Ahenobarbus, who had assailed and threatened him during the previous ten years. Without exacting a promise not to take up arms against him in the future, Caesar dismissed all the aristocrats and restored to Ahenobarbus a payroll chest with six million sesterces, declaring that "he had as little eagerness to take money as to take human life."[14] Ahenobarbus' cohorts Caesar put under oath and enrolled into his own army.

Having delayed only seven days in the capture of Corfinium, Caesar set out by forced marches to prevent Pompeius from embarking for the East. En route, seeking to exploit the propaganda advantage in his capture of a major optimate force and in his clemency to so many senators and other aristocrats, he drafted letters for dissemination to leading personalities. Caesar knew that the mistrustful optimates would denounce Pompeius for abandoning Ahenobarbus and losing a substantial army. So suspicious of Pompeius were his optimate allies that some even charged that Pompeius "thought [the] massacre would be good propaganda for his own side," a lesson to his associates henceforth to yield to his judgment. On the other hand, Balbus wrote to Cicero that Caesar "would like nothing more than to live without fear under Pompeius' primacy,"[15] and Balbus' nephew stopped to visit the orator on his way with a letter and an oral message from Caesar to the current consul Lentulus Crus (who had sponsored the grant of citizenship to Balbus during the Sertorian war) to persuade him to return to Rome. Caesar promised the bankrupt consul aid in obtaining a lucrative province for the coming year.

In response to Balbus' letter and to a note enclosed from Caesar, Cicero declared that "peace became a man of [Caesar's] wisdom." Caesar sent a copy of Cicero's letter to Rome to be read in the Forum. At the same time, writing to Atticus, Cicero excoriated Pompeius: "His plan from the first has been to ransack every land and sea, to stir up foreign kings, to bring savage races in arms to Italy, to raise enormous armies." He recalled, belatedly, that Pompeius had been "hankering for a long while after despotism on the Sullan model."[16]

Optimate sympathizers were offering grudging praise of Caesar's accomplishments and even expressing the hope that he would arrive at Brundisium in time to compel Pompeius to engage in peace negotiations. "Do you see what sort of man this is into whose hands the state has fallen," exclaimed Cicero, reviving for a moment his admiration for Caesar of a few years earlier, "how clever, alert, well prepared?" Ever naive about popular sentiment, Cicero expressed astonishment that in towns and in the country, people "really think of nothing except their fields and their bits of farms and investments. . . . They fear the man they used to trust [Pompeius] and love the man they used to dread [Caesar]." Thus in a few weeks by his swift victories, by the disciplined behavior of his troops, by his own repeated representations of his desire merely for justice and for an end to the tyranny of a privileged coterie and especially by his clemency to defeated enemies, Caesar had reversed popular sentiment. No longer did people blame him for crossing the Rubicon, all anger was centered on Pompeius. As Caesar sped southward, word spread that in the towns he entered "they make a god of him and no pretense about it either, as there was when they were offering prayers for Pompeius' recovery [a year earlier]. People [were] delighted with [Caesar's] artful clemency and fear[ed] the other's wrath." On the other hand, the Pompeians were not convinced that Caesar would persist in his "artful" clemency. "How can Caesar behave otherwise than as a desperado?" exclaimed Cicero. "That is precluded by his life, his character, his past, the nature of his present enterprise, his associates, the strength of the honest [optimate] party or just their persistence."[17]

Apprized of these shifts in sentiment, Caesar issued a policy statement appropriate to the new stage in the conflict. In a letter addressed to Balbus and Oppius for reproduction and dissemination, he expressed satisfaction with their approval of his generosity to his foes at Corfinium and of his continuing efforts to reconcile himself with Pompeius. Above all, pursuing the call for consensus he had first broached in his opening address as consul more than a decade earlier, Caesar proclaimed a new direction for Rome: a termination of the factional violence that had disrupted the life of the city and brought anxiety and suffering to the citizenry since the days of the Gracchi:

> Let us try whether by this means [general amnesty] we can win back the goodwill of all and enjoy a lasting victory, seeing that others have not managed by cruelty to escape hatred or to make their victories endure, except only L. Sulla, whom I do not propose to imitate. Let this be the new style of conquest to make mercy and generosity our shield.

Caesar had not formulated a detailed program for achieving this radical shift in Roman politics. "As to how that is to be done," he declared, "certain possibilities occur to me and many more can be found." He asked for counsel: "I request you to apply your thoughts to these matters." As evidence of the seriousness of his intentions, he freed two Pompeian officers. "If they wish to show themselves grateful," he noted, "they should urge Pompeius to prefer my friendship to that of those who have always been his and my bitter enemies, by whose machinations the country has been brought to its present pass."[18]

Although addressed to Balbus and Oppius, the letter, composed with tact and the mastery of propaganda Caesar had acquired during many years of political and military experience, would strike all as a direct and personal appeal. Caesar displayed modesty, receptivity to counsel, gratitude for approval, eagerness for reconciliation and resolution in vindicating his just demands and in rejecting the ruthless vengeance of predecessors like Sulla. He played upon the mutual suspicions of Pompeius and Cato's faction, placed the blame for the civil war on the optimates and invited Pompeius to a renewed friendship.

Like the previous letter sent to Pompeius and the consuls through Lucius Caesar and Roscius, this letter arrived too late.

Reaching Brundisium on March 9, Caesar discovered that the consuls and a large number of senators along with thirty cohorts had sailed from the port and that young Balbus had not arrived in time to present Caesar's proposals to the consul Lentulus Crus. To Caesar's peace envoy, a freed Pompeian officer, Pompeius announced that "in the absence of the consuls, no negotiations about a settlement could be conducted."[19]

XLIV

MASTER OF ITALY?

POSSESSING no fleet, Caesar could not blockade Brundisium, and despite a desperate effort at extending a causeway to shut off the narrow entrance to the port, he could not prevent Pompeius from sailing away with his remaining forces during the night of March 17, 49. Caesar was left in control of Italy, the two Gauls and Illyricum, but the rest of the empire remained under Pompeius' dominion, and the war henceforth would involve the entire Mediterranean world and not just the peninsula. For the moment Caesar was a hero, a savior against Pompeius, whose intention to ape Sulla had been exposed—"first to strangle Rome and Italy with hunger, then to carry fire and sword through the countryside and dip into the pockets of the rich." Indifferent to the general threat to society, Pompeius enrolled shepherd slaves into his army, and at Capua (where Spartacus had initiated the servile revolt) the consul Lentulus Crus armed gladiators belonging to Caesar. Caesar, on the other hand, refused to accept slaves into his own forces; and whereas he declared that he "counted all men [his] adherents who were not against him," Pompeius issued "threats to the municipalities, to honest men individually named, to everyone who stayed behind" and failed to evacuate Italy with him. Pompeius did not disguise his intentions to conduct proscriptions of his foes and boasted, "What Sulla could do, I can do." On the other hand, Spinther, the consular released at Corfinium, was writing to friends "glowing expressions of gratitude to Caesar," and Caesar himself gave assurance that he would not be shaken from his policy of clemency even by reports that aristocrats he had freed at Corfinium and elsewhere had "departed [with Pompeius] to wage war on [him] again, for there is nothing [he] like[d] better than that [he] should be true to [himself] and they to themselves."[1]

As Caesar had discovered in the past, his every action provoked a counteraction, often unpredictable. Confirmed optimates, embittered at their miscalculations and projecting upon Caesar their own vindictiveness, disseminated rumors that Caesar, nephew of Old Marius and one-time son-in-law to Cinna, was threatening to "avenge the deaths of Gnaeus Carbo and Marcus Brutus and of all the other victims of Sulla's cruelty, in [whose deaths] Pompeius . . . participated." Other hostile or uncommitted aristocrats reasoned that if Caesar pardoned an Ahenobarbus, an obstinate foe of many years, no one else who opposed Caesar in speech or writing had cause to fear, and they ignored the placards Caesar posted at Rome and in the suburbs announcing a Senate meeting. Stopping on his way to Rome at Cicero's villa at Formiae (halfway between Naples and Rome), Caesar found the orator willing to attend a Senate meeting only on condition that Caesar permit him to speak out against any continuation of the war. Infuriated at the obstinacy of a man who trembled at Pompeius' aspirations to be a second Sulla and yet would permit Pompeius to mobilize for an invasion of Italy while depriving him of the right to defend himself and Italy, Caesar snapped that "if he could not avail himself of [Cicero's] counsels, he would take those he could get and stop at nothing."[2] Nevertheless, he threatened no reprisals when the orator elected to remain at his seaside villa.

Arriving at Rome on April 1, almost precisely nine years after his departure for Gaul, Caesar searched the crowd assembled at the fifth milestone to conduct him into the city. He saw only two consulars, Volcatius and Servius, both of whom had sons serving as officers on Caesar's staff. He looked in vain for his father-in-law, Calpurnius. More encouraging was the number of equestrians, far less concerned about factional rivalries than about the security of their property. Weeks earlier Atticus had announced to Cicero that "if Caesar continues as he has begun with sincerity, moderation and prudence, I shall think hard and look more attentively to our interests."[3] In the city Caesar found money scarce and prices, especially of foodstuffs, inflated beyond the reach of the poor. People dreaded a famine from a Pompeian blockade.

To a silent rump Senate with fewer than half the members in attendance, Caesar declared that "he sought no extraordinary office, but waiting for the legitimate time of his consulship, was content with privileges open to all citizens." Indeed, he had no further demands requiring a test of arms. "His own wish," Caesar said, "was to be superior to others in justice and equity as he had striven to surpass them in action."[4] (His audience recalled Pompeius' frequent warnings that *he* would brook no rivals in prestige and power.) Caesar urged the Senate to choose a delegation to treat of peace with Pompeius and the consuls. Convinced of Caesar's clemency (though muttering doubts privately) and fearful of Pompeius' vindictiveness, no senators volunteered for the mission. On the other hand, the consular Servius, the renowned jurisconsult, denounced as unconstitutional Caesar's forthcoming campaign against the Pompeian legions in Spain.

Mindful that all these senators were aware of Pompeius' Sullan aspirations as well as of the flagrant opportunism of the Cato faction during the previous three months and infuriated at the pomposity of men whose chief defense lay in their weakness and in his policy of reconciliation, Caesar adjured the senators "to take up the burden of state and administer it with his help. . . . If they [shrank] from fear," he warned, "he [would] not burden them and [would] administer the state himself." Unable to count on older and experienced senators for important posts, Caesar was compelled to employ young aristocrats eager for high office but of varying capacities. To assure the grain supply, he appointed Curio commander with propraetorian rank of an army to expel Cato from Sicily and then to capture Africa from the optimates. He entrusted Antonius with the defense of Italy, also as a propraetor; he appointed Antonius' younger brother Gaius, a mere quaestorian, governor of Illyricum; young Marcus Crassus, governor of Cisalpina; and Cicero's thirty-year-old son-in-law Dolabella and Hortensius' son of a similar age admirals of fleets to be constructed for deployment in the Adriatic and Tyrrhenian seas. The twenty-seven-year-old Asinius Pollio, a friend to the recently deceased poets Catullus and Calvus, he dispatched forthwith to Sicily in advance of Curio. Elder statesmen who had refused to accept responsibilities grumbled that "the provinces and the state [were] to be governed by people not one of whom had the capacity to look after his own family property."[5]

In departing from Italy Caesar could be confident that entrepreneurs would be content with contracts for arms, equipment, supplies, warships and transports. He had reassured the grain dealers and the populace by dispatching troops to regain the grain-producing provinces of Sicily, Sardinia and Africa. He pacified anxious oligarchs by prohibiting the confiscation of the property of the Pompeians and by undertaking no radical reforms. He did not restore the civil rights of sons and grandsons of those proscribed by Sulla or of men recently condemned in optimate courts or blacklisted by the censor Appius Claudius though many of these men volunteered their services to him. Furthermore, he proposed no legislation for the relief of debtors, mollifying the commons by a grain distribution and a promise of 300 sesterces in individual largess upon completion of the present war. He did prompt a praetor to pass a bill granting the Transpadanes full citizenship, a measure he had first championed almost twenty years earlier and a reward for their support of his Gallic campaigns and in the present struggle.

Although unable to compete with Pompeius in mobilizing overseas clients, Caesar could appeal for aid from princes and cities upon whom he had been bestowing largess out of his Gallic booty. To embroil Pompeius' father-in-law, governor of Syria, in a costly diversion, Caesar sent back to rouse a rebellion a king of Judea captured by Pompeius. To Jews everywhere Pompeius, the desecrator of the Holy of the Holies in the Temple and the enslaver of thousands of Jewish captives, represented the arch fiend, and Caesar could hope to rally this numerous people to his own camp.

After eight days of feverish activity at Rome, Caesar was ready to set out for Spain. Before confronting Pompeius in the East, he had to eliminate the threat from the seven Pompeian legions in the Iberian peninsula. A tractable popular assembly authorized his expropriation of the public treasury and the votive offerings in the temples (previously assigned to Pompeius by the Senate but abandoned in the hasty flight from Rome). The tribune Metellus, a son-in-law of Caesar's deceased foe Lucullus, posted himself at the door to the treasury at the base of the Temple of Saturn and forbade Caesar's men to take the gold and silver stored there. "Arms and laws had not the same season," Caesar reminded the brash tribune. "If you are displeased at what is going on," he declared, "for the present get out of the way since war has no use for free speech; when, however, I have come to terms and laid down my arms, then you shall come before the people with your harangues." When the tribune insisted that under a time-honored tradition the funds were reserved against a possible threat from the Gauls and protected by a curse, Caesar scoffed, declaring that he had eliminated that threat for all time. He would kill the tribune if he did not cease his interference. "Surely you know, young man," he declared, "that it is more unpleasant for me to say this than to do it."[6]

The populace of Rome, notoriously short of memory and excitable in the constant anxiety of their miserable existence, knew only that Caesar had attacked a tribune, the supposed defender of their rights. Now, Caesar's enemies proclaimed, he had displayed his true character and demonstrated the expediency of his clemency. He had also exposed his desperate need for money, and the optimates were convinced that upon his victory, like a Marius, if not a Sulla, he would introduce his own proscriptions and confiscations.

During his absence in Spain Caesar would have to fear not only a possible Pompeian invasion of Italy but also a revival of opposition at Rome. Caesar gambled that Pompeius, cautious and uncertain of the loyalty of his associates or his troops, would not undertake such a bold action, and he relied upon Antonius to maintain order in the city.

As he marched from the city to give battle to the Pompeian legions in Spain, Caesar proclaimed: "I go to meet an army without a leader, and I shall return to meet a leader without an army."[7]

XLV

MASTER OF THE WEST

AT Massilia, where with characteristic speed he arrived in twelve days, Caesar was barred at the border. The Council of Six Hundred, the ruling oligarchy, declared that the city was beholden to both Caesar and Pompeius for benevolences and they were resolved "to show equal goodwill to both and . . . not to help one against the other, nor admit either to [their] city and harbors."[1] Pompeius had sent instructions to the oligarchs to replenish their grain reserves and to summon to their defense ferocious mountain tribesmen, and from atop the hills encircling the city Caesar could see the townspeople repairing walls and gates and fitting out warships in naval yards.

During negotiations with the council, Ahenobarbus, "arriving by sea at Massilia, [was] received by the inhabitants and put in command of the city; the whole control of the war [was] placed in his hands." Ahenobarbus brought "seven merchant vessels which he had requisitioned" at the Etrurian coast north of Rome "and had manned with his own slaves, freedmen and tenants" from his plantations in that region.[2] By delaying Caesar, the Massiliots afforded Pompeius additional time to mobilize and, as was rumored, to march across North Africa to meet Caesar in the Spains. The Massiliots were retaliating for Caesar's threat to their traditional economic and political supremacy throughout Gaul. Their resistance might inspire a rebellion in Gaul, where the city's influence remained strong.

Unable to tolerate a hostile stronghold astride his communications, Caesar prepared to besiege the city. He sent orders to Gaius Fabius to advance into Spain with the three legions with which he had been investing the passes of the Pyrenees. Simultaneously, to reinforce his cavalry, Caesar dispatched heralds throughout the Province and the newly subjugated states of Gaul, "summoning individually all the noblest and bravest members of the Gallic tribes." Furthermore, "he borrowed money from the tribunes and centurions and distributed it among the troops, thus killing two birds with one stone—he took a security for the loyalty of the centurions and won the goodwill of the troops by his bounty."[3] He also summoned the three legions he had left along the southern coasts of Italy. Gambling on Pompeius' caution, he dared to denude the peninsula of a defense garrison.

News from Italy and elsewhere was mixed. Antonius was conducting himself with characteristic flamboyance, flaunting his authority and yielding to his old habits of debauchery. Optimate sympathizers, disgruntled at his ability to maintain order in Italy, reported that he traveled about with an entourage of revelers, actors and courtesans along with his mother, the indomitable Julia, and humiliated municipal authorities by failing to awaken in time for conferences after late-night revels. Caesar was reassured regarding the Roman grain supply. Upon his invasion of Italy, the Sardinians, viciously exploited for generations, expelled their optimate governor. Four years earlier in a cynical parody of justice, the leaders of the Senate, including nine consulars headed by Pompeius, appearing as character witnesses, had won the acquittal of Sulla's stepson on a charge of plundering the province. Cicero, as chief defense counsel, mocked the provincial plaintiffs for a "national character so utterly worthless that they imagine that freedom is to be distinguished from slavery only by the license which it gives for the telling of lies . . . devoid of honor, devoid of any fellowship or bond with our race."[4] On the other hand, the Sardinians associated Caesar with his clansman Caesar Strabo, who a half century earlier obtained the conviction of a corrupt governor of the province, a rare victory for the savagely oppressed islanders; and like other provincials throughout the empire, the Sardinians were mindful of Caesar's repeated defense of provincials in the courts and of his passage as consul of a comprehensive bill aimed at curbing imperial corruption. It is likely, too, that Caesar had distributed Gallic plunder as largess to the island. Recognizing Caesar as a champion and anticipating in the event of his victory a radical transformation in their condition, they rose up as the first people to come to his aid.

Cato, the optimate commandant of grain-rich Sicily, challenged Asinius Pollio to declare "whether he brought the order of the Senate or of the people to take possession of a government that had been assigned to another." The brash young man responded to the imperious Stoic: "The master of Italy has sent me on this business."[5] On April 23, grumbling that Pompeius had deserted him by abandoning Italy and protesting his desire to avoid bloodshed, the Man of Virtue, who bore especial responsibility for provoking the civil war, stole away from Syracuse. Pollio's superior, Curio, finding the island liberated from optimate control, prepared to embark with his legions for Africa, another major source of grain for Rome.

In June, despite his doubts about Pompeius' aspirations, Cicero fled Italy to join the optimates. "I foresee a massacre," he wrote to Atticus, "if [Caesar] wins, and an onslaught on private property and a return of exiles and cancellation of debts and elevation of rapscallions to office and despotism worse than any Persian, let alone Rome, could endure."[6] Since Caesar had forbidden anyone to depart from Italy without special dispensation, Cicero slipped off in secret, taking with him his laurel-wreathed lictors in anticipation of the triumph the Senate had authorized for his victories as governor of Cilicia.

Early in June with the siege works far advanced and with Decimus Brutus ready with a fleet of warships constructed in a mere thirty days at nearby Arelate (Arles), Caesar departed from Massilia with an escort of nine hundred Gallic horse. In Spain he found his two legates, Fabius and Plancus, adroitly applying military and diplomatic tactics they had mastered in Gaul. "Fabius was attempting, by letters and emissaries, to suborn the neighboring tribes," exploiting individual and factional rivalries.[7] Both officers were encouraged by the incompetence of the enemy commanders. As his personal agent Pompeius had sent an officer freed by Caesar at Corfinium, a certain Vibullius, with instructions for a division of the forces. Varro, the renowned intellectual, was to retain two of the seven legions in reserve in Further Spain, while Afranius, a consular renowned for his skill in social dancing, and Petreius, the professional soldier who had defeated Catilina, advanced to the Pyrenees. Apparently learning nothing from Caesar's communiqués from Gaul or from Caesar's victory at Corfinium, Vibullius concentrated an army at Ilerda, a mountain fortress overlooking the Sicoris (Segre) river. Even more surprising was the failure of Pompeius and his lieutenants to apply lessons from the Sertorian war. They did not, for example, employ Spanish auxiliaries in the mobile warfare for which Sertorius had demonstrated their special capability.

Nevertheless, Caesar's legionaries were bewildered by "the method of fighting employed by the Pompeian troops . . . to charge violently at the outset and seize a position [with] no particular concern about keeping their ranks. . . . If they were being worsted, they did not think it shame to retreat and give ground. They had grown accustomed to this sort of fighting with the Lusitanians and other barbarian tribes—naturally, since it usually happens that troops are influenced by the habits of the natives of any region in which they have spent a long period of service."[8] In response, with the veteran IXth legion Caesar evolved a special tactic and routed the enemy. Impatient after so many years of service (since Caesar's first campaign in Gaul), the legion pursued the Pompeians up a precipitous hill. When the enemy wheeled about, the legionaries suffered a near repetition of the disaster at Gergovia against Vercingetorix, with seventy dead and more than six hundred wounded. Caesar refrained from chastizing his troops. Since the last campaigns in Gaul, he had dealt cautiously with his war-weary veterans.

Rains of unprecedented duration swelled the Sicoris and disrupted Caesar's communications and cut off his supply trains. In a surprise attack, Afranius fell upon a column of Gauls with wagons loaded with baggage, slaves, wives and children along with young Italians coming to join Caesar. Gallic horsemen repelled the assault but only after some two hundred had been slain. To bring the backed-up column across the river, Caesar's legionaries constructed boats with keels and ribs of light timber and hulls wattled and sheathed in hides like those they had seen in Britain and conveyed these on wagons by night twenty-two miles upstream. On the far bank they fortified a hill and working from both sides completed a bridge in two days. Advancing downstream, Caesar surprised the enemy, unsuspecting of the resourcefulness and engineering skill of his veterans. He wrought great slaughter among the Pompeians.

The reversal in fortune at Ilerda was matched by a victory at Massilia. A center of advanced technology with arsenals well stocked with engines of war, Massilia effectively resisted Roman attacks on land, but employing the skill and imagination that had brought victory over the Gallic sea peoples, Decimus Brutus and his engineers "prepared hooks and grappling throwing-darts and other missiles" and overcame an enemy fleet superior in numbers, speed and seamanship.[9] Caesar had selected from among volunteers the bravest and most experienced veterans to serve as marines, and their superior discipline and the ingenuity of the engineers proved decisive.

Meanwhile, upon reports from Afranius and Petreius of their initial success in repelling the IXth legion and in attacking Caesar's supply train and of his hardships from the flooding of the Sicoris—reports embroidered "with plenty of exaggerations and amplified detail"—at Rome "it was thought that the war was almost over [and] great crowds gathered at Afranius' house and congratulations were lavished on him; many people left Italy to join Pompeius, some in

order to have the credit of being the first to bring such news, others to avoid
turning up last of all and appearing to have waited for the outcome of the
war."[10]

On the other hand, news of Caesar's success in bridging the Sicoris and
routing the Pompeian troops as well as of the victory at Massilia impelled
defections in nearby Iberian towns and tribes. Among the first to promise "to
obey [Caesar's] commands" were Osca (Huesca), once Sertorius' capital, and
Calagurris (Calahorra) and Tarraco (Tarragona), formerly Sertorian strongholds. They offered grain to ease the shortage in Caesar's camp, and a detachment of a defecting tribe crossed the lines to join him. In despair, the Pompeians resolved to retire to a new defense line below the Iberus (Ebro). To pursue
them (his only passage across the Sicoris lay at the bridge twenty-two miles
upstream), Caesar dug diversionary ditches to lower the level of the river and
sent cavalry to harry the retreating enemy. Seeing how the Pompeians fled
before the horsemen, the legionaries sent messages through centurions and
military tribunes to "tell Caesar not to hesitate to expose them to toil or
danger; they said they were ready, able and bold enough to cross the river in
the same place as the cavalry had crossed." Although "anxious about exposing
the army to so powerful a river,"[11] Caesar feared even more the frustration of
the legionaries. Assigning weaker men as guards at the camp and setting pack
animals across the river both upstream to break the force of the current and
downstream as a barrier to catch men carried off their feet, he led a force to the
far bank without a casualty. The troops insisted upon pursuing the enemy
without resting, and by forced marches they caught up with the Pompeians.

Scouts reported that at narrow defiles ahead Caesar could trap the retreating
army. Caesar informed his troops that the war would be indefinitely prolonged
if the Pompeians crossed the Ebro and established a defense line in the south
among a population disposed to their cause, and the legionaries raced the
enemy toward the chasm. One night at word that the Pompeians were stealing
off in small groups, Caesar sounded the signal for advance, and the enemy,
apprehensive, withdrew to its camp. At dawn Caesar began to lead his army
off in apparent retreat. The enemy turned to pursue, jeering. Suddenly Caesar
wheeled his column about, and the Pompeians realized that Caesar was out-
flanking them. Abandoning their baggage, the Pompeians scrambled off in the
direction of the defiles. Caesar outdistanced them and blocked their forward
movement. Both armies watched as Gallic and German horsemen annihilated
companies of Pompeian light-armed auxiliaries holding a strategic height. Immediately, "all sections of [Caesar's] army urgently demanded an engagement;
the lieutenants, centurions and military tribunes crowded round him urging
him to engage at once, as the troops were all keyed up in readiness." It had
always been Caesar's practice to seize such a moment for attack, and he could
hardly expect his men, yearning for an end to the conflict, to be impressed with
his determination to win goodwill in Spain after victory so as to forestall any
uprisings here. "Why," he asked his officers, "should I sacrifice some of my

men, even for victory? Why should I allow the troops who have done me such excellent service to be wounded? Why, in fine, should I tempt providence?— especially as I know that a good commander should be able to gain as much by policy as by the sword. Besides, I am stirred by pity for the citizens who I see must be killed: I would rather gain my ends without any harm befalling them." After pursuing a policy of terror during the final campaigns in Gaul, Caesar could not easily persuade his troops of his new approach. "Indeed, the soldiers openly avowed to each other that since such a chance of victory was being thrown away, they would not fight even when he wanted them to." [12] Prudently ignoring this mutinous sentiment, Caesar withdrew a short distance to reduce the fears of the enemy and established a tight blockade against them.

The next day while Afranius and Petreius were off supervising the defense of water carriers against Caesar's cavalry, troops of both armies emerged from their fortifications and advanced to within shouting distance; some called out names of acquaintances and of fellow townsmen. In the exchanges Pompeians acknowledged that they owed their lives to Caesar's restraint, while Caesar's men praised him as a man of good faith. In response to an inquiry from the Pompeians Caesar sent word that he would spare the lives of the enemy commanders in the event of a surrender. Upon this announcement, men passed freely from camp to camp. Military tribunes, centurions and Spanish chieftains came to pledge their faith to Caesar.

Returning to the camp, Afranius, reassured by his son, who had obtained Caesar's promise of safety, resigned himself to the change in circumstances, but Petreius, a hardened campaigner, armed his retainers and fell upon Caesar's legionaries in the camp and killed all he caught. Assembling troops and officers, he administered a new oath of allegiance and ordered that Caesarian soldiers hiding in the camp be brought forth and slain in the view of all. Caesar sent back Pompeians unharmed, allowing military tribunes and centurions to remain with him of their own accord.

Afranius and Petreius resolved to return to Ilerda. Worn down by harassment from Caesar's cavalry, by hunger and despair and demoralized by their commanders' ineptness, the Pompeian troops could not prevent Caesar from cutting off their retreat. When they offered battle, however, Caesar, posed with a delicate morale problem with his legionaries, did not dare to refuse, aware that "his reputation would suffer a severe setback if he gave the appearance of shunning a battle, contrary to the general feeling among his troops and to his reputation in the world at large." At best he would "offer resistance if the enemy came against him but not . . . take the initiative in starting a battle." After holding positions for the entire day, both armies withdrew. Now, as Caesar had anticipated, Afranius and Petreius requested a parley, and in view of both armies Afranius proclaimed that he and his men had fulfilled their oath to Pompeius and confessed themselves beaten. "We earnestly beg," he declared, "if there is any room for pity left that you will not feel obliged to exact the supreme penalty." [13]

Caesar formulated his reply to Afranius as a policy statement appropriate for the new stage of war initiated in this first defeat of a Pompeian army outside Italy. He called attention to the contrast between his own restraint and the vindictiveness of the Pompeian commanders. While soldiers and centurions had urged negotiations after conferring with his troops and with him, "you alone," he declared to Afranius and Petreius, "shrank from peace. It was you who did not observe the conventions of a truce and a conference." Nevertheless, he continued, "I do not intend to take advantage of your humiliation and of the present circumstances so as to increase my own resources." To the amazement of the armies on both sides, he announced: "I require only the disbanding of those armies which you have maintained against me these many years."[14] To confirm his desire for peace and to encourage the surrender of enemy troops in the future, he proclaimed that he would not incorporate the Pompeian troops into his own forces as he had done previously with captured enemy soldiers.

Exuberant, the Pompeian troops clamored for discharge, and Caesar ordered that those living in Spain be released immediately; those from Italy would be demobilized upon reaching the river Var, the border between the Province and Italy. Refusing to permit plundering of Roman citizens, Caesar offered to compensate his legionaries for any enemy property they had seized.

COMPLICATIONS OF CIVIL WAR

Disseminated by Balbus and Oppius, Caesar's speech would serve as a directive for Caesar's partisans throughout the empire. It would confirm the goodwill of neutrals and, like his policy of clemency, undermine the resistance of his enemies. The impact of the message was reinforced by the announcement of a second naval victory at Massilia. If Pompeius had dispatched a sizable contingent of his vast fleet to aid Ahenobarbus instead of a mere sixteen armorplated vessels, Decimus Brutus' force might have been overwhelmed. As it was, the crews of the relief ships, who "had not the sight of their homeland nor the injunctions of their kinsfolk to urge them on into mortal danger," withdrew at a crucial moment in the battle and sailed off to Further Spain.[15]

The Massiliots continued to mount a stubborn resistance. With artillery and various machines they harried legionaries constructing an earthen rampart eighty feet high topped by machines rising an additional sixty feet. "When the ram tortoise came to demolish the wall," declares Vitruvius, one of Caesar's engineers, "they let down a rope and caught the head of the ram. Then they wound the rope around a drum, using a windlass, and by keeping the ram raised they prevented it from touching the wall. In the end they demolished the whole engine with fiery missiles and blows from the ballista [a catapult]."[16]

Confident of imminent victory at Massilia, Caesar ordered the tribune Quintus Cassius to advance into Further Spain with two legions, while he himself, with a bravado certain to impress the Spaniards, rode ahead with an escort of a mere six hundred cavalry. Dispatching heralds to all the towns of Further Spain, he summoned leading citizens to an assembly at Corduba. One after another the communities of the province expelled Pompeian garrisons. The people of Gades drove out the commandant, a friend of Ahenobarbus', and informed the governor, Varro, that he, too, would be locked out of the city. Varro appealed for terms, and Caesar ordered his young cousin Sextus Caesar to take over Varro's legions. At Corduba Caesar thanked citizens and officers who had shown loyalty to him, remitted monies sequestered by Varro, returned confiscated properties and rewarded towns that had opposed the Pompeians.

Hailed as a liberator at Gades, Caesar restored treasures Varro had seized from the Temple of Hercules (where twenty years earlier Caesar had been goaded to new exploits at the sight of a bust of Alexander) and announced that he would propose to the Senate a grant of full citizenship to the Gaditans, the first extension of the franchise outside the borders of Italy. Along with Caesar's earlier sponsorship of a similar bill in favor of the Transpadanes, this momentous action heralded a new policy for the gradual association of dependent peoples in the administration of the empire, a policy certain to rouse resistance among Caesar's opponents as well as hope among oppressed provincials everywhere.

Within forty days Caesar had accomplished the defeat of Afranius and Petreius. By the end of September, little more than three months since he had crossed the Pyrenees, he had eliminated a threat from the West by wresting the Spains, long a Pompeian stronghold, from his enemies.

Caesar continued to suffer from a shortage of capable administrators both because he required the services of his most competent and devoted associates as army commanders and because of the continuing refusal of older and more experienced senators to collaborate with him. Though undoubtedly aware of Quintus' greed and cruelty during his recent quaestorship in Further Spain, Caesar was indebted to the former tribune. He could hope that he had learned from experiences of the last months and that he would follow the policies Caesar had laid down in his addresses to the defeated Pompeian army and to the leading citizens of Further Spain at Corduba. He appointed Quintus Cassius governor of the province—a decision he would soon regret.

Sailing to Tarraco (Tarragona), Caesar conferred there with deputations from throughout Nearer Spain, formerly the base of Sertorius' power and now firmly loyal to him. Proceeding north, Caesar paused to gaze once again at Pompeius' monument to the victory over Sertorius. He did not destroy the pretentious trophy, but with a nice irony he erected nearby a modest altar with an inscription attesting to his defeat of the builder of the mammoth memorial.

Caesar sent orders ahead that Massilia was not "to be stormed by force in case the combined effects of resentment against the rebels, the contempt displayed towards themselves and their prolonged labors should inflame the soldiers' feelings to such a degree that they should kill all the men of military age."[17] No matter what terms Caesar imposed on Massilia he would be denounced for harsh treatment of an ancient ally. Nevertheless, he had to provide a warning to the other hostile cities and to render the haughty local oligarchy impotent to cause him further harm. Although upon the town's surrender, he did not permit his troops to pillage or vent their anger on the populace, he did deprive the town of its arms, treasury and the greater part of its domains. Shrunken in size, bereft of its fleet and deprived of its privileged relationship with Rome, Massilia would suffer a decline in influence in Gaul and Spain and lose its commercial supremacy to Roman towns in the Province and to Cisalpina. Throughout the Western Mediterranean, towns would contrast Caesar's treatment of hostile Massilia with that he accorded loyal Gades.

Before the city's surrender, Ahenobarbus escaped with his ships. Caesar would encounter him again.

Except for Spain and for Massilia, where Trebonius, an experienced legate of the Army of Gaul, held supreme command, Caesar suffered reverses. In Illyricum a veteran legate of the Army of Gaul ferried to safety on makeshift rafts part of an army Marcus Antonius' brother Gaius had left on an island at the mercy of a Pompeian fleet. Swimming to escape the attacking Pompeians, most of the troops were trapped in nets spread across the waters by pirates who had been captured and freed years earlier by Pompeius. Caesar grieved especially over the raw Cisalpine recruits who had slain each other rather than submit to capture. With the loss of this force, Illyricum was open to Pompeian attack and the northern flank of Italy was exposed.

More grievous to Caesar was Curio's fate. Upon landing in Africa he had reported dissension among the local Pompeians, the dispersal of an enemy fleet, the rout of Numidian cavalry and the capture of some two hundred merchant vessels loaded with supplies. On the other hand, Curio's troops, Pompeian recruits captured at Corfinium, had no stomach for a power struggle among oligarchs, "men . . . of a class which was permitted to do freely what it liked." After recalling them to discipline and driving the enemy within the walls of the city of Utica, Curio succumbed to a ruse and was overwhelmed by a horde of Numidian cavalry. He "declared that he would never go and face Caesar again after losing the army that Caesar had entrusted to him; and so he fought on and was killed."[18] A few of his men, including young Pollio, escaped and made their way to Sicily. King Juba of Numidia slaughtered most of the prisoners and then, escorted by Roman senators and equestrians, the haughty monarch rode in triumph into Utica as though lording it in his own domain.

Almost as disquieting was the news of a mutiny in the IXth legion, "real veterans of incomparable courage."[19] Caesar had had warning of weariness and disaffection in this legion in their rash pursuit of the enemy up to the walls of Ilerda that almost brought destruction to Caesar's entire army. They had grumbled at his procrastination in attacking the demoralized Pompeians, at his prohibition against plundering the camp of a defeated enemy and at his general policy of clemency. Accompanying the defeated Pompeian troops back to Italy, they had submitted to the mockery of an enemy force returning to be discharged while they remained in service. In their encampment at Placentia (Piacenza) in

Cisalpina, they muttered against further deployment overseas. They had no desire to contest the rule of the world in the East with Pompeius and the great host of men and ships he had supposedly assembled during the last months.

Not since the first year of the Gallic wars had Caesar confronted mutiny in his legions. On occasions when he had castigated troops for breaches of discipline, they had accepted rebuke, aware that with his remonstrances he sought to inspire them to excellence as soldiers. After ten years of service, however, they had passed the prime of youth. No longer could they be roused to Caesar's unflagging enthusiasm. If Caesar did not recall the legionaries from mutiny, he would become their prisoner. Hastening to their encampment and disregarding warnings about the angry mood of the troops, Caesar ordered a general assembly. From his platform he eyed the men. They returned his stare with apprehension, for they knew that he would not yield to insubordination, and they were not certain they could resist his will. Caesar denounced them for their ingratitude and greed and challenged them to declare that their present behavior was worthy of their past exploits. Soldiers who pillaged fellow citizens (as they had been doing in the environs of Placentia) were of no use to him, and he no longer wanted them in his service. Nevertheless, he would not permit mutiny to go unpunished and he ordered the distribution of lots for the execution of every tenth man. After the punishment, he declared, he would discharge the rest. The legionaries looked to their officers, and one by one tribunes and centurions came forward and appealed to Caesar for mercy. The legionaries fell to their knees, wailing and berating themselves and joining their pleas to their officers'. Yielding a little, Caesar demanded that they deliver up one hundred and twenty ringleaders, twelve men from each cohort. From these he would choose by lot one of ten for execution. After executing the mutineers in view of the assembled troops, Caesar received the legion back into his service.

LEGITIMACY

Caesar arranged for the praetor Lepidus (younger son of the rebel consular of thirty years earlier), the senior magistrate remaining at Rome, to nominate him as dictator with the responsibility of holding elections for the coming year. Under his own auspices Caesar obtained a second consulship. As his colleague he chose Publius Servilius Isauricus, son of the consular under whom Caesar had served as a youth in Cilicia. One of the most distinguished of the nobles loyal to Caesar, Servilius was, like Lepidus, a son-in-law of Caesar's mistress Servilia, and it is to be suspected that this politically astute woman was instrumental in promoting the careers of the two men.

On January 1, 48, with the expiration of the terms of the optimate consuls, Caesar's anomalous status was at an end. Now, too, his war aims had been achieved: his election to a consulship, the lapsing of the ultimate decree, the restoration of the tribunician authority and the termination of optimate domination of the Senate, the courts and the electoral process. At the New Year, if they remained in arms, Pompeius and his associates would become the rebels. Nevertheless, before departing from Rome, Caesar took measures to protect his rear while he encountered his foes in the East. To broaden his base of support, he prompted Antonius, tribune until December 10, 49, to pass a law restoring the civil rights of the sons and grandsons of those proscribed by Sulla more than three decades earlier, rehabilitating men blacklisted by the censor Appius Claudius and recalling from exile those condemned in recent years by optimate juries. Among those amnestied were men who "had offered their services to Caesar . . . at the beginning of the civil war,"[20] including the consulars Gabinius and Messalla and the litterateur Sallustius.

Caesar recognized the festering economic crisis as a grave threat to civil peace in Italy. Overseas commerce was almost at a standstill, money was in short supply, moneylenders were pressing for payment and debtors were suffering bankruptcy and disgrace. In his youth Caesar had seen how his father-in-law Cinna had reestablished stability in the economy after years of violent civil strife. With a law far more moderate than a comparable measure promoted by Cinna's colleague Valerius (Caesar's bill provided relief of one-quarter of all debts as against three-quarters in the earlier bill), Caesar permitted debtors to pay off part of their obligations by selling property at prewar values. He appointed arbiters under the supervision of the urban praetor Trebonius (the victor over Massilia) to adjudicate disagreements between debtors and creditors. Although he satisfied neither moneylenders, who had been enjoying a windfall in the deflation and in the collapse of real estate prices, nor debtors, who had anticipated a more radical solution of their problems, Caesar considered these proposals "as the most effective way to remove or lessen the fear of a total abolition of debts which usually accompanies wars or civil wars and to preserve the credit of debtors." Caesar's measure represented the first attempt in decades at a solution to a chronic and fundamental problem undermining the republic, for neither the hidebound optimates nor self-proclaimed libertarians like Cicero or Cato proposed remedies other than the violent suppression of the desperate. In the current relationship of political forces in the commonwealth only a statesman with Caesar's authority could impose a solution to the debt crisis, a solution inevitably displeasing to bankers and unsatisfying to debtors. To ease the credit shortage, Caesar forbade the hoarding of more than 60 thousand sesterces in silver or gold. He rejected, however, the popular clamor for a reward to slaves who denounced masters for hoarding. Recalling the general but impotent fury at Sulla's use of slaves as informers, Caesar announced that he would "invoke destruction against himself if he should ever trust a slave when speaking against his master."[21] In newly minted coins Caesar advertised his will for peace. Optimates might bridle at a representation of Liberty on a coin commemorating the deliverance of Rome from the domination of an arrogant clique, but other Romans would consider the coin a memorial to the popular hero Clodius, who had erected a shrine to Liberty on the site of Cicero's razed mansion. Few could cavil at images on coins of Concord and Pietas or of Liber (Bacchus) and Ceres (symbols of Caesar's commitment to a secure food supply).

Out of respect for tradition, Caesar, the pontifex maximus, delayed his departure for battle in order to celebrate the Latin Festival on the Alban Mount, a festival of appeal for divine sanction for military campaigns that dated to the formation of the alliance between Rome and neighboring Latin communities many centuries earlier. When a hawk dropped a sprig of laurel as he crossed the Forum, Caesar reassured the superstitious by proclaiming the event a good omen, and at alarm that "while he was sacrificing to Fortune the bull escaped before being wounded, rushed out of the city and coming to a certain lake swam across it," Caesar encouraged soothsayers (they were now in his service, not in his enemies') to declare "that destruction should be his portion if he remained at home but safety and victory if he crossed the seas."[22] Caesar announced that he would henceforth display a bull on his standard, a decision certain to please many of his legionaries, for the beast was not only a symbol of might but also the device of the Italian rebels four decades earlier.

In this brief stopover at Rome, in a series of swift and decisive moves, Caesar had brought a sense of order to the city. He had also given an indication of where he would seek his prime support. Though providing relief to the most depressed elements of the population, the nucleus of Clodius' party, and reassuring the wealthiest landowners, bankers and entrepreneurs, it was the middle stratum among the landowners, the artisans and the Italian municipal aristocracy whose interests Caesar catered to above all. Caesar had undermined the clientships of the optimates; his measures in defense of the provincials would result in a curb upon the extortions of the public corporations and upon the magistrates. To the middle stratum of Italy and the productive elements of the provinces, Caesar offered security against oppression and violence. In Aristotle's Politics Caesar found authority for his political stance. "Surely the ideal of the state," wrote the Greek sage, "is to consist as much as possible of persons that are equal and alike, this similarity is most found in the middle classes . . . this class of citizens . . . do not themselves covet other men's goods as do the poor, nor do the other classes covet their substance as the poor covet that of the rich; and because they are neither plotted against nor plotting they live free from danger."[23]

To the bewilderment of unreconciled optimates, who had been assuring each other that like Sulla, Caesar would retain the dictatorship indefinitely, he resigned the emergency magistracy after holding it a mere eleven days, and without awaiting formal installation as consul he departed for Brundisium. Within the compass of two market days (less than three weeks) Caesar had accomplished more than the most assiduous consuls of the last generation (except for Caesar himself) had accomplished in a full year in office: elections, passage of vital economic legislation, restoration of political outcasts, replenishment of his war chest and the enactment of provisions for administering the city, Italy and the provinces under his control.

XLVI
THE CONSUL AND THE REBEL

A T Brundisium Caesar discovered that Dolabella, Cicero's son-in-law, and Hortensius, two young officers who had bungled naval engagements in the Adriatic, had failed to assemble sufficient transports to convey Caesar's army across the sea. Nor had they accumulated adequate stores of grain, arms and materiel. In addition, not all the twelve legions Caesar had ordered to march to Brundisium had arrived, and as they straggled into the port city Caesar saw that they were woefully undermanned. "Many had been lost during all the campaigns in Gaul, the long march from Spain had removed a great many, and the unhealthy autumn weather in Apulia and around Brundisium, after the wholesome regions of Gaul and Spain, had seriously affected the health of the whole army."[1]

On the other hand, according to Caesar's intelligence, during the months since his flight from Italy Pompeius had mobilized, in addition to the troops from the peninsula (five legions and a personal bodyguard of eight hundred slaves), four legions among veterans and other citizens, the legionaries captured in Illyricum with Marcus Antonius' younger brother along with three thousand archers, twelve hundred slingers and seven thousand cavalry, including mounted bowmen from various clients. From throughout the Eastern Mediterranean Pompeius assembled more than five hundred ships and was constructing many more. He had amassed an inexhaustible war chest and a great store of provisions. In Syria after poisoning the Judean prince Caesar had dispatched to raise a rebellion, Pompeius' father-in-law Scipio was preparing to join Pompeius with two additional legions. On the other hand, Pompeius could not be confident of the loyalty of the two legions he had obtained from Caesar or of the infantry recruited from client states and cities, and his untested legions clearly were no match for Caesar's veterans.

Caesar was handicapped by a shortage of transport. In addition, every legionary was accompanied by at least one slave, and officers traveled with entire retinues, grooms, muleteers and armor bearers (dignity was reckoned according to the size of one's baggage and the number of one's retainers). To reduce the impedimenta and the number of noncombatants, Caesar issued an appeal. "We have come almost to the end of our toils and dangers," he declared. "You may therefore leave your slaves and baggage behind in Italy with easy minds. You must embark with only basic kit to allow a great number of troops to be put on board. When we win, my generosity in reward will answer all your hopes." In response, even the IXth legion, punished for mutiny only weeks earlier, joined in shouting their approval, "bidding him give what orders he liked; they would carry them out cheerfully."[2] Accordingly, on January 4, 48 (actually, because of a six-week disparity from the solar calendar, toward the end of November 49), Caesar embarked with seven legions (some twenty thousand men) and six hundred horse. Reaching land the next morning, he disembarked the men on the double so as to return the ships that very night for the remaining troops. Caesar's foes consistently underestimated him. They hardly anticipated that he would sail from Italy immediately after the exhausting Spanish and Massiliot campaigns or that he would risk a sea passage with a large army before the spring sailing season. Informed of Caesar's arrival, Bibulus, the Pompeian admiral in these waters, however, sailed out of Corcyra (Corfu), not far south from the rocky stretch where Caesar had disembarked, and captured and set afire thirty of Caesar's empty transports with their crews aboard. Caesar had surprised his enemies with his first contingent; now he was cut off from reinforcements.

Ignoring Bibulus' savage vindictiveness toward the crews of the transports, Caesar undertook a new peace effort, for his landing in Pompeian territory signaled the initiation of yet another phase in the conflict. To carry his proposals Caesar had retained Pompeius' officer Vibullius, captured and released at Corfinium and then recaptured in Spain. In a personal communication to Pompeius, Caesar noted that each had won significant victories and sustained substantial defeats. At this point of parity, "both of us," he urged, "ought to stop being obstinate, disarm and not tempt fortune further.... Let us ... spare both ourselves and Rome; our own losses have given us enough proof of the power of fortune in war. This is the best time of all to discuss peace, while we are both confident and appear equally matched; but if fortune should favor one, only a little, the one who seems the better off will have nothing to do with terms of peace, nor will he be satisfied with an equal share, when he believes he can have everything." Having dismissed as irrelevant the claims of vanity, Caesar offered a proposal difficult to reject by men who pretended to be defending the traditional institutions of the commonwealth. "As for the conditions of peace," Caesar declared, "since we ourselves have been unable to reach a settlement up till now, we should ask the Senate and people at Rome to frame terms."[3] By posing fair and honorable terms without conditions to his personal advantage or to the detriment of his adversary, Caesar certainly sought to gain a propaganda edge over Pompeius. It is to be suspected, however, that despite his many years of maneuvering in politics Caesar still harbored a confidence, perhaps not fully conscious and certainly unjustified by experience, in the power of rational discourse. In this instance, Caesar's continued insistence upon the restoration of the independence of the Senate and of the People and, implicitly, upon the elimination of the domination of an arrogant optimate clique and of Pompeius' special role as arbiter of the commonwealth rendered unlikely an acceptance of his terms.

Caesar did not procrastinate while awaiting a response from Pompeius. On the very day of disembarkation he expanded his bridgehead northward. He reaped the first advantage of his new status as duly elected consul when at the port of Oricum the townspeople "refused to fight against someone who had an official command from the Roman people."[4] Other Epirote towns sent deputations with promises to obey the consul's orders. From deserters Caesar learned that, apprized of his landing, Pompeius, who had been marching at a leisurely pace from his headquarters at Thessalonica (at the northern extremity of the Aegean) to the Adriatic, stepped up his advance in order to outrace Caesar to Dyrrachium, the chief port of the region and the entrepôt of his military supplies and provisions. As Caesar anticipated, Pompeius confronted morale problems more serious than his own. Men recruited locally deserted en masse, and Labienus, now Pompeius' closest associate, repeating Petreius' tactic in Spain, assembled the army and compelled officers and men to renew their oath of allegiance to Pompeius.

Pompeius' forces, for all his problems, outnumbered Caesar's at least two to one, and Pompeian admirals, galled at Caesar's outwitting their surveillance, now patrolled the strait between Italy and Epirus with renewed resolution. Caesar, in fact, dispatched a warning to Brundisium against incautious embarkation. One vessel that set sail before the arrival of his message was captured by Bibulus, "who took his vegeance on everyone aboard, slave and free, even the youngsters, killing every one of them."[5] Apparently it was optimate policy to terrorize foes into submission (standard practice among defenders of outmoded political orders).

Within days of Vibullius' release, a messenger arrived from Bibulus and his vice-admiral Libo (father-in-law to Pompeius' younger son) with a request for a conference. Assuming this to be a response to his letter to Pompeius, Caesar complied. Libo appeared alone. Bibulus, he said, was "a very hot-tempered man and had besides certain private quarrels with Caesar dating from the time of his aedileship and praetorship [he and Caesar had been colleagues in both offices as well as in the consulship]; for these reasons he avoided a meeting in case his temper should be a hindrance in such important and salutary negotiations."[6] Rejecting negotiations for peace, the Pompeians merely proposed an armistice during which their ships would replenish their supplies along the coast under Caesar's control without at the same time relaxing their blockade against Caesar.

When Caesar established a camp on the south bank of the Apsus river just north of the town of Apollonia, Pompeius set his camp on the opposite bank. Despite his superiority in numbers, he failed to attack. Gradually, vigilance relaxed on both sides of the stream, and men began to call across to each other. Recognizing an opportunity for the fraternization that had proved so effective in Spain, Caesar sent to the riverbank the rough-and-ready Vatinius, whose stentorian boom and tavern-house wit roused chortles among the soldiers. Vatinius played on a single theme, "asking whether, as between citizens, they might send two envoys to discuss peace—a privilege which had been granted even to the fugitives from the Pyrenean mountains [at the end of the Sertorian war] and to the pirates [crushed by Pompeius some fifteen years earlier] and which ought especially to be granted as the aim was to stop citizens from bearing arms against each other." Vatinius "was heard in silence by the troops on both sides," and the Pompeians could not ignore the general sentiment. Someone shouted that an officer would appear the next day to arrange for a conference of envoys. On the next day great throngs assembled on both sides. Labienus stepped forward. He sought to goad Vatinius into an argument. Suddenly a shower of missiles fell among Caesar's men, wounding young Balbus, several other officers and numerous legionaries. "Now then," shouted Labienus, "stop talking about an agreement. Until Caesar's head is delivered to us, there can be no peace."[7]

The Pompeians had not been foolhardy in their rejection of peace negotiations. They had received news from Italy that roused their hopes.

A NEW CLODIUS

Caesar had no illusions regarding partisans like Caelius, who had joined his party after the censor Appius Claudius attempted to blacklist him and because he adjudged Caesar's Army of Gaul invincible. Like other profligate aristocrats, Caelius had tolerated Caesar's policy of clemency as a temporary tactic to undermine enemy resistance. He looked forward to proscriptions and confiscations in which he would enrich himself and seize a position of power. "As bankrupt in property as in character and unable to save himself by paying even a reasonable proportion of his debts," he had expected a cancellation of his debts as a reward for his support—a reward over and above the praetorship to which Caesar had advanced him. Calculating that Caesar would be preoccupied in a long struggle without certainty of victory and acting out of "pure chagrin and a sense of humiliation, which," he admitted, "as a rule influenced [him] more than anything,"[8] Caelius sought to revive Clodius' party. Clodius' political machine had disintegrated following his assassination and the repression introduced by Pompeius in alliance with the optimates, but his leaderless partisans remained. A skilful demagogue, Caelius set his praetorian curule chair next to Trebonius' and announced that he would support appeals to the urban praetor's rulings on disagreements between debtors and creditors. Caelius discovered, however, that the populace had no heart for new disorders and that even the majority of the debtors considered Caesar's bill equitable and Trebonius' administration of the law humane. Failing in this maneuver, Caelius proposed a law for deferring all debts for six years without interest. When this measure evoked no response, he proposed, also unsuccessfully, a one-year moratorium on rents and a general cancellation of debts. He now tried violence, instigating a riot in which Trebonius was hustled off his tribunal and several people were injured. Fortunately, Caesar had made a wise choice in his consular colleague. Upon Servilius' motion, the Senate suspended Caelius from office, and Caelius departed from the city, announcing he would appeal to Caesar. In fact, he had already entered into communication with Pompeius and summoned from exile in Massilia his old friend Milo, Clodius' murderer. Milo hastened to southern Italy to rouse the herdsmen, the dispossessed smallholders and the remnants of Spartacus' following, while Caelius established himself at Capua, where Spartacus had initiated his rebellion.

Upon word of this uprising, Pompeius and his optimate councilors, hardly finicky about their alliances, dispatched the troubleshooter Vibullius to Italy. At Vibullius' urging, Milo recruited an army by breaking into slave stockades on plantations and latifundia. Caesar's nephew, the praetor Pedius, however, marched to the south, defeated and killed Milo, while Caelius was slain by Gallic and Spanish cavalrymen he sought to suborn. In the suppression of the putsch Caesar won goodwill among the men of property; on the other hand, Caelius had exposed the discontent among Clodius' old following, and they would respond to appeals by other demagogues.

Caesar had more pressing concerns.

Antonius and the legate Calenus failed to embark the remaining legions from Brundisium. With the advent of spring the Pompeian admirals would tighten their surveillance of the strait. Furthermore, Caesar had word that Scipio was on the march from Asia Minor with a relief army; he would entrap Caesar in a pincers movement. Receiving no responses to messages to Brundisium, one night, disguised and with an escort of only three slaves, Caesar sailed out into high winds and rough surf in a twelve-oared smack. When, after several hours of fruitless battling against the waves, the owner of the boat ordered the oarsmen to turn about, Caesar disclosed himself and cried: "Why are you afraid? You have Caesar on board." Impressed with the resolution of their distinguished passenger, the sailors heaved on their oars. At last, with the boat taking water and making no headway in the swell, Caesar yielded.[9]

At word of Caesar's recklessness, tribunes and centurions gathered at his headquarters with resolutions from the legionaries reproving him for doubting that "with them alone he was able to conquer." Upon a change in weather Caesar dispatched a devoted officer, Postumius, with an order to Antonius and Calenus not to miss the first favorable wind. Wary of adventurist associates since the Caelius affaire, Caesar entrusted Postumius with a message to be read before the assembled legionaries in which he exhorted "everyone who was willing to do so [to] follow Postumius on board and sail to any place where the wind might carry them and not to mind what happened to the ships because Caesar did not want ships but men."

"With the men themselves expressing eagerness and ready to face any danger to save Caesar," Antonius and Calenus set sail. Lookouts reported that the transports were being carried north by a strong wind with a Pompeian squadron in pursuit. Caesar sent scouts to follow the fleet to its landing place. At a further report that Pompeius was advancing with his army to cut off Antonius, Caesar, compelled to follow a circuitous route in order to ford the Apsus, by forced marches outdistanced Pompeius. Battered by a sudden shift in gale-force winds, part of the enemy squadron was blown ashore. Rhodian sailors captured by his patrols Caesar freed and sent home to their island. (Caesar would be rewarded by the Rhodians for this gesture.) The Pompeians, on the other hand, displayed their usual ruthlessness with prisoners. After promising to spare lives of men captured on ships driven ashore in the storm, a Pompeian commander slaughtered a detachment of new recruits. Veterans on another vessel fought their way free and joined Caesar.

Caesar's legionaries rejoiced at linking up with Antonius and Calenus. Resolved to avenge the massacre of the new recruits, they carried out with their customary discipline the ruse Caesar had employed successfully against Afranius and Petreius in Spain. Caesar led the army away from Dyrrachium only to veer in a contrary direction under cover of night so as to reach the outskirts of the town in the morning. He had cut his foe off from his base. Henceforth Pompeius would be forced to rely upon ships for delivery of grain, forage and materiel.

In Gaul Caesar had learned never to commence a campaign without securing his food supply. In the present circumstances he had had no choice, and blockaded by enemy fleets, he confronted a crisis. Local grain would not ripen for months, and reserves were low. Both to expedite the delivery of foodstuffs and to intercept Scipio advancing from the southeast, Caesar dispatched a legion of new recruits to Thessaly in northern Greece under the command of Lucius Cassius.* A half legion and some horse Caesar sent into Central Greece under a legate of the Army of Gaul along with two veteran legions and five hundred horse under the consular Calvinus.

With Pompeius refusing to give battle, Caesar resolved upon a dramatic strategy. Though blockaded by a superior army and by a fleet in control of the seas, he set to constructing siege works so as to blockade Pompeius in turn. Because of the numerical superiority of the Pompeians and the rugged terrain, the task was more complicated than at Alesia. After surveying the area, Caesar and his engineers planned the erection of a series of forts on hilltops with a line of connecting works. As soon as Caesar's men began the construction, Pompeius initiated counterworks, and with archers and slingers he harassed Caesar's troops. Commanding greater manpower and working within a smaller inner ring, he outstripped Caesar in completing his defenses. Nevertheless, Caesar's action represented a bold psychological stroke. He recognized the demoralization that would set in among his troops if Pompeius continued to

---

*Brother to Servilia's son-in-law Gaius Cassius, a Pompeian admiral (and Caesar's future assassin).

avoid giving battle, and he was confident they would recover their élan when engaged in a mammoth construction. Despite their reduced rations, the legionaries exhibited "remarkable endurance, for they recollected that when they suffered the same hardships the previous year in Spain by their efforts and their fortitude they had brought an end to a great war. They remembered that they had endured severe privation at Alesia and even more at Avaricum and had come off victorious over very powerful tribes. They did not refuse barley when it was offered, nor vegetables; and meat, of which there was a very large supply from Epirus, they held in great esteem," for they had acquired a taste for flesh in Gaul. Priding themselves on their ingenuity, they discovered that a root called "chara" mixed with milk could be baked into a kind of bread, and "when the Pompeians . . . taunted [them] with famine, they used frequently to throw these loaves at them."[10]

The report spread throughout the Mediterranean that "Pompeius was blockaded . . . and did not dare to join battle." Simultaneously Caesar evolved various long-range strategies. He sent a messenger to Further Spain to order the governor Quintus Cassius to recruit an army for an invasion of Africa in order that the Pompeian forces there might be subdued at the same time as their main army in Epirus. Caesar also renewed his diplomatic efforts, sending an old acquaintance of Scipio's with a shrewdly drafted message to Pompeius' father-in-law. Noting that Scipio commanded an army of his own and enjoyed great personal influence, Caesar addressed the pompous mediocrity as a man whose "authority was such that he could not only state his own views freely, he could even to a large extent control Pompeius and direct him when he went astray." Playing upon the persistent rivalry among the optimates, Caesar suggested that in undertaking a settlement to the current hostilities "his alone would be the credit of securing a respite for Italy, peace for the provinces and salvation for the empire."[11] (In this formulation Caesar defined his war aims in a new stage of the conflict.)

Upon his arrival at Scipio's headquarters, Caesar's emissary was given a ready hearing. Abruptly, however, he was excluded from further discussions. Later Caesar would learn that the praetorian Favonius, a contentious optimate who imagined himself a second Cato, expostulated so severely with Scipio as to compel him to back away from his initial receptivity. Favonius sensed, of course, the contradiction in conception of the empire between Caesar and the optimates. In his message to Scipio, Caesar had not even mentioned Rome, alluding only to Italy, the provinces and the empire—a formulation certain to invite suspicion among the Pompeian leadership with its parochial, city-state mentality.

Caesar also sought to exploit the dissension within Pompeius' camp. Morale ebbed among the enemy troops when Caesar's engineers traced the sources of their water supply and diverted streams away from Pompeian territory, and within their beachhead the Pompeians "were finding their health affected by their cramped conditions, the foul smell from the large number of corpses and the daily toil, as they were unaccustomed to construction work." In their discomfort, aristocrats began snapping at each other. They sneered at Pompeius for his inactivity during the months following Caesar's landing, for his dawdling in marching to head off Antonius' newly arrived force, for allowing himself to be cut off from Dyrrachium and for submitting to a blockade by a force much inferior to his own. From spies, deserters and prisoners, Caesar learned that his old foe, the consul of 51, Marcus Marcellus, "disapproved of . . . Pompeius' troops and the composition of his army [and] utterly distrusted it."[12] Assuming that other optimates more susceptible to offers of reconciliation shared this suspicion of Pompeius' client troops, Caesar sent young Balbus several times on a dangerous mission across the lines to negotiate with Lentulus Crus, the bankrupt consul of the previous year. Unfortunately, Lentulus still demanded an exorbitant price for defecting.

Cicero offered a more promising subject for blandishments. He openly mocked Pompeius for incompetence and for shrinking "in horror at any suggestion of peace negotiations" and proclaimed his dismay at the noblemen in the camp "greedy for loot . . . bloodthirsty in the way they spoke." Furthermore, he could not understand why Pompeius made no particular use of his talents. At Caesar's instance, Dolabella wrote to urge Cicero now that "the scales have inclined toward our victory" to accept "such advice as I could not as a dutiful son-in-law leave unspoken." He warned that Pompeius, no longer shielded "by the glamor of his name and achievements nor by his patronage of diverse kings and peoples," could not hope for "the possibility of escape without dishonor," and he appealed to Cicero to consult his own interests and take a stand "where the new constitution is" [under Caesar's consulship] and retire from the war zone.[13]

Within Dyrrachium Caesar's agents arranged for an incursion through the gates, and one night Caesar led an assault party to a rendezvous at a temple just outside the walls. He was ambushed and saved only by the timely arrival of Publius Sulla with two legions. Sulla's nephew Publius had been deprived of his civil rights after conviction for malfeasance in the consular elections for 65. Like many others in similar circumstances, he had offered his services to Caesar. Now veterans grumbled that if Sulla, who had not fought in Gaul, "had been willing to pursue more keenly, the war might have been concluded on that day." Indeed, on that very day in six engagements of extraordinary ferocity, the Pompeians had suffered heavy casualties. At one redoubt in Caesar's presence, legionaries counted out some thirty thousand enemy arrows, "and they brought him the shield of the centurion Scaeva, in which were found one hundred and twenty holes. Caesar gave Scaeva 200 thousand sesterces and promoted him from the eighth rank up to the first centurionate—for it was certain that it was largely thanks to him that the fortress had been saved; and later he lavishly rewarded the cohort with double wages, corn, clothes, food allowances and military decorations."[14]

With such troops victory seemed assured.

PERIPETEIA (Reversal of Fortune)

Two Allobrogian chieftains, brothers who had fought under Caesar in Gaul and enjoyed rewards of influence, lands and money, "carried away by stupid, barbarian vanity . . . began to look down on their own people, to cheat the cavalry of their pay and appropriate all the plunder for themselves." Gallic troops complained that by "making a false return of the numbers of cavalry they were embezzling the pay of several men."[15] Caesar took the offenders to task privately and won from them a promise of restitution. One night, however, the two Gallic chiefs crossed the lines with a band of clients and a train of horses.

The loyalty of Caesar's auxiliaries roused universal wonderment, and before his army an exultant Pompeius paraded the Allobrogians, whose tribe was Caesar's favorite among the Gauls. Interrogating them closely, Pompeius learned of a breach in Caesar's as yet incomplete siege works (the Gauls may have recalled how an uncompleted segment of the Alesia fortifications had almost brought defeat to Caesar). Sailing by night with an overwhelming force, Pompeius attacked this sector at dawn with a barrage of javelins, arrows and other missiles and panicked Caesar's outflanked legionaries. Veteran soldiers mobbed centurions who sought to stem the rout, and if Antonius had not marched to the rescue, the entire army might have been engulfed. Informed of the peril by smoke signals, Caesar brought up reinforcements and stemmed the attack. Then upon a report of an enemy legion established in an isolated camp abandoned by his own troops, Caesar surprised his foes, and victory would have been his except for the intervention of Fortune.

Catching sight of Pompeius advancing with a relief force in serried ranks, Caesar's cavalry, cut off from the legionaries by a rampart and blocked in a cul-de-sac, wheeled in terror, jostling and trampling each other. When legionaries saw the horsemen in flight, they were seized with fright and within minutes "everywhere was full of turmoil, panic and rout; so much so that when Caesar grabbed the standards of the men fleeing and ordered them to halt, some gave their horses rein and continued in their course of flight, while others in their fear actually let the standards drop, but no one halted at all." Caesar himself almost perished. "As a tall and sturdy man was running away past him, he laid his hand upon him and bade him stay and face about upon the enemy; and the fellow full of panic at the threatening danger raised his sword to smite Caesar, but before he could do so Caesar's shieldbearer lopped off his arm at the shoulder."[16]

Salvation came from Pompeius, who did not press on to certain and total victory. "Pompeius," Caesar commented to his officers, "I believe, feared an ambush because the situation was so contrary to his expectations, [and he] did not venture for some time to go near the entrenchments." He added wryly: "Today victory would have been with the enemy if they had had a victor in command."[17]

Casualties in this rout totaled nearly a thousand men, including thirty-two military tribunes and centurions; thirty-two standards were lost. The honor of the army had been preserved only by certain valorous individuals like the standard bearer of the formerly mutinous IXth legion. Mortally wounded, he had appealed to cavalrymen in flight, crying: "I have faithfully guarded this eagle for many years in my lifetime and now, dying, I restore it, with equal faithfulness, to Caesar. I beg you, do not allow our military honor to be disgraced—something which has never happened before in Caesar's army— and bear the eagle to him safely."[18] Nevertheless, the defeat was the most calamitous of Caesar's career, far more grievous than the destruction of the fifteen cohorts in Belgium or the repulse at Gergovia.

Pompeius' soldiers hailed him as Imperator, and Labienus, who considered this victory as a vindication of his defection, lined up prisoners, his former comrades-in-arms, and demanded with a sneer "whether veteran troops were in a habit of running away."[19] He killed them all in the sight of the Pompeian army.

Assembling his troops Caesar urged the men "not to be disheartened or afraid of what happened but to balance against this one setback . . . all the many successful engagements they had had"—the victories in Italy, in Spain and their successful landing in Epirus. "We must help fortune," he declared, "by some efforts of our own." As at Gergovia, he noted that they could readily turn "loss to gain" as a result of the lesson of this day. Instead of executing standard bearers who abandoned their standards, as custom prescribed, he merely degraded them. Mortified at their ignominy and at his restraint, the legionaries "demanded that they be decimated according to the traditional rule." Upon Caesar's refusal, they begged to be led forthwith against the enemy and "on their own . . . took an oath by companies . . . that they would not leave the field of battle except as victors." Caesar, however, "had little confidence in his demoralized troops and thought they should be given time to rally their spirits."[20]

With his staff Caesar analyzed the events of the day. He had long recognized that "Fortune, whose power is very great in all spheres, but particularly in warfare, often brings about great reversals by a slight tilt of the balance"—an insight with which the Epicureans on his staff would sympathize, believing, as they did, that atoms falling in ceaseless motion through space "swerve a little from their course," collide and produce novel combinations.[21] Thus in appre- hending the general motion within nature, men come to appreciate "the slight tilt of the balance" and the continuous mobility in human affairs. Caesar's enemies, Stoics, viewing nature as immutable, did not in the present circum- stances "recall how things commonly happen in war, how small causes—false alarm or sudden panic or a religious scruple—had often inflicted great damage, how often through the inadequacy of a commander, or the fault of a tribune an army had come to grief." Confident that all had been resolved, the Pompeians "broadcast that day's victory through the world by word of mouth and by dispatches just as if they had conquered by their own valor and as if no reversal could occur."[22]

Caesar never persisted beyond season in any strategy. With no more delay than was required to tend to the sick and wounded, he dispatched his baggage train southward with an escort of a single legion. The remaining legions he sent forth one by one so as to delay the enemy's awareness of his general retreat. Celebrating their victory, the Pompeians took up the pursuit belatedly and in their overoptimism suffered a repulse with great losses at a river crossing. Both armies reoccupied the camps they had constructed on opposite banks of the Apsus prior to the battle of Dyrrachium. Instead of resting, however, Caesar waited one day until the enemy troops dispersed for foraging and then sounded the signal for departure. Before Pompeius could reassemble his troops, Caesar gained a secure head start. Once again by setting himself in the character and the thinking of his opponent, Caesar had anticipated Pompeius, while Pompeius, out of conceit and limited imagination and as incapable as other optimates of learning from experience, projected his own mindset upon Caesar.

After four days Pompeius abandoned pursuit.

Though in retreat, Caesar had regained the initiative.

XLVII

THE TOPPLING OF POMPEIUS

H
AD Caesar been in Pompeius' place, he might have embarked for Italy, occupied Rome and recaptured the western provinces, but the Great Man was uncertain of the morale of his troops and the loyalty of his associates. While Pompeius and his counselors haggled over strategy, Caesar deposited his wounded at Apollonia, paid his troops, installed garrisons in loyal towns and marched inland, drawing Pompeius away from his supply lines on the sea. Fortune this time intervened in Caesar's favor. Advancing to unite their forces, Caesar and the consular Calvinus, who had earlier been sent into Macedonia, were ignorant of each other's precise positions. Gallic horsemen who had deserted from Caesar with the two Allobrogian chiefs warned Calvinus' Gallic scouts of Pompeius' imminent approach, and he withdrew in time to escape destruction and link up with Caesar. After marching some two hundred miles, Caesar's exhausted legions arrived at the village of Pharsalus. They were in low spirits when Pompeius, now joined by Scipio and commanding a force almost double Caesar's, set up camp on a nearby hill. When Pompeius consistently

refused to descend for combat, however, Caesar's men took heart. To compensate for his inferiority in cavalry, outnumbered seven to one by the Pompeians, Caesar assigned younger legionaries, lightly armed, to support the cavalry and trained them in tactics he had learned from the Germans and had employed against British charioteers. Thus reinforced, Caesar's cavalry repulsed the enemy in a skirmish and killed one of the Allobrogian deserters.

On August 9 (early June by the solar calendar), facing a shortage in provisions, suffering from the intense heat of this marshy region and convinced that Pompeius would not offer battle, Caesar gave orders to break camp. He counted on wearying the pursuing Pompeians, unaccustomed to long marches, and on compelling them to give battle on some occasion advantageous to himself. With the tents already struck, sentinels reported that on this morning Pompeius had advanced his line farther than usual from his ramparts. Caesar immediately displayed his scarlet cloak before his command post, the signal for battle. Assembling the legions, he asked whether to delay an engagement pending arrival of reinforcements from Illyricum and southern Greece. The legionaries shouted an adamant "no." "Our spirits are ready for battle,"[1] declared Caesar, and he ordered tallies circulated with the watchword of the day: Venus Victrix (the Victorious). Usurping the deity to whom Pompeius had dedicated the temple in his theater at Rome, Caesar vowed another temple to his divine ancestress in the event of victory. To oppose Ahenobarbus, commanding the enemy right wing, he appointed Antonius, honored for his valor at Dyrrachium, anchoring Antonius' flank on a stream with steep banks. In the center Caesar set the loyal consular Calvinus against Pompeius' father-in-law Scipio; on the right against the consular Lentulus Crus he placed Publius Sulla; he himself took his stand at the flank in opposition to Pompeius with the Xth legion, his bodyguard since the first campaign in Gaul.

Surveying the enemy host, Caesar noted that the cavalry under Labienus, reinforced by archers and slingers, was massed against his right wing. (After the battle Caesar was to learn that in a council of war Pompeius had announced that Caesar's army would be routed even before the collision of the infantry lines. "I know that what I promise is almost incredible," Pompeius declared, "but listen to my tactical plan so that you may go to battle with more confidence. I have advised the cavalry, when the armies come within fairly close range, to attack Caesar's right wing on its exposed flank, surround the line in the rear and thus throw his army into confusion and rout it before a missile is thrown from our side at the enemy. They have undertaken to do so, and in this way we shall bring the war to an end without danger to the legions and almost without bloodshed. It is not difficult in view of our superiority in cavalry.")[2] Apprehending that just such a stratagem had been proposed by Labienus, Caesar withdrew six cohorts from his third line and concentrated them behind the Xth legion, facing them sideways and not full face toward the enemy. He instructed them as to their responsibility and charged them that victory might depend upon their response to orders and upon their valor.

At Alesia two civilizations had confronted each other in a contest to decide the fate of Gaul. Now two parties with contradictory views of the world were about to decide the fate of the world. On the side of the Pompeian forces stood the defenders of the oligarchic city-state and its client princes under the slogan "No change!"; with Caesar stood those who gave assent to the slogan "There is nothing but change!"—receptive to some new, as yet unformulated, imperial order. The Pompeians dismissed as a transitory manifestation of a decline in moral fibre the corruption pervading the institutions of the city-state and recognized no correlation between the profligacy and greed of the oligarchy and the famine and misery in Italy and the provinces. Fearing even to discuss remedies for the crisis threatening their hegemony, they dismissed all proposals for reforms and could "endure neither [their own] vices nor the cure [for these vices]."[3]

The ideological contrast was mirrored within the two armies. On the side of the Pompeians, a devious commander aspired to leadership of an oligarchy confirmed in its imperial hegemony, while his associates, scheming to curb his supremacy, even gloated over his defeats. Like all other beleaguered aristocracies, they entertained no qualms about suppressing opposition with terror. They massacred prisoners and threatened uncommitted aristocrats with proscriptions and confiscations. Apart from legions formerly in Caesar's service and of dubious loyalty, Pompeius commanded feckless recruits and Eastern peasants dragooned into service by princelings whom they detested. In Caesar's service, on the other hand, a cadre of devoted legates trained in years of campaigning in Gaul commanded the unquestioning respect of legionaries and auxiliaries who had fought under Caesar for as long as ten years. "Caesar's men," they could hardly imagine their lives apart from his, emulating him in discipline, versatility, initiative and valor. Caesar had made them larger as men, more fulfilled as human beings, and introduced them into the theater of history.

In primary confrontation, however, were Roman aristocrats related by blood and marriage or otherwise connected by a mesh of intricate ties, men who had exercised together on the Campus Martius, exchanged congratulations at the assumption of the toga of manhood, at marriages and at births, marched together in funeral processions or in triumphs, collaborated or battled in the Senate, assisted at ceremonies of priestly colleges—partners in ruling a city and an empire. By manipulation they had involved Italian yeomen and foreign dependents in a struggle in which the troops had only minimal concerns. Even Caesar maintained ties primarily of personal loyalty with his men, and the troops were not convinced of the propriety of his clemency or his respect for enemy property, and they gave little thought to his long-range aspirations regarding the city, Italy and the empire.

Caesar delivered a customary exhortation, recalling to the troops "the good service they had done him at all times" and calling them "to witness the earnestness with which he had sought peace." Never, he insisted, had it been "his wish to expose his troops to bloodshed nor to deprive the State of either army."[4]

The troops required no exhortation. They clamored for battle.

When Caesar signaled the trumpeters to sound the attack, a centurion named Crastinus, formerly of the crack Xth legion, stepped forward. "Follow me," he cried, "you who were formerly in my company and give your general the service you have promised. Only this one battle remains; after it, he will recover his position and we our freedom." Then looking at Caesar, he declared: "General, today I shall earn your gratitude, either dead or alive."[5] Roaring a battle cry and led by Crastinus, the first and second lines advanced.

To Caesar's dismay, as the legionaries approached the Pompeians, they hesitated. Pompeius had apparently ordered his men to hold their position in order to conserve energy for the shock of the encounter. He had not taken to heart the axiom that "there is a certain eagerness of spirit and an innate keenness in everyone which is inflamed by desire for battle." Thus "the practice began in antiquity of giving the signal on both sides and everyone's raising a war-cry . . . both to frighten the enemy and to stimulate one's own men." Although Caesar feared that his men would be exhausted upon reaching the enemy lines, he did not dare to break the momentum of their advance by issuing new orders.

Caesar need not have been apprehensive.

"Thanks to the practical experience and training they had had in earlier battles, they checked their charge and halted about half-way so as not to approach worn out. Then after a short interval they renewed the charge, threw their javelins and, as ordered by Caesar, quickly drew their swords."[6]

The collision of the two lines provided the signal for Labienus' cavalry. With a multitude of archers and slingers, they galloped forward, princes of client states and young Roman aristocrats, "impatient for the battle since they had a splendid array of shining armor, well-fed horses and handsome persons . . . in high spirits, too, on account of their numbers."[7] They overwhelmed Caesar's squadrons.

Acquainted with these dandies, Romans as boastful on the battlefield of supposed exploits as in the stews and whorehouses at home, or princelings "insolent in bearing, yielding to none in zeal and ardor for the cause" (or so they vaunted among themselves), Caesar had prepared for this attack. He ordered his standardbearer to display his commander's flag to the two thousand legionaries crouched in reserve in a fourth line behind the right flank. They sprang up and darted forth, "not hurling their javelins as usual, nor yet stabbing the thighs and legs of their enemies with them but aiming at their eyes and wounding their faces." As Caesar had foreseen, "these blooming and handsome war dancers would not stand their ground for fear of having their youthful beauty marred, nor would they face the steel when it was right at their eyes."[8] Howling in terror the foppish horsemen wheeled back toward their own lines, while in serried ranks behind their standards Caesar's legionaries assailed the unprotected archers and slingers and slew them all. Pressing forward, they outflanked the melee and struck the Pompeians from the rear.

Meanwhile, Caesar's third line had been shifting on their feet, resentful at their exclusion from the triumph of Venus Victrix over Hercules Invictus (Pompeius' patron for the day). At a signal from Caesar they shot forth, fueling the embroilment with fresh zeal. Upon the rout of the cavalry, amongst the Pompeians "the panic extended further and one body of troops spreading confusion to another, the slaughter of the rest was accomplished as though by one sweep of the hand. . . . Spare your fellow citizens!" cried Caesar.[9]

With Caesar at their head, a band of legionaries attacked Pompeius' camp, overwhelming the Thracian guards and bursting through the gates. They halted in astonishment as they beheld tents wreathed with ivy, "a great weight of silver plate laid out, tents spread with fresh turf . . . and many other indications of extravagant indulgence and confidence in victory; so that it could readily be judged that they had had no fears for the outcome of the day." Exhorted by their centurions, other legionaries sped after the demoralized foe. In the advancing twilight, ignoring their exhaustion, the legionaries dug a moat and raised a rampart against a large band atop a hill. When enemy troops attempted to withdraw at the far side of the elevation, Caesar blocked their escape, and in the depths of the night a deputation arrived for terms. At dawn, in obedience to Caesar's instructions, all the Pompeians descended. They threw down their arms and prostrated themselves, "weeping and begging . . . for their lives." Caesar "reassured them, told them to get up and spoke briefly to them about his own leniency." In an implicit response to Pompeius' threat to execute all oligarchs who failed to take arms on his side, he announced: "Those have not wronged me who supported the cause of Pompeius their friend without having received any benefit from me."[10] Roman aristocrats previously captured and released he ordered executed, permitting each of his officers, however, to participate in his general policy of clemency by saving the life of a friend or connection. The princes and officers of the client troops Caesar freed, and they departed, astonished at his generosity and pledging their allegiance to him. The Pompeian legionaries, including the troops of the two legions formerly in the Army of Gaul as well as the soldiers captured in Illyricum with Antonius' brother, Caesar enrolled in his own army.

One hundred and eighty standards and nine eagles (one for each of Pompeius' legions) were brought to Caesar, and an initial count disclosed six thousand Pompeian dead, including ten senators. Some twenty-four thousand were numbered among the prisoners. An additional twenty thousand had fled. Ahenobarbus was overtaken and slain by Caesar's cavalry, but his son was among those spared and freed. Pompeius' father-in-law Scipio, the consular Lentulus Crus, Labienus and Pompeius himself along with many other oligarchs were not to be found.

Surveying the thousands of bodies on the battlefield, Caesar recalled the years the optimates had threatened him with prosecution and disgrace, their rejection of his offers of negotiation and their obstinate refusal to compromise. "They would have it so," Caesar mused to his staff officers. "Even I, Gaius Caesar, after so many great deeds, should have been found guilty if I had not turned to my army for help."[11]

Among the thirty centurions who fell that day was Crastinus, the brave soldier who had led the attack with his ringing exhortation to his comrades, "killed, fighting staunchly, by a sword thrust full in the face."[12] Caesar ordered a burial mound erected in honor of this hero in recognition of the contribution of the dedicated noncoms to Caesar's victories.

Letters Caesar discovered in Pompeius' files he "neither read nor had copied but burned immediately in order not to be forced by what was in them to take severe measures,"[13] for Caesar had no intention of instituting a hunt for "subversives." From prisoners Caesar learned that Pompeius, despairing at the rout of the cavalry upon whom he relied for victory, had retired and brooded in his tent until he heard the sounds of fighting at the ramparts of the camp. Tearing off his insignia, he sent for his horse and galloped out a rear gate in the direction of Larisa, a day's ride to the northwest.

THE CHASE

Caesar granted his troops a day of rest. They had long since come to take it for granted that under such circumstances he would not allow himself an equal indulgence. He was preoccupied with plans drafted in advance of the battle, dispatching heralds by fast relays and swift galleys to report the victory and to warn islands and coastal towns against offering asylum to enemies. He conferred with Antonius, who was to conduct most of the legions back to Italy. He discussed with Calvinus the deployment of legions enrolled from among the Pompeian prisoners; with Fufius Calenus, entrusted with the governorship of Greece, the disposition of Pompeian senators and equestrians in refuge there. He drafted orders for Gabinius, the consul of 58 condemned to exile in a politically motivated trial and rehabilitated by Caesar, to march north with reserves he had been drilling at Brundisium, to relieve Cornificius beleaguered in Illyricum by Pompeian fleets and soon to be threatened by troops that had escaped from Pharsalus. He sent orders to Quintus Cassius to cross the Strait of Gibraltar to attack the Pompeians in Africa.

The war was not over. Pompeian fleets controlled the seas. They had destroyed or captured most of Caesar's vessels beached along the Adriatic coast and were raiding Illyricum and Italy. In Dyrrachium Cato commanded a substantial garrison reinforced with refugees from Pharsalus. Burebista, the king of the Dacians, aware of Caesar's plans to invade and conquer his kingdom, had offered Pompeius an alliance, and Pompeius had been in negotiation, too, with the king of the Parthians. Had circumstances been reversed, Caesar would have continued the war, but in defeat Pompeius fell into despair. Questions of prestige took precedence for him over military considerations. He recalled his boasts that all he had to do was to stamp his foot to rouse all Italy to arms, that having built up Caesar he would pull him down with equal ease and that with his cavalry he would overwhelm Caesar at Pharsalus. His optimate associates would blame him for the deaths of Ahenobarbus and other nobles at Pharsalus. Caesar, on the other hand, was subject to the judgment of only one man regarding his achievements and failures, a severe judgment, nevertheless.

Caesar, immediate task was to capture or destroy Pompeius, and on the second day after Pharsalus with a small escort of Gallic and German cavalry he set out in pursuit of his enemy. To his great joy on the road he came upon Marcus Brutus. Caesar had ordered that the life of Servilia's son be spared, and he had searched for Brutus in vain after the battle. Though a morose and dour Stoic like his uncle Cato and scarcely attractive with his bony, flat and sharply incised face, untidy beard, protruding lips, blunt nose and mottled complexion, Brutus was still a favorite of Caesar; Caesar embraced the younger man and invited him to join him as a companion.

During the months of the Epirote campaign and at Pharsalus, disgusted by the intrigues in Pompeius' camp, Brutus had withdrawn to his tent to draft an epitome of the many-volumed history of the Greek Polybius (an analysis of the factors that raised Rome to preeminence in the Mediterranean world). He could describe to Caesar the pettiness and savage bickering that sapped the will of the Pompeians. Upon receiving Caesar's proposal for negotiations immediately after Caesar's landing in Epirus, for example, Pompeius had exclaimed, "What do I want with life or citizenship which I shall appear to possess by Caesar's good grace? And that will be the ineradicable impression if people think that I have been brought back to Italy, which I left voluntarily." Pompeius' associates projected upon the Great Man their own selfish aspirations. He "was loudly denounced, and charges were rife that he was directing his campaign not against Caesar but against his country and the Senate in order that he might always be in office and never cease to have as his attendants and guards men who claimed to rule the world." Ahenobarbus, who had sought to deprive Pompeius of the glory of victory by opposing Caesar at Corfinium and then at Massilia, "by calling him Agamemnon and King of Kings made him odious." Most of the noblemen spent their time squabbling over properties and offices. The bankrupt consular Lentulus Crus "had promised himself Hortensius' house, Caesar's gardens and a place at [the seaside resort of] Baiae." Ahenobarbus, Scipio and Spinther (the consul of 57, freed by Caesar at Corfinium and initially grateful to Caesar for his liberty) disputed as to which of them would replace Caesar as pontifex maximus. Some noblemen canvassed for votes among fellow officers for magistracies and priesthoods. It was rumored that Scipio prodded Pompeius into giving battle at Pharsalus against Pompeius' judgment because Scipio "wished to appropriate to his own use the greater part of the treasure which he had brought from Asia and therefore hid it away and then hastened on the battle on the plea that there was no longer any money." Aristocrats harried by moneylenders looked forward to a new Sullan

Terror, and Cicero was appalled that "cruelty was rampant . . . a plan was sketched out for a proscription not of persons but of whole classes," including men of property who had failed to evacuate Italy with Pompeius, one of whom was Cicero's friend Atticus. The scheming oligarchs had, in fact, behaved like Gallic chieftains. Like the Gauls after Caesar's defeat at Gergovia, Labienus took an oath that "he would not come back from the battle unless he routed the enemy" and compelled all the others to swear similarly.[14] For all their vaunting, the Pompeians took fright at omens—lightning flashes as they marched from Dyrrachium, a swarm of bees on the standards, a disquieting dream of Pompeius' and the sight of a flaming torch rising from Caesar's camp and darting down into Pompeius'.

Pausing only long enough at Larisa to reward local aristocrats who had supported him (Caesar never neglected to reward partisans for outstanding service, whether legionaries or civilians), Caesar pressed on after Pompeius, who had fled not west to his fleet or northwest to his base at Dyrrachium but northeast to Amphipolis, a port at the head of the Aegean. Here he had boarded a merchant vessel.

In the pursuit Fortune once again threatened Caesar.

As the flotilla of small boats Caesar had commandeered to ferry his cavalry and the veteran VIth legion across the Hellespont approached the middle of the narrow waterway, ten warships hove into view from the west. It was too late to flee, and Caesar ordered his oarsmen to race to the enemy flagship. He summoned the optimate admiral and demanded his surrender. Nonplussed, the officer invited Caesar aboard and offered to turn over his ships. On orders from a council convened by Cato at Dyrrachium, he was on his way to the north shore of the Black Sea to call to war Pharnaces, son of Rome's stubborn foe Mithridates. Once again the optimates, including the Man of Virtue, Cato, were inviting an enemy to join them against Caesar.

At Ilium, the legendary home of his ancestors, a village atop a hill within sight of the Hellespont, Caesar sacrificed at the altar before the ruins of the Temple of Athena, destroyed during the Mithridatic wars. In renewing his claim to descent from the Trojan hero Aeneas and the goddess Venus, Caesar was proclaiming his links both to the Greek East and the Roman West. Starting on his conquest of Persia, Alexander, a youth in his twenties, had raced naked about Akhilleus' barrow (he claimed the hero as his ancestor). Now, some two and a half centuries later, the weatherbeaten middle-aged Roman gazed across the plain of the Scamander. He could picture the camp of the Achaeans disposed along the shore and hear the cry of the Trojan priest singing of Caesar's forbear:

> O you children of Priam, the king whom the gods love, how long
> will you allow the Achaeans to go on killing your people?
> Until they fight beside the strong-builded gates? A man lies
> fallen whom we honored as we honor Hektor the brilliant,
> Aineias, who is son of great-hearted Anchises.[15]

Caesar confirmed the exemption from tribute accorded Ilium four decades earlier by his clansman, the censor Lucius Caesar, and extended the territory under the town's jurisdiction. He must have smiled to see the statue of the censor's daughter, Marcus Antonius' mettlesome mother, amid the ruins of the town.

Learning of Caesar's arrival, envoys of towns and principalities hastened to beg forgiveness for their aid to his enemy. They reported unconscionable depredations by Pompeian leaders. Pompeius' father-in-law Scipio had confiscated the treasures of the Temple of Artemis at Ephesus but was forestalled in hauling them off only by an urgent summons from Pompeius. Scipio had quartered his troops in the towns and granted them license to pillage under the standard rationale of emigrés that having "been driven from home and country [they] lacked all the necessities of life." Scipio invented new methods of extortion. "Many different kinds of devices were thought up to satisfy avarice. A poll-tax was imposed on slaves and free men; there were taxes on pillars and on doors; there were requisitions of grain, troops, weapons, rowers, missile engines, transport. So long as a name could be found for the object, this was held to justify the exaction."[16] The Pompeians had acted as though enjoying a final opportunity for plunder, and the provincials were eager for a radical change in imperial rule.

As a youth Caesar had seen the ruin from untrammeled Roman exploitation in Asia. Risking the wrath of the publicans, he decreed that the towns of the region would henceforth collect their own tribute. Further to promote their economic recovery he reduced assessments by one-third and responded generously to individual petitions for relief. Upon the pleas of the Mityleneans (formerly Pompeius' clients) he deprived the town's rich citizens of immunity from taxation. Exasperated with the Athenians for resisting even after Pharsalus, he reminded the city's envoys of the many occasions in which Athens had allied itself with losing causes. "How often," he exclaimed, "will the glory of your ancestors save you from self-destruction?"[17] Nevertheless, he pardoned the city.

Notorious sycophants, the Greeks readily transferred the succession of Alexander from Pompeius to Caesar. The Ephesians acclaimed him as a descendant of Ares and Aphrodite, "a god in epiphany and common savior of mankind." Others vied in reporting miracles occurring at the moment of victory at Pharsalus. At Elis in the Peloponnesos, a statue of Victory in the Temple of Athena supposedly had turned on its base. At Antioch and Ptolemais in Syria "so loud a sound of trumpet signals" rang forth "that the population armed themselves and ran to their various posts on the walls." From the sanctuary of the Temple of Dionysos at Pergamum (where a supposed bastard and namesake of Mithridates, an agent of Caesar's, served as priest) a sound of drums echoed forth, and at Tralles in front of a statue erected to Caesar three decades earlier upon his repulse of a Mithridatic incursion, "a palm [symbol of victory] was displayed which had grown up inside the building out of the pavement, in the joint of the paving stones." Back in Italy, ever-faithful Cisalpina was not to be outdone. "At Patavium [Padua] a seer discerned the time of the battle and said to those present that even then the event was in progress and the men were going into action, and when he looked again and observed the sign, he sprang up in a rapture crying: 'Thou art victorious, O Caesar!' The bystanders being amazed, he took the chaplet from his head and declared with an oath that he would not put it on again until the event had borne witness to his art."[18]

Reports from other fronts were mixed. Upon news of Pharsalus, Gaius Cassius, brother to a Caesarian officer and son-in-law to Servilia, withdrew his fleet from raiding Sicily and southern Italy; and in Illyricum Cornificius aided by fishermen from a town that "had always displayed outstanding loyalty" routed a Pompeian fleet;[19] but of far greater significance was word that Cato and Scipio had sailed off to Africa with sizable remnants of the Pompeian forces.

Pompeius himself had sailed from Cyprus with some two thousand troops, many of them slaves, and with a sizable sum extorted from local tax-farmers. "Caesar took a long walk with Brutus alone and sounded him on the subject. Certain considerations advanced by Brutus made his opinion concerning Pompeius' flight seem the best, and Caesar therefore renounced all other courses and hastened towards Egypt."[20] He embarked with two understrength veteran legions (some three thousand men) and eight hundred cavalry on the ships that had defected to him at the Hellespont and on others provided by the Rhodians, who recalled with gratitude his release of sailors captured near Dyrrachium.

On the eve of October 1, less than two months after Pharsalus, lookouts descried a steady light in the distance. The captain assured Caesar that it was no unearthly flame, no portent, but the flare atop the lighthouse on the island of Pharos, offshore from Alexandria. As the fleet hove toward shore, the light-house appeared in all its grandeur—one of the Seven Wonders of the world, a fortress and signal tower in one, reaching some four hundred feet into the air. It was equipped, some said, with a reflecting mirror (others told of a huge magnify-ing glass) and with hydraulic machinery for raising the fuel for the signal fire. At the apex Poseidon gazed out over the god's watery domain. Beneath was the fire room and below that a platform adorned with tritons. A round story stood above a hexagonal one, and in a lower square story were windows of the living quarters of the three hundred mechanics and other attendants.

Passing through a channel alongside the lighthouse, Caesar's fleet entered the Great Harbor. A mole, the Heptastadion, almost a mile in length, con-nected the island of Pharos with the mainland and divided the harbor into two ports. The quay was crowded with merchant ships, and fifty naval vessels withdrawn from service under Pompeius' elder son were beached at dock-yards. To the left, toward the east, a sprawling compound of parks belonging to the Ptolemies occupied the shore. Beyond, the rim of a huge theater could be descried. Somewhere within stood the tomb of the founder of the city, the great Macedonian.

On the mole and along the quay a silent crowd waited. No one gave a sign of welcome. A lighter flying the royal standard approached, and a Greek attended by a large escort of slaves boarded Caesar's ship. The visitor introduced himself as Theodotos, tutor to the boy-king, and apologized for Ptolemaios' absence. The monarch was with his army at the gate to the Sinai engaged in warding off an invasion by rebels under his sister-wife, Cleopatra.

Ptolemaios had sent Caesar a gift.

Summoning a slave bearing a bundle on a tray, Theodotos removed the wrapping and revealed—the head of Pompeius.

XLVIII

EGYPT

CAESAR wept.

On the signet ring Theodotos offered him, Caesar recognized the seal commemorating the would-be Alexander's triumphs over three corners of the world. Pompeius had been slain, said Theodotos, three days earlier, on September 28, the anniversary of the day thirteen years earlier on which Pompeius, wearing a cloak purportedly once belonging to Alexander, had celebrated the first day of a double triumph, unprecedented in magnificence, for victories over the pirates and over Mithridates. September 29 was Pompeius' birthday; he would have entered his fifty-ninth year. Pompeius had been one of Caesar's companions through life. In Caesar's youth they had been connected through the marriage of Caesar's younger sister to Pompeius' first cousin. Upon Caesar's entrance into the progress of magistracies, Caesar had associated himself with Pompeius, and Pompeius had assisted Caesar in winning a consulship. They had established an alliance through Pompeius' marriage to Caesar's only daughter, an alliance confirmed through their mutual affection for that bright and loving young woman and through their anxiety at her miscarriage and sorrow at her death in childbirth. Pompeius' head represented the guerdon of the vicious struggle in which the fate of millions was joined to the strife of few dozen ambitious oligarchs, including Caesar and Pompeius, a strife, according to the Epicureans, as barren to the individual protagonists as it was destructive to the world whose destiny they involved with their own. Pompeius' miserable end recalled the schoolboy parable in Herodotus—the advice of the Athenian statesman Solon to the Lydian king Croesus: "Until he is dead, keep the word 'happy' in reserve. . . . Whoever has the greatest number of good things . . . and keeps them to the end and dies a peaceful death, that man, my lord Croesus, deserves . . . to be called happy."[1] The greedy bankrupt, Lentulus Crus, the consul of the previous year who had demanded an exorbitant bribe for defection, provided another exemplum of the vanity of oligarchic aspirations. Unaware of Pompeius' fate, he had landed and also been executed by the Egyptians. Other aristocrats, Theodotos reported, awaited Caesar's disposition.

Caesar ordered the release of all Roman prisoners and dismissed the astonished Greek.

Caesar had Pompeius' head bathed in perfumes and burned in a solemn ceremony.

A year earlier at Pompeius' prompting the rump Senate at Thessalonica had recognized Ptolemaios XIII, the adolescent heir to the Piper, as the lawful ruler of Egypt, and in the dynastic war between the king and his twenty-one-year-old queen and sister, Cleopatra, Caesar recognized an opportunity for his intervention. Ptolemaios the Piper had bequeathed the throne to both children and appealed to Rome to respect his testament. As consul Caesar could now assume this responsibility as well as his obligation to punish the murderers of Roman consulars. Furthermore, Caesar had a claim to an indemnity for the assignment of fifty Egyptian warships to Pompeius' elder son for deployment against him as well as to the unpaid portion of the 6 thousand talents the recently deceased Ptolemaios had engaged to pay during Caesar's consulship for recognition of his crown. In Egypt, the wealthiest land in the Mediterranean world, Caesar could replenish his war chest.

In his hasty pursuit of Pompeius Caesar had neglected to obtain intelligence about the kingdom. Landing with a small escort, he confronted angry soldiers, who shouted and gesticulated their objections to his lictors with their fasces, symbols of Roman authority and an offense to the majesty of the rulers of the ancient kingdom. Caesar was compelled to scurry within the royal compound, and during the next days several legionaries were set upon and slain by mobs. They had much cause for resentment against Rome: the supervision of their economy by a Roman knight for the collection of the late king's debts to Roman moneylenders, the murder of much of a large delegation sent to petition the Senate and the compulsion to furnish a fleet in support of one Roman warlord against another. Furthermore, whether because of a failure of the flooding of the Nile or because of the late king's obligations to Roman bankers, a royal decree forbade shipment of grain anywhere except to Alexandria, and grain was fetching premium prices. In this time of rancor and trouble a second Roman warlord had descended on the country to display his arrogance and to meddle in the affairs of the kingdom.

Summoning the boy-king from his army camp, Caesar announced that he would arbitrate the quarrel rending the kingdom. Simultaneously Caesar sent couriers to the consular Calvinus, his appointee as governor of Asia, to request reinforcements, a legion by sea and another by land. Caesar also ordered his client, Mithridates of Pergamum, the bastard son of the former king of Pontus, to lead an army of auxiliaries through Syria and to recruit reinforcements on his way. With the boy-king in the palace, Caesar had a hostage for the security of his four thousand troops and paltry squadron in a hostile city of more than a half-million inhabitants protected by a fleet of seventy-two men-of-war.

The eunuch Pothinus, one of the king's tutors and his chief councilor, scarcely concealed his defiance. At banquets he served Alexandrian delicacies on common crockery with the plea that the gold and silver plate were being melted down to meet Caesar's exactions. He furnished the legionaries with mildewed grain and "bade them put up with it and be content since they were eating what belonged to others." Seizing offerings in the temples, he announced to the people, notorious as the most superstitious in the world, that he was acting on Caesar's orders. With the wiliness of an Egyptian courtier, he proposed that Caesar not await the collection of the monies he demanded of the Egyptians but depart immediately to attend to his wars elsewhere. Caesar retorted that he "had no need whatever of Egyptians as advisors."[2]

Soliciting the goodwill of the Alexandrians, Caesar visited the various quarters of the city, ostensibly as an admiring tourist. Actually he was reconnoitering so as to prepare a defense in the event of an attack. Of course, ever curious, Caesar was eager to investigate "the first city of the civilized world . . . certainly far ahead of all the rest in elegance . . . riches and luxury,"[3] a leading commercial and industrial center, the chief emporium of the Mediterranean in trade with the East, as far off as China.

A century earlier the Greek historian Polybius had observed: "Up to this time the world's history has been . . . a series of disconnected transactions as widely separated in their origin and results as their localities. But from this time forth history becomes a connected whole; the affairs of Italy and Libya are involved with those of Asia and Greece, and the tendency of all is to unity."[4] It was inevitable, as Caesar recognized, that Egypt one day be incorporated into the empire. Certainly he could not tolerate at his back a fractious Egypt susceptible to optimate blandishments. In any event, Etesian winds barred sailing westward for the next weeks, and Caesar was trapped here.

An imperial city and a monument to the spirit of rationalism with which Aristotle, the mightiest intellect of Greece, imbued his conqueror pupil, Alexandria was the cultural capital of the Greek world. In contrast to Rome, which had burgeoned with no other impetus than private greed and whim, Alexandria had been laid out in a geometric pattern based on two perpendicular boulevards, each almost fifty feet wide and flanked by colonnades and handsome public buildings of finely hewn stone. Cross streets identified by Greek letters were broad enough for chariot traffic. At the intersection of the two boulevards stood Alexander's mausoleum, a shrine to the hero as tutelar demigod of the city.

The Ptolemies maintained their power by balancing the three major elements of the city and kingdom: the Greeks (descendants of the conquering Macedonians and of subsequent Greek settlers), the Jews and the indigenous Egyptians. Centers of the Greek intellectual life were the Museum and Library (largest in the world), unique institutions founded by one of the first Ptolemies with the assistance of one of Aristotle's disciples. At the Museum scholars with royal stipends from all over the Greek world studied and lectured. Many of the greatest minds of the previous three centuries had achieved momentous discoveries here: Euclid, father of geometry, Erasistratos, pathfinder in anatomy and physiology, Aristarchos, proponent of a heliocentric theory of the universe, Hipparchos, cataloguer of the stars and formulator of the concept of latitude and longitude, and Eratosthenes, calculator of the size of the earth from observations of the declination of the sun.

Haughty about the cultural preeminence of their city, Alexandrians discovered that this "barbarian" could not only listen attentively at esoteric lectures but also engage in learned discussions with distinguished scholars and scientists. In the laboratories and exhibit halls Caesar could pose searching questions about experiments with compressed air and steam and with vacuum in force pumps and siphons (he had seen applications in the Spanish mines) as well as in the dissection of corpses and in vivisection. With Theon, author of treatises on Greek syntax and compiler of lexica and commentator on Alexandrian poets, Caesar could range over the fields of literature and language, discussing the experiments in Alexandrian verse traditions by poets of Catullus' circle and citing from his own work on the Latin tongue. He could captivate mechanics with descriptions of the Rhine bridges, siege works and artillery engines. He could evaluate model catapults superior to any in use and a device for measuring distances with an attachment on the axle of a vehicle. With Sosigenes, a mathematician and astronomer, Caesar could discuss his measurement of the day in Britain as well as his observations on the influence of the sun, the moon and the winds on the tides of the ocean. As pontifex maximus, charged with ordering the Roman lunar calendar, he could question Sosigenes on the Egyptian solar calendar. With his experience with tradition-bound Roman aristocrats he would not have been astonished to learn that Egyptian priests barred the institution of leap years as a dangerous innovation.

In the Egyptian quarter Caesar could gratify the pious by a pilgrimage to the Temple of Serapis, another of the Seven Wonders of the world, an imposing structure overlooking the city and surrounded by a monumental colonnade and broad park, where quadrennial games were celebrated in honor of the god. With his insight into the political uses of religion, Caesar would be impressed to learn that the first Ptolemaios had entrusted a committee of Egyptian priests and Greek philosophers with the invention of a deity suitable for worship by both his Egyptian and Greek subjects, an amalgam of two popular local gods, Osiris and Apis, endowed with attributes of Olympian deities, a god that promised a mystical union in another life, in keeping with the spiritual temper of the post-Alexandrian era. The new god had won disciples throughout the Mediterranean world, especially in Italy.

Always on the lookout for commercial opportunities (Italian businessmen had established a thriving colony in the city), Caesar noted the varied goods produced in the city or transshipped from distant places. The streets of Alexandria teemed with merchants, sailors and caravan drivers. Egypt exported papyrus, linen, scents, ivory and gems and might one day become a major supplier of grain to Rome.

The center of the Jewish community was the Diploston, "a sort of great basilica, stoa in front of stoa." Here merchants and artisans boasted that throngs "at times twice as many as left Egypt [in the exodus to Palestine centuries before the founding of Rome] did not sit intermingled, but the goldsmiths by themselves, the silversmiths and the weavers by themselves." Caesar was acquainted with the impoverished Jewish community at Rome—tanners, dockworkers and common laborers. He had encountered Jews (perhaps comprising as much as ten per cent of the population of the Mediterranean world) in Gades and in populous communities in Asia Minor, where many had been settled as garrison troops by various kings. Alexandria, however, was the major center of Jewish culture of the day as well as the largest single Jewish community. Nevertheless, Jews here and throughout Egypt experienced a sense of insecurity. As elsewhere in the Eastern Mediterranean, they suffered taunts from Greek neighbors regarding their dietary laws, their practice of circumcision, their subservience to their priests, their worship of a god never represented in images, their mockery of other deities and their conviction that they were chosen by their god for a special mission on earth. Non-Jews resented both their refusal to participate in pagan rituals central to community life and the special privileges they were granted by various kings and princes. The Jews deserved Caesar's attention, scattered as they were throughout the Mediterranean in communities in communication with each other and with Jerusalem. Caesar had, of course, noted their peculiar clannishness. At the Diploston, as elsewhere, "when a poor man entered, he recognized the members of his own craft and applied to them and derived his livelihood and that of his family."[5] For all their caviling against the Jews, Greeks never accused them of decadence or scoffed at their philanthropy to co-religionists. They admired the Jews, too, as the only other people who could boast of great philosophers. Non-Jews in many lands, including Italy, had taken to observing the Jewish sabbath, and many were converting to Judaism (more women than men because of the prescription regarding circumcision). At Alexandria the Jewish community prided itself on its amalgam of Greek and Hebraic cultures and boasted of epics and histories composed in Greek. Every year on the island of Pharos, they commemorated the translation into Greek of the scriptures, the Septuagint.

Caesar, who had investigated the institutions of Gauls and Germans with avidity, now had an opportunity to discuss with Jewish scholars principles of Jewish belief. Impressive was their veneration of the law. "And what great nation is there," it was written in their scriptures, "that both hath statutes and ordinances so righteous as all this law, which I set before you this day?" In their harsh historical experience, they had evolved a rich code of morality. "And a stranger thou shalt not oppress, for ye know the heart of a stranger, seeing ye were strangers in the land of Egypt."[6]

Caesar could point out to the leaders of the Jewish community that he enjoyed the goodwill of the Jews at Rome, that he had returned to Judea Aristobolus, a king deposed by Pompeius, and that after Pharsalus he had granted clemency to Judean troops in Pompeius' army. Simply as Pompeius' foe, however, he could claim their friendship, for they remembered Pompeius' siege of the Temple, his violation of the Holy of Holies and his dismemberment of the kingdom of Judea. Indeed, a Jewish poet exulted at Pompeius' assassination:

> And I had not long to wait before God showed me the insolent one
> Slain on the mountains of Egypt,
> Esteemed of less account than the least on land and sea;
> His body too borne hither and thither on the billows with much insolence,
> With none to bury him because He had rejected him with dishonor.
> He reflected not that he was a man,
> And reflected not on the latter end.
> He said: "I will be lord of land and sea,"
> And he recognized not that it is God who is great,
> Mighty in His great strength.[7]

One night during these days of "tourism," with peremptory obstinacy, a Syrian merchant demanded entrance to Caesar's quarters. Declaring that he brought a gift of a rug for Caesar, he pushed his way into the palace. In Caesar's presence he ordered his slaves to unroll the rug. A young woman sprang forth—a fitting entrance for a descendant of Alexander, heiress to the ancient pharaohs, queen of Egypt and incarnation of the goddess Isis. With the glee of a twenty-one-year-old who had outsmarted the most cunning of tricksters, Cleopatra related how she had eluded the patrol vessels posted by the eunuch Pothinus and bribed the sentries at the entrance to the harbor and at the postern gate to the palace.

Caesar saw no beauty before him, but Cleopatra embellished nature with art. Antimony and lamp black on eyebrows and eyelids magnified her eyes and drew attention from a nose too long and aquiline; ochre on lips softened a pouting mouth, and seaweed and mulberry juice brightened full cheeks and a blunt chin; henna on her nails accentuated the delicacy of her hands and feet, and her hair shimmered with a metal band tied by a ribbon at the chignon low on her neck. In a licentious court Cleopatra had studied how to charm. She moved with grace and spoke in a low music. Ready with a saucy wit or a pretense at helplessness, she also knew the seduction of gorgeous attire and feline guile. She communicated with a glance, and she exchanged glances with Caesar. How, indeed, could a balding, harried military man, a connoisseur of womanhood, resist the youth, the wiles?

Philodemos, the Epicurean poet and companion to Caesar's father-in-law, had written a poem on the love of an aging roué:

I loved. Who has not? I made revels in her honor.
Who is uninitiated in those mysteries? But I was distraught.
By whom? Was it not by a god? Goodbye to it; for already
the gray locks hurry on to replace the black and tell me
I have reached the age of discretion. While it was playtime
I played; now it is over I will turn to more worthy thoughts.[8]

"More worthy thoughts" for Caesar were always political thoughts. At least until he had crushed his enemies Caesar would need reliable agents in this complex country. Caesar and Cleopatra took each other's measure. At Alexandria Caesar would, it appeared, play at more than politics.

Apprized of his sister's stealing through the patrols, the infuriated boy-king ran out of the palace crying that he had been betrayed. He tore the royal diadem from his head and cast it into the street, and at his shouts the people massed at the palace gates. Caesar appeared on a balcony and assured the demonstrators that he would carry out their will. He produced the young people at a public assembly, read their father's testament and promised to fulfil the dead king's wishes by uniting them on the throne. To celebrate the reunion of the royal couple and the conclusion to civil strife, Caesar granted a gift to the royal house—restoring Cyprus with the younger brother and sister as king and queen of the island—an action gratifying to the Alexandrians, nostalgic for the ancient greatness of their kingdom.

Caesar mollified the Egyptians not merely because he was fearful of turmoil in the city but also because of mixed news he received from Balbus. Conditions, it was true, at Rome were satisfactory. After Pharsalus senators who had previously resisted Caesar vied in proposing honors for him. The people overturned statues of Sulla and Pompeius, and Balbus and Oppius were overwhelmed with assurances of loyalty and requests for intercession with Caesar for pardon or for favors. The consul Servilius nominated Caesar to a second dictatorship, this time for a full year, and postponed the elections for the higher magistracies pending his return. In response Caesar nominated Antonius as master of horse, deputy to a dictator, and entrusted Antonius with the administration of Italy and preparations for an invasion of Africa. On the other hand, Balbus urged Caesar to hasten to deal with crises in both Africa and Spain. Pompeius' death had not demoralized the optimates. Massing in Africa, the Pompeians had recouped their strength, and in raids on Sicily and southern Italy they had destroyed half of Caesar's newly constructed fleet. A threat had arisen, too, in Further Spain, where by extortions, requisitions, arrogance and villainy, Quintus Cassius, Caesar's appointee as governor, had provoked an uprising. Far from invading Africa, as Caesar had ordered, Quintus was battling provincial rebels, and Lepidus, governor of Nearer Spain, negotiated an uneasy truce between loyal legions and mutineers who openly proclaimed their allegiance to Pompeius' elder son.

Caesar would have to pacify anew a province he had considered safely in his own camp. Would he have to repress revolts in other pacified provinces because of the incompetence and greed of his lieutenants? Would he spend his remaining years as a harried policeman? Confident at least in the legates of the Army of Gaul, he ordered Trebonius, the victor at Massilia, to depart for Further Spain without awaiting the expiration of his praetorship. From Asia Minor Calvinus reported that Mithridates' son, Pharnaces, had crossed the Black Sea to reconquer his father's kingdom. For lack of an adequate army, Calvinus had suffered a defeat. Nevertheless, "more alarmed at Caesar's danger than his own,"[9] he dispatched two of his three legions to Alexandria, as Caesar had requested.

Already in his fifty-second year and committed, after crushing the optimates, to subduing the Dacians in the Balkans and to repelling the Parthians beyond the Euphrates, Caesar dared not leave Egypt unpacified.

THE PACIFICATION OF EGYPT

Achillas, the Egyptian king's general, was marching from the Sinai to Alexandria with twenty thousand infantry and two thousand horse, a force outnumbering Caesar's more than five to one. The nucleus of the royal army was legionaries and cavalry left by Gabinius after he had restored the Piper to his throne. Unlike legionaries stationed in the Spains or the Gauls, who retained their language and customs, these troops "had grown accustomed to the lax way of life at Alexandria [and] ceased to think of themselves as Roman, forgotten the standards of discipline of the Roman people and had married and mostly had children by the marriages." Their ranks had been increased with runaway slaves and other desperate men. "These men had been accustomed to demand the execution of royal favorites, to plunder the property of the wealthy, to besiege the palace for a rise in pay, to drive some from the throne and summon others to fill it."[10] Three years earlier, when Bibulus as governor of Syria had sent his sons to summon the legionaries to service against the Parthians, they had murdered the youths. One of their officers had engineered Pompeius' assassination.

At Caesar's instructions the king dispatched two courtiers to order Achillas to halt his advance on Alexandria, but the troops killed one of the royal envoys and wounded the other. Fearing blockade by the Egyptian fleet, Caesar burned the men-of-war in the harbor and seized part of the island of Pharos, thereby securing access to the harbor for his supply ships and for the transports with reinforcements he was awaiting from Asia Minor. He transformed the buildings about the palace compound, including the theater, into fortresses and extended defense works through the middle of the city from the harbor to a marsh to the south, athwart the Jewish quarter, where he expected support from the populace.

An attempt by Pothinus to poison Caesar was aborted when Caesar's barber, "who left nothing unscrutinized, owing to a timidity in which he had no equal, but kept his ears open and was here, there and everywhere, perceived that Achillas the general and Pothinus the eunuch were hatching a plot against Caesar."[11] Intercepting messages from the royal tutor to Achillas, Caesar ordered the eunuch's execution.

Caesar sent couriers to urge Calvinus to hasten the dispatch of reinforcements, and he summoned archers from Crete, cavalry from Arabia and ships and materiel from Cilicia and Syria. At the same time, the Alexandrian oligarchs dispatched recruiting agents throughout the kingdom, assembled missiles and ballistic machines, established arsenals and armed their slaves. They fortified the streets and alleyways and constructed movable towers ten stories in height. "They showed such smartness in copying what they observed our men doing that it seemed almost as if our men were imitating their operations; they also devised many expedients for themselves." In war councils and public assemblies their leaders exhorted the population to resistance, declaring: "If we do not drive [Caesar] out, the kingdom will be turned into a province. We must act quickly," they insisted, "for while he is cut off by storms owing to the season of the year he cannot receive reinforcements from overseas."[12]

Caesar responded to the aggression of the Alexandrians by conniving at the escape from the palace of the princess Arsinoe, a sister of the king and queen. As Caesar anticipated, Achillas and Arsinoe's councilor, a wily eunuch named Ganymede, quarreled over the command of the army, and Achillas was murdered. The cunning Ganymede, however, proved a formidable foe. He constructed machines to flood with sea water the aqueducts leading into the palace compound, and Caesar's legions would have panicked if Caesar had not realized that fresh water often seeps into beaches at the seaside and sunk wells to replenish the supply of drinking water. The legionaries were encouraged, too, by the arrival of transports with the XXVIIth legion, dispatched by Calvinus along with grain, weapons and artillery.

While countering the enemy attack with his customary ingenuity and valor, Caesar was heartened by news from Rome. Upon the arrival of his messenger with Pompeius' signet ring, a list of Pompeians Caesar had rescued from Egyptian captivity along with a letter assuring the Senate and the people that "the greatest and sweetest pleasure he derived from his victory [was] from time to time to save the lives of fellow citizens who had fought against him," the Senate heaped new honors upon him. Balbus reported that "by their shouts and by their gestures, they all, as if Caesar were present and looking on, showed the very greatest zeal and thought that in return for it they would get immediately—as if they were doing it to please him and not at all from necessity—one an office, another a priesthood and a third some pecuniary reward."[13] On the other hand, in a pretense at asserting their former authority, the senators voted Caesar powers he was already exercising or could usurp without consulting them—the right to declare war and make peace and to dispose of the Pompeians and their property. Furthermore, they granted Caesar the consul ship for five consecutive years and permitted him to sit among the tribunes with a right of veto of any of his colleagues—measures that effectively repealed the old constitution and endowed Caesar with powers far broader than those he had sought upon crossing the Rubicon two years earlier. Anticipating Caesar's prompt return from Egypt and his immediate assault on his remaining foes, the senators decreed in advance a triumph for his victory over Juba, the ally to the Pompeians in Africa. Yet, in a disquieting presage of future resistance, the college of augurs, a bastion of optimate resistance, attempted, unsuccessfully, to block Antonius' appointment as Caesar's master of horse.

With these generally favorable developments at Rome and in the desultory fighting in Alexandria, Caesar set himself to disarming wavering opponents and preparing a climate for his assumption of absolute authority throughout the empire at the conclusion of hostilities. He began to compose a commentary on the cause and events of the civil war as he saw them or as they reflected best upon him. He emphasized how he had been compelled to defend his dignity and security against the arrogance of an optimate clique and how he had displayed generosity in negotiations and persistence in pressing for a peaceful settlement. He contended that he had invaded Italy in order to free the Senate and the people from the domination of an obstinate and power-hungry clique and to restore the rights of the tribunes. He had exercised unfailing clemency toward fellow-citizens, resisted pressure for radical measures regarding debt and property rights, encouraged fraternization between his troops and the Pompeians in the hope of ending hostilities without bloodshed and outgeneraled his opponents on the battlefield with troops of surpassing valor, discipline and skill.

Such a document of psychological warfare is particularly effective, of course, when victory seems assured.

Awaiting further reinforcements, Caesar benefited from the dissensions among his foes. Arsinoe, a presumptuous young woman in her late teens, proclaimed herself queen of Egypt. Her legionaries, bewildered by the assassination of their commander, Achillas, felt no esprit de corps with troops newly recruited throughout Egypt, and the Alexandrian oligarchs viewed with ambivalence the lawless elements in the army. Against these forces of a divided and decadent monarchy Caesar's men compensated for their numerical inferiority by feats of extraordinary valor. In a supreme test with a reconstituted Egyptian navy, the élan of Caesar's troops proved decisive, and Caesar determined to win control of both harbors by occupying the entire island of Pharos as well as the mole connecting it to the mainland. In a single day he accomplished most of his objectives. On the next day, however, Fortune intervened. Frightened by sounds of combat at their rear, three cohorts abandoned an entrenchment and scrambled in panic aboard their vessels. Ships capsized, and Caesar, throwing off his commander's cape but weighed down by his armor, swam some two hundred yards to a warship, from which he sent small boats to rescue legionaries wallowing in the water.

Within minutes some four hundred troops perished along with a great number of seamen.

In this crisis Caesar determined upon a desperate maneuver, granting a petition from the Alexandrians for the release of their king. "They said that the whole people was ready to obey the king's commands; they were weary of a girl [Arsinoe] who ruled by proxy and of the cruel despotism of Ganymede." Despite the opposition of his officers, who insisted that no trust could be placed in any Egyptian, Caesar decided to gamble. The king, professing loyalty to Caesar, wept as he left the palace, but "well trained in wiles,"[14] once freed, he immediately proclaimed his leadership in the war against the invader.

In mid-February 47, three months after Achillas' initial attack, a courier reported that Caesar's client Mithridates of Pergamum was approaching with a relief army. Marching from Asia Minor, he had assembled a sizable force as he advanced southward. Hyrkanos, High Priest of Jerusalem, and his general, Antipater, provided troops and supplies and summoned additional forces from neighboring princes. Upon crossing the Egyptian frontier they persuaded Jewish garrisons to defect and Jewish communities to furnish soldiers and grain. In an engagement in the Nile delta, the Jewish troops transformed defeat into victory.

Learning that the king had withdrawn from Alexandria with all his forces to head off the relief force, Caesar by forced marches linked up with Mithridates and Antipater. The united army routed and annihilated the royal forces, and on March 27, escorted by a small squadron of Gallic cavalry, Caesar returned victorious into Alexandria. "On his arrival . . . the entire populace of the town threw down their weapons and abandoned the fortifications. They adopted the garb usually worn by suppliants attempting to turn the wrath of despots, brought out all the sacred objects to the sanctity of which they were accustomed to appeal in trying to placate the enmity and wrath of their kings and coming to meet Caesar they surrendered to him." No oriental despot, Caesar reassured the populace and "proceeded through the enemy lines to his own part of the town, where he received the congratulations of his own men, who were delighted not only at the successful outcome of this great war with all its fighting but also at the happy nature of his arrival."[15]

News from abroad, however, reminded Caesar of the many battles he had yet to fight. In Illyricum Gabinius, infirm with age, had died after ferocious battles against local tribes supported by a Pompeian fleet, and Vatinius was marching to the relief of Cornificius, the governor of the province. In Asia Minor Calvinus, with a single legion and a motley force of native auxiliaries, had suffered a defeat from Pharnaces, and in Further Spain Trebonius was unable to restore order.

An enduring pacification of Egypt was imperative.

XLIX
MASTER OF THE EAST?

CAESAR sent Arsinoe off to Rome as a prisoner to march in his triumph. Cleopatra he married to her surviving brother, a helpless ten-year-old. In Cleopatra's womb he left a hostage, for she was pregnant with his child.[1] At lavish banquets to celebrate the restoration of peace, dignitaries in brilliant robes colored according to their rank and headbands and gold brooches according to their degree of intimacy with the god-king and god-queen, in wide-brimmed felt hats, small oblong mantles and high laced boots (the attire of their Macedonian forbears), and Egyptian priests with shaved heads in white gowns paid homage to Caesar. He had ended an era of camarilla intrigue and brought Egypt effectively under Roman tutelage.

Cleopatra ordered the construction of a mammoth colonnade at the harbor, a Caesareum celebrating the genius of her patron, his termination of the strife in her country and his confirmation of its independence. It would serve as a reminder of Caesar's authority after his departure. In keeping with the traditional Roman policy of divide et impera Caesar singled out for special privileges the Jewish community, one-seventh or -eighth of the population of the kingdom, a vigorous minority militant in defending its identity and its rights, numerous enough to provide support to his rule but too small to dispense with his protection. He erected a bronze pillar in Alexandria with an inscription proclaiming his ratification of the autonomy accorded the Jews by the Ptolemies in religion, law and communal administration.

Seeking to determine what would be an appropriate relationship of Egypt to the rest of the empire, Caesar set himself to the kind of extensive investigation he had made of Gallic civilization. Egypt, he understood, was unique among Mediterranean lands. "In density of population it far surpassed of old all known regions of the inhabited world. The total population . . . was of old about seven millions, and the number remained no less down to [Caesar's] day."[2] Concentrated along the Nile valley, these millions were regimented within a corporate state without parallel elsewhere. The realm was divided, as it had been for millennia, into regions, districts and villages administered as a single royal estate by an army of hereditary civil servants organized within a complex hierarchy that made lavish use of the local resource, papyrus, in maintaining detailed registers of land holdings, dwellings, agricultural implements, slaves, cattle and free labor. Local censuses were transmitted to central bureaus at Alexandria for use in drafting a yearly economic plan embracing every aspect of agricultural, commercial and industrial activity. From the capital, production quotas were apportioned, and civil servants meticulously fulfilled norms without concern for the welfare of the fellaheen working the soil. Royal monopolies controlled the prices and set standards in all branches of the economy, and a central bank with offices in districts and with village substations arranged loans and collected taxes.

Ptolemaios IV, an ancestor of Cleopatra's, had constructed a barge three hundred feet long, forty-five feet wide and sixty feet high with luxurious apartments along arcaded courts, and to inspect the countryside, view the renowned antiquities and confirm Cleopatra's authority (under his patronage), Caesar traveled up the Nile with the young queen. At each stop the countryfolk prostrated themselves before the goddess and attended her every utterance as though harking to an oracle. Well informed about the country, its traditions and its administrative machinery and fluent in the native tongue (unlike others of her Greek-speaking dynasty), in Hebrew and in the languages of various minority and neighboring peoples, Cleopatra served as an able guide for her middle-aged lover.

By assigning the fellaheen to the maintenance of irrigation ditches and dikes in their spare hours, the bureaucrats kept them from mischief; and to avert discontent in times of labor surplus, the Ptolemies, like "the ancient kings of Egypt built great marvelous works with the aid of so many hands and left in them immortal monuments to their glory." Caesar viewed wonders about which he had read as a schoolboy in Herodotus—enormous statues and grandiose temples. Now he saw them, of course, with the insight of a mature statesman. Egyptian monarchs averted problems with the demoralized unemployed by promoting public works on a vast scale, including constructions of use only as symbols of royal power. Of the pyramid of Cheops, indeed, Herodotus had written: "The work went on in three-monthly shifts, a hundred thousand men in a shift. It took ten years of this oppressive slave-labor to build the track along which the blocks were hauled. . . . To build the pyramid itself took twenty years." With Cleopatra as his interpreter, Caesar could check the hieroglyphic inscription cited by the Greek historian four hundred years earlier, "recording the amount spent on radishes, onions and leeks for the laborers . . . sixteen hundred talents of silver"; and wonder with Herodotus "how much must have been spent in addition on bread and clothing for the laborers during all those years the building was going on."[3]

During the Gallic campaigns and even during the current civil war, Caesar had been able to compare the labor efficiency of free legionaries imbued with a sense of mission with that of slaves on private estates or on public constructions. No forced laborers could match the ingenuity and efficiency of the troops in bridging the Rhine, building transport vessels and men-of-war, gir-

dling fortresses with siege works or designing engines for particular circumstances. Freeborn Italians, of course, could not be dragooned into constructing
monuments to guarantee the immortality of a monarch. Could Caesar rally
enthusiasm among the unemployed and underemployed at Rome and throughout Italy in large-scale projects for promoting the general economy?

With local officials Caesar could discuss the implementation of central office
directives for maintaining a balance of production of oil, grain and industrial
crops, in apportioning state-owned agricultural tools and domestic animals
and supervising fish-curing stations and brickworks. Particularly impressive
was the association of the Museum and Library at Alexandria with the economy and with the application of the latest agricultural methods and devices,
like the Archimedean screw in irrigation. Physicians from the Museum supervised the medical services of the armed forces and advised on public health. An
example of technology applied to public use was the Nilometer, "a well on the
bank of the Nile constructed with close-fitting stones in which [were] marks
showing the greatest, least and mean rises of the Nile." Inspectors made nota-
tions and dispatched messengers down river with reports on the annual flooding. More impressive was "an ingenious lock, which opened when ships passed
and quickly closed again" on a canal that connected one of the mouths of the
Nile to the Red Sea, a canal one hundred and fifty feet wide and sixteen to
seventeen feet deep.[4] The delta of the Nile was crisscrossed with canals, and
because of its canal connections the harbor of Alexandria on a large lake to the
south of the city was busier than the seaport.

The corporate state had proved appropriate for a country consisting of a
desert-bound strip of arable land dependent upon the annual flooding of a single
great river, but it afforded no model for Italy or for any of the imperial provinces. Because of its unique social and political structure and intense xenopho-
bia, Egypt could not easily be assimilated into an imperial system in which
provinces were milked as the private plantations of a tiny oligarchy; another
form of association with Rome would have to be evolved for the country.

Especially after the rebellion in Further Spain against Quintus Cassius, Caesar did not dare to entrust the large population and vast wealth of Egypt to an
ambitious Roman nobleman. On the other hand, because the royal couple
enjoyed "neither the affection of their own people because they had remained
loyal supporters of Caesar, nor the authority of long usage since they had been
made rulers only a few days before," Caesar decided to leave a garrison under
the command of the son of one of his freedmen. This Rubio would be mindful
that his patron "thought it important for the prestige of our empire and for the
common good, if the rulers were to remain loyal, that they should have the
protection of our forces, while if they proved ungrateful, these same forces
could constrain them."[5]

With the many crises throughout the empire requiring Caesar's prompt
intervention, people at Rome were bewildered as to why Caesar tarried so

long and, apparently, to little purpose in Egypt. That Cleopatra, a woman of extraordinary talents and charm, was an attraction to the middle-aged Caesar is a likely but hardly sufficient explanation in regard to a man who all his life had been driven by relentless ambition and by a stern sense of his responsibilities. Nevertheless, for all his heroic qualities, peerless self-discipline and death-defying dedication to his aspirations, Caesar was a man, and now he was a man in his fifties. All his life he had worked hard at living, but it was in middle age that the tempo of his life had attained its maximum intensity. Since his praetorship thirteen years earlier he had scarcely known a day of relaxation. Frequently he had traveled great distances with impetuous speed, often in heat and cold and storms. When granting his legionaries, far younger than he, deserved respites after battles, he had not spared himself, continuing to march and to fight without pause. In addition, despite his philosophic acceptance of death, he was scarcely immune to the ravages of sorrow—for his mother, his sisters, his beloved child, his friends of years' standing, his comrades-in-arms. Nor was he impervious to onslaughts of oligarchic enemies, men with whom he had grown up and shared many experiences. He was hardly unmoved at the alienation of his father-in-law after the crossing of the Rubicon, at the slaughter at Pharsalus, at Pompeius' assassination and at the treachery of Labienus and Caelius. In Egypt after a year of constant battling in Italy, in Spain, in Epirus and finally at Pharsalus, Caesar had found himself hemmed in by a numerous and vengeful Egyptian foe. In a near defeat he had been forced to swim two hundred yards in his armor and then, panting with weariness, he had had to rally his troops out of their panic. After so many years in unlettered Gaul, he found himself in the capital of Mediterranean civilization, able to give rein to his intellectual enthusiasms. All these factors, along with Cleopatra, induced the exhausted Caesar to yield a little, to beguile himself with rationalizations only slightly illusory, to grant himself a refreshment of body and soul, a pause.

Nevertheless, Caesar could not permit himself to tarry in Egypt until Cleopatra gave birth, and with the remnant of the veteran VIth legion, a mere thousand men, he set out for Syria.

THE PACIFICATION OF SYRIA, JUDEA AND ASIA MINOR

In Syria Caesar was joined by Hirtius with disturbing news from Rome. Rumors of Caesar's death in the near-disaster in the harbor of Alexandria had provoked disturbances in the city and in Italy. The troublemaker this year was Cicero's son-in-law, Dolabella. For shifting to Caesar's party before the civil war he had been rewarded with command of a fleet, in which post he had acquitted himself with no distinction. After serving in the Epirus campaign and at Pharsalus, he had been sent back to Rome, where, transferring from the patriciate to the plebs, he had won election to a tribuneship. Rallying Clodius' old following along with disgruntled aristocratic profligates, he revived Caelius' program of the previous year for the cancellation of debts and remission of rents. Another tribune, equally as demagogic, took up the defense of property and mobilized gangs to battle Dolabella's partisans. It seemed as though Rome had relapsed to the time of the riots between Clodius' followers and Milo's armed henchmen. With the disintegration of authority, "no part of the government was being properly conducted."[6] Even more disquieting was Hirtius' report of mutiny among the legions in Italy, including veterans of the Army of Gaul. Fearing that with Caesar dead, as rumor held, they would not collect back pay or win promised bonuses, they mutinied. Marcus Antonius proved incapable either of supressing the disorders at Rome or of restoring discipline among the troops. By his vacillation and bohemianism, he earned universal contempt. Once, drunk, he vomited at the Rostra.

Hirtius urged Caesar to return to Italy immediately, but Caesar insisted that "Priority must be given to organizing the provinces and districts into which he had just come so that they would be free from internal disturbances, would adopt laws and judicial procedures and would cease to fear external enemies." Stopping in "most of the communities of standing" in Syria, Caesar rewarded those towns and individuals that merited his gratitude and gave judgment on long-standing disputes. "He formally received under his protection the kings, tyrants and dynasts . . . who had all come flocking to him, on condition that they would accept responsibility for guarding and defending the province, then sent them away as firm friends of himself and of the Roman people."[7] Once again he singled out the Jews, not just that he was grateful for their decisive role in the victory in Egypt but also because he recognized that they could provide a substantial bulwark to his authority in their settlements scattered about the Mediterranean. Although proclaiming the High Priest Hyrkanos Ethnarch (ruler of a people) over a state restricted to the boundaries of 162, the year Judah Maccabaeus entered into an alliance with Rome, he granted him authority without precedent—protection of Jews throughout the Roman dominions—and extended to Jews everywhere as "friends and allies of the Roman people" unique extraterritorial privileges: exemption from military service and from responsibility for billeting legionaries, an onerous chore which all provincials sought to evade. As spokesman for the Jewish people, the Ethnarch could petition the Senate for redress of grievances occurring anywhere in the empire. Antipater, the Judean general who had fought so effectively in Egypt, Caesar granted Roman citizenship and appointed Procurator of Judea, Rome's special representative in Jerusalem and a counterweight to the Ethnarch. Thus Caesar resolved problems with an aggressive, numerous people difficult to subsume within the administrative authority of an imperial state. (By his actions he showed himself to be the outstanding benefactor of the Jews until the French Revolution.)

In Syria by distinguishing his behavior from that of the former governor, Pompeius' father-in-law, Caesar won local gratitude. By extorting "large sums of money from local communities and rulers" and by exacting "from the tax-farmers . . . the arrears of money for the last two years as well as an advance on the next year's payments," Scipio had caused great hardship. Furthermore, "he required the whole province to supply cavalry" and roused apprehension by denuding the province of troops in face of a threatened Parthian invasion. In contrast, Caesar reformed the method of tax collection and granted relief in tribute as he had done the previous year in Asia Minor. He left in command of the province his young cousin Sextus Caesar with a single legion and hastened north to Tarsus, the chief city of the province of Cilicia. Here he found a crowd of Pompeians assembled to seek his pardon, with Brutus seconding the appeal of their spokesman, Brutus' brother-in-law Gaius Cassius. Caesar granted clemency to all and welcomed Servilia's son and son-in-law to his staff. Hurrying through the Cilician gate, Caesar paused to read the inscription commemorating Alexander's passage in the opposite direction on the way to give battle to the Persian king. At Comana, a renowned center of pilgrimage visited by both Marius and Sulla, Caesar gave audience to Deiotarus, the most powerful monarch of the client principalities of Asia Minor, a wily princeling who had aided Pompeius generously with money and troops. Caesar was taken aback when Brutus pleaded with great passion on behalf of the sly and duplicitous potentate. "It's a great question what [Brutus] wants," remarked Caesar; "but whatever he wants, he wants it with a will."[8] (It is to be suspected that Deiotarus was another of Brutus' debtors.) Ordering the king to provide troops for the forthcoming campaign against Mithridates' son, Pharnaces, Caesar delayed judgment, a tactic he was to follow henceforth with individuals of dubious reliability.

At Caesar's approach Pharnaces sent him a gold crown to signify his goodwill and with insulting affrontery offered Caesar his daughter in marriage. Aware of the disorders in Italy and of the mounting optimate power in Africa, he was confident that Caesar would overlook his recent castration and massacre of Roman citizens and permit him to reoccupy his father's kingdom. The battle took place precisely on the second anniversary of Caesar's victory over the Pompeians in Spain. At first Caesar's men, including the VIth legion, proud of its victory in Egypt, were discomfited by chariots armed with scythes, but after hand-to-hand combat lasting four hours with heavy casualties on both sides, the legionaries routed the enemy, and the king escaped with only a few horsemen. "At such a victory Caesar, though many times victorious, was filled with incredible joy because he had finished a great war so quickly; and he was made the more joyful by the recollection of the peril in which he had suddenly been placed." In his exultation, he cried out, "O fortunate Pompeius, who was named the Great for warring against such men as these!" To his friend Matius, an Epicurean banker at Rome, he sent the famous vaunt: "I came, I saw, I conquered."[9]

Caesar dispatched the VIth legion back to Italy generously rewarded. He confirmed administrative arrangements in Asia Minor by entrusting tested partisans with governorships of the several provinces. He instructed them to investigate sites for colonies at commercial centers and seaports in order to

revive the economy. To Mithridates of Pergamum, commander of the relief
army that had rescued him in Egypt, he assigned a portion of Deiotarus'
domain as well as the kingdom of Bosphorus, part of Pharnaces' realm. "By
interposing a friendly king, Caesar was protecting the provinces of the Roman
people against barbarian and hostile kings." Having settled these matters,
Caesar sped to the Aegean escorted by a single squadron of Gallic cavalry. On
the way, he "heard and judged all the disputes . . . [and] assigned powers to
kings, tetrarchs and states." In return for pardons Caesar exacted indemnities
to replenish his war chest. Wealthy landowners and princelings who had
rallied to Pompeius he fined heavily, reducing their power and influence without rendering them desperate for revenge. Thus he punished one provincial
magnate "with the wealth of a king, worth more than two thousand talents,"
by auctioning off his landed estates. Roman fugitives he pardoned. To a Pompeian provincial official he "said nothing harsh, nothing bitter, but simply
ordered him to Rome."[10]

Having assured himself of the stability of Asia Minor, "he stayed nowhere
longer than the needs of the troubles at Rome seemed to warrant."[11]

At Rome, expecting that Caesar would be preoccupied for months in the war
with Pharnaces, Dolabella had intensified his campaign for the cancellation of
debts and remission of rents. Learning of Caesar's approach and fearful that
Caesar would punish him for his adventurism, Dolabella saw to his defenses.
In the Forum he set up a statue of Clodius, and his armed bands terrorized the
city. In an appeal for a restoration of civil tranquility, the vestal virgins
emerged from their cloister and paraded through the Forum with their sacred
vessels, and the Senate enacted the ultimate decree empowering Antonius, the
master of horse, to employ all measures to restore order. In his ferocious
repression of the rioters, Antonius was said to be motivated by more than
concern for the tranquility of the city, for rumor held that Dolabella had
seduced Antonius' wife. In an attack on Dolabella's partisans, Antonius left
eight hundred corpses strewn about the Forum.

The situation in the legionary camps was also deteriorating. Two of Caesar's
legates ordered to ready the troops for the forthcoming African campaign were
stoned; one of them was besieged by a mutinous centurion.

Despite disquieting reports from Rome, Caesar refused to be hurried. He
stopped in Greece to resolve local problems. Greeted as "savior and benefactor" at Athens, he outdid Pompeius in his largess to the city, providing for the
construction of a new market place at the foot of the Acropolis. At Athens,
too, he found a distinguished architect for new building projects he was planning at home, for he had resolved to follow the policy of the kings of Egypt in
providing public works projects for the unemployed. At the Isthmus of Corinth
Caesar inspected the diolkos, an ancient causeway for hauling vessels overland
from the Saronic Gulf on the Aegean to the Gulf of Corinth and the Adriatic to
the west. Large ships, however, were compelled to make a dangerous circuit
around the Peloponnesos. In the past plans had been drafted but never carried

out for the digging of a canal through the four-mile neck of land. Caesar could summon Alexandrian engineers to supervise such a project, a canal far shorter than that linking the Nile to the Red Sea though in considerably more difficult terrain. At the nearby site of ancient Corinth, formerly a center of culture and industry renowned as "wealthy Corinth," plundered and leveled by a Roman general a century earlier, Caesar was "moved by compassion" at the wilderness.[12] Impressed by the commercial potential for a new city, especially in connection with the construction of a canal through the nearby isthmus, he marked it as a site for a new settlement.

As he embarked for Italy, Caesar could reflect with satisfaction upon his achievements during the thirteen months since Pharsalus—pacification of the most ancient and wealthy state in the Mediterranean as well as of the other Eastern territories, winning the goodwill of the Jews and crushing the last substantial foe in Asia Minor. On the other hand, he had not dealt with the Parthian menace, nor had he resolved the threat from the Dacians in the Balkans. Above all, his foes had regrouped in Africa, and new crises had arisen in Illyricum, Further Spain and in Italy.

Caesar had learned years earlier that life consists of unremitting struggle. He did not despair at challenges. Congratulating himself upon "accomplishing all his business with great success and great speed, [he] arrived in Italy sooner than anyone expected."[13]

L

SUBMISSION AND MUTINY

A T Tarentum (Taranto) in the heel of Italy late in September (47), Caesar found a crowd of silent Pompeians awaiting him at the harbor. They feared that now with the defeat and death of his rival, Caesar, like Sulla, would undertake a final solution with his enemies. A timorous Cicero approached. He knew that in Greece his brother and nephew had denounced him as an opportunist and irreconcilable foe and had blamed him for their defection to Pompeius. Caesar dismounted. He hailed Cicero as imperator, an indication of his willingness to grant the orator the triumph he had so long been awaiting. (Yearning for this ultimate achievement, Cicero had been traveling about with laureled lictors for three years.) Abruptly, Caesar rushed forward and embraced Cicero as though an old friend from whom he had too long been separated. To encourage all the others who were watching with desperate anticipation, Caesar walked with Cicero for a considerable distance in earnest but amicable conversation.

Moved by Caesar's graciousness and relieved at the termination of months of nightmare (Antonius had forbidden him to leave southern Italy without Caesar's authorization), Cicero assured Caesar that during the last weeks "amid the groans of Italy and the piteous lamentations of the city," he and others devoted to the republic would "have done something to alleviate them . . . if only the man in authority [Caesar] had been there."[1] Caesar listened and knew that Cicero believed for the moment what he was saying. Caesar remembered, of course, how Cicero had once praised him as a nonpareil of generosity and kindness and as his dearest friend, only to reverse his sentiments and to attack him as a monster of cruelty and treachery. Caesar could wonder how long Cicero would persist in his present goodwill.

Hastening to Rome Caesar organized and conducted two sets of elections, choosing magistrates both for the remainder of the current year and for the coming year. Rewarding faithful associates, he nominated for the consulship Fufius Calenus (father-in-law to Caesar's devoted councilor Pansa), a legate who had served with distinction in Epirus and as military governor of Greece, along with the trusty Vatinius, who despite a painful ailment in his legs had routed a rebel force far superior to his own and pacified Illyricum, rendering unnecessary Caesar's presence at least in that province. For temporarily pacifying the mutineers in Further Spain, Caesar rewarded Lepidus with a triumph. With the flight or death of so many nobles, priesthoods were available for the deserving, and Caesar nominated Sulpicius Rufus, a legate of the Army of Gaul, for a pontificate; and for augurships Vatinius (who years earlier had been mocked for daring to aspire to this exalted priesthood) as well as Cornificius, the young officer who had defended Illyricum for many months. Caesar himself assumed an augurship, determined to end the domination of this college by the ultra-conservatives. To replenish the decimated Senate, Caesar as dictator appointed several centurions (presumably those who had acquired equestrian wealth as rewards for military valor) as well as equestrians like his closest associate, Balbus. Nevertheless, not even the most obdurate of Caesar's opponents could accuse him of reserving high posts solely to his partisans, as Sulla had done. Though taken by surprise, Servius, the consular and noted jurisconsult who had condemned Caesar early in the civil war for carrying the war into Spain, accepted the governorship of Greece. Unlike Sulla again, Caesar provided no windfalls to immediate relatives though he "knocked down some fine estates to [Servilia] in a public auction at a nominal price."[2] Servilia now enjoyed greater political influence than ever with her son Marcus Brutus a governor of Cisalpina and her three sons-in-law appointed to important posts: Lepidus, honored with a consulship for the coming year; Servilius Isauricus, Caesar's colleague in the consulship of 48, appointed governor of Asia; and Gaius Cassius, a legate.

"There are two things," Caesar, no hypocrite, frequently declared, "which created, protected and increased sovereignties—soldiers and money—and these two are dependent upon each other."[3] Now he solicited "loans" from wealthy optimates, and these responded with alacrity, relieved at not seeing their names posted in a new proscription. On the other hand, he set up the auctioneer's spear at the Temple of Jupiter the Stayer and sold off Pompeius' properties as well as those of other enemy aristocrats who had died in the war or were continuing the rebellion in Africa.

Romans awaited Caesar's reaction to Dolabella's recent demagogic adventurism. Having pardoned Pompeians, Caesar could hardly exact severe punishment from a man who had fought valiantly, if not always effectively, in his own forces. Caesar was aware, too, of Dolabella's popularity with Clodius' former partisans and with young aristocratic prodigals. Above all, for the reconstruction of the society and the state, Caesar had to make do with whatever cadre was available within a degenerate oligarchy. He could expect that Dolabella, an incorrigible opportunist, would prove the more loyal henceforth for receiving a pardon. Nevertheless, Caesar would not permit adventurers to profiteer as though this civil war was being fought for private aggrandizement. When at auctions Dolabella and Antonius seized Pompeius' properties through inflated bids, Caesar insisted upon immediate and full payment. "Is it of me Gaius Caesar asks for money?" Antonius protested. "Why not rather I from him? Was it without me he conquered?" In chagrin he announced that he would not participate in the forthcoming African campaign "since he got no recompense for his previous successes."[4] Caesar ignored Antonius' sulking. Dolabella he ordered to ready himself for service. He was not leaving this demagogue unattended.

Antonius may have been disgruntled at more than Caesar's demands for payment for properties, for Caesar was displaying extraordinary favor to his great-nephew. Octavius was handsome with "clear, bright eyes . . . hair slightly curly and inclining to golden. His eyebrows met, his ears were of moderate size and his nose projected a little at the top and then bent slightly inward. His complexion was between dark and fair." Though "he was short of stature . . . this was concealed by the fine proportion and symmetry of his figure." Yet his appearance was marred by teeth set "wide apart, small and ill-kept." Like Caesar as a youth, Octavius was delicate, suffering from a weak stomach and frequent catarrhs, and he limped as the result of an infirmity of his left side.[5] In September, when Caesar attended the ceremony at Octavius' donning of the toga of manhood, to Caesar's delight Octavius asked to participate in the African war. Caesar's niece Atia, an anxious mother, refused permission, and Caesar contented himself with raising the young man to lofty honors in anticipation of involving him in state and military affairs in the future. He nominated him as a pontifex in place of Ahenobarbus, dead at Pharsalus, and appointed him prefect of the city while the consuls Vatinius and Fufius journeyed to the Alban Mount to celebrate the Latin festival.

With Pompeius' defeat and subsequent assassination and the capitulation of a substantial number of Pompeius' partisans, the civil war had degenerated into a mere factional rebellion. It was time for Caesar to institute a sense of order and direction in the commonwealth. He had to deal first with the continuing economic crisis, putting an end to demagogic agitation and reassuring the stable elements of society. To alleviate immediate distress he distributed grain, oil and money among the plebs. Simultaneously he decreed severe penalties for incitement to riot. To an unruly crowd clamoring for a cancellation of debts, he snapped: "I, too, owe large amounts." Nevertheless, "he made a present to the multitude of all the interest they were owing from the time he had gone to war with Pompeius, and he released them from all rent for one year, up to the sum of two thousand sesterces; furthermore he revised the valuation on the goods, in terms of which it was required by law for loans to be paid, to their worth at the time the loan had been made, in view of the fact that everything had become much cheaper as a result of the great amount of confiscated property."[6] Partisans of Clodius, Caelius and Dolabella accused Caesar of selling out his former supporters. To no avail! Caesar adopted policies on the basis of a strict calculation of the relationship of forces. Although he both sought reconciliation with individual disgruntled oligarchs and desired as well to provide relief to the most depressed elements among the citizenry, Caesar considered that it was the productive elements—medium and large land-owners, manufacturers, traders and shipowners—whose support was decisive for the reconstruction of the commonwealth.

Caesar had left the problem of the mutiny of his legionaries for last. Disaffection was widespread; the veteran XIIth legion had been joined in open rebellion by the Xth, Caesar's former bodyguard. Mutineers had murdered two senators of praetorian rank dispatched to negotiate with them, and the newly elected praetor Sallustius sent to offer them a bonus of one thousand denars per man and further rewards at the conclusion of hostilities barely escaped assassination. An angry mob tracked him back to Rome and bivouacked in the Campus Martius, declaring that they would not move until their demands were met.

One day, unannounced, Caesar appeared at the encampment.

The legionaries had not seen Caesar for almost a year and a half, since Pharsalus. When Caesar demanded to know what they wanted of him, they were abashed. Saying not a word of the bonuses for which they had been clamoring during the previous months, spokesmen for the troops complained only of wounds, weariness and old age and of years of endless travail. They requested immediate discharge.

"Why, of course, Quirites," replied Caesar. "What you say is right. You are naturally weary and worn out with wounds. I discharge you."[7]

The soldiers looked at each other. They had expected an appeal for patience for yet one more "final" battle. When Caesar addressed them as "Quirites"— standard to an assembly of civilians—they realized all at once the meaning of the title "fellow soldiers." When Caesar sympathized with their weariness, they recalled how he had alternated them in service during the final winter campaigns in Gaul without permitting himself any respite. During the last year, while they had been recuperating from the exertions of Epirus and Pharsalus, he had been fighting without rest in the East. Their senior in age, he never spared himself.

"I shall give you all that I have promised," Caesar continued, "when I triumph with other soldiers."

The men of the Xth remembered how more than eleven years earlier, in the first Gallic campaign, Caesar had quelled a mutiny by declaring that against the German Ariovistus he would march, if necessary, with the Xth legion alone, such trust had they enjoyed with him then. Now as Caesar eyed them, the legionaries recollected the many occasions on which with "incredible powers of endurance" he marched before them "sometimes on horseback, but oftener on foot, bareheaded both in the heat of the sun and in rain . . . swimming the rivers which barred his path or crossing on inflated skins." They recalled, too, how "when his army gave way, he often rallied it single-handed, planting himself in the way of the fleeing men, laying hold of them one by one and even catching them by the throat and forcing them to face the enemy." They knew that "he valued his soldiers neither for their personal character nor their fortune but solely for their prowess, and he treated them with equal strictness and indulgence; for he did not curb them everywhere and at all times but only in the presence of the enemy. Then he required the strictest discipline, not announcing the time of a march or a battle but keeping them ready and alert to be led on a sudden at any moment wheresoever he might wish. He often called them out even when there was no occasion for it, especially on rainy days and holidays. And warning them every now and then that they must keep close watch on him, he would steal away suddenly by day or night and make a longer march than usual to tire out those who were tardy in following." They had always been mindful that "he did not take notice of all their offenses or punish them by rule, but he kept a sharp look out for deserters and mutineers and chastised them most severely, shutting his eyes to other faults. . . . Sometimes after a great victory he relieved them of all duties and gave them full license to revel, being in the habit of boasting that his soldiers could fight well even when reeking of perfumes."[8] They remembered, too, how, grieving, he had let his hair and beard grow until he had, with them, avenged the fifteen cohorts massacred by Belgian tribesmen.

Noting that the soldiers stood silent in their confusion, Caesar's "friends urged him to say something more . . . and not leave his old comrades of so many campaigns with a short and austere word." When he spoke again, he addressed them yet once more as "Quirites" and not as "fellow soldiers."

Now the troops begged Caesar, shameful not merely at deserting him but also at abandoning the image of themselves Caesar had evoked in them over the years—as men of superior daring, men who strove for excellence in fulfilment of their responsibilities as his chosen companions. Their shame was "mingled with jealousy that while they would be thought to be abandoning their commander in the midst of so many enemies, others would join in the triumph instead of themselves, and they would lose the gains of the war in Africa . . . and become hateful to Caesar himself as well as to the opposite party."

As the troops lamented and cried for his pardon, Caesar left the platform. Fearful that he was abandoning them, they appealed to him to punish the ringleaders of the mutiny and to receive them back into his service as he had done with the IXth legion after the Spanish campaign.

Caesar hesitated.

Confident that he was softening, the men renewed their pleas.

Returning to the podium, Caesar recalled the mutiny during the first Gallic campaign. He was especially grieved, he said, at the present disloyalty of the Xth legion. Reversing the events of that old mutiny, he declared that he would discharge this legion alone since their betrayal seemed to him more disgraceful than that of the others. The other legionaries congratulated themselves on their good fortune, but the men of the Xth, in despair, begged Caesar to choose by lot a portion of their number for execution. Only then did Caesar yield, like a father unable to resist the importunings of outcast sons, but those who had been leaders in the mutiny understood that Caesar would demand proof of their loyalty on the battlefield.

Assured that he could rely on the veterans during the next and, once again, final campaign, Caesar could depart from Rome.

In April 49, after Pompeius' flight from Brundisium Caesar had tarried eight days in the city; returning from Spain on his way to fight Pompeius he had remained eleven days; on this, his third sojourn he remained two months. On each occasion he astounded the citizenry with his swift accomplishment of manifold tasks. Romans contrasted the months of disorder under Caelius and Dolabella with the constructive activity during Caesar's presence in the city. Citizens sensed that between the arrogance and corruption of the former ruling clique and the violence of the disgruntled commons, Caesar offered the only alternative. Former Pompeians, fearful of the vindictiveness of those continuing the struggle in Africa, whose cause they had deserted, were encouraged by Caesar's restoration of order and his continuing clemency. Caesar could hope that upon the defeat of the optimates in Africa, he would enjoy the collaboration of broad elements of the senatorial and equestrian orders in instituting a wide-ranging program for the restoration of tranquility and prosperity in Italy and throughout the empire.

LI

MASTER OF AFRICA

O N December 17 (actually early October since the lunar calendar was running more than two full months ahead of the sun), Caesar arrived at Lilybaeum at the western tip of Sicily, the point on the island closest to the province of Africa (roughly modern Tunisia). On tenterhooks to complete this final campaign, he pitched his tent on the beach and would have embarked with the single legion of green recruits and the six hundred cavalry he found awaiting him if the weather had been favorable. Once again officers had failed to prepare for his arrival, and he boarded legionaries as they arrived and kept rowers and crews at the ready. On December 25, with newly arrived transports and a total of six legions and two thousand horse, Caesar set sail. Three days later with the remaining transports scattered by strong winds, Caesar landed near the fortified town of Hadrumetum (Sousse in Tunisia, some sixty miles south of Carthage). He had only three thousand legionaries and about one hundred and fifty cavalrymen. Lacking firm intelligence on the enemy fleets or on landing conditions, Caesar had given ship captains no precise orders as to a rendezvous. The inexperienced troops, fearful of entering upon unknown perils and aware that an army under Curio had been annihilated in a previous invasion of this country, grew panicky when a victim escaped during a sacrifice before they disembarked. They shuddered as Caesar stumbled upon stepping ashore and were scarcely reassured when he exclaimed, "I hold thee fast, Africa."[1]

Caesar counted upon catching the optimates once again by surprise, confident that they would not expect an invasion just before winter. He had intelligence of fierce bickering among the enemy leaders. A praetorian freed by Caesar at Corfinium had seized the governorship of Africa. Having participated in Curio's defeat, he now contested the supreme command with the latecomer Scipio. In turn, to win the support of Juba, King of Numidia, an ally whose assistance had been decisive in destroying Curio's army, Scipio agreed to the destruction of Utica, the capital of the province and a city whose commercial influence and popular sympathies were resented by the king. Only Cato's intervention averted a massacre of the townspeople. Despite his resentment at Scipio's conspiring with the Numidian potentate and an old personal enmity, the Stoic insisted that Scipio, a consular and the Roman of highest rank in the optimate camp, serve as supreme commander. Hardly grateful, the arrogant Scipio scoffed at Cato's indignation at his "extravagant and dread-ful" threats of proscriptions and confiscations in the event of their victory. He denounced Cato, too, as a coward for advising him "not to give battle to a man who was versed in war and of formidable ability, but to trust to time"—advice Cato had given Pompeius before Pharsalus.[2]

The optimates were further divided between those, like Labienus, whose first loyalty had been to Pompeius and those who rejoiced that with Pompeius' death the conflict was no longer primarily between rival warlords but between defenders of the oligarchic constitution and a "tyrant." Some resented the deference paid by Roman oligarchs to Juba and muttered that they "did not consider it right to defend the nation with the barbarian auxiliaries of a treach-erous nation."[3] Caesar was confident that, uneasy about the superior discipline and capacities of his veterans, the optimate troops would crack after the first setbacks. Caesar had confronted mutinies, but he had not suffered the break-down of morale that occurred among the optimate troops after Pharsalus, when the garrison at Dyrrachium pillaged granaries and set fire to transports in protest against a continuation of the war. The rebel generals could scarcely rely upon the remnants of Curio's army incorporated into their ranks or Gallic and German auxiliaries who had accompanied Labienus in his defection from Caesar. Nor could optimates count on the local population. The province was scarcely Romanized; Punic remained the predominant language, and the cul-ture, more Hellenistic than Roman. Imbued with intense local patriotism, descendants of the original Phoenician settlers, Berbers and Italian colonists regarded the optimates as a foreign occupation force. During the previous civil war, a Marian governor had appealed to the smallholders and the urban plebs for support against the bankers, large landowners and entrepreneurs, and the antagonism between the rich and poor remained intense. In Africa as else-where, Caesar had cultivated clientships, and he enjoyed the goodwill of a sizable party in the capital city of Utica.

Caesar had made preparations against Juba. Serving with Caesar was the son of the pretender to the Numidian throne whose cause Caesar had champi-oned fifteen years earlier. This prince would be useful in rousing dissension within the Numidian camp. Caesar had also contracted alliances with mon-archs of neighboring kingdoms and with Sittius, a soldier of fortune (once an associate of Catilina's) who commanded a sizable, battle-trained private army and fleet. On the other hand, for more than two years the rebels had been drilling their troops, stocking arsenals and granaries and extorting monies from the wealthy province. Labienus commanded a cavalry force of sixteen hundred Gauls and Germans and eight thousand Numidians; Petreius, whom Caesar had defeated and freed in Spain, had an additional sixteen hundred horsemen; and Scipio, eight legions with three thousand cavalry along with thousands of light-armed infantry, archers, slingers and mounted archers. King Juba could call up inexhaustible reserves.

At this stage of the war, in every move Caesar had to assess the morale of his war-weary veterans and of new recruits of uncertain loyalty. In the perilous days immediately after the landing, as the unknown officer who wrote the account of this campaign noted, Caesar confronted a crisis:

> The entire army were ignorant of their commander's intentions and anxious to find them out; and in their distress they were tormented by fear and unhappiness; for they saw themselves set down in Africa with a small force, and a newly recruited one at that and not all of them disembarked, to face large forces, including the countless cavalry of a treacherous nation; they could find no comfort in their present situation and no help in the advice of their comrades; their one comfort was in the bearing of their commander himself, in his energy and his remarkable cheerfulness—for he displayed an exalted and alert spirit. The men found reassurance in this, and they all hoped that his experience and foresight would make everything plain sailing.[4]

Caesar was, however, fortunate in his officers, by now a sizable corps of experienced men. Vatinius, for example, rounded up Caesar's scattered transports and led them to Caesar's bridgehead. Morale improved both with the arrival of these reinforcements and with a display of Caesar's characteristic versatility. To counter Labienus' tactic of intermingling light-armed auxiliaries with Numidian cavalry (a tactic mastered in the Gallic campaigns), Caesar formed units of light-armed troops, three hundred per legion, and trained them in gladiatorial skills, teaching them "how many feet they were to retreat from the enemy; the manner in which they must wheel round upon their adversary; the restricted space in which they must offer him resistance—now doubling forward, now retiring and making feint attacks; and almost the spot from which and the manner in which they must discharge their missiles."[5] He also familiarized the troops and the horses with elephants, of which the enemy possessed a great number, training the legionaries with dummy javelins in the repulse of the monster beasts.

At panic upon a report that Juba was approaching with a great horde of barbarians, Caesar relieved the fears of the troops with hyperbolic irony. "Let me tell you," he declared, "that within the next days the king will be here with ten legions, thirty thousand horsemen, a hundred thousand light-armed troops and three hundred elephants. Therefore some of you may as well cease to ask further questions or make surmises and may rather believe me since I know all about it. Otherwise, I shall surely have them shipped on some worn-out craft and carried off to whatever lands the winds may blow them." Caesar raised guffaws, too, at an optimate oracle declaring that "it was always the prerogative of the family of the Scipios to conquer in Africa." He presented a legionary with the name Scipio to the troops and set him "in the forefront of his battles as if commander of the army."[6]

Despite the general war fatigue Caesar permitted no relaxation in discipline. He discharged ship captains negligent in protecting transports from enemy raiders. Parading ringleaders of the recent disaffection before the troops, he admonished the IXth and Xth legions that he would tolerate no new mutinies.

A tribune of the Xth who had commandeered an entire transport for his slaves and horses he accused of fomenting the mutiny in Italy. "I discharge you with ignominy from my army," he declared, "and order you to remove yourself today from Africa and do so with all possible speed." Other officers he dismissed from service as "neither brave in warfare nor loyal and serviceable in peace." In a near rout in face of an overwhelming enemy force, he seized a standard bearer by the neck, faced him about and shouted, "Yonder is the enemy!"[7]

Caesar succeeded in reviving the initiative and spirit of emulation among the veterans. At Dyrrachium they had overcome famine by making bread out of some strange root; here, cut off from foraging by enemy cavalry, they collected seaweed and washed it in fresh water as feed for horses and mules. As in previous campaigns, Caesar's troops submitted to almost intolerable privations. Because Caesar had reduced impedimenta to a minimum in order to transport a maximum number of troops, "only a very few men were sleeping under proper tents; the rest were camping under makeshift shelters made of clothes or reeds and branches woven together. And so these tents were weighed down by the sudden rain and the hail that succeeded it; they were ripped to shreds by the force of the water. . . . All the foodstuffs were spoiled; and the men went wandering about the camp holding their shields over their heads." Frustrated by these conditions and eager to conclude the conflict, the men exhibited the impatience they had shown in the last campaigns. In one engagement, cavalry and light-armed troops "advanced . . . recklessly and without orders . . . and after crossing . . . marshy ground proved incapable of withstanding the superior numbers of the enemy. The cavalry were deserted by the light infantry and sustained severe damage before fleeing back to their own forces." In general, however, Caesar had not miscalculated regarding the comparative morale of the two forces. The enemy armies were composed in great part of "the very men whom he himself had often routed, beaten back and utterly demoralized, only to spare their lives and forgive their misdemeanors. . . . His name and prestige had a sobering effect upon the reckless spirit of their army," and when he fired leaflets into their lines with a promise to preserve the property and persons of local draftees and offering amnesty and rewards to Italians, many defected. Scipio's leaflets, on the other hand, displayed the standard optimate illusions, and his call to "liberate the Roman people and the Senate" evoked laughter.[8] Labienus' ambushes were foiled by deserters who crossed the lines to warn Caesar, and when Labienus did surprise Caesar's men, he could not prod his troops to follow up on their initial success.

Caesar was also the beneficiary of his family and other connections. When he sent nomadic Gaetulian deserters back to their homes to rouse rebellion, a thousand of their cavalry crossed the lines en masse. The chiefs explained that their "fathers had . . . served under Marius and been rewarded by him with grants of territory."[9] Juba was forced to dispatch an army to suppress a

Gaetulian revolt, and to discourage flight on the battlefield he crucified soldiers who panicked. Before he could deploy his forces against Caesar, he was
compelled to relieve a city under siege by Caesar's ally, the adventurer Sittius.
Inhabitants of an island off the coast, descendants of Marian legionaries settled
by Caesar's father and his clansman Caesar Strabo, welcomed Sallustius and
delivered to him a huge supply of grain that had been stored there by the
rebels. Nor could the optimates control the provincials. Towns, including
some founded by Marius for his legionaries, sent deputations to Caesar to
request garrisons for their defense.

   Whereas Caesar forbade looting and kept his cavalry aboard transports to
prevent depredations against the civilian population, the rebels behaved like an
occupation force. Scipio's officers "had collected corn from all over Africa into
a few well-fortified towns so that the whole territory of Africa was exhausted
of corn." Employing a tactic that would be revived in twentieth-century colonial pacification campaigns, the optimates "were also razing and abandoning
all the towns except those few which they could hold with garrisons of their
forces and had forced the inhabitants to move into the garrisons so that the
fields were now deserted and laid waste." In Utica, Cato, uncertain of the
loyalty of the population, interned all men of military age. Prosperous civilians
fleeing to Caesar's camp "recounted the cruelty and harshness of his opponents," and Caesar himself "saw that farmhouses were being burned down,
fields devastated, flocks plundered and killed, towns and forts razed and abandoned, and the leading citizens slain or kept in chains while their children were
carried off, ostensibly as hostages, and enslaved."[10] It was even reported that
Scipio, desperate at Juba's procrastination in dispatching reinforcements, had
promised to cede the province to the king in return for prompt deployment of
his troops.

   As much concerned about establishing a lasting peace in Africa as in securing
victory, Caesar changed his strategy. Instead of delaying battle in anticipation
of the disintegration of enemy morale, he invested the town of Thapsus and
challenged Scipio, at last reinforced with Juba's army, to give battle or to
accept the humiliation of the capture of a major optimate garrison. Caesar
ordered his fleet to approach the shore so as to attack the enemy's rear and,
repeating a tactic employed at Pharsalus, he posted five cohorts of the Vth
legion (Gauls recruited in the Province and in long-haired Gaul) as a fourth line
behind either wing to repel a flank attack by Scipio's one hundred and twenty
elephants.

   A remarkable event ensued.

   While Caesar was making the rounds to exhort his troops, a commotion was
seen outside the enemy camp. Caesar "observed the enemy in frantic movement around the rampart, running here and there in confusion and sometimes
withdrawing inside the gates, sometimes coming out in a disorderly and reckless fashion." Caesar's troops cried out for the signal. In response Caesar
shouted "that he did not approve of engaging in battle by an impromptu

sally." With difficulty he checked the line from advancing. "Suddenly a trumpeter on the right wing, yielding to pressure from the troops and without Caesar's orders, began to sound the charge. This was taken up by all the cohorts and they began to advance on the enemy; but the centurions faced about and vainly attempted to restrain their men, urging them not to engage without their commander's orders."[11]

Caesar "realized that it was impossible to resist his troops' impetuosity; he gave the word, 'Good Luck!' and set his horse at a gallop against the enemy front line." Under the pelting of Caesar's slingers and archers, Scipio's elephants reared, wheeled about and stampeded into their own troops. The enemy cavalry broke into a rout. Caesar's men overran first Scipio's camp and then Juba's, and enemy troops lowered their weapons in surrender. Caesar's legionaries, however, were in no mood to grant mercy. The veterans, in particular, "were in such a blaze of indignation that not only could they not be induced to spare their enemies," but in a sudden fury at all the aristocrats whose rivalries had caused this long and bloody civil war, "they even wounded or killed several refined and distinguished Romans on their own side, calling them agitators." Pompeius Rufus, brother to Caesar's second wife, was struck in the arm with a sword and would have been killed if he had not fought his way to Caesar's side. All Scipio's soldiers who sought to surrender were slaughtered "under Caesar's very eyes and despite his entreaties to the troops to spare them."

Once again Caesar dared not reprimand his veterans. Assembling them the next day, he "praised them, gave cash gratuities to all the veterans and from his tribunal issued decorations to all who had rendered conspicuously good service."[12]

CONFIRMING THE PEACE IN AFRICA

Thus on April 9 (February 6, according to the solar calendar), little more than three months after his landing with three thousand raw recruits and one hundred and fifty horsemen, Caesar liberated Africa and, of decisive importance, crushed the optimate clique whose threats and insults had compelled him to cross the Rubicon. Dispatching lieutenants to obtain the surrender of rebel garrisons, he tactfully entrusted Valerius Messalla, a consular and a nephew to Cato's deceased connection Hortensius, with the task of treating with the Stoic at Utica. Caesar followed, accepting the capitulation of towns and seeking to forestall atrocities by marauding bands of rebel soldiers. At one town, refused admittance, cavalrymen stormed inside, built a pyre and flung the citizens alive into the flames.

On the road Caesar encountered his clansman Lucius Caesar, the young man sent as an emissary by Pompeius at the outbreak of the civil war. Lucius "fell at [Caesar's] feet and begged him for one favor alone—to spare his life. Caesar readily assented, as both his inclination and his general policy dictated." When

Lucius reported that Cato had taken his own life, Caesar exclaimed: "O Cato, I begrudge you your death, for you did begrudge me the preservation of your life." Cato had failed to rally to continued resistance the three hundred local men of property who served as his advisory council. When fugitive horsemen demanded a massacre of the Uticans for their sympathy for Caesar, Cato and Faustus Sulla bribed them to depart from the city. Cato supervised the embarkation of senators and others who feared Caesar, but when Lucius Caesar asked permission to appeal to Caesar for him, Cato responded: "If I were willing to be saved by grace of Caesar, I ought to go to him in person and see him alone; but I am unwilling to be under obligations to the tyrant for his illegal acts, and he acts illegally in saving, as if their master, those over whom he has no right at all to be the lord."[13]

For more than fifteen years, Caesar and Cato had fought, sometimes out of petty jealousy, generally out of a fundamental ideological antagonism. Though Cato bore especial responsibility for the civil war, during the conflict he had sought to restrain his fellow optimates from cruelty. Such was Cato's prestige that if he had accepted Caesar's clemency, the other optimates might have surrendered. By his suicide Cato proclaimed enmity from the grave. In death he would prove a greater threat than in life.

Lucius confirmed other rumors. Fearing the irascibility and presumption of Pompeius' elder son, Cato had sent him off with a fleet to attack Caesar's allies along the African coast. Repulsed, he went on to seize the Balearic islands. When rebels in Further Spain invited him to take command in their uprising, he established a foothold on the Iberian peninsula. To him the remaining optimates were now fleeing.

The war was not over.

Caesar had yet to deal with a second Gnaeus Pompeius and to pacify Further Spain for a second time.

How would he exhort the veterans of the Army of Gaul to follow him once again in search of a final victory?

All the more pressing, therefore, was the pacification of Africa.

At Utica Caesar thanked the local citizenry for their loyalty. To the delight of the commons, he read a detailed accusation against the assembly of the three hundred local oligarchs, but he astonished everyone by inviting them and the other rebel sympathizers to come forth without fear. He granted them their lives and the right to repurchase properties he put up for auction. Here, as in Asia Minor, Caesar filled his own war chests and deprived wealthy foes of influence by confiscation of much of their riches. Relieved at Caesar's generosity, the oligarchs petitioned him to impose an indemnity upon them as a group, and he set a sum of 200 million sesterces to be paid in six instalments, an amount only slightly less than the tribute he had imposed on all of conquered Gaul.

At a report that the son of the pretender to the Numidian throne "held possession of the whole lands" of a major Numidian city and was under siege by Juba, Caesar set out to his relief. Tidings of Caesar's leniency preceded him, "and when he reached Zama pretty well all the cavalry of the kingdom came to him and were released from their fears and danger."[14] The disintegration of resistance proceeded apace. A rebel general was murdered by his Gaetulian escort. Juba and Petreius died in a suicide pact. Sittius captured Afranius and Faustus Sulla, and the two men were subsequently murdered under unexplained circumstances. Sittius' fleet captured Scipio and other leading optimates in flight to Spain, and all these aristocrats either killed themselves or were slain.

Caesar sold off the royal property and the holdings of wealthy Roman rebels, decreed indemnities against towns that had supported his enemies, large sums against the communities and separate penalties against the corporations of wealthy citizens, collecting thereby quantities of oil and grain for relief of the poor at Rome. He rewarded Sittius with a portion of Juba's territory and entrusted the rest to Sallustius to reorganize into the province of Africa Nova, hopeful that the pedantic litterateur with his ready homilies on oligarchic corruption would display greater responsibility than Quintus Cassius had shown in Further Spain.

Caesar instructed the newly appointed governor of the old province of Africa, a legate of the Army of Gaul, to select areas for settlement of veterans and the poor of Rome. He himself surveyed the site of old Carthage, destroyed precisely a century earlier by Scipio Africanus the Younger, who sowed the ground with salt and laid a curse against any new habitation there. Gaius Gracchus had projected a colony nearby, and Caesar saw that a new town could become a center of commerce and industry for the entire region. To counter fears of Scipio's curse, he gave out that encamped at the ruins he dreamed of an army weeping (as though in regret for the destruction of the original city) and proclaimed his intention to refound the former Punic capital. (It would become one of the most prosperous cities of the Mediterranean world.)

Confident that by breaking up the kingdom of Numidia, by undermining the influence of the men of property and by establishing garrison colonies, he had secured the peace in Africa so that he would not have to return for another pacification campaign, Caesar dispatched a legate named Didius with a fleet to engage Gnaeus Pompeius and ordered his nephew Pedius along with his longtime political ally Fabius Maximus to march to Spain from Italy to put down the rebellion on land.

In mid-June Caesar set sail for Sardinia, the island which had rallied early to his cause. Landing at Caralis (Cagliari) and greeted as a liberator, Caesar granted citizenship to the townspeople, even as he had done with the Gaditans in Further Spain. In other towns Caesar thanked the indigenous Sards and the descendants of Punic settlers for the grain and other supplies they had shipped to him in Africa. He eliminated inequities in the local tribute, rewarded deserving individuals and punished with fines collaborators with the rebels. After arranging for the establishment of a colony of veterans, Caesar departed on June 27. In this province at least he would not face rebellion upon his departure. To the Sardinians Caesar was not merely a patron but a champion and a liberator.

Adverse winds delayed Caesar for twenty-seven days. Finally, seven months after setting out from Sicily for Africa, Caesar arrived at Rome.

LII
"THE OLD ORDER THRUST OUT BY THE NEW"

ON July 25, 46, Caesar arrived at Ostia. His agents had assembled what appeared to be all Italy to greet him—magistrates and senators, equestrians, officers, legionaries, officials of the tribes and of the collegia and a host of commoners and foreigners. Oppius and Balbus had warned, however, that optimate sympathizers, projecting upon Caesar their own vindictiveness, still entertained uncertainty regarding Caesar's intentions now that he had defeated the optimate leaders and was the unchallenged master of the empire. The new stage in the political developments required a new policy statement, and in a speech at the city gate Caesar reassured those who feared proscriptions and confiscations by recalling how at every turn in the civil war he had remained faithful to his policy of clemency. Not only had he no intention of instituting persecutions of "subversives," but, on the contrary, even as at the beginning of his consulate he had called for a consensus to replace factional antagonisms, so now he proclaimed the inauguration of a new era of reconciliation and reconstruction and called upon all citizens "to join with him and confidently unite our interests, forgetting all past events . . . and beginning to love each other without suspicion as if we were in some sort new citizens."[1]

While still in Africa, Caesar had received reports of almost daily shifts in attitude in Italy. As long as the outcome on the battlefield remained uncertain and rumors told of Caesar's being threatened by an overwhelming enemy force, optimates at home advised each other to take no public stand. At the initial report of Caesar's victory at Thapsus, Cicero counseled Varro, the Pompeian governor of Further Spain defeated by Caesar, to "lie low just where you are until all this rejoicing cools down." When the defeat of the optimates had been confirmed, Cicero advised capitulation. "Since all is over and done, we must not hesitate to go over 'horse and foot.' " A month later, awaiting Caesar's return to Rome, he was expressing hostile resignation. "To bear what must be borne is not at all the same thing as to approve what must not be approved," Cicero now wrote to Varro. "The republic we live in is in a state of chaos."[2]

Caesar discovered that his reconfirmed clemency at first evoked relief and then resentment as his enemies repeated Cato's charge that Caesar was presumptuous in granting pardon. Among themselves they complained of violations of the old constitution in Caesar's repeated dictatorships and his control of legislation and of the election of magistrates. Particularly resented was the favor he showed to "new men" and to officers of the Army of Gaul.

For the varied tasks of the empire Caesar was not able to assemble a substantial cadre of competent associates. The entrepreneurs whose prosperity Caesar had consistently promoted—wine growers, oil producers, cattlemen, produce farmers, manufacturers, contractors, shipowners and men engaged in import and export trade—were loath to be diverted from profit making; they often lacked experience in administration; and, of greater importance in tradition-bound Rome, they did not enjoy the prestige of the old oligarchs. In Egypt Caesar could challenge traditional prejudices by appointing a reliable and capable son of a freedman in command of the garrison, but he dared not make similar appointments to magistracies at Rome.

After Thapsus, mindful of the fate of previous reformers destroyed by vindictive enemies, Balbus and his associates implemented a program to confirm Caesar as the unchallenged arbiter of the commonwealth. (The spate of honors accorded Caesar after Pharsalus until his death reflects an obsessive concern with Caesar's security and with the shoring up of his authority.) At their prompting, the Senate hailed the victory at Thapsus with a public thanksgiving of forty days, twice as long as that after Alesia. Caesar was granted the right to an unprecedented escort of seventy-two lictors. To associate Caesar with Rome's patron god and to terminate the association of the Old Guard with the deity, Catulus' name was erased from the dedication of the Temple of Capitoline Jupiter and Caesar's substituted for it. To symbolize Caesar's hegemony over the Mediterranean world, the Senate ordered the erection beside the image of Jupiter of a statue of Caesar standing on a globe, and within the temple they stationed a triumphal chariot for his use. Caesar was proclaimed dictator with the right of annual renewal for a period of ten years as well as prefect of morals (a new office with censorial authority). He was granted the right to sit with the consuls in the Senate when not holding the office himself and to deliver his opinion first in all debates.

Over a period of a month, from late August through September, Caesar presented a series of magnificent triumphs to celebrate his victories in Gaul, Egypt, Asia Minor and Africa. Thousands thronged the city to hail the victor who had brought peace without vengeance. Ever the master regisseur, Caesar did not disappoint his public. Four times, garbed in a painted toga, his face reddened like the ancient Etruscan image of Jupiter that had been destroyed in the Capitoline temple in the fire during the previous civil war, he rode in his chariot with a slave bearing a gold wreath over his head and another walking behind and crying, to ward off jealousy of the gods, "Look behind yourself and remember that you are a man!" By Senate decree Caesar's chariot was drawn by four white horses, an honor reserved to Jupiter and to the Sun god and granted only to one other mortal, three centuries earlier, the hero Camillus, hailed as a new Romulus and Second Founder of Rome for repelling a Gallic invasion. Having brought to an end the Gallic peril, the new Romulus and Fourth Founder of Rome (Marius was the Third for his defeat of the Germans) surpassed Camillus in glory.

Fortune almost undid the magic of the first, the Gallic, triumph. As Caesar passed the Temple of Fortune, the axle of his chariot buckled and he was nearly thrown to the ground. Onlookers gasped, but the superstitious forgot the dire presage when Caesar, in homage to the divine author of his victory, mounted the steps to the Temple of Jupiter on his knees. To the applause of the multitude he ordered the pretentious inscription "Demigod" erased from his statue in the temple.

To impress the citizenry with the varied glory in his triumphs, Caesar constructed the trophies of different materials—lemonwood for Gaul, tortoise shell for Egypt, acanthus for Asia Minor and ivory for Africa. In the Gallic triumph he displayed representations of the great waters—the Rhone, the Rhine and the Ocean (depicted with fetters of gold); in the Egyptian he displayed a replica of the lighthouse at Pharos (equipped with a flame) and a statue of the fabulous Nile. With models of captured towns and fortresses and paintings of battle scenes, Caesar recalled exotic places that had appeared over the years in his communiqués. People cheered a depiction of the death of the treacherous Achillas, jeered at a representation of the ignominious flight of Mithridates' son and applauded a poster with Caesar's vaunt, "I came, I saw, I conquered." A view of Massilia, however, evoked frowns from old-fashioned Romans, chagrined at the humiliation of an ally "without whose help the ancestors never triumphed over Transalpine tribes."[3] In the parade of captives behind Caesar's chariot marched Vercingetorix, whose subsequent strangulation signified the termination of centuries of terror of the Gauls; Arsinoe, Cleopatra's sister, a symbol of the subjugation of the last independent kingdom of Alexander's successors; and Juba's four-year-old son, assurance of the end of the threat from the perfidious Numidians. Thus Caesar proclaimed the triumph of Rome in the Mediterranean and the imperial expansion to the Channel and the Rhine.

Respecting tradition, Caesar celebrated no triumph over fellow-citizens, ignoring his victory over the Pompeian armies in Spain, at Pharsalus and at Thapsus. On the other hand, to mock the obstinacy of oligarchs who prolonged the civil war after Pharsalus and subordinated themselves to a barbarian king against Rome's duly elected consul, Caesar displayed posters of Scipio throwing himself into the sea, of Petreius killing himself at a banquet and of Cato tearing at his own entrails. If aristocrats were angered by this mockery of optimate leaders, the populace was delighted with Caesar's good humor at the traditional bantering of his legionaries, a warding off of divine jealousy at human boasting. Those who had fought at Dyrrachium gibed at him for compelling them to live on wild cabbage. All hooted at his amorous prowess, naming Gallic princesses, a queen of Mauretania and, especially, the artful Cleopatra. They chanted:

Men at Rome, keep close your consorts, here's a bald adulterer.
Gold in Gaul you spent in dalliance, which you borrowed here in Rome.

Only at mockery of his supposed seduction as a youth by the king of Bithynia did Caesar blush and protest:

All the Gauls did Caesar vanquish, Nicomedes vanquished him;
Lo! now Caesar rides in triumph, victor over all the Gauls.
Nicomedes does not triumph, who subdued the conqueror.[4]

The troops lampooned Caesar for appointing officers and noncoms to the Senate and in a parody of a children's jingle proclaimed the lesson of the civil war and jeered at optimates for goading Caesar into usurping autocratic power:

If you do right, you will be punished;
but if wrong, you will be king.[5]

Since the major industry of the commonwealth was war, nothing impressed Romans more than booty, and Caesar dazzled the citizens with a display unparalleled in Roman history. He paraded nearly three thousand gold crowns (gifts from towns and princes), heaps of coins along with countless additional treasures and captured weaponry, all of which was subsequently converted into 60 thousand talents (1,552 million sesterces). With a prodigality that would eradicate memory of all such previous entertainments, Caesar hosted the populace at a mammoth banquet, serving at each of the twenty thousand tables both Falernian (Italy's finest) and Chian wine from the Aegean along with six thousand lampreys (affording a substantial profit for the equestrian who furnished them from his hatcheries). He also regaled the people with the games he had promised years earlier in honor of his daughter, games reminding Romans of his pietas and profound affection for those close to him.

Employing hundreds of workmen, contractors dredged a huge pool in the Tiber at the Campus Martius for naval games involving Egyptian and Tyrian fleets manned by four thousand oarsmen and one thousand marines. In a temporary amphitheater Caesar offered a Pyrrhic victory dance of Asian princes as well as British chariot vaulting and a Thessalian bull fight in which horsemen seized the horns of the beasts and twisted back the neck. Ever entranced by exotic animals, Romans gaped at their first cameleopard, a gift from Cleopatra—"like a camel in all respects except that its legs are not all of the same length, the hind legs being the shorter. . . . Towering high aloft, it supports the rest of its body on its front legs and lifts its neck to turn to an unusual height. Its skin is spotted like a leopard's."[6]

In these festivities Caesar was instructing Romans to think of themselves no longer as citizens of a dominant city-state but of an imperial capital. To revive Roman aristocratic traditions, on the other hand, Caesar mounted the Trojan Games, in which young Romans of distinguished families conducted a mock cavalry battle involving intricate maneuvers. Then in recognition of the dual founts of the imperial culture (and of the mixed origins of the population), Caesar presented theatrical performances simultaneously in Latin and in Greek, assigning supervision of the Greek theatricals to his grandnephew Octavius, now in his eighteenth year. People had noted that Octavius walked behind Caesar's chariot in the triumphal processions (a place ordinarily reserved for a triumpher's son) resplendent with military decorations though he had never participated in a battle. In addition, Caesar allowed Octavius to transmit petitions from former Pompeians, a task in which Octavius displayed extraordinary tact. "Looking out for the opportune moment he respectfully asked and was successful. . . . He took care never to ask a favor at an inopportune time nor when it was annoying to Caesar."[7] Gossips reported that upon hearing that Octavius, a sickly young man, had fallen ill from his exertions in the theater, Caesar jumped from his dining couch and ran barefoot to Octavius' house to be at the youth's bedside.

At the culmination of the victory festivities, on September 26, Caesar dedicated the temple he had vowed at Pharsalus, not, however, to Venus Victrix, the war goddess, but to Venus Genetrix, a goddess of peace and prosperity and divine progenitress of Rome, mother of Aeneas, ancestress of the Julian clan. Joining Jupiter, the patron deity of the city-state, this goddess, a protectress of imperial Rome, represented the fruitful power invoked by Lucretius in the opening lines of his Epicurean masterpiece:

> Mother [Genetrix] of Aeneas and his race, darling of men and gods, nurturing Venus, who beneath the smooth-moving heavenly signs fillest with thyself the sea full-laden with ships, the earth with her kindly fruits.

In its architecture the temple exemplified Caesar's intention to transform the shabby and cluttered metropolis into a majestic imperial capital, a rival to Alexandria and other royal capitals in the East. The temple shimmered with Carraran marble from newly opened Italian quarries. The cult statue, unveiled though still unfinished, the work of a renowned sculptor of the day, represented the goddess not in Greek nudity but as a chaste Roman matron in belted tunic and long mantle. A breastplate of British pearls stood at her side, and in the cella Caesar placed six cabinets of precious stones, for the temple was to serve also as an art gallery. Within the portico, with the purpose of "giving public importance to pictures,"[8] Caesar hung two paintings by Timomachus, a Medea and an Ajax, which he had purchased for the breathtaking sum of 80 talents.

Instead of constructing a mere extension to the cluttered old Forum, Caesar provided a new and independent center for public business and commerce, a new Forum for a New Era of an imperial capital. Within this architectural complex, the temple set the dynamic. Handsome colonnades enclosed a square with arcades of stone blocks revetted with marble and embellished with gold. In the center of the square stood a fountain adorned with nymphs and at the entrance to the plaza a statue of Caesar in full armor astride his famous steed with hoofs split like hands. The symmetry and simplicity in the ensemble reflected Caesar's style in all things—in personal intercourse, in oratory and writing as well as in military strategy and statesmanship. Sophisticated Romans recognized in the Forum a skilful amalgam of Greek and Roman architecture and sensed that with this construction Roman cultural expression was entering upon a new direction. So awed were the citizens by the artistic and civic achievement that at the conclusion of the dedication ceremonies a crowd escorted Caesar to the domus publica through darkened streets illuminated by forty torchbearing elephants—an imperial procession!

THE NEW ERA

In his speech upon his return to Rome, Caesar had reaffirmed his policy of clemency, asserted his political and military supremacy in the empire and proclaimed the inauguration of a new era. Romans awaited a comprehensive policy statement detailing the programs and reforms Caesar intended to initiate. After Thapsus while reorganizing the African provinces Caesar engaged, of course, in discussions regarding the future of the empire. He would have talked at length with the governor of New Africa, the leading political theoretician of his party and the author of the programmatic open letter published just before the outbreak of the civil war. Apparently, Sallustius agreed to summarize his conversations with Caesar in a platform statement for Caesar's policies in the coming period. Formulating his epistle as a speech addressed to Caesar,[9] Sallustius opened with the warning that "however virtuous and merciful one may be, one who has more power is nevertheless feared." He was alluding, of course, to the danger mentioned in his earlier letter, when he spoke of the assassination suffered by Drusus for proposing reforms opposed by a segment of the optimates. Sallustius was troubled, however, by a more immediate threat to Caesar's long-range plans. Implicitly contrasting Caesar to Sulla, Sallustius noted: "For you it is harder than for all before you to administer your conquests because your war was more merciful than their peace. Moreover, the victors demand booty, the vanquished are fellow citizens. Amidst these difficulties you have to make your way and strengthen the state for the future, not in arms only and against the enemy but also in the kindly arts of peace, a task far, far thornier." Threatening Caesar's "far, far thornier task," according to Sallustius, were the opportunists in his own camp, "men whose whole lives were stained with infamy and debauchery," who associated themselves with Caesar in the hope of gaining "control of the state" and of winning a repudiation of their debts and an appropriation of the properties of their foes. Reassuring those who continued to fear Sullan-like proscriptions, Sallustius pretended to counsel Caesar to follow a policy to which, in fact, Caesar had already committed himself. "A cruel rule is always more bitter than lasting," Sallustius warned, "and . . . no one is fearful to the many but fear from the many recoils upon his head," while, contrarily, "those who have tempered their rule with kindness and mercy have found everything happy and prosperous."

In regard to social problems, Sallustius offered few specific proposals. He advised Caesar to provide the commons, "demoralized by largess and by the free distribution of grain," with occupations "by which they may be kept from public mischief," called for strengthening security throughout Italy and the provinces to protect life and property and proposed more equitable regulations governing military service along with adequate rewards for veterans. In the current crisis, according to Sallustius, money was "the root of all evil," and moneylenders the villains. "Frenzied indulgence in extravagance," he insisted, "subverts the established order of things" and leads to "revolution." He advised Caesar to fix "the amount of each man's income as the limit of his expenditure" and to deprive money "of its advantage and honor" through sumptuary laws against conspicuous consumption. For the restoration of peace and prosperity in the empire, Sallustius found the sole hope in Caesar himself, a man who "excelled others to such a degree that men are sooner wearied in singing the praises of [his] deeds than [he] in doing deeds worthy of praise." He exhorted Caesar directly: "I conjure you by the gods, take the commonwealth in hand and surmount all difficulties, as you always do. For either you can cure our ills or else all must give up the attempt." Caesar alone, he said, could "set the whole world in order by land and sea." With his propensity to epigram, Sallustius posed succinctly a thought obsessing Caesar: "Unless you bring about a lasting peace, what mattered victory or defeat?"

Thus with the viewpoint of the country squires and of other men of moderate property, the elements among whom Caesar enjoyed his firmest support, Sallustius exposed the general lines of Caesar's policy: clemency for the defeated, curbs on the adventurers among his own partisans, avoidance of radical reforms, restraint of profligacy and political corruption and the inauguration of an imperial rather than a city-state approach to problems. In proclaiming the utter dependence of the commonwealth upon the actions and statesmanship of a single man, Sallustius was not indulging in sycophancy but was expressing a general belief of a population weary of civil war and of domestic dissensions and seeing no faction or other leadership capable of establishing lasting peace, achieving reconstruction and instituting belated, essential reforms.

Very likely at the time of the Sallustius epistle, Philodemos, the philosopher-poet and companion of Caesar's father-in-law Calpurnius, published an apology for Caesar's autocracy entitled On the Good King, a treatise directed to fellow Epicureans—an influential segment of the propertied classes. Extrapolating from the Homeric epics the Bard's prescriptions for a benevolent ruler, Philodemos by implication praised Caesar as the fulfilment of the Homeric ideal. In his catalogue of Homeric royal virtues: magnanimity, intellect, willingness to accept advice, military genius and leadership ability, readers would inevitably think of Caesar. In his private life, Homer's good ruler was abstemious (Caesar's moderation at the table was well known), discreet in his love affairs (as was Caesar, by contemporary standards) and unstinting in clemency and benevolence (cardinal Caesarian virtues). Philodemos posed as the principal responsibility of the ideal monarch the establishment of ataraxia, an Epicurean term that could be translated into such political terms as "tranquility," "peace" and "security" (Caesar's stated aims in the civil war).[10]

With Balbus, Oppius and Matius, Caesar analyzed the sentiments and aspirations of the various elements of the population and evolved strategies for winning goodwill or appeasing discontent. To eliminate the threat of disorders among the urban plebs, Caesar dissolved Clodius' political ward collegia and authorized the continuation of only the long-established professional and community associations, singling out as exceptions to his decree the disciples of Isis and Osiris, persecuted by the optimates before the civil war, the Dionysiacs (also with a large following among the people) and, of course, the Jews. In proposing legislation, he ignored the tribal assembly, often dominated by mobs bribed for their votes and fists, turning instead to the centuriate assembly controlled by the men of property. He also restricted nominations to the jury panels to senators and equestrians, relying on men he had promoted into the two aristocratic orders to outvote his opponents. He abolished provocatio, the right of appeal to the people in capital cases, a right he had often defended against the optimates, on the rationale that with the election of jurors, the people required no special protection against the courts.

In the city Caesar confronted seemingly overwhelming problems. Few tenements had been constructed since a huge conflagration had ravaged entire districts a few years earlier. Concerned only with achieving a maximum rate of profit, landlords milked buildings without maintaining them, and the housing shortage grew daily more critical. Debt and unemployment posed other burdens. Thousands, resigned to living on the dole and handouts, spent their days at barbarous spectacles in which both men and beasts were slaughtered or sought solace in mystical cults promising a paradise in an afterlife or wasted their lives otherwise in loafing, violence and crime. Sallustius denounced the dole as "a reward of idleness." During the recent turmoil, the list of recipients of free grain had been swollen through fraud until the appropriation for the program had climbed to 75 million sesterces annually. Caesar established new criteria for eligibility, ordered a census by district and tenement block and arbitrarily reduced the number of recipients from three hundred and twenty thousand (almost the entire free male population) to one hundred and fifty thousand. Pending the development of long-range programs for relieving the misery of the poor and ending generational poverty, Caesar provided distributions of grain and oil and a donation of 400 sesterces to each citizen (a hundred more than he had promised during the first year of the civil war and the equivalent of more than three months' wages for a laborer). By granting his veterans bonuses of 20 thousand sesterces, an unprecedented sum, Caesar assured their prosperity during their readjustment to civilian life and for years thereafter. Offering prizes for large families, Caesar inaugurated a population policy designed to check the alarming decline in the Italian birthrate. He passed a bill securing boundary stones of smallholders against encroachments by great landowners, and to provide employment to the rural poor and to decrease the threat of violence from armed slaves, he decreed that owners of herds hire free men as at least one half of their shepherds.

In Egypt Caesar had observed the results of make-work programs in the construction of temples and pyramids as well as in the building and maintenance of irrigation works, canals and handsome public buildings. In his as yet uncompleted projects at Rome Caesar was providing employment on a small scale. Now he and his aides drafted plans to put tens of thousands to work in the city and throughout Italy. The Senate assigned him the responsibility of building a new Senate house in place of the one burned down after Clodius' death. He also undertook to reorder the old Forum. Affording employment for thousands were his projects of dredging the harbor at Ostia to accommodate larger vessels and of draining the Pomptine marshes, which extended some forty miles along the coast south of Rome. With this project Caesar would make available a vast tract of land for settlement and encourage commerce through the construction of a canal connecting the Tiber with a deep-water port at Terracina—a canal as ambitious as those linking Alexandria with the Nile and the Nile with the Red Sea. With this undertaking, too, Caesar would relieve a major health threat, for the marshes exuded "mala aria," "a heavy pestilent moisture." Varro advised farmers living near swamp land to "see that the stead does not face in the direction from which the infected wind usually comes," warning that "in the neighborhood of swamps . . . there are bred certain minute creatures which cannot be seen by the eyes, which float in the air and enter the body through the mouth and nose and hereby cause serious diseases." Caesar also planned to tunnel into a large mountain lake in central Italy for an increase in the city water supply, an operation that would afford employment to thirty thousand for more than a decade. In addition, he planned the construction of additional roads in the peninsula. As supervisors for these projects he could assign officers and legionaries who had acquired skills in building the Rhine bridges and in constructing siege works in his various campaigns.[11]

To avoid the nearly disastrous disruption of property relations in Sulla's confiscations and colonization schemes, Caesar offered veterans plots out of lands confiscated from Pompeians who had died in battle or were still in arms as well as from public lands and from his personal properties. For the thousands of civilians deprived of the dole Caesar drafted plans for overseas colonization unprecedented in scope and organized with a rationality and humanity unknown in previous history (and rarely, if ever, matched subsequently). Entire legions were to be dispatched under their officers to Cisalpina, Transalpina and to Africa. They would be joined by landless Italians. Greek-speaking Romans, primarily freedmen or descendants of freedmen, were to be sent to the Greek-speaking East, to colonies at Corinth and in devastated regions of Asia Minor and Syria and as far off as Sinope, once Mithridates' capital on the south shore of the Black Sea, more than a thousand miles from Rome. With this enormous movement of populations Caesar would provide an impetus to the Romanization of the empire, strengthen the security in areas of doubtful loyalty (rendering less likely the necessity of repacification campaigns) and promote commerce and industry, especially in war-ravaged or otherwise depopulated areas. For this mammoth effort (eventually to involve eighty thousand civilians or some ten per cent of the population of Rome)* logistical organization was many times more complex than for the greatest military operation until that time. Governors in the provinces had to assemble teams of surveyors, accountants, clerks and technicians for establishing plot assignments; they had to arrange for the feeding and housing of settlers and the provision of tools, draft animals and seed. Thousands of transports (including naval vessels freed from war duty) would be required for the settlers, their possessions and provisions. Way stations would have to be established for stops on journeys that might take months of hardship and suffering. Organizers for each colony interviewed and registered applicants, held orientation meetings and arranged for transport, accommodations and supplies and for the selection of a mix of craftsmen and workers, separating those able to wrest a living from the soil from those better adapted to town life. To inspire greater enthusiasm among the freedmen, Caesar granted them the right to hold magistracies in the new communities, a right denied them in Italy.

The excitement and ferment and the extraordinary sense of community evoked in this momentous enterprise can hardly be imagined; contemporaries who left accounts of that time and the historians who followed them were not impressed with a program that concerned primarily the poor (or the contractors who stood to gain huge profits). It was a program not only of little interest but even suspect to people like Cicero (whose sole concern in regard to this historic action was to safeguard Atticus' investments in a region where a colony was planned).

Simultaneously, to accelerate the integration of the western provinces into the commonwealth, Caesar granted limited citizenship in the Province and in Sicily, providing these dependencies with new protection against rapacious

---

*For a comparable effort in the twentieth century, the United States would have to settle seven hundred thousand New Yorkers receiving public assistance as far away as Alaska and Hawaii.

Roman officials and setting them on a course to the full citizenship already awarded the Transpadanes. Caesar also had the Senate ratify his treaties guaranteeing the Jews extraterritorial rights throughout the empire, and he set a copy of these treaties, engraved on bronze tablets, on the Capitol.

To establish Rome as an imperial center of culture and learning, a rival to Alexandria, Caesar appointed Varro (as a gesture of reconciliation the learned polymath had dedicated to Caesar a major opus on Roman religious traditions) to serve as Rome's first librarian, charged with assembling comprehensive collections of Greek and Latin manuscripts. Further to stimulate the intellectual life of the city, Caesar offered citizenship to teachers and physicians who would settle in Rome.

The new imperial era required a scientific calendar. Throughout the Mediterranean even small towns recorded time with local calendars. Rome's lunar calendar, inefficient, subject to political manipulation, not readjusted for years, lagged ninety days behind the sun. Holidays were falling out of season, and Romans experienced inconveniences in many aspects of life. Caesar established a commission to submit recommendations to the Alexandrian astronomer and mathematician Sosigenes. Upon completion of this effort, Caesar decreed the insertion of two intercalary months totaling sixty-three days between November and December. Since in February of that year, 46, Caesar had already added a standard intercalary month, he now synchronized the calendar with the sun, and for the coming year he instituted for the entire Mediterranean world a solar calendar in which seven months had thirty-one days, the remaining months thirty, apart from February, sacred to the gods of the underworld, which remained unchanged at twenty-eight except for leap years. On January 1, 45, for the first time in many years, the Roman calendar matched the solar calendar—and forever thereafter (except for a minor revision instituted during the Renaissance). To publicize the new calendar Caesar issued an almanac, Concerning the Stars, with advice for planting, harvesting and other agricultural activities.

RECONCILIATION

Preoccupied with so many projects, Caesar chafed at diversions, especially resenting the time he devoted to problems of personal dignity, influence and profit. No matter how often he reiterated and demonstrated his commitment to a policy of clemency, oligarchs, disgruntled at their loss of influence and exclusion from his varied projects (for which, in any event, they expressed minimal enthusiasm), continued to mutter that with his autocratic power Caesar could reverse himself at any juncture and institute proscriptions and confiscations. They pointed to sabotage of his clemency policy by disgruntled members of his own party as well as to Caesar's refusal to proclaim a general amnesty for exiled foes who had opposed him most stubbornly.

To eliminate all doubts as to his dedication to a policy of reconciliation, Caesar mounted a theatrical coup. One day in the Senate Calpurnius rose and appealed to Caesar to recall Marcus Marcellus from exile. As consul in 51, Marcellus had initiated the attack on Caesar that eventually culminated in the civil war. After Pharsalus he had withdrawn to Mitylene on the island of Lesbos, resolved never to beg for mercy from Caesar. Upon Calpurnius' plea, Gaius Marcellus, cousin to the exile and husband of Caesar's grandniece Octavia (as consul in 49 Gaius had retired into hostile neutrality in Italy), "flung himself at Caesar's feet and the Senate, as it had previously arranged to do, rose in a body and approached Caesar with an air of supplication."[12] Caesar feigned bewilderment and protested that he had intelligence of plots against his life and feared to recall such an implacable foe. Nevertheless, he declared, he would not pose his personal safety against the general will, and he called upon the senators one by one to advise him, in effect, rendering each responsible for his security in the event of Marcellus' return.

Caesar's charade proved more successful than he could have anticipated. Cicero, who since returning to Rome had remained aloof in Senate debates and other public business and had dismissed his laurel-wreathed lictors, rejecting Caesar's offer of a triumph, rose and declared himself overwhelmed by "Caesar's magnanimity and the Senate's devotion." Comparing Caesar "not to the greatest of men, but to a god," he delivered a panegyric surpassing in adulation the praise he had lavished on Caesar during their earlier close friendship. So moved was he by Caesar's clemency to an unrepentent enemy that he associated himself with Caesar's view of the civil war, alleging that the Pompeians for the most part had been "induced to enter the war rather by ignorance and by a false and groundless apprehension." He avowed that since Caesar's victory "in the city we have never seen the sword bared of its scabbard," whereas "the universal fears would have been realized in the passionate excesses that would have attended [a Pompeian] victory." Like Sallustius, he reminded Caesar that he had not completed his task. "If this city is never to be tranquilized by your measures and your institutions," he warned, "the passage of your name to the ends of the earth will be but a wayward roaming." As to Caesar's fears of assassination plots, speaking for all the senators, Cicero promised "not merely sentinels and bodyguards but the shelter that our own breasts can afford."[13]

Thus in his first speech since his return to Rome, Cicero, like Sallustius and Philodemos, was, in effect, acclaiming Caesar as "the good, wise and skilful guardian and protector" who should, according to Cicero's treatise On the Republic published five years earlier, "maintain the safety of the state both by counsel and by action." Cicero called upon Caesar "to reanimate all that you see shattered and laid low as was inevitable by the shock of the war itself; courts of law must be set on foot, licentiousness must be checked and the growth of population fostered; all that has become disintegrated and dissipated must be knit together by stringent regulation."[14]

Following up this unexpected triumph, Caesar offered Cicero the privilege of serving as chief intermediary for suppliant Pompeians and staged a second pageant to assure aristocrats still in arms in Spain of his readiness to grant them clemency. Cicero accepted the defense of a certain Ligarius, the first

Pompeian exile indicted on a capital charge. "What is to prevent our hearing a speech from Cicero after all this while," exclaimed Caesar with delight, "since Ligarius has long since been adjudged a villain and an enemy?"[15]

Before Caesar in a crowded Forum, Cicero performed with his old virtuosity. He pleaded for Ligarius, charged with war crimes, as for a wayward child and appealed to Caesar as "before a father" to repeat for the people the clemency he had exhibited to Marcellus for the Senate. "Nothing is so dear to the people as kindness," declared Cicero, speaking as though an old "popular." Cicero succeeded in "moving his hearers beyond measure, and his speech, as it proceeded, showed varying pathos and amazing grace. Caesar's face often changed color and it was manifest that all the emotions of his soul were stirred; and at last, when the orator touched upon the struggles at Pharsalus, he was so greatly affected that his body shook and he dropped from his hand some of his documents." Caesar acquitted Ligarius, and former optimates were remarking in the Forum, at the baths and at dinner parties how he was "moving insensibly towards a position of equipoise and the natural order of things." They congratulated each other that "every day . . . fears are falsified by some unexpectedly mild and liberal measures." Nevertheless, Caesar had had much experience with the vacillation of his former enemies, and he had no illusions that he resolved fundamental problems by dramatic spectacles. Stability, he knew, is an illusion; an inexorable dynamic is ever at work:

> Neither can death-dealing motions lord it forever and forever bury existence, nor further can motions that generate and give increase to things forever preserve them when made. Thus war waged from infinity on the first beginnings [atoms] is carried on with doubtful issue: now here, now there the vital elements gain the mastery and in like manner are mastered.[16]

For the moment it appeared that Caesar had gained mastery at Rome. In fact, he had achieved "doubtful issue."

LIII

"EVERLASTING CONFLICT . . ."

DURING the very days Caesar was securing his hegemony and engaging at last in the constructive work of peace, couriers brought news of new wars. In the East a Pompeian officer named Bassus had roused a mutiny against Caesar's cousin Sextus, whom Caesar had left in charge of Syria; and when Herod, son of Antipater, Caesar's appointee as Procurator of Judea, arrived with a relief army, he discovered that Sextus had been assassinated. With Bassus rousing Pompeius' former clients throughout the East and appealing to the king of Parthia for assistance, Caesar ordered Cornificius, now governor of Cilicia in Asia Minor, to march against the rebel. In the West Caesar's admiral had routed the rebel fleet, but Pedius, Caesar's nephew, and Fabius Maximus, pressed hard on land by Pompeius' two sons and the fugitives from Africa, begged Caesar to come quickly to Further Spain.

In the four years since he had crossed the Rubicon, indeed in the thirteen years since his first campaign in Gaul, Caesar had scarcely known a day without war. Every "decisive" victory had proved a prelude to a new campaign, and even during his "peaceful" sojourns at Rome he had been badgered by intrigues and, recently, by assassination plots. He found himself as tempest-tossed as Lucretius' atoms:

> in everlasting conflict, struggling, fighting, battling in troops without any pause, driven about with frequent meetings and partings . . . the first-beginning of things [atoms] . . . ever tossed about in the great void.

Romans knew nothing of Caesar's weariness. Ever astonished at the speed and multiplicity of his accomplishments, they took for granted his "native vigor and quickness, winged as it were with fire" and related with wonder anecdotes about his ability to "write or read and dictate or listen simultaneously and to dictate to his secretaries four letters at once." People were amazed at how after uninterrupted conferences, discussions, debates, consultations—reading, dictating, talking, listening, questioning—Caesar maintained unflagging attention to details of the manifold problems referred to him. Even former enemies praised him for his "sobriety and justice and wisdom."[1]

Ever vain of his appearance (his handsomeness, he said, evidenced his descent from Venus), in his mirror Caesar saw mortality—a scraggly neck, distended Adam's apple, pointed chin, tense lips, beaked nose, jutting cheekbones, puffs under the eyes, wrinkled forehead and wisps of lifeless hair. At fifty-five, at the zenith of his power, Caesar found himself lapsing into the state "when the body is . . . wracked with the mighty strength of time and the frame has succumbed with blunted strength, the intellect limps, the tongue babbles, the intelligence totters, all is awanting and fails at the same time . . . the spirit . . . falling to pieces." Driving himself unsparingly, always with the expectation of someday devoting himself to constructive effort, he now learned he would have to pacify for a second time provinces at the two ends of the Mediterranean. The exhaustion at the prospect evoked Epicurean questions:

> What is this great and evil lust of life that drives us to be agitated amidst doubt and peril? . . . While we have not what we crave, that seems to surpass all else; afterwards when we have attained that, we crave something else.

He who had accomplished so much in life against perpetual challenges now entertained Epicurean counsel about retirement from struggle:

If your former life now past has been to your liking, if it is not true that all your
blessings have been gathered as it were into a riddled jar and have run through and
been lost without gratification; why not like a banqueter fed full of life withdraw
with contentment and rest in peace?

Frequently Caesar was remarking to associates, "I have lived long enough
either for nature or for glory." Reports of his despair dismayed even former
Pompeians, men who only recently had been conspiring at his death. They
looked to him to protect them from young Gnaeus Pompeius, who, they declared among themselves, "deems cruelty a virtue . . . in his boorish way . . .
inclined to reply [to the defection of former comrades-in-arms] by wiping
[their] noses with the sword." After Pharsalus the young Pompeius had threatened to kill Cicero for counseling surrender. Now in the Senate Cicero exclaimed to Caesar: "What man on earth is there so ignorant of life, so unversed
in politics, so utterly careless of his own well-being and that of the community,
as not to realize that his own well-being is bound up in yours and that on your
sole life hang the lives of all?" Aware that in expressing his readiness for death
Caesar was echoing the Epicureans, Cicero went on to appeal: "Speak not to
us of the wisdom of philosophers who make light of death; let it not be at our
peril that you play the sage. . . . So far are you from consummating your
chiefest labors that you have not yet laid the foundation of all your plans."[2]

This anxiety regarding Caesar's security represented, of course, mere opportunism. Convinced at least for the moment of Caesar's commitment to clemency and his revulsion at vindictive punishments of opponents, optimates
grumbled openly at any clumsiness from their harried protector. They professed outrage, for example, at his summoning a venerable poet named Laberius, an equestrian, to compete in verse with a Syrian-born freedman. By
appearing on the stage an equestrian automatically forfeited his enrolment in
the order, and the optimates applauded when the aged poet attacked Caesar in
a song in praise of Necessity: "To what depths has she thrust me down, now
all but at the ending of my life? I, whom no soliciting, no bribe, no threat, no
violence, no influence could ever have moved from my rank when I was young,
see how easily I am made to fall from my place now, in my old age, by a man of
high position." To the audience Laberius cried: "O citizens of Rome, we lose
our liberty!" and turning to Caesar he warned, "Many he needs must fear
whom many fear."[3]

Recognizing a serious lapse in tact, Caesar, with characteristic graciousness,
awarded Laberius a gold ring as a token of his reinstatement in the equestrian
order along with a munificent gift of 500 thousand sesterces. Caesar enjoyed a
good witticism, and he could guffaw at a humorous exchange immediately
after this ruckus. When the poet returned to the rows of the theater reserved
for the aristocracy, "everyone huddled up so as not to let the newcomer in." As
Laberius passed, Cicero sent a message reading, "I should have let you in, but I
was rather cramped in my seat"—a snide allusion to Caesar's numerous ap-

pointments to the senatorial and equestrian orders. "Yet," replied Laberius to the notorious trimmer, "you generally sit on two seats."[4]

Caesar sought to soothe hurt feelings of the impotent optimates, but he suffered no mutinous disaffection from veterans whom he was about to call out to yet another "final" campaign. When troops discovered that he had stretched silken awnings in a theater against the sun, they rioted at his squandering of monies they insisted should have been distributed among them. Caesar seized one of the demonstrators along with two ringleaders and brought them in solemn procession with the pontifices and the priest of Mars to the Campus Martius, where he sacrificed them in place of the animal in the ancient ritual of the October Horse.

As for himself, even as he had quickly restored his spirits after the death of his daughter, so now he recalled himself to new effort. Had not Homer permitted his indomitable hero to give vent to tears and to complain that "the sweet days of his life time / were running out in anguish over his exile"? Nevertheless, steeling himself, Odysseus proclaimed to the nymph Calypso:

> If any god has marked me out again
> for shipwreck, my tough heart can undergo it.
> What hardship have I not long since endured
> at sea, in battle! Let the trial come.[5]

SPAIN—THE SECOND PACIFICATION

In the second intercalary month of 46 (November by the solar year), some nine months after Thapsus and little more than five months after his return to Rome, Caesar departed for Spain. As the springless coach jolted along the paving stones or lurched in mire or groaned up steep inclines, Caesar, chary of losing a moment, dictated a verse account of his trip, The Journey, a description of the countryside, the people and the vicissitudes of the road across the Province—"easy to travel in summer [but] muddy and also flooded by the rivers in winter . . . some of the streams crossed by ferries, others by bridges—some made of timber and others stone."[6] In twenty-seven days Caesar reached Obulco, not far from Corduba, so surprising Pedius and Fabius by his speed that they failed to dispatch cavalry to escort him through hostile territory. Immediately Caesar ordered a force to the relief of a loyal town under siege by Gnaeus Pompeius, while he himself advanced on Corduba, a stronghold occupied by Gnaeus' younger brother, Sextus. Caesar had no illusions about the current struggle. Over the centuries wars in Spain had always been ferocious. Furthermore, here in contrast to Africa, where the optimates had alienated the population by their marauding, a governor appointed by Caesar had committed outrages, rousing to rebellion all the elements that had once supported Sulla and fought against Sertorius. Moneylenders recalled measures Caesar had introduced as governor to relieve the debtors; and old settlers, his grant of

citizenship to Punic Gades. Nor would these rebels capitulate without a ferocious struggle. Local oligarchs who had promoted the uprising against Caesar's governor and invited Gnaeus Pompeius to assume command over their
revolt had heard of the heavy indemnities Caesar had imposed on his enemies
in Africa. Fugitives like Labienus would not accept mercy from Caesar. In
addition, the morale of the rebels had been bolstered by successes against
Caesar's lieutenants, and they were confident of their defenses. Heavily fortified towns perched atop steep hills would have to be assaulted one by one by
legionaries with no stamina for prolonged sieges.

On the other hand, only four of the enemy's thirteen legions were battle
worthy. Others had been assembled out of runaway slaves and adventurers.
Though inferior in numbers, Caesar's army was superior in quality as well as
in light-armed auxiliaries and cavalry, and he could draw upon the entire
empire for reinforcements and supplies. He could also count upon the arrogance, greed and unstable morale among his foes to antagonize the civilian
population. Labienus, however, was aware of the feverish mood of Caesar's
legionaries, and the rebels tantalized Caesar's troops by avoiding decisive encounters and needling them with raids and ambushes. With Caesar's men
enraged and the Pompeians desperate, neither side granted quarter. Prisoners
were summarily beheaded, runaway slaves crucified and captured messengers
had their hands lopped off.

At Rome former Pompeians once again were reassessing their loyalties. Arriving in January, Caesar's devoted councilor Pansa reported that in the city
enemies were saying that "though the results of battles are always uncertain,
on this occasion so great are the forces on each side and so well equipped . . .
that nobody will be surprised which of the two commanders proves the victor." Cicero, who only months earlier had been proclaiming his readiness to
defend Caesar's life with his own and advising other aristocrats that "we
should do nothing but what we think Caesar most desires," now was asserting
that in the current struggle the choice seemed to be massacre in the event of
Gnaeus Pompeius' victory or slavery under Caesar. To guarantee his security
in the event of a Pompeian victory, he published a treatise undisguisedly hostile
to Caesar. He had written the work months earlier with the intention of
demonstrating his sympathy to the optimates in case of a rebel victory in
Africa, but he was forestalled in publishing it by news of Caesar's victory at
Thapsus. Thereafter, while he was praising Caesar and begging Caesar not to
give way to despair, he had held it in reserve. Upon Caesar's departure from
Rome and under the protection of Marcus Brutus, to whom he dedicated the
treatise, he issued the work. A survey of Roman eloquence, the book appeared
innocent enough, but by lauding Caesar's enemies (many of them as yet unde-
feated at the time of composition) Cicero proclaimed his opposition to Caesar
and offered himself as a leader of a new party of resistance. He exhorted
Brutus to follow the example of his tyrannicide forbears, a Brutus "who drove
from the state a powerful king . . . and freeing it from the domination of an

absolute ruler fixed its constitution by establishing annual magistrates, laws and courts" (a jibe at Caesar's appointment of consuls for short terms, his control of legislation and domination of the courts); and a Servilius (a maternal ancestor of Brutus') who murdered a man accused of aspiring to tyranny for distributing grain among the starving commons. In a scarcely disguised appeal to Brutus to assume leadership of a rebellion against Caesar, Cicero declared, "We crave such a constitution of public affairs as shall make it possible for you to maintain the fame of two great houses and add to them a new luster."[7]

Confident of Brutus' loyalty both because of his faith in Brutus' mother, Servilia, and because of the young man's declarations, Caesar had appointed Brutus governor of Cisalpine Gaul though by law Brutus was not eligible to hold such a high post. As for Cicero, Caesar had no doubts that with victory in Spain the orator would again sing his praises.

The task at hand, in any case, was the war. Caesar moved against Ategua, the main supply depot of the rebels and a key enemy stronghold. Within this natural fortress atop a steep mountain, the garrison, like garrisons in many towns, was hampered by the presence of a sizable pro-Caesar faction. One day the commandant paraded a line of civilians on the wall and announcing the names of his victims to Caesar's besieging force he put the "traitors to the sword and flung their bodies from the battlements, including wives of those in [Caesar's] camp. . . . He massacred children in their mothers' arms. The smallest he trampled underfoot or had hurled into the air to be caught on the javelins of the soldiers." After a desperate sortie in an attempt to break through Caesar's siege works, however, the townspeople asked for terms. "As I have behaved to foreign people," Caesar responded, "even so will I show myself to my fellow citizens when they surrender." To a further request for a guarantee of personal security, he replied "that he was Caesar and would keep his word."[8] On February 19, 45, less than two months after his arrival in Spain, Caesar led his troops through the gates of the enemy stronghold.

While besieging Ategua, Caesar received from Rome new compositions by the recalcitrant orator, an encomium on the dead Cato and a technical treatise entitled The Orator. Begun during the African war and completed during the summer but prudently withheld until Caesar's departure for Spain, the Cato work was a pronunciamento for rebellion. Cicero had decided that he could not "properly" eulogize the Man of Virtue if he "kept clear of his speeches in the Senate and his whole political outlook and opinions," and he set out to demonstrate that "that remarkable man . . . foresaw our present situation and strove to avert it and abandoned his life rather than witness it in actuality." In the treatise on the ideal orator published simultaneously with the Cato eulogy, Cicero protested that he had written the Cato eulogy upon Brutus' urging:

I would never have undertaken [this work] through fear of this age so unfriendly to virtue had I not considered it base not to yield when you urged so strongly and kindled the memory of one so dear to me. I call you to witness that it was because you asked me that I dared, albeit reluctantly, to write this book. For I wish that you should share the reproach with me so that if I cannot defend myself against so weighty a charge, you may take the blame for imposing an excessive task on me, as I take the blame for accepting it.[9]

Cicero was testing the limits of Caesar's clemency, inspiring friction between Brutus and Caesar and guaranteeing his own security in the event of a Pompeian victory in Spain.

Caesar understood Cicero's frustration. In praising him for pardoning Marcellus, Cicero had called upon Caesar to restore the antebellum Republic. "This act yet remains to be played," he had declared, "to this you must summon all your powers—to plant the constitution firmly."[10] Cicero, like other oligarchs sharing his sentiments, entertained no interest in, or sympathy for, Caesar's reforms, building projects and vision of a new era; they aspired to a restoration of the old leadership of the Senate with its rivalries, intrigues, corruption, social and political myopia and proclivity to violent repression of opponents.

In the Cato eulogy, rancorous at his own fall from eminence, Cicero wrote not as a historian but as an advocate, as though arguing a case in court, where truth was rarely of consequence. He praised Cato, for example, for "his unwavering constancy," ignoring his own repeated accusations of Cato for pigheaded obstinacy, his despair at Cato's abandonment of him at the time of his exile and his dismay at Cato's sabotage of his mediation efforts before the outbreak of the civil war. Cicero did not decry Cato's folly in continuing the war after Pharsalus when he himself had urged negotiations with Caesar or Cato's bad judgment in nominating Scipio supreme commander in Africa despite Scipio's bloodthirsty threats of proscriptions and confiscations (in which Cicero and his friends would certainly have suffered). Instead, Cicero transformed the acerbic reactionary into a Roman Socrates, a martyr to what the oligarchs called "liberty." Cato himself had invited the comparison, fortifying his resolution before stabbing himself by reading Plato's Phaedo, a dialogue in which Socrates preaches the release of the soul "into the realm of purity and eternity and immortality and unchangeableness." Embellishing the pathos of Cato's suicide, Cicero proclaimed: "When god himself has given a valid reason as he did in the past to Socrates and in our day to Cato . . . then your true wise man will joyfully pass forthwith from the darkness here into the light beyond." With no witnesses present when Cato plunged his sword into his chest, Cicero invented last words for his hero: "Fortune, you have accomplished nothing by resisting all my endeavors. I have fought till now for my country's freedom and not for my own. I did not strive so doggedly to be free but only to live among the free. Now since the affairs of mankind are beyond hope, let Cato be withdrawn to safety."

As for Cato's suicide, extolled by Cicero as the supreme moment of the Stoic's life, Caesar would never die in his bed nor give up his life without a struggle, and he could recount deaths among his own officers and men far more valorous. A quaestor whose life Scipio offered to spare, for example, scoffed that "it was the custom with Caesar's soldiers not to receive but to offer mercy" and plunged his sword into himself, not as he lay on his bed reading Plato but in face-to-face defiance of the enemy.[11]

Preoccupied with more pressing tasks, Caesar entrusted Hirtius, an associate with literary talent, with the task of rebutting Cicero.

Following the fall of Ategua, the enemy leaders, distrustful of their own troops and of the civilian population, engaged in savage repression. Villages blazed from hilltop to hilltop, and deserters streamed into Caesar's camp with tales of atrocities far more savage than those committed by Scipio in Africa. At last on March 17, the fourth anniversary of his father's departure from Italy at the start of the civil war, Gnaeus Pompeius drew up his forces outside the walls of the town of Munda. In response, Caesar displayed the flag of battle, and with his old bodyguard the Xth legion in the place of honor on the right and the IIIrd and Vth on the left, he advanced across a five-mile plain. The Pompeians, more than fifty thousand strong, were positioned atop a steep incline— thirteen legions screened by cavalry, six thousand light-armed troops and an equal number of auxiliaries. In an apparent repetition of his father's strategy at Pharsalus, Gnaeus ordered his men to hold their places, challenging Caesar to attack across a stream and a marsh and then up a slope. Caesar, "observing this . . . began to restrict the area of maneuver in order to avert the danger of a blunder through rashness or error." The legionaries had noted in this campaign that Caesar had become "slower to engage through a conviction that the oftener he had been victor, the less he ought to tempt fate and that he could not possibly gain as much by success as he might lose by a defeat." The troops had heard rumors, too, that at Corduba Caesar had suffered an attack of the sacred disease (epilepsy). Now, when the men saw how Caesar was restraining them from advancing, "they were very annoyed and bitter because in their view they were being hindered from bringing the fight to an issue," and once again, as at Thapsus a year earlier, they disregarded his orders. "The shout was raised and the battle joined."[12]

Though outnumbered and handicapped by the sharp incline, the legionaries pinned down the Pompeians with javelins and artillery. The Xth, reduced to only a few hundred men after almost fifteen years of campaigning, fought with especial gallantry. Nevertheless, the enemy's numbers and advantageous position began to tell, and Caesar's army wavered. Throwing off his helmet to reveal himself, Caesar seized a shield and raced down the line and at the top of his voice demanded of his men "whether they felt no shame to take him and put him in the hands of these boys [Pompeius' sons]," and he exhorted them, crying, "This shall be the end of my life and of your military service." Grouping themselves about their commander, centurions and military tribunes burst into the fray. The combat turned grim. "Neither sound of paean nor groan was to be heard . . . but both sides merely shouted 'Strike! Kill!' " At last with a strange irony, Fortune chose Labienus, the treacherous defector, as her instrument. "All would have perished or at nightfall they would have parted with honors even, had not Bogud [an African king and Caesar's ally], who was somewhere outside the conflict, set out for Pompeius' camp, whereupon Labienus, observing this, left his station and proceeded against him. Pompeius' men, then, supposing him to be in flight, lost heart. . . . Some fled to the city and some to the rampart."[13] Caesar's legionaries advanced to the carnage. They heaped up captured shields and javelins as a palisade around the town and piled corpses and bodies of the dying as a rampart about the wall and ranged heads on sword points atop these strange siegeworks. They brought Caesar thirteen legionary eagles and a vast collection of varied insignia along with the heads of Labienus and of other leading Pompeians, but Gnaeus Pompeius' was not among them.

Leaving a siege force at Munda, Caesar sped off to Corduba. At his arrival sounds of rioting were heard within the walls, and when the garrison set fire to the town Caesar's men burst through the gates and massacred the enemy troops.

Sextus Pompeius escaped to a warlike tribe in the hinterland, but Caesar's admiral bottled Gnaeus in the port of Carteia (some four miles from Gibraltar) and then tracked him, wounded in the leg and unable to walk, to a cave and killed him. On April 12 Gnaeus' head arrived at Hispalis (near Seville) and was posted in the forum. Here Caesar came to deliver a victory address.

The wealthy men who had promoted the rebellion, ranchers, owners of sprawling estates and mine operators accustomed to lording it over private armies of slaves, would not easily be pacified. These men vied in displaying masculine vigor and mistook effrontery for valor. They saw themselves as princes, and after Caesar's victory at Munda, one of the ringleaders of the initial mutiny mounted a theatrical suicide with all the pretensions of an oriental potentate: "He summoned his slaves and freedmen, had himself built a lofty pyre and ordered a banquet to be served on the most lavish possible scale and the finest tapestries likewise to be spread out . . . he presented his slaves with money and silver. . . . In due course he fell to upon the banquet and . . . anointed himself with resin and nard. . . . At the latest possible moment, he bade a slave and a freedman—the latter was his catamite—the one to cut his throat, the other to light the pyre."[14]

Whether Caesar could compel such arrogant provincials to yield indefinitely was moot. At Hispalis, he recalled his benefactions as quaestor and governor of Further Spain and upbraided his audience for their rebelliousness and especially for inviting Gnaeus Pompeius to "seize the rods of office and military power for himself." As though bewildered at their unreason, he chided the rebels. "Did you not realize," he asked, "that even if I were destroyed, the Roman people has legions which could not only stop you but could even bring the skies tumbling down about you?"[15] Caesar's officers knew that this statement represented a delusion. Without Caesar, no skies would come tumbling down. Caesar himself had had experience enough to know it. Although he had always acted as though men made history, some men more than others, now, despite these bold words, Caesar was coming to realize that, in fact, in the current balance of forces within the empire, it was doubtful that without him the Roman people could bring the skies tumbling down. It was equally doubtful that they could do so with him.

At Rome Cicero's eulogy of Cato created more of a stir than anticipated. Others, including Brutus, followed with additional eulogies, and Hirtius' rebuttal, reflecting the indignation at Caesar's headquarters, failed. His blackening of the character of the Man of Virtue rebounded, and Cicero urged Atticus to disseminate Hirtius' work as a weapon for the opposition party. Caesar was compelled to issue his own reply, a hastily composed two-volume Anti-Cato. He had effective arguments to cite—instances when the Stoic acted upon the pettiest of motivations, even with obtuse vindictiveness; his abandonment of principle to benefit a relative or to gain advantage in a factional conflict and his antagonizing with "his arrogance, haughtiness and tyranny . . . investing himself with the powers of Senate, courts and magistrates." Often Cato had provoked Caesar to intemperance, and now Caesar was carried away by passion. Though he mocked Cato's addiction to wine with such finesse as to seem to be praising him for his fault, he dealt clumsily with matters like Cato's surrender of his wife to Hortensius and remarriage to her after Hortensius' death. "Why," Caesar sneered, "should Cato give up his wife if he wanted her, or why, if he did not want her, should he take her back again? Unless it was true that the woman was at the first set as a bait for Hortensius and lent by Cato when she was young that he might take her back when she was rich [with a legacy from the wealthy orator]?"[16] If true, this accusation was paltry, and its inclusion in the tirade made it appear that Caesar lacked arguments of substance against his enemy.

Caesar failed with his Anti-Cato, but he did succeed in bringing Cicero to heel. Recalling Cicero's alarm after Pharsalus at reports that his brother and nephew were denouncing him, Caesar now instructed various officers to inform Cicero of how young Quintus Cicero, serving on Caesar's staff, was charging at every opportunity that his orator uncle was "thoroughly hostile to Caesar and not to be trusted" and calling him "actually dangerous." Pretending to sympathize, each of these correspondents assured Cicero of their support. Of Caesar's reaction to Quintus' tirades, however, they gave no word. Further to confuse Cicero, in a letter to Balbus, Caesar expressed admiration for Cicero's eulogy of Cato, declaring that "reading and rereading it [had] improved his powers of expression, whereas after reading Brutus' Cato he [had begun] to fancy himself a writer."[17] On the content of Cicero's work Caesar made no comment. On the other hand, to demonstrate that he would not permit political differences to interfere with their personal friendship, at a report of the death in childbirth of Cicero's daughter, a grief Caesar understood, Caesar sent Cicero a letter of condolence.

After these threats and blandishments, Caesar demanded proof of the orator's submission. At his instructions Balbus and Oppius suggested to Atticus that Caesar would welcome a letter of political counsel from Cicero, a document like Sallustius' two open letters. Caesar was offering Cicero an opportunity to display his eloquence and political acumen as a second Aristotle with a new Alexander. In drafting the document, Cicero would confront and evaluate his own policies during his career on issues like land reform, extension of the franchise and amnesty for political dissidents. In addition, he would investigate the implications of Caesar's reforms, his building projects and program of colonization and explore the import of his own injunction to Caesar the previous fall in his speech on Marcellus' pardon: "It is the welfare of the community, it is the whole range of public life that your achievements have embraced; so far are you from consummating your chiefest labors that you have not yet laid the foundation of all your plans."[18] Finally, Cicero would reexamine what he had meant in his work On the Republic regarding the need for an arbiter to resolve critical commonwealth problems.

Apprehending Caesar's intentions and helpless to refuse the request, Cicero fell into despair. For a letter that he drafted, Balbus and Oppius suggested so many changes (part of the reeducation process) that Cicero was beside himself with grief. Despite urging from Brutus, he could not bring himself to draft another letter. He was shrewd enough to sense that Caesar would be as impatient with his nostalgia for the republic of the days of Scipio Africanus as was Alexander, the empire builder, with Aristotle's preachments about the ideal city-state. Cicero did muster sufficient will, however, to write a letter complimenting Caesar on the Anti-Cato, and he was relieved when Balbus and Oppius declared that they had "never read anything better."[19] In effect, never having expected anything significant from Cicero in a letter of counsel to Caesar, they were content with any clear statement of capitulation from the orator. For the moment and without hullabaloo, Cicero had been curbed.

GROOMING AN HEIR

One day at Carteia a frail and careworn youth appeared at the door. Caesar leaped up. It was Octavius. His mother had refused to allow him to accompany Caesar on the African campaign, and illness had kept him from traveling to Spain with his great-uncle. Upon recuperating he set out with a few companions and suffered shipwreck on the way. Caesar embraced the young man and established him in his own billets, set him on his own dining couch and kept him constantly at his side.

Rome had long wondered whom Caesar would choose as his heir—whether Antonius, now out of favor; Sempronia's son, Caesar's capable legate, Decimus Brutus; or Marcus Brutus, Servilia's son. Then suddenly Caesar had begun heaping honors on Octavius, a blood relative, intelligent, disciplined and affable, simple in his tastes and like Caesar sparing in his use of wine. A good student, he copied out precepts in his reading. Like Caesar, and perhaps in imitation of Caesar, he cultivated a chaste and clear style in speaking and writing. His mother had trained him in the old virtues, and he was unsophisticated about the vices of the fast set at Rome, and, unlike men of Antonius' generation, he was young enough to be groomed in Caesar's ways and policies. Caesar permitted the young man to intercede in favor of provincials, enabling him to begin to assemble an overseas clientship. He exposed Octavius to his program of reconciliation and to his policy of attacking foes in their money chests rather than in their persons. He explained his attempt to promote the economic recovery of Further Spain by ramifying the Via Herculea, the highway from the Pyrenees to Gades, by monetary reforms and by providing security in hostile areas through the establishment of colonies of veterans. (In confirmation of his political supremacy, Caesar gave new settlements the Julian name except for Carisa Aurelia, named in memory of his mother.)

Upon sailing north to Tarraco (Tarragona), Caesar received petitions and settled the affairs of the less Romanized (and more loyal) province of Nearer Spain. At Emporion (Ampurias), an ancient Massiliot colony at the foothills of the Pyrenees, he established a veterans colony in order to reinforce the Roman influence in the region. As in Further Spain, he rewarded loyal communities with limited franchise. As they progressed through the Province, Octavius saw the enthusiastic reception Caesar received everywhere. Caesar rewarded Gauls who had supported him in the civil war, conscious that he could not have triumphed without their aid. He singled out individuals for special honors and granted communities limited citizenship pursuant to his policy of assimilating deserving Romanized towns into a close relationship with the metropolis. Caesar conferred with Tiberius Nero (father of the future emperor), an admiral during the Egyptian war, who was founding colonies of veterans in the Province. At Narbo (Narbonne) Caesar bade farewell to the survivors of the Xth legion, men with whom he had shared life and death for so many years. His leave-taking represented the closing of an era, and both he and his comrades understood that no longer would they rally at his command. They were finishing out their years close to the frontier of the vast territory they and he had conquered. At Arelate (Arles) Caesar took leave of the VIth legion, veterans not only of Gaul but also of Egypt and Asia Minor. For the capital of all Gaul, Caesar fixed on Lugdunum (Lyons) in the territory of the Allobroges, Caesar's particular ally among the Gauls.

As Caesar approached Italy, he encountered Romans who had hastened from the city to accompany him on the last stage of his journey. Many came in hope of preferment, but Caesar could not question the devotion of a Decimus Brutus or a Trebonius, the two victors over Massilia, or of Marcus Brutus, about whose fairness in administering Cisalpina Caesar had heard gratifying reports. Among these men was a contrite and wary Antonius. Almost two years had elapsed since Caesar excluded him from his inner council. Now Caesar had a guarantor for Antonius' future behavior, for Antonius had married the widow of two successive allies of Caesar's, Clodius and Curio—Fulvia, a woman capable of taming the flamboyant roué. Caesar had heard the tale about how on his hasty return to Rome in the spring, Antonius arrived at night disguised as a slave and announced that he carried a letter for Fulvia. "Fulvia in great distress before taking the letter asked whether Antonius was still alive; and he, after handing her the letter without a word, as she began to open and read it, threw his arms about her and kissed her." Not a woman to dawdle all morning with a hairdresser or to burst into tears at frustration in choosing a gown or a piece of jewelry and less at home at a soiree than at a mass demonstration, Fulvia "wished to rule a ruler and command a commander,"[20] and she would not tolerate Antonius' banishment from Caesar's circle.

Antonius was a brave and capable officer. He had performed with valor in the Epirus campaign and at Pharsalus. Next to Caesar, he was probably Rome's most capable general. Having forgiven and advanced to high posts so many enemies, how could Caesar persist in hostility to Antonius? Still handsome, if overweight from dissipation, as ever he exuded good nature and generosity. Besides, over the years Caesar had discerned what is common to all men as well as the small measure distinguishing one man from another. He had learned the difficulty of reforming men's characters. Antonius was not a man who would relentlessly refine his qualities in order to achieve an integration of his personality. He did not understand the Homeric exploration of capacities in struggle. Few men pursue Lucretius' counsel: "So trivial are the traces of different natures . . . beyond reason's power to expel, that nothing hinders our living a life worthy of gods."[21]

Caesar embraced Antonius and invited him to ride in his coach. Octavius and Decimus Brutus followed behind.

LIV

"SUBVERSIVE"

O N every hand, oligarchs complained of fresh indignities. Some were forced to accept as new neighbors men of no birth or breeding, Caesar's officers and other partisans who had taken over properties of Pompeian oligarchs, men like the centurion Scaeva (a hero of the battle of Dyrrachium, where he had lost an eye). More generally they suffered petty frustrations where they had formerly enjoyed free exercise of their authority, frustrations like those Cicero encountered in planning a monument to his recently deceased daughter. After pestering Atticus for five months to find him a site, he discovered on his own "some gardens across the Tiber," of which he declared that he could not see "any other place that can be so much frequented." As usual, Cicero lacked cash, and he dared not dun men in Caesar's service who owed him money nor delay payments on a debt of his own to Balbus. Upon obtaining a loan from a wealthy woman, he discovered that under Caesar's sumptuary law, "if anything is spent on a monument in excess of whatever it is that the law allows, one had to give an equal sum to the public funds." After hitting upon the expedient of constructing a shrine instead of a tomb, Cicero learned that he would have to abandon the site, for a friend informed him that "the course of the Tiber [was] to be diverted from the Mulvian bridge along the Vatican hills; the Campus Martius [was] to be built over and the Vatican plain to be a sort of Campus Martius." Caesar's project of joining the two halves of the city was interfering with Cicero's memorial. "The law will be passed," the friend assured him; "Caesar wants it."[1] In despair, Cicero abandoned his project.

In the new era the oligarchs were discovering that birth, wealth and prior honors no longer guaranteed old privileges. Caesar controlled elections, and men accustomed to compete for office with intrigue, bribery and even violence complained, like the consular Servius in a letter of condolence on the death of Cicero's daughter, of "being robbed of all that should be no less dear to men than their offspring—of country, of an honorable name, of position, of all the preferments of state." A nobleman could no longer be certain that his daughter "might become the mother of sons in whose brilliant success she might rejoice . . . who might by their own merit [as interpreted by the oligarchs] maintain the position bequeathed them by her father . . . who would be likely to stand for the offices of state in their due order and to exercise their independence in politics and in promoting the interests of their friends."[2]

Great landowners who had illegally taken possession of public lands or seized lands of neighboring smallholders now found commissioners expropriating holdings without clear title for distribution to veterans. Migrant laborers were drifting off to seek employment on Caesar's public works projects and leaving estates shorthanded. Others were demanding hire as shepherds under Caesar's decree requiring employment of free herdsmen along with slaves.

Before Caesar returned to Rome from Spain, Balbus and Oppius had proposed a series of new measures to guarantee both Caesar's security and the continuation of his varied programs. Representing him now as a living Romulus, the founder of a new Rome, they withheld the announcement of the victory at Munda until April 21, the Palilia, the traditional birthday of the founding of Rome. Munda was to be celebrated as a second birthday, the inauguration of a new era in the city's history, and in the Senate Caesar's partisans voted to institute annual games to commemorate Caesar's final triumph in the five-year civil war. They proclaimed him Parens patriae (Father of the Country) and set up his statue in the Temple of Quirinus (the deified

Romulus). Caesar's agents publicized the legend (possibly revived or invented by Caesar's antiquarian clansman, the consular Lucius Caesar) of the Julian contemporary of Romulus, who, encountering the shade of the recently deceased hero atop the Quirinal hill, hastened to assemble the citizens and announced: "Quirites, the Father of the City, Romulus, descended suddenly from the sky at dawn this morning and appeared to me. . . . 'Go,' said he, 'and declare to the Romans the will of heaven that my Rome shall be the capital of the world; so let them cherish the art of war and let them know and teach their children that no strength can resist Roman arms.' "[3]

The Senate erected two busts of the new Romulus on the Rostra, one bearing the wreath of a savior of the citizenry and the other the wreath of a savior of the state, and atop the Capitol they set his statue among the kings and the regicide Lucius Brutus. Senators vied in proposing honors for the new Founder of the City: the erection of a new residence adorned like a temple with an architrave and portico (appropriate for the head of the state religion); an unprecedented thanksgiving of fifty days for his latest victory; and the right both to wear a laurel crown of victory at all times (wiseacres would joke that the aging commander would be able to hide his baldness without brushing his spare locks forward) and to appear at games in triumphal garb. The Senate hailed him as triumpher and imperator for life with the privilege of bequeathing the latter title to his heir. All future triumphs were to be assigned to him as permanent commander-in-chief. In processions his ivory image was to be paraded along with those of the gods, next to the statue of Victory. He was awarded the right to dedicate war spoils in the Temple of Jupiter Feretrius (an ancient and forgotten honor dating to Romulus and granted in the past only to generals who slew enemy commanders with their own hands). In addition, towns throughout Italy and the empire were ordered to erect his statue in some prominent place, for Caesar was not the Founder of a new city-state but of a new empire. With these measures Caesar's partisans associated him with Romulus and ancient traditions as well as with the patron deities and established him not only as Fourth Founder of Rome but as unchallenged leader of a united Italy and of a consolidated empire.

To ratify Caesar's call for reconciliation among former opponents in the civil war, Caesar's supporters voted to construct a temple of Concordia Nova. In their view, the old temple had been defiled by its association with the massacre of Gaius Gracchus and his followers and with the execution of the Catilinarians. The decisions to build a temple of Liberty with a statue of Caesar as the Liberator reminded the populars of Clodius and the shrine to Liberty he had built on the site of Cicero's razed mansion. The new temple would both gratify the enemies of the optimates and memorialize the optimates' loss of Liberty, as recently defined by Cicero—"the power to live as you will,"[4] a euphemism for oligarchic license in both running the republic for personal profit and in plundering the empire.

THE FINAL PHASE

With the elimination of Pompeius, the overthrow of the optimate clique and the crushing of the rebel adventurers, Caesar had brought all corners of the Mediterranean under his private patronage. Now he confronted new questions: How was he to rule the empire? Was he to revive the old constitution and seek to infuse antiquated institutions with new vitality to respond to the dynamics of political and social change?

Caesar could count securely on no single element in the population. The commons, beneficiaries of the public works and colonial projects, were disgruntled at the dissolution of the aggressive collegia, at Caesar's failure to decree a cancellation of debts and at his limitation on the number of grain recipients. Unfailingly rational and eloquent, Caesar, with his promises to transform their lives, frightened men long accustomed to existing on handouts. When a veterinarian, a certain Herophilus, proclaimed himself the illegitimate son of the younger Marius, he was hailed as a hero. Towns passed resolutions acclaiming him, and grizzled veterans thought they recognized in him the tough manner of Old Marius. Accosting Octavius at the Janiculum hill hurrying home ahead of Caesar, Herophilus badgered the young man to acknowledge him as a relative. Bewildered at the aggressive importuning of the crowd accompanying the imposter and admonished that his mother had repudiated Herophilus, Octavius replied that it was for Caesar as head of the family to rule on the man's claim. Subsequently, when Caesar opened his gardens across the Tiber to the people, the False Marius received as much applause as Caesar himself. Caesar ordered Herophilus out of the city and forbade him to continue his agitation, preferring to buy off such a potential nuisance than to increase his popularity by harsh measures. The response to Herophilus, however, provided a warning regarding unfulfilled aspirations among the plebs.

By expediting and expanding his public works projects, Caesar could alleviate discontent among both the poor and the investors in the tax-gathering corporations whom Caesar had deprived of provincial plunder. He announced plans for the construction of a second stone theater to rival Pompeius', of a temple to Mars that was to be the largest in the world and of another to Felicitas, a monument to his own good fortune and an oblique response to Sulla's claim of particular felicity—projects that would provide employment as well as profit to entrepreneurial corporations. To reassure the commons regarding the food supply, a constant concern, he appointed two additional aediles charged solely with this responsibility.

As for the veterans, Caesar was confident of their devotion, but many of these aging soldiers were scattered throughout Italy or in colonies in the provinces. Caesar was reminded of the loosening of his relationship with his former comrades-in-arms when one day a cantankerous old fellow with a hideously disfigured face and a patch over a vacant eye appeared before his tribunal.

Seeing that Caesar was about to dismiss his complaint against neighbors who had trespassed on his farm, the man asked, "Do you remember, general, the time in Spain when you sprained your ankle near the river Sucro?" At Caesar's nod, he continued, "Do you remember too when because of the powerful heat of the sun you wanted to rest under a certain tree that cast very little shade that one of your fellow soldiers spread out his cloak for you because the ground in which that solitary tree had sprung up was very rough?"

"I would have perished with thirst," Caesar recalled, "if my companion . . . had not brought me some water in his helmet."

"Could you recognize that man," the old man insisted, "or the helmet?"

Caesar nodded. "You at any rate," he said, "are not he."

"You have good reason, Caesar," said the man, "not to recognize me. When this happened I was a whole man. Later, during the battle of Munda, one of my eyes was torn out and some bones were taken from my skull, and you would not recognize that helmet if you saw it, for it was split by a Spanish sword."

Moved by the recollection of the incident and the man's devotion, Caesar ordered that the old soldier suffer no further inconvenience and awarded him an additional strip of land.[5]

It was, of course, the vacillating sentiment among the leading oligarchs that worried Caesar. As a patrician, he had always taken it for granted that men of birth, noble heritage, wealth and education be entrusted with the administration of the city and the empire. Now his experience not only with former Pompeians but also with opportunists within his own party inspired him with caution. The many eulogies of Cato, Cicero's provocative writings as well as reports of assassination plots exposed the complexity of the problem of associating the aristocratic orders with the new era for the empire.

Sulla's spate of legislation appeared paltry in comparison to Caesar's, and in the decades after Sulla all the consuls combined had scarcely matched Caesar's manifold activities. Oligarchs were bewildered by the flood of bills, reports of construction projects, awards of citizenship and appointments to the Senate. They chafed at Caesar's regulation of the pettiest aspects of life at Rome and throughout Italy like his edict proclaiming that with the new year (44): "No one shall drive a wagon along the streets of Rome or along those streets in the suburbs where there is continuous housing after sunrise or before the tenth [daylight] hour." They grumbled at his restrictions on the use of litters and at regulations concerning the paving, repair and cleaning of streets at Rome and of public roads throughout the peninsula. In their general disillusionment, oligarchs even expressed pique at his calendar, insisting that the lunar calendar had served well enough since King Numa instituted it six centuries earlier. Romans repeated Cicero's witticism upon hearing someone remark that the constellation Lyra would rise the next day—"Yes, by decree."[6]

Associating their status with the supremacy of the city-state, the old nobility resented Caesar's measures for expanding the autonomy of the Italian municipalities (in recognition of the increasing role local aristocrats were playing in the empire), decentralizing censorial and judicial functions and promoting administrative uniformity throughout the peninsula. They bridled at the preference granted to veterans in election to local office. Even his plan "to reduce the civil code to fixed limits and of the vast and prolix mass of statutes to include only the best and most essential in a limited number of volumes," a project long overdue, they opposed as a limitation on oligarchic hegemony.[7]

Cleopatra, too, provoked annoyance. Summoned to Rome with her boy-king husband as royal hostages, she infuriated Roman aristocrats by maintaining the rigid ceremonial of the Alexandrian court and generally behaving with royal arrogance. Aristocrats pretended indignation at Caesar's open display of affection for the Egyptian and grumbled at paying court to eunuchs in order to win the queen's favor in the luxurious villa across the Tiber that Caesar had put at the disposal of the royal couple.

Exhausted by the Spanish campaign and overwhelmed by the varied enterprises to which he was about to reapply himself and by the unrelenting effort required to deal with the many elements of the population, Caesar shut himself up in his villa in the Alban hills and drafted a new will on the Ides of September (45). Caesar did not subscribe to the Epicurean teaching that nothing matters after death. As a child, he had been indoctrinated as to his responsibility to his patrician house and to Rome's divine mission, and he had a sufficient sense of history (he who had made so much history) to desire the continuity of his work. With no son of his own, he fixed upon Octavius as his first heir and adopted him in his will. As secondary heirs he named his nephews, Pedius and Pinarius, and singled out for expressions of gratitude Antonius and Decimus Brutus. He sent the document, sealed, to the chief vestal for safekeeping.

Returning to his varied projects, Caesar astonished his associates with his renewed energy, for they recalled his lassitude before the Spanish campaign. He approached civil occupations with military discipline. Instead of meeting with his staff officers at dawn, he conferred with his "cabinet" as a group or individually. They discussed all manner of concerns, deciding, for example, whether one of the magistrates should replace Caesar in proposing a new piece of legislation to the Senate or the people; what public functions Caesar had to attend, including religious ceremonies in his capacities as pontifex maximus and augur; whether it was important that he be present at the assumption of the toga of manhood of the son of an influential oligarch; what approach should be taken at a trial at which he was presiding; how much of his schedule he could spare for visiting veterans eager to reminisce over old campaigns or for audiences with aristocrats petitioning for the return of exiled relatives or disgruntled over matters of prestige. He had to allocate time to grant awards to men and women who had won prizes for large families, to receive a delegation of Jews complaining of violations of their special privileges on some Aegean island, to hear a dispute between the organizing committee for an overseas colony and contractors procrastinating in furnishing ships and equipment or to rule on the request of a wealthy equestrian to shift a colony away from a town of which he was a patron.

More and more of the cluttered day had to be reserved to strategy sessions for Caesar's forthcoming campaigns. In Dacia in a coup possibly abetted by Caesar's agents, Burebista had been overthrown. Frightened by word of Caesar's warlike preparations, Illyrian tribes that had supported Pompeius and had continued to battle Vatinius after Pharsalus dispatched envoys to Rome "to crave pardon for what they had done and to offer their friendship and alliance, vaunting themselves as a very brave race."[8] The assault on the Balkans could be delayed until after the defeat of Parthia. That kingdom only recently had suffered dissension between two princes, and Caesar and his legates interrogated traders about the possibility of promoting a new insurrection. Considering themselves the defenders of Hellenistic civilization, Romans assumed that Greek cities in Parthia could be roused to support them. Hyrkanos, High Priest at Jerusalem, could call upon the numerous Jewish communities to assist Caesar, even as they had done in Egypt. Meanwhile, Caesar and his legates held planning sessions on the assemblage and movement of troops, the levying of auxiliary forces, the establishment of mints for the paymasters, the coordination of the movements of transport vessels, the dispatch of pack animals and the purchase and storage of materiel and foodstuffs.

In this exhausting whir, day after day, with rarely a moment of relaxation, on the qui vive for grave decisions, wearing out one secretary after another, Caesar found relief in attending to his favorite projects—the draining of the Pomptine marshes, the canal to Terracina, the Corinth canal and other engineering works in Italy and abroad.

THE WINNOWING FAN

Caesar was sensitive to the humiliation of leading figures excluded from the seats of power. Catching sight of Cicero sitting patiently one day in the antechamber awaiting his turn for an interview, Caesar remarked to Matius, "I must be a most unpopular man. There's Marcus Cicero sitting waiting and can't get to see me at his own convenience. He is the most easy-going of mankind, but I don't doubt he detests me."[9] Like other leading senators, Cicero had been accustomed to finding his own antechamber thronged by petitioners every morning; now to petition Caesar he was forced to court a foreigner like Balbus or "new men" like Hirtius and Oppius (Cicero had forgotten his own equestrian origin).

Caesar was aware, of course, of the unbridgeable ideological difference that separated him from men like Cicero. In fact, the orator was publishing a series of attacks on Epicureanism. "What greater or better service," he asked rhetorically in one of his treatises, "can I render to the commonwealth than to instruct and train the youth—especially in view of the fact that our young men have gone so far astray because of the present moral laxity that the utmost effort will be needed to hold them in check and direct them in the right way?" Cicero was, in fact, concerned more with politics than morality. Wary of attacking Caesar and his councilors, he assailed the philosophy to which they adhered. Pious out of political expediency, he expressed alarm at Caesar's disavowal of traditional religious manipulation. "With philosophers who hold that the gods exercise no control over human affairs whatever," he asked, "can piety, reverence or religion exist? The disappearance of piety towards the gods," he warned, "will entail the disappearance of loyalty and social union among men as well as of justice itself." Religion was the bulwark of the social order; and the world as it was, he insisted, following the Stoic view, was divinely ordained, perfect and requiring no modifications. "The study of the heavenly phenomena," Cicero declared, "bestows a power of self-control that arises from the perception of the consummate restraint and order that obtains even among the gods; also loftiness of mind is inspired by contemplating the creations of the actions of the gods and justice by realizing the will, design and purpose of the Supreme Lord and Ruler to whose nature we are told by philosophers that the True Reason and Supreme Law are conformed."[10]

Eloquent words, these, but of little avail in the digging of canals, the tunneling of mountains or the resettlement of tens of thousands in distant colonies.

In fact, Epicureanism was in the ascendancy, and Cicero was alarmed at the dissemination of popular Epicurean tracts. "The crowd had its interest stirred and flocked to the teaching in preference to any other." The school, he admitted, "[had taken] all Italy by storm." Epicurus' picture was everywhere—on personal jewelry, on cups, on walls. . . . Cicero attributed Epicurean success to "the seductive allurements of pleasure" and to the ease with which the doctrine could be grasped, an advantage "so much to the taste of the unlearned." He accused the Epicureans of canvassing "the country villages for the assemblage of doubtless respectable but certainly not very learned adherents," that is, the farmer-entrepreneurs introducing scientific methods in farming, viniculture and animal husbandry. "For my part," he sneered, "I hold that what is popular is often positively base."[11]

The ideological conflict pervaded every aspect of life. Cicero accused the Epicureans of subverting traditional education. He chided them for their lack of intellectual rigor and for their impatience with "any education worth the name that did not help to school [them] in happiness." He scoffed at the Epicurean dogmatist, "afraid of nothing so much as lest he should appear to have doubts about anything,"[12] an arrogance not unusual among proponents of radical change; but, as Cicero knew very well, his tirade hardly befit his friend Atticus (certainly influenced by the Epicureans if not a disciple of the school) or his sometime friends in Caesar's circle—Balbus, Oppius, Hirtius, Pansa, Matius and the jurist Trebatius—or the former Pompeian Gaius Cassius, who had succumbed recently to the appeal of the philosophy. Nor was Cicero's invective appropriate to Lucretius, to whose poem Cicero alluded not once in his polemics.

Urging passivity in the face of a general crisis, insisting upon the exploitation of religion for the preservation of property rights, exhorting to submission to Providence rather than to corrective action, Cicero could find no rapport with Caesar's councilors, grappling day by day, as they were, with real problems and with little time for disquisitions on divine design and purpose. For them the first task was to understand the world, a world in flux, the next to change it; for them progress and creation, progress without dependence upon gods, not stability and retrogression; for them man creating himself in struggle with his environment and with other men, a struggle for the survival of the fittest in institutions as well as in nature; for them no future life but annihilation in death (with a concomitant intensity in exploiting one's capacities in the brief career on earth).

Nevertheless, appreciative of the variety of human experience and no dogmatist, Caesar did not allow philosophical differences to interfere with personal friendship, and on an excursion into Campania in December he stopped at Cicero's villa. Entertaining Caesar was an onerous occupation, for he traveled with two thousand Spanish bodyguards and a retinue of civilians. On the other hand, Caesar could never spare more than a brief visit with each of his hosts. In the morning at the villa of Octavius' stepfather, he conferred with Balbus, then, as previously arranged, he moved on to Cicero's villa. Passing the rest of the day on a precise schedule, he walked briefly along the shore, took a bath, received reports, dressed and took his place at dinner, eating more than was his custom inasmuch as his physician had prescribed an emetic after meals. Tactfully avoiding topics that might give rise to disagreement but delighting in conversation with the witty and learned orator, Caesar discoursed with Cicero "of nothing serious but a good deal on literary matters."[13] With his wide-ranging curiosity, eloquence, acumen and graciousness, Caesar could always charm Cicero, but Cicero was not unhappy to see him leave.

Confronting problems both in finding reliable collaborators and in rewarding old partisans and reconciled Pompeians, monstrously overworked and distracted by dozens of simultaneous activities, Caesar ignored constitutional niceties. Resigning as sole consul, he appointed as consuls for the last three months of the year Trebonius, the victor over Massilia, and Fabius Maximus, a legate in the recent Spanish campaign. While thus obliging two associates and adding to the number of friendly consulars in the Senate, Caesar outraged opponents by failing to submit his candidates to the vote, and when Fabius' lictor announced his entrance into the theater, voices hooted, "He's no consul!"[14] For praetorships Caesar nominated men without qualifications of age or prior magistracies, men who had demonstrated loyalty and capacities in his service, like the two intellectuals Pollio and Cornificius as well as young Hortensius and Decimus Brutus. Though Caesar increased the number of quaestors from ten to forty, of aediles from four to six and of praetors from ten to fourteen, he could not satisfy all aspirants for office.

Eager to attend to other problems, Caesar grew weary of the litany of personal complaints:

He gave me the praetorship, but I had hoped for the consulship, he gave me the twelve fasces [as consul], but he did not make me a regular [full-term] consul; he was willing that my name should be attached to the year [as consul], but he disappointed me with respect to the priesthood; I was elected a member of the college, but why of one only? What he gave me he had to give to somebody—he took nothing out of his pocket.[15]

For the next year, 44, Caesar prudently avoided appointing consuls and held elections. Of his two candidates, Dolabella and Antonius, the latter was at least close to the required age for a consulship. Neither man had held the prerequisite magistracies. The wilful Antonius had qualifications as a general and experience in administering Italy as Caesar's master of horse (deputy dictator). Oligarchs resented Dolabella for his demagogy as a tribune two years earlier and mocked him as an incurable profligate and womanizer. Caesar recognized, however, that Dolabella enjoyed popularity among elements of the commons lukewarm to himself. Besides, in the African and Spanish campaigns Dolabella had made amends for his adventurism. Nevertheless, to impress upon this obvious opportunist the necessity for judgment and loyalty, Caesar gave him a curious warning. To the astonishment of the citizenry, at the elections Caesar presented Antonius and himself as candidates for the consulship and ignored Dolabella. Subsequently, he announced that he would nominate Dolabella to replace him upon his departure for the war against the Parthians. Antonius, however, with no love lost on Dolabella, advised that as an augur he would find the auspices unfavorable for Dolabella's election. The two adventurers would check each other.

With Marcus Brutus and Brutus' brother-in-law Gaius Cassius, Caesar played another game. Servilia had lost influence with her son after he, in defiance of her wishes, divorced his wife and married Porcia, Cato's daughter and widow of Caesar's equally resolute foe Bibulus, a woman as single-minded as her father and as vindictive against Caesar as her late husband. Cassius, Servilia's son-in-law, had a history of adventurism. During the ill-fated campaign against the Parthians, he had proved insubordinate to Crassus and subsequently as acting governor of Syria had profiteered so rabidly as to earn the sobriquet "the date man." It was also charged that he had "let loose a horde of Arabs into Syria and reported these to the Senate as being Parthians in order that his own depredations might pass as the devastations of the enemy." Nevertheless, pursuant to his policy of reconciliation, Caesar advanced these two leading optimates of dubious morality to high office, playing one against the other, as he had done with Antonius and Dolabella. When the two men, newly elected praetors, submitted claims to the urban praetorship (the foremost of the praetorships), Caesar encouraged their rivalry. Although as the elder and more experienced, Cassius was confident of being chosen, Caesar declared: "Cassius makes the juster plea, but Brutus must have the first praetorship"[16]—an illogical decision certain to please Brutus and to anger Cassius. To appease the irascible Cassius, Caesar promised him the governorship of Syria for 43, when Cassius would assist him against the Parthians with an expectation of generous booty.

Optimates murmured that though Caesar had declined the authority to nominate candidates for the lesser as well as the higher magistrates, he nevertheless circulated memoranda among the tribes reading: "Caesar the dictator to this or that tribe. I commend to you so and so, to hold their positions by your votes." Caesar increased the number of consulars, a ruling circle within the Senate, both by providing consulships even for brief portions of the year and by arbitrarily promoting praetorians to the higher rank. He reduced thereby the prestige of older consulars like Cicero, hardly to their satisfaction. To the further indignation of his opponents he deprived the Senate of its exclusivity by expanding its membership from six hundred to nine hundred, appointing men who had never held magistracies, officers of the Army of Gaul, sons of those proscribed by Sulla and men condemned by optimate courts as well as citizens from Italian towns, Cisalpina, the Province and the Spains, some of them newly enfranchised. To the dismay of old-fashioned Romans, Gauls and Spaniards in outlandish dress and speaking a broken Latin took their places in what had formerly been a Roman conclave of princes. In the Forum defiant posters appeared with the legend: "God bless the republic! Let no one consent to point out the Senate to a newly made senator!" In the streets people sang a snide ditty: "Caesar led the Gauls in triumph, led them to the Senate house. Then the Gauls put off their breeches and put on the laticlave [the broad purple stripe of the senatorial order]." Exasperated, Caesar snapped that "if he had been helped in defending his honor by brigands and cutthroats, he would have requited even such men in the same way."[17]

Indifferent to resentment at his celebrating his victory over fellow-citizens, Caesar held a triumph for the campaign in Spain, and conservative Romans muttered at his vaunting not at a victory "over foreign commanders or barbarian kings but [at] the utter annihilation of the sons and the family of the mightiest of the Romans." As his triumphal chariot rolled past the bench from which the ten tribunes were reviewing the procession, Pontius Aquila, a pardoned Pompeian, failed to rise. Caesar was in no humor to submit to open defiance. "Come then, Aquila," he cried, "take back the republic from me, you tribune."[18]

Thus, at last, Caesar publicly proclaimed what all had known but had preferred not to voice: Caesar was Rome, the oligarchic republic was no more.

The commons were indifferent to such oligarchic complaints, and the people rejoiced when Caesar announced that the victory banquet "had not been served with a liberality creditable to his generosity" and ordered a second, more lavish public repast. Freedmen and other foreigners were delighted at Caesar's staging theatrical productions in various languages in different quarters of the city—an unprecedented honoring of the cultural variegation at Rome (beyond the two official languages of Latin and Greek). On the other hand, the crowd murmured with displeasure when at gladiatorial games Caesar sat leafing through documents and ignoring the combats except to rescue with a wave of his handkerchief gladiators consigned to death by the down-turned thumbs and hooting of the audience. Cicero accepted these "cruel and inhuman" spectacles as a vent for the frustration of the plebs. "There is no school at least for the eyes," he declared, "where one can learn better to confront grief and death." Caesar had, however, confronted grief and death too often, and he found the shouting repulsive: "Kill him! Lash him! Burn him! Why does he meet the sword in so cowardly a way? Why does he strike so feebly? Why doesn't he die game? Whip him to meet his wounds! Let them receive blow for blow, with chests bared and exposed to the stroke!"[19]

One day Caesar committed an egregious blunder, offending friends as well as foes among both the aristocracy and the commons. As he was reviewing contracts for constructions and for his prospective military campaigns seated in the porch of the Temple of Venus, a vast concourse of magistrates, senators, equestrians and commons approached bearing to the Temple of Jupiter silver tablets on which were engraved in gold the latest honors decreed him by the Senate. Whether deep in thought, exhausted or simply out of patience with incessant distractions, Caesar failed to note the procession until it was upon him. Laying down his documents and extending his hand in greeting, like an oriental monarch, he neither rose immediately nor during the sycophantic speeches. Enemies denounced him for his arrogance to the Senate and the People. It was rumored that Balbus had restrained him by whispering, "Remember you are Caesar and permit yourself to be courted as a superior,"[20] and that Caesar had glowered when Trebatius urged him to stand. Apparently regretting his tactlessness, Caesar gave out that he had not been well, but the apology seemed lame and belated.

Caesar concluded the year with the worst defiance of tradition of all. On the last day of December, the end of the term of the current consuls, Fabius failed to appear at the quaestorian elections for the coming year. When a messenger brought word that he had died suddenly, Caesar seized the opportunity to reward another of his partisans. Regrouping the citizens from a tribal assembly (for the quaestorian elections) into a centuriate assembly, he nominated Caninius Rebilus, a legate of the Army of Gaul and governor of Africa after Thapsus, to serve as suffect consul for the single day remaining to the year. Old-fashioned Romans were indignant at this denigration of the highest magistracy of the republic, but Caesar was delighted at Cicero's sarcastic quip (of which Caesar kept a private collection) that "in the consulship of Caninius nobody lunched . . . nothing untoward occurred . . . for so wonderfully wide awake was he that during the whole of his consulship he saw no sleep."[21]

Caesar was pressured by more important concerns. Dispatches from Spain reported a renewal of the rebellion under Pompeius' surviving son, Sextus. Caesar's garrisons were beleaguered. With no life to spare for a third pacification of the Iberian peninsula, Caesar asked the praetor Pollio to accept the governorship of Further Spain. A handsome thirty-year-old, articulate, witty and a loyal associate for almost ten years, Pollio had crossed the Rubicon, served with Curio in the disastrous first campaign in Africa, accompanied Caesar to Epirus and participated in the battles of Pharsalus and Munda. As a tribune, he had resisted Dolabella's demagogy. Though he yearned to retire to his true calling, literature and the arts, and opposed the current concentration of "all power in the hands of one man,"[22] grateful for the affection and trust Caesar had always displayed toward him, Pollio accepted the charge.

In Syria Cornificius' replacement had locked the insurgents in a siege but had been forced to retreat before a Parthian relief force. That rebellion would have to await Caesar's campaign against the Parthians.

Day by day, to the dismay of his councilors, Caesar grew ever more gaunt and haggard. Frequently he stared into space, as though searching for something far off. He was burning himself into an old man. For him life granted no reprieves, and he could recall to an anxious Calpurnia Odysseus' words to Penelope after the Homeric hero had won his way home through countless perils:

> My dear, we have not won through to the end.
> One trial—I do not know how long is left for me
> to see fulfilled. Teiresias' ghost [in the underworld] . . .
> told me I must take an oar
> and trudge the mainland, going from town to town,
> until some traveler falling in with me will say:
> "A winnowing fan, that on your shoulder, sir?"
> Then I must plant my oar, on the very spot,
> with burnt offerings to Poseidon of the Waters . . . Thereafter
> when I come home again, I am to slay
> full hekatombs to the gods who own broad heaven,
> one by one. Then death will drift upon me
> from seaward, mild as air, mild as your hand,
> in my well-tended weariness of age,
> contented folk around me on our island.[23]

LV

THE IDES OF MARCH

THE winter of 45–44 was harsh, with frequent snowfalls, unusual for Rome, and in drafty, poorly illuminated halls Caesar attended to preparations for his final military campaigns, the culmination of his career and the achievement of his ultimate goal: the security of the empire. In this venture

Caesar would avenge Crassus' defeat and recapture the legionary standards from the Parthians. Soldiers and officers of the Caesarian and Pompeian armies who had lost zest for civil pursuits during the many years of conflict would fight as comrades-in-arms, overcoming the bitterness of the civil war in recouping the honor of the republic. Senators deprived of hope of extortions in the provinces on account of Caesar's administrative reforms would win personal booty; and wealthy equestrians no longer able to reap huge profits through tax-farming would enjoy huge contracts for ships and materiel as well as opportunities in buying and selling plunder and in slavetrading. Caesar would capture treasure to pay for his varied construction and settlement projects. Furthermore, in fighting alongside legionaries in a grandiose enterprise guaranteeing peace for generations, troops levied in the provinces and the dependencies would take pride as participants.

For Caesar himself war offered, strangely, a respite. For almost fifteen years, war rather than peace had become a way of life for him, a life with fewer frustrations, simpler, than that at Rome with its constant jockeying for equilibrium among antagonistic elements, a battle in which no resolution, no final victory, could be foreseen. On the battlefield, issues were clear; commands were obeyed; factionalism and cynicism were not tolerated; and Caesar enjoyed universal respect, safe from hostile maneuvers of unreconciled foes, from intrigue and threats of assassination. Above all, Caesar had not unlimited time. If his recent fits were not the sacred disease (epilepsy), they were certainly symptoms of utter exhaustion, as were his outbursts of rage and his general neurasthenia. During his remaining years he would achieve more in campaigns than in maneuvering at Rome. Yet even his war plans evoked resistance; Romans did not disguise their resentment at the call to new adventures, especially against the dreaded Parthians.

In December, after engaging Octavius to Servilia's grandchild, the daughter of Servilius Isauricus, Caesar's colleague in the consulship of 48, thereby strengthening his own ties to his mistress and his grandnephew's status in the oligarchy, Caesar sent Octavius across the Adriatic to Apollonia. As the young man's tutor Caesar appointed a certain Apollodorus of Pergamum, a distinguished Epicurean who had dedicated a treatise on rhetoric to Caesar's close associate Matius. Octavius would benefit as much from the scholar's Epicureanism as from his mastery of rhetoric, for the young man was credulous about omens, fearful of thunder and lightning and even carried a sealskin talisman. To prepare Octavius for combat (he was to assume important responsibilities in the forthcoming campaigns), Caesar arranged for him to drill with troops of horse and to learn the arts of war from experienced officers.

Caesar had mobilized twelve legions and ten thousand cavalry. If there was time, he would confirm the esprit de corps of those assembling from Cisalpina, Illyricum and Macedonia in the construction of the canal through the Isthmus of Corinth. (He had already selected an engineer to supervise the project.) These legions would eventually join up with the three legions battling Pompeian rebels in Syria and four legions marching from Egypt. Relying on the counsel of Gaius Cassius and others who had served in Crassus' campaign, Caesar would follow a different invasion route and, as was his custom, test the Parthians with probing attacks before engaging them in a decisive encounter. Having assured the frontier on the Euphrates and opened trade routes to India with the defeat of the Parthians, Caesar would proceed through the Caucasus into uncharted regions never invaded by any Roman general. Explorations effected by Pompeius had "ascertained that a seven days' journey from India into the Bactrian country reaches the river Bactrus, a tributary of the Amu Darya, and that Indian merchandise can be conveyed from the Bactrus across the Caspian to the Kur and thence with not more than five days' portage by land can reach Phasis in Pontus" on the Black Sea.[1] After confirming this trade route, Caesar would circle north of the Black Sea and advance through the heart of Europe to link up with his trusted legate Plancus, marching to meet him from Gaul. He would fix the imperial frontier along the Danube.

In the tumultuous events of these last years Caesar had begun to apprehend the limits of his capacities. No matter what his dedication, he would not implement all his plans; and more and more he wondered at his own frenzied efforts. Paradoxically, Caesar had persevered as though he had time without end and as though his every act was decisive not only for himself, but for humanity as well. Immediately after the hard-won victory in Spain, exhausted, he "made up his mind to stay in Rome," alleging that he feared "that his laws might be disregarded in his absence."[2] Within months of his return to Rome, he reversed himself and was adamant about departing for the East. To objections that in the previous three years no one but him had been able to keep the peace in Italy or to maintain his initiatives, Caesar could argue, though hardly with conviction, that his varied projects were sufficiently advanced to be left in the hands of technicians.

During the three years Caesar would be away from Rome beyond the reach of communications, how would Caesar's councilors maintain order, much less carry on his undertakings?

Unable to persuade Caesar to delay his departure, his associates insisted upon new measures to render his authority inviolable even in his absence. In a series of Senate decrees, they provided him with an aura of sanctity. Despite his earlier erasure of the inscription "demigod" on his statue in the Temple of Jupiter, Caesar's associates extended his prior identification with the hero Romulus to an identification with the deified Romulus, exalting him into a demigod, the violation of whose acts would be sacrilege. They proclaimed Caesar's birthday a public holiday and decreed that the vestals and priests offer quadrennial prayers for his health and safety. They renamed the seventh month in his honor and dedicated a day to him in the Roman Games, sacred to Jupiter. Henceforth official oaths were to be taken in the name of Caesar's genius, the spirit that brought him victory and good fortune. One of the thirty-five tribes was renamed after his clan and a Julian college was established as one of the priesthoods entrusted with the celebration of the Luper-calia, a festival commemorating the founding of Rome. After his death a cult was to honor his genius with Antonius (already chief priest of the Julian Lupercals) as flamen. To confirm his political supremacy, the Senate voted Caesar a dictatorship for life instead of for ten years, and with no require-ment for annual renewal. To assure the loyalty of the magistrates during his absence, he was permitted to appoint half of those below the rank of consul and to hold elections for all the magistracies for the coming year (43) and of the consuls, praetors and tribunes for 42, that is, for the period of his antici-pated absence.

For 43 Caesar nominated for the consulship Hirtius and Pansa, two mem-bers of his "cabinet," and for 42 the equally reliable legate Plancus, who was to lead an army out of Gaul to link up with him in Germany, along with Caesar's protégé of many years, Decimus Brutus, also experienced in war in the north countries. For the coming year, to succeed Lepidus as master of horse, deputy to the dictator, Caesar appointed the loyal consular Calvinus, who had proved his devotion at Pharsalus and afterwards in Asia Minor, as well as young Octavius, the two to serve either concurrently or in succession.

The Senate granted Caesar control of the mint and permitted him, against all tradition, to stamp his image on coins at Rome; and to pay for the war preparations, moneyers employing Caesar's slaves and freedmen began issuing a flood of specie greater than at any other comparable period of Roman history, with representations of Caesar in his various capacities—as dictator, as Father of the Country, as pontifex maximus, augur and imperator. On the reverse they stamped an image of his divine ancestress Venus or symbols of peace and prosperity. Similar coins were minted by provincial governors so that Caesar was proclaimed the unchallenged ruler throughout the empire.

Through other measures Caesar's associates rendered large numbers of citi-zens beholden to him. The Senate granted him authority (not exercised since the days of the kings) to name new patricians in place of the many who had died in the civil war, and Caesar advanced Marcus Antonius, Octavius and others to the privileged status. Of broader appeal and decisive evidence of his determination for reconciliation with his former enemies were his proclama-tion of a general amnesty and the return from exile of all but a few of his most compromised foes. In addition, he restored dowries to widows of deceased enemies and a share of confiscated properties to their children, "thus putting Sulla's cruelty mightily to shame and gaining for himself a great reputation not alone for bravery but also for goodness." In a symbolic termination of fac-tional antagonisms, he ordered the restoration of the statues of Sulla and Pompeius, overturned by the people after Pharsalus, and even Cicero, who scarcely disguised his hostility to Caesar any longer, conceded that "by this act of generosity Caesar did indeed set up the statues of Pompeius but firmly planted his own also,"[3] and the orator joined in sponsoring a resolution to commemorate Caesar's magnanimity with the construction of a temple of

Clementia, in which the goddess would be represented as reaching out her hand to Caesar.

Defense measures promulgated to protect him and to reinforce his authority also intensified the opposition against him. Alone among the senators, Gaius Cassius had opposed honors for Caesar (a disturbing portent), but other hostile senators followed Cicero in devising all kinds of excessive honors for him, "thus rendering Caesar odious and obnoxious even to the mildest citizens because of the pretension and extravagance of what was decreed for him." Caesar's foes could be confident that his partisans would vote for every such measure and that Caesar himself would not "dare to thrust all honors aside for fear of being thought contemptuous." Thereafter, these same foes "found fault with him . . . and spread slanderous reports on how glad he was to accept them and how he behaved haughtily as a result." Frustrated in their intention, Caesar's councilors wondered whether the proposals of Caesar's enemies "were, as it were, decorations heaped upon a victim doomed to die; for the envy which he inspired influenced men more than his clemency."[4]

CAESAR, NOT REX!

Caesar had always preferred persuasion to compulsion in regard to his legislative proposals. As consul, fifteen years earlier, he had consulted opponents in advance on a land reform bill and then invited discussion in the Senate, appealing for a consensus on the issue. Upon his reassumption of power, once again he sought to persuade the Senate and the people regarding his measures. With constant public speaking he achieved an eloquence impressive even to Cicero. "Come now," wrote Cicero to the historian Nepos, "what orator would you rank above him of those who have devoted themselves to nothing else? Who has cleverer or more frequent epigrams? Who is either more picturesque or more choice in diction?"[5] Conscious of the delicate balance of forces under which he operated, Caesar engaged in no harsh repression. He did not call Cicero to account for publishing seditious works nor did he take action against those who he knew were plotting against his life. In face of constant sniping and scarcely disguised subversive activities, however, more and more Caesar found himself simply imposing his will and behaving, indeed, like a tyrant.

Having no program to oppose to his, Caesar's enemies employed a timeworn maneuver against him, charging him with aspiring to a throne, an accusation that had brought death to many ambitious oligarchs in Roman history. Shortly before the end of the year (45), in pleading the case of an Eastern monarch before Caesar, Cicero listed as an accusation against the king the charge that his envoy "was in the habit of writing to the king, saying that you [Caesar] were under a cloud, that you were looked upon as a tyrant, that public feeling had been gravely affronted by the placing of your statue amongst those of the kings, and that no applause greeted you." Cicero added slyly: "We, free men born in freedom's fairest clime, so far from finding you a tyrant, have seen in you a leader of unbounded mercy in the day of victory." Caesar and his associates were, of course, aware of Cicero's actual sentiments. They knew that among themselves Caesar's enemies spoke of him as "the king" or "the tryant." Reacting mechanically, Caesar had "forbidden [this title] with threats, saying that it was an inauspicious name by reason of the curse of their ancestors."[6]

The issue could not be resolved by the outlawing of a word.

On January 26, 44, as he was riding into Rome after conducting the Latin Festival at the Alban Mount, amid the cheers of welcome, Caesar heard cries of "Hail, king! Caesar rex!" He signed for silence. "I am Caesar," he declared, "and no Rex!"[7] Almost twenty-five years earlier at the funeral of his aunt, Caesar had boasted of her descent (and his own) from the king Marcius Rex. But many were the kings whom Romans saw as suppliants in the antechambers of their magistrates, and the power and prestige of none of these monarchs matched that of a consul, much less a dictator for life, and Caesar certainly had no reason to be desirous of a title held by an Egyptian boy imprisoned in his villa across the Tiber. Now in rejecting the title of rex, an epithet of opprobrium, he was not merely denying his aspiration to a title abolished four and a half centuries earlier but insisting that his own name, Caesar, was superior in dignity. Indeed, unlike Sulla (Felix) and Pompeius (Magnus) but like Gaius Marius (modestly content with two names), Caesar never assumed a cognomen.

Already in his fifty-sixth year and committed to the most ambitious military campaign in history, a campaign from which he might not return, Caesar had other concerns than setting another ornament on his brow.* The incident after the Latin Festival would have been forgotten had not someone during the night placed a laurel wreath entwined with a white fillet (an insignia of royalty) on one of Caesar's statues on the Rostra. On the pretext of enforcing Caesar's decree prohibiting any proposal of a crown, two tribunes arrested both the man who had first hailed Caesar as king as well as those who set the fillet on the statue, and in a "spontaneous" demonstration, they were acclaimed as Bruti (after the tyrannicide ancestor of Marcus Brutus who had compelled his countrymen to forswear all future thoughts of kings).

Exasperated by the incessant caviling of his detractors, Caesar reacted to this incident with hyperbolic fury. He denounced the tribunes as "brutes," not Brutuses, and when they complained on the Rostra that "they were unable to speak their minds freely and safely on behalf of the public good," he charged them with a provocation (hardly unlikely!). The loyal tribune, the poet Helvius Cinna, moved their expulsion from office, and Caesar deleted their names

---

*Napoleon, who found it desirable to crown himself Emperor of the French, rejects the charge that Caesar schemed for a crown as "absurd and calumnious," a canard inspired by Caesar's assassins, p. 214.

from the Senate rolls. Upon reflection, however, Caesar regretted his impetuosity. Summoning the father of one of the tribunes, he offered to advance the
man's two other sons if he disowned the recalcitrant one. "Caesar," replied the
man, "sooner will you snatch from me all my sons than that I should drive one
of these away."[8] In the tensions of the time, the incident had been inflated out
of all proportion, and Caesar had behaved like a testy monarch. Abashed at his
clumsiness, Caesar prompted the praetor Cinna (son of the consul and brother
to Caesar's first wife) to move that the exiled tribunes be permitted to return to
Rome as private citizens.

No action by Caesar could put an end to the sniping of his enemies.
Relentlessly, disgruntled oligarchs yipped at Caesar's heels. They goaded him
to anger and then embellished his retorts. He was said to have mocked Sulla
as an illiterate for retiring from his dictatorship, to have sneered that the
Republic was "a mere name without body or form" (a fact which few recognized and fewer admitted), and even to have asserted that "men ought now
to be more circumspect in addressing him and to regard his word as law." It
was said, too, that he constantly quoted a menacing verse of Euripides:

> If one must be unjust, it is best to be unjust in regard to tyranny, for other things
> one must be just.[9]

Caesar's enemies also spread the tale that the tribune Helvius Cinna was about
to propose a law authorizing Caesar to take more than one wife, like some
barbarian potentate, and that he would then marry the unpopular Cleopatra.
With her as his queen Caesar purportedly would transfer the capital of the
empire to Alexandria or to Ilium.

Caesar was aware that hostile oligarchs were provoking him to behavior
which he did not admire in himself, that they sought to drive him into the
moral degeneration tyrants suffered once they grew fearful for their lives. To
refute once and for all the charge of aspiring to a crown, the most damaging
and effective accusation against him, Caesar mounted the final theatrical coup
of his life.

At the festival of the Lupercalia on February 15, the day after the Senate
voted him the dictatorship for life, Antonius, chief of the Julian college of
Lupercalian priests, racing half naked through the streets in the ancient fertility
rite, halted before the Rostra, where Caesar sat enthroned on a gilded chair
attired in a purple robe and the high red shoes of the ancient Alban kings and
wearing a gold wreath. Events followed so quickly that observers could not
agree on what then ensued. Some declared that a certain Licinius (others said
one of the Lupercals) leaped up and placed a wreath with a royal diadem on
Caesar's head and that Antonius cried, "The people offer this to you through
me." All agreed that Caesar removed the wreath and turned to Lepidus for
assistance. Gaius Cassius reached down and set the diadem on Caesar's lap,
and the tribune Casca, another individual of doubtful loyalty, joined Cassius in
urging Caesar to accept it. Each time Caesar rejected the wreath, the people

applauded, and when Antonius leaped up and placed the diadem on Caesar's head, many gasped, but a few shouted, "Hail, king!" Lepidus, it was said, burst into tears. Finally, Caesar rose, removed the wreath and diadem from his head and tossed them from the Rostra. Declaring that a crown belonged only to Jupiter, he ordered that this one be taken to the temple on the Capitoline. He further announced that he would publish a notice in the public record reading: "To Gaius Caesar, perpetual dictator, Marcus Antonius, the consul, by command of the people offered the kingship; Caesar was unwilling."[10]

If Caesar had desired to assume a crown, his decision would have been made on the basis of political expediency, not out of vainglory, and he certainly would not have chosen a frenetic festival and a sweaty, half-naked Antonius for such a momentous announcement. In abandoning a triumph after his praetorship, Caesar had demonstrated his appreciation of the difference between the trappings of power and actual power. If he had sought a crown, he would have prepared carefully, mobilizing overwhelming support before braving both foes and lukewarm partisans by such a move. His enemies, of course, circulated the tale that in seeking a crown Caesar had been rebuffed by the people.

As the date (March 18) for Caesar's departure for his campaign against the Parthians approached, his enemies intensified their badgering. Playing on popular superstition, they reported that in the newly discovered grave of the ancient founder of the city of Capua men came upon a bronze tablet bearing the warning: "Whenever the bones of Capys shall be moved, it will come to pass that a son of Ilium shall be slain at the hands of his kindred." They made much also of the failure to find a heart in the vitals of a votive ox and of the seer's warning to Caesar to "beware lest thought and light should fail him, both of which . . . proceeded from the heart." They pretended outrage when Caesar scoffed, declaring: "The omens will be more favorable when I wish it."[11]

WHOSE VIOLENCE?

To the incessant reports of assassination plots Caesar would make no response beyond proclaiming through heralds the information relayed to him of conspiratorial meetings. To an accusation of treachery against Antonius and Dolabella, he responded, "I am not much in fear of these fat, long-haired fellows but rather of those pale, thin ones," and he pointed to Brutus and Cassius. Caesar could not disregard, however, graffiti scrawled on the statue of the regicide Lucius Brutus, "O, that you were alive!"; and on Caesar's statue nearby, "First of all was Brutus consul since he drove the kings from Rome. Since this man [Caesar] drove out the consuls he at last is made our king." Nor could he ignore handbills with such exhortations as: "Brutus, are you dead? You should be living at this hour! Your posterity is unworthy of you!"; and on Brutus' praetorian tribunal someone had scribbled, "Brutus, you're asleep!"

and "You are not Brutus!"; and as Brutus conducted his praetorian court, men chanted, "Brutus, Brutus, we need a Brutus!"[12]

Hirtius and Pansa, two associates of unquestioned devotion and men universally respected for their leniency to foes, advised Caesar "that that . . . won with the sword must be maintained with the sword," only to have Caesar reply "that he would rather die than be feared." He refused to employ informers or provocateurs against would-be assassins. "There is nothing more unlucky than perpetual watching," he declared, "that is the part of one who is always afraid," and musing to himself he added, "The recollection of cruelty is a wretched support for old age."[13]

Caesar's councilors investigated new expedients for safeguarding Caesar's initiatives in his absence. Five centuries earlier, after drafting a code of laws and compelling his fellow-citizens to swear not to amend any law without his approval, the Athenian sage Solon had deliberately set out on travels lasting ten years. He had been successful with his maneuver. Caesar's associates promoted more comprehensive measures, enjoining all senators to swear "to guard Caesar and Caesar's body with all their strength" and all magistrates to swear to uphold his acts, past and future, and the entire citizenry to take an oath to him as between troops and commander.[14]

In regard to his personal safety Caesar proved less than cooperative. He was aware that his enemies marveled at his "genius, calculation, memory, letters, industry, thought, diligence" and that they stood in awe of the "great labor, great dangers" by which he had attained supreme power. Whether out of bravado, lassitude or naive trust, Caesar refused to believe that he was threatened by men whose lives he had spared and whose careers he had advanced. When his councilors warned him of Marcus Brutus, Caesar put his hand upon his chest and said: "What, do you think that Brutus cannot wait for this poor flesh?" It had been reported to him, too, that Favonius, formerly Cato's most loyal collaborator, had rebuffed an invitation to join a conspiracy, declaring: "Better an illegitimate sovereign than civil war." Caesar was confident that he was not alone in apprehending that "it was not so much to his own interest as to that of his country that he remain alive" and that "if aught befell him, the commonwealth would have no peace but would be plunged into civil strife under much worse conditions."[15]

To the dismay of his councilors, Caesar dismissed his Spanish guard of two thousand men and walked through the Forum accompanied only by his lictors and a small entourage. "When his friends thought it best that he should have a bodyguard, and many of them volunteered for this service, he would not consent, saying that it was better to die once for all than to be always expecting death." Instead, he insisted that "the effort to surround himself with men's goodwill [was] the fairest and at the same time the securest protection." His associates wondered whether he was deliberately courting death or issuing a challenge to would-be assassins in accordance with Lucretius' injunction "to scrutinize a man in danger or peril and to discern in adversity what manner of man he is; for then are the words of truth drawn up from the very heart, the mask is torn off, the man remains."[16]

Weary of the incessant and fruitless battling against his own kind, Caesar had lost his zest. As much as Odysseus after the slaughter of the suitors, he yearned for an end to factional struggle. As the Homeric hero prepared for his final battle, Athena cried to him:

> Son of Laertes and the gods of old,
> Odysseus, master of land ways and sea ways,
> command yourself. Call off this battle now,
> or Zeus who views the wide world may be angry.

In the succeeding, and final, lines of his epic, Homer ends the conflict:

> Both parties later swore to terms of peace
> set by their arbiter, Athena, daughter
> of Zeus who bears the storm cloud as a shield.[17]

But Caesar could not count on divine intervention to end his conflict.

WHY, THIS IS VIOLENCE!

In the last days before Caesar's departure, hostile rumors and reports of dire omens multiplied. It was said, for example, that Caesar's cousin, Lucius Cotta, "one of the interpreters [of the Sibylline] verses was going to declare in the Senate that for . . . safety the man whom we had as king in fact should be made king also in name," a report later proved false.[18] On March 14, a little king bird bearing a sprig of laurel (the symbol of a triumpher) flew into the Hall of Pompeius, where the Senate was to convene the next morning. It was pursued by other birds and torn to pieces.

The evening of March 14, accompanied by Decimus Brutus, Caesar dined at the home of Marcus Lepidus. During the meal, while the others conversed, Caesar, as was his custom, read and signed correspondence. After dinner, however, over wine, Caesar proposed as a topic for discussion, "What is the best kind of death?" He himself commented on Xenophon's description of the death of Cyrus, a cynosure of kingship. Caesar could approve the sentiment in the king's deathbed instructions, an epitome of the Homeric view of life:

> You must always speak and act in regard to me as one blessed of fortune, for when I was a boy, I think I plucked all the fruits that among boys count for the best; when I became a youth, I enjoyed what is accounted best among young men; and when I became a mature man, I had the best that men can have. And as time went on, it seemed to me that I recognized that my own strength was always increasing with my years so that I never found my old age growing any more feeble than my youth had been; and, so far as I know, there is nothing that I ever attempted or desired and yet failed to secure.

On the other hand, Caesar found Cyrus' lingering death appalling and expressed a desire for a death "swift and sudden."[19]

With another intense day of activity to begin at dawn, Caesar left the gathering early. That night he suffered a seizure of vertigo, and Calpurnia tossed, murmuring and groaning in her sleep. A sudden blast of wind burst open doors and windows, and the sacred spears of Mars, lodged in the house of the pontifex maximus, shifted with an awesome clamor. Caesar awakened, however, to sounds of revelry, for it was the feast of Anna Perenna, goddess of the year, whose festival was celebrated on the first full moon of the first month (March under the ancient lunar calendar). According to legend, Anna, sister of Dido, queen of Carthage, followed Aeneas to Italy and became mistress to Caesar's ancestor. On her holiday, the Ides of March, the commons streamed to the banks of the Tiber and set up tents or huts of twigs draped with togas and prayed for as many years of life as the cups of wine they swilled, singing and dancing, the women letting down their long hair. On this festival day the crowds were augmented by hundreds of veterans who had streamed into town to accompany their old commander part way on the road to Brundisium for his final campaign.

Daughter of an Epicurean, Calpurnia had never displayed "womanish superstition." Now, distressed after weeks of rumors of assassination plots, she insisted that Caesar summon a soothsayer to interpret her nightmare. She had dreamed that Caesar lay on her bosom all bloody and that the house had collapsed about them. The seers alarmed her by not finding the upper part of the entrails in the sacrificial animal. Caesar laughed. He had received a similar warning from a seer during his last campaign in Spain. But after other victims proved equally unpropitious, at Calpurnia's insistence Caesar was about to send Antonius to dismiss the Senate, when Decimus Brutus arrived. A sober and unsmiling soldier, Decimus chided Caesar for keeping the senators waiting. "Come, sir," he exclaimed, "turn your back on these peoples' nonsense and do not postpone the business that deserves the attention of Caesar and of the great empire but consider your own worth a favorable omen."[20]

Caesar reminded himself of important matters to be dealt with. The question of Dolabella's assumption of the consulship in Caesar's place, for example, could not be postponed. As he rode in a litter through the street, the crowd, ignoring criers and lictors, swarmed about him. Commoners were eager to kiss his hand. Veterans came forward to be recognized by name, calling wishes for long life and success in battle. Petitioners pushed toward him, including the Greek philosopher Artemidoros, an old acquaintance of Caesar's and a former tutor to Marcus Brutus. He thrust a scroll into Caesar's hand and implored him to read it forthwith. At sight of Spurinna the soothsayer, Caesar cried, "Where are your prophecies now?" for Spurinna had warned him of the Ides of March. "Do you but see," said Caesar, "that the day which you feared is come and that I am alive?" "Ay, it is come," replied the soothsayer, "but it is not yet past."[21]

From Pompeius' theater came cheers and hooting, for Decimus Brutus was presenting gladiatorial games. At the adjacent meeting hall Caesar was greeted by more than a score of senators. Among them were men Caesar had advanced to high magistracies—the praetors Marcus Brutus and Gaius Cassius, the consular Trebonius, the tribune Casca, Tullius Cimber, governor designate of Bithynia and Pontus, the Ligarius Caesar had pardoned two years earlier and Aquila, the tribune who had refused to rise at Caesar's last triumph. Caesar could barely congratulate Cassius on his son's adoption of the toga of manhood that very morning, for a senator, reassured regarding an old petition, kissed Caesar's hand. As Caesar entered the hall, he noted that Trebonius detained Antonius at the door. Inside, the senators rose in greeting, and Caesar advanced to the podium near a statue of Pompeius recently restored at his orders. Cimber walked with Caesar and implored once again for the release of his brother from exile. As Caesar took his place on his gilded ceremonial chair, a group of senators pressed about him, joining in Cimber's plea. They clasped Caesar's hands and kissed his chest and head. Stifled, Caesar cried out that he would not rule on Cimber's brother at this moment. Cimber seized Caesar's purple toga and wrenched it from the shoulder.

"Why, this is violence!" cried Caesar.

Casca, who stood behind Caesar, struck Caesar with a dagger, grazing his shoulder.

"Accursed Casca, what are you doing?" exclaimed Caesar, jumping up and jabbing a stylus into Casca's hand. Casca cried to his brother for help. Someone stabbed Caesar in the side. Caesar turned about and flailed with his fists. He saw a whirl of desperate faces—Decimus Brutus, Marcus Brutus, Cassius, Ligarius, Galba (the legate who failed of election to a consulship), Basilus (a praetor awarded with a purse instead of a province) and the insolent tribune Aquila. As Caesar fought, the assassins struck wildly, wounding each other. Caesar heard Cassius cry to a fellow conspirator, "If you will it so, strike through me," and he thrust his dagger into Caesar's body.[22]

Caesar glimpsed Calvisius Sabinus and Marcius Censorinus, devoted officers, pushing toward the platform shouting encouragement to him, but Marcus Brutus plunged a dagger into Caesar's groin.

"You, too, child?" said Caesar.

Caesar muffled his head. He felt the assassins, frenzied, jab their daggers into him, and the blood spurting over his toga.

Caesar reached and drew his toga down toward his feet with his left hand, his final thought and action—"in order to fall more decently, with the lower part of his body also covered."[23]

EPILOGUE

L ONG live the Republic!" shouted the assassins. "The tyrant is dead."
"Run! Bolt the doors!" cried senators, scurrying from the hall.

Bewildered by the panic, instead of carrying off the corpse to dump it into the Tiber, as they had intended to do, the conspirators "wrapped their togas around their arms to serve as shields and with swords still reeking of blood"[1] ran to the Forum, proclaiming their deed as they went and calling out the name of their mentor—Cicero. One of the murderers bore a liberty cap on a spear and shouted the name of Lucius Brutus, the ancient hero who had expelled the last of the kings.

Word of Caesar's death reached the gladiatorial games and the holiday crowds carousing at the Campus Martius, and the people stampeded through the streets to their homes. Everywhere shutters were rung down and gates clanged.

The conspirators, dismayed, hurried to the Capitol and summoned gladiators to guard them.

In the empty hall Caesar's corpse lay abandoned. Three slaves lifted him and carried him to the domus publica, one arm flapping over the side of the litter.

Lepidus hastened to the Tiber island and put on alert the legion he maintained there as master of horse, Caesar's deputy. Ever a subaltern, he sent word to Antonius of his readiness to march into the city to arrest the assassins. Antonius and Fulvia, feverishly fortifying their mansion, urged Lepidus to caution. A messenger from the conspirators assured Antonius that he faced no danger. Antonius summoned the Senate, and Cicero, aware of the general dread of a new civil war, proposed an amnesty for the conspirators. The assassins, demoralized by their failure to win the immediate approval of the citizenry, did not dare to demand the annulment of Caesar's acts; and, claiming they had opposed a tyrant and not his laws, they accepted a Senate resolution honoring both those already in force and those Caesar had projected. (Of course, the only man who could implement these acts was dead.) Furthermore, the assassins acceded to a funeral and to Caesar's burial in the Campus Martius, next to his daughter.

A gilded model of the Temple of Venus Genetrix erected on the Rostra reminded Romans both of Caesar's divine ancestry and of the monuments with which he had been adorning the city. Underneath lay his corpse on a couch of

ivory with coverlets of purple and gold, and his purple robe, bloody and
tattered from dagger strokes, hung on a pillar beside him. So numerous were
the individuals and groups bringing offerings for his pyre that they "were
directed to bring them to the Campus by whatsoever streets of the city regardless of any order of precedence." At funeral games, "to rouse pity and indignation at his death, these words from the Contest of Arms by Pacuvius, a tragedian of the previous century, were sung: "Saved I these men that they might
murder me!" At the reading of the oath taken by all senators to guard Caesar's
safety, ordered by Antonius in lieu of a eulogy, and then of Caesar's will, the
people stirred uneasily. Caesar had honored some of his murderers and left his
gardens across the Tiber as a public park as well as a bequest of 300 sesterces
to every citizen of Rome.

As the bier, carried by magistrates and ex-magistrates, was lowered from the
Rostra, two men with torches in sudden passion rushed forward and set it
afire. As though jolted to a realization that Caesar was no more, men and
women seized branches and frantically heaped up benches from the tribunals
to feed the flames. "The musicians and actors tore off their robes, which they
had taken from the equipment of his triumphs and put on for the occasion,
rent them to bits and threw them into the flames; and the veterans of the
legions, the arms with which they had adorned themselves for the funeral;
many of the women, too, offered up the jewels which they wore and amulets
and robes of their children."[2]

"Kill Brutus, kill Cassius!" men and women cried, and seizing brands a
crowd raced off to the mansions of the leaders of the conspiracy. On the way
they encountered Helvius Cinna, the tribune ever faithful to Caesar, and mis-
taking him for Caesar's former brother-in-law, they tore the hapless poet
apart. (The other Cinna had pulled off his praetorian toga declaring that he
would no longer wear insignia granted him by "the tyrant," his one-time
brother-in-law and constant benefactor.)

Emerging from retirement, the False Marius exhorted the people to erect a
column of Numidian marble in the Forum with the inscription "To the Father
of His Country," and as though sensing Caesar's continuing presence among
them, the people settled disputes there, taking oaths in Caesar's name. The
various nationalities paraded to the spot where Caesar had been slain, each
lamenting in its own tongue and according to its own rites, "above all the Jews,
who even flocked to the spot for several nights."[3]

Apart from the brief riot following upon Caesar's funeral, the city was tense
but quiet. Without the arbiter and mainstay of peace among the varied conflicting elements, no one knew what to do; all factions feared the others and
trembled in expectation of some uncontrollable upheaval. It was as though all
elements of the population and all factions sensed that unless they pretended
that Caesar was still among them, an explosion might erupt in which no party
could muster strength to achieve dominance, and violence would rage without
cease.

Undoubtedly prodded by Fulvia,* Antonius initiated the inevitable struggle for the murdered leader's power. Angry that Octavius and not he had been set down as Caesar's heir, Antonius nevertheless represented himself as Caesar's successor. He brought before the Senate and the People a series of radical bills, drafts of which he claimed to have discovered among Caesar's papers. In addition, he seized 700 million sesterces deposited in the Temple of Wealth for Caesar's projects and campaigns.

The assassins, having decided simply to rely on Fortune after killing Caesar, had prepared no program. They found themselves helpless to establish control over the commonwealth or even to offer proposals for the restoration of the antebellum Republic. Incapable of viewing the world in a dynamic of unremitting struggle and change, Cicero and the conspirators had been convinced that upon Caesar's death his policies and programs would disappear with him. They spoke of liberty and meant plunder, and with boundless arrogance they assumed that the populace would not merely accept but even welcome the restoration of the oligarchic city-state, under whose constitution and military power a coterie of aristocratic pirates had pillaged a helpless empire.

Less than a month after the murder, Cicero, the self-proclaimed mentor of the opposition party, a statesman who prided himself on being Rome's leading political theoretician, the man who for two years had exhorted others to assassinate "the tyrant," was expressing perplexity to his friend Atticus at "what never happened in any other state—that the constitution has not been recovered when freedom has." Two weeks later he was wondering whether in exhorting others to the assassination of Caesar he might not have committed an error. "At times," he exclaimed, "one almost wishes for Caesar back again." Paradoxically, however, he expressed bewilderment at the despair of far wiser men. Matius, for example, astonished him by exclaiming: "If Caesar with his genius could not find a solution [to the imperial crisis], who will find it now?" By May, forgetting his own role in abetting the murder, Cicero was complaining that "the deed was done with the courage of men but with the blind policy of a child." Three days later he was expressing astonishment when Hirtius charged that "a most distinguished person had been killed, that by his death the whole state has been thrown into disorder; that [Caesar's] acts will be null and void as soon as the [assassins] have ceased to fear; that his clemency was his destruction and that if he had not practiced clemency such a thing could not have happened to him."[4] Cicero did not recognize that Hirtius' complaint pertained particularly to him.

In June, three months after Caesar's murder, at a conference called by Ser-

---

*One of the most remarkable women of her time, Fulvia was to persuade one of her husband's brothers to join her in a rebellion against Octavius in the hope of recalling Antonius from his philandering with Cleopatra. She apparently counted on support from followers of each of her three husbands: Clodius, Curio and Antonius. The rebellion failed. Shakespeare's line in Antony and Cleopatra upon Antony's learning of her death, "Can Fulvia die?" sums up the vigor and resolution of this extraordinary woman.

vilia, Cicero listened in silence as Caesar's former mistress promised to obtain Senate authorization for the prompt departure of her son and son-in-law for the provincial governorships to which Caesar had appointed them, for neither Brutus nor Cassius could remain safely at Rome. Servilia had been estranged from her son for more than a year, and he had undoubtedly not taken her into his counsel regarding the conspiracy. At the meeting, to Cicero's chagrin, Servilia was not interested in his advice, and he reported to Atticus: "I found a ship breaking up or rather already in wreckage." A week after this conference, Cicero was berating the "liberators" for having accomplished their "heroic deed" with "no plan, no reason, no system."[5]

Now past sixty, after almost four decades of involvement in Roman politics, Cicero had not yet learned that the party to which he committed himself twenty years earlier never had a program, unless Sulla's attempt some thirty-five years earlier to return the republic to its condition before the Gracchan reforms could be considered such. Balking at any modification in the traditional city-state institutions, the Old Guard had shown themselves myopic in policy, corrupt in private and public affairs and quick to violence in face of any challenge to their hegemony. Vainly seeking to shore up the Sullan order, the dictator's successors had sabotaged the registration of new citizens, resisted sharing the imperial plunder with the entrepreneurs and municipal aristocracy, opposed restoration of the civil rights of their political opponents and reform of the courts and of the provincial administration and sought to block all measures for alleviating the misery of the urban and rural plebs. They proved lethargic in dealing with the menace of piracy and incompetent in crushing a servile rebellion in Italy and rebellions in the provinces. Only twice after Sulla's death had they exhibited energy and initiative, in Cicero's consulship and in Pompeius' second consulship, and on both occasions they exercised their power for repression.

Why, therefore, should Cicero have expressed bewilderment at the failure of his protégés to offer a political program in place of Caesar's? And Cicero was the most thoughtful of Caesar's foes.

When Antonius initiated a new civil war, Octavius, cheated of much of his inheritance by Antonius, turned to Cicero and the optimates, and once again Cicero found himself in the best of all possible worlds. As mentor to Caesar Octavianus, as Caesar's heir now was called, Cicero saw himself anew as the arbiter of the republic. In a series of polemics against Antonius, he revived the invectives of his consulship and regaled Rome with the bombast of the old anti-subversive campaign—"that greatest struggle in the history of mankind!" "We are defending the temples of the immortal gods," he cried, "our homes and the abodes of the Roman people, the altars, hearths and the sepulchers of our ancestors; we are defending our laws, law courts, liberty, wives, children, fatherland." In his exultation, he could not understand why the aged Lucius Cotta, the last of Aurelia's three cousins, "yielding to a sort of irresistible despair [as Lucius himself described his state]" rarely attended the Senate.[6]

Abruptly, Lepidus reconciled Octavius and Antonius, and the three warlords compelled the Senate to recognize them as a ruling directorate. Under the pretense of avenging Caesar, they drew up a proscription list of their enemies, marking one hundred and four senators for death. In explanation of their rejection of Caesar's policy of clemency, the triumvirs declared:

> Had not perfidious traitors begged for mercy and when they obtained it become the enemies of their benefactors and conspired against them, neither would Gaius Caesar have been slain by those whom he saved by clemency after capturing them in war, whom he admitted to his friendship and upon whom he heaped offices, honors and gifts. . . . Now seeing that the malice of those who have conspired against us and by whose hands Gaius Caesar suffered, cannot be mollified by kindness, we prefer to anticipate our enemies rather than suffer at their hands.[7]

With a vindictiveness reminiscent of the Sullan era, each of the triumvirs demanded of the others the death of a close connection. Antonius surrendered his uncle Lucius Caesar; Lepidus, his brother, Paullus; and Octavianus, his mentor, Cicero. Julia, Antonius' mother, interceded successfully for her brother, Lucius Caesar, but this time there was no Caesar to pardon Cicero and to raise him up. He was overtaken in flight, and an officer sent Antonius the orator's head and hands, the appurtenances of his eloquence. Antonius exulted: "Now let our proscriptions have an end."[8]

Arguments among scholars regarding the motivations for Caesar's clemency have little meaning unless his actions are set in perspective with Sulla's before him and with the triumvirs' after him. The only answer to the question whether Caesar's clemency represented his genuine sentiments or mere opportunism is that motivations for such profound policies are always complex. For the beneficiaries of this clemency, the question had no meaning, for they discovered that after he achieved supreme power he did not reverse his policy. He permitted Cicero to publish exhortations for his overthrow and refused to initiate a hunt for the subversives who were conspiring to kill him.

What other autocrat, past or present, has matched Caesar's clemency?

When Hirtius and Pansa, thoughtful men and protagonists in that tumultuous time, declared to Caesar "that that had been won by the sword must be maintained by the sword"; they were posing a realistic and fundamental question for which history provides no certain answer: whether Caesar would have acted with more humanity and served the empire better by executing a hundred or so irredeemable oligarchs or, if he was incapable of promoting a proscription, he had at least rendered these men powerless by confiscating their property and exiling them to some distant corner where they could foment no rebellions.

If Caesar had acted upon the advice of Hirtius and Pansa to look to his defenses, would scholars then have denounced him for cruelty?

Caesar recognized and warned that civil war would ravage the empire if he was killed, but the self-proclaimed champions of liberty and defenders of the constitution, the subversive-hunters, the praters of piety, of patriotism and of the ancestral virtues were prepared to pull down the world if their outmoded privileges were not restored. In the end, in a further series of civil wars along with all the conspirators thousands were to perish throughout the empire and vast regions were to suffer devastation.

On the other hand, though Caesar might have conducted a proscription of his enemies, he seems to have recognized that under no circumstances could he succeed in the years remaining to him in transforming the city-state into an imperial state. Within less than a year (the discontinuous months he was able to spend in Rome from the crossing of the Rubicon until his murder) with characteristic deliberation and decision he gave the impulse to a transformation in the empire politically, socially, economically and culturally. Nevertheless, another major upheaval was required to establish the conditions for the achievement of the changes which he dimly envisioned. That task was left for Caesar's heir.

Weary of turmoil at the conclusion of the renewed civil war, the empire hailed the victorious Caesar Octavianus as the peacemaker. Profiting from his adoptive father's experience and from the annihilation of the Old Guard nobility in proscriptions and on the battlefield, the new Caesar revived the outward forms of the old oligarchic republic and made a pretense of restoring the constitution. Only thirty-two, with four decades in which to effect Caesar's projects and his own, Octavianus, later called Augustus, continued Caesar's colonization plans and beautified Rome. He abandoned, however, Caesar's major engineering projects and his codification of the laws. He did serve as a patron of the arts, which flourished under his rule as never before or after in the empire. He completed the conquest of Spain, reached an agreement with Parthia, suffered a catastrophic defeat in Germany and gave up Caesar's bold plan to secure indefinitely the eastern and northern frontiers. He reconstructed temples and shrines, for in "the loss of nerve" throughout the Mediterranean world in the period following upon Caesar the enlightened Epicurean philosophy yielded before superstition in a triumph of astrology and, especially, of cults preaching subservience in this world and a blessed life in the hereafter.

Generations were to pass before the role of the emperors was defined and nostalgia for the oligarchic republic faded. Meanwhile, indicative of the rising influence of peoples whose role in the empire Caesar augmented was the assumption of imperial rule first by representatives of the Italian, rather than the Roman, aristocracy and then by Spaniards and thereafter by natives of Gaul and then of Africa. With the extension of the franchise and of the participation of provincials in the management and benefits of the empire, there began a period of peace and prosperity of a vast common market reaching eventually from Scotland to the Red Sea. Everywhere towns were erected with skilful planning, furnished with aqueducts, baths, theaters, markets, temples, sports complexes and majestic public squares, all adorned with fountains and statuary. With wars banished to distant frontiers, the empire enjoyed an apparently permanent peace, and, writing from the perspective of the eighteenth century, Edward Gibbon could rightly proclaim: "If a man were called to fix the period in the history of the world during which the condition of the human race was most happy and prosperous, he would without hesitation name that which elapsed from the death of Domitian [a cruel emperor assassinated in 96 A.D.] to the accession of Commodus [a monster who ascended the throne in 180 A.D.]."

The difference between Caesar and the Ciceros and the Catos of his day and of all subsequent times is that unlike them Caesar saw society as an integrity in motion; he was not confused by the apparent disconnection among social, economic, political and cultural developments. Thus he did not vacillate from week to week or even day to day in his judgments, and he was able both to evolve grandiose plans and to effect them. Caught up in profound and impelling personal experiences interrelated with the fundamental struggles of his day, Caesar evolved into an instrument of history. Eventually he was locked into his role so that he could not diverge from the course of action that history was effecting through him. As an instrument of history, he awed his contemporaries with his energy, imagination and varied and stupendous achievements. No one of his day sensed the future as he did or explored as many aspects of life experience, testing the limits of human capacities and seeking, in effect, to compel the world to adapt itself to his personal vision and aspirations. At the zenith of his power, he discovered, of course, that the world yields to the will of no single man or even to any assemblies of men, that out of the conflicting wills of all men a synthesis, neither anticipated nor fully desired, emerges.

What renders Caesar so compelling, even to those who reject what he represented as a historical force, was his refusal to accept the limitations of a lifetime; he sought to accomplish in his single day what, in fact, was to require generations. Throughout a career embracing almost four decades, he gambled repeatedly with his very life. In his final gamble, he failed by a mere three days (he would have been out of reach of his assassins, safe among his legions).

Among tyrants and dictators, Caesar stands unique. Ever conscious of the corruption that threatens men commanding absolute power, he disdained to enforce conformity through repression, rejected terror as a political weapon, refused to be alarmed by rumors, scorned the use of informers and despised the hunting of "subversives." Though harried into short temper and badgered by fools, he remained Caesar to the moment of his death. A man of extraordinary complexity, he possessed a penetrating intelligence coupled with a universal curiosity, an unyielding will and inexhaustible energy as well as an exuberance about the dynamic variety in life. As a foe he proved fierce and cunning, yet with an irresistible charm and a trenchant wit he captivated (and still captivates) even his enemies. Writing to the orator in the summer of 44, Caesar's friend Matius sought in vain to convey a sense of Caesar's greatness to an uncomprehending Cicero:

They put it down to my discredit that I am sorely grieved at the death of a very intimate friend and resent the fall of one I loved; for they declare that patriotism must come before friendship just as if they have already demonstrated that his death has been of benefit to the state. But I shall use no ingenious arguments; I frankly confess I have not reached their high level of philosophy. . . . I strove that mercy should be shown to our defeated fellow-citizens. . . . Is it possible then that I who desired the security of all should feel no resentment at the fall of him from whom that boon was obtained? . . . My desire is that all the world should feel the bitterness of Caesar's death.[9]

Caesar did engage in the unscrupulous tactics of the politics of his day. He caused savage bloodshed in Gaul, and his failures and shortcomings have been precisely catalogued. But the Classical ideal as propounded by Homer, the Greek tragedians and Aristotle extolled heroes, not saints—men who tested the frontiers of human capacities in this world, not in a hereafter. In the epic Caesar created of his life, he achieved a coalescence of the Greek Odysseus (who explored himself within all the varieties of experience and challenged the very powers of nature) and the Roman dedication and civic service of Aeneas, Caesar's own legendary ancestor.

Caesar is the greatest personality of the thousand years of Roman history. Rightfully do we continue to commemorate him in the seventh month of the year.

ANCIENT SOURCES

The following is a list of texts referred to in the notes, not a complete list of ancient sources consulted. Unless otherwise noted, all texts are from the Loeb Classical Library. Abbreviations employed in the notes are at the right.

Ammianus Marcellinus, John C. Rolfe, 3 vols.
The Apocrypha and Pseudepigrapha of the Old Testament in
    English Translation, ed. R. H. Charles, 2 vols., Ox-
    ford, 1913.
Appian, Roman History, Horace White, 4 vols.
    Celtica
    The Civil Wars   Appian
    The Illyrian Wars
    The Mithridatic Wars   Appian, Mithr.
Aristotle, H. Rackham
    Nicomachean Ethics
    Politics
Athenaeus, The Deipnosophistae, C. B. Gulick, 6 vols.   Athenaeus
Sextus Aurelius Victor, Liber de viris illustribus, ed. Fr.   Aurelius Victor
    Pichlmayr, Leipzig, 1961.
Caesar
    Gallic War, H. J. Edwards   BG (I–VIII)
    Civil Wars, A. G. Peskett   BC (I–III)
    (Corpus Caesarianum), A. G. Way
        Alexandrian War   B. Alex.
        African War   B. Afr.
        Spanish War   BH
Cato, De re rustica (and Varro), H. B. Ash and W. D. Hooper   Rustica
Catullus, The Poems of, tr. Horace Gregory, New York,   Catullus
    1956.
Cicero
    Orations:
        1. John Henry Freese
        Pro Quinctio
        Pro Sextio Roscio Amerino   Rosc. Am.
        Contra Rullum (De lege agraria) I, II, III   Leg. Agr.

2. The Verrine Orations, L. H. G. Greenwood, 2 vols.
Divinatio
Part I   Verr., I
Part II   II Verr. i–v
3. H. Grose Hodge
Pro Caecina
Pro lege Manilia   Leg. Man.
Pro Cluentio
Pro Rabirio Perduellionis   Pro Rab.
4. Louis E. Lord
In Catilinam   Cat., I–IV
Pro Flacco
Pro Murena
5. N. H. Watts
Pro Archia
Post reditum in Senatu   Red. Sen.
Post reditum ad Quirites   Red. Quir.
De domo sua   Dom.
De haruspicum responsis   Har. resp.
6. R. Gardner
Pro Sestio
In Vatinium   In Vat.
7. R. Gardner
Pro Caelio
De provinciis consularibus   Prov. Cons.
Pro Balbo
8. N. H. Watts
Pro Milone
In L. Calpurnium Pisonem   In Pis.
Pro M. Aemilio Scauro   Pro Scauro
Pro M. Fonteio   Pro Fonteio
Pro C. Rabirio Postumo   Rab. Post.
Pro M. Marcello   Pro Marcello
Pro Q. Ligario   Pro Ligario
Pro rege Deiotaro   Pro Deiotaro
9. C. A. Ker
Philippics
Scholia in Ciceronis Orationes Bobiensia, ed. Paul
    Hildebrandt, Leipzig, 1907.
Ciceronis Orationum Scholiastae II, ed. Thomas Stangl,   Schol. Gronovianus
    Vienna, 1912.
Asconius, Orationum Ciceronis quinque enarratio, A. C.   Asconius
    Clark, London, 1907 (1966).
Letters:
1. To Atticus
Cicero's Letters to Atticus, tr. D. R. Shackleton Bailey,   Att.
    New York, 1978.
2. To His Friends, W. Glynn Williams, 3 vols.   Fam.

3. Letters to Quintus, W. Glynn Williams — QFr.
and: Q. Cicero, Handbook of Electioneering — Comment. Pet.
(Commentariolum petitionis), Mary Henderson
Rhetorical, Philosophical and Other Works:
De inventione, H. M. Hubbell
De oratore — De or.
I and II, E. W. Sutton and H. Rackham
III, H. Rackham
Paradoxa stoicorum, H. Rackham — Parad. stoic.
Brutus, G. L. Hendrickson
and: Orator, H. M. Hubbell
De natura deorum, H. Rackham — Nat. D.
De officiis, Walter Miller — Off.
De re publica — R. P.
and: De legibus, Clinton Walker Keyes — Leg.
De divinatione, William Armistead Falconer — Div.
Tusculan Disputations, J. E. King — Tusc. Disp.
De finibus bonorum et malorum, H. Rackham — De fin.

Dio Cassius, Roman History, E. Cary, 9 vols. — Dio Cassius
Diodorus Siculus, R. M. Geer, C. H. Oldfather, C. L. — Diod. Sic.
   Sherman, F. R. Walton, C. B. Welles, 12 vols.
Diogenes Laertius, R. D. Hicks, 2 vols.
Dionysius of Halicarnassus, Roman Antiquities, Spelman,
   rev. E. Cary, 7 vols.
Florus, Epitome of Roman History (and Nepos), E. S. Forster — Florus
Fronto, The Correspondence of, C. R. Haines — Fronto
Aulus Gellius, The Attic Nights, John C. Rolfe, 3 vols. — Gellius
Greek Anthology, W. R. Paton, 5 vols.
Herodotus, The Histories, tr. Aubrey De Selincourt, — Herodotus
   Harmondsworth, Middlesex, 1954 (1960).
Hippocrates, W. H. S. Jones, 4 vols.
Homer
   The Iliad, tr. Richmond Lattimore, Chicago, 1951 (1967).
   The Odyssey, tr. Robert Fitzgerald, Garden City, N.Y., — Odys.
   1961 (1963).
Horace, Satires, Epistles, Ars Poetica, H. R. Fairclough
   Odes and Epodes, C. E. Bennett
Juvenal, G. G. Ramsay
Livy, Ab urbe condita, B. O. Foster, Russel M. Geer, Frank — Livy
   Gardner Moore, Evan T. Sage, Alfred C. Schlesinger,
   14 vols.
Lucretius, De rerum natura, W. H. D. Rouse — Lucretius
Macrobius, The Saturnalia, tr. Percival Vaughan Davies, — Macrobius
   New York, 1969.
Cornelius Nepos, De viris illustribus (and Florus), John C. — Nepos
   Rolfe

Nicholas of Damascus' Life of Augustus, tr. Clayton Morris   Nicholas of Damascus
    Hall, Smith College Classical Studies, IV,
    Northampton, Mass., 1923.
Obsequens (in Livy, vol. 14)
Paulus Orosius, The Seven Books of History against the   Orosius
    Pagans, tr. Roy Defarrari, Washington, 1964.
Ovid, Amores, Grant Showerman
Plato, Phaedo, tr. Jowett
Plautus, Paul Nixon, 5 vols.
Pliny, Natural History, H. Rackham, W. H. S. Jones, D. E.   Pliny
    Eichholtz, 10 vols.
Plutarch, Lives, Bernadotte Perrin   Plut. (with
    individual life
    in italics)
Polybius, The Histories of, tr. Evelyn S. Shuckburgh,   Polybius
    Bloomington, 1962.
Quintilian, Institutio oratoria, H. E. Butler, 4 vols.   Quintilian
Remains of Old Latin, E. H. Warmington, vols. 1 and 2.
Sallust, J. C. Rolfe
    Bellum Catilinae   B. Cat.
    Bellum Jugurthinum   B. J.
    Histories
    Invectives
    Epistles to Caesar, I and II
C. Sallusti Crispi Historiarum Reliquiae, ed. Bertoldus
    Maurenbrecher, 2nd ed., Stuttgart, 1967.
The Elder Seneca, Controversiae, Suasoriae, Michael
    Winterbottom, 2 vols.
Seneca, Moral Essays, John W. Basore, 3 vols.
    Epistulae morales, R. M. Gummere, 3 vols.
Strabo, The Geography, H. L. Jones, 8 vols.   Strabo
Suetonius, J. C. Rolfe, 2 vols.
    The Lives of the Caesars   Suet. (with
    individual life
    in italics)
    (the Life of
    Caesar is simply:
    Suet.)
    Grammarians and Rhetoricians
Tacitus, The Histories and The Annals, Clifford H. Moore
    and John Jackson, 4 vols.
    Dialogus, Sir Wm. Peterson
Terence, John Sargeaunt, 2 vols.
Thucydides, The Peloponnesian War, tr. Crawley, ed. John   Thucydides
    H. Finley, Jr., New York, 1951.
Valerius Maximus, Factorum et Dictorum Memorabilium,   Val. Max.
    ed. Karl Kempf, Stuttgart, 1888 (1966).

Varro (and Cato), Rerum Rusticarum, Wm. Davis Hooper   RR
    and Harrison Boyd Ash
Velleius Paterculus, Frederick W. Shipley   Velleius
Vitruvius, De architectura, F. Granger, 2 vols.   Vitruvius
Xenophon, Cyropaedia, Walter Miller, 2 vols.
    Memorabilia and Oeconomicus, E. C. Marchant
    Scripta minora, E. C. Marchant
Zonaras, Fragmenta Historicorum Graecorum, III, ed. Carl   FGrH
    Mueller, Paris, 1874.

Miscellaneous: anthologies, etc.
A Book of Latin Quotations, ed. Norbert Guterman, New   Latin Quotations
    York, 1966.
The Complete Greek Tragedies, 4 vols., ed. David Grene and
    Richmond Lattimore, 1959–1960.
Corpus Inscriptionum Latinarum, Berlin, 1863–   CIL
Oratorum Romanorum Fragmenta, H. Malcovati, Turin,
    1953.
The Oxford Book of Greek Verse in Translation, ed. T. F.
    Higham and C. M. Bowra, Oxford, 1938 (1958).
Sources for Roman History, 133–70 B.C., A. H. J. Greenidge
    and A. M. Clay, 2nd ed., rev., E. W. Gray, Oxford,
    1961 (1966).

NOTES

Abbreviations match those in the Ancient Sources list. Notes contain the sources for all quoted material within a paragraph.

PREFACE

1. This approach has dominated much of British and American Roman historiography although it has undergone penetrating criticism by scholars like Arnaldo Momigliano, who wrote as long ago as 1940: "History is the history of problems, not of individuals or of groups. If the tacit assumption of much prosopographical research is that people are moved by personal or family ambition, the assumption is not merely one-sided, it substitutes generic trends for concrete situations." (In a review of *The Roman Revolution* by Ronald Syme, a leading proponent of the prosopographical approach to Roman history, *The Journal of Roman Studies,* XXX, 1940, 75–80.)
2. Isaiah Berlin, "The Concept of Scientific History," *Concepts and Categories,* New York, 1979.
3. E. H. Carr, *What Is History?* (New York, 1962), 163.
4. Christopher Lasch, *The Culture of Narcissism: American Life in an Age of Diminishing Expectations* (New York, 1979), 25.
5. *The City in History* (New York, 1961), 262.

I: AURELIA

1. Posidonius, cited by Athenaeus, VI, 274.
2. Livy, XXXIV ii–vii.
3. Probably relying upon some lost biography of Caesar, Tacitus, writing a century and a half later (Dialogus, 28), cites Aurelia as an example of an outstanding mother of an earlier day; Seneca thus describes (De ira, II, 8) the upbringing of previous generations.
4. Plut., *Marius,* VIII.
5. Velleius, II xiv.

II: GAIUS

1. Plut., *Cato Maior,* XXIII; Macrobius, III xiv, 6 ff.
2. Translated by Lionel Casson, *Classical Age* (New York, 1965).
3. The first two appear in Caesar's own writings: BG III, 18 and BC II, 27 for the first

459

and BC II, 8 for the second. The remainder are from Latin Quotations: Naevius, Ennius, Plautus and Lucilius, respectively; *Oxford Book of Greek Verse*, translated by Sir Wm. Marris, 138.
4. Plut., *Cato Maior*, XXI.
5. Rustica, Preface.
6. In a dialogue set early in the century, Cicero puts these words in the mouth of the censor Marcus Antonius (De or., I, 249); Plut., *Cato Maior*, V.
7. Politics, I, 1253b.
8. Cicero, R. P., II, 39.
9. Juvenal, XIV, 47.

III: THE PRAETOR'S SON

1. De fin., V, 65; Livy, II iii, 4.
2. Suet., *Nero*, II.
3. De or., III, 94; Plut., *Cato Maior*, XXIII; De or., II, 265.
4. Plut., *Marius*, XXVIII.
5. CIL, I (2), 15.
6. De or., II, 162; Gellius, XIX, 14.
7. Suet., Grammarians, VII.
8. Latin Quotations, 3; Gellius, XVI i, 4; Heauton Timorumenos, 77.
9. Xenophon, II, 21 ff.
10. Epistle II ii.

IV: THE GRAND DESIGN

1. Cicero, Nat. D., II, 5; De fin., II, 46.
2. Cicero, Dom. 14.
3. Cicero, Brutus, 173; De or., II, 220.
4. Livy, II i, 9.
5. Cicero, De or., III, 4; Velleius, II xiv.
6. Asconius, p. 22.

V: THE ITALIAN REVOLT

1. Appian, I, 43.
2. Cicero, Rosc. Am., 47; Odys., VIII, 470; XI, 488–491.
3. Remains of Old Latin, I, Annales, 200–202.
4. Cicero, Brutus, 305.
5. Plut., *Tiberius Gracchus*, IX.
6. Plut., *Marius*, XXXI.
7. Latin Quotations, 41; Plut., *Cato Maior*, XXI.
8. Plut., *Sulla*, VII.

VI: MURDERED CLANSMEN AND JUPITER'S PRIEST

1. Odys., VIII, 182–185; Plut., *Marius*, XXXIV.
2. Quintilian, VI iii, 65.

3. Plut., *Marius,* XXXV; Cicero, De or., III, 31; II, 152.
4. Appian, I, 57.
5. Val. Max., III viii, 5.
6. Plut., *Marius,* XXXIX.
7. Appian, I, 65.
8. Plut., *Sertorius,* IV.
9. Cicero, Tusc. Disp., V, 56.
10. Annales, VIII.

VII: THE CONSUL'S SON-IN-LAW

1. Cicero, Leg., II, 47; Off., II, 57; Brutus, 148.
2. Telamo, Latin Quotations, 23; Cicero, De fin., II, 74.

VIII: PERIPETEIA

1. Velleius, II xxvi.
2. Seneca, De clementia, XII, 2.
3. Appian, I, 94 (a quotation from Aristophanes' Knights, 542).
4. Plut., *Sulla,* XXI.
5. A fragment from the Atreus quoted by Seneca, De ira, I, 4; Orosius, V, 21; Plut., *Sulla,* XXXI.
6. Cicero, Pro Archias, 14; Prometheus Bound, 1002–1006.
7. Epidemics, I, 24.
8. VII, 204.
9. Phoenix, Latin Quotations, 23.
10. Seneca, Epistle XI, 4.

IX: THE OAK WREATH

1. Suetonius and Plutarch both recount this anecdote in the first chapters of their biographies of Caesar. The tale may have been invented by Caesar's enemies years after this event. It would have enjoyed credence because it conformed to general knowledge about the dictator's vexation at any braving of his will and about Caesar's mettlesome resolve even as a youth.
2. Plut., *Caesar,* LXIX.
3. Strabo, V iv, 11.
4. Odys., I, 296–302; II, 276–280; Cicero, Fam., I i, 28.
5. Appian, Mithr., IX, 63.
6. Plut., *Sulla,* XXXVI, XXIII; Cicero, Rosc. Am., 135.
7. Dio Cassius, XXVI, 16.

X: THE OUTSIDER

1. Plut., *Pompeius,* XIV.
2. De inventione, II, 173 ff.
3. Pro Quinctio, 51. It cannot be ascertained either in this or in other speeches

whether Cicero published the text he had actually delivered or modified the text subsequently to serve some purpose of the moment.

4. Rosc. Am., 36; 127; 130; 139.
5. Plut., *Sulla*, XXXV.
6. Among the fragments of Sallust's Histories is a speech supposedly delivered by Lepidus. This and other speeches of the decade of the seventies are to be accepted as representative of the political positions of that period if not as authentic reproductions of actual speeches (I, 55).
7. Plut., *Pompeius*, XV.
8. Cited without a source by J. M. Cobban in *Senate and Provinces, 78–49 B.C.*, 4. From the ancient sources it is impossible to fix precisely the date of Sulla's resignation of the dictatorship.
9. Appian, I, 104.
10. Plut., *Sulla*, XXXVIII.

XI: DEBUT IN THE FORUM

1. From the Lepidus speech in the fragments of Sallust's Histories, I, 55.
2. Sallust, Histories, I, 71.
3. Cicero, Leg. Man., 62.
4. Cicero, Brutus, 216, 127.
5. Plut., *Sertorius*, XVIII.
6. Ibid. XIV.
7. Cicero, Har. resp., 19.
8. Cicero, Brutus, 317; ibid.
9. Suet., XLV; Brutus, 261; Suet., IV; XLIX.
10. Gellius, XI xviii; Cicero, Verr., I, 38.
11. Cicero, Brutus, 317; Comment. Pet., 8.
12. Plut., *Caesar*, IV.

XII: THE PONTIFEX

1. Q. Cicero, Comment. Pet., 47–48.
2. Ibid.
3. Sallust, Histories, II, 47. All selections from the Cotta speech are from this source.
4. Cicero, Brutus, 178.
5. Plut., *Lucullus*, V.
6. Cicero, Brutus, 316.
7. Sallust, Histories, II, 98.

XIII: WARLORDS

1. Hiero, IV, 3.
2. Plut., *Sertorius*, XXII.
3. Macrobius, Saturnalia, III, 13.
4. Livy, XXI lxiii, 4; Plut., *Comparison of Crassus and Nicias*, I; Cicero, Parad. stoic., VI, 43.

5. Gellius, V xiii, 6.
6. Cicero, Pro Fonteio, 42–43; Plut., *Caesar*, V.
7. Cicero, Brutus, 238.
8. Histories, II, 48 ff.
9. Cicero, II Verr. iii, 91.
10. Cicero, Off., I, 25; Plut., *Crassus*, VII.
11. BG I, 40: "We made trial of them of late in Italy in the slave revolt . . . men whom you had feared without cause during a long time when they had no arms, you subsequently subdued though they had taken up arms and won victories."
12. Plut., *Crassus*, XI.
13. Ibid.

XIV: THE OLD MAN'S SUCCESSOR

1. Nicomachean Ethics, I, 7.
2. Cicero, Verr. I, 45; 44–45; Gellius, XIII iii, 5.
3. Verr. I, 40.
4. Ibid. Div., 7.
5. Ibid. I, 18.
6. II Verr. iii, 223–224; ibid.
7. Ibid. v, 126.
8. Plut., *Pompeius*, XXIII.
9. Plut., *Sertorius*, XXVI.
10. Plut., *Caesar*, V.
11. Suet., VI.
12. Robert Coles, *Erik H. Erikson: The Growth of His Work* (Boston, 1970), 243; Plut., *Caesar*, V.

XV: ALEXANDER

1. BC I, 61.
2. V, 37–39.
3. Strabo, III i, 6.
4. Ibid. III ii, 9.
5. Odys., XI, 617–624; Suet., VII.
6. Odys., XI, 636–639; Suet., VII.
7. Ibid.
8. Plut., *Marius*, VIII.
9. Cicero, Off., 88.
10. Cicero, almost twenty-five years later, Philippic III, 13.

XVI: POMPEIUS' ASSOCIATE

1. Sallust, B. J., 63.
2. Plut., *Sertorius*, XXII.
3. Plut., *Caesar*, V; Suet., XLV.
4. Plut., *Caesar*, V.

5. Cicero, II Verr. v, 126.
6. Cicero, Pro Flacco, 22.
7. Plut., *Lucullus*, XX; ibid.
8. Ibid. XXXIV.
9. Dio Cassius, XXXVI, 24; Plut., *Pompeius*, XXXV.
10. Dio Cassius, XXXVI, 25 ff.
11. Plut., *Tiberius Gracchus*, XV.
12. Plut., *Pompeius*, XXXVI.

XVII: THE OLIGARCHY DIVIDED

1. B. Cat., XXXIX; Val. Max., VII, 8.
2. Epidicus, 735.
3. Plut., *Cicero*, IX.
4. Cicero, Att., I iv, early 66; Plut., *Cicero*, IX.
5. Cicero, Leg. Man., 35.
6. Ibid. 4; 14; 18; 19.
7. Ibid. 59; 69.
8. Plut., *Cicero*, IX.

XVIII: MARIUS AGAIN

1. Cicero, Div., I, 20.
2. Quintilian, VIII iii, 3.
3. Plut., *Caesar*, VI.
4. Suet., X.
5. Plut., *Caesar*, VI.
6. Ibid.

XIX: PRELUDE TO BATTLE

1. Herodotus, I, 33.
2. Politics, 1307b.
3. Plut., *Cato*, XVII.
4. Ibid.
5. Ibid.; Cicero, Pro Murena, 61 ff.; Plut., *Cato*, XVII.
6. Pro Ligario, 12.
7. Q. Cicero, Comment. Pet., 10; Sallust, B. Cat., V.
8. Cicero, II Verr. v, 182.
9. Cicero, Att., I ii, July 65; Cicero, Pro Caelio, 14.
10. Att., I i, before July 27, 65.
11. Nepos, The Life of Atticus, 6.
12. Att., I ii.
13. B. Cat., XXIII.
14. Comment. Pet., 2. Although some scholars deny the authenticity of the document, none denies its value in illuminating the problems confronted by Cicero in this campaign and his strategy for resolving them.

15. Cicero, Pro Cluentio, 111; II Verr. iii, 81.
16. Quintilian, XI iii, 93.

XX: LEADER OF THE RESISTANCE

1. II, 1164–1169; Odes II, xviii, 23–28.
2. Leg. Agr. II, 12.
3. Ibid. II, 13; I, 22.
4. Ibid. II, 55.
5. Ibid. II, 10.
6. Ibid. I, 18.
7. Ibid. I, 23–24.
8. Ibid. I, 26; II, 23.
9. Ibid. II, 15; 10; Off. II, 43; Leg. Agr. II, 12; 15.
10. Ibid. 70; Varro, RR II, Pref., 3; Leg. Agr. II, 71.
11. Ibid. III, 7; II, 65; 103.
12. Ibid. I, 27.
13. Ibid. II, 91.

XXI: COUNTERATTACK

1. Leg. Agr. II, 82; 100; 103.
2. Cicero, II Verr. i, 151.
3. Livy recounts the tale, I xxvi.
4. A description of a portion of the procedure appears in the extant passages of Cicero's defense speech (Pro Rab., 13).
5. Macrobius, III xiii, 4.
6. Pro Rab., 2, 3.
7. Ibid. 12; 18.
8. Ibid. 24.
9. Ibid. 25.
10. Cicero, Pro Flacco, 98.
11. Cicero, Off. II, 78; In Pis., 4.
12. I, 60.
13. Plut., Caesar, VII.

XXII: CATILINA'S TORMENT

1. Pro Quinctio, 49.
2. B. Cat., XX.
3. Pro Caelio, 13; B. Cat., XXV.
4. Cat., II, 22 ff.
5. Plut., Cato, XX.
6. Suet., Augustus, V. The anecdote is probably a later invention, but it provides evidence in any case of the growing popularity of astrology among the aristocracy at this time.
7. Pro Murena, 50; Dio Cassius, XXXVII, 29.

8. Pro Murena, 51.
9. Ibid.
10. Dio Cassius, XXXVI, 29.
11. Cat., I, 27.

XXIII: THE CONSPIRACY OF CICERO AND CATILINA

1. Cicero, Div., I, 105.
2. B. Cat., XXXIII.
3. Ibid. XXXIV.
4. Cat., I, 2.
5. Ibid. 5, 6 and 9.
6. Ibid. 10.
7. Ibid. 13.
8. Ibid. 20.
9. Ibid. 21; 30.
10. Ibid. 32.
11. Sallust, B. Cat., XXXI.
12. Cat., II, 1; 3; 4; 8.
13. Cicero, Off., II, 84; Cat., II, 11.
14. Ibid. 14; 25.
15. Ibid. III, 70.
16. Ibid. II, 28.

XXIV: THE PROMISE OF EVERLASTING PEACE

1. Sallust, B. Cat., XXXIV–XXXV.
2. Cicero's admission many years later regarding his behavior at the trial—De fin., IV, 74; Pro Murena, 65; Plut., Cato, XXI.
3. Pro Murena, 78; 85.
4. Pro Sestio, 12.
5. Plut., Gaius Gracchus, XVII.
6. Sallust, B. Cat., XL.
7. Pro Fonteio, 27, 44; Pro Murena, 42.
8. Cat., III, 10.
9. Ibid. 9.
10. Ibid. 12; Schol. Gronovianus, p. 290; Cat., IV, 13.
11. Ibid. III, 14–15.
12. Ibid. 25. A suggestive comparison can be made with Senator Joseph R. McCarthy's denunciation of the Communists as "a conspiracy on a scale so immense as to dwarf any previous such venture in the history of man" (America's Retreat from Victory [New York, 1951], 169).
13. Cat., III, 26. Cicero would have his wish. Century upon century school children would plod through his four orations against Catilina, persuaded by awe-struck teachers (themselves persuaded by equally awe-struck professors) of Cicero's supposed defense of liberty against the forces of anarchy.
14. Cat., III, 29.

XXV: CAESAR GIVES WARNING

1. Plut., *Cicero*, XX. Plutarch recounts a similar tale in connection with a figure of Greek history, but Cicero was as familiar with Greek history as Plutarch and might have been inspired by the earlier legend to concoct a similar miracle in collaboration with his wife and sister-in-law. We are under no obligation to ape the Cicero-worshipers through the ages in doubting that Cicero would engage in such trickery.
2. Cat., IV, 6.
3. In his monograph on the Catilinarian conspiracy (LI), the contemporary historian Sallust provides a précis of Caesar's speech which concurs with Cicero's summation in the fourth Catilinarian speech. Indeed, Sallust may have had available the stenographic notes of the proceedings and, perhaps, a copy of the speech that Caesar published himself.
4. "The Mitylenean Incident," III, 42–51.
5. Cat., IV, 9; 10.
6. Ibid. 11–12; 16.
7. Plut., *Cato Maior*, VIII; Sallust (B. Cat., LII) presents a summary of this speech, which in Plutarch's day was the only speech by the Man of Virtue still extant; Polybius, VI, 56.
8. Plut., *Cicero*, XXII.
9. Leg. Agr., I, 27.
10. Plut., *Brutus*, V.
11. Plut., *Lucullus*, XXXI; Plut., *Cato Maior*, VIII.
12. Cicero, Fam., V ii, to Metellus Celer, January or February 62.
13. Plut., *Cato*, XXVI.
14. Plut., *Caesar*, VIII.
15. Odys., III, 121–122.

XXVI: POMPEIUS MISCALCULATES

1. Sallust, B. Cat., LXI; Florus, II xii; B. Cat., LXI.
2. Ibid. XXII.
3. Ibid. XXIII.
4. Fam., VII xxvi.
5. Att., I xiii, January 25, 61.
6. Pliny, VII, 97–99.
7. Suet., LXXI.
8. Ibid. XLVI.
9. Plut., *Caesar*, X.
10. Velleius, II xl, 2.
11. Plut., *Cato*, XXX.
12. Plut., *Pompeius*, XLIII; Att., I xiv, February 13, 61.
13. Seneca, Epistle CXXII, 2.
14. LXXXVI.
15. IV, 1121–1140.
16. Att., I xiv, February 13, 61.

17. Ibid.
18. Appian, II, 8.

XXVII: DEPRIVED OF A TRIUMPH

1. Plut., *Caesar,* XI.
2. Zonaras (FGrH), X v.
3. Strabo, III, 3.
4. Lucretius, V, 34–36.
5. Cicero, Pro Balbo, 43.
6. Att., I xviii, January 20, 60; Dio Cassius, XXXVII xl.
7. Att., I xviii, January 20, 60.
8. Pro Caelio, 60.
9. Att. I xx, May 60; II i, June 60.
10. Ibid.
11. Plut., *Lucullus,* XXXIX; Att., I xviii, January 20, 60.
12. Plut., *Lucullus,* XLI.
13. Varro, RR, III xii, 2.
14. Suet., XIX.
15. Ibid.
16. Dio Cassius, XXXVII lxiii.

XXVIII: POMPEIUS' CONSUL

1. Velleius, II xli.
2. Dio Cassius is the chief source for this and subsequent events in this chapter. He provides a credible account of the session, XXXVIII, l ff.
3. This anecdote is recounted by Dio Cassius, XXXVIII, cxi.
4. Cicero, In Vat., 23.
5. The scene appears in Dio Cassius, XXXVIII, lvii.
6. Plut., *Pompeius,* XLVII.
7. Cicero, In Pis., 9; Lucretius, VI, 83–91.
8. Appian, II, 11.
9. Att., II i, June 60; QFr., I i, end of 60.
10. Appian, II, 3.
11. Cat., IV, 20.
12. Catullus, LXXVII.
13. Quintilian, IV ii, 124.
14. Att., II v, April 59.

XXIX: FATHER-IN-LAW TO THE GREAT MAN

1. Att., II xvi, April 29 or May 1, 59.
2. Greek Anthology, XI, 44. The Phaeacians were the inhabitants of a utopian kingdom visited by Odysseus, where he competed in athletic contests.
3. In an imaginary dialogue Cicero puts these words in Cato's mouth, De fin., 74.

4. The quotations are from Lucretius' Epicurean epic, De rerum natura (The Nature of Things), respectively: II, 118–120; III, 964–965; II, 578–580; V, 857–859; I, 151–154; II, 7–15.
5. Plut., *Caesar,* XIV.
6. Suet., XX.
7. Suet., XX–XXII.; Seneca the Elder, Controversiae, VII iv, 7; Suet., XLIX; Att., II xix, July 59.
8. Att., II xxiv, before October 18, 59.
9. Catullus, XCVIII. Tenny Frank's emendation of "Victius" is plausible (*American Journal of Philology,* XL, 1919, 405).
10. Cicero, In Pis., 37.
11. Pro Flacco, 1 and 5.
12. Ibid. 12 and 67.
13. Ibid. 94 and 104.
14. Ibid. 25.

XXX: CONSOLIDATING DEFENSES

1. Velleius, II xlv.
2. Appian, II, 15.
3. Cicero, Har. resp., 47.
4. In Pis., 12
5. Plut., *Cato,* XXXIV.
6. Cicero, Red. Sen., 13; Pro Sestio, 28; Dio Cassius, XXXVIII xvi, xvii.
7. Att., I xx, May 6, 60.
8. In Pis., 75; Plut., *Cato,* XXXV.
9. Suet., XX.
10. Velleius, II xli.

XXXI: MASTERING THE ARTS OF WAR

1. BG I, 8.
2. Sallust or Pseudo-Sallust, Invective against Cicero.
3. Tusc. Disp., II, 37. Cicero presents a brief description of basic training in the legions.
4. Cicero, Dom., 16.
5. Ibid. 22.
6. BG I, 13.
7. Ibid. 14.
8. Ibid. 19.
9. Ibid. 21.
10. Ibid. 29. Such statistics in ancient sources are always suspect, but these figures represent a census, and Camille Jullian, dean of French scholars on ancient Gaul, notes (II, 6) that "the cantons where the Helvetians lived in 1850 contained a population of one and a half millions and . . . a population of a quarter of a million in 58 B.C. does not therefore seem unlikely."

XXXII: APPRENTICESHIP IN IMPERIALISM

1. BG I, l.
2. Diogenes Laertius, I, 6.
3. Pro Fonteio, 11.
4. Diod. Sic., V, 26.
5. Cicero, Off. I, 38; BG I, 33.
6. Ibid. 35.
7. Ibid. 36.
8. Livy, XLV xii, 5–6; BG I, 39.
9. Ibid. 39: Thus several years later, in October 54, Cicero wrote to a protégé he had recommended to Caesar: "Your letters during the first months used to worry me that you were sometimes . . . capricious in your longings for the city and city life, sometimes indolent, sometimes timorous in your military duties and too often . . . just a little presumptuous." This Trebatius was the kind of junior officer of whom Caesar was complaining at Vesontio.
10. Nicomachean Ethics, II vi, 3.
11. BG I, 40.
12. Ibid. 41.
13. Ibid. 43; Appian, Celtica, XIII; BG I, 44.
14. Ibid. 46.
15. Ibid. 40.
16. Ibid. 53.

XXXIII: CONSOLIDATION IN GAUL AND AT ROME

1. Plut. Caesar, XX; Cicero, Har. resp., 48.
2. BG I, 1.
3. Ibid. II, 15.
4. Ibid. 20; 25.
5. Ibid. 28; 31.
6. Red. Sen., 29; Red. Quir., 16; Pro Domo, 15.
7. Red. Sen., 8.
8. Ibid. 32.
9. QFr., 5.
10. BG II, 27.
11. Ibid. 35.
12. Ibid. III, 1; 7.
13. Strabo, VI vii, 12.
14. Although Strabo (III v, 11) does not state whether the Publius Crassus whom he mentions in this connection is the father or the son of Marcus Crassus, it seems more likely that the son is meant. He, after all, had the assignment of compelling the Gallic tribes of the Channel region to accept Roman dominion; his grandfather as proconsul of Spain would have had a less direct impetus to make the journey to the "tin islands." BG III, 8.
15. QFr., II iii, February 12–15, 56.
16. Lucretius, VI, 417–422.

17. Plut., *Pompeius,* XLIX.
18. Pro Sestio, 128; the discussion of the "two classes" appears at 96 ff.
19. Dom. 95; Macrobius, II i, 12; II iii, 5.
20. Har. resp., 40; 59.
21. Ibid. 22.
22. QFr., II v, April 11, 56.
23. Plut., *Pompeius,* LI.

XXXIV: "SHATTER THE CONFINING BARS OF NATURE'S GATES . . ."

1. Plut. *Caesar,* XX; QFr., II iv, March 5–6; Plut., *Caesar,* XXI; Att., IV vi, c. April 19, 56; Prov. Cons., 33–34.
2. Prov. Cons., 38, 42.
3. BG III, 10.
4. Ibid. 13.
5. Ibid. 14.
6. Ibid. 16–17.
7. Ibid. 23.
8. Val. Max., VI ii, 6; Plut., *Cato,* XXXIX.
9. Plut., *Cato,* XLIII.
10. BG IV, 7.
11. Catullus, XXVIII; XLVII.
12. Varro, RR, I, 7. R. Dion refers to fossilized wood submerged along much of the coast from Brittany to Denmark from which a small quantity of salt can be obtained by burning ("Les campagnes de César en l'année 55," *Revue des études latines,* XLI, 1963); BG IV, 16.
13. Ibid. 17.
14. Ibid. 19.
15. Ibid. 20; Plut., *Caesar,* XXIII; BG IV, 20; Odys., IX, 174–176; BG IV 21.
16. Ibid. 21; 25.
17. Strabo, III, 8; BG IV, 2; Lucretius, VI, 1106–1107.
18. BG IV, 33.
19. Fam., VII i, September or October 55; Dio Cassius, XXXIX, 38; Pliny, VIII, 20.
20. Lucretius, I, 68–71.
21. Plut., *Caesar,* XXII.

XXXV: "MIGHTY IN HONOR AND FAME"

1. Plut., *Cato,* LI.
2. Plut., *Crassus,* XVI; Div., II, 84.
3. BG V, 1.
4. QFr., II xiii, February 14, 54; Fam., VII v, April (?) 54.
5. Pro Caelio, 39–41.
6. Cicero, Leg., II, 39.
7. Quintilian, X i, 114; Cicero, Brutus, 262.
8. Catullus, XII, XIV, XXXVIII, XCV; Fam., X xxxi, March 16, 43, Asinius Pollio in a letter to Cicero explaining his attitude toward the assassinated Caesar.

9. QFr., II xi, February 10 or 11, 54. The translation of Cicero's obscure comment has been subject to much interpretation; the text may be corrupt. Lucretius, III, 260.
10. Cicero, Brutus, 235.
11. Ibid.; Gellius, I, 4; Brutus, 258.
12. Fam., VII v, April 54; Brutus, 253; 252.
13. Two centuries later, writing to his former pupil the Emperor Marcus Aurelius, Fronto expressed wonderment at Caesar's literary achievements, including this treatise (II, 29): "Gaius Caesar, while engaged in a most formidable war in Gaul wrote besides many other military works two books of the most meticulous character, On Analogy, discussing amid flying darts the declension of nouns and the aspiration of words and their classification mid the blare of bugles and trumpets." Only scanty fragments of Caesar's work remain.

XXXVI: NEW VICTORIES, NEW GLORY

1. Lucretius, I, 72–73; BG V, 2–3.
2. Ibid. 5; 6–7.
3. QFr., II xi, August 54; BG V, 13; Lucretius, I, 127–129.
4. Strabo, IV, 200.
5. Dio Cassius, XXXIX, 64.
6. QFr., III viii, November 54.
7. Cicero, Brutus, 247.
8. QFr., III iv, October 24, 54.
9. Seneca, De consolatione, XIV, 3.
10. BG V, 29.
11. Ibid. 54.
12. Att., IV xvii, October 1, 54; QFr., III ix.
13. Athenaeus, VI, 273; Plut., Cato, IX; Catullus, XI.
14. Dio Cassius, XXXIX, 61.
15. Att., IV xix, end of November.
16. Rab. Post., 42; 44; R. P., II, 20.
17. R. P., II, 69.

XXXVII: COLLAPSE OF THE TRIUMVIRATE

1. Seneca the Elder, Controversiae, X i, 8; Quintilian, IX iii, 95.
2. BG VI, 1; Plut., Cato, XLV.
3. BG VI, 8.
4. Plut., Pompeius, LIV.
5. BG VI, 34.
6. Ibid. 43.
7. Lucretius, VI, 9–19.
8. BG VI, 44.
9. Fam., VII xii.
10. Lucretius, V, 1448–1457.
12. BG VI, 19; 13.

13. Ibid. 15.
14. Ibid. 22.
15. Obsequens, 63.
16. Appian, II, 22.
17. Plut., *Pompeius,* LIV.
18. Ibid. LV.

XXXVIII: AT BAY

1. BG VII, 1.
2. Ibid. 17.
3. Ibid. 19.
4. Ibid. 21.
5. Pro Milone, 37; 76; 77; 80; 103.
6. BG VII, 29.
7. Ibid. 52.
8. Ibid. 54.
9. Ibid.
10. Ibid. 66.
11. Ibid. 69.
12. Ibid. 75.
13. Ibid. 76.
14. Ibid. 77.
15. Ibid. 80.
16. Ibid. 88.
17. Dio Cassius, XL, 41.
18. Florus, I xlvi, 26; Dio Cassius, XL, 41.

XXXIX: AN OUTSIDER ONCE AGAIN

1. Plut., *Cato,* L.
2. Fam., V xviii, undated.
3. BG VIII, 3.
4. Ibid. 6–8. Excavations in peat bogs at Brieul-le-Sec have disclosed two bridges with a roadway constructed of prefabricated sections laid on bundles of brush-wood and fastened by stakes driven into a riverbed (J.-J. Hatt, *Celts and Gallo-Romans* [London, 1979], fn., p. 139); BG VIII, 22.
5. Suet. XXVIII; Fam., IV iii. In this letter written in September 46 Cicero recalled Servius' warning.
6. Fam., VIII i, June 51. This is the first of a series of reports of events in Rome written by Caelius to Cicero, absent as governor in Cilicia, reports providing first-hand information about developments for more than a year; Appian, II, 26.
7. Fam., VIII i, June 51.
8. Att., V xvi, August 9–11, 51.
9. Fam., VIII i, June; Suet., XXX.
10. BG VIII, 38.
11. Ibid. 39.
12. Fam., VIII xi, September 2, 51; ibid. viii, October 51.

13. Ibid.
14. Ibid.
15. BG VIII, 41–42. Hirtius' praise exemplifies the adulation of Caesar's officers for their commander.
16. Ibid. 42; 32; 44.
17. Ibid. 48.

XL: RECONCILIATION IN GAUL, ISOLATION AT ROME

1. BG VIII, 49.
2. Plut., *Pompeius*, LI; Suet., XXVII; XXVII–XXVIII; Att., VI i, February 24, 50.
3. BG VIII, 52; Appian, II, 28.
4. Fam., VIII iv, August 1, 51; Velleius, II xlviii.
5. Att., VI i, February 20, 50; Fam., VIII vi, February 50.
6. Att., VII xxi, February 13, 50; V i, February 24, 50.
7. Fam., VIII xi, April 50.
8. Plut., *Pompeius*, LVII.
9. BG VIII, 54.
10. Plut., *Pompeius*, LVII.
11. BG VIII, 50.
12. Ibid.; Fam., VIII xiv, August 50.
13. BG VIII, 51.

XLI: CIVIL WAR?

1. Fam., VIII xiv, early August 50.
2. Macrobius, III xiv; Fam., VIII xiv, August 50.
3. This document (called the Second Epistle to Caesar because it follows another, similar letter in the extant manuscript though obviously referring to prior events) is a subject of controversy among scholars. Those who doubt its authenticity do not, generally, question its accuracy as a reflection of the political debate at Rome at the end of the year 50.
4. Att., VI viii, October 1, 50.
5. Att., VII i, October 16, 50, written during Cicero's journey from the East.
6. Suet., XXIX; Plut., *Caesar*, XXIX.
7. The events of these days are described in Appian (II, 30 ff.), very likely summarized from a comtemporary account. Though embellished, the scene resembles scenes described in Caelius' letters to Cicero earlier the same year.
8. Att., VII iii, December 9, 50.
9. Ibid. v, mid-December; VII vi, December 18, 50; VII vii, December 19, 50.
10. Ibid.
11. Suet., XXIX; Att., VII viii, December 25 or 26, 50.
12. Ibid.; ibid., ix, December 27, 50.

XLII: "THE DIE IS CAST"

1. BC I, 1.
2. Plut., *Caesar*, XXX.

3. BC I, 3.
4. Fam., IV i, April 49: Cicero recalling his experiences in a letter to Servius, consul of 51.
5. Fam., IV i, April 49; Suet., XXX; Plut., *Cato,* LI.
6. Suet., XXVII.
7. Fam., IV i, April 49; XVI xi, January 12, 49.
8. BC I, 7.
9. Lucretius, I, 38–40; Catullus, III, 70–74.
10. Velleius, II xlix.
11. Lucretius, II, 257.
12. Suet. XXXI; Plut., *Caesar,* XII. Plutarch cites Asinius Pollio, an officer on Caesar's staff, a historian and a friend of the poet Catullus; ibid. XXII; Suet., XXXI.

XLIII: MORE THAN DIGNITY

1. BC I, 7.
2. Suet., LVIII.
3. Plut., *Pompeius,* LX.
4. Appian, II, 37; Plut., *Pompeius,* LXI.
5. BC I, 8.
6. Ibid. 9.
7. Att., VII xv, January 26, 48.
8. Att., VII xv, February 8, 49.
9. Ibid.
10. BC I, 15.
11. Att., VII xii, February 9, 49; ibid. xxiii, February 10, 49; ibid. VIII i, February 15 or 16, 49; ibid. iii, February 18–19, 49.
12. Amores, III xv, 8–10; BC I, 18.
13. Ibid. 22.
14. Ibid. 23.
15. Att., VIII ix, February 25, 49.
16. Ibid. xi, February 27, 49.
17. Ibid. xvi, March 4, 49; ibid. IX iia, March 8, 49.
18. Ibid. viic, March 5, 49.
19. BC I, 26.

XLIV: MASTER OF ITALY?

1. Att., IX vii, March 13, 49; Cicero, Pro Ligario, 33; Att., IX x, March 18, 49; ibid. xi, March 20, 49; ibid. xvi, March 26, 49.
2. Ibid. xiv, March 24 or 25, 49; ibid. xviii, March 28, 49.
3. Ibid. x, March 18, 49.
4. BC I, 32.
5. Ibid.; Att., X viii, May 2, 49.
6. Plut., *Caesar,* XXXV.
7. Suet., XXXIV.

XLV: MASTER OF THE WEST

1. BC I, 35.
2. Ibid. 36; 34.
3. Ibid. 39.
4. Cicero, Pro Scauro, 38; 44.
5. Appian, II, 40.
6. Att., X viii, May 2, 49.
7. BC I, 40.
8. Ibid. 44.
9. Ibid. 58.
10. Ibid. 53.
11. Ibid. 50; 54; 64.
12. Ibid. 71; 72.
13. Ibid. 82; 84.
14. Ibid. 85.
15. Ibid. II, 7.
16. De arch., X xvi, 11–12. This work, written by Vitruvius many years after this battle, would have enormous influence on Renaissance architects.
17. BC II, 13.
18. Ibid. 29; 38.
19. BG VIII, 8.
20. BC III, 1.
21. Ibid.; Dio Cassius, XLI, 38.
22. Ibid. 39.
23. Politics, 1295b.

XLVI: THE CONSUL AND THE REBEL

1. BC III, 2.
2. Ibid. 6.
3. Ibid. 10.
4. Ibid. 11.
5. Ibid. 14.
6. Ibid. 16.
7. Ibid. 19.
8. Velleius, II lxviii; Cicero, Fam., VIII xvii, February 48—Caelius writing about himself to Cicero.
9. The incident is related by Appian (II, 58).
10. BC III, 47–48.
11. Ibid. 43; 57.
12. Cicero, Fam., IV vii, September 46.
13. Ibid. VIII iii, Cicero recollecting in May(?) 46; ibid. IX ix, May 48.
14. BC III, 51; 53.
15. Ibid. 59.
16. Ibid. 69; Plut., *Caesar,* XXXIX.
17. BC III, 70; Plut., *Caesar,* XXXIX.

NOTES TO PAGES 355–374

18. BC III, 64.
19. Ibid. 71.
20. Ibid. 73; Appian, II, 63; BC III, 74.
21. Ibid. 68; Lucretius, II, 217–224.
22. BC III, 72.

XLVII: THE TOPPLING OF POMPEIUS

1. BC III, 85.
2. Ibid. 86.
3. Livy, I, Preface, 9.
4. BC III, 90.
5. Ibid. III, 91.
6. Ibid. 92; 93.
7. Plut., *Caesar,* LXII.
8. Cicero, Pro Deiotaro, 28; Plut., *Caesar,* LXII.
9. Florus, II xiii, 49.
10. BC III, 96; 98; Dio Cassius, XLI, 62.
11. Suet., XXX, quoting Pollio, who was present at the battle.
12. BC III, 99.
13. Dio Cassius, XLI, 63.
14. BC III, 18; Plut., *Pompeius,* LXVII; Plut., *Comparison of Agesilaus and Pompeius,* IV; Att., XI vi, November 27, 48; Plut., *Pompeius,* LXVIII.
15. Iliad, Homer, V, 464–469.
16. BC III, 32.
17. Appian, II, 88.
18. BC III, 105; Plut., *Caesar,* XLVII. Plutarch comments: "At any rate Livy [a native of Patavium and a youth at this time] insists that this was so."
19. B. Alex., 42.
20. Plut., *Brutus,* VIII.

XLVIII: EGYPT

1. Herodotus, I, 38–39.
2. Plut., *Caesar,* XLVIII.
3. The description of the historian Diodorus of Sicily, who visited Alexandria a few years before Caesar, XCII lii, 5.
4. I, Preface, 3.
5. Tcherikover, *Hellenistic Civilization and the Jews* (Philadelphia, 1959), 337, applies this description written centuries later in the Talmud to the Alexandria of Caesar's day.
6. Deuteronomy, 4, 8; Exodus, 23, 9.
7. Apocrypha, Psalm of Solomon, II.
8. Greek Anthology, XI, 44.
9. B. Alex., 39.
10. BC III, 110.
11. Plut., *Caesar,* XLIX.
12. B. Alex., 3.

13. Plut., *Caesar,* XLVIII; Dio Cassius, XLII, 19.
14. B. Alex., 23–24.
15. Ibid. 32.

XLIX: MASTER OF THE EAST?

1. Scholars disagree as to whether this was actually Caesar's child. The boy was called "Caesarion" (Caesar's son) by the Alexandrians. Ancient sources do not pose the question of his paternity.
2. Diod. Sic., I xxxi, 6 ff.
3. Ibid. 9; Herodotus, II, 125.
4. Strabo, XVII i, 48.
5. B. Alex., 33.
6. Ibid. 63.
7. Ibid.; ibid. 65.
8. BC III, 31; Att., XIV i, April 7, 44, a month after Caesar's assassination.
9. B. Alex., 77; Appian, II, 91; Plut., *Caesar,* L.
10. B. Alex., 78; Strabo, XIV i, 42; Fam., XIII xxix, early in 46, Cicero writing to Plancus, one of Caesar's legates.
11. B. Alex., 78.
12. Diod. Sic., XXXII xxvii, 3.
13. B. Alex., 78.

L: SUBMISSION AND MUTINY

1. Fam., XV xv, August 3, 47, Cicero writing to Gaius Cassius little more than a month before Caesar's arrival at Taranto.
2. Suet., L.
3. Dio Cassius, XLII, 49.
4. Plut., *Antonius,* X.
5. Suet., *Augustus,* LXIX–LXXX.
6. Dio Cassius, XLII, 50–51.
7. This scene, described by both Appian (II, 92 ff.) and Dio Cassius (XLII, 53), undoubtedly derives from a contemporary account, very likely the history written by Caesar's staff officer Pollio.
8. Suet., LVII; LXII; LXV; LXVII.

LI: MASTER OF AFRICA

1. Suet., XLIX.
2. Plut., *Cato,* LVII.
3. Att., XI vii, December 17, 48.
4. B. Afr., 10.
5. Plut., *Caesar,* LII.
6. Suet., LXVI; Plut., *Caesar,* LII.
7. B. Afr., 54; Plut., *Caesar,* LII.
8. B. Afr., 47; 61; 31; Dio Cassius, XLIII, 5.

9. B. Afr., 56.
10. Ibid. 20; 26.
11. Ibid. 82.
12. Ibid. 83–85.
13. Suet., LXXV; B. Afr., 89; Plut., *Cato*, LXXII; LXVI.
14. Vitruvius, VIII iii, 25; B. Afr., 92.

LII: "THE OLD ORDER THRUST OUT BY THE NEW"

1. If Dio Cassius embellished an account contemporary with Caesar or invented this scene (XLIII xvii), Caesar's speech, as he reports it, conforms in content and tone with contemporary documents and with Caesar's subsequent actions.
2. Fam., IX ii, late April 46; ibid. vii; ibid. vi.
3. Cicero after Caesar's assassination—Philippic VIII, 18.
4. Suet., LI; XLIX.
5. Dio Cassius, XLIII, 20.
6. Ibid. 23.
7. Nicholas of Damascus, VIII.
8. Lucretius, I, 1–14; Pliny, XXXV, 26.
9. Called the First Epistle because it precedes the earlier letter in the extant manuscript, this document, like the Second Epistle, is not universally accepted as Sallustius'. No one questions, however, the insights it affords into issues of the period immediately after Thapsus. The letter finds echoes in Cicero's letters and speeches and conforms to Caesar's actions at this time. All subsequent Sallustian passages are from this epistle.
10. The date and content of this work, discovered among scrolls in Calpurnius' house in Herculaneum, are investigated by Pierre Grimal, *Revue des études latines*, XLIV, 1966, 254–285.
11. Vitruvius, I v; Cato the Elder, Rustica, I xii. The Pomptine marshes were not drained until Mussolini's day. The tunnel project, abandoned after Caesar's death, was taken up by Claudius a century later with thirty thousand workers engaged for eleven years (Pliny, XXXVI, 124).
12. Fam., IV, i, late September 46, Cicero writing to Servius, Marcellus' colleague in the consulship and Caesar's current appointee as governor of Greece.
13. Pro Marcello, 8, 16, 17, 28–29.
14. R. P., II, 51; Pro Marcello, 23.
15. Plut., *Cicero*, XXIX.
16. Pro Ligario, 30; 37; Plut. *Cicero*, XXX; Fam., VI xv, September 24, 46, Cicero to Ligarius before the trial; Lucretius, II, 569–575.

LIII: "EVERLASTING CONFLICT . . ."

1. Lucretius, II, 116–122; Pliny, VII, 91 ff.; Fam., VI vi, end of September 46—Cicero to an unpardoned Pompeian.
2. Lucretius, III, 451–458; 1076–1090; 935–939; Pro Marcello, 23; Fam., XV xix, late January 45—Gaius Cassius to Cicero; Pro Marcello, 25; 32.
3. Macrobius, II vii.

4. Seneca the Elder, Controversiae, VII iii, 9.
5. Odys., V, 153–154; 221–224.
6. Strabo, IV i, 12.
7. Fam., VI iv, January 45; IV iv, September 46; Brutus, 251; 213; 118; 331.
8. Val. Max., IX ii, 4; BH, 17; 19.
9. Att., XII iv, May (?) 46, at the time of the composition of the eulogy; Orator, 35.
10. Pro Marcello, 27.
11. Plut., Cato, LXV; Phaedo, 79D; Tusc. Disp., I, 74 (this quotation from a subsequent work by Cicero probably echoes the Cato eulogy); Seneca, Epistle XXIV, 7 (though almost a century later, Seneca's quotation is derived either from Cicero's eulogy or from one of the others that appeared after Cicero's or is composed in the spirit of the Cato-worshipers inspired by Cicero and the others who lauded Cato as a martyr to freedom); B. Afr., 45.
12. BH, 30; Suet., LX; BH, 30.
13. Plut., Caesar, LVI; Dio Cassius, XLIII, 37–38.
14. BH, 33.
15. Ibid. 42.
16. Gellius, IV xvi, 8 (like Cicero's and other eulogies, Caesar's work has been lost except for brief citations); Plut., Cato, XLIV; LII.
17. Att., XIII xxxvii, August 12, 45; ibid. xl, August 7 or 8, 45.
18. Pro Marcello, 25.
19. Att., XIII i, August 24, 45.
20. Plut., Antonius, X.
21. Lucretius, III, 310–322.

LIV: "SUBVERSIVE"

1. Att., XII xix, March 14, 45; ibid. xxxv, May 1 or 2, 45; ibid. XIII xxxiiia, July 9, 45; Fam., IV v, mid-March 45.
2. Fam., IV v, mid-March 45.
3. Livy, I xvi.
4. Parad. stoic., V, 34.
5. Seneca, De benevolentia, V xxiv.
6. A. C. Johnson et al., Ancient Roman Statutes (Austin, 1961), p. 95; Plut., Caesar, LIX.
7. Suet., XLIV.
8. Appian, Illyrian Wars, 13.
9. Att., XIV i, April 7, 44, Cicero citing Matius after Caesar's death.
10. Div., II, 5; Nat. D., I, 3; De fin., IV, 11.
11. Tusc. Disp., IV, 6; De fin., II, 12; 49.
12. De fin., I, 71; Nat. D., I, 18.
13. Att., XIII iii, December 19, 45.
14. Suet., LXXX.
15. Seneca, De ira, III xxxi, apparently a quotation or paraphrase of a document of Caesar's day.
16. Aurelius Victor, LXXXIII, 3; Plut., Brutus, VII.
17. Suet., XLI; LXXX; LXII.

18. Suet., LXVIII, citing the historian Tanusius Geminus, an unreconciled Pompeian.
19. Ibid. XXXVIII; Tusc. Disp., II, 41; Seneca, Epistle VII, 4.
20. Plut., *Caesar*, LX.
21. Fam., VII xxx, early January 44.
22. Fam., IX xxxi, March 16, 43, writing to Cicero a year after Caesar's assassination.
23. Odys., XXIII, 248–284.

LV: THE IDES OF MARCH

1. Varro ap. Pliny, VI, 52.
2. Att., XIII vii, June 10, 45.
3. Dio Cassius, XLIII, 50; Plut., *Caesar*, LVII.
4. Ibid.; Dio Cassius, XLIV, 3; Florus, II xiii.
5. Suet., LV.
6. Pro Deiotaro, 33–34; Appian, II, 107.
7. Suet., LXXIX.
8. Dio Cassius, XLIV, 10; Val. Max., V vii, 2.
9. Suet., LXVII, citing a Pompeian historian; Phoenissae, 525, cited by Cicero, Off., III, 82.
10. Dio Cassius, XLIV, 9; the source is unimpeachable in this instance, Cicero, Philippic II, 87.
11. Suet., LXXXI; Cicero, Div. I, 119; Suet., LXVII.
12. Suet., LXXX; Appian, II, 112; Dio Cassius, XLIV, 12.
13. Velleius, II lvii; Ammianus Marcellinus, XXIX ii, 18.
14. Plut., *Caesar*, LVII.
15. Philippic II, 116; Plut., *Brutus*, VIII; XII; Suet., LXXXVI.
16. Plut., *Caesar*, LVII; Lucretius, III, 58–59.
17. Odys., XXIV, 542 ff.
18. Div., II, 110.
19. Cyropaedia, VIII vii, 6; Suet., LXXXVII.
20. Plut., *Caesar*, LXIII; Nicholas of Damascus, XXIV.
21. Dio Cassius, XLIV, 18.
22. Suet., LXXXII; Plut., *Caesar*, LXVI; Aurelius Victor, V, 83, 5.
23. Suet., LXXXII.

EPILOGUE

1. Appian, II, 119.
2. Suet., LXXXIV.
3. Ibid.
4. Att., XIV iv, April 10, 44; ibid. i, April 7, 44; ibid. xxi, May 11, 44; ibid. xxii, May 14, 44.
5. Ibid. XV xi, June 8, 44; ibid.
6. Philippic VIII, 8; Fam., XII ii, September 44.
7. Appian, IV, 8.
8. Plut., *Cicero*, XLIX.
9. Fam., XI xxviii, August (?) 44.

SELECTED BIBLIOGRAPHY

To reduce the bibliography to reasonable proportions, wholesale eliminations have had to be made. Articles from standard reference works have been omitted as well as articles published in journals and collections (including festschriften and reports of conferences). As a result, numerous distinguished scholars (particularly those from Eastern Europe) are either underrepresented or do not appear at all. The titles of full-length studies in the following selected bibliography represent approximately one-fifth of the titles a complete bibliography would contain.

Abbott, Frank Frost, and Johnson, Allan Chester. *Municipal Administration in the Roman Empire.* New York, 1926.

Abrams, Philip, and Wrigley, E. A. *Towns in Societies.* Cambridge, 1978.

Adcock, F. E. *Marcus Crassus, Millionaire.* Cambridge, 1966.

———. *The Roman Art of War under the Republic.* Martin Classical Lectures, VIII. Cambridge, Mass., 1940.

Africa, Thomas W. *Science and the State in Greece and Rome.* New York, 1968.

Aigner, H. *Gedanken zur sog. Heeresreform des Marius.* Innsbrucker Beitr. z. Kulturwiss., XVIII, 1974.

———. *Die Soldaten als Machtfaktor in der ausgehenden roem. Republik.* Innsbrucker Beitr. z. Kulturwiss., XXXV, 1974.

Altheim, Franz, ed. *Untersuchungen z. roem. Geschichte,* I. Frankfurt, 1961.

———, and Stiehl, R. *Die Araber in der alten Welt,* I. Berlin, 1964.

André, J. M. *L'otium.* Paris, 1966.

Auguet, Roland. *Cruelty and Civilization: The Roman Games.* London, 1972.

Aymard, André. *Etudes d'histoire ancienne.* Paris, 1967.

———, and Auboyer, Jeannine. *Rome et son empire.* Histoire gén. des civilisations, II. Paris, 1954.

Badian, Ernst. *Foreign Clientelae, 264–70 B.C.* Oxford, 1958.

———. *Publicans and Sinners.* Oxford, 1972.

———. *Roman Imperialism in the Late Republic.* Ithaca, 1968.

———. *Studies in Greek and Roman History.* Oxford, 1964.

Balsdon, J. P. V. D. *Life and Leisure in Ancient Rome.* New York, 1969.

———. *Roman Women.* London, 1962.

———. *Romans and Aliens.* London, 1979.

Bardon, Henry. *La littérature latine inconnue.* Paris, 1952.

Bauman, Richard A. *The Crimen Maiestatis in the Roman Republic and Augustan Principate.* Johannesburg, 1967.

————. *The Duumviri in the Roman Criminal Law and in the Horatius Legend.* Historia Einzelschrift, 12. Wiesbaden, 1969.

Bayet, Jean. *Histoire politique et psychologique de la religion romaine.* Paris, 1957.

————. *Littérature latine.* Paris, 1965.

Becher, Ilse. *Das Bild der Kleopatra in der griechischen und lateinischen Literatur.* Berlin, 1966.

Beesly, Edward Spencer. *Catiline, Clodius and Tiberius.* (Repr. London, 1878, ed.) New York, 1924.

Bengston, Hermann. *Zur Geschichte des Brutus.* Bay. Akad. d. Wiss, Philos.-hist. Kl. Sitzungsber., I, 1970.

Bennett, Harold. *Cinna and His Times.* Diss., Univ. of Chicago, Menasha, Wis., 1923.

Berciu, D. *Romania before Burebista.* London, 1967.

Berti, Enrico. *Il 'De re publica' di Cicerone e il pensiero politico classico.* Pubb. della Scuola di Perfezionamento in Filosofia, Univ. di Padova, I, 1963.

Bertman, Stephen, ed. *The Conflict of Generations in Ancient Greece and Rome.* Amsterdam, 1976.

Bianchi Bandinelli, Ranuccio. *L'origine del ritratto in Grecia e in Roma.* Rome, 1960.

————. *Rome: The Center of Power.* New York, 1970.

————. *Storicità dell'arte classica.* Florence, 1950.

Bickerman, E. J. *Chronology of the Ancient World.* Ithaca, 1968.

Billeter, Gustav. *Gesch. des Zinsfusses in gr.-roem. Altertum bis auf Justinian.* Leipzig, 1898.

Binder, Julius. *Die Plebs.* Leipzig, 1909.

Binder, Max. *Studien zur Gesch. des zw. Buergerkriegs.* Diss., Freiburg, Ueberlingen am Bodensee, 1928.

Blake, Marion Elizabeth. *Ancient Roman Construction in Italy from the Prehistoric Period to Augustus.* Washington, 1947.

Blazquez, Jose Maria. *Historia economica de la Hispania romana.* Madrid, 1978.

Bleicken, Jochen. *Staatliche Ordnung und Freiheit in der roem. Republik.* Frankfurter Althist. Studien, VI, 1972.

Bloch, Gustave. *M. Aemilius Scaurus.* Mél. d'hist. anc. Paris, 1909.

————, and Carcopino, Jérôme. *Histoire romaine, II: la République romaine de 133 à 44 av. J.-C.* Paris, 1940.

Bloch, Leo. *Soziale Kaempfe im alten Rom.* Leipzig, 1908.

Boemer, Franz. *Untersuch. u. die Religion der Sklaven in Griechenland und Rom.* Akad. d. Wiss. und der Lit. Mainz, I, 1957; IV, 1963.

Boissier, Gaston. *Cicéron et ses amis.* Paris, 1865.

Borda, Maurizio. *La scuola di Pasiteles.* Bari, 1953.

Bouché-Leclerq, A. *Histoire des Lagides, II.* Paris, 1904.

Botsford, George Willis. *The Roman Assemblies.* (Repr. 1909 ed.) New York, 1968.

Boyancé, Pierre. *Etudes sur l'humanisme cicéronien.* Coll. Latomus, 121. Brussels, 1970.

Bradford, John. *Ancient Landscapes.* London, 1957.

Breckenridge, James D. *Likeness: A Conceptual History of Ancient Portraiture.* Evanston, 1968.

Brewster, Ethel Hampson. *Roman Craftsmen and Tradesmen of the Early Empire.* (Repr. 1917 ed.) New York, 1972.

SELECTED BIBLIOGRAPHY

Brion, Marcel. *De César à Charlemagne*. Paris, 1949.

Brisset, Jacqueline. *Les idées politiques de Lucain*. Paris, 1964.

Brisson, J.-P., ed. *Problèmes de la guerre à Rome*. Paris, 1969.

———. *Spartacus*. Paris, 1959.

Brockmeyer, Norbert. *Arbeitsorganisation u. oek. Denken in der Gutswirtschaft des roem. Reiches*. Diss., Bochum, 1968.

Brogan, Owen. *Roman Gaul*. Cambridge, Mass., 1953.

Broughton, T. R. S. *The Romanization of Africa Proconsularis*. Johns Hopkins Studies in Historical and Pol. Science, N.S. 5, 1929.

Bruhl, Adrien. *Liber Pater*. Bibl. des écoles fr. d'Athènes et de Rome, fasc. 165. Paris, 1953.

Bruhns, Hinnerk. *Caesar u. die roem. Oberschicht in den Jahren 49–44 v. Chr.* Hypomnemata, Heft 53. Goettingen, 1978.

Brunt, P. A. *Italian Manpower, 225 B.C.–A.D. 14*. Oxford, 1971.

———. *Social Conflicts in the Roman Republic*. Cambridge, 1967.

Brutscher, Cordula. *Analysen zu Suetons Divus Julius u. der Parallelueberlieferung*. Noctes Romanae, 8. Bern, 1958.

Burford, Alison. *Craftsmen in Greek and Roman Society*. Ithaca, 1972.

Canali, Luca. *Personalità e stile di Cesare*. Rome, 1966.

Carandini, Andrea. *L'anatomia della scimmia: La formazione economica della società prima del capitale*. Turin, 1979.

———, and Settis, Salvatore. *Schiavi e padroni nell'Etruria romana*. Bari, 1979.

Carcopino, Jérôme. *Cicero: The Secrets of His Correspondence*. London, 1951.

———. *Jules César*. Paris, 1968.

———. *Points de vue sur l'imperialisme romain*. Paris, 1934.

———. *Promenades historiques aux pays de la Dame de Vix*. Paris, 1957.

———. *Sylla ou la monarchie manquée*. Paris, 1931.

Carney, Thomas F. *A Biography of C. Marius*. Proceedings of the Afr. Cl. Ass., Suppl. No. 1. Assen, The Netherlands, 1961.

Cassola, Filippo. *I gruppi politici romani nel III secolo a.C.* Trieste, 1962.

Casson, Lionel. *The Ancient Mariners*. New York, 1959.

———. *Ships and Sailing in the Ancient World*. Princeton, 1971.

Castagnoli, Ferdinando, et al. *Topografia e urbanistica di Roma*. Istituto di studi romani, Vol. 22. Bologna, 1958.

Cauer, Friedrich. *Ciceros politisches Denken*. Berlin, 1903.

Celli, Angelo. *The History of Malaria in the Roman Campagna*. London, 1933.

Cesare nel bimillenario della morte. Turin, 1956.

Chadwick, Nora K. *Early Brittany*. Cardiff, 1969.

———. *The Druids*. Cardiff, 1966.

Charlesworth, M. P. *Trade-Routes and Commerce of the Roman Empire*. Cambridge, 1924.

Chilver, G. E. F. *Cisalpine Gaul*. Oxford, 1941.

Ciaceri, Emanuele. *Cicerone e suoi tempi*. Milan, I, 1926; II, 1930.

Cichorius, Conrad. *Roemische Studien*. Leipzig, 1922.

Clemente, Guido. *I Romani nella Gallia meridionale*. Bologna, 1974.

Cobban, J. Macdonald. *Senate and Provinces, 78–49 B.C.* Cambridge, 1935.

Coles, Robert. *Erik H. Erikson: The Growth of His Work*. Boston, 1970.

Combes, R. *Imperator*. Paris, 1966.

Cowell, F. R. *The Revolutions of Ancient Rome*. London, 1962.

Cramer, Frederick H. *Astrology in Roman Law and Politics*. Philadelphia, 1954.

Crawford, Michael H. *Roman Republican Coinage*. Cambridge, 1974.

Crook, John. *Law and Life of Rome*. Ithaca, 1967.

Daicoviciu, C. *Die Daker und die Antike*. Coll. Latomus, 102, II. Brussels, 1969.

————. *La Transylvanie dans l'antiquité*. Bucharest, 1945.

D'Arms, John. *Commerce and Social Standing in Ancient Rome*. Cambridge, Mass., 1981.

————. *Romans on the Bay of Naples*. Cambridge, Mass., 1970.

————, and Kopff, E. C. *Seaborne Commerce of Ancient Rome*. Mem. of the Am. Acad. in Rome, XXXVI, 1980.

Dechelette, Joseph. *Manuel d'archéologie préhistorique celtique et gallo-romaine*, II iii. Paris, 1914.

De Martino, Francesco. *Diritto e società nell' antica Roma*. Rome, 1979.

————. *Storia della costituzione romana*. Naples, II, 1955; III, 1958.

De Reuck, Anthony, and Knight, Julie. *Caste and Race: Comparative Approaches*. London, 1967.

De Robertis, Francisco M. *Lavoro e lavoratori nel mondo romano*. Bari, 1963.

De St. Croix, G. E. M. *The Class Struggle in the Ancient World*. Ithaca, 1981.

De Saint-Denis, E. *Du nouveau sur la bataille d'Alésia*. Coll. Latomus, 102. Brussels, 1969.

De Solla Price, Derek. *Gears from the Greeks: The Antikythera Mechanism—a Calendar Computer from c. 80 B.C.* Trans. Am. Philos. Soc., LXIV, 7, 1974.

Dieckhoff, Max. *Krieg und Frieden im griechisch-roemischen Altertum*. Berlin, 1962.

Diesner, H.-J., Barth, H. and Zimmermann, H.-D., eds. *Afrika u. Rom in der Antike*. Halle, 1968.

Dobesch, Gerhard. *Caesars Apotheose zu Lebzeiten und sein Ringen um den Koenigstitel*. Oesterreichische Arch. Inst., 1966.

Dodge, Theodore A. *Caesar*. Cambridge, Mass., 1892.

Donnadieu, A. *La prétendue épilepsie de Jules César*. Mém. de. la Soc. Nat. des Antiquaires de France, X, 1937.

Drachmann, Anders B. *Atheism in Pagan Antiquity*. London, 1922.

Drexler, Hans. *Die Catilinarische Verschwoerung: Ein Quellenheft*. Darmstadt, 1976.

————. *Die Entdeckung des Individuums*. Salzburg, 1966.

Drinkwater, John. *Roman Gaul: The Three Provinces, 58 B.C.–A.D. 260*. London, 1983.

Duff, A. M. *Freedmen in the Early Roman Empire*. 2nd rev. ed., New York, 1958.

Earl, Donald. *The Moral and Political Traditions of Rome*. Ithaca, 1967.

————. *The Political Thought of Sallust*. Cambridge, 1961.

Ebel, Charles. *Transalpine Gaul: The Emergence of a Roman Province*. Studies of the Dutch Arch. and Hist. Soc., IV. Leiden, 1976.

Ehrenberg, Victor. *Ost und West*. Brno, 1935.

Erdmann, Elisabeth H. *Die Rolle des Heeres in der Zeit von Marius bis Caesar*. Neustadt/Aisch, 1972.

Erikson, Erik H. *Gandhi's Truth*. New York, 1969.

————. *Identity: Youth and Crisis*. New York, 1968.

————. *Young Man Luther: A Study in Psychoanalysis and History.* New York, 1958.

Esser, Albert. *Caesar und die Julisch-Claudischen Kaiser im biologischaerztlichen Blickfeld.* Janus, Suppl. I. Leiden, 1958.

Etienne, Robert. *Les Ides de Mars: l'assassinat de César ou de la dictature?* Paris, 1973.

Farrington, Benjamin. *The Faith of Epicurus.* London, 1967.

Ferenczy, E. *From the Patrician State to the Patricio-plebeian State.* Budapest, 1976.

Ferguson, John. *Utopias of the Classical World.* London, 1975.

Finley, Moses I. *The Ancient Economy.* Sather Classical Lectures, 43. Berkeley, 1973.

————. *Ancient Slavery and Modern Ideology.* London, 1980.

————, ed. *Slavery in Classical Antiquity.* Cambridge, 1960.

Foertsch, Barbara. *Die politische Rolle der Frau in der roem. Republik.* Wuerzburger Studien zur Altertumswiss., V. Stuttgart, 1935.

Forster, Edward M. *Alexandria.* Garden City, N.Y., 1961.

Fowler, W. Warde. *The Religious Experience of the Roman People.* London, 1911.

————. *Roman Essays and Interpretations.* Oxford, 1920.

————. *Roman Ideas of Deity.* London, 1914.

————. *Social Life at Rome in the Age of Cicero.* Chatauqua, N.Y., 1909.

Frank, Tenney. *An Economic History of Rome.* 2nd ed., Baltimore, 1927.

————. *An Economic Survey of Ancient Rome, I: Rome and Italy of the Republic;* editor remaining volumes on individual provinces. Baltimore, 1933.

————. *Roman Buildings of the Republic.* Papers & Monographs of the Am. Acad. in Rome, III, 1924.

————. *Roman Imperialism.* New York, 1914.

Fruechtl, Alois. *Die Geldgeschaefte bei Cicero.* Diss., Erlangen, 1912.

Fuchs, Harald. *Der geistige Widerstand gegen Rom in der Antiken Welt.* Berlin, 1938.

Fustel de Coulanges, N. D. *The Ancient City.* (Tr. of 1864 ed.) New York, 1955.

————. *Histoire des institutions politiques de l'ancienne France: La Gaule romaine,* I. Paris, 1891.

Gabba, Emilio. *Appiano: La storia delle guerre civili.* Florence, 1956.

————. *Esercizio e società nella tarda Repubblica romana.* Florence, 1973.

————. *Sulle strutture agrarie dell'Italia romana fra III e I sec. A.C.* Pisa, 1979.

Gagé, Jean. *Apollon romain.* Bibl. des écoles fr. d'Athènes et de Rome. Paris, 1955.

————. *Les classes sociales dans l'empire romain.* Paris, 1964.

————. *Matronalia.* Coll. Latomus, 60. Brussels, 1963.

Gallini, Clara. *Protesta e integrazione nella Roma antica.* Bari, 1970.

Galsterer, Helmut. *Untersuchungen zum roemischen Staedtewesen auf der iberischen Halbinsel.* Berlin, 1971.

Garcia Bellido, Antonia, et al. *Conflictos y estructuras sociales en la Hispania antigua.* Madrid, 1977.

Garlan, Yvon. *War in the Ancient World.* New York, 1975.

Garnsey, Peter. *Social Status and Legal Privilege in the Roman Empire.* Oxford, 1970.

————, et al., eds. *Trade in the Ancient Economy.* London, 1983.

Garzetti, Albino. *Vita Caesaris Plutarchi.* Florence, 1954.

Geffcken, Katherine A. *Comedy in the "Pro Caelio."* Mnem. Suppl., 30, 1973.

Gelzer, Matthias. *Caesar.* Oxford, 1968.

————. *Cicero und Caesar.* Sitzungsber. d. wiss. Ges. an d. J. W. Goethe-Univ., Frankfurt/Main, VII, nr. 1. Wiesbaden, 1968.

————. *Cn. Pompeius Strabo und der Aufstieg seines Sohnes Magnus.* Abh. d. Preuss. Akad. d. Wiss., Philos.-hist. Kl., Nr. 14. Berlin, 1942.

————. *Kleine Schriften,* 2 vols. Wiesbaden, 1962–1963.

————. *Pompeius.* Munich, 1949.

————. *The Roman Nobility.* New York, 1969.

————. *Vom roemischen Staat.* Leipzig, 1944.

Gesche, Helga. *Caesar.* Ertraege der Forschung, 51. Darmstadt, 1976.

————. *Die Vergottung Caesars.* Frankfurter Althistorische Studien, I, 1968.

Giardina, A., and Schiavone, A., eds. *Società romana e produzione schiavistica,* 3 vols. Bari, 1981.

Gil, Juan, ed. *Estudios de literatura latina.* Madrid, 1969.

Ginsburg, Michel S. *Rome et la Judée.* Paris, 1928.

Giovannetti, Eugenio. *La religione di Cesare.* Milan, 1937.

Giuffre, Vincenzo. *Aspetti costituzionali del potere dei militari nella tarda "respublica."* Naples, 1973.

Giuffrida, Pasquale. *L'epicureismo nella letteratura latina nel I sec. a.C.,* 2 vols. Turin, 1940–1950.

Glodariu, Ioan. *Dacian Trade with the Hellenistic and Roman World.* BAR Suppl. Series 8, 1976.

Grant, Michael. *The Army of the Caesars.* London, 1974.

————. *Cleopatra.* London, 1972.

————. *From "Imperium" to "Auctoritas."* Cambridge, 1946.

————. *Gladiators.* New York, 1967.

————. *The Jews in the Roman World.* New York, 1972.

Greenidge, A. H. J. *Roman Public Life.* London, 1911.

Grenier, Albert. *La Gaule celtique.* Paris, 1945.

————. *L'opera di Cesare e di Augusto nella Gallia.* Quadrani Augustei, Ist. di studi stranieri, IX. Spoleto, 1938.

Grimal, Pierre. *La civilisation romaine.* Paris, 1960.

————. *Etudes de chronologie cicéronienne.* Paris, 1967.

Gros, Pierre. *Architecture et societé à Rome et en Italie centroméridionale aux deux derniers siècles de la République.* Coll. Latomus, 156. Brussels, 1978.

Gruen, Erich S. *Roman Politics and the Criminal Courts, 149–78 B.C.* Cambridge, Mass., 1968.

Guarino, Antonio. *La democrazia a Roma.* Naples, 1979.

————. *Spartaco.* Naples, 1979.

Guenther, Rigobert, and Schrot, Gerhard, eds. *Sozialoekonomische Verhaeltnisse im alten Orient und im Klassischen Altertum.* Berlin, 1961.

Gwynn, Aubrey. *Roman Education from Cicero to Quintilian.* (Repr. 1926 ed.) New York, 1966.

Hahlweg, Werner, ed. *Klassiker der Kriegskunst.* Darmstadt, 1960.

Hall, W. H. *The Romans on the Riviera and the Rhone.* London, 1898.

Hammond, M. *City State and World State.* Cambridge, Mass., 1951.

Hands, A. R. *Charities and Social Aid in Greece and Rome.* Ithaca, 1968.

Hanfmann, G. M. A. *Observations on Roman Portraiture.* Coll. Latomus, 11. Brussels, 1953.

Harcum, Cornelia G. *Roman Cooks.* Diss., Johns Hopkins Univ., 1913.

Hardy, E. G. *The Catilinarian Conspiracy in its Context: A Re-study of the Evidence.* Oxford, 1924.

———. *Some Problems in Roman History.* Oxford, 1924.

Harmand, Jacques. *L'armée et le soldat à Rome.* Paris, 1967.

———. *Une campagne césarienne: Alésia.* Paris, 1967.

———. *Les Celtes au second âge du fer.* Paris, 1970.

———. *Les origines des recherches françaises sur l'habitat rural gallo-romain.* Coll. Latomus, 51. Brussels, 1961.

Harmand, Louis. *L'occident romain.* Paris, 1960.

Harris, Harold A. *Sport in Greece and Rome.* London, 1972.

Harris, W. V. *Rome in Etruria and Umbria.* Oxford, 1971.

———. *War and Imperialism in Republican Rome, 327–70 B.C.* Oxford, 1979.

Hatt, Jean-Jacques. *Celts and Gallo-Romans.* London, 1970.

Hatzfeld, Jean. *Les trafiquants italiens dans l'Orient héllenique.* Paris, 1919.

Heaton, John Wesley. *Mob Violence in the Late Roman Republic.* Urbana, 1939.

Heitland, W. E. *Agricola.* Cambridge, 1921.

Hellegouarc'h, J. *Le vocabulaire latin des relations et des partis politiques sous la république.* Paris, 1963.

Hellenismus in Mittelitalien. Pontignano, 1969; Goettingen, 1976.

Herrmann, Claudine. *Le rôle judiciaire et politique des femmes sous la République romaine.* Coll. Latomus, 67. Brussels, 1964.

Herrmann, Joachim, and Sellnow, Irmgard, eds. *Die Rolle der Volksmassen in der Gesch. der vorkapitalistischen Gesellschaftsformationen.* XIVth Int'l. Hist. Congress. San Francisco, 1975; Berlin, 1975.

Heuss, Alfred. *Roemische Geschichte.* Braunschweig, 1960.

Hill, H. *The Roman Middle Class in the Republican Period.* Oxford, 1952.

Holland, Louise Adams. *Lucretius and the Transpadanes.* Princeton, 1979.

Holmes, T. Rice. *Ancient Britain and the Invasions of Julius Caesar.* Oxford, 1917.

———. *Caesar's Conquest of Gaul.* 2nd ed., London, 1911.

———. *The Roman Republic and the Founder of the Empire,* II. Oxford, 1923.

Homo, Léon. *Problèmes sociaux de jadis et à présent.* Paris, 1922.

———. *Roman Political Institutions.* New York, 1962.

Hopkins, Keith. *Conquerors and Slaves.* Cambridge, 1978.

Hubert, Henri. *Les Celtes.* Paris, 1950.

Jal, Paul. *La guerre civile à Rome.* Paris, 1963.

Jashemski, Wilhelmina F. *The Origins and History of the Proconsular and the Propraetorian Imperium to 27 B.C.* Chicago, 1950.

John, Constantin. *Die Entstehungsgeschichte der Catilinarischen Verschwoerung.* Jahrb. f. Klass. Philol., Suppl. Bd. VIII, Heft 3, 1876.

Johnson, Allan Chester, Coleman-Norton, P. R., and Bourne, Frank C. *Ancient Roman Statutes.* Austin, 1961.

Joliffe, Richard O. *Phases of Corruption in Roman Administration in the Last Half-Century of the Roman Republic.* Diss., Univ. of Chicago, 1919.

Jones, A. H. M. *Ancient Empires and the Economy,* ed. P. A. Brunt. Oxford, 1974.

Jonkers, E. J. *Social and Economic Commentary on Cicero's "De imperio Cn. Pompei."* Leiden, 1959.

————. *Social and Economic Commentary on Cicero's "De lege agraria orationes tres."* Leiden, 1963.

Jucker, Hans. *Vom Verhaeltnis der Roemer zur bildenden Kunst der Griechen.* Frankfurt, 1950.

Judeich, Walther. *Caesar im Orient.* Leipzig, 1885.

Jullian, Camille. *Histoire de la Gaule.* Paris, II, 1908; III, 1931.

Juster, Jean. *Les juifs dans l'empire romain.* Paris, 1914.

Kelly, J. M. *Roman Litigation.* Oxford, 1966.

Klass, Justinus. *Cicero und Caesar.* Hist. Studien, 354. Berlin, 1939.

Klein, Richard, ed. *Das Staatsdenken der Roemer.* Darmstadt, 1966.

Knapowski, Roch. *Die Staatsrechnungen der roem. Rep. in den Jahren 49–45 v. Chr.* Untersuchungen z. Roem. Ges., IV. Frankfurt/Main, 1967.

Koch, Carl. *Religio: Studien zu Kult und Glauben der Roemer.* Nuremberg, 1960.

Kolendo, Jerzy. *L'agricoltura nell'Italia romana.* (Tr. fr. Polish.) Rome, 1980.

Konstan, David. *Some Aspects of Epicurean Psychology.* Philosophia Antiqua, XXV. Leiden, 1973.

Kovaliov, S. I. *Storia di Roma.* (Tr. fr. Russian.) Rome, 1953.

Kraft, Konrad. *Zur Entstehung des Namens "Germania."* Sitzungsber. d. wiss. Ges. an d. J.W. Goethe-Univ., IX, nr. 2. Wiesbaden, 1970.

Kroll, Wilhelm. *Die Kultur der Ciceronischen Zeit.* Leipzig, 1933.

Kuchle, Franz. *Sklavenarbeit u. technischer Fortschritt im roem. Reich.* Forschungen z. antiken Sklaverei, III. Wiesbaden, 1969.

Kuczynski, Juergen. *Allgemeine Wirtschaftsgeschichte von der Urzeit bis zur sozialistischen Gesellschaft.* Berlin, 1951.

Kunkel, Wolfgang. *An Introduction to Roman Legal and Constitutional History.* London, 1966.

Lambrechts, F. *Les Lupercales, une fête prédéiste?* Coll. Latomus, 2. Brussels, 1948.

Lanciani, Rodolfo. *Ancient and Modern Rome.* (Repr. 1925 ed.) New York, 1963.

Lanzani, Carolina. *Lucio Cornelio Silla, Dittatore: Storia di Roma negli anni 87–78 a.C.* Milan, 1936.

————. *Mario e Silla.* Catania, 1915.

La Penna, Antonio. *Aspetti del pensiero storico latino.* Turin, 1978.

————. *Sallustio e la 'rivoluzione' romana.* Milan, 1968.

Larsen, J. A. O. *Representative Government in Greek and Roman History.* Sather Classical Lectures, 28. Berkeley, 1955.

Last, Hugh, ed. *Cambridge Ancient History,* IX. Cambridge, 1951.

Lavedun, P., and Huguenay, J. *Histoire de l'urbanisme dans l'antiquité.* Paris, 1966.

Le Gall, Joel. *Le Tibre dans l'antiquité.* Paris, 1953.

Legio VII Gemina. Inst. Leones de Estud. romano-visigoticos. Leon, 1968.

Lenaghan, John O. *A Commentary on Cicero's Oration "De haruspicum responso."* Mouton, 1969.

Leon, Harry. *The Jews of Ancient Rome.* Philadelphia, 1960.

Lepore, Ettore. *Il princeps ciceroniano.* Naples, 1954.

Lévi, Mario Attilio. *Political Power in the Ancient World.* (Tr. of 1955 ed.) New York, 1968.

Lévy, Jean-Philippe. *The Economic Life of the Ancient World.* Chicago, 1967.

Lewis, I. M., ed. *History and Social Anthropology*. London, 1968.

Liebeschuetz, J. H. W. G. *Continuity and Change in Roman Religion*. Oxford, 1979.

Linderski, Jerzy. *Der Senat und die Vereine*. Gesellschaft u. Recht im griechisch-roemischen Altertum, I. Berlin, 1969.

Lintott, A. W. *Violence in Republican Rome*. Oxford, 1968.

Littleton, A. C., and Yamey, B. S., eds. *Studies in the History of Accounting*. Homewood, Ill., 1965.

Loane, Helen J. *Industry and Commerce of the City of Rome, 50 B.C.–200 A.D.* Johns Hopkins Univ. Studies in Historical and Pol. Science, Ser. 56, No. 2. Baltimore, 1938.

Lossmann, Friedrich. *Cicero und Caesar im Jahre 54*. Hermes Einzelschr. 17. Wiesbaden, 1962.

Lot, Ferdinand. *La Gaule*. Paris, 1947.

McGushin, P. C. *Sallustius Crispus, Bellum Catilinae: A Commentary*. Mnemosyne Suppl. 45. Leiden, 1977.

MacMullen, Ramsay. *Roman Social Relations, 50 B.C. to A.D. 284*. New Haven, 1974.

———. *Soldier and Civilian in the Later Roman Empire*. Cambridge, Mass., 1963.

Magie, David. *Roman Rule in Asia Minor*. Princeton, 1950.

Malaise, Michel. *Les conditions de pénétration et de diffusion des cultes égyptiens en Italie*. Leiden, 1972.

Manni, Eugenio. *Lucio Sergio Catilina*. Florence, 1939.

Mansuelli, Guido. *I Cisalpini*. Florence, 1962.

———. *Il problema delle relazioni culturali fra la Cisalpina e le Gallie*. Problemi attuali di sc. e di cultura, 158, Accad. naz. dei Lincei, 1973.

———. *Les civilisations de l'Europe ancienne*. Paris, 1967.

———. *Urbanistica e architettura della Cisalpina romana fino al III sec. e. n.* Coll. Latomus, 111. Brussels, 1971.

Marsden, E. W. *Greek and Roman Artillery*. Oxford, 1969.

Marshall, B. A. *Crassus: A Political Biography*. Amsterdam, 1976.

Martin, René. *Recherches sur les agronomes latins et leur conceptions économiques et sociales*. Paris, 1971.

Maschkin, A. *Zwischen Republik u. Kaiserreich*. (Germ. tr.) Leipzig, 1954.

Mattingly, Harold. *Roman Coins*. London, 1967.

Mazzarino, Santo. *Il pensiero storico classico*, II. Bari, 1966.

Mazzolani, Lidia S. *The Idea of the City in Roman Thought*. Bloomington, 1970.

Meier, Christian. *Entstehung des Begriffs "Demokratie."* Frankfurt, 1970.

———. *Res Publica Amissa*. Wiesbaden, 1966.

Menendez Pidal, Ramon, ed. *Historia de Espana*, II. Madrid, 1935.

Meyer, Eduard. *Caesars Monarchie und das Principat des Pompeius*. (Repr. 1919 ed.) Stuttgart, 1963.

Michel, Dorothea. *Alexander als Vorbild fuer Pompeius, Caesar und Marcus Antonius*. Coll. Latomus, 94. Brussels, 1967.

Michels, Agnes Kirsopp. *The Calendar of the Roman Republic*. Princeton, 1967.

Misch, Georg. *Geschichte der Autobiographie*, I i, ii. 3rd ed., Bern, 1949.

Mishulin, A. V. *Spartakovskoye Vosstaniye: Revolutsia Rabov v Rimye v 1 Vekye do N.E.* Moscow, 1936.

Moore, Frank Gardner. *The Roman's World.* (Repr. 1936 ed.) New York, 1971.

Mueller, Reimar. *Die epikureische Gesellschaftstheorie.* Schriften z. Gesch. u. Kultur der Antike, 5, Akad. d. Wiss. der DDR, Zentralinst. f. alte Geschichte u. Archaeologie. Berlin, 1972.

Muenscher, Karl. *Xenophon in der griech.-roem. Literatur.* Philologus Suppl. Bd. 13, 1920.

Muenzer, Friedrich. *Roemische Adelsparteien und Adelsfamilien.* Stuttgart, 1920.

Napoleon I. *Précis des Guerres de Jules César,* ed. M. Marchand. Paris, 1836.

Nash, Ernest. *Pictorial Dictionary of Ancient Rome.* 2nd ed., New York, 1968.

Niccolini, Giovanni. *I fasti dei tribuni della plebe.* Milan, 1934.

————. *Il tribunato della plebe.* Milan, 1932.

Nichols, James H., Jr. *Epicurean Political Philosophy: The "De rerum natura" of Lucretius.* Ithaca, 1976.

————, and McLeish, Kenneth. *Through Roman Eyes.* Cambridge, 1976.

Nicolet, Claude. *Les idées politiques à Rome sous la République.* Paris, 1964.

————. *Le métier de citoyen dans la Rome républicaine.* Paris, 1976.

————. *L'ordre équestre à l'époque républicaine.* Paris, 1966.

————. *Rome et la conquête du monde méditerranéen: 267–27 av. J.-C.,* 2 vols. Paris, 1977–1978.

Nisbet, Robert G. M. *Tulli Ciceronis: "De domo sua."* Oxford, 1939.

————. *M. Tulli Ciceronis: "In L. Calpurnium Pisonem oratio."* Oxford, 1961.

Oliver, E. H. *Roman Economic Conditions to the Close of the Republic.* Toronto, 1917.

Omerod, Henry A. *Piracy in the Ancient World.* Liverpool, 1924.

Oppermann, Hans, ed. *Roemertum.* Wege d. Forschung, 18. Darmstadt, 1962.

————, ed. *Roemische Wertbegriffe.* Wege d. Forschung, 34. Darmstadt, 1967.

Otto, A. *Die Sprichwoerter und sprichwoertlichen Redensarten der Roemer.* Leipzig, 1890.

Paoli, Ugo Enrico. *Rome: Its People, Life and Customs.* New York, 1963.

Paratore, Ettore. *L'epicureismo e la sua diffusione nel mondo latino.* Rome, 1960.

Pareti, Luigi. *Storia di Roma, IV: Dal primo triumvirato all'avvento di Vespasiano.* Turin, 1955.

————. *Studi minori di storia antica.* Rome, 1965.

Parvan, Vasile. *Dacia.* Cambridge, 1928.

Pasquinucci, Marinella. *La transumanza dell'Italia romana.* Pisa, 1979.

Patsch, Carl. *Beitraege zu Voelkerkunde von Suedosteuropa.* Sitzungsber. Philos.-hist. Kl., 214, Akad. der Wiss. in Wien, 1932.

Percival, John. *The Roman Villa.* London, 1976.

Perowne, Stewart. *The Life and Times of Herod the Great.* London, 1956.

Perret, Jacques. *Les origines de la légende troyenne de Rome (281–31).* Paris, 1942.

Petrochilos, Nicholas. *Roman Attitudes to the Greeks.* Athens, 1974.

Peyre, Christian. *La Cisalpine gauloise du IIIième au Ier siècle av. J.-C.* Paris, 1979.

Picard, Gilbert. *Roman Painting.* Greenwich, Conn., 1968.

Picard, Gilbert-Charles. *Nordafrika und die Roemer.* Stuttgart, 1962.

————. *Les trophées romains.* Bibl. des éc. fr. d'Athènes et de Rome, fasc. 187. Paris, 1957.

Piganiol, André. *La conquête romaine.* 5th ed., Paris, 1967.

Piggott, Stuart, et al. *France before the Romans*. London, 1973.

Pin, Benjamin. *Jérusalem contre Rome*. Paris, 1938.

Platner, S. B., and Ashby, T. *A Topographical Dictionary of Ancient Rome*. Oxford, 1929.

Pocock, L. G. *A Commentary on Cicero's "In Vatinium."* Amsterdam, 1967.

Poeschl, Viktor, ed. *Sallust*. Wege d. Forschung, 94. Darmstadt, 1970.

Polay, Elemer. *Differenzierung der Gesellschaftsnormen im antiken Rom*. Budapest, 1964.

Posner, Ernst. *Archives in the Ancient World*. Cambridge, Mass., 1972.

Raaflaub, K. *Dignitatis contentio*. Vestigia, XX. Munich, 1974.

Radin, Max. *The Jews among the Greeks and Romans*. Philadelphia, 1915.

Ramage, Edwin S. *Urbanitas: Ancient Sophistication and Refinement*. Norman, Okla., 1973.

Rambaud, Marcel. *L'art de la déformation historique dans les commentaires de César*. Paris, 1966.

Ramsay, Sir Wm. M. *The Social Basis of Roman Power in Asia Minor*. Amsterdam, 1967.

Rasmussen, Detlef, ed. *Caesar*. Wege d. Forschung, 43. Darmstadt, 1967.

Reinach, Theodore. *Mithridates Eupator, Roi de Pont*. Paris, 1890.

Reinhold, Meyer. *History of Purple as a Status Symbol in Antiquity*. Coll. Latomus, 116. Brussels, 1970.

Renardot, Etienne. *Vie et croyances des Gaulois avant la conquête romaine*. Paris, 1975.

Rickman, Geoffrey. *The Corn Supply of Ancient Rome*. Oxford, 1980.

Righini, Valeria. *Lineamenti di storia economica della Gallia cisalpina: la produttività fittile in età repubblicana*. Coll. Latomus, 119. Brussels, 1970.

Ripostelli, J., and Marucchi, H. *La Via Appia*. Rome, 1908.

Robinson, Frederich W. *Marius, Saturninus und Glaucia*. Bonn, 1912.

Rodgers, Wm. L. *Greek and Roman Naval Warfare*. Annapolis, 1937.

Rodriguez Neila, Juan Francisco. *Los Balbos de Cadiz*. Seville, 1973.

Romanelli, Pietro. *Storia delle province romane dell'Africa*. Rome, 1959.

Rose, J. Holland. *The Mediterranean in the Ancient World*. Cambridge, 1933.

Rossi, Ruggiero F. *Nuove questioni di storia antica*. Milan, 1968.

———. *Marco Antonio nella lotta politica della tarda Repubblica Romana*. Trieste, 1959.

Rostovtzeff, M. *Rome*. (Repr. 1928 ed.) Oxford, 1962.

———. *The Social and Economic History of the Hellenistic World*. Oxford, 1941.

———. *The Social and Economic History of the Roman Empire*. Oxford, 1926.

Rouland, Norbert. *Les esclaves romains en temps de guerre*. Aix-en-Provence, 1975.

Rouge, Jean. *Recherches sur l'organisation du commerce maritime en la Méditerranée sous l'empire romain*. Paris, 1966.

Rudolph, H. *Stadt und Staat im roemischen Italien*. Leipzig, 1935.

Salmon, E. T. *The Making of Roman Italy*. Ithaca, 1982.

———. *Roman Colonization under the Republic*. Ithaca, 1970.

———. *Samnium and the Samnites*. Cambridge, 1967.

Salvioli, Giuseppe. *Le capitalisme dans le monde antique*. Paris, 1906.

Samter, Ernst. *Geburt, Hochzeit und Tod.* Leipzig, 1911.

Sands, P. C. *The Client Princes of the Roman Empire under the Republic.* Cambridge, 1908.

Scarborough, John. *Roman Medicine.* Ithaca, 1972.

Schefold, Karl. *Pompejanische Malerei.* Basel, 1952.

Schiavone, Aldo. *Nascità della giurisprudenza.* Bari, 1976.

Schilling, Robert. *La religion romaine de Vénus.* Bibl. des éc. fr. d'Athènes et de Rome, 178, fasc. 1. Paris, 1954.

Schmidt, Joel. *Vie et mort des esclaves dans la Rome antique.* Paris, 1973.

Schmidt, Otto M. *Der Briefwechsel des M. Tullius Cicero.* Leipzig, 1893.

Schmitt, Hatto H. *Rom und Rhodos.* Munich, 1957.

Schmittlein, R. *Avec César en Gaulle.* Paris, 1970.

Schneider, Helmuth. *Wirtschaft und Politik: Unters. z. Gesch. der spaeten roem. Republik.* Erlangen Studien, 3, 1974.

Schulte-Holtey, Gabriele. *Unters. z. gallischen Widerstand gegen Caesar.* Diss., Westfaelischen Wilhelms-Univ., 1969.

Schulten, Adolf. *Sertorius.* Leipzig, 1926.

Schulz, Fritz. *History of Roman Legal Science.* Oxford, 1946.

Schweitzer, Bernhard. *Die Bildniskunst der roem. Republik.* Weimar, 1948.

Seel, Otto. *Cicero: Wort, Staat, Welt.* Stuttgart, 1953.

———. *Caesar Studien.* Der altsprachliche Unterricht, I x. Stuttgart, 1967.

———. *Hirtius: Unters. ueber die Pseudocaesarischen Bella und den Balbusbrief.* Klio Beih. XXXV, 1935.

Sereni, Emilio. *Communità rurali nell'Italia antica.* Rome, 1955.

Shatzman, Israel. *Senatorial Wealth and Roman Politics.* Coll. Latomus, 142. Brussels, 1975.

Sherwin-White, A. N. *Racial Prejudice in Imperial Rome.* Cambridge, 1967.

———. *The Roman Citizenship.* Oxford, 1939.

Shtaerman, E. M. *Die Bluetezeit der Sklavenwirtschaft in der roem. Republik.* (Tr. from Russian.) Wiesbaden, 1969.

Singer, Chas., et al. *A History of Technology,* II. New York, 1956.

Smallwood, E. Mary. *The Jews under Roman Rule.* Leiden, 1976.

Smith, R. E. *Service in the Post-Marian Roman Army.* Manchester, 1958.

Sordi, Marta, ed. *Aspetti dell'opinione pubblica nel mondo antico.* Milan, 1978.

Sprague de Camp, L. *The Ancient Engineers.* New York, 1963.

Stahl, William H. *Roman Science.* Madison, 1962.

Stampacchia, Giulia. *La tradizione della guerra di Spartaco.* Pisa, 1976.

Stark, Freya. *Rome on the Euphrates.* New York, 1966.

Starks, Rudolf, ed. *Politeia u. Res Publica.* Wiesbaden, 1969.

Staveley, E. S. *Greek and Roman Voting and Elections.* London, 1972.

Stein, Arthur. *Der roemische Ritterstand.* Muenchener Beitr. z. Papyrusforschung u. antiken Rechtsgeschichte, X, 1927.

Steinmetz, P., ed. *Res Publica.* Wiesbaden, 1969.

Stillwell, Richard, et al., eds. *The Princeton Encyclopaedia of Classical Sites.* Princeton, 1976.

Stoffel, Col. E. G. H. C. *Histoire de Jules César,* 2 vols. Paris, 1887.

Strasburger, Hermann. *Caesars Eintritt in die Geschichte*. Darmstadt, 1966.

Sumner, G. V. *The Orators in Cicero's "Brutus": Prosopography and Chronology*. Phoenix Suppl., Vol. 11. Toronto, 1973.

Suolahti, Jaakko. *The Junior Officers of the Roman Army in the Republican Period*. Helsinki, 1955.

———. *The Roman Censors: A Study on Social Structure*. Helsinki, 1963.

Sutherland, C. H. V. *Roman Coins*. New York, 1974.

Syme, Ronald. *Roman Papers*, ed. Ernst Badian. New York, 1980.

———. *The Roman Revolution*. Oxford, 1939.

———. *Sallust*. Sather Classical Lectures, 33. Berkeley, 1964.

Szemler, G. J. *The Priests of the Roman Republic*. Coll. Latomus, 127. Brussels, 1972.

Szidat, Joachim. *Caesars diplomatische Taetigkeit im gallischen Krieg*. Historia-Einzelschrift, 14. Wiesbaden, 1970.

Taeger, Fritz. *Das Altertum*. Stuttgart, 1942.

———. *Charisma*, II. Stuttgart, 1960.

Tarn, Sir Wm., and Griffith, G. T. *Hellenistic Civilization*. 3rd ed., London, 1952.

Taylor, Lily Ross. *The Divinity of the Roman Emperor*. A.P.A. Philol. Monograph, 1. Middletown, Conn., 1931.

———. *Party Politics in the Age of Caesar*. (Repr. 1949 ed.) Berkeley, 1971.

———. *Roman Voting Assemblies from the Hannibalic War to the Dictatorship of Caesar*. Ann Arbor, 1966.

———. *The Voting Districts of the Roman Republic*. Am. Acad. in Rome Papers and Monographs, 20, 1960.

Tcherikover, Victor. *Hellenistic Civilization and the Jews*. Philadelphia, 1959.

Teggart, Frederick J. *Rome and China: A Study of Correlations in Historical Events*. Berkeley, 1939.

Thevenot, Emile. *Les Eduens n'ont pas trahi*. Coll. Latomus, 1. Brussels, 1960.

———. *Les Gallo-Romains*. Paris, 1948.

Thiel, J. H. *Studies on the History of Roman Seapower in Republican Times*. Amsterdam, 1946.

Tibiletti, Gianfranco. *L'ambiente politico-familiare di Cesare*. Turin, 1956.

———. *Lo sviluppo del latifondo in Italia dall'epoca graccana al principio dell'impero*. Relazioni del X Congr. Internaz. di scienze storiche. Roma 1955; Florence, 1955.

———, et al. *Arte e civiltà romana nell'Italia settentrionale*, I. Bologna, 1964.

Toynbee, Arnold J. *Hannibal's Legacy*, II. London, 1965.

Tozzi, Pierluigi. *Storia padana antica*. Pubb. d. fac. di lett. e filos., Univ. di Pavia, Ist. di storia greca e romana. Milan, 1972.

Treggiari, Susan. *Roman Freedmen During the Late Republic*. Oxford, 1969.

Ueberweg, Friedrich. *Grundriss der Gesch. der Philosophie*, I. Berlin, 1926.

Ungern-Sternberg von Puerkel, Juergen. *Untersuchungen z. spaetrep. Notstandsrecht*. Munich, 1970.

Ussani, Vincenzo, ed. *Guida allo studio della civiltà romana antica*, 2 vols. Naples, 1952, 1954.

Utchenko, Sergei L. *Drevnii Rim*. Moscow, 1969.

Valgiglio, E. *Plutarcho, Vita di Mario*. Florence, 1956.

———. *Silla e la crisi repubblicana*. Florence, 1956.

van Ooteghem, J. *Caius Marius*. Ac. roy. de Belg., Cl. des Lettres et des Sc. Morales et Politiques, Mémoires 56, fasc. 6, 1964.

———. *Lucius Licinius Lucullus*. Mém. 53, fasc. 4, 1959.

———. *Lucius Marcius Philippus et sa famille*. Mém. 55, fasc. 3, 1961.

———. *Pompée le Grand*. Mém. 49, 1954.

Vessberg, Olof. *Studien z. Kunstgesch. der roem. Republik*. Skrifter, Svenska Institutet i Rom, VIII. Lund, 1941.

Vigneron, Paul. *Le cheval dans l'antiquité greco-romaine*. Nancy, 1968.

Vittinghoff, Friedrich. *Roem. Kolonisation u. Buergerrechtspolitik*. Akad. d. Wiss. u. d. Lit. in Mainz, Abh. d. Geistes-und Soz.wiss. Kl., 14, 1951.

Vogt, Joseph. *Cicero und Sallust ueber die Catilinarische Verschwoerung*. Frankfurt/Main, 1938.

———. *Orbis: Ausgewaehtle Schriften zur Gesch. des Altertums*. Freiburg, 1960.

———. *Struktur d. antiken Sklavenkriege*. Akad. d. Wiss. u. d. Lit. in Mainz, Abh. der Geistes-und Soz.wiss. Kl., 1, 1957.

Volkmann, Hans. *Cleopatra*. New York, 1958.

———. *Die Massenversklavungen der Einwohner eroberter Staedte in der hellenistisch-roem. Zeit*. Akad. d. Wiss. u. d. Lit. in Mainz, Abh. der Geistes-und Soz.wiss. Kl., 3. Mainz, 1961.

———. *Sullas Marsch auf Rom*. Munich, 1958.

von Fritz, Kurt. *The Theory of the Mixed Constitution in Antiquity*. New York, 1954.

von Luebtow, Ulrich. *Das roemische Volk: Sein Staat u. Sein Recht*. Frankfurt/Main, 1955.

von Poehlmann, Robert. *Aus Altertum und Gegenwart*. Munich, 1911.

———. *Geschichte der Sozialen Frage und des Sozialismus in der Antiken Welt*, II. 3rd ed. Munich, 1925.

von Premerstein, Anton. *Vom Werden und Wesen des Prinzipats*. Abh. d. Bayr. Akad. d. Wiss., Philosophisch-hist. Abt., NF 15, 1937.

von Wiese, Leopold, ed. *Die Entwicklung der Kriegswaffe und ihr Zusammenhang mit der Sozialordnung*. Cologne, 1953.

Vretska, Karl. *Sallust; Invektive und Episteln*. Heidelberg, 1961.

Wagenvoort, H. *Roman Dynamism*. Oxford, 1947.

Walser, Gerold. *Caesar und die Germanen*. Historia Einzelschrift, 1. Wiesbaden, 1956.

Waltzing, J.-P. *Etude historique sur les corporations professionnelles chez les Romains*. Brussels, 1895.

Ward, Allen M. *Marcus Crassus and the Late Roman Republic*. Columbia, Mo., 1977.

Wardman, Alan. *Religion and Statecraft among the Romans*. Baltimore, 1982.

Ward-Perkins, J. B. *Cities of Ancient Greece and Italy: Planning in Classical Antiquity*. New York, 1974.

Watson, Alan. *The Law of the Ancient Romans*. Dallas, 1970.

———. *Law Making in the Later Roman Republic*. Oxford, 1974.

———. *Rome of the XII Tables*. Princeton, 1975.

Weinstock, Stefan. *Divus Julius*. Oxford, 1971.

Weische, Alfons. *Studien zur politischen Sprache der roem. Republik*. Muenster, 1966.

Welskopf, Elisabeth Charlotte, ed. *Neue Beitr. z. Gesch. der Alten Welt*. Berlin, 1965.

————. *Die Produktionsverh. im Alten Orient und in der Griechisch-roemischen Antike.* Deutsche Akad. der Wiss. zu Berlin, 5, 1957.

Westerman, William L. *The Slave Systems of Greek and Roman Antiquity.* Philadelphia, 1955.

Wheeler, Sir Mortimer. *Rome Beyond the Imperial Frontiers.* London, 1954.

White, K. D. *Roman Farming.* Ithaca, 1970.

Willems, Pierre. *Le sénat de la République romaine.* (Repr. 1883–1885 ed.) Darmstadt, 1968.

Wilson, A. J. N. *Emigration from Italy in the Republican Age of Rome.* New York, 1966.

Wilson, Lillian M. *The Clothing of the Ancient Romans.* Johns Hopkins Univ. Studies in Arch., 24. Baltimore, 1938.

Wirszubski, C. *Libertas as a Political Idea at Rome during the Late Republic and Early Principate.* Cambridge, 1950.

Wirz, Hans. *Catilinas und Ciceros Bewerbung um den Consulat fuer das Jahr 63.* Zurich, 1864.

Wiseman, F. J. *Roman Spain.* London, 1956.

Wiseman, T. P. *Cinna the Poet and Other Roman Essays.* Leicester, 1974.

————. *New Men in the Roman Senate, 139 B.C.–A.D. 14.* Oxford, 1971.

Wistrand, Erik. *Caesar and Contemporary Roman Society.* Acta Regiae Soc. Sc. & Litt. Gothoburgensis, Humaniora 15, 1979.

————. *Sallust on Judicial Murders in Rome.* Studia Graeca et Latina Gothoburgensia, XXIV, 1968.

Wood, E. and N. *Class Ideology and Ancient Political Theory.* New York, 1978.

Yawetz, Zwi. *Plebs and Princeps.* Oxford, 1969.

Zecchini, Giuseppe. *Cassio Dione e la guerra gallica di Cesare.* Milan, 1978.

Zenker, Paul. *Forum Romanum.* Tuebingen, 1972.

CONFERENCE REPORTS

Besançon, Univ. de, Actes du colloques sur l'esclavage: 1970 (Ann. litt., CXXVIII; 1971 (Ann. litt., CXL); 1972 (Ann. litt., CLXIII); 1974 (Ann. litt., CLXXXVII).

Colloque d'histoire sociale, St. Cloud, 1967.

Colloque d'histoire sociale, Besançon, 1970.

Colloques nationaux du Centre national de la recherche scientifique (Sc. humaines), Paris, 1970.

Ve Congrès international d'études classiques, Madrid, 1974. Besançon, 1976.

XCIIIe Congrès nationale des sociétés savantes, Paris, 1968.

Congresso internazionale di studi ciceroniani, Rome, 1959.

Conventus IX, "Eirene," Warsaw, 1968.

Conventus XI, "Eirene," Warsaw, 1971.

Dialoghi di archeologia. Incontro di studi su "Roma e l'Italia fra i Gracchi e Silla," 1970–1971.

IInd International Conference of Economic History, Paris, 1962.

IIIrd International Conference of Economic History, Munich, 1965.

IVth International Conference of Economic History, Bloomington, 1968.

International Congress of Historical Sciences, Rome, 1955.
XIth International Congress of Historical Sciences, Stockholm, 1960.
XIIIth International Congress of Historians, Moscow, 1970.
Konferentsiya po izucheniyu problem antichnosti, Moscow, 1967.
Soziale Probleme im Hellenismus u. im roemischen Reich, Konferenz, Liblice, 1972.

FESTSCHRIFTEN

Festschrift fuer Franz Altheim, eds. Ruth Stiehl and Hans Erich Stier. Berlin, 1969.
Ricerche storiche ed economiche in memoria di C. Barbagallo, ed. L. Di. Naples, 1970.
Hommage à Jan Bayet, eds. M. Renard and R. Schilling. Coll. Latomus, 70. Brussels, 1964.
Hommages à Joseph Bidez et à Franz Cumont. Coll. Latomus, 2. Brussels, 1948.
Mélanges d'archéologie, d'épigraphie et d'histoire offerts à J. Carcopino. Paris, 1966.
Hommage à la mémoire de Jérôme Carcopino, ed. R. de Thomasson. Paris, 1977.
Studi in onore di Giuseppe Grosse, III. Turin, 1968.
Studies in Roman Economic and Social History in Honor of Allan Chester Johnson, ed. P. R. Coleman-Norton. Princeton, 1951.
Festgabe fuer Paul Kirn, ed. Ekkehard Kaufmann. Berlin, 1961.
Classical Essays Presented to James A. Kleist, S.J. St. Louis, 1946.
Antidosis: Festschrift W. Kraus, eds. R. Hanslik, A. Lesky, H. Schwabl. Wiener Studien Beih. V. Vienna, 1972.
Ciceroniana: Hommages à Kazimierz Kumaniecki, eds. A. Michel and R. Verdière. Leiden, 1975.
Etudes offertes à Jean Macqueron. Aix-en-Provence, 1970.
Essays in Roman Coinage Presented to Harold Mattingly, eds. R. A. G. Carson and C. H. V. Sutherland. London, 1956.
Mélanges d'archéologie et d'histoire offerts à André Piganiol, ed. R. Chevalier. Paris, 1966.
Hommages à Marcel Renard. Coll. Latomus, 102. Brussels, 1969.
Polis and Imperium: Studies in Honour of Edward Togo Salmon, ed. J. A. S. Evans. Toronto, 1974.
Mélanges Paul Thomas. Bruges, 1930.
Studies Presented to George Thomson, eds. L. Varcl and R. F. Willetts. Graecolatina Pragensia, II. Prague, 1963.
Studien zur antiken Sozialgeschichte: Festschrift Friedrich Vittinghoff, ed. Werner Eck. Cologne, 1980.
Aufstieg und Niedergang der roemischen Welt: Geschichte und Kultur Roms im Spiegel der neueren Forschung: Festschrift Joseph Vogt, I i–iv, ed. Hildegard Temporini. Berlin, 1972–1973.
Studi in onore di E. Volterra, IV. Milan, 1971.
Festgabe Friedrich von Bezold. Bonn and Leipzig, 1921.
Sein und Werden im Recht: Festgabe fuer Ulrich von Luebtow, eds. Walter G. Becker and Ludwig Schnorr von Carolsfeld. Berlin, 1970.

INDEX